W9-BGS-156

ETHICS
THEORY AND CONTEMPORARY ISSUES

Concise, Eighth Edition

Barbara MacKinnon
University of San Francisco, Professor of Philosophy, Emerita

Andrew Fiala
California State University, Fresno, Professor of Philosophy

CENGAGE
Learning·

Australia • Brazil • Mexico • Spain • United Kingdom • United States

For Edward, Jennifer, and Kathleen

CENGAGE
Learning

Ethics: Theory and Contemporary Issues, Concise, Eighth Edition

Barbara MacKinnon

Andrew Fiala

Product Director: Suzanne Jeans

Product Manager: Debra Matteson

Content Developer: Ian Lague

Content Coordinator: Joshua Duncan

Media Developer: Phil Lanza

Senior Content Project Manager: Catherine G. DiMassa

Art Director: Kristina Mose-Libon, PMG

Manufacturing Planner: Sandee Milewski

Rights Acquisition Specialist: Shalice Shah-Caldwell

Production Service & Compositor: Cenveo® Publisher Services

Text and Cover Designer: PreMediaGlobal

Cover Images: © Elliott & Fry/Stringer/Hulton Archive/Getty Images

© ADEK BERRY/Stringer/AFP/Getty Images

© Scott Olson/Staff/ Getty Images News/ Getty Images

© Rob Melnychuk/DigitalVision/Getty Images

© iStockphoto/dra_schwartz/Vetta Collection

© iStockphoto/GeorgiosArt

© iStockphoto/Thinkstock

© 2015, 2012, 2009, Cengage Learning

WCN: 01-100-101

ALL RIGHTS RESERVED. No part of this work covered by the copyright herein may be reproduced, transmitted, stored, or used in any form or by any means graphic, electronic, or mechanical, including but not limited to photocopying, recording, scanning, digitizing, taping, Web distribution, information networks, or information storage and retrieval systems, except as permitted under Section 107 or 108 of the 1976 United States Copyright Act, without the prior written permission of the publisher.

For product information and technology assistance, contact us at **Cengage Learning Customer & Sales Support, 1-800-354-9706**

For permission to use material from this text or product, submit all requests online at **www.cengage.com/permissions.** Further permissions questions can be emailed to **permissionrequest@cengage.com.**

Library of Congress Control Number: 2014943332

ISBN-13: 978-1-305-07750-8
ISBN-10: 1-305-07750-4

Cengage Learning
200 First Stamford Place, 4th Floor
Stamford, CT 06902
USA

Cengage Learning is a leading provider of customized learning solutions with office locations around the globe, including Singapore, the United Kingdom, Australia, Mexico, Brazil and Japan. Locate your local office at **international.cengage.com/region.**

Cengage Learning products are represented in Canada by Nelson Education, Ltd.

For your course and learning solutions, visit **www.cengage.com.**

Purchase any of our products at your local college store or at our preferred online store **www.cengagebrain.com.**

Instructors: Please visit **login.cengage.com** and log in to access instructor-specific resources.

Printed in the United States of America.
Print Number: 01   Print Year: 2014

Contents

Preface

This concise version of the eighth edition of *Ethics: Theory and Contemporary Issues* represents an extensive revision of the text and reflects the input of a new co-author. This new edition provides increased coverage of ethical theory in Part I and a thorough introduction to contemporary ethical issues in Part II. As in past editions, each chapter begins with a detailed, accessible introduction. In this, it not only remains a comprehensive introduction to ethics but also continues to emphasize pedagogy through clear summaries, engaging examples, and various study tools—such as review exercises, discussion cases, and the appendix on how to write an ethics paper. Each chapter now begins with a list of learning objectives, and the book now ends with an extensive glossary of key terms.

ADDITIONS AND CHANGES

Although the basic elements remain the same, this edition includes the following additions and changes from the seventh edition. Part I has been revised to include a new chapter on religion and global ethics, as well as increased coverage of naturalistic approaches to ethics and natural law. All introductions in Part II have been updated to incorporate contemporary issues and current affairs. These updates include recent statistics, relevant cases, and contemporary examples.

In this edition there is expanded coverage of the following topics: global (non-Western) philosophy and religion, the prisoner's dilemma and the tragedy of the commons, social justice and economic inequality, mass incarceration and restorative justice, environmental justice, biotechnology and bioengineering, vegetarianism and the ethics of hunting, race and racism, pacifism, gay marriage, and global poverty.

Key Elements

Each chapter of *Ethics: Theory and Contemporary Issues* contains an extended summary of key concepts and issues, written in clear, accessible prose. These detailed summaries go beyond the short introductions found in most ethics anthologies, to provide students with a thorough grounding in the theory and practical application of philosophical ethics.

As noted above, these discussions have been thoroughly updated to include detailed information on current events, statistics, and political and cultural developments.

The theory chapters in Part I present detailed summaries of the theories and major concepts, positions, and arguments. The contemporary issues chapters in Part II include summaries of:

> current social conditions and recent events, with special emphasis on their relevance to students' lives;
> conceptual issues, such as how to define key words and phrases (for example, cloning, terrorism, and distributive justice); and
> arguments and suggested ways to organize an ethical analysis of each topic.

Throughout this text, we seek to engage readers by posing challenging ethical questions and then offering a range of possible answers or explanations. The aim is to present more than one side of each issue so that students can decide for themselves what position they will take. This also allows instructors more latitude to emphasize specific arguments and concepts, and to direct the students' focus as they see fit.

Where possible throughout the text, the relation of ethical theory to the practical issues is indicated. For example, one pervasive distinction used throughout the text is that between consequentialist and nonconsequentialist considerations and arguments. The idea is that if students are able to first situate or categorize a philosophical reason or argument, then they will be better able to evaluate it critically in their thinking and writing. Connections to related concepts and issues in other chapters are also highlighted throughout the text, to help students note similarities and contrasts among various ethical positions.

Pedagogical Aids This text is designed as an accessible, "user-friendly" introduction to ethics. To aid both instructor and student, we have provided the following pedagogical aids:

> a list of learning objectives at the beginning of each chapter (this is new to this edition);
> a real-life event, hypothetical dialogue, or updated empirical data at the beginning of each chapter;
> diagrams, subheadings, boldface key terms and definitions that provide guideposts for readers and organize the summary exposition;
> review exercises at the end of each chapter that can be used for exams and quizzes;
> a glossary of definitions of key terms (this is new to this edition);
> discussion cases that follow each chapter in Part II and provide opportunities for class or group discussion;
> topics and resources for written assignments in the discussion cases; and
> an appendix on how to write an ethics paper, which gives students helpful advice and brief examples of ethics papers.

Online Student and Instructor Resources This text is accompanied by an innovative online resource center that offers animated simulations that give you the opportunity to engage with dilemmas and thought experiments commonly presented in your introduction to ethics class. The resource center also includes Aplia, an interactive learning solution that provides automatically graded assignments with detailed, immediate explanations on every question. You will get immediate feedback on your work (not only what you got right or wrong, but why), and you can choose to see another set of related questions if you want more practice. A searchable eBook (MindTap Reader) is also available inside the resource center, for easy reference, and includes links to a host of assets.

The Instructor's Manual is available online on the password-protected Instructor's Companion Site. It provides useful suggestions for lectures and classroom activities, based directly on the content in this book. Answers to any review exercises or study questions are provided, as well as questions for further thought. Interested instructors can find it by looking up this edition of the book on cengage.com.

IN SUMMARY

We have sought to make this edition of *Ethics: Theory and Contemporary Issues* the most comprehensive ethics text available. It combines theory and issues. It is designed to be flexible, user-friendly, current, pedagogically helpful, and balanced.

> The flexible structure of the text allows instructors to emphasize only those theories and applied ethical topics which best suit their courses.
> The text is user-friendly while at the same time philosophically reliable. It employs pedagogical aids throughout and at the end of each chapter, and provides extensive examples from current events and trends. The exposition challenges students with stimulating questions and is interspersed with useful diagrams, charts, and headings.
> The text provides up-to-date coverage not only of developments in the news and in scientific journals but also on ethical issues as they are discussed in contemporary philosophy.

> *Ethics: Theory and Contemporary Issues* is accompanied by a broad range of online and textual tools that amplify its teachability and give instructors specific pedagogical tools for different learning styles.

ACKNOWLEDGMENTS

We wish to thank the many people who have made valuable suggestions for improving the text, including Nicoleta Apostol, College of DuPage; Amy Beaudry, Quinsigamond Community College; Joanna Crosby, Morgan State University; Michael Emerson, Northwestern Michigan College; Richard Greene, Weber State University; Jeremy Hovda, Minneapolis Community & Technical College; Richard McGowan, Butler University; Robert Milstein, Northwestern College; and Ted Stryk, Roane State Community College.

Barbara MacKinnon especially wants to thank the students in her classes at the University of San Francisco. Over the years they have also contributed greatly to this text by challenging her to keep up with the times and to make things more clear and more interesting. She also appreciates the support of her husband and fellow philosopher, Edward MacKinnon. She dedicates this book to her two wonderful daughters, Jennifer and Kathleen. Andrew Fiala is thankful for Barbara's hard work throughout the previous editions of this book and for the opportunity to transform his classroom teaching experience into a useful text for teaching ethics.

We also wish to acknowledge the many professional people from Cengage Learning and its vendors who have worked on this edition, including Joann Kozyrev–Senior Sponsoring Editor, Debra Matteson–Product Manager, Ian Lague–Development Editor, Lauren MacLachlan–Production Manager, Cathie DiMassa–Senior Content Project Manager, Kristina Mose-Libon–Art Director, and Joshua Duncan–Assistant Editor.

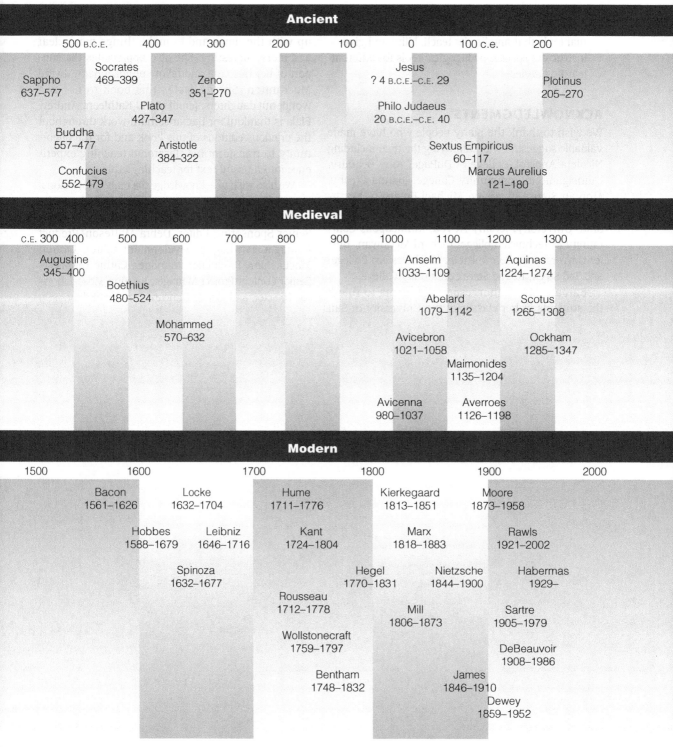

Ancient

| 500 B.C.E. | 400 | 300 | 200 | 100 | 0 | 100 c.e. | 200 |

Sappho
637–577

Socrates
469–399

Zeno
351–270

Jesus
? 4 B.C.E.–C.E. 29

Plotinus
205–270

Plato
427–347

Philo Judaeus
20 B.C.E.–C.E. 40

Buddha
557–477

Aristotle
384–322

Sextus Empiricus
60–117

Confucius
552–479

Marcus Aurelius
121–180

Medieval

| C.E. 300 | 400 | 500 | 600 | 700 | 800 | 900 | 1000 | 1100 | 1200 | 1300 |

Augustine
345–400

Anselm
1033–1109

Aquinas
1224–1274

Boethius
480–524

Abelard
1079–1142

Scotus
1265–1308

Mohammed
570–632

Avicebron
1021–1058

Ockham
1285–1347

Maimonides
1135–1204

Avicenna
980–1037

Averroes
1126–1198

Modern

| 1500 | 1600 | 1700 | 1800 | 1900 | 2000 |

Bacon
1561–1626

Locke
1632–1704

Hume
1711–1776

Kierkegaard
1813–1851

Moore
1873–1958

Hobbes
1588–1679

Leibniz
1646–1716

Kant
1724–1804

Marx
1818–1883

Rawls
1921–2002

Spinoza
1632–1677

Hegel
1770–1831

Nietzsche
1844–1900

Habermas
1929–

Rousseau
1712–1778

Mill
1806–1873

Sartre
1905–1979

Wollstonecraft
1759–1797

DeBeauvoir
1908–1986

Bentham
1748–1832

James
1846–1910

Dewey
1859–1952

Ethics and Ethical Reasoning

Learning Outcomes

After reading this chapter, you should be able to:

- Describe the philosophical study of ethics.
- Understand the difference between normative and descriptive claims.
- Define key terms: intuitionism, emotivism, objectivism, and subjectivism.
- Explain the difference between metaethics and normative ethics.
- Decide whether naturalistic explanations of ethics commit the naturalistic fallacy.
- Differentiate between instrumental and intrinsic values.
- Distinguish consequentialist from non-consequentialist approaches to ethics.
- Use the distinctions among motives, acts, and consequences to analyze ethical phenomena.

© Jack Hollingsworth/Digital Vision/Thinkstock

WHY STUDY ETHICS?

It is clear that we often disagree about questions of value. Should homosexuals be allowed to marry? Should women be permitted to have abortions? Should drugs such as marijuana be legalized? Should we torture terrorists in order to get information from them? Should we eat animals or use them in medical experiments? These sorts of questions are sure to expose divergent ideas about what is right or wrong.

Discussions of these sorts of questions often devolve quite rapidly into name-calling, foot-stomping, and fallacious argumentation. One common fallacy or error in reasoning that occurs in ethical argument is *begging the question* or arguing in a circle. If someone says that abortion should (or should not) be permitted, she needs to explain why this is so. It is not enough to say that abortion should not be permitted because it is wrong or that women should be allowed to choose abortion because it is wrong to limit women's choices. To say that these things are wrong is merely to reiterate that they should not be permitted. Such an answer begs the question. We need further argument and information to know *why* abortion is wrong or *why* limiting free choice is wrong. We need a theory of what is right and wrong, good or evil, justified, permissible, and unjustifiable; and we need to understand how our theory applies in concrete cases. The first half of this text will discuss various theories and concepts that can be used to help us avoid begging the question in debates about ethical issues. The second half of the book looks in detail at a number of these issues.

It is appropriate to wonder, at the outset, why we need to do this. Why isn't it sufficient to simply state your opinion and assert that "x is wrong (or evil, just, permissible, etc.)"? One answer to this question is that such assertions can do nothing to solve the deep conflicts of value that we find in our world. We know that people disagree about abortion, **gay marriage**, animal rights, and other issues. If we are to make progress toward understanding each other, if we are to make progress toward establishing some consensus about these topics, then we have to understand *why* we think certain things are right and other things are wrong. We need to make arguments and give reasons in order to work out our own conclusions about these issues and in order to explain our conclusions to others with whom we disagree.

It is also not sufficient to appeal to custom or authority in deriving our conclusions about moral issues. While it may be appropriate for children to simply obey their parents' decisions, adults should strive for more than conformity and obedience to authority. Sometimes our parents and grandparents are wrong—or they disagree among themselves. Sometimes the law is wrong—or the laws conflict. And sometimes religious authorities are wrong—or

the authorities do not agree. To appeal to authority on moral issues, we would first have to decide which authority is to be trusted and believed. Which religion provides the best set of moral rules? Which set of laws in which country is to be followed? Even within the United States, there is currently a conflict of laws with regard to some of these issues: some states have legalized medical marijuana and gay marriage, and others have not. The world's religions also disagree about a number of issues: for example, the status of women, the permissibility of abortion, and the question of whether war is justifiable. Many of these disagreements are internal to religions, with members of the same religion or denomination disagreeing among themselves. To begin resolving the problem of laws that conflict and religions that disagree, we need critical philosophical inquiry into basic ethical questions. In the next chapter, we discuss the world's diverse religious traditions and ask whether there is a set of common ethical ideas that is shared by these traditions. In this chapter, we clarify what ethics is and how ethical reasoning should proceed.

Member of the international animal rights group PETA demonstrates in a human-sized meat packaging tray.

WHAT IS ETHICS?

On the first day of an ethics class, we often ask students to write one-paragraph answers to the question, "What is ethics?"

How would you answer? Over the years, there have been significant differences of opinion among our students on this issue. Some have argued that ethics is a highly personal thing, a matter of private opinion. Others claim that our values come from family upbringing. Other students think that ethics is a set of social principles, the codes of one's society or particular groups within it, such as medical or legal organizations. Some write that many people get their ethical beliefs from their religion.

One general conclusion can be drawn from these students' comments: We tend to think of ethics as the set of values or principles held by individuals or groups. I have my ethics and you have yours, and groups have sets of values with which they tend to identify. We can think of ethics as the study of the various sets of values that people have. This could be done historically and comparatively, for example, or with a psychological interest in determining how people form their values and when they tend to act on them. We can also think of ethics as a critical enterprise. We would then ask whether any particular set of values or beliefs is better than any other. We would compare and evaluate the sets of values and beliefs, giving reasons for our evaluations. We would ask questions such as, "Are there good reasons for preferring one set of ethics over another?" As we will pursue it in this text, ethics is this latter type of study. We will examine various ethical views and types of reasoning from a critical or evaluative standpoint. This examination will also help us come to a better understanding of our own values and the values of others.

Ethics is a branch of *philosophy*. It is also called *moral philosophy*. In general, philosophy is a discipline or study in which we ask—and attempt to answer—basic questions about key areas or subject matters of human life and about pervasive and significant aspects of experience. Some philosophers, such as Plato and Kant, have tried to do this systematically by interrelating their philosophical views in many areas. According to Alfred North Whitehead, "Philosophy is the endeavor to frame a coherent, logical, necessary system of general ideas in terms of which every element of our experience can be interpreted."[1] Other people believe that philosophers today must work at problems piecemeal, focusing on one particular issue at a time. For instance, some might analyze the meaning of the phrase "to know," while others might work on the morality of lying. Some philosophers are optimistic about our ability to address these problems, while others are more skeptical because they think that the way we analyze the issues and the conclusions we draw will always be influenced by our background, culture, and habitual ways of thinking. Most agree, however, that these problems are worth wondering about and caring about.

We can ask philosophical questions about many subjects. In **aesthetics**, or the philosophy of art, for example, philosophers do not merely interpret a certain novel or painting. Rather, philosophers concerned with aesthetics ask basic or foundational questions about art and objects of beauty: What kinds of things do or should count as art (rocks arranged in a certain way, for example)? What makes something an object of aesthetic interest its emotional expressiveness, its peculiar formal nature, or its ability to show us certain truths that cannot be described? In the philosophy of science, philosophers ask not about the structure or composition of some chemical or biological material, but about such matters as whether scientific knowledge gives us a picture of reality as it is, whether progress exists in science, and whether it is meaningful to talk about the scientific method. Philosophers of law seek to understand the nature of law itself, the source of its authority, the nature of legal interpretation, and the basis of legal responsibility. In the philosophy of knowledge, called **epistemology**, we try to answer questions about what we can know of ourselves and our world, and what it means to know something rather than just to believe it. In each area, philosophers ask basic questions about the particular subject matter. This is also true of moral philosophy.

> Ethics, or moral philosophy, asks basic questions about the good life, about what is better and worse, about whether there is any objective right and wrong, and how we know it if there is.

One objective of ethics is to help us decide what is good or bad, better or worse, either in some general way or with regard to particular ethical issues. This is generally called **normative ethics**. Normative ethics defends a thesis about what is good, right, or just. Normative ethics can be distinguished from **metaethics**. Metaethical inquiry asks questions about the nature of ethics, including the meaning of ethical terms and judgments. Questions about the relation between philosophical ethics and religion—as we discuss in Chapter 2—are metaethical. Theoretical questions about ethical relativism—as discussed in Chapter 3—also belong most properly to metaethics. The other chapters in Part I are more properly designated as ethical theory. These chapters present concrete normative theories; they make claims about what is good or evil, just or unjust.

From the mid-1930s until recently, metaethics predominated in English-speaking universities. In doing metaethics, we often analyze the meaning of ethical language. Instead of asking whether the death penalty is morally justified, we would ask what we meant in calling something "morally justified" or "good" or "right." We analyze ethical language, ethical terms, and ethical statements to determine what they mean. In doing this, we function at a level removed from that implied by our definition. It is for this reason that we call this other type of ethics *metaethics—meta* meaning "beyond." Some of the discussions in this chapter are metaethical discussions—for example, the analysis of various senses of "good." As you will see, much can be learned from such discussions.

ETHICAL AND OTHER TYPES OF EVALUATION

"That's great!" "Now, this is what I call a delicious meal!" "That play was wonderful!" All these statements express approval of something. They do not tell us much about the meal or the play, but they do imply that the speaker thought they were good. These are evaluative statements. Ethical statements or judgments are also *evaluative*. They tell us what the speaker believes is good or bad. They do not simply *describe* the object of the judgment—for example, as an action that occurred at a certain time or that affected people in a certain way. They go further and express a positive or negative regard for it. However, factual matters are often relevant to our moral evaluations. For example, factual judgments about whether capital punishment has a deterrent effect might be quite relevant to our moral judgments about it. So also would we want to know the facts about whether violence can ever bring about peace; this would help us judge the morality of war and terrorism. Because ethical judgments often rely on such *empirical* or experientially based information, ethics is often indebted to other disciplines such as sociology, psychology, and history. Thus, we can distinguish between empirical or **descriptive claims**, which state factual beliefs, and evaluative judgments, which state whether such facts are good or bad, just or unjust, right or wrong. Evaluative judgments are also called **normative judgments**. Moral judgments are evaluative because they "place a value," negative or positive, on some action or practice, such as capital punishment.

> Descriptive (empirical) judgment: Capital punishment acts (or does not act) as a deterrent.
> Normative (moral) judgment: Capital punishment is justifiable (or unjustifiable).

We also evaluate people, saying that a person is good or evil, just or unjust. Because these evaluations also rely on beliefs in general about what is good or right—in other words, on norms or standards of good and bad or right and wrong—they are also normative. For example, the judgment that people ought to give their informed consent to participate as research subjects may rely on beliefs about the value of human autonomy. In this case, autonomy functions as a norm by which we judge the practice of using people as subjects of research. Thus, ethics of this sort is **normative**, both because it is evaluative and not simply descriptive, and because it grounds its judgments in certain norms or values.

"That is a good knife" is an evaluative or normative statement. However, it does not mean that the knife is morally good. In making ethical judgments, we use terms such as *good, bad, right, wrong, obligatory*, and *permissible*. We talk about what we ought or ought not to do. These are evaluative terms. *But*

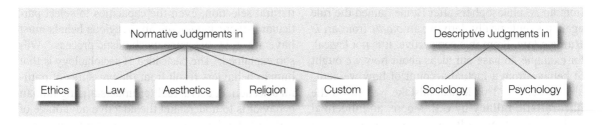

not all evaluations are moral in nature. We speak of a good knife without attributing moral goodness to it. In so describing the knife, we are probably referring to its practical usefulness for cutting or for impressing others. People tell us that we ought to pay this amount in taxes or stop at that corner before crossing because that is what the law requires. We read that two styles ought not to be worn or placed together because such a combination is distasteful. Here someone is making an aesthetic judgment. Religious leaders tell members of their communities what they ought to do because it is required by their religious beliefs. We may say that in some countries people ought to bow before the elders or use eating utensils in a certain way. This is a matter of custom. These various normative or evaluative judgments appeal to practical, legal, aesthetic, religious, or customary norms for their justification.

How do other types of normative judgments differ from moral judgments? Some philosophers believe that it is a characteristic of moral "oughts" in particular that they override other "oughts," such as aesthetic ones. In other words, if we must choose between what is aesthetically pleasing and what is morally right, then we ought to do what is morally right. In this way, morality may also take precedence over the law and custom. The doctrine of civil disobedience relies on this belief, because it holds that we may disobey certain laws for moral reasons. Although moral evaluations are different from other normative evaluations, this is not to say that there is no relation between them. In fact, moral reasons often form the basis for certain laws. But law—at least in the United States—results from a variety of political compromises. We don't tend to look to the law for moral guidance. And we are reluctant to think that we can "legislate morality" as the saying goes. Of course, there is still an open debate about whether the law should enforce moral ideas in the context of issues such as gay marriage or abortion.

There may be moral reasons supporting legal arrangements—considerations of basic justice, for example. Furthermore, the fit or harmony between forms and colors that ground some aesthetic judgments may be similar to the rightness or moral fit between certain actions and certain situations or beings. Moreover, in some ethical systems, actions are judged morally by their practical usefulness for producing valued ends. For now, however, note that ethics is not the only area in which we make normative judgments. Whether the artistic worth of an art object ought to be in any way judged by its moral value or influence is another interesting question.

SOCIOBIOLOGY AND THE NATURALISTIC FALLACY

The distinction between descriptive and normative claims is a central issue for thinking about ethics. Philosophers have long been aware that we tend to confuse these issues in our ordinary thinking about things. Many people are inclined to say that if something is natural to us, then we ought to do it. For example, one might argue that since eating meat is natural for us, we ought to eat meat. But vegetarians will disagree. Another example is used by the eighteenth-century philosopher David Hume, who noticed that incest appears to be quite natural—animals do it all the time. But human beings condemn incest. It is thus not true that what is natural is always good. But people often make the mistake of confusing facts of nature and value judgments. Most of the time, we are not attentive to the shift from facts to values, the shift from *is* to *ought*. Hume pointed out the problem of deriving an *ought* from an *is*; philosophers after Hume named the rule against simplistically deriving an *ought* from an *is* **Hume's law**. From this perspective, it is not logical, for example, to base our ideas about how we ought to behave from a factual account of how we actually do behave. This logical mistake was called the **naturalistic fallacy** by G.E. Moore, an influential philosopher of the early twentieth century. Moore maintained that moral terms such as *good* are names for non-empirical properties that cannot be reduced to some other natural thing. Moore claimed that to attempt to define *good* in terms of some mundane or natural thing such as pleasure is to commit a version of this fallacy. The problem is that we can ask whether pleasures are actually good. Just because we desire pleasure does not mean that it is good to desire pleasure. As Moore suggested, there is always an open question about whether what is natural is also good.

Now not everyone agrees that naturalism in ethics is fallacious. There are a variety of naturalistic approaches to thinking about ethics. One traditional approach to ethics is called natural law ethics (which we discuss in detail in a subsequent chapter). Natural law ethics focuses on human nature and derives ethical precepts from an account of what is natural for humans. Natural law ethicists may argue, for example, that human body parts have natural functions and that by understanding these natural functions, we can figure out certain moral ideas about sexuality or reproduction. Opponents might argue that this commits the naturalistic fallacy, since there is no obvious moral content to be seen in the structure and function of our body parts.

A more recent version of naturalism in ethics focuses on evolutionary biology and cognitive science. From this perspective, to understand morality, we need to understand the basic functions of our species, including the evolutionary reasons behind moral behavior. We also need to understand how our brains function in order to explain how pleasure works, why some people are psychopathic, and why we struggle to balance egoistic and altruistic motivations. One version of this naturalism is known as **sociobiology**—an idea that was introduced by the biologist E.O. Wilson.[2] "If the brain evolved by natural selection, even the capacities to select particular esthetic judgments and religious beliefs must have arisen by the same mechanistic process," Wilson explained.[3] The basic idea of sociobiology is that human behaviors result from the pressures of natural selection. A useful tool for understanding human behavior is to understand the adaptive advantage of certain behaviors. We can study this by comparing human behaviors with the behavior of other social animals—from insects to chimpanzees.

Sociobiology attempts to understand altruism, for example, in terms of evolutionary processes. From this perspective, altruistic concern develops through natural selection because altruistic animals will help each other survive. Biologist Richard Dawkins explains a related idea in terms of "the selfish gene." Dawkins's idea is that our genes use our altruistic and other behaviors to spread themselves. Thus, when we cooperate within groups that share a genetic endowment, we help to preserve the group and help to disseminate our shared genetic characteristics, often in competition with rival genetic groups.[4]

In discussing sociobiology and interpreting biological evidence, we must be careful, however, not to anthropomorphize.[5] The problem is that when we look at the natural world, we often interpret it in anthropomorphic terms, seeing in animals and even in genes themselves the motivations and interests that human beings have. In other words, we must be careful that our value judgments do not cloud or confuse our description of the facts.

While the naturalistic approach of sociobiology is provocative and insightful, we might still worry that it commits the naturalistic fallacy. Just because altruistic behavior is natural and useful in the evolutionary struggle for survival does not mean that it is good, just, or right. To see this, let us return to Hume's example of incest. Incest might be useful as a method for disseminating our genetic material—so long as the negative problems associated with inbreeding are minimized. We do inbreed animals in this way in order to select for desirable traits. But it is still appropriate to ask whether incest is morally permissible for human beings—the question of *ought* might not be settled by what *is*.

ETHICAL TERMS

You might have wondered what the difference is between calling something "right" and calling it "good." Consider the ethical meaning for these terms. Right and wrong usually apply to actions, as in "You did the right thing," or "That is the wrong thing to do." These terms prescribe things for us to do or not to do. On the other hand, when we say that something is morally good, we are not explicitly recommending doing it. However, we do recommend that it be positively regarded. Thus, we say things such as "Peace is good, and distress is bad." It is also interesting that with "right" and "wrong" there seems to be no in-between; it is either one or the other. However, with "good" and "bad" there is room for degrees, and some things are thought to be better or worse than others.

We also use other ethical terms when we engage in moral evaluation and judgment. For example, we sometimes say that something "ought" or "ought not" to be done. There is the sense here of urgency. Thus, of these things we may talk in terms of an obligation to do or not do something. It is something about which there is morally no choice. We can refrain from doing what we ought to do, but the obligation is still there. On the other hand, there are certain actions that we think are permissible but that we are not obligated to do. Thus, one may think that there is no obligation to help someone in trouble, though it is "morally permissible" (i.e., not wrong) to do so and even "praiseworthy" to do so in some cases. Somewhat more specific ethical terms include *just* and *unjust* and *virtuous* and *vicious*.

To a certain extent, which set of terms we use depends on the particular overall ethical viewpoint or theory we adopt. This will become clearer as we discuss and analyze the various ethical theories in this first part of the text.

ETHICS AND REASONS

When we evaluate an action as right or wrong or some condition as good or bad, we appeal to certain norms or reasons. Suppose, for example, I say that affirmative action is unjustified. I should give reasons for this conclusion; it will not be acceptable for me to respond that this is just the way I feel. If I have some intuitive negative response to **preferential treatment** forms of affirmative action, then I will be expected to delve deeper to determine whether there are reasons for this attitude. Perhaps I have experienced the bad results of such programs. Or I may believe that giving preference in hiring or school admissions on the basis of race or sex is unfair. In either case, I also will be expected to push the matter further and explain *why* it is unfair or even what constitutes fairness and unfairness.

To be required to give reasons to justify one's moral conclusions is essential to the moral enterprise and to doing ethics. However, this does not mean that making ethical judgments is and must be purely rational. We might be tempted to think that good moral judgments require us to be objective and not let our feelings, or emotions, enter into our decision-making. Yet this assumes that feelings always get in the way of making good judgments. Sometimes this is surely true, as when we are overcome by anger, jealousy, or fear and cannot think clearly. Biases and prejudice may stem from such strong feelings. We think prejudice is wrong because it prevents us from judging rightly. But emotions can often aid good decision-making. We may, for example, simply feel the injustice of a certain situation or the wrongness of someone's suffering. Furthermore, our caring about some issue or person may, in fact, direct us to more carefully examine the ethical issues involved. However, some explanation of why we hold a certain moral position is still required. Simply to say "X is just wrong," without explanation, or to merely express strong feelings or convictions about "X" is not sufficient.

INTUITIONISM, EMOTIVISM, SUBJECTIVISM, OBJECTIVISM

Philosophers differ on how they know what is good. They also differ on the question of whether our moral judgments refer to something objective to us or are simple reports of subjective opinions and dispositions.

To say that something is good is often thought to be different from saying that something is yellow or heavy. The latter two qualities are empirical, known by our senses. However, good or goodness is held to be a non-empirical property, said by some to be knowable through intuition. A position known as **intuitionism** claims that our ideas about ethics rest upon some sort of intuitive knowledge of ethical truths. This view is associated with G.E. Moore, whom we discussed above.[6] Another philosopher, W.D. Ross, thinks that we have a variety of "crystal-clear intuitions" about basic values. These intuitions are clear and distinct beliefs about ethics, which Ross explains using an analogy with mathematics: just as we see or intuit the self-evident truth of "2 + 2 = 4," we also see or intuit the truth of ethical truths such as that we have a duty to keep our promises. As Ross explains,

> Both in mathematics and in ethics we have certain crystal-clear intuitions from which we build up all that we can know about the nature of numbers and the nature of duty … we do not read off our knowledge of particular branches of duty from a single ideal of the good life, but build up our ideal of the good life from intuitions into the particular branches of duty.[7]

A very important question is whether our intuitions point toward some objective moral facts in the world or whether they are reports of something subjective. A significant problem for intuitionism is that people's moral intuitions seem to differ. Unlike the crystal-clear intuitions of mathematics—which are shared by all of us—the intuitions of ethics are not apparently shared by all of us.

Another view, sometimes called **emotivism**, maintains that when we say something is good, we are showing our approval of it and recommending it to others rather than describing it. This view is associated with the work of twentieth-century philosophers such as A.J. Ayer and C.L. Stevenson. But it has deeper roots in a theory of the moral sentiments, such as we find in eighteenth-century philosophers Adam Smith and David Hume. Hume maintains, for example, that reason is "the slave of the passions," by which he means that the ends or goals we pursue are determined by our emotions, passions, and sentiments. Adam Smith maintains that human beings are motivated by the experience of pity, compassion, and sympathy for other human beings. For Smith, ethics develops out of natural sympathy toward one another, experienced by social beings like ourselves.

Emotivism offers an explanation of moral knowledge that is subjective, with moral judgments resting upon subjective experience. One version of emotivism makes ethical judgments akin to expressions of approval or disapproval. In this view, to say "murder is wrong" is to express something like "murder—yuck!" Similarly, to say "courageous self-sacrifice is good" is to express something like "self-sacrifice—yeah!" One contemporary author, Leon Kass, whom we study in a later chapter, argues that there is wisdom in our experiences of disgust and repugnance—that our emotional reactions to things reveal deep moral insight. Kass focuses especially on the "yuck factor" that many feel about advanced biotechnologies such as cloning.

One worry, however, is that our emotions and feelings of sympathy or disgust are variable and relative. Not only do our own emotional responses vary depending upon our moods but these responses vary among and between individuals. We will discuss **relativism** in more detail later, but the problem is that these emotional responses are relative to culture and even to the subjective dispositions of individuals. Indeed, our own feelings change over time and are not reliable or sufficient gauges of what is going on in the external world. The worry here is that our emotions merely express our internal or subjective responses to things and that they do not connect us to some objective and stable source of value.

Other moral theories aim for more objective sources for morality. From this standpoint, there must be objective reasons that ground our subjective and emotional responses to things. Instead of saying that the things we desire are good, an **objectivist** about ethics will argue that we ought to desire things that are good—with an emphasis on the goodness of the thing-in-itself apart from our subjective responses. The ancient Greek philosopher Plato was an objectivist in this sense. Objectivists hold that values have an objective reality—that they are objects available for knowledge—as opposed to **subjectivists**, who claim that value judgments are merely the expression of subjective opinion. Plato argues that there is some concept or idea called "the Good" and that we can compare our subjective moral opinions about morality with this objective standard.

Those who want to ground morality in God are objectivists, as are those who defend some form of natural law ethics, which focuses on essential or objective features of bodies and their functions. Interestingly, the approach of sociobiology tends not to be objectivist in this sense. Although the sociobiologist bases her study of morality on objective facts in the world, the sociobiologist does not think that moral judgments represent moral facts. Instead, as Michael Ruse puts it,

> Objective ethics, in the sense of something written on tablets of stone (or engraven on God's heart) external to us, has to go. The only reasonable thing that we, as sociobiologists, can say is that morality is something biology makes us believe in, so that we will further our evolutionary ends.[8]

One of the issues introduced in Ruse's rejection of objectivity in ethics is the distinction between **intrinsic** and **instrumental** goods. Instrumental goods are things that are useful as instruments or tools—we use them and value them as a means toward some other end. Intrinsic goods are things that have value in themselves or for their own sake. For example, we might say that life is an intrinsic good—it is just fundamentally valuable. But food is an instrumental good because it is a means or tool that is used to support life. From Ruse's perspective, morality itself is merely an instrumental good that is used by evolution for other purposes. Morality is, from this perspective, simply a tool that helps the human species to survive. According to Hume's law, there is no higher value that can be derived from the factual description of how morality is developed by evolutionary forces. The selfish gene hypothesis of Richard Dawkins understands individual human beings instrumentally, as carriers of genetic information: "We are survival machines—robot vehicles blindly programmed to serve the selfish molecules known as genes."[9] This conception of human beings runs counter to our usual moral view, which holds that human beings have intrinsic or inherent value. The idea that some things have intrinsic value is an idea that is common to a variety of approaches that claim that ethics is objective. The intrinsic value of a thing is supposed to be an objective fact about

that thing, which has no relation to our subjective response to that thing. Claims about intrinsic value show up in arguments about **human rights** and about the environment. Do human beings or ecosystems or species have intrinsic value, or is the value of these things contained within our subjective responses and in their instrumental uses? This question shows us that the metaethical theories are connected to important practical issues.

ETHICAL REASONING AND ARGUMENTS

It is important to know how to reason well in thinking or speaking about ethical matters. This is helpful not only in trying to determine what to think about controversial ethical matters but also in arguing for something you believe is right and in critically evaluating positions held by others.

The Structure of Ethical Reasoning and Argument

To be able to reason well in ethics you need to understand something about ethical arguments and argumentation, not in the sense of understanding why people get into arguments but rather in the sense of what constitutes a good argument. We can do this by looking at an argument's basic structure. This is the structure not only of ethical arguments about what is good or right but also of arguments about what is the case or what is true.

Suppose you are standing on the shore and a person in the water calls out for help. Should you try to rescue that person? You may or may not be able to swim. You may or may not be sure you could rescue the person. In this case, however, there is no time for reasoning, as you would have to act promptly. On the other hand, if this were an imaginary case, you would have to think through the reasons for and against trying to rescue the person. You might conclude that if you could actually rescue the person you ought to try to do it. Your reasoning might go as follows:

> Every human life is valuable.
> Whatever has a good chance of saving such a life should be attempted.
> My swimming out to rescue this person has a good chance of saving his life.
> Therefore, I ought to do so.

Or you might conclude that you could not save this person, and your reasoning might go like this:

> Every human life is valuable.
> Whatever has a good chance of saving such a life should be attempted.
> In this case, there is no chance of saving this life because I cannot swim.
> Thus, I am not obligated to try to save him (although, if others are around who can help, I might be obligated to try to get them to help).

Some structure like this is implicit in any ethical argument, although some are longer and more complex chains than the simple form given here. One can recognize the reasons in an argument by their introduction through key words such as *since*, *because*, and *given that*. The conclusion often contains terms such as *thus* and *therefore*. The reasons supporting the conclusion are called **premises**. In a sound argument, the premises are true and the conclusion follows from them. In the case above, then, we want to know whether you can save this person and also whether his life is valuable. We also need to know whether the conclusion actually follows from the premises. In the case of the examples given above, it does. If you say you ought to do what will save a life and you can do it, then you ought to do it. However, there may be other principles that would need to be brought into the argument, such as whether and why one is always obligated to save someone else's life when one can.

To know under what conditions a conclusion actually follows from the premises, we would need to analyze arguments in much greater detail than we can do here. Suffice it to say, however, that the connection is a logical connection—in other words, it must make rational sense. You can improve your ability to reason well in ethics first by being able to pick out the reasons and the conclusion in an argument. Only then can you subject them to critical examination in ways we suggest below.

Evaluating and Making Good Arguments

Ethical reasoning can be done well or done poorly. Ethical arguments can be constructed well or constructed poorly. A good argument is a **sound argument**. It has a **valid** form in which the conclusion actually follows from the premises, and the premises or reasons given for the conclusion are true. An argument is poorly constructed when it is fallacious or when the reasons on which it is based are not true or are uncertain. This latter matter is of particular significance with ethical argumentation because an ethical argument always involves some claim about values—for example, that saving a life is good. These value-based claims must be established through some theory of values. The rest of Part I of this book examines different theories that help establish basic values.

Ethical arguments also involve conceptual and factual matters. Conceptual matters are those that relate to the meaning of terms or concepts. For example, in a case of lying, we would want to know what lying actually is. Must it be verbal? Must one have an intent to deceive? What is deceit itself? Other conceptual issues central to ethical arguments may involve questions such as, "What constitutes a 'person'?" (in arguments over abortion, for example) and "What is 'cruel and unusual punishment'?" (in death penalty arguments, for example). Sometimes, differences of opinion about an ethical issue are a matter of differences not in values but in the meaning of the terms used.

Ethical arguments often also rely on factual claims. In our example, we might want to know whether it was actually true that you could save the drowning person. In arguments about the death penalty, we may want to know whether such punishment is a deterrent. In such a case, we need to know what scientific studies have found and whether the studies themselves were well grounded. To have adequate factual grounding, we will want to seek out a range of reliable sources of information and be open-minded. Each chapter in Part II of this book begins with or includes factual material that may be relevant to ethical decisions on the particular issue being treated.

It is important to be clear about the distinction between facts and values. It is especially helpful when dealing with moral conflict and disagreement. We need to ask whether we disagree about the values involved, about the concepts and terms we are employing, or about the facts connected to the case.

Those who analyze good reasoning have categorized various ways in which reasoning can go wrong or be fallacious. One of the most familiar examples of this is called the **ad hominem** fallacy. In this fallacy, people say something like, "That can't be right because just look who is saying it." They look at the source of the opinion rather than the reasons given for it. Another fallacy is called **begging the question** or **circular argument**. Such reasoning draws on the argument's conclusion to support its premises, as in "Lying in this case is wrong because lying is always wrong." You can find out more about these and other fallacies from almost any textbook in logic or critical thinking.

You also can improve your understanding of ethical arguments by making note of a particular type of reasoning that is often used in ethics: **arguments from analogy**. In this type of argument, one compares familiar examples with the issue being disputed. If the two cases are similar in relevant ways, then whatever one concludes about the first familiar case one should also conclude about the disputed case. Thus, in a famous use of analogy by Judith Jarvis Thomson, one is asked whether it would be ethically acceptable to "unplug" a famous violinist who had been attached to you and your kidneys to save his life. She argues that if you say, as she thinks you should, that you are justified in unplugging the violinist and letting him die, then a pregnant woman is also justified in doing the same with regard to her fetus. The reader is prompted to critically examine such an argument by asking whether or not the two cases were similar in relevant ways—that is, whether the analogy fits.

Finally, we should note that giving reasons to *justify* a conclusion is also not the same as giving an *explanation* for why one believes something. One might explain that she does not support euthanasia because that was the way she was brought up or that she is opposed to the death penalty because she cannot stand to see someone die. To justify such beliefs, one would need rather to give reasons that show not why one does, in fact, believe something but why one should believe it. Nor are rationalizations justifying reasons. They are usually reasons given after the fact that are not one's true reasons. *Rationalizations* are usually excuses, used to explain away bad behavior. These false reasons are given to make us look better to others or ourselves. To argue well about ethical matters, we need to examine and give reasons that support the conclusions we draw.

ETHICAL THEORY

Good reasoning in ethics usually involves either implicit or explicit reference to an ethical theory. An *ethical theory* is a systematic exposition of a particular view about what is the nature and basis of good or right. The theory provides reasons or norms for judging acts to be right or wrong and attempts to give a justification for these norms. It provides ethical principles or guidelines that embody certain values. These can be used to decide in particular cases what action should be chosen and carried out. We can diagram the relationship between ethical theories and moral decision-making as follows.

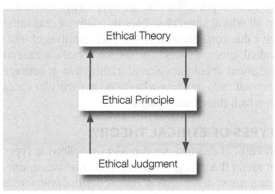

We can think of the diagram as a ladder. In practice, we can start at the ladder's top or bottom. At the top, at the level of theory, we can start by clarifying for ourselves what we think are basic ethical values. We then move downward to the level of principles generated from the theory. The next step is to apply these principles to concrete cases. We can also start at the bottom of the ladder, facing a particular ethical choice or dilemma. We can work our way back up the ladder, thinking through the principles and theories that implicitly guide our concrete decisions. Ultimately and ideally, we come to a basic justification, or the elements of what would be an ethical theory. If we look at the actual practice of thinking people as they develop their ethical views over time, the movement is probably in both directions. We use concrete cases to reform our basic ethical views, and we use the basic ethical views to throw light on concrete cases.

An example of this movement in both directions would be if we start with the belief that pleasure is the ultimate value and then find that applying this value in practice leads us to do things that are contrary to common moral sense or that are repugnant to us and others. We may then be forced to look again and possibly alter our views about the moral significance of pleasure. Or we may change our views about the rightness or wrongness of some particular act or practice on the basis of our theoretical reflections. Obviously, this sketch of moral reasoning is quite simplified. Moreover, feminists and others have criticized this model of ethical reasoning, partly because it shows ethics to be governed by general principles that are supposedly applicable to all ethical situations. Does this form of reasoning give due consideration to the particularities of individual, concrete cases? Can we really make a general judgment about the value of truthfulness or courage that will help us know what to do in particular cases in which these issues play a role?

TYPES OF ETHICAL THEORY

In Part I of this text, we consider the following types of moral theory: *egoism* and *contractarianism*, *utilitarianism*, *deontological ethics*, *natural law*, *virtue ethics*, and *feminist ethics*. These theories represent different approaches to doing ethics. Some differ in terms of what they say we should look at in making moral judgments about actions or practices. For example, does it matter morally that I tried to do the right thing or that I had a good motive? Surely it must make some moral difference, we think. But suppose that in acting with good motives I violate someone's rights. Does this make the action a bad action? We would probably be inclined to say yes. Suppose, however, that in violating someone's rights I am able to bring about a great good. Does this justify the violation of rights? Some theories judge actions in terms of their motive, some in terms of the character or nature of the act itself, and others in terms of the consequences of the actions or practices.

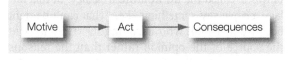

We often appeal to one of these types of reason. Take a situation in which I lie to a person, Jim. We can make the following judgments about this action. Note the different types of reasons given for the judgments.

> That was good because you intended to make Jim happy by telling him a white lie—or it was bad because you meant to deceive him and do him harm. (Motive)
> That was good because it is good to make people happy—or it was bad because it is always wrong to tell a lie. (Act)
> That was good because it helped Jim develop his self-esteem—or it was bad because it caused Jim to believe things about himself that were not true. (Consequences)

Although we generally think that a person's motive is relevant to the overall moral judgment about his or her action, we tend to think that it reflects primarily on our moral evaluation of *the person*. We also have good reasons to think that the results of actions matter morally. Those theories that base moral judgments on consequences are called **consequentialist** or sometimes **teleological** moral theories (from the Greek root *telos*, meaning "goal" or "end"). Those theories that hold that actions can be right or wrong regardless of their consequences are called **nonconsequentialist** or **deontological** theories (from the Greek root *deon*, meaning "duty").

One moral theory we will examine is *utilitarianism*. It provides us with an example of a consequentialist moral theory in which we judge whether an action is better than alternatives by its actual or expected results or consequences; actions are then judged in terms of the promotion of human happiness. Kant's moral theory, which we will also examine, provides us with an example of a nonconsequentialist theory, according to which acts are judged right or wrong independently of their consequences; in particular, acts are judged by whether they conform to requirements of rationality and human dignity. The other ethical theories that we will examine stress human nature as the source of what is right and wrong. Some elements of these theories are deontological and some teleological. So, also, some teleological theories are consequentialist in that they advise us to produce some good. But if the good is an ideal, such as virtue or self-realization, then such theories differ from consequentialist theories such as utilitarianism.[10] As anyone who has tried to put some order to the many ethical theories knows, no theory completely and easily fits one classification, even those given here. Feminist theories of care provide yet another way of determining what one ought to do (see Chapter 9). In Part II of this text, we will examine several concrete ethical issues. As we do so, we will note how various ethical theories analyze the problems from different perspectives and sometimes reach different conclusions about what is morally right or wrong, better or worse.

CAN ETHICS BE TAUGHT?

It would be interesting to know just why some college and university programs require their students to take a course in ethics. Does this requirement stem from a belief that a course in ethics or moral philosophy can actually make people good?

On the question of whether ethics can be taught, students have given a variety of answers. "If it can't be taught, then why are we taking this class?" one wondered. "Look at the behavior of certain corporate executives who have been found guilty of criminal conduct. They surely haven't learned proper ethical values," another responded. Still others disagreed. Although certain ideals or types of knowledge can be taught, ethical behavior cannot because it is a matter of individual choice, they said.

The ancient Greek philosopher Plato thought that ethics could be taught. He argues that "All evil is ignorance." In other words, the only reason we do what is wrong is because we do not know or believe it is wrong. If we come to believe that something is right, however, it should then follow that we will necessarily do it. Now, we are free to disagree

with Plato by appealing to our own experience. If I know that I should not have that second piece of pie, does this mean that I will not eat it? Ever? Plato might attempt to convince us that he is right by examining or clarifying what he means by the phrase "to know." If we were really convinced with our whole heart and mind that something is wrong, then we might be highly likely (if not determined) not to do it. However, whether ethics courses should attempt to convince students of such things is surely debatable.

Another aspect of the problem of teaching ethics concerns the problem of motivation. If one knows something to be the right thing to do, does there still remain the question of why we should do it? One way to teach ethics to youngsters, at least, and in the sense of motivating them, may be to show them that it is in their own best interest to do the right thing.

With regard to teaching or taking a course in ethics, most, if not all, moral philosophers think that ethics, or a course on ethics, should do several other things. It should help students understand the nature of an ethical problem and help them think critically about ethical matters by providing certain conceptual tools and skills. It should enable them to form and critically analyze ethical arguments. It is up to the individual, however, to use these skills to reason about ethical matters. A study of ethics should also lead students to respect opposing views because it requires them to analyze carefully the arguments that support views contrary to their own. It also provides opportunities to consider the reasonableness of at least some viewpoints that they may not have considered.

In this opening chapter, we have questioned the value of ethics and learned something about what ethics is and how it is different from other disciplines. We have considered a few metaethical issues. We have provided a description of ethical reasoning and arguments and have examined briefly the nature of ethical theories and principles and the role they play in ethical reasoning. We will examine these theories more carefully in the chapters to come, and we will see how they might help us analyze and come to conclusions about particular ethical issues.

NOTES

1. Alfred North Whitehead, *Process and Reality* (New York: Macmillan, 1929), 4.
2. E.O. Wilson, *Sociobiology: The New Synthesis* (Cambridge, MA: Harvard University Press, 1975).
3. E.O. Wilson, *On Human Nature* (Cambridge, MA: Harvard University Press, 1978), 2.
4. See Richard Dawkins, *The Selfish Gene* (Oxford: Oxford University Press, 1989).
5. See Frans de Waal, *Good Natured: The Origins of Right and Wrong in Humans and Other Animals* (Cambridge, MA: Harvard University Press, 1996). Also see Morton Hunt, *The Compassionate Beast: What Science is Discovering about the Human Side of Humankind* (New York: William Morrow, 1990).
6. G. E. Moore, *Principia Ethics* (Buffalo, NY: Prometheus, 1903).
7. W.D. Ross, *Foundations of Ethics* (Oxford: Clarendon Press, 1939), 144–45.
8. Michael Ruse, *Sociobiology: Sense or Nonsense?* (New York: Springer, 1985), 237.
9. Richard Dawkins, *The Selfish Gene*, 30th Anniversary Edition (Oxford: Oxford University Press, 2006), xxi.
10. I thank reviewer J. E. Chesher for this distinction.

REVIEW EXERCISES

1. Determine whether the following statements about the nature of ethics are true or false. Explain your answers.
   a. Ethics is the study of why people act in certain ways.
   b. The solution to moral conflicts and ethical disputes is to accurately describe the way the world actually is.
   c. The statement "Most people believe that cheating is wrong" is an ethical evaluation of cheating.
2. Label the following statements as either *normative* (N) or *descriptive* (D). If normative, label each as *ethics* (E), *aesthetics* (A), *law* (L), *religion* (R), or *custom* (C).
   a. One ought to respect one's elders because it is one of God's commandments.
   b. Twice as many people today, as compared to ten years ago, believe that the death penalty is morally justified in some cases.
   c. It would be wrong to put an antique chair in a modern room.
   d. People do not always do what they believe to be right.
   e. I ought not to turn left here because the sign says "No Left Turn."
   f. We ought to adopt a universal health insurance policy because everyone has a right to health care.
3. Discuss the differences between the ideas that ethics is subjective and that it is objective.
4. Explain emotivism and intuitionism in ethical theory.
5. Discuss the advantages and disadvantages of using naturalistic explanations in ethics.
6. As they occur in the following statements, label the reasons for the conclusion as appeals to the *motive* (M), the *act* (A), or the *consequences* (C).
   a. Although you intended well, what you did was bad because it caused more harm than good.
   b. We ought always to tell the truth to others because they have a right to know the truth.
   c. Although it did turn out badly, you did not want that, and thus you should not be judged harshly for what you caused.

Religion and Global Ethics

2

Learning Outcomes

After reading this chapter, you should be able to:

- Describe the challenge of developing a global ethical perspective.
- Understand the idea of universal human rights.
- Explain the meaning of key terms: cosmopolitan, civil disobedience, pluralism, secularism, humanism, Eurocentrism.

- Evaluate the divine command theory of ethics.
- Differentiate between humanistic and religious approaches to ethics.
- Defend your own ideas about ethics, religion, and global cultural diversity.

© iStockPhoto.com/Scott Hailstone

We live in an increasingly integrated world. With the click of the mouse, you can instantly interact with people from a variety of cultures and religions. It is inspiring to see how well we human beings get along despite our differences. But we should also admit that diversity—especially religious diversity—can create tension and difficulty.

In the summer of 2012, a video titled "The Innocence of Muslims," which mocked and condemned the Islamic religion, was put up on YouTube. Muslims around the world soon reacted to this video with protests, rallies, and occasional violence. The violence peaked on September 11, when terrorists in Benghazi, Libya, murdered the American ambassador there, Christopher Stevens. Although later reports indicated that the Benghazi attack was planned as a response to the anniversary of the September 11, 2001, terrorist attacks, the world was focused on the question of the anti-Islamic video. U.S. President Barack Obama delivered an address at the United Nations on September 25, 2012, in which he defended the principle of freedom of expression.

> The United States government had nothing to do with this video, and I believe its message must be rejected by all who respect our common humanity. It is an insult not only to Muslims, but to America as well—for as the city outside these walls makes clear, we are a country that has welcomed people of every race and every faith. We are home to Muslims who worship across our country. We not only respect the freedom of religion, we have laws that protect individuals from being harmed because of how they look or what they believe.[1]

In response to Obama's speech, leaders from the Muslim world gave speeches at the United Nations that called for restrictions on the freedom to criticize religion. Egypt's president stated, "Insults against the prophet of Islam, Muhammad, are not acceptable. We will not allow anyone to do this by word or by deed." Yemen's president said, "These behaviors find people who defend them under the justification of the freedom of expression. These people overlook the fact that there should be limits for the freedom of expression, especially if such freedom blasphemes the beliefs of nations and defames their figures." Pakistan's president said, "The international community must not become silent observers and should criminalize such acts that destroy the peace of the world and endanger world security by misusing freedom of expression."[2]

It is remarkable that this discussion of freedom of religion took place at the General Assembly of the United Nations, a body whose founding after World War II was dedicated to the goals of world peace, harmony, and understanding. In 1948, the UN's member nations ratified the Universal Declaration of Human Rights, which lays out a set of basic moral principles. The nations of the world are supposed to share these principles despite our vast cultural, religious, and political differences. One important symbol of the hope of cross-cultural agreement about basic values is the United Nations' Universal Declaration of Human Rights. The preamble to the UN Declaration begins by affirming the "inherent dignity" and "inalienable rights" of all members of the human family. It explains that disregard for these rights has resulted in barbarous acts that outrage the moral conscience of mankind. It continues, "the advent of a world in which human beings shall enjoy freedom of speech and belief and freedom from fear and want has been proclaimed as the highest aspiration of the common people." It goes on to state that the purpose of the United Nations is to promote universal respect for human rights and fundamental freedoms.[3]

The UN Declaration aims for global agreement about basic rights, the inherent dignity of human beings, and equal rights for men and women, with the broader goals of fostering world peace and harmony. As the dispute over the "Innocence of Muslims" video demonstrates, however, there are

U.S. President Barack Obama addressing the United Nations in September 2012.

Jason Szenes/EPA/Newscom

outstanding disagreements about the nature of these basic rights. The UN document asserts the importance of freedom of speech and freedom of religion. Article 18 of the UN Declaration explicitly states, "Everyone has the right to freedom of thought, conscience and religion; this right includes freedom to change his religion or belief, and freedom, either alone or in community with others and in public or private, to manifest his religion or belief in teaching, practice, worship and observance."

But does freedom of speech run up against a limit when such speech defames important religious figures or when such speech advocates for practices and social arrangements that are viewed by religious people as immoral? In some parts of the world, freedom of religion is viewed as leading to apostasy and blasphemy, which is a punishable offense. In previous centuries, Christians burned witches and heretics alive. And today, according to some interpretations of Islam, blasphemy and apostasy are punishable by death. An Egyptian court sentenced the creators of the "Innocence of Muslims" to death in November 2012. Another famous example of this is the *fatwa*, or religious decree, announced by the Iranian cleric and supreme leader Ayatollah Ruhollah Khomeini, which called for the death of novelist Salman Rushdie in 1989 for writing a novel the Ayatollah considered blasphemous. This fatwa was renewed in 2012, as a further response to the anti-Islamic film discussed above. The Ayatollah Hasan Sanei added a $500,000 inducement to the price on Rushdie's head, bringing the bounty on Rushdie's life to $3.3 million.[4]

These examples suggest a serious clash of values, with the basic idea of freedom of expression running up against rigid religious convictions. Lest we think that this is only a problem for Muslims, it is important to note that American Christians are not always tolerant of different religious viewpoints. Consider the perspective of Dennis Terry, a Christian pastor in Louisiana who introduced presidential candidate Rick Santorum, with the following words:

> This nation was founded as a Christian nation … there's only one God and his name is Jesus.… Listen to me, if you don't love America, and you don't like the way we do things, I have one thing to say: Get Out! We don't worship Buddha, we don't worship Mohammed, we don't worship Allah, we worship God, we worship God's son Jesus Christ.[5]

While many Americans would disagree with Pastor Terry, religious differences continue to be flashpoints for conflict. From some religious perspectives, the basic ideas of toleration and freedom of religion may be seen as immoral. It might be that the ideas we find in the First Amendment to the American Constitution or in the UN Declaration only make sense within the context of Western secular democracies. Are these values shared by people who adhere to Buddhism, Confucianism, or Islam? Are these values shared by Christians such as Pastor Terry?

This points to the important question of how ethics relates to religion. While recent events continue to bring these matters to the forefront, there are deep historical precedents for this discussion. It is important to recall that Socrates—the father of the Western philosophical tradition—ran into trouble with the religious and political authorities of Athens. Socrates

Protestors in Pakistan in 2012 respond to the anti-Islam movie, "Innocence of Muslims."

© Musa Farman/EPA/Newscom

asked people how they defined moral terms, trying to understand ideas such as justice, courage, love, and friendship. But his philosophical inquiries were tinged with skepticism. He questioned traditional religion, traditional political authority, and conventional wisdom. He called himself a "gadfly," by which he meant that he buzzed around Athens, nipping at and probing things. He believed that his effort would help Athenians understand morality and help to make them virtuous. Many Athenians found Socrates to be offensive and even immoral. Some viewed him as a dangerously subversive figure. Eventually he was brought to court and formally charged with not believing in the gods of the city and with corrupting its youth. Many suspected him of being an atheist. As a result, he was sentenced to death.

FREEDOM, COSMOPOLITANISM, AND THE EUROPEAN ENLIGHTENMENT

The story of Socrates demonstrates the inherently controversial nature of philosophical inquiry and the complicated relationship between philosophy and religion. If it is difficult for us to imagine how Socrates could have been sentenced to death for asking questions about Athenian morality and religion, that is because we are used to extensive freedom when it comes to religion and morality. Americans like to believe that our freedom is unique—a product of a distinctly Western tradition of tolerance and pluralism. However, we should be careful when making sweeping generalizations about history. There have been many tolerant and open-minded epochs in the history of the world. The Buddhist emperor Ashoka is known for sponsoring a tolerant regime, as is the Muslim emperor Akbar. And under Confucianism, China was tolerant toward a variety of religious perspectives. We forget that China proclaimed an "Edict of Toleration" in 1692, which permitted Christian missionary work—at around the same time that Protestants were still being persecuted in Europe. Indeed, at the time, the philosopher Leibniz and other Europeans praised China and Confucianism for its open and tolerant spirit. As the economist and philosopher Amartya Sen explains,

> The claim that the basic ideas underlying freedom and tolerance have been central to Western culture over the millennia and are somehow alien to Asia is, I believe, entirely rejectable. The allegedly sharp contrast between Western and Asian traditions on the subject of freedom and tolerance is based upon very poor history.[6]

World history includes a number of free thinkers—both within the lineage that follows after Socrates and in others of the world's traditions. Nonetheless, much of our terminology for understanding these sorts of issues is rooted in Western thinking. The terms *philosophy*, *politics*, and *ethics* come to us from the Greek language. And we still tend to tell a Eurocentric or Western-focused story about the development of tolerance, liberty, and individual rights.

That standard story often begins with Socrates, his trial and execution, and the development of his ideas by his student, Plato, and Plato's student, Aristotle—both of whom will be discussed in greater detail below. But we might also begin with one of Socrates's other followers, Diogenes the Cynic. Diogenes was a free spirit who refused to conform to social conventions and had an antagonistic relationship with the authorities of his time. One ancient legend explains that when Alexander the Great was a young man, about to embark on his conquest of the ancient world, he went to see Diogenes, who was lounging in the sun. After demanding that the young prince stop blocking his sunbath, Diogenes asked Alexander what he was up to. Alexander explained that he was about to depart with his armies to conquer the world. Diogenes asked, "Then what?" and Alexander said that he supposed he would relax after that. Diogenes said, "Why not sit in the sun with me now and relax, and save yourself all of the trouble?" When the astonished Alexander asked Diogenes where he was from, Diogenes replied, "I am a citizen of the world" or a "cosmopolitan."

In this anecdote, Diogenes displays skepticism toward conventional authority, while asserting his freedom and claiming independence from any particular nation or culture—values that we have come to associate with the Western philosophical approach. This approach is often seen to emphasize individual freedoms over traditional hierarchies and universal morality over local customs and traditions. Like Diogenes, it makes a **cosmopolitan** claim—for a single moral community of humanity not bound by national, cultural, or, in many cases, religious traditions. And it questions many things we take for granted. Why do we salute superiors? Why do we drive on the right? Why do we eat with knives and forks? Or, for that matter, why do we adopt certain religious beliefs and practices rather than others? Is it simply a matter of where and to whom we were born?

While it is true that there are a variety of differences across the globe, including vast religious differences, the cosmopolitan perspective holds that certain ethical principles are universally valuable, such as respect for life and for liberty. In the Western world, we have institutionalized these ideas in the laws of the modern nation state. And a growing body of international law, including the UN Declaration, emphasizes a set of basic ideas about individual liberties and human rights.

Although we've noted above that toleration and freedom are not uniquely Western values, the usual historical account emphasizes the development of these values during the seventeenth and eighteenth centuries in Europe. This era is known as the **Enlightenment.** It is the period during which many of the philosophers we'll discuss in the book were active: Locke, Hume, Kant, Bentham, and others. These philosophers tended to think that liberty and tolerance were key values. They were optimistic that history was developing in a progressive direction. They thought that progress would occur through the employment of human reason. And they were interested in discovering common values and learning from other cultures. Also during this time, many philosophical ideas were put into practice in revolutionary politics, as was the case in the American and French revolutions.

The American Revolution can be seen to begin with a famous phrase from the Declaration of Independence: "We hold these truths to be self-evident, that all men are created equal, that they are endowed by their Creator with certain unalienable Rights, that among these are Life, Liberty and the pursuit of Happiness." Drawing on the natural law tradition as developed by John Locke (see Chapter 7), the Declaration enshrines individual liberties at the core of American society. The Constitution of the United States goes further, detailing areas of individual liberty upon which government must not intrude. The most important example, for our purposes, is the First Amendment to the Constitution, which reads, "Congress shall make no law respecting an establishment of religion, or prohibiting the free exercise thereof; or abridging the freedom of speech, or of the press; or the right of the people peaceably to assemble, and to petition the Government for a redress of grievances." The First Amendment makes religious liberty the law of the land (in the so-called "free exercise" clause), while also prohibiting government from getting involved in religion (in the so-called "establishment clause"). The American system can thus be seen to explicitly reject the kind of society that executed Socrates, where an "established" state religion allowed the authorities to punish (by death) speech perceived to be blasphemous. We've come a long way from ancient Athens.

It should not be surprising that philosophers emphasize individual liberty. Philosophical speculation involves wide-ranging inquiry into an ever-expanding set of topics. We cannot philosophize properly unless we are free to question, argue, and think. Nor is it surprising that philosophical reflection on morality points in a cosmopolitan direction. When Jefferson claims that "all men are created equal," he implies that inalienable rights—of life, liberty, and the pursuit of happiness—are the endowment of all people, from all cultures.

But a quick glance at world history or today's paper makes it clear that no such consensus exists. For a long time, even in the United States, there was a substantial disagreement about whether all men really were created equal, with slavery and racism as an obvious problem. And even after slavery was abolished, we continued to disagree about the status of women. In the global context, these issues are far from resolved.

Philosophical freedom can lead to conflicts with authority, especially religious authorities. At around the same time that the American revolutionaries were fighting in the name of liberty, the German philosopher Immanuel Kant defined enlightenment in terms of freedom. He thought that progress would occur when we were permitted freedom to argue and when we were courageous enough to use this freedom to imagine ways to improve society. Kant wrote,

> Enlightenment is man's emergence from his self-incurred immaturity. Immaturity is the inability to use one's own understanding without the guidance of another. This immaturity is self-incurred if its cause is not lack of understanding, but lack of resolution and courage to use it without the guidance of another. The motto of enlightenment is therefore: *Sapere Aude!* (dare to know) "Have courage to use your own understanding!"[7]

Kant thought that history would develop in a cosmopolitan direction, with European nations forming a confederation based upon shared moral ideas. This federation—an idea that foreshadowed the development of the United Nations—would ensure perpetual peace. It would take two long centuries of war and misery for Europe and the rest of the world to finally achieve Kant's idea. And the idea still seems a bit naive, given remaining cultural and religious differences across the globe.

RELIGION, CIVIC LIFE, AND CIVIL DISOBEDIENCE

Like Socrates, Kant advocated gradual reform through public argument about morality, politics, and religion. This philosophical approach can seem naive when faced with entrenched and powerful unjust systems, such as slavery, serfdom, colonialism, and apartheid. What if the rulers simply have no interest in listening to the ruled?

After Kant, a variety of thinkers and activists—from Henry David Thoreau to Mohandas K. Gandhi to Martin Luther King Jr.—concluded that principled resistance to an unjust system required something more than argument. Rather than advocate the violent overthrow of the regime, these thinkers called for **civil disobedience**, the open, nonviolent refusal to obey unjust law, with the intent of accepting the penalty and arousing the conscience of the community as a whole. King developed his ideas about nonviolent civil disobedience from Gandhi, the Indian political activist and religious leader who advocated **ahimsa** (or nonviolence) as a key to the struggle for Indian independence. King also drew inspiration from Jesus and from Socrates. As Martin Luther King argues in his "Letter from Birmingham Jail,"

> Just as Socrates felt that it was necessary to create a tension in the mind so that individuals could rise from the bondage of myths and half truths to the unfettered realm of creative analysis and objective appraisal, so must we see the need for nonviolent gadflies to create the kind of tension in society that will help men rise from the dark depths of prejudice and racism to the majestic heights of understanding and brotherhood.[8]

The "tension in the mind" that King refers to is a product of philosophical reflection, focused here on the injustices of institutionalized segregation and racism of the 1960s America. King appears to inherit the Enlightenment dream, by which individuals and societies strive to achieve moral maturity through rational inquiry. Like Socrates, King expresses faith in logical questioning of accepted dogmas as a means of overcoming injustice. And like Kant, King also sees his efforts in explicitly cosmopolitan terms, famously declaring that "Injustice anywhere is a threat to justice everywhere."[9]

But while King and other advocates of civil disobedience seek to criticize existing traditions and institutions, they also demonstrate that one need not reject those traditions and institutions in order to scrutinize them. Thus, King saw his reasoned criticism of unjust laws as "expressing the very highest respect for law"[10] and considered ethical critique as a means of helping America realize the full promise of its founding documents.

This last point is particularly important to bear in mind as we consider the relationship between philosophical inquiry and religious traditions and institutions. Sometimes, it might seem that the most serious impediment to free-ranging philosophical criticism is religion—especially those forms of religious belief that want to limit freedom in the name of conformity to the will of God. With regard to morality, it is often thought that what is required is obedience to God's commandments, his laws, his prophets, and the institutions that have developed to defend and disseminate the faith. (We will hear more about this view of morality in the next section.) And

Martin Luther King Jr., in his Atlanta office, standing in front of a portrait of Mohandas K. Gandhi.

it may seem that philosophy has nothing to offer a faith-centered worldview, that it has no interest in the sacred and views human life in exclusively secular terms. (A recent survey of nearly 1,000 philosophers indicates that 15 percent of the philosophers surveyed accept or lean toward *theism* [belief in the existence of god or gods], while 73 percent accept or lean toward atheism.[11])

But such a stark opposition between philosophy and religion ignores the fact that for most of human history, the two subjects have been deeply intertwined or even indistinguishable. Both are concerned with the most fundamental questions of human existence: Why are we here? What is the meaning of life? How should we treat one another? And both have frequently challenged ruling powers and conventional ways of thinking. The example of Martin Luther King is a case in point; King was a devout Baptist minister who also thought that philosophical critique was necessary to make moral progress. King drew his primary inspiration from Jesus's teachings on poverty, tolerance, and love. King also valued Socrates's example. It is not necessarily true that philosophical ethics is atheistic or opposed to religious belief. The philosophers mentioned here—Socrates, Locke, and Kant—remained committed to some form of theistic belief.

Religion remains at the center of many of the applied ethical topics that we will discuss later in this text: same-sex marriage, euthanasia, abortion, the status of women, and the death penalty, to name a few. Religious perspectives on such topics are not easy to categorize as "liberal" or "conservative." Religion is not one thing. There are a variety of sects and denominations, just as there are a variety of religious people who belong to these sects and denominations. And this reminds us of the importance of religious liberty. Religious liberty along with the freedom of philosophical inquiry is essential in a world that includes a wide variety of people who disagree about religious, political, and moral questions.

ETHICS, RELIGION, AND DIVINE COMMAND THEORY

Many people get their ethical or moral views from their religion. Although religions include other elements, most do have explicit or implicit requirements or ideals for moral conduct. In some cases, they contain explicit rules or commandments: "Honor thy father and mother" and "Thou shalt not kill." Some religions recognize and revere saints or holy people who provide models for us and exemplify virtues we should emulate. And most religions have a long history of internal arguments and interpretations about the nature and content of moral law.

Most contemporary philosophers, however, believe that ethics does not necessarily require a religious grounding. Rather than relying on holy books or religious revelations, philosophical ethics uses reason and experience to determine what is good and bad, right and wrong, better and worse. In fact, even those people for whom morality is religiously based may want to examine some of their views using reason. They may want to examine various interpretations of their religious principles for internal consistency or coherence. Or they may want to know whether elements of their religious morality—some of its rules, for example—are good or valid ones given that other people have different views of what is right and wrong, and given that the problems of contemporary times may be different from those of the past.

If moral right and wrong can be grounded only in religious belief, then nonbelievers could not be said to have moral views or make legitimate moral arguments. But even religious believers should want to be able to engage in constructive dialogue with nonbelievers and evaluate their claims. In fact, even religious believers regularly make moral judgments that are not based strictly on their religious views but rather on reflection and common sense.

Thinking further about religious morality also raises challenges for it. A key element of many religious moralities is the view that certain things are good for us to do because this is what God wants. This conception is often referred to as the **divine command theory**. The idea is that certain actions are right because they are what God wills for us. Plato's dialogue *Euthyphro* examines this view. In this dialogue, Socrates asks whether things are good because they are approved by the gods or whether the gods approve of them because they are good. To say that actions are good just because they are willed or approved by the gods or God seems to make morality arbitrary. God could decree anything to be good—lying or treachery, for example. It seems more reasonable to say that lying and treachery are bad, and for this reason the gods or God condemns or disapproves of them, so we should also. One implication of this view is that morality has a certain independence; if so, we should be able to determine whether certain actions are right or wrong in themselves and for what reason.

This argument does not imply, however, that religion cannot provide a motivation or inspiration to be moral. Many believe that if life has some eternal significance in relation to a supreme and most perfect being, then we ought to take life and morality extremely seriously. This is not to say that the only reason religious persons have for being moral or doing the morally right thing is so that they will be rewarded in some life beyond this one. Such a view might be seen to undermine morality, since it suggests that we should be good only if we are "bribed" to do so. Rather, if something is morally right, then this is itself a reason for doing it. Thus, the good and conscientious person is the one who wants to do right just because it is right.

Questions about the meaning of life, however, often play a significant role in a person's thoughts about the moral life. Some people might even think that atheists have no reason to be moral or to be concerned with doing the morally right thing. However, this is not necessarily so. For example, a religious person may be inclined to disregard the moral stakes of what occurs in this life if he or she thinks of it as fleeting and less important than the afterlife. And an atheist who believes that this life is all there is may in fact take this life more seriously and care more about living morally. Furthermore, the religious as well as the nonreligious live in contemporary society and have pressing practical reasons to think clearly and reason well about morality.

For at least three reasons, we should all seek to develop our moral reasoning skills. First, we should be able to evaluate critically our own or others' views of what is thought to be good and bad or just and unjust, including religious views. Second, believers of various denominations as well as nonbelievers ought to be able to discuss moral matters

together. Third, the fact that many of us live in organized secular communities, cities, states, and countries requires that we be able to develop and rely on widely shared reason-based views on issues of justice, fairness, and moral ideals. This is especially true in political communities with some separation of church and state, where no religion can be mandated, and where one has freedom within limits to practice a chosen religion or practice no religion at all. In these settings, it is important to have nonreligiously based ways of dealing with moral issues. This is one goal of philosophical ethics.

The Russian novelist Fyodor Dostoevsky provides the kernel of one argument that is often used in defense of divine command ethics. Dostoevsky's writings contain the famous claim that, "If God is dead, then everything is permissible."[12] This expresses the worry that if there were no God then there would be no morality. There are two concerns here: one about religion as the source of morality and another about religion as providing a motivation for morality. The first concern is that without God as a source for morality, there would be no eternal, absolute, or objective basis for morality. We will deal with the first worry in more detail in Chapter 3 when we consider *relativism*—which is the claim that there are no eternal, absolute, or objective values. Theists often hold that God is the source of moral law, provided through the words of a prophet, such as Moses, who receives the moral law directly from God. Some theists worry that if that prophetic origin of morality is denied, we are left without any objective moral principles. Most of the rest of the first half of this book focuses on providing an account of values that avoids this criticism; the ethical theories we will study try to provide reasons and justifications for ethical principles without reference to God.

The second concern is that without a divine judge who gives out punishments and rewards in the afterlife, there would be no motivation to be ethical. A version of this concern led Kant to postulate God and immortality as necessary for morality—so that we might at least hope that moral actions would be rewarded (and immoral actions would be punished) in an afterlife. In response, atheists might argue that the demands, rewards, and punishments of human social life are sufficient to provide motivation to be ethical. We turn to the issue of motivation in our discussion of egoism in Chapter 4. In that chapter, we consider a story from Plato about Gyges, a man who can literally get away with murder. If you were able to do whatever you wanted, without fear of getting caught, would you commit immoral deeds? Or do you think that we need some idea of a God who observes our deeds and punishes us or rewards us accordingly?

One of the most important problems for defenders of divine command ethics is the fact of religious diversity. Even if we agree with Dostoevsky that God is required for ethics, we still have to figure out which God or religious story is the one that provides the correct teaching about morality. Saying that ethics is based in religion does not really help us that much because we must also determine which religion is the correct one. Given the incredible amount of religious diversity in the world, it is easy to see that the divine command approach is not really very helpful without a much broader inquiry into the truth of various religions.

The problem of diversity holds even within specific religious traditions. This problem was recognized at the time of Socrates and Plato. Plato asks us to consider which versions of the Greek religious stories are the correct or proper ones. Although no religion currently professes faith in the Greek myths, the same consideration applies to contemporary religions. Not only do we have to determine which religion is correct, we also have to determine which version of this religion is the correct one. Consider, for example, that Christianity includes a range of denominations: Eastern Orthodox, Roman Catholic, and Protestant (which includes a range of groups from Mennonites and Quakers to Methodists, Presbyterians, and Southern Baptists). Similar diversity can be found within Islam, Judaism, and the religious traditions that come out of South Asia. Even if we think that ethics comes from God, how can we decide which account of God's commands is the correct one? The philosophical approach reminds us that we would have to use reason and experience—including especially our own human insight into ethics—to decide among the world's religious traditions.

PLURALISM AND THE GOLDEN RULE

One approach to resolving the problem of diversity is to look for common ground among the world's cultural and religious traditions. This general idea is known as **religious pluralism**. A more specific philosophical view is often called **value pluralism**, which argues that there are multiple and conflicting goods in the world, which cannot be reduced to some other good. (We will discuss pluralism again when we deal with relativism in Chapter 3.) Pluralists about religion often make a different sort of argument. Religious pluralists, such as John Hick, claim that there is a common core of ideas found among the world's religious traditions. As Hick puts it, quoting the Islamic poet Rumi, "the lamps are many, but the light is one."[13]

The usual candidate for this common core among religions is something like the **Golden Rule:** "Do unto others as you would have them do unto you" or "treat others as you would like to be treated." Many people have claimed that each of the world's religious and cultural systems includes something like the Golden Rule. John Hick argues that, "all the great traditions teach the moral ideal of generous goodwill, love, compassion, epitomized in the Golden Rule."[14] The Tibetan Buddhist leader, the Dalai Lama, put it this way: "All of the different religious faiths, despite their philosophical differences, have a similar objective. Every religion emphasizes human improvement, love, respect for others, sharing other people's suffering. On these lines every religion has more or less the same viewpoint and the same goal."[15] A similar idea has inspired a number of people, including Mohandas K. Gandhi, a well-known defender of religious pluralism. The religious pluralist idea is a friendly and optimistic one; it hopes to be able to reconcile the world's religious traditions around an ethical core.

Unfortunately, this hopeful reconciliation must ignore much; the very deep differences that exist among religions, the fact of apparently immoral elements in some of the world's religious traditions, the reality of religious conflict, and the moral importance of our deep differences over metaphysical questions. As religion scholar Stephen Prothero suggests, the idea that all religions are basically the same "is a lovely sentiment but it is dangerous, disrespectful, and untrue."[16]

Consider for example, the Hindu idea of *dharma*, which is a complex concept that refers to laws of natural order, justice, propriety, and harmony. The idea of *dharma* is connected to the traditional Indian caste system. Now there are parallels between the idea of destiny and caste in India and medieval Christian ideas about natural law and the great chain of being. But the differences between these ideas are as important as the similarities. The end goal of Hindu ethics is to attain some form of self-realization and connection with the eternal soul of *Brahman*. While this may sound like the kind of insight and beatification (or holiness) that occurs in Christian unity with God, the differences are again quite important. Other differences and similarities exist among the world's traditions. For example, Islam emphasizes *zakat* or alms-giving as one of its five pillars. This includes a universal duty to build a just society, help the poor, and eliminate oppression. While this sounds quite a bit like the idea of charity and tithing in the Christian tradition, *zakat* may be more important and more obligatory than mere charity—more close to a tax than a gift. And so on. The differences are as important and pervasive as the similarities among the world's traditions.

Now the pluralists want to reduce all of these differences to something like love, compassion, and the Golden Rule. But it is easy to see that religious ethics is not simply about love and compassion. If all the world's religions agree about compassion, love, and the Golden Rule, then how do we explain holy wars and religious violence? If all religions are basically variations on the theme of love and compassion, then how do we explain religious texts and ideas that are not very compassionate? Would a purely compassionate and loving God destroy the earth with a flood, threaten punishment in Hell, or require gruesome tests of faith? Would compassionate and loving religious believers stone adulterers and homosexuals and burn witches alive? While interpreters of religion can explain these things in various ways, the specific details of religious ethics matter as much as the general principle of compassion or love.

THE PROBLEM OF EVIL AND FREE WILL

A further ethical question arises in the context of thinking about religion and ethics: the **problem of evil**. This issue provides a concrete example of the problem of religious diversity, since different religions will deal with the problem of evil in different ways. How do we explain the presence of suffering and evil in the world? Buddhists explain that life is characterized by suffering or *dukha*. They explain that suffering comes from attachment to the fleeting goods of this world and from wrongful actions. Christians also struggle with the problem of evil. But for Christians, the existence of evil creates a metaphysical problem. How can evil exist in a world that is supposedly created by a benevolent and all-powerful God? The Christian tradition developed elaborate **theodicies**, or arguments that attempt to justify God as all-powerful and all-knowing, despite the problem of evil. Important thinkers such as Saint Augustine and Leibniz responded to this problem by focusing on sin and on freedom of the will. For Augustine, **original sin** is passed down from Adam to the rest of us. Leibniz clarifies that God provided us with free will so that we might choose between good and evil, and he argues that the best of all possible worlds is one that contains both freedom and the related possibility of evil.

Humanistic philosophers have subjected these sorts of disputes to skeptical criticism. How do we know that all life is suffering and that suffering is caused by attachment? How do we know that there is a God, that this God created freedom, and that original sin is passed down? The metaphysical complexities introduced by religion point toward mysteries and paradoxes that give humanistic philosophers reasons to be skeptical.

Even leaving God out of the picture, it remains an open question, for example, as to whether we possess the sort of free will that is presumed in these accounts of evil. We should note that free will is crucially important for ethics, since free choice is typically correlated with responsibility. Unless we have the freedom to choose between good and evil, it is not clear that we are responsible for our actions—in which case, the enterprise of moral philosophy begins to seem shaky. As the well-known atheist author Sam Harris explains,

> Morality, law, politics, religion, public policy, intimate relationships, feelings of guilt and personal accomplishment—most of what is distinctly human about our lives seems to depend upon our viewing one another as autonomous persons, capable of free choice.… Without free will, sinners and criminals would be nothing more than poorly calibrated clockwork, and any conception of justice that emphasized punishment (rather than deterring, rehabilitating, or merely containing them) would appear utterly incongruous.[17]

Despite this admission, Harris denies the idea of free will—based upon natural scientific account of human beings—while still arguing that morality makes sense. Philosophers have pondered the problem of free will for millennia. Some deny that there is free will in an entirely deterministic universe. Others have argued that free will remains compatible with determinism.

Free will is a puzzle even within Christianity, where there are questions about how much freedom we can have in a universe that is created by an omnipotent (all-powerful) and omniscient (all-knowing) God. Different Christian denominations have different ideas about this issue, with some emphasizing the idea of predestination, by which God ordains things in advance, and others responding to this issue differently. Other religions have responded to the problem of free will in a variety of ways. Buddhists and Hindus, for example, appear to believe in free will—although there are differences within these vast and complex traditions. But Buddhists, at least, do not believe in a God who punishes evil. Rather, they believe that suffering results from the laws of *karma,* the law of continuity between causes and effects: bad deeds lead to suffering and good ones lead to reward—whether in this life or the next. Whether the idea of karma is compatible with free will is an open question. The Confucian and Taoist traditions also maintain that human beings have the freedom to choose. But Confucianism holds that such free choices are constrained by destiny or fate, while the Taoists emphasize freedom experienced in harmony with nature. In the Chinese traditions, there is, again, no God who judges or punishes.

As noted, the idea of religious pluralism focuses on the ethical "core" of the world's religions. But it is difficult to see how such radically different ideas could converge. As Stephen Prothero acknowledges, "the world's religious traditions do share many ethical precepts.… The Golden Rule can be found not only in the Christian Bible and the Jewish Talmud but also in Confucian and Hindu books."[18] But the Golden Rule is a very weak common link. Philosophers have also subjected the Golden Rule to criticism. One problem for the Golden Rule is that if it tells us to love our neighbors as ourselves, we need a definition of "neighbors." Does this mean we should love only those who are related to us—our co-religionists, for example? Or do we have obligations to distant human beings and future generations who do not live in our geographic (or temporal) neighborhood? Even if we all accept the Golden Rule as a basic moral starting point, there are still very difficult questions of application. How does the Golden Rule apply to sexual ethics, abortion, euthanasia, or the death penalty? And what does the Golden Rule tell us to do about evil? Should we punish evil-doers? Or should we follow Jesus, who explained that in addition to loving our neighbors, we should love our enemies and refrain from returning evil for evil? The problem of responding to wrongdoing and evil is a complex moral issue, one that is subject to multiple interpretations even within specific religious traditions. Different traditions—even different sects and denominations within the same tradition—give divergent answers about these applied ethical issues, including the very deep question of where evil comes from and how we should deal with it.

We will see that the normative theories defended by philosophers also suffer from a similar problem: they appear to conflict and can be applied in various ways. But the conflicts among the different theories in philosophical ethics may be easier to reconcile, since philosophical arguments are usually not subject to the same ambiguities of interpretation and translation that tend to plague ancient scriptural sources.

It may be possible to imagine a pluralistic convergence of the world's religions around certain key moral principles and central human values. However, until this convergence occurs, we will have to find some way to coexist despite our differences. The challenge of coexistence is exacerbated by our growing diversity. As more and different religious people come to share our common life, we have to find some set of values that can allow us to live together even though we disagree about religion.

SECULAR ETHICS AND TOLERATION

The effort to find ways to coexist despite our religious differences gives rise to **secular ethics**. *Secular* is an adjective that means "based in this world or this age" (as opposed to the eternal and other-worldly focus of religion). When we say that an ethical idea or theory is secular, we mean that it is divorced from any source in religion. A secular ethic can develop out of religious conflict, as members of different religious groups agree to coexist despite their differences. Indeed, this is how the secular system that we currently have in the Western world developed through the course of several centuries of religious wars beginning with the Protestant Reformation. By the end of the seventeenth century, European philosophers of the Enlightenment era were arguing that public **toleration** of religious diversity was necessary. A hallmark of secularism is the idea of freedom of religion and toleration of religious diversity. For many, the progress of **secularization** is a central aspect of modernization: as cultures and polities modernize, they also become more secular. One recent study concludes that secularization "suggests a trend, a general tendency toward a world in which religion matters less and various forms of secular reason and secular institutions matter more. It is a trend that has been expected at least since modernity and has been given quasi-scientific status in sociological studies advancing a secularization thesis."[19] While this same study presents a somewhat critical perspective on the secularization thesis, the idea does help to explain much of recent history, including the spread of secular cosmopolitan ideas such as those we find in the UN document discussed at the outset of this chapter. Of course, in some parts of the world

(even in some parts of the United States), religious fundamentalism—whether it be Christian, Muslim, Jewish, Hindu, etc.—still remains a potent force, with some religious leaders arguing for the subordination of women, arguing against scientific naturalism, and trying to defend traditional ideas from previous centuries.

One of the most important philosophical sources for thinking about secularism is John Locke, who is discussed in greater detail in Chapter 7. In the 1680s, Locke published his influential "Letter Concerning Toleration," which has served as an important touchstone. Locke argues that the state should tolerate religious dissenters. For Locke, religious belief must be a matter of inward persuasion, which is not amenable to the use of force. Locke's basic point is that force is simply not effective to produce genuine religious belief. If that's the case, then political efforts to establish conformity of belief by the use of coercion will ultimately be ineffective. Locke goes on to argue that spiritual and civil authorities must operate in wholly different spheres—the former through persuasion and conversion and the latter through laws backed by coercive force. Religions are to be left alone to deal with spiritual issues. And the state is supposed to focus only on issues related to public order. This argument forms the basis of the constitutional doctrine that is often called "separation of church and state."

Locke's ideas had a significant impact on Jefferson and the other founders of the United States—and they have gone on to influence ethical and political thought, including the ideas found in the UN Declaration of Human Rights. The question of toleration and religion has also been taken up by a number of important philosophers. The great American political philosopher John Rawls has argued that societies need to work to develop "overlapping consensus" among people who adhere to divergent religious and moral worldviews. He calls these deeply held worldviews "comprehensive doctrines." According to Rawls, societies should focus on agreement in the political realm, instead of trying to force a deeper agreement about these comprehensive moral and religious ideas. This leads to a theory of political justice that Rawls calls "political liberalism," as well as a basic conception of human rights that emphasizes toleration for religious diversity. Rawls describes the problem of political liberalism as follows:

> The problem of political liberalism is: How is it possible that there may exist over time a stable and just society of free and equal citizens profoundly divided by reasonable religious, philosophical, and moral doctrines? This is a problem of political justice, not a problem about the highest good. For the moderns the good was known in their religion; with their profound divisions, the essential conditions of a viable and just society were not.[20]

The point here is that while religion describes "the highest good," we've got to find a means of peaceful coexistence in a viable and just society among people who disagree about the highest good. Rawls's solution is to suggest that there can be "overlapping consensus" among people who disagree about religion. This overlapping consensus about political issues would leave us with something like a secular ethic: a system of values and fair rules that can be agreed upon by people who come from quite different religious traditions or by people who have no religion at all. (Rawls's influential theory of justice is discussed in greater detail in Chapters 4 and 14.)

In contrast to Rawls's view, there are some who have a more radical understanding of the term *secular* that equates it with atheism. Some religious people denounce "secular humanism" as nothing more than atheism. One of the most influential proponents of the idea of secular humanism, Paul Kurtz, has worked hard to clarify that secular humanism can remain open to religious believers, even though it is grounded in a nonreligious approach to ethics. Kurtz has recently focused on what he calls "neo-humanism," which is an attempt to reconcile atheists and religious believers around a global ethics. Kurtz's "Neo-Humanist Manifesto" states, "The challenge facing humankind is to recognize the basic ethical principle of planetary civilization—that every person on the planet has equal dignity and value as a person, and this transcends the limits of national, ethnic, religious, racial, or linguistic boundaries or identities."[21] Kurtz's idea hearkens back to the Enlightenment ideal of a cosmopolitan world grounded in shared ethical values.

CRITICISMS OF SECULARISM AND GLOBAL ETHICS

The dream of global consensus around secular principles may seem like an appealing solution to centuries of violent conflict and contention over religion. But it remains an open question as to whether this is possible. One significant problem is that some religious people reject any taint of secularism on doctrinal grounds. For religious believers who think that God requires absolute obedience to his commandments, or that those commandments must be embodied in the laws of the state, a secular ethic that does not explicitly embrace God as the source of morality will appear to be morally suspect and blasphemous.

Such responses can present advocates of tolerance with a problem called the **paradox of toleration**. The paradox revolves around the question of whether there is a good reason to tolerate those who are intolerant or those who reject the very idea of toleration. Some defenders of toleration simply bite the bullet here and admit that there are limits to toleration. Locke, for example, did not extend toleration to atheists or to Catholics. He thought atheists were untrustworthy since they did not believe in God, and he thought that Catholics were too loyal to Rome to be trusted. Although Locke defended toleration, he clearly thought that there were some people who could not be tolerated. We've come a long way since the time of Locke. But the rise of new fundamentalist movements within such religions as Judaism, Christianity, and Islam has posed new challenges for the idea of tolerance. (**Fundamentalism** is characterized by rigid adherence to a literal interpretation of religious doctrines and a reaction against compromise with secularism and modernity.) The political philosopher Jürgen Habermas argues that "a fundamentalism that leads to a practice of intolerance is incompatible with the democratic constitutional state."[22] He concludes, "in multicultural societies, the national constitution can tolerate only forms of life articulated within the medium of such non-fundamentalist traditions."[23] Habermas is saying that we cannot tolerate those who reject liberal-democratic principles of toleration on fundamentalist religious grounds. Indeed, it is not difficult to imagine circumstances in which religious fundamentalists violate the shared principles of secular ethics. What do we do about religious pacifists who refuse to serve in the military or pay their taxes, pastors who think that it is acceptable for thirteen-year-old girls to be married to older men, or religious communities that mutilate the genitals of their daughters? And what of religious groups who get involved in democratic politics to advance intolerant agendas—or who may be explicitly opposed to democracy itself? In many cases, even those who want to embrace religious diversity will have to say that there are ethical limits to what they are willing to tolerate in terms of religious belief and practice.

A further problem is that secularization, **cosmopolitanism**, and modernization sometimes appear to spring directly from the post-Reformation philosophy and politics of the West. One charge against secular and cosmopolitan ethics is that it is Eurocentric, meaning that it is an idea that makes sense only within the context of European culture and history. The sociologist of religion, José Casanova, explains:

> Cosmopolitanism builds upon developmental theories of modernization that envision social change as a global expansion of Western modernity.... In the cosmopolitan accounts, religion either does not exist or it is 'invisible'.... If and when religion emerges in the public sphere and has to be taken seriously, it is usually branded either as anti-modern fundamentalism resisting processes of secularization, or as a form of traditionalist collective identity reaction to the threat of globalization. In other words, religion, in the eyes of the cosmopolitan elites, is either irrelevant or reactive.... Cosmopolitanism remains a faithful child of the European Enlightenment.[24]

A significant point of such a criticism has to do with the role of political and economic power. According to this way of thinking, European culture, with its emphasis on individualism and the separation of church and state, spread across the world along with European colonial power. While some may think that this is a progressive development, critics will view it as an imposition of European culture and values that comes at the expense of alternative ideas about

morality and politics. A related criticism develops from Karl Marx's critique of "bourgeois morality" as the product of a certain strand of European thinking, associated with the ruling class. (Marxists, by the way, tend to view religion as "the opiate of the people," that is, as a drug that reconciles oppressed people to the injustices of the social order by promising an other-worldly reward.) More recently, scholars such as Enrique Dussel have expanded this critical perspective to argue that **Eurocentrism** is at the heart of continual cultural divisions and economic inequalities that plague the globe (as we discuss in more detail in Chapter 20 on globalization). An influential Latin American philosopher, Dussel critiques the traditional Anglo-American and European approach to philosophy and ethics. For Dussel, European philosophy begins with conquest—as the colonial conquests of the Americas, Asia, and Africa coincide with the dawning of European Enlightenment.[25] Dussel gives voice to the concern that there may be a connection between European imperialism and European ethics—that moral ideas about a variety of topics from sex and gender to individualism and human rights, to the use of drugs and the morality of war have a lot to do with the economic and political power structures at work in the world.

For people who identify with non-Western religions and cultures, the approaches to ethics that we are taking in this book can appear to be Eurocentric. From this standpoint, one might argue that the approach of this book reflects the biases of a predominantly Christian and European worldview. Indeed, the main normative traditions discussed in this book—utilitarianism, virtue ethics, natural law, and Kantian deontology—are rooted in the ideas of European philosophers.

In response, one might admit that even though the goal of understanding ethics in an objective and universal fashion, without reference to religion, is a goal that is widely shared by many in the Western world, this goal is not uniquely Christian or European. Indeed, it is a goal that is shared by many people around the world. As Amartya Sen and others have pointed out, the move toward philosophical and cosmopolitan ethics is also deeply rooted in non-Western intellectual traditions. It is true that we must be sensitive to the diverse cultural and religious starting points from which we begin reflecting on ethics. But this does not mean that we should not attempt to move beyond narrow allegiances and prejudices toward a broader, more impartial, and more objective perspective—that is, toward a cosmopolitan and pluralist point of view that would incorporate the insights of the world's great moral and religious traditions. Whether we can attain this goal is an open question. In the next chapter, we confront this problem more directly as a question of relativism. The question of the next chapter will be whether there really is such a thing as a universal, objective point of view or whether we are hopelessly stuck within a perspective and worldview that we inherit from our culture or religion.

NOTES

1. The White House, "Remarks by the President to the UN General Assembly," press release, September 25, 2012, http://www.whitehouse.gov/the-press-office/2012/09/25/remarks-president-un-general-assembly
2. Neil MacFarquhar, "At U.N., Egypt and Yemen Urge Curbs on Free Speech," *New York Times*, September 27, 2012, http://www.nytimes.com/2012/09/27/world/united-nations-general-assembly.html
3. http://www.un.org/en/documents/udhr/
4. Robert Tait, "Iran Resurrects Salman Rushdie Threat," *Telegraph*, September 16, 2012, http://www.telegraph.co.uk/news/worldnews/middleeast/iran/9546513/Iran-resurrects-Salman-Rushdie-threat.html
5. "Pastor Dennis Terry Introduces Rick Santorum, Tells Non-Christians and Liberals to Get Out," *Huffington Post*, March 19, 2012, http://www.huffingtonpost.com/2012/03/19/dennis-terry-rick-santorum_n_1364414.html
6. Amartya Sen, *The Argumentative Indian* (New York: Macmillan, 2006), 136.
7. Immanuel Kant, "An Answer to the Question: 'What Is Enlightenment?'" in *Kant: Political Writings* (Cambridge: Cambridge University Press, 1991), 54.
8. Martin Luther King Jr., "Letter from Birmingham Jail," in *Why We Can't Wait* (New York: Penguin, 2000; originally published 1964), 67–8.
9. Ibid., 65.
10. Ibid., 72.
11. http://philpapers.org/surveys/results.pl
12. Although this claim is often attributed to Dostoevsky, it is not directly stated by any one of Dostoevsky's characters. Nonetheless, it is the basic idea of his atheist characters: Ivan Karamazov in *The Brothers Karamazov* and Kirilov and Stavrogin in *Devils*.
13. John Hick, *An Interpretation of Religion: Human Responses to the Transcendent*, 2nd ed. (New Haven, CT: Yale University Press, 2005), xl.
14. Ibid., 316.
15. Dalai Lama, *Kindness, Clarity, and Insight* (Ithaca, NY: Snow Lion Publications, 2006), 58.
16. Stephen Prothero, *God Is Not One: The Eight Rival Religions That Run the World—And Why Their Differences Matter* (New York: HarperCollins, 2010), 2.
17. Sam Harris, *Free Will* (New York: Free Press, 2012), 1.
18. Prothero, *God Is Not One*, 2.
19. Craig Calhoun, Mark Juergensmeyer, and Jonathan Van Antwerpen, *Rethinking Secularism* (New York: Oxford University Press, 2011), 10.
20. John Rawls, *Political Liberalism* (New York: Columbia University Press, 2005), xxv.
21. Paul Kurtz, "Neo-Humanist Statement of Secular Principles and Values," http://paulkurtz.net/
22. Jürgen Habermas, "Struggles for Recognition in the Democratic Constitutional State," in *Multiculturalism: Examining the Politics of Recognition*, ed. Amy Gutmann (Princeton, NJ: Princeton University Press, 1994), 132–33.
23. Ibid., 133.
24. José Casanova, "Public Religions Revisited," in *Religion: Beyond a Concept*, ed. Hent de Vries (New York: Fordham University Press, 2007), 119.
25. See Enrique Dussel, *Beyond Philosophy: Ethics, History, Marxism, and Liberation Theology* (Lanham, MD: Rowman & Littlefield, 2003).

REVIEW EXERCISES

1. Describe the challenge of developing a global ethical perspective in light of religious and national differences.
2. What is the history of the idea of universal human rights? And how is this history susceptible to the charge that it is Eurocentric?
3. If we could develop a global ethic, what would its basic values be?
4. Explain arguments in favor of the divine command theory of ethics, as well as arguments against that theory. Is it true that if there were no God, then everything would be permitted?
5. Is the humanistic or secular approach to ethics better or worse than religious approaches to ethics? Is the humanistic or secular approach antagonistic to religion?
6. Are you optimistic about our ability to develop a global ethical consensus across our national and religious differences? Why or why not?
7. Do you think that all religions and cultures are pointing in a similar direction, or are there irreconcilable differences among the world's religions?

3

Ethical Relativism

Kisialiou Yury/Alamy

Learning Outcomes

After reading this chapter, you should be able to:

- Describe the difference between descriptive relativism and metaethical relativism.
- Understand criticisms of objectivism, subjectivism, relativism, and moral realism.
- Explain how relativism poses a problem for moral judgment.
- Explain the connections between relativism and pluralism.

- Evaluate the arguments in favor of and against relativism.
- Differentiate between relativism and a commitment to tolerance.
- Understand how relativism might come up in conversations about concrete moral issues.
- Defend your own ideas about relativism.

The previous chapter introduced the difficulty of trying to discover a set of universal values that are valid for people who come from diverse religious and cultural backgrounds. This points toward the problem of relativism. Relativism means that our judgments about ethics are relative to (or dependent upon) something else. Cultural relativism holds that ethical judgments are relative to cultural contexts. Individualistic versions of relativism hold that judgments about morality are relative to an individual's point of view. In saying that judgments are relative to individuals or cultures, we mean that they are a function of, or dependent on, what those individuals or cultures happen to believe. Relativism can be based upon **epistemological** claims about what we know. Relativism can also be based upon a claim about the nature of values (as discussed in Chapter 1). The epistemological approach maintains that knowledge about values is derived from or dependent upon a cultural context or worldview. A metaphysical approach claims that there just are no absolute, transcendent, or universal values. For the metaphysical relativist, there are only individual perspectives and culturally defined values—there are no absolute or objective values.

Relativism is a very difficult metaethical issue. It asks us to consider how we know things in the realm of morality. And it asks us to consider the ultimate nature or reality of moral values. The belief that guides this text—indeed, the belief that guides most philosophical discussions of ethics—is that better and worse choices can be made, and that morality is not simply a matter of what we feel to be morally right or wrong; nor is morality simply a matter of what our culture tells us. If this were not the case, then there would not seem to be much point in studying ethics. The purpose of studying ethics, as noted in Chapter 1, is to improve one's ability to make good ethical judgments. If ethical relativism were true, then this purpose could not be achieved.

DESCRIPTIVE VS. NORMATIVE ETHICAL RELATIVISM

Ethical relativism is a kind of skepticism about ethical reasoning—it is skeptical of the idea that there are right and wrong answers to ethical questions. There are some good reasons why we might be skeptical about the existence of universal or objective values (or that we can know what the objective or universal values are). One reason for skepticism is the empirical and historical fact that different cultures disagree about moral values. As a descriptive fact, relativism appears to be true: it is evident that there are different ideas about ethics at large in the world. What we call **descriptive ethical relativism** is the factual or descriptive claim that there are different ideas about values.

In support of descriptive relativism, we might list some of the ways that cultures vary with regard to morality. Some societies hold bribery to be morally acceptable, but other societies condemn it. Views on appropriate sexual behavior and practices vary widely. Some societies believe that cannibalism, the eating of human flesh, is good because it ensures tribal fertility or increases manliness. Some groups of the Inuit, the native peoples of northern Canada and Alaska, believed that it was appropriate to abandon their elderly when they could no longer travel with the group, whereas other groups once practiced ritual strangulation of the old by their children. The anthropologist Ruth Benedict documented the case of a Northwest Indian group that believed it was justified in killing an innocent person for each member of the group who had died. This was not a matter of revenge but a way of fighting death. In place of bereavement, the group felt relieved by the second killing.[1]

There are a variety of examples of descriptive relativism. In some countries, it is acceptable for women to wear short skirts; in others, women are expected to cover their legs and hair. Indeed, relativism shows up in the language we use to describe contested practices. Consider the practice of cutting women's genitals. Those who are sympathetic to the practice might call it *female circumcision*. But that practice is illegal in other societies, which condemn

it by calling it *female genital mutilation* (as we discuss in Chapters 9 and 12). You should be able to think of many other examples of such differences.

Descriptive relativism might appear to lead to a normative rule of thumb, that "When in Rome," we should "do as the Romans do." This phrase originated from a discussion between Augustine and Ambrose—two important Christian saints of the fourth century. Augustine noticed that the Christians in Rome fasted on a different day than the Christians in Milan. Ambrose explained that when in Rome, he does what the Romans do. In many cases, it does appear to be wise to go along with local practices. The issue of the appropriate day for fasting is a minor point and it is easy enough to "go along" with such minor details. But should we also go along with local practices that could include slavery, female genital mutilation, child sacrifice, or cannibalism?

Different cultures do have different values. But it might still be the case that some of these cultures are wrong about certain values. Recall the "fact/value" distinction discussed in Chapter 11. Just because something is a fact of the world (as descriptive relativism is a fact) does not mean that it is a good thing. It is possible that we *ought* to strive to overcome our cultural differences. And it is possible that some cultures (or individuals) are wrong—despite the fact that cultures and individuals vary in their moral judgments. We want to say, for example, that cultures that practice slavery (as the United States did until the 1860s) are wrong to do so. The mere fact that cultures disagree about values should not immunize cultures from moral criticism. But to say that a culture is wrong, we need an objective or non-relativist account of the values that would allow us to criticize that culture.

A stronger version of relativism goes beyond merely descriptive relativism and claims that there are no objective or absolute values that would allow us to make such criticisms. We call this version of relativism **metaethical relativism**. Metaethical relativism holds that there are no universal or objective norms (or that human beings cannot know such objective values). Rather, from this point of view, values are simply the beliefs, opinions, practices, or feelings of individuals and cultures. In saying that values are "relative" to individuals or societies, we mean that they are a function of, or dependent on, what those individuals or societies do, in fact, believe. According to metaethical relativism, there is no objective right and wrong. The opposite point of view, that there is an objective right and wrong, is often called **objectivism**, or sometimes simply nonrelativism.

We can understand more about ethical relativism by comparing ethics with science. Most people believe that the natural sciences (biology, chemistry, physics, geology, and their modern variants) tell us things about the natural world. Throughout the centuries, and modern times in particular, science seems to have made great progress in uncovering the nature and structure of our world. Moreover, science seems to have a universal validity. Regardless of a person's individual temperament, background, or culture, the same natural world seems accessible to all who sincerely and openly investigate it. Modern science is thought to be governed by a generally accepted method and seems to produce a gradually evolving common body of knowledge. Although this is the popular view of science, philosophers hold that the situation regarding science is much more complex and problematic. And it is possible for there to be relativism with regard to theories of the natural world. Not everyone agrees, for example, that Western biomedicine holds all the answers to good health. Nevertheless, it is useful to compare the ordinary view of science as providing objective truth about the physical world with common understandings of morality.

Morality, in contrast to science, does not seem so objective. Not only is there no general agreement about what is right and wrong, but some people doubt that ethical judgments are the sorts of things about which we could agree. Some people think of morality as a matter of subjective opinion. This is basically the conclusion of ethical relativism: morality is simply a function of the moral beliefs that people have. There is nothing beyond this. Specifically, no category of objective moral truth or reality exists that is comparable to that which we seem to find in the world of nature investigated by science.

INDIVIDUAL VS. CULTURAL RELATIVISM

In further exploring the nature of ethical relativism, we should note that it has two basic and different

forms.[2] According to one form, called personal or **individual relativism** (also called **subjectivism**), ethical judgments and beliefs are the expressions of the moral outlook and attitudes of individual persons. Rather than being objective, such judgments are subjective. I have my ethical views, and you have yours; neither my views nor yours are better or more correct. I may believe that a particular war was unjust, and you may believe it was just. Someone else may believe that all war is wrong. According to this form of relativism, because no objective right or wrong exists, no particular war can be said to be really just or unjust, right or wrong, nor can *all* wars. We each have our individual histories that explain how we have come to hold our particular views or attitudes. But they are just that—our own individual views and attitudes. We cannot say that they are correct or incorrect because to do so would assume some objective standard of right and wrong against which we could judge their correctness. Such a standard does not exist, according to ethical relativism.[3]

The second form of ethical relativism, called social or cultural **relativism**, holds that ethical values vary from society to society and that the basis for moral judgments lies in these social or cultural views. For an individual to decide and do what is right, he or she must look to the norms of the society. People in a society may, in fact, believe that their views are the correct moral views. However, a cultural relativist holds that no society's views are better than any other in a transcultural sense. Some may be different from others, and some may not be the views generally accepted by a wider group of societies, but that does not make these views worse, more backward, or incorrect in any objective sense.

STRONG AND WEAK RELATIVISM

While it is obvious that different cultures or societies do in fact often have different views about what is morally right and wrong, ethical relativism goes further. For the stronger versions of ethical relativism, what is morally right for one just depends on what his or her society holds is right. There are no transcultural moral principles, even ideally. One author often associated with relativism is Friedrich Nietzsche. Nietzsche maintains that words like *good* and *evil* are defined by different people based upon their own perspectives on the world. Indeed, Nietzsche is often viewed as a proponent of **perspectivism**, the idea that there are only perspectives on the world—and nothing beyond these perspectives. Nietzsche also thinks that moral judgments reflect power relations and basic instinctual needs. For example, those who are in power tend to call themselves "good" because they instinctively view themselves as superior to those who are less powerful than themselves. As Nietzsche explains, "It is our needs that interpret the world; our drives and their For and Against. Every drive is a kind of lust to rule; each one has its perspective that it would like to compel all the other drives to accept as a norm."[4] For Nietzsche, there is no truth beneath these perspectives, instincts, and norms other than the "will to power." Such a strong version of relativism makes it quite difficult to judge or criticize across cultural divides.

A weaker version of relativism holds that there are some abstract and basic norms or values that are shared but that these abstract values are expressed in different cultures in different ways. Thus different cultures may share the idea that "life should be valued," for example, but they will disagree about what counts as "life" and what counts as "valuing life." It might be that both human and animal lives count and so no animal lives can be taken in order to support human beings. Or it might be that some form of ritual sacrifice could be justified as a way of valuing life.

One version of this kind of "weak relativism" or "soft universalism" is the "capabilities approach" to ethics and human welfare—as developed by the economist Amartya Sen and the philosopher Martha Nussbaum. Nussbaum maintains that there are certain central features of human flourishing or human well-being, including life, bodily health, bodily integrity, and so on. But she admits the possibility of "multiple realization" of these basic capabilities. As Nussbaum explains, "each of the capabilities may be concretely realized in a variety of different ways, in accordance with individual tastes, local circumstances, and traditions."[5] Nussbaum's approach leads to a sort of pluralism. Nussbaum writes that "legitimate concerns for diversity, pluralism, and personal freedom are not incompatible with the recognition of

Philosopher Martha C. Nussbaum during an event at Oveido University in Spain.

universal norms; indeed, universal norms are actually required if we are to protect diversity, pluralism, and freedom, treating each human being as an agent and an end."[6] But critics will argue that so long as there is no universal agreement about the specific sorts of values that count for human flourishing and an ethical life, we are still left with a kind of relativism.

Nussbaum's Central Capabilities[7]

1. Life
2. Bodily health
3. Bodily integrity
4. Senses, imagination, and thought
5. Emotions
6. Practical reason
7. Affiliation
8. Other species
9. Play
10. Control over one's environment: political and material

REASONS SUPPORTING ETHICAL RELATIVISM

There are many reasons for believing that what ethical relativism holds is true. We will first summarize the three most commonly given reasons and then evaluate their related arguments.[8]

The Diversity of Moral Views

One reason most often given to support relativism is the existence of moral diversity among people and cultures. In fields such as science and history, investigation tends to result in general agreement despite the diversity among scientists. But we have not come to such agreement in ethics. Philosophers have been investigating questions about the basis of morality since ancient times. With sincere and capable thinkers pursuing such a topic for millennia, one would think that some agreement would have been reached. But this seems not to be the case. It is not only on particular issues such as abortion that sincere people disagree but also on basic moral values or principles.

Tolerance and Open-Mindedness

Related to the fact of diversity is the desire to be tolerant and open-minded. Often people maintain relativism in an attempt to refrain from judging and condemning others. Since we know that there are problems with regard to ethnocentrism and bias in judging, we may want to prevent these problems by espousing relativism. From this perspective, the idea is that since there are a variety of cultures with different values, we are in no place to judge which culture is right and wrong. Furthermore, a defender of relativism may argue that those who try to judge are being ethnocentric, closed-minded, and intolerant.

Moral Uncertainty

A second reason to believe that what relativism holds is true is the great difficulty we often have in knowing what is the morally right thing to believe or do. We don't know what is morally most important. For example, we do not know whether it is better to help one's friend or do the honest thing in a case in which we cannot do both. Perhaps helping the friend is best in some circumstances, but being honest is best in others. We are not sure which is

best in a particular case. Furthermore, we cannot know for sure what will happen down the line if we choose one course over another. Each of us is also aware of our personal limitations and the subjective viewpoint that we bring to moral judging. Thus, we distrust our own judgments. We then generalize and conclude that all moral judgments are simply personal and subjective viewpoints.

Situational Differences

Finally, people and situations, cultures and times differ in significant ways. The situations and living worlds of different people vary so much that it is difficult to believe that the same things that would be right for one would be right for another. In some places, overpopulation or drought is a problem; other places have too few people or too much water. In some places, people barely have access to the basic necessities of life; in other places, food is plentiful and the standard of living is high. Some individuals are healthy, others are seriously ill. Some are more outgoing, and others are more reserved. How can the same things be consistently right or wrong under such different circumstances and for such different individuals? It seems unlikely, then, that any moral theory or judgment can apply in a general or universal manner. We thus tend to conclude that they must be relative to the particular situation and circumstance and that no objective or universally valid moral good exists.

ARE THESE REASONS CONVINCING?

Let us consider possible responses by a non-relativist or objectivist to the preceding three points.

The Diversity of Moral Views

We can consider the matter of diversity of moral views from two different perspectives. First, we can ask, how widespread and deep is the disagreement? Second, we may ask, what does the fact of disagreement prove?

How Widespread and Deep Is the Disagreement?   If two people disagree about a moral matter, does this always amount to a moral disagreement? For example, Bill says that we ought to cut down dramatically on carbon dioxide emissions, while Jane says that we do not have a moral obligation to do this. This looks like a basic moral disagreement, but it actually may result from differences in their factual, rather than ethical, beliefs (as indicated in the following table). Bill may believe that the current rate of carbon emissions is causing and will cause dramatically harmful global climate effects, such as rising sea levels and more severe weather. Jane may see no such connection because she believes that scientists' assessments and predictions are in error. If they did agree on the factual issues, then Bill and Jane would agree on the moral conclusion. It turns out that they both agree on the basic moral obligation to do what we can to improve the current human condition and prevent serious harm to existing and future generations.

It is an open question how many of our seemingly moral disagreements are not basic moral disagreements at all but disagreements about factual or other beliefs. But suppose that at least some of them are about moral matters. Suppose that we do disagree about the relative value, for example, of health and peace, honesty and generosity, or about what rights people do and do not have. It is this type of disagreement that the moral relativist would need to make his or her point.

What Would Disagreement about Basic Moral Matters Prove?   In past years, we have asked students in our ethics classes to tell us in what year George Washington died. A few brave souls venture a guess: 1801, or at least after 1790? No one is sure. Does this disagreement or lack of certitude prove that he did not die or that he died on no particular date? Belief that he did die and on a particular date is consistent with differences of opinion and with uncertainty. So also in ethics: people can disagree about what constitutes the right thing to do and yet believe that there is a right thing to do. "Is it not because of this belief that we try to decide what is

Arguments over moral matters often stem from factual disagreements, such as whether CO_2 emissions from cars and other sources are causing catastrophic climate change.

right and worry that we might miss it?" the non-relativist would ask.

Or consider the supposed contrast between ethics and science. Although a body of knowledge exists on which those working in the physical sciences agree, those at the forefront of these sciences often profoundly disagree. Does such disagreement prove that no objectivity exists in such matters? If people disagree about whether the universe began with a "big bang" or about what happened in its first millisecond, then does this prove that no answer is to be found, even in principle, about the universe's beginning? Not necessarily.

Tolerance and Open-Mindedness

While some people think that relativism goes hand in hand with tolerance and open-mindedness, it is not necessarily true that these things are mutually implied. It is possible to hold that since there are a variety of different cultures, we should simply ignore the other cultures or show them no respect whatsoever. If relativism holds that there are no universal norms that tell us how to deal with cross-cultural interaction, then tolerance and open-mindedness

Basic Moral Agreement	Factual Disagreement	Different Moral Conclusions
We ought not to harm.	CO_2 emissions harm.	We ought to reduce emissions.
We ought not to harm.	CO_2 emissions do not harm.	We need not reduce emissions.

themselves must be seen as culturally relative values, no more legitimate than intolerance or aggression. Moreover, if Nietzsche is correct that the moral world consists of perspectives and struggles for power, then there is no good reason to remain open-minded and tolerant. Indeed, relativism might be used to support the use of power in order to defend and expand your own worldview or perspective when it comes into conflict with others.

Moral Uncertainty

Let us examine the point that moral matters are complex and difficult to determine. Because of this, we are often uncertain about what is the morally best thing to do. For example, those who "blow the whistle" on unscrupulous employers or coworkers must find it difficult to know whether they are doing the right thing when they consider the potential costs to themselves and others around them. However, this sort of dilemma is not strictly a question of relativism but of **skepticism**. Skepticism is the view that it is difficult, if not impossible, to know something. However, does the fact that we are uncertain about the answer to some question, even a moral question, prove that it lacks an answer? One reason for skepticism might be the belief that we can see things only from our own perspective and thus, in ethics and other inquiries, can never know things as they are. This is a form of subjectivism (as defined earlier). The non-relativist could argue that in our very dissatisfaction with not knowing and in our seeking to know what we ought to do, we behave as though we believe that a better or worse choice can be made.

In contrast, matters of science and history often eventually get clarified and settled. We can now look up the date of George Washington's death (1799), and scientists gradually improve our knowledge in various fields. "Why is there no similar progress in ethical matters?" relativists might respond. Answers to that question will depend upon a variety of issues, including our ideas about ethical theory (as discussed in the first half of this book) and ideas about progress on social issues (as discussed in the second half). The fact of continued disagreement about moral theory and moral issues reminds us that ethical inquiry is different from inquiry in history and the social sciences or in the natural sciences.

Situational Differences

Do dramatic differences in people's life situations make it unlikely or impossible for them to have any common morality? Suppose that health is taken as an objective value. Is it not the case that what contributes to the health of some is different than what contributes to the health of others? Insulin injections are often good for the diabetic but not for the nondiabetic. A non-relativist might reply as follows: Even though the good in these specific cases differs, there is still a general value—health—that is the goal. Similarly, justice involves "giving to each his or her due," and what is due people in justice is not the same. Those who work might well deserve something different from those who do not, and the guilty deserve punishment that the innocent do not. But these different applications of justice do not mean that justice is not an objective moral value. (See the table below.)

One reason situational differences may lead us to think that no objective moral value is possible is that we may be equating objectivism with what is sometimes called **absolutism**. Absolutism may be

Objective Value	Situational Differences	Different Moral Conclusions
Health	Diabetic	Insulin injections are good.
Health	Nondiabetic	Insulin injections are not good.
Justice	Works hard	Deserves reward.
Justice	Does not work hard	Does not deserve reward.

described as the view that moral rules or principles have no exceptions and are context-independent. One example of such a rule is "Stealing is always wrong." According to absolutism, situational differences such as whether or not a person is starving would make no difference to moral conclusions about whether she is justified in stealing food—if stealing is wrong.

However, an objectivist who is not an absolutist can argue that although there are some objective goods—for example, health or justice—what is good in a concrete case may vary from person to person and circumstance to circumstance. She or he could hold that stealing might be justified in some circumstances because it is necessary for life, an objective good, and a greater good than property. Opposing absolutism does not necessarily commit one to a similar opposition to objectivism.

One result of this clarification should be the realization that what is often taken as an expression of relativism is not necessarily so. Consider this statement: "What is right for one person is not necessarily right for another." If the term *for* means "in the view of," then the statement simply states the fact that people do disagree. It states that "What is right in the view of one person is not what is right in the view of the other." However, this is not yet relativism. Relativism goes beyond this in its belief that this is all there is. Relativists will claim that there only are various points of view and that there is no way to reconcile what's right for one person with what's right for another. Similarly, if *for* is used in the sense "Insulin injections are good for some people but not for others," then the original statement is also not necessarily relativistic. It could, in fact, imply that health is a true or objective good and that what leads to it is good and what diminishes it is bad. For ethical relativism, on the other hand, there is no such objective good.

IS RELATIVISM SELF-CONTRADICTORY?

One significant argument against relativism is that it is self-contradictory. If relativists claim that all values or truths are relative, then it is possible to ask whether the claim of relativism is itself merely a relative truth or value judgment. But it might be that

such an argument against relativism sets up a **straw man**, an easy-to-defeat version of the opposing position. The philosopher Richard Rorty argues that there are no relativists in the sense that is aimed at by this sort of an argument. Rorty explains,

> Relativism is the view that every belief on a certain topic, or perhaps about any topic, is as good as every other. No one holds this view. Except for the occasional cooperative freshman, one cannot find anybody who says that two incompatible opinions on an important topic are equally good. The philosophers who get called 'relativists' are those who say that the grounds for choosing between such opinions are less algorithmic than had previously been thought.[9]

Rorty does not claim that any belief is as good as any other. Instead, he says that it is not so easy to figure out what is better or worse—as he puts it here, there are no "algorithms" that can be used to give precise answers about these things. His version of relativism attempts to avoid the charge of self-contradiction by connecting relativism to skepticism. Rorty has described his approach to things as "pragmatism" or "anti-foundationalism," by which he means that we find ourselves in the middle of things without access to any final account of ultimate reality or absolute values. For pragmatists such as Rorty, our judgments about things (including our judgment about ideas such as relativism) are provisional and embedded in contexts, cultures, and ways of life.

A related objection holds that a relativist has no way to define the group or perspective to which things are relative. With which group should my moral views coincide: my country, my state, my family, or myself and my peers? And how would we decide? Different groups to which I belong may have different moral views. Moreover, if a society changes its views, does this mean that morality changes? If 52 percent of its people once supported some war but later only 48 percent, does this mean that earlier the war was just but it became unjust when the people changed their minds about it?

One problem that individual relativism faces is whether its view accords with personal experience. According to individual relativism, it seems that I should turn within and consult my moral feelings to solve a personal moral problem. This is often just the source of the difficulty, however; for when I look within I find conflicting feelings. I want to know not how I *do* feel but how I *ought* to feel and what I *ought* to believe. But the view that there is something I possibly ought to believe would not be relativism.

As we saw above, a problem for both types of relativist lies in the implied belief that relativism is a more tolerant position than objectivism. The cultural relativist can hold that people in a society should be tolerant only if tolerance is one of the dominant values of their society. He or she cannot hold that all people should be tolerant because tolerance cannot be an objective or transcultural value, according to relativism. We can also question whether there is any reason for an individual relativist to be tolerant, especially if being tolerant means not just putting up with others who disagree with us but also listening to their positions and arguments. Why should I listen to another who disagrees with me? If ethical relativism is true, then it cannot be because the other person's moral views may be better than mine in an objective sense, for there is no objectively better position. Objectivists might argue that their position provides a better basis for both believing that tolerance is an objective and transcultural good and that we ought to be open to others' views because they may be closer to the truth than ours are.

Relativism is sometimes simply a kind of intellectual laziness or a lack of moral courage. Rather than attempting to give reasons or arguments for my own position, I may hide behind some statement such as, "What is good for some is not necessarily good for others." I may say this simply to excuse myself from having to think about or be critical of my own ethical positions. Those who hold that there is an objective right and wrong may also do so uncritically. They may simply adopt the views of their parents or peers without evaluating those views themselves.

The major difficulty with an objectivist position is the problem it has in providing an alternative to the relativist position. The objectivist should give us reason to believe that there is an objective good. To pursue this problem in a little more detail, we will briefly examine two issues discussed by contemporary moral philosophers. One is the issue of the reality of moral value—**moral realism**; and the other concerns the problem of deciding among plural goods—**moral pluralism**.

MORAL REALISM

Realism is the view that there exists a reality independent of those who know it. Most people are probably realists in this sense about a variety of things. We think, for example, that the external world is real in the sense that it actually exists, independently of our awareness of it. If a tree falls in the woods and no one is there, the event is still real and it still makes a sound. The sound waves are real, even if the subjective perception of them depends upon a variety of contingent factors.

Now compare this to the situation regarding ethics. If I say that John's act of saving a drowning child was good, then what is the object of my moral judgment? Is there some real existing fact of goodness that I can somehow sense in this action? I can observe the actions of John to save the child, the characteristics of the child, John, the lake, and so forth. But in what sense, if any, do I observe the goodness itself? The British philosopher G. E. Moore (discussed in Chapter 1) held that goodness is a specific quality that attaches to people or acts.[10] According to Moore, although we cannot observe the goodness of acts (we cannot hear, touch, taste, or see it), we intuit its presence. Philosophers such as Moore have had difficulty explaining both the nature of the quality and the particular intuitive or moral sense by which we are supposed to perceive it.

Some moral philosophers who seek to support a realist view of morality attempt to explain moral reality as a relational matter—perhaps as a certain fit between actions and situations or actions and our innate sensibilities.[11] For example, because of innate human sensibilities, some say, we just would not be able to approve of torturing the innocent. The problem, of course, is that not everyone agrees. To continue with this example, some people would be willing to torture an innocent person if they thought that by torturing that person they could elicit information about a terrorist attack or send a message to frighten would-be terrorists. And some activities that we might describe as torture—starvation, sleep deprivation, even beatings—can be viewed as valuable in religious contexts, in cultural initiation rituals, and even in hazing that occurs on sports teams or fraternities. Moral realists will claim that such disagreements can be resolved by consulting the real objects of morality which are supposed to make judgments about good and evil true. But relativists wonder whether there are any actual or objective qualities of actions that are intuited in the same way by all observers, just as they doubt that moral truth rests upon objective moral reality.

MORAL PLURALISM

Another problem non-relativists or objectivists face is whether the good is one or many. According to some theories, there is one primary moral principle by which we can judge all actions. However, suppose this were not the case, that there were instead a variety of equally valid moral principles or equal moral values. For example, suppose that autonomy, justice, well-being, authenticity, and peace were all equally valuable. In this case, we would have a plurality of values. One version of this is Nussbaum's capabilities approach, discussed earlier. Nussbaum implies that a variety of basic goods can be realized in multiple ways in different cultural contexts. Another version is W. D. Ross's account of what he calls *prima facie* duties. According to Ross, there are a variety of duties—listed below. To say that these duties are ***prima facie*** (which means "at first face" or "on first look") means that they are duties that are important and valuable at first blush, all other things being equal. It might be, however, that these duties conflict—because there are more than one of them. The fact of a plurality of goods or duties means that there will be conflicts of values.

W. D. Ross's Prima Facie Duties[12]

1. Fidelity
2. Reparation
3. Gratitude
4. Beneficence
5. Nonmaleficence
6. Justice
7. Self-improvement

The difficulty of this pluralistic account is that we face a problem when we are forced to choose between competing duties or values. For example, what do we do when we've made a promise to someone (and have a duty of fidelity) but that promise conflicts with the opportunity to do something good for someone else (in order to fulfill the duty of beneficence)? In such cases when duties or values conflict, we may be forced simply to choose one or the other for no reason or on the basis of something other than reason. Whether some rational and nonarbitrary way exists to make such decisions is an open question. Whether ultimate choices are thus subjective or can be grounded in an assessment of what is objectively best is a question not only about how we do behave but also about what is possible in matters of moral judgment.

Pluralism about morality may be understood as a form of relativism, which holds that there is no single objective or universal standard. In response, pluralists might hold that there are several equally plausible standards of value. But—as we saw in our discussion of religious pluralism in the previous chapter—it is possible for a pluralist to hold that there is some sort of convergence toward something unitary and universal in the realm of values. It might be that there is a hierarchy of values. But genuine pluralism points toward a sort of equality among values, which does not admit to a hierarchical organization of duties.

In subsequent chapters, we will examine several major ethical theories—utilitarianism, deontology, natural law theory, and the ethics of care. These theories are articulated from an objectivist or non-relativist standpoint: defenders of these theories claim that the theory presents a substantive definition of what is good. But the problem of relativism returns as soon as we ask whether there is some way to compare or unite these normative theories—or whether we are left with incompatible accounts of the good.

NOTES

1. Ruth Benedict, "Anthropology and the Abnormal," *Journal of General Psychology* 10 (1934): 60–70.
2. We could also think of many forms of ethical relavism from the most individual or personal to the universal. Thus, we could think of individual relativism, or that based on family

values, or local community or state or cultural values. The most universal, however, in which moral values are the same for all human beings, would probably no longer be a form of relativism.

3. According to some versions of individual ethical relativism, moral judgments are similar to expressions of taste. We each have our own individual tastes. I like certain styles or foods, and you like others. Just as no taste can be said to be correct or incorrect, so also no ethical view can be valued as better than any other. My saying that this war is or all wars are unjust is, in effect, my expression of my dislike of or aversion to war. An entire tradition in ethics, sometimes called emotivism (as discussed in Chapter 1), holds this view.

4. Friedrich Nietzsche, *Will to Power* (New York: Random House, 1968) no. 481, p. 267.

5. Martha C. Nussbaum, *Women and Human Development* (Cambridge: Cambridge University Press, 2001), 105.

6. Ibid., 106.

7. Ibid., 78–80.

8. These are not necessarily complete and coherent arguments for relativism. Rather, they are more popular versions of why people generally are inclined to what they believe is relativism.

9. Richard Rorty, "Pragmatism, Relativism, and Irrationalism," *Proceedings and Addresses of the American Philosophical Association* 53, no. 6 (1980): 727.

10. G. E. Moore, *Principia Ethica* (Cambridge: Cambridge University Press, 1903).

11. Bruce W. Brower, "Dispositional Ethical Realism," *Ethics* 103, no. 2 (January 1993): 221–49.

12. W. D. Ross, *The Right and the Good* (Oxford: Oxford University Press, 1930), Chapter 1.

REVIEW EXERCISES

1. Explain the definition of ethical relativism given in the text: "the view that there is no objective standard of right and wrong, even in principle."

2. What is the difference between individual and social or cultural relativism?

3. What is the difference between the descriptive claim that people do differ in their moral beliefs and the metaethical theory of relativism?

4. What are the differences among the three reasons for supporting ethical relativism given in this chapter? In particular, what is the basic difference between the first and second? Between the first and third?

5. How would you know whether a moral disagreement was based on a basic difference in moral values or facts? As an example, use differences about the moral justifiability of torture.

6. What is moral realism? How does your understanding about the reality of the external world differ from your intuitions about morality?

Egoism, Altruism, and the Social Contract

4

Learning Outcomes

After reading this chapter, you should be able to:

- Describe the differences between descriptive (or psychological) egoism and ethical egoism.
- Explain criticisms of altruism and the importance of reciprocal altruism.
- Understand disputes about the sources of morality and reasons to be moral.
- Explain the prisoner's dilemma and how it relates to the discussion of egoism and the social contract.

- Understand how egoism shows up in discussions of laissez-faire capitalism and economics.
- Evaluate the challenge that egoism poses for the moral point of view.
- Understand and apply concepts such as ethical egoism and altruism to real world cases.
- Defend your own ideas about egoism, altruism, and the social contract.

© Getty Images/Photos.com/Thinkstock

Morality seems to require that individuals sacrifice their own selfish interests for the benefit of others. We tend to praise altruists and condemn egoists. **Altruism** means, most basically, concern for the well-being of others. Some versions of altruism may even appear to hold that truly self-sacrificial behavior is the peak of moral development. Unlike altruists, **egoists** are primarily concerned with their own well-being. Sometimes egoists are purely selfish, even to the point of being willing to take advantage of others. But less selfish defenders of egoism may claim that egoism is not about taking advantage or being uncaring. Rather, egoism may be a descriptive thesis about human behavior, which claims that even apparently altruistic behavior is ultimately motivated by self-interest. From this perspective, people behave altruistically because they hope to gain something in return, even behaving altruistically in hope of developing social relations of cooperation, which are valuable in the long run. A further form of egoism holds that we would all be better off if people just looked out for themselves and left other people alone. From an egoistic perspective, social rules can be understood as resulting from agreements among rational and self-interested individuals. That idea is known as the **social contract theory**. This chapter considers egoism, altruism, and the theory of the social contract.

Popular culture is full of examples of the conflict between egoism and altruism. Television programs like *Survivor* create circumstances in which people are forced to forge short-term alliances to maximize their own self-interest. The film and book *The Hunger Games* shows us a life-and-death competition in which children struggle for survival in a war of all against all. In these contexts, egoism is to be expected and altruism is an exceptional and heroic virtue.

Our disagreements about ethics and political life often rest upon divergent ideas about human nature. We wonder whether people are basically egoistic or altruistic, whether we are motivated by self-interest, or whether we are able to genuinely concern ourselves with the interests of others. Our conception of social organizations, politics, and the law often rests upon what we think about the motives of individuals. Are individuals basically cooperative or competitive? Are individuals motivated primarily by egoistic or altruistic concerns? Should social organizations be set up to minimize the dangers of an inevitable cutthroat competition? Or is there a more cooperative and altruistic basis for social cooperation?

To think about these issues, we need to consider a basic empirical question: Are people basically selfish and primarily motivated by self-interest or are people altruistic and motivated by concern for others? We also have to ask a normative question: Is selfishness good or bad? These two issues illustrate two different versions or meanings of egoism and altruism. One version is descriptive and answers the empirical question. According to this version, egoism (or altruism) is a theory that describes what people are like. Simply put, **descriptive egoism** holds that people

are basically self-centered or selfish; that is, people primarily pursue their own self-interest. It is a view about how people behave or why they do what they do. It is often referred to as **psychological egoism**.

Egoism is opposed to altruism. Altruism is often viewed as pure concern for the well-being of others. Sometimes altruism is thought to require entirely unselfish behavior, even to the point at which we sacrifice ourselves for others. But a broader conception of altruism involves a variety of what psychologists call **pro-social behaviors**—that is, behaviors that are not primarily self-interested and that are motivated by basic concern for others.

The empirical question is whether human beings are motivated by self-interest or whether they are also motivated by non-self-interested concern for others. That empirical question is not so easy to answer. How do we really know what motivates others? Indeed, are you sure that you know what motivates you all of the time? Scientists have examined this question from various perspectives. Psychological studies, including accounts of developmental psychology, can give us some insight into what actually motivates people. Another line of inquiry looks at pro-social behavior from an evolutionary

Films such as *The Hunger Games* illustrate conflicts between egoism and altruism.

© Pictorial Press Ltd/Alamy

perspective. It turns out that pro-social cooperation produces an evolutionary advantage, especially in social species of animals such as our own. Individuals who cooperate with others tend to be able to pass on their genes better than selfish egoists and those who cheat. This is especially true when we cooperate with and support those who are related to us. Our genes get passed on when we are altruistic toward our close relations, helping those who share our genes to survive. This might explain why parents are willing to sacrifice for their own children—but not so willing to sacrifice for children to whom they are not related. It might also explain why we may be more willing to help a cousin than a stranger. Such an evolutionary explanation points toward instinctive forces that lie below the surface of our more explicit motivations and intentions.

Of course, an account of human behavior that is solely focused on the ways that pro-social behavior functions in evolutionary contexts fails to consider the subjective side of experience and human freedom. Sometimes our motivations and intentions run at cross-purposes to attitudes and behaviors that provide evolutionary advantage. Furthermore, it is possible to ask a normative question with regard to the descriptive science of pro-social behavior. We may be instinctively motivated to help those to whom we are more closely related. But should we really help our close relations and only our close relations? Maybe we should ignore everyone else and focus only on our own needs and interests. Or maybe we should focus our concern more broadly on humanity at large, possibly even extending moral concern to members of other species.

We must, then, ask a moral question with regard to the empirical science of egoism and altruism. *Should* we be motivated by self-interest or *should* we be concerned with the well-being of others? As a normative theory, **ethical egoism** holds that it is good for people to pursue their own self-interest. Some versions of ethical egoism also hold that altruism is misguided and wrong. In this view, not only should people pursue their own self-interest but they should also mind their own business and not reach out to help others. In defense of this idea, ethical egoists may argue that altruism breeds dependency

and undermines the self-esteem of those who receive benefits and gifts from do-gooder altruists.

Various authors have defended egoism. One of the most influential is the novelist and essayist Ayn Rand. Rand's ideas have had a significant influence on the thinking of a variety of American politicians—including former Texas Congressman Ron Paul (who ran for president in 2012), his son Senator Rand Paul (from Kentucky), and Wisconsin Congressman Paul Ryan (who was Mitt Romney's vice presidential running mate in 2012). Paul Ryan has explained that his reading of Ayn Rand is "the reason I got involved in public service."[1] These politicians tend to hold to a libertarian ideology, which emphasizes laissez-faire capitalism and limited government intervention (these political and economic issues are discussed in more detail in Chapter 14).

A fiercely individualistic émigré from Bolshevik Russia, Ayn Rand thought that altruism was pernicious. She argues that altruistic morality "regards man as a sacrificial animal" and that altruism "holds that man has no right to exist for his own sake, that service to others is the only justification of his existence, and that self-sacrifice is his highest moral duty, virtue and value." Her argument goes on to present the altruistic idea of self-sacrifice as a kind of death wish: "altruism holds *death* as its ultimate goal and standard of value—and it is logical that renunciation, resignation, self-denial, and every other form of suffering, including self-destruction, are the virtues it advocates."[2]

While Rand condemns altruism, most mainstream moralists tend to hold that altruism is better than egoism. We tend to praise self-sacrifice. And we tend to agree with the basic principle of altruism that is outlined in the Golden Rule—that you should "do unto others as you would have them do unto you." One might say that the moral point of view is one that involves some basic level of altruism. While altruists need not go to the extremes that Rand criticizes—in advocating suicidal self-sacrifice, for example—most people tend to think that pro-social and cooperative behavior are morally praiseworthy. Indeed, philosophers such as Kurt Baier, James Sterba, and Alan Gewirth have argued in various ways that egoism is basically inconsistent. As Gewirth explains, the egoist's moral claims do not apply to all other people in the same way that they apply to himself.[3] Furthermore, one might claim that the moral point of view simply ought to point toward altruism. Baier explains that one of our "most widely held moral convictions" is that "in certain circumstances it is morally wrong to promote one's own best interest or greatest good."[4] We tend to think that morality involves overcoming egoism and learning to develop an altruistic (or at least impartial and non-self-interested) point of view.

A further issue has to do with the question of how social cooperation is supposed to occur. Defenders of altruism can argue that there is something natural about developing and nurturing caring relationships with others—perhaps grounded in an account of natural family bonds or group belonging. It may appear to be more difficult for egoists to explain how self-interested egoists can avoid brutal and counterproductive competition and develop a system of cooperation. But cooperation can be explained as paying off in terms of self-interest. From the perspective of

Ayn Rand (1905–1982) was a well-known proponent of egoism.

egoism, it is rational for self-interested persons to cooperate, since cooperation tends to produce good outcomes for those who cooperate. One way of describing this is in terms of **reciprocal altruism**, which holds that altruistic behavior makes sense for self-interested persons when it is repaid in kind. A more elaborate development of reciprocal altruism is found in the social contract theory which holds that it is in each person's self-interest to join with others in a social contract, which serves to help us each to maximize our self-interest in community with others. We discuss the social contract theory in more detail at the end of this chapter.

PSYCHOLOGICAL EGOISM
What Is Psychological Egoism?

In general, psychological egoism is a descriptive theory about what people are like, but we can understand what it asserts in several ways. In one interpretation, it might be taken to say that people are basically selfish. Here, psychological egoism holds that people usually or always act for their own narrow and short-range self-interest. But a different formulation of this theory asserts that although people do act for their own self-interest, this self-interest is to be understood more broadly and as being more concerned with long-term outcomes. Thus, we might distinguish between acting selfishly and acting in our own self-interest.

In the broader view, many things are in a person's interest: good health, satisfaction in a career or work, prestige, self-respect, family, and friends. Moreover, if we really wanted to attain these things, we would need to avoid shortsighted selfishness. For example, we would have to be self-disciplined in diet and lifestyle to be healthy. We would need to plan long-term for a career. And we would need to be concerned about others and not be overbearing if we wanted to make and retain friends.

However, as some people have pointed out, we would not actually need to be concerned about others but only to *appear* to be concerned. Doing good to others, in this view, would be not for the sake of others but, rather, to enable one to call on those friends when they are needed. This would be helping a friend not for the friend's sake but for one's own sake.

Putting the matter in this way also raises another question about how to formulate this theory. Is psychological egoism a theory according to which people always act in their own best interests? Or does it hold that people are always motivated by the desire to attain their own best interests? The first version would be easily refuted; we notice that people do not always do what is best for them. They eat too much, choose the wrong careers, waste time, and so forth. This may be because they do not have sufficient knowledge to be good judges of what is in their best interests. Or it may be because of a phenomenon known as **weakness of will**. For example, I may want to lose weight or get an A in a course but may not quite get myself to do what I have to do in order to achieve my goal. Philosophers have puzzled over this problem, which is also called the problem of **akrasia** (to use the Greek term for the problem of weakness of will). This is a complex issue in moral psychology; to treat it adequately would take us beyond what we can do here.[5] But the basic concern is why we fail to do the things we know we ought to do. If we really know what we ought to do, it might seem that we would never fail to do what we ought.

On the other hand, it might well be true that people always do what they *think* is best for them. This version of psychological egoism, which we will address next, asserts that human beings act for the sake of their own best interests. In this version, the idea is not that people sometimes or always act in their own interests, but that this is the only thing that ultimately does motivate people. If they sometimes act for others, it is only because they think that it is in their own best interests to do so. A stronger version of psychological egoism asserts that people cannot do otherwise than act for the sake of their own interests. But how would we know this? We know how people do act, but how could we show that they cannot act otherwise? Perhaps we could appeal to certain views about human nature. We could argue that we always seek our own best interests because we are depraved by nature or perhaps by a religious "fall" such as the one described in the biblical book of Genesis.

Is Psychological Egoism True?

In the early 1990s, a study was done in which people were asked whether they believed in or supported the jury system; that is, should people be judged guilty or not guilty by a group of peers? Most responded that they do support the jury system. However, when asked whether they would serve on a jury if called, significantly fewer said they would.[6] Those who answered the two questions differently might have wanted justice for themselves but were not willing to extend it to others. Some of our most cherished social values may involve more selfish motivation than we generally like to admit. Consider the following story about Abraham Lincoln.[7] It is reported that one day as he was riding in a coach over a bridge he heard a mother pig squealing. Her piglets were drowning after having fallen into the creek and she could not get them out. Lincoln supposedly asked the coachman to stop, waded into the creek, and rescued the piglets. When his companion cited this as an example of unselfishness, Lincoln responded that it was not for the sake of the pigs that he acted as he did. Rather, it was because he would have no peace later when he recalled the incident if he did not do something about it now. In other words, although it seemed unselfish, his action was quite self-centered. Advocates for psychological egoism often draw on such accounts of underlying selfish motivations to bolster their arguments.

But how are we to evaluate the claims of psychological egoism? As a theory about human motivation, it is difficult, if not impossible, to prove. How do we assess the motivations of people? We cannot just assume that apparently altruistic individuals are acting for the sake of the selfish satisfaction they receive from what they do. Nor can we ask them, for individuals are often poor judges of what actually motivates them. We commonly hear or say to ourselves, "I don't know why I did that!"

Furthermore, it is difficult to distinguish different sources of our motivations. Are we innately egoistic or altruistic—that is, are we born with a tendency toward egoism or altruism? Or do our cultural values contribute to our egoistic (or altruistic) tendencies? For example, we might consider differences in socialization between boys and girls. It might be that female children, for example, are expected to be altruistic and caring, while male children are taught to be independent and self-motivated. And it might be that these differences in socialization are also dependent upon other cultural differences, with boys and girls from different cultures growing up with divergent dispositions toward altruism or egoism.

Leaving aside the issue of socialization, suppose that people do, in fact, get satisfaction from helping others. This is not the same thing as acting for the purpose of getting that satisfaction. What psychological egoism needs to show is not that people do get satisfaction from what they do, but that achieving such satisfaction is their aim. Now we can find at least some examples in our own actions to test this theory. Do we read the book to get satisfaction or to learn something? Do we pursue that career opportunity because of the satisfaction that we think it will bring or because of the nature of the opportunity? Do we volunteer to help the sick or the needy because we think it will give us personal satisfaction or because we think it will actually help someone? In addition, directly aiming at satisfaction may not be the best way to achieve it. Henry Sidgwick described this as the **paradox of hedonism**: "The impulse toward pleasure, if too predominant, defeats its own aim."[8] We probably have a better chance of being happy if we do not aim at happiness itself but obtain happiness while pursuing other worthwhile objects.

Thus, we have seen that the most reasonable or common form of psychological egoism, a theory about human motivation, is especially difficult to prove. It also can't be disproved or falsified. Even if it were shown that we *often* act for the sake of our own interest or satisfaction, this is not enough to prove that psychological egoism is true. According to this theory, we must show that people *always* act to promote their own interests. We need next to consider whether this has any relevance to the normative question of how we *ought* to act.

ETHICAL EGOISM
What Is Ethical Egoism?

Ethical egoism is a normative theory. It is a theory about what we *ought* to do, how we *ought* to act. As with psychological egoism, we can formulate ethical egoism in different ways. One version is *individual ethical egoism*. According to this version, I ought to look out only for my own interests. I ought to

be concerned about others only to the extent that this concern also contributes to my own interests. A slightly broader formulation of ethical egoism, sometimes called *universal ethical egoism*, maintains that people ought to look out for and seek only their own best interests. As in the individual form, in this second version people ought to help others only when and to the extent that it is in their own best interests to do so. It is possible to explain cooperation from this perspective as a kind of reciprocal altruism: we cooperate because we each see that it is in our own self-interest to cooperate. As the saying goes, I'll scratch your back, if you scratch mine. From this point of view, what I really want is to get my back scratched (something I cannot do for myself), and I realize that in order to get what I want, I have to give you something you want in return.

Is Ethical Egoism a Good Theory?

We can evaluate ethical egoism in several ways. We will consider its grounding in psychological egoism and its consistency or coherence. We will also consider how it explains social cooperation in the social contract theory as well as its derivation from economic theory. We will finally consider its conformity to commonsense moral views.

Grounding in Psychological Egoism   Let us consider first whether psychological egoism, if true, would provide a good foundation for ethical egoism. It might be that we should affirm egoism because people are basically and unavoidably egoistic. But recall the discussion of the naturalistic fallacy in Chapter 1: it is not clear that we can derive the *value* of ethical egoism from the *fact* of psychological egoism. If people were in fact always motivated by their own interests, then would this be a good reason to hold that they *ought* to be so motivated? It seems superfluous to tell people that they ought to do what they always do anyway or will do no matter what. One would think that at least sometimes one of the functions of moral language is to try to motivate ourselves or others to do what we are not inclined to do. For example, I might tell myself that even though I could benefit by cheating on a test, it is wrong, and so I should not do it.

Furthermore, the fact that we do behave in a certain way seems a poor reason for believing that we ought to do so. If people always cheated or lied, we ask, would that in itself make these acts right? Thus, although it may at first seem reasonable to rely on a belief about people's basic selfishness to prove that people ought to look out for themselves alone, this seems far from convincing.

Consistency or Coherence   Universal ethical egoism in particular is possibly inconsistent or incoherent. According to this version of ethical egoism, everyone ought to seek his or her own best interests. However, could anyone consistently support such a view? Wouldn't this mean that we would want our own best interests served and at the same time be willing to allow that others serve their interests—even to our own detriment? If food were scarce, then I would want enough for myself and yet at the same time would have to say that I should not have it for myself when another needs it to survive. This view seems to have an internal inconsistency. We might compare it to playing a game in which I can say that the other player ought to block my move, even though at the same time I hope that she or he does not do so.

The Prisoner's Dilemma   A serious problem plaguing agreements that are made among egoists is the temptation to cheat. If I agree to scratch your back, after you scratch mine, what guarantee do you have that I will follow through on my promise, once I've gotten my back scratched? If we are both convinced that human beings are basically egoistic, then you will suspect that I will cheat (and I'll suspect that you will cheat), in which case it will be difficult to cooperate. For this reason, there is a worry that egoism will lead to conflict and war. To prevent this from happening, even egoists might agree that we need something external to ourselves to guarantee that we do not renege on our promises. This is the basis for the development of the social contract, which can be interpreted as an agreement made by self-interested persons who want to establish a legal system that ensures that promises are kept and that prevents cheating by egoists.

The problem for egoism can be clarified with reference to a thought experiment known as **the prisoner's dilemma**. Imagine that the cops arrest two suspects, X and Y. The cops have the prisoners in two separate rooms. They offer each prisoner the following deal: If you betray the other suspect, you will go free instead of getting a twenty-year term in prison; but if you both betray each other, you will each end up with ten years in prison. On the other hand, if both prisoners keep their mouths shut and refuse to betray each other, there will be no conviction and they will both go free. The choices look like this:

	Y betrays X	**Y does not betray X**
X betrays Y	Each ends up with 10 years	X goes free; Y gets 20 years
X does not betray Y	Y goes free; X gets 20 years	Each goes free

For the prisoners, the best option is if they coordinate their choices and both refuse to betray each other. But if the prisoners suspect each other of being self-interested egoists, they will not trust each other. Each will suspect that the other prisoner will betray him in pursuit of a better deal. And so it is likely that self-interested prisoners will end up with less-than-optimal outcomes. Each prisoner will suspect the other of operating out of self-interested motives that will lead toward cheating and reneging on prior promises. The prisoner's dilemma thought experiment is often used as a model to show why we need some larger structure to ensure that we do not break our promises. It might be that morality itself provides that larger structure: if we would just agree to comply with the dictates of morality, we would be able to guarantee cooperation. But if there are egoists who would break moral rules when they think that they can get away with it, we might need something stronger than morality—we might need an enforcement mechanism, that is, something like a legal and political system that helps to guarantee cooperation. It is possible, then, that rational, self-interested individuals would agree to something like a social contract.

The Social Contract   Theory provides a justification of the legal system that is grounded in the rational self-interest of human beings. The idea of the social contract is that it is rational for self-interested individuals to join together and submit to the rule of law in order to ensure that promises are kept and that social cooperation will occur. One of the earliest versions of this idea is found in the writings of the seventeenth-century English philosopher Thomas Hobbes. Hobbes holds that individuals are self-interested; that is, they seek to fulfill their interests and desires and above all seek self-preservation. Hobbes maintains that in the state of nature, individuals would be equal in terms of strength, since even weak individuals can band together with others or use sneak attacks to overpower stronger individuals. Conflict arises when these equally powerful individuals seek the same thing. The individuals competing will thereby become enemies. As a result, the state of nature will be one of war, of all against all, and the results, as Hobbes describes them, are quite bleak,

> In such condition there is no place for industry, because the fruit thereof is uncertain, and consequently, no culture of the earth, no navigation, nor the use of commodities that may be imported by sea, no commodious building, no instruments of moving and removing such things as require much force, no knowledge of the face of the earth, no account of time, no arts, no letters, no society, and which is worst of all, continual fear and danger of violent death, and the life of man, solitary, poor, nasty, brutish, and short."[9]

The solution is peace via an agreement in which one gives up as much liberty "as against other men, as he would allow other men against himself."[10] For Hobbes, the social contract is an agreement to give up certain things to better secure one's own self-interest. Thus, individuals will agree to certain rules, which would be in each individual's best interest to accept and obey. To secure the peace and ensure that these rules are obeyed, Hobbes believes that an absolute sovereign ruler is required.

Hobbes's social contract theory is based on a desire of each person to secure his own advantage while agreeing to social rules enforced by a sovereign; it is a view of how society should function and thus both a political and a moral position. Other versions of the social contract idea were proposed by philosophers such as John Locke and Jean-Jacques Rousseau. Contemporary moral and political theories that appeal to contract ideas can be found in the works of Thomas Scanlon, David Gauthier, and John Rawls.[11] Gauthier's idea is that we should imagine basic moral rules that rational, self-interested parties would voluntarily agree to. Gauthier suggests that rational, self-interested agents would recognize the need for mutual restraint: it is in the interest of self-interested agents to agree to restrain the unbridled pursuit of self-interest.

John Rawls's views are especially influential and will be treated further in Chapter 14. For Rawls, justice is fairness. How would we know if a particular distribution of goods in a society is fair? Rawls argues that to know if a distribution is fair, we would need to ask what people would accept, if they were ignorant of the position they actually occupy in society. What would rational self-interested people agree to, in terms of laws and institutions, if they did not know if they were young or old, rich or poor, male or female, healthy or disabled? Rawls imagines an ideal form of social contract, which is supposed to help us see what rational, self-interested people would agree to in terms of justice.

Derivation from Economic Theory One argument for ethical egoism is taken from economic theory—for example, that proposed by Adam Smith. He and other proponents of **laissez-faire capitalism** (a form of capitalism with minimal government regulation or intervention) argue that self-interest provides the best economic motivation. The idea is that when the profit motive or individual incentives are absent, people will either not work or not work as well. If it is my land or my business, then I will be more likely to take care of it than if the profits go to others or to the government. In addition, Smith believed that in a system in which each person looks out for his or her own economic interests, the general outcome will be best, as though an "invisible hand" were guiding things.[12]

Although this is not the place to go into an extended discussion of economic theory, it is enough to point out that not everyone agrees on the merits of laissez-faire capitalism. Much can be said for the competition that it supports, but it does raise questions, for example, about the breakdown of "winners" and "losers" in such a competition.

Is it acceptable if the same individuals, families, or groups consistently win or lose, generation after generation? What if there are many more economic "losers" than a few extremely wealthy "winners?" And what about those with innate or inherited disadvantages that prevent them from competing? Is care for these people a community responsibility? Recent community-oriented theories of social morality stress just this notion of responsibility and oppose laissez-faire capitalism's excessive emphasis on individual rights.[13] (Further discussion of capitalism can be found in Chapter 14.) In any case, a more basic question can be asked about the relevance of economics to morality. Even if an economic system worked well or efficiently, would this prove that morality ought to be modeled on it? Is not the moral life broader than the economic life? Are all human relations economic relations?

Furthermore, the argument that everyone ought to seek his or her own best interests because this contributes to the general well-being is not ethical egoism at all—since self-interest is, here, merely used as a means to pursuing a broader collective value. As we will come to see more clearly when we examine it, this is a form of utilitarianism. (We evaluate this issue in our discussion of utilitarianism in the next chapter.)

Conformity to Commonsense Morality Finally, is ethical egoism supported by commonsense morality? On the one hand, some elements of ethical egoism seem to be contrary to commonsense morality. For example, doesn't it assume that anything is all right as long as it serves an individual's best interests? Torturing human beings or animals would be permitted so long as this served one's interests. When not useful to one's interests, traditional virtues of honesty, fidelity, and loyalty would have no value. Ethical egoists could argue on empirical or factual grounds that the torturing of others is never in one's best interests because this would make one less sensitive, and being sensitive is generally useful to an individual's objectives. Similarly, they might argue that the development of traditional virtues is often in one's own best interests because these traits are valued by society. For example, my possessing these traits may enable me to get what I

want more readily. Whether these are good enough reasons to value these virtues or condemn torture is something you must judge for yourself.

Part of the intuitive appeal of egoism may derive from the sense that people ought to take better care of themselves. By having a high regard for ourselves, we increase our self-esteem. We then depend less on others and more on ourselves. We might also be stronger and happier. These are surely desirable traits. The altruist, moreover, might be too self-effacing. He might be said to lack a proper regard for himself. There is also some truth in the view that unless one takes care of oneself, one is not of much use to others. This view implies not ethical egoism, however, but again a form of utilitarianism.

THE MORAL POINT OF VIEW

Finally, we will consider briefly two issues related to ethical egoism that have puzzled philosophers in recent decades. One is whether one must take a particular point of view to understand things morally and whether that point of view is incompatible with egoism. The other, which is treated in the next section, is whether there are self-interested reasons to be moral.

Suppose that a person cares for no one but herself. Would you consider that person to be a moral person? This is not to ask whether she is a morally good person, but rather whether one can think of her as even operating in the moral realm, so to speak. In other words, the question concerns not whether the person's morality is a good one but whether she has any morals at all.

To take an example from W. D. Falk, suppose we want to know whether a person has been given a moral education.[14] Someone might answer that she had because she had been taught not to lie, to treat others kindly, not to drink to excess, and to work hard. When asked what reasons she had been given for behaving thus, suppose she responded that she was taught not to lie because others would not trust her if she did. She was taught to treat others well because then they would treat her well in return. She was taught to work hard because of the satisfaction this brought her or because she would then be better able to support herself. Would you consider her to have been given a moral education?

Falk thinks not. He suggests that she was given counsels of prudence, not morality. She was told what she probably should do to succeed in certain walks of life. She was taught the means that prudence would suggest she use to secure her own self-interest. According to Falk, only if she had been taught not to lie because it was wrong to do so, or because others had a right to know the truth, would she have been given a moral instruction. Only if she had been taught to treat others well because they deserved to be so treated, or that it would be wrong to do otherwise, would the counsel be a moral one. Similarly with working hard, if she had been told that she ought not to waste her talents or that she ought to contribute to society because it was the right thing to do, the teaching would have been a moral one. In summary, the education would not have been a moral one if it had been egoistically oriented. Do you agree?

Taking the moral point of view, on this interpretation, would then involve being able to see beyond ourselves and our own interests. It may also mean that we attempt to see things from another's point of view or to be impartial. Morality would then be thought of as providing rules for social living—ways, for example, of settling conflicts. The rules would apply equally to all, or one would have to give reasons why some persons would be treated differently than others. One reason might be that some persons had worked harder than others or their particular roles demanded differential treatment.

But this view of morality as a set of neutral and impartial social rules raises a number of tricky questions. We do not think that we have to justify treating those close to us differently and more favorably than others. If we care more for our own children or our own friends than we do for strangers, does this mean that we are not operating in the moral domain? Questions can be raised about the extent to which impartiality influences the moral domain or is required in order to be moral. Some feminists, for example, would rather define morality in terms of sympathy and caring. (See Chapter 9 for further treatment of this issue.)

WHY BE MORAL?

Let us assume that morality does involve being able at least sometimes to take the other's point of view and at some level to treat people equally or impartially. Why should anyone do that, especially when it is not in her or his best interests to do so? In other words, are there any reasons we can give to show why one should be moral? One reason is that doing what one ought to do is just what being moral means. One should not ask why one ought to do what one ought to do! However, perhaps something more can be said.

Notice that this is a question about why I as an individual ought to be moral. This is not the same as asking why everyone ought to be moral. We could argue that it is generally better for people to have and follow moral rules. Without such rules, our social lives would be pretty wretched. As Hobbes suggests, a life of egoism in the state of nature would be one of constant conflict and war. However, this does not answer the question concerning why I should be moral when it is not in my best interests to do so.

If you were trying to convince someone why he should be moral, how would you do it? You might appeal to his fear of reprisal if he did not generally follow moral rules. If he is not honest, then he will not be trusted. If he steals, he risks being punished. Plato's dialogue, *The Republic*, includes a story about a shepherd named Gyges. Gyges comes into possession of a ring that he discovers makes him invisible when he turns it around on his finger. He proceeds to take advantage of his invisibility and take what he wants from others. Plato wonders whether we all would not do the same if we, like Gyges, could get away with it. Some believe we would. But is that right? Is avoiding punishment the only reason that people do the right thing?

There are other more positive but still self-interested reasons you might offer someone to convince her that she ought to be moral. You might tell her that, as in Falk's moral education example, being virtuous is to one's own advantage. You might recall some of the advice from Benjamin Franklin's *Poor Richard's Almanac*.[15] "A stitch in time saves nine." "Observe all men, thyself most." "Spare and have is better than spend and crave." Many of the moral aphorisms put forward by motivational speakers and self-help gurus—from Dr. Phil and Oprah Winfrey to Deepak Chopra—are focused on maximizing self-interest. These are the self-interested counsels of a practical morality. It turns out, as the philosopher Philippa Foot and others have argued, that most of the traditional virtues are in our own best interests. It is in our interests to be temperate, courageous, thrifty, kind, honest, and so on—because these virtues help us live a stable life in a world that we share with others. Indeed, it does appear to be in our interests to be altruistic, since concern for others is often reciprocated.

You might go even further in thinking about reasons to be moral. You might make the point that being moral is ennobling. Even when it involves sacrifice for a cause, being a moral person gives one a certain dignity, integrity, and self-respect. Only humans are capable of being moral, you might say, and human beings cannot flourish without being moral. You can give more thought to this question when you read about Kant's moral theory in Chapter 6. For Kant, human dignity and worth is wholly bound up with being able to act for moral reasons.

Nevertheless, one can point to many examples in which people who break the moral rules seem to get away with it and fare better than those who follow them. "Nice guys [and gals?] finish last," as baseball great Leo Durocher put it. If being moral seems too demanding, then some say this is too bad for morality. We ought to have a good life, even if it means sacrificing something of morality. In another view, if being moral involves sacrificing something of the personally fulfilling life and perhaps even "finishing last" sometimes, then this is what must be done. No one ever said being moral was going to be easy![16]

NOTES

1. Stephen Prothero, "You Can't Reconcile Ayn Rand and Jesus," *USA Today*, June 5, 2011, accessed March 13, 2013, http://usatoday30.usatoday.com/news/opinion/forum/2011-06-05-Ayn-Rand-and-Jesus-dont-mix_n.htm

2. Ayn Rand, "The Objectivist Ethics," available at the Ayn Rand Institute website: http://www.aynrand.org/site/PageServer?pagename=ari_ayn_rand_the_objectivist_ethics

3. Alan Gewirth, *Reason and Morality* (Chicago: University of Chicago Press, 1981), 85.

4. Kurt Baier, *The Rational and the Moral Order* (Open Court, 1995), 159. Also see James P. Sterba, "Morality and Self-Interest," *Philosophy and Phenomenological Research* 59, no. 2 (June 1999).

5. For a discussion of "weakness of will," see Gwynneth Matthews, "Moral Weakness," *Mind* 299 (July 1966): 405–19; Donald Davidson, "How Is Weakness of the Will Possible?" in *Moral Concepts*, ed. Joel Feinberg (New York: Oxford University Press, 1970), 93–113.

6. Amitai Etzioni, a presentation at the University of San Francisco, December 1, 1992.

7. From the *Springfield Monitor* (ca. 1928), cited in Louis Pojman, *Ethics* (Belmont, CA: Wadsworth, 1990), 41.

8. Henry Sidgwick, *The Methods of Ethics* (London: MacMillan and Co., 1884), 47.

9. Thomas Hobbes, *Leviathan*, in *The English Works of Thomas Hobbes*, ed. Sir William Molesworth (London: John Bohn, 1839), 2:38–41, 85.

10. Ibid., Chapter 14.

11. Tom Scanlon, *What We Owe Each Other* (Cambridge, MA: Harvard University Press, 1998); David Gauthier, *Morals by Agreement* (Oxford: Oxford University Press, 1987); John Rawls, *A Theory of Justice* (Cambridge, MA: Harvard University Press, 1971).

12. See Adam Smith, *The Wealth of Nations* (New York: Edwin Cannan, 1904).

13. See the communitarian views in Robert Bellah, *Habits of the Heart* (Berkeley: University of California Press, 1985), and Amitai Etzioni, *The Spirit of Community: Rights, Responsibilities, and the Communitarian Agenda* (New York: Crown, 1993).

14. W. D. Falk, "Morality, Self, and Others," in *Morality and the Language of Conduct*, ed. Hector-Neri Castaneda and George Nakhnikian (Detroit: Wayne State University Press, 1963), 25–67.

15. Benjamin Franklin, "Poor Richard's Almanac," in *American Philosophy: A Historical Anthology*, ed. Barbara MacKinnon (New York: State University of New York Press, 1985), 46–47.

16. See Thomas Nagel's discussion of these different possibilities of the relation between the good life and the moral life in "Living Right and Living Well," in *The View from Nowhere* (New York: Oxford University Press, 1986), 189–207. Also see David Gauthier, "Morality and Advantage," *The Philosophical Review* (1967): 460–75.

1. Explain the basic difference between psychological egoism and ethical egoism.
2. Give two different formulations or versions of psychological egoism and ethical egoism.
3. To prove that the motivational version of psychological egoism is true, what must be shown?
4. How is psychological egoism supposed to provide support for an argument for ethical egoism? What is one problem for this argument?
5. Summarize the arguments regarding the consistency or inconsistency of ethical egoism.
6. In what sense does the argument for ethical egoism based on economics support not egoism but utilitarianism? in other words, the view that we ought to do what is in the best interest of all or the greatest number?
7. Explain how the prisoner's dilemma can be used in discussions of egoism and cooperative endeavor.
8. What is meant by taking the "moral point of view?"
9. Is Hobbes's proposed solution to the problem of egoism, via the social contract, acceptable?
10. How might a discussion of evolution inform your understanding of the conflict between egoism and altruism?

Utilitarianism and John Stuart Mill

5

Getty Images/Photos.com

Learning Outcomes

After reading this chapter, you should be able to:

- Understand the differences between utilitarianism and egoism as kinds of consequentialism.
- Explain the difference between act utilitarianism and rule utilitarianism.
- Explain the trolley problem and how it exemplifies the challenge of utilitarianism.
- Identify key components of the utilitarian assessment of pleasure: intensity, duration, fruitfulness, likelihood.

- Articulate ways that utilitarianism is connected with hedonism and Epicureanism.
- Apply utilitarian reasoning to a variety of cases in the real world.
- Provide an overview of John Stuart Mill's defense of utilitarianism.
- Defend your own thesis with regard to the value of utilitarianism.

In 2011, the global population hit the seven billion mark. Demographers predict that another billion people will be added to the world's population by 2025.[1] The increase in human population during the past two centuries has been explosive. Causes for this growth include industrialization, a revolution in agriculture and other technologies, and better political organization. This growing population has created problems, however, as soils are depleted, oceans are overfished, and pollution has increased. Industrialization and technology have led to massive use of carbon-based fuels, which contribute to global climate change. If the world's population keeps growing at the current pace—and if the growing human population eats, drives, and consumes at current rates—we may be headed for a worldwide environmental and humanitarian crisis. A United Nations report published in 2012 argued,

> As the population grows from 7 billion to almost 9 billion by 2040, and the number of middle-class consumers increases by 3 billion over the next 20 years, the demand for resources will rise exponentially. By 2030, the world will need at least 50 per cent more food, 45 per cent more energy and 30 per cent more water—all at a time when environmental boundaries are throwing up new limits to supply.[2]

Some argue that a prudent solution would be to take steps to limit consumption, population growth, or both. In China, policies are already in place that seek to limit reproduction to one child per family. Such policies obviously impinge upon a basic liberty—the freedom to reproduce. The means that are used to control population include morally controversial technologies such as abortion. Moral concerns also haunt proposals to limit consumption: each of us wants the freedom to earn, spend, and consume as we wish. Even though individuals enjoy expanding their families and consuming products, the cumulative choices of individuals pursuing their own happiness can lead to less happiness for all—as the overall increase in population, pollution, and environmental degradation may well decrease opportunities and life prospects for everyone. When we think about issues from this perspective—one that takes into account the general happiness of everyone—we are adopting a utilitarian point of view.

Utilitarian reasoning can be used to justify a variety of actions and policy decisions. How do we justify speed limits on the highways? It might seem that each of us should be free to go as fast as we want. However, unbridled speed would result in more accidents, which not only kill people but also slow the rest of us down. Speed limits satisfy the utilitarian goal of maximizing the greatest happiness for the greatest number. Some will be unhappy because they can't drive 100 mph. But when we each drive at 65 mph and arrive safely, we are each more likely to be better off. Some may be less happy because they are forced to drive more slowly, but overall more of us are happier.

Some uses of utilitarian reasoning are controversial because they seem to run counter to our intuitions about basic principles of right and wrong. Consider, for example, the use of torture in interrogations of terror suspects. If a terrorist had planted a bomb in a public place that would threaten to kill thousands of innocent people, would it be justifiable to torture the terrorist to force him to reveal the location of the bomb? On the one hand, some assert that torture is never permissible because it violates basic moral principles. The Geneva Conventions regulating warfare prohibit torture and define it as "any act by which severe pain or suffering, whether physical or mental, is intentionally inflicted on a person for such purposes as obtaining from him or a third person information or a confession."[3] On the other hand, suppose, for example, that torture could save many lives. Would it then be justified? Former Vice President Dick Cheney maintains that "enhanced interrogation techniques" including waterboarding (a process that simulates drowning) have produced useful information. According to the *New York Times,* the CIA waterboarded terror suspect Khaled

Crowded village ferry crossing the River Hooghly, West Bengal, India.

Annie Owen/Robert Harding World Imagery/Passage/Corbis

Sheikh Mohammed 183 times.[4] In a speech on the tenth anniversary of September 11, Cheney claimed that by waterboarding terrorists such as Mohammed, information was extracted that led to the assassination of Osama bin Laden.[5] Cheney and other members of the Bush administration justify torture on utilitarian grounds, and their view is shared by many. A Pentagon study of "the ethics of troops on the front line" in Iraq found that 41 percent said that "torture should be allowed to save the life of a soldier or Marine," and about the same number said that it "should be allowed to gather important information from insurgents."[6] From a utilitarian standpoint, it may make good sense to inflict pain on someone to prevent pain that would be inflicted on a greater number of others. From the same standpoint, however, one may argue that practices such as torture cause greater harm than good—by frequently extracting false confessions and lowering a country's standing with potential allies. In any event, the question remains: Does a good end justify otherwise objectionable means?

WEIGHING CONSEQUENCES

One way of thinking about this is to compare the benefits and costs of each alternative. Whichever has the greater net benefit is the best alternative. Such an approach begins with the belief that we can measure and compare the risks and benefits of various actions. The idea is that actions are morally better or worse depending on whether they produce pleasure or pain or, more abstractly, on how they affect human well-being and happiness. Unlike egoism, utilitarianism focuses on the *sum* of individual pleasures and pains. It is not my pleasures or pains that matter—but the cumulative happiness of a number of people.

Another aspect of utilitarianism is the belief that each of us counts equally—no one counts for more than others. Peter Singer, perhaps the most influential contemporary defender of utilitarianism, derives utilitarianism from the basic idea that each person's interests ought to be given equal consideration. Related to this is the idea that "my own interests cannot count for more, simply because they are my own, than the interests of others."[7] The basic procedure for utilitarianism is to add up the interests of everyone who is affected by an action without privileging the interests of anyone in particular. Utilitarianism is thus opposed to racist or sexist ideas, for example, which often hold that the interests of some people matter more than the interests of others.

Utilitarianism suggests that we ought to consider the totality of consequences of a policy or action. Forms of utilitarianism will differ depending on how we understand what sorts of consequences or interests matter. Complexities arise in defining key concepts such as happiness, interest, and well-being. Singer, for example, wants to focus on *interests* instead of pleasures or happiness. This indicates that it is possible that some pleasures are not really in our interest. Drug use, for example, can produce pleasure; but it is not in anyone's long-term interest to be addicted to cocaine or heroin. We might also focus on people's *preferences*—that is, what people themselves state that they prefer. But again there is an important question of whether our preferences actually coordinate with our interests—or can we prefer things that are not in our interest? In different terms, we might wonder whether pleasure is a good thing or whether genuine happiness can be reduced to pleasure. In any case, utilitarians have to provide an account of what matters when we try to add up benefits and harms—whether it is subjective feeling, taste and preference, or whether it is something deeper and more objective such as well-being or other interests (in health, longevity, fulfillment, accomplishment, etc.).

Utilitarianism also has to provide an account of *whose* interests or happiness matters. Jeremy Bentham, one of the founding fathers of utilitarianism, extended his utilitarian concern in a way that included all suffering beings, including nonhuman animals. Peter Singer would agree. He is well-known as an advocate of animal welfare. Like Bentham, he claims that the interests of nonhuman animals ought to be taken into account. We discuss the issue of animal ethics further in Chapter 17.

One important point to bear in mind when discussing utilitarianism is that utilitarians generally do not think that actions or policies are good or bad in themselves. Rather, for the utilitarian, the goodness or badness of an action is solely a function of its consequences. Thus, even killing innocent people may be acceptable if it produces an outcome that saves a greater number of others from harm.

HISTORICAL BACKGROUND
Jeremy Bentham and John Stuart Mill

The classical formulation of utilitarian moral theory is found in the writings of Jeremy Bentham (1748–1832) and John Stuart Mill (1806–1873). Jeremy Bentham was an English-born student of law and the leader of a radical movement for social and legal reforms based on utilitarian principles. His primary published work was *Introduction to the Principles of Morals and Legislation* (1789). The title itself indicates his aim—namely, to take the same principles that provide the basis for morals as a guide for the formation and revision of law. Bentham believed that the same principles guided both social and personal morality.

James Mill, the father of John Stuart Mill, was an associate of Bentham's and a supporter of his views. John Stuart was the eldest of James's nine children. He was educated in the classics and history at home. By the time he was twenty, he had read Bentham and had become a devoted follower of his philosophy. The basic ideas of utilitarian moral theory are summarized in Mill's short work *Utilitarianism*, in which he sought to dispel the misconception that morality has nothing to do with usefulness or utility or that morality is opposed to pleasure. Mill was also a strong supporter of personal liberty, and in his pamphlet *On Liberty* he argued that the only reason for society to interfere in a person's life was to prevent him or her from doing harm to others. People might choose wrongly, but he believed that allowing bad choices was better than government coercion. Liberty to speak one's own opinion, he believed, would benefit all. However, it is not clear that utility is always served by promoting liberty. Nor is it clear what Mill would say about cases in which liberty must be restricted to promote the general good, as in the case of speed limits or airport security rules. In his work *On the Subjection of Women*, Mill also emphasized the general good and criticized those social treatments of women that did not allow them to develop their talents and contribute to the good of society. Consistent with these views, he also supported the right of women to vote. Later in life he

The Print Collector/Alamy

A portrait of the utilitarian philosopher John Stuart Mill (1806–1873).

married his longtime companion and fellow liberal, Harriet Taylor. Mill also served in the British Parliament from 1865 to 1868.

The original utilitarians were democratic, progressive, empiricist, and optimistic. They were democratic in the sense that they believed that social policy ought to work for the good of all persons, not just the upper class. They believed that when interests of various persons conflicted, the best choice was that which promoted the interests of the greater number. The utilitarians were progressive in that they questioned the status quo. They believed that if, for example, the contemporary punishment system was not working well, then it ought to be changed. Social programs should be judged by their usefulness in promoting the greatest happiness for the greatest number. Observation would determine whether a project or practice succeeded in this goal. Thus, utilitarianism is part of the empiricist tradition in philosophy, which holds that we know what is good only by observation or by appeal to experience. Bentham and Mill were also optimists. They believed that human wisdom and science would improve the lot of humanity. Mill wrote in *Utilitarianism*, "All the grand sources of human suffering are in a great degree, many of them almost entirely, conquerable by human care and effort."[8]

In this chapter, you will learn about the basic principle of utilitarianism and how it is used to make moral judgments in individual cases. You will also learn something about different forms of utilitarianism. Finally, you will get a chance to examine a few criticisms of utilitarianism so as to judge for yourself whether it is a reasonable theory.

THE PRINCIPLE OF UTILITY

The basic moral principle of utilitarianism is called the **principle of utility** or the **greatest happiness principle**. As John Stuart Mill explained it, "actions are right in proportion as they tend to promote happiness, wrong as they tend to produce the reverse of happiness."

Utilitarianism is a form of consequentialism. It focuses on the consequences of actions. Egoism is also a form of consequentialism. But unlike egoism, utilitarianism focuses on the consequences for all persons impacted by an action. Consider the diagram used to classify moral theories provided in Chapter 1.

According to classical utilitarian moral theory, when we evaluate human acts or practices, we consider neither the nature of the acts or practices nor the motive for which people do what they do. As Mill put it, "He who saves a fellow creature from drowning does what is morally right, whether his motive be duty or the hope of being paid for his trouble."[9] It is the result of one's action—that a life is saved—that matters morally. According to utilitarianism, we ought to decide which action or practice is best by considering the likely or actual consequences of each alternative. For example, over the years people have called for a suicide barrier on the Golden Gate Bridge to prevent people from using it to commit suicide. More than 1,400 people have jumped from the bridge to their deaths.[10] Building a suicide barrier on a bridge is neither good nor bad in itself, according to utilitarianism. Nor is it sufficient that people supporting the building of such a barrier be well intentioned. The only thing that matters for the utilitarian is whether,

by erecting such a barrier, we would actually increase happiness by preventing suicides.

PLEASURE AND HAPPINESS

Of course, there is an open question about whether suicide is good or bad. Some will argue that there is something inherently or intrinsically wrong with suicide. The deontologist Immanuel Kant provides this sort of argument, as you will see in the next chapter, maintaining that suicide is wrong in principle. But utilitarians cannot argue that suicide is intrinsically wrong—since they do not focus on the intrinsic rightness or wrongness of acts. Instead, utilitarians have to consider the impact of suicide on the happiness of all those it affects.

Since utilitarians reject the idea that certain acts are intrinsically good or evil, they are open to experimentation and evidence. And they are open to various ways of conceiving the goodness of consequences. Any sort of consequences might be considered good—for example, power or fame or fortune. However, classical utilitarianism is a *pleasure* or *happiness* theory, meaning that it tends to reduce all other goods to some form of pleasure or happiness. Utilitarianism was not the first such theory to appear in the history of philosophy. Aristotle's ethics, as we shall see in Chapter 8, also focuses on happiness, although it is different from utilitarianism in its focus on virtue. Closer to utilitarianism is the classical theory that has come to be known as **hedonism** (from *hedon*, the Greek word for pleasure) or **Epicureanism** (named after Epicurus, 341–270 BCE). Epicurus held that the good life was the pleasant life. For him, this meant avoiding distress and desires for things beyond one's basic needs. Bodily pleasure and mental delight and peace were the goods to be sought in life.

Utilitarians believe that pleasure or happiness is the good to be produced. As Bentham put it, "Nature has placed mankind under the governance of two sovereign masters, *pain* and *pleasure*. It is for them alone to point out what we ought to do, as well as to determine what we shall do."[11] Things such as fame, fortune, education, and freedom may be good, but only to the extent that they produce pleasure or happiness. In philosophical terms, they are **instrumental goods** because they are useful for attaining the goals of happiness and pleasure. Happiness and pleasure are the only **intrinsic goods**—that is, the only things good in themselves.

In this explanation of utilitarianism, you may have noticed the seeming identification of pleasure and happiness. In classical utilitarianism, there is no difference between pleasure and happiness. Both terms refer to a kind of psychic state of satisfaction. However, there are different types of pleasure of which humans are capable. According to Mill, we experience a range of pleasures or satisfactions from the physical satisfaction of hunger to the personal satisfaction of a job well done. Aesthetic pleasures, such as the enjoyment of watching a beautiful sunset, are yet another type of pleasure. We also can experience intellectual pleasures such as the peculiar satisfaction of making sense out of something. Mill's theory includes the idea that there are higher, uniquely human pleasures—as we will explain below.

In Mill's view, we should consider the range of types of pleasure in our attempts to decide what the best action is. We also ought to consider other aspects of the pleasurable or happy experience. According to the greatest happiness or utility principle, we must measure, count, and compare the pleasurable experiences likely to be produced by various alternative actions in order to know which is best.

CALCULATING THE GREATEST AMOUNT OF HAPPINESS

Utilitarianism is not an egoistic theory. As we noted in the previous chapter's presentation on egoism, those versions of egoism that said we ought to take care of ourselves because this works out better for all in the long run are actually versions of utilitarianism, not egoism. Some philosophers have called utilitarianism *universalistic* because it is the happiness or pleasure of all who are affected by an action or practice that is to be considered. We are not just to consider our own good, as in egoism, nor just the good of others, as in altruism. Sacrifice may be good, but not in itself. As Mill puts it, "A sacrifice which does not increase or tend to increase the sum total of happiness, (utilitarianism) considers as wasted."[12] Everyone affected by some action is to be counted equally. We ourselves hold no privileged place, so our own happiness

counts no more than that of others. I may be required to do what displeases me but pleases others. Thus, in the following scenario, Act B is a better choice than Act A:

Act A makes me happy and two other people happy.
Act B makes me unhappy but five others happy.

In addition to counting each person equally, Bentham and his followers identified five elements that are used to calculate the greatest amount of happiness: the net amount of pleasure or happiness, its intensity, its duration, its fruitfulness, and the likelihood of any act to produce it.[13]

Pleasure Minus Pain Almost every alternative that we choose produces unhappiness or pain as well as happiness or pleasure for ourselves, if not for others. Pain is intrinsically bad, and pleasure is intrinsically good. Something that produces pain may be accepted, but only if it causes more pleasure overall. For instance, if the painfulness of a punishment deters an unwanted behavior, then we ought to punish but no more than is necessary or useful. When an act produces both pleasure or happiness and pain or unhappiness, we can think of each moment of unhappiness as canceling out a moment of happiness so that what is left to evaluate is the remaining or *net* happiness or unhappiness. We are also to think of pleasure and pain as coming in bits or moments. We can then calculate this net amount by adding and subtracting units of pleasure and displeasure. This is a device for calculating the greatest amount of happiness even if we cannot make mathematically exact calculations. The following simplified equation indicates how the net utility for two acts, A and B, might be determined. We can think of the units as either happy persons or days of happiness:

Act A produces twelve units of happiness and six of unhappiness ($12 - 6 = 6$ units of happiness).
Act B produces ten units of happiness and one of unhappiness ($10 - 1 = 9$ units of happiness).

On this measure, Act B is preferable because it produces a greater net amount of happiness, namely, nine units compared with six for Act A.

Intensity   Moments of happiness or pleasure are not all alike. Some are more intense than others. The thrill of some exciting adventure—say, running river rapids—may produce a more intense pleasure than the serenity we feel standing before a beautiful vista. All else being equal, the more intense the pleasure, the better. All other factors being equal, if I have an apple to give away and am deciding which of two friends to give it to, I ought to give it to the friend who will enjoy it most. In calculations involving intensity of pleasure, a scale is sometimes useful. For example, we could use a positive scale of 1 to 10 degrees, from the least pleasurable to the most pleasurable. In the following scenario, then, Act B is better (all other things being equal) than Act A, even though Act A gives pleasure to thirty more people; this result is because of the greater intensity of pleasure produced by Act B:

> Act A gives forty people each mild pleasure
> ($40 \times 2 = 80$ degrees of pleasure).
> Act B gives ten people each intense pleasure
> ($10 \times 10 = 100$ degrees of pleasure).

Duration   Intensity is not all that matters regarding pleasure. The more serene pleasure may last longer. This also must be factored in our calculation. The longer lasting the pleasure, the better, all else being equal. Thus, in the following scenario, Act A is better than Act B because it gives more total days of pleasure or happiness. This is so even though it affects fewer people (a fact that raises questions about how the number of people counts in comparison to the total amount of happiness):

> Act A gives three people each eight days of happiness ($3 \times 8 = 24$ days of happiness).
> Act B gives six people each two days of happiness ($6 \times 2 = 12$ days of happiness).

Fruitfulness   A more serene pleasure from contemplating nature may or may not be more fruitful than an exciting pleasure such as that derived from running rapids. The fruitfulness of experiencing pleasure depends on whether it makes us more capable of experiencing similar or other pleasures. For example, the relaxing event may make one person more capable of experiencing other pleasures of friendship or understanding, whereas the thrilling event may do the same for another. The fruitfulness depends not only on the immediate pleasure but also on the long-term results. Indulging in immediate pleasure may bring pain later on, as we know only too well! So also the pain today may be the only way to prevent more pain tomorrow. The dentist's work on our teeth may be painful today, but it makes us feel better in the long run by providing us with pain-free meals and undistracted, enjoyable mealtime conversations.

Likelihood   If before acting we are attempting to decide between two available alternative actions, we must estimate the likely results of each before we compare their net utility. If we are considering whether to go out for some sports competition, for example, we should consider our chances of doing well. We might have greater hope of success trying something else. It may turn out that we ought to choose an act with lesser rather than greater beneficial results if the chances of it happening are better. It is not only the chances that would count but also the size of the prize. In the following equation, A is preferable to B. In this case, "A bird in the hand is worth two in the bush," as the old saying goes:

> Act A has a 90 percent chance of giving eight people each five days of pleasure (40 days $\times$ 0.90 = 36 days of pleasure).
> Act B has a 40 percent chance of giving ten people each seven days of pleasure (70 days $\times$ 0.40 = 28 days of pleasure).

QUANTITY VS. QUALITY OF PLEASURE
Bentham and Mill are in agreement that the more pleasure or happiness, the better. However, there is one significant difference between them. According to Bentham, we ought to consider only the *quantity* of pleasure or happiness brought about by various acts: how much pleasure, to how many people, how intense it is, how long-lasting, how fruitful, and how likely the desired outcome will occur. Consider

Bentham's own comment on this point: The "quantity of pleasure being equal, pushpin (a children's game) is as good as poetry."[14] The aesthetic or intellectual pleasure that one might derive from reading and understanding a poem is no better in itself than the simple pleasure of playing a mindless game.

Mill agreed with Bentham that the greater amount of pleasure and happiness, the better. But Mill also believed that the *quality* of the pleasure should also count. In his autobiography, Mill describes a personal crisis in which he realized that he had not found sufficient place in his life for aesthetic experiences; he realized that this side of the human personality also needed developing and that these pleasures were significantly different from others. This experience and his thoughts about it may have led him to focus on the quality of pleasures. Some are intrinsically better than others, he believed. Intellectual pleasures, for example, are more valuable in themselves than purely sensual pleasures. Although he does not tell us how much more valuable they are (twice as valuable?), he clearly believed this greater value ought to be factored into our calculation of the "greatest amount of happiness." Although I may not always be required to choose a book over food (for example, I may now need the food more than the book), the intellectual pleasures that might be derived from reading the book are of a higher quality than the pleasures gained from eating.

Mill attempts to prove or show that intellectual pleasures are better than sensual ones. We are to ask people who have experienced a range of pleasures whether they would prefer to live a life of a human, despite all its disappointments and pains, or the life of an animal, which is full of pleasures but only sensual pleasures. He believes that people generally would choose the former. They would prefer, as he puts it, "to be a human being dissatisfied than a pig satisfied; better to be Socrates dissatisfied than a fool satisfied."[15] Socrates, as you may know, was often frustrated in his attempts to know certain things. He struggled to get a grasp on true beauty and true justice. Because human beings have greater possibilities for knowledge and achievement, they also have greater potential for failure, pain, and frustration. The point of Mill's argument is that the only reason we would prefer a life of fewer net pleasures (the dissatisfactions subtracted from the total satisfactions of human life) to a life of a greater total amount of pleasures (the life of the pig) is that we value something other than the *amount* (quantity) of pleasures; we value the *kind* (quality) of pleasures as well.[16] When considering this argument, you might ask yourself two questions. First, would people generally prefer to be Socrates than a pig? Second, if Mill is correct in his factual assessment, then what does this fact prove? Could it be that people are mistaken about what kinds of pleasures are the best, as Socrates himself often implied? This points us back to the question of whether happiness is merely a subjective preference or whether happiness resides in a more objective standard.

EVALUATING UTILITARIANISM

The following are just some of the many considerations raised by those who wish to determine whether utilitarianism is a valid moral theory.

Application of the Principle

One reaction that students often have to calculating the greatest amount of happiness is that this theory is too complex. When we consider all of the variables concerning pleasure and happiness that are to be counted when trying to estimate the "greatest amount of pleasure or happiness," the task of doing so looks extremely difficult. We must consider how many people will be affected by alternative actions, whether they will be pleased or pained by them, how pleased or pained they will be and for how long, and the likelihood that what we estimate will happen will, in fact, come to be. In addition, if we want to follow Mill rather than Bentham, we must consider whether the pleasures will be the more lowly sensual pleasures, the higher types of more intellectual pleasures, or something in between. However, in reality we may at any one time have to consider only a couple of these variables, depending on their relevance to the moral question we are considering.

The point of this criticism is that no one can consider all of the variables that utilitarianism requires us to consider: the probable consequences of our action to all affected in terms of duration, intensity, fruitfulness, likelihood, and type or quality of pleasure. It also requires us to have a common unit of measurement of pleasure. (Elementary units called *hedons* have been suggested.) The difficulty is finding a way to reduce pleasures of all kinds to some common or basic unit of measurement. A utilitarian could respond to these criticisms by arguing that while this complexity indicates no one can be a perfect judge of utility, we do make better judgments if we are able to consider these variables. No moral theory is simple in its application.

A more difficult problem in how to apply the principle of utility comes from Mill's specific formulation of it. It may well be that in some cases, at least, one cannot both maximize happiness and make the greatest number of people happy. Thus, one choice may produce 200 units of happiness—but for just one person. The other alternative might produce 150 units of happiness, 50 for each of three people. If the maximization of overall happiness is taken as primary, then we should go with the first choice; if the number of people is to take precedence, then we should go with the second choice. Most readings of Mill, however, suggest that he would give preference to the overall maximization of utility. In that case, how the happiness was distributed (to one versus three) would not in itself count.

Utilitarianism and Personal Integrity

A more substantive criticism of utilitarianism concerns its universalist and maximizing agenda; that we should always do that which maximizes overall happiness. Many critics have noted that utilitarian theory does not allow us to privilege our own happiness over that of others. Nor can we privilege the happiness of those we love. In determining what to do, I can give no more weight to my own projects or my own children than other people's similar projects or others' children. For some philosophers, the idea that I must treat all persons equally is contrary to common sense, which tells us that we ought to care for our own children more than we care for the children of distant others. Utilitarians might respond that we should probably give more attention to our own projects and our own children, but only because this is likely to have better results overall. We know better how to promote our own projects and have more motivation to do so. Thus, giving preference to ourselves will probably be more effective.

A further objection maintains that there is something wrong if utilitarianism requires us to not give preference to ourselves and to our own personal moral commitments. Utilitarianism appears to be an affront to our personal integrity.[17] The idea is that utilitarianism seems to imply that I am not important from my own point of view. However, a utilitarian might respond that it is important that people regard themselves as unique and give due consideration to their own interests because this will probably have better consequences both for these individuals and the broader society.

Ends and Means

A second criticism concerns utilitarianism's consequentialist character. You may have heard the phrase "The end justifies the means." People often utter this phrase with a certain amount of disdain. Utilitarianism, as a consequentialist moral theory, holds that it is the consequences or ends of our actions that determine whether particular means to them are justified. This seems to lead to conclusions that are contrary to commonsense morality. For example, wouldn't it justify punishing or torturing an innocent person, a "scapegoat," in order to prevent a great evil or to promote a great good? Or could we not justify on utilitarian grounds the killing of some individuals for the sake of the good of a greater number, perhaps in the name of population control? Or could I not make an exception for myself from obeying a law, alleging that it is for some greater long-term good? Utilitarians might respond by noting that such actions or practices will probably do more harm than good, especially if we take a long-range view. In particular, they might point out that practices allowing the punishment of known innocents would undermine the legitimacy and deterrent effect of the law—and thus reduce overall utility.

THE TROLLEY PROBLEM

One particular problem for utilitarianism is exemplified by what has come to be called the **trolley problem**.[18] According to one version of this scenario, imagine you find yourself beside a train track, on which a trolley is speeding toward a junction. On the track ahead of the trolley are five workers who will all be killed if the trolley continues on its current course. You have access to a switch, and if you pull it the trolley will be diverted onto another track where it will kill only one worker. According to utilitarianism, if nothing else is relevant, you would not only be permitted but *required* to pull the switch, which would result in one death and five lives saved. From a utilitarian standpoint, it is obvious that you should pull the switch, since not pulling the switch would result in greater net loss of life. Now compare this scenario with another. In this case, you find yourself on a bridge over a single trolley track with the five workers below you. Next to you on the bridge is an enormously fat man. The only way to stop the trolley in this case is to push the fat man off the bridge and onto the tracks ahead of the workers. Would you be permitted to do this? In both cases, five lives would be saved and one lost. But are the cases the same morally? It would seem that according to utilitarianism, in which only the results matter, the cases would morally be the same. However, it is the intuition of most people that the second case is significantly different. You can't kill one person to save five. To take another example, it seems clear that a doctor who has five patients needing organ transplants to save their lives should not be permitted to take those organs out of another healthy patient, causing his death.

It is important to note that versions of the trolley problem have been employed by psychologists to probe human decision-making procedures. Some of this research examines how different parts of the brain are involved in different ways of making decisions that involve moral dilemmas.[19] This sort of research investigates the psychological sources of our decisions—whether emotional responses predominate, whether we actually do calculate costs and benefits, and whether we tend to feel bound to abstract moral rules. One recent study (2012) used a virtual reality version of the trolley problem to pursue this question. It found that 89 percent of people chose the utilitarian option when confronted with a 3-D virtual reality representation of a runaway boxcar that threatened to crash into a group of people.[20] One issue exposed by these sorts of studies is that people respond differently when confronted with the choice of doing something (pulling the lever to divert the train into the group of people) or not doing something (allowing the train to crash into the group). One conclusion of this sort of research is that sometimes there are conflicts in how we actually react and how we think we *should* react to morally fraught situations. Other inquiries have considered whether utilitarian calculation involves a sort of "coldness" that runs counter to empathy and other emotional responses.[21] One recent study (2011) by Daniel Bartels and David Pizarro concludes, "participants who indicated greater endorsement of utilitarian solutions had higher scores on measures of psychopathy, Machiavellianism, and life meaninglessness."[22] This conclusion appears to follow from the fact that the utilitarian decision—to kill one in order to save others—asks us to overcome an emotional

One version of the trolley problem.

or instinctual aversion to harming others. And yet, it might be that—from the utilitarian point of view—this is exactly what we should do in order to bring about greater happiness for the greatest number. The psychological research into the dilemmas generated by utilitarianism is interesting. But the normative or moral question remains. Moral philosophy is not merely interested in the psychological question of how we react in these situations, it is also concerned with the question of how we *ought* to react.

ACT AND RULE UTILITARIANISM

Utilitarianism may appear to justify any action just so long as it has better consequences than other available actions. Therefore, cheating, stealing, lying, and breaking promises may all seem to be justified, depending on whether they maximize happiness in some particular case. In response to this type of criticism, contemporary utilitarians often focus on general rules instead of on individual acts. The version of utilitarianism that focuses on rules is usually called **rule utilitarianism**. This is contrasted with **act utilitarianism**, which focuses solely on the consequences of specific individual acts.

Both are forms of utilitarianism. They are alike in requiring us to produce the greatest amount of happiness for the greatest number of people. They differ in what they believe we ought to consider in estimating the consequences. Act utilitarianism states that we ought to consider the consequences of *each act separately*. Rule utilitarianism states that we ought to consider the consequences of the act performed as a *general practice*.[23]

Take the following example. Sue is considering whether to keep or break her promise to go out to dinner with Ken. She believes that if she breaks this promise in order to do something else with other friends, then Ken will be unhappy—but she and the other friends will be happier. According to act utilitarianism, if the consequences of her breaking the promise are better than keeping it, then she ought to break it.

Act utilitarianism: Consider the consequences of some particular act such as keeping or breaking one's promise.

A rule utilitarian, on the other hand, would tell Sue to consider what the results would be if everyone broke promises or broke them in similar situations. The question "What if everyone did that?" is familiar to us. According to rule utilitarianism, Sue should ask what the results would be if breaking promises in similar circumstances became a general practice or a general rule that people followed. It is likely that trust in promises would be weakened. This outcome would be bad, she might think, because if we could not trust one another to keep promises, then we would generally be less capable of making plans and relating to one another—two important sources of human happiness. So, even if there would be no general breakdown in trust from just this one instance of promise-breaking, Sue should still probably keep her promise according to rule utilitarian thinking.

Rule utilitarianism: Consider the consequences of some practice or rule of behavior—for example, the practice of promise-keeping or promise-breaking.

Another way to understand the method of reasoning used by the rule utilitarian is the following: I should ask what would be the best practice. For example, regarding promises, what rule would have the better results when people followed that rule? Would it be the rule or practice "Never break a promise made"? At the other end of the spectrum would be the rule or practice "Keep promises only if the results of doing so would be better than breaking them." (This actually amounts to a kind of act utilitarian reasoning.) However, there might be a better rule yet, such as "Always keep your promise unless doing so would have very serious harmful consequences." If this rule were followed, then people would generally have the benefits of being able to say, "I promise," and have people generally believe and trust them. The fact that the promise would not be kept in some limited circumstances would probably not do great harm to the practice of making promises.

Some utilitarians go further and ask us to think about sets of rules. It is not only the practice of promise-keeping that we should evaluate but also a broader set of related practices regarding truthfulness and bravery and care for children (for example).

Moreover, we should think of these rules as forming a system in which there are rules for priority and stringency. These rules would tell us which practices are more important and how important they are compared to the others. We should then do what the best system of moral rules dictates, where *best* is still defined in terms of the maximization of happiness.[24]

Which form of utilitarianism is better is a matter of dispute. Act utilitarians can claim that we ought to consider only what will or is likely to happen if we act in certain ways—not what *would* happen if we acted in certain ways but will not happen because we are not going to so act. Rule utilitarians can claim that acts are similar to one another and so can be thought of as practices. My lying in one case to get myself out of a difficulty is similar to others' lying in other cases to get themselves out of difficulties. Because we should make the same judgments about similar cases (for consistency's sake), we should judge this act by comparing it with the results of the actions of everyone in similar circumstances. We can thus evaluate the general practice of "lying to get oneself out of a difficulty." You can be the judge of which form of utilitarian reasoning is more persuasive.

"PROOF" OF THE THEORY

One of the best ways to evaluate a moral theory is to examine carefully the reasons that are given to support it. Being an empiricist theory, utilitarianism must draw its evidence from experience. This is what Mill does in his attempt to prove that the principle of utility is the correct moral principle. His argument is as follows: Just as the only way in which we know that something is visible is its being seen, and the only way we can show that something is audible is if it can be heard, so also the only proof that we have that something is desirable is its being desired. Because we desire happiness, we thus know it is desirable or good. In addition, Mill holds that happiness is the only thing we desire for its own sake. All else we desire because we believe it will lead to happiness. Thus, happiness or pleasure is the only thing good in itself or the only intrinsic good. All other goods are instrumental goods; in other words, they are good insofar as they lead to happiness. For example, reading is not good in itself but only insofar as it brings us pleasure or understanding (which is either pleasurable in itself or leads to pleasure).

There are two main contentions in this argument. One is that good is defined in terms of what people desire. The other is that happiness is the only thing desired for itself and is the only intrinsic good. Critics have pointed out that Mill's analogy between what is visible, audible, and desirable does not hold up under analysis. In all three words, the suffix means "able to be," but in the case of *desirable*, Mill needs to prove not only that we can desire happiness (it is able to be desired) but also that it is *worth* being desired. Furthermore, just because we do desire something does not necessarily mean that we *ought* to desire it or that it is good. There is a risk of the naturalistic fallacy (as defined in Chapter 1) here. Is this a case of illegitimately deriving an *ought* from an *is*?

Mill recognizes the difficulty of proving matters in ethics and that the proofs here will be indirect rather than direct. On the second point, Mill adds a further comment to bolster his case about happiness. He asserts that this desire for happiness is universal and that we are so constructed that we can desire nothing except what appears to us to be or to bring happiness. You may want to consider whether these latter assertions are consistent with his empiricism. Does he know these things from experience? In addition, Mill may be simply pointing to what we already know rather than giving a proof of the principle. You can find out what people believe is good by noticing what they do desire. In this case, they desire to be happy or they desire what they think will bring them happiness.[25]

Utilitarianism is a highly influential moral theory that also has had significant influence on a wide variety of policy assessment methods. It can be quite useful for evaluating alternative health care systems, for example. Whichever system brings the most benefit to the most people with the least cost is the system that we probably ought to support. Although Mill was perhaps too optimistic about the ability and willingness of people to increase human happiness and reduce suffering, there is no doubt that the ideal is a good one. Nevertheless, utilitarianism has difficulties, some of which we have discussed here. You will know better how to evaluate this theory when you can compare it with those treated in the following chapters.

NOTES

1. United Nations Department of Economic and Social Affairs, http://esa.un.org/wpp/other-information/faq.htm
2. United Nations Panel on Global Sustainability, "Resilient People, Resilient Planet: A Future Worth Choosing" (2012): 11, http://www.un.org/gsp/sites/default/files/attachments/GSP_Report_web_final.pdf
3. Office of the United Nations High Commissioner for Human Rights, "Convention Against Torture and Other Cruel, Inhuman, or Degrading Treatment or Punishment," http://www.un.org/millennium/law/iv-9.htm
4. Scott Shane, "Waterboarding Used 266 Times on 2 Suspects," *New York Times,* April 19, 2009, http://www.nytimes.com/2009/04/20/world/20detain.html?_r=0
5. Chris McGreal, "Dick Cheney Defends Use of Torture on Al-Qaida Leaders," *Guardian,* September 9, 2011, http://www.guardian.co.uk/world/2011/sep/09/dick-cheney-defends-torture-al-qaida
6. *San Francisco Examiner,* February 2, 1993, A4; *San Francisco Chronicle,* May 5, 2007, A5.
7. Peter Singer, *Writings on an Ethical Life* (New York: HarperCollins, 2001), 16.
8. John Stuart Mill, *Utilitarianism,* ed. Oskar Priest (Indianapolis, IN: Bobbs-Merrill, 1957), 20.
9. Ibid., 24.
10. Scott James, "A Year of Rising Suicides on Bridge and Tracks," *New York Times,* August 26, 2011, accessed March 17, 2012, http://www.nytimes.com/2011/08/26/us/26bcjames.html?pagewanted=all&_r=0
11. Jeremy Bentham, *An Introduction to the Principles of Morals and Legislation* (New York: Oxford University Press, 1789).
12. Mill, *Utilitarianism,* 22.
13. These elements for calculation of the greatest amount of happiness are from Bentham's *Principles of Morals and Legislation.*
14. Bentham, *Principles of Morals and Legislation.*
15. Mill, *Utilitarianism,* 14.
16. Note that this is an empiricist argument. It is based on an appeal to purported facts. People's actual preferences for intellectual pleasures (if true) are the only source we have for believing them to be more valuable.
17. J. J. C. Smart and Bernard Williams, *Utilitarianism: For and Against* (New York: Cambridge University Press, 1973). Also see Samuel Scheffler, *The Rejection of Consequentialism* (New York: Oxford University Press, 1984). In *The Limits of Morality* (New York: Oxford University Press, 1989), Shelley Kagan distinguishes the universalist element of utilitarianism—its demand that I treat all equally—from the maximizing element—that I must bring about the most good possible. The first element makes utilitarianism too demanding, whereas the second allows us to do anything as long as it maximizes happiness overall.
18. Philippa Foot, "The Problem of Abortion and the Doctrine of Double Effect," in *Virtues and Vices* (Oxford: Basil Blackwell, 1978); and Judith Jarvis Thomson, "Killing, Letting Die, and the Trolley Problem," *The Monist* (1976), 204–17.
19. See, for example, work done by Joshua Greene and the Moral Cognition Lab at Harvard University, http://wjh.harvard.edu/~mcl/
20. C. David Navarrete, Melissa M. McDonald, Michael L. Mott, and Benjamin Asher, "Virtual Morality: Emotion and Action in a Simulated Three-Dimensional 'Trolley Problem,'" *Emotion* 12, no. 2 (April 2012): 364–70.
21. K. Wiech, G. Kahane, N. Shackel, M. Farias, J. Savulescu, and I. Tracey, "Cold or Calculating? Reduced Activity in the Subgenual Cingulate Cortex Reflects Decreased Emotional Aversion to Harming in Counterintuitive Utilitarian Judgment," *Cognition* 126, no. 3 (March 2013): 364–72.
22. Daniel M. Bartels and David A. Pizarro, "The Mismeasure of Morals: Antisocial Personality Traits Predict Utilitarian Responses to Moral Dilemmas," *Cognition* 121, no. 1 (October 2011): 154–61.
23. See, for example, the explanation of this difference in J. J. C. Smart, "Extreme and Restricted Utilitarianism," *Philosophical Quarterly* (1956).
24. Richard Brandt, "Some Merits of One Form of Rule Utilitarianism," in *Morality and the Language of Conduct,* ed. H. N. Castaneda and George Nakhnikian (Detroit: Wayne State University Press, 1970), 282–307.
25. This explanation is given by Mary Warnock in her introduction to the Fontana edition of Mill's *Utilitarianism,* 25–26.

REVIEW EXERCISES

1. State and explain the basic idea of the principle of utility or the greatest happiness principle.
2. What does it mean to speak of utilitarianism as a consequentialist moral theory?
3. What is the difference between intrinsic and instrumental good? Give examples of each.
4. Which of the following statements exemplify consequentialist reasoning? Can all of them be given consequentialist interpretations if expanded? Explain your answers.
   a. Honesty is the best policy.
   b. Sue has the right to know the truth.
   c. What good is going to come from giving money to a homeless person on the street?
   d. There is a symbolic value present in personally giving something to another person in need.
   e. It is only fair that you give him a chance to compete for the position.
   f. If I do not study for my ethics exam, it will hurt my GPA.
   g. If you are not honest with others, you cannot expect them to be honest with you.
5. Is utilitarianism a hedonist moral theory? Why or why not?

6. Using utilitarian calculation, which choice in each of the following pairs is better, X or Y?
   a. X makes four people happy and me unhappy. Y makes me and one other person happy and three people unhappy.
   b. X makes twenty people happy and five unhappy. Y makes ten people happy and no one unhappy.
   c. X will give five people each two hours of pleasure. Y will give three people each four hours of pleasure.
   d. X will make five people very happy and three people mildly unhappy. Y will make six people moderately happy and two people very unhappy.
7. Is there a difference in value between intellectual and sensual pleasures or some other qualitative difference between higher and lower pleasures? Explain your answer with specific reference to the discussion in this chapter.

8. Which of the following is an example of act utilitarian reasoning and which is an example of rule utilitarian reasoning? Explain your answers.
   a. If I do not go to the meeting, then others will not go either. If that happens, then there would not be a quorum for the important vote, which would be bad. Thus, I ought to go to the meeting.
   b. If doctors generally lied to their patients about their diagnoses, then patients would lose trust in their doctors. Because that would be bad, I should tell this patient the truth.
   c. We ought to keep our promises because it is a valuable practice.
   d. If I cheat here, I will be more likely to cheat elsewhere. No one would trust me then. So I should not cheat on this test.

Deontological Ethics and Immanuel Kant

6

Georgios Kollidas/Alamy

Learning Outcomes

After reading this chapter, you should be able to:

- Understand the difference between consequentialist and non-consequentialist approaches to ethics.
- Describe different deontological approaches to ethics.
- Explain the difference between hypothetical and categorical imperatives.
- Describe two formulations of the categorical imperative.

- Explain the difference between perfect and imperfect duties.
- Apply Kantian reasoning to a variety of cases in the real world.
- Provide an overview of Immanuel Kant's moral philosophy.
- Defend your own thesis with regard to the value of deontological ethics.

Between 1932 and 1972, experiments were conducted in Tuskegee, Alabama, in which 390 poor and illiterate African American men who had syphilis were followed in order to determine the progress of the disease, whether it was always fatal, and how it was spread. The researchers even failed to give the men penicillin treatment for syphilis, when it became available in the early 1940s. The study was ended in 1972 when it became public and a source of major controversy. The reasons were by now obvious; these men had not been treated with respect but had been used for the purpose of obtaining information.

According to utilitarian thinking, the Tuskegee experiments could perhaps be justifiable. If the harm done to the participants was minimal and the study had no other negative effects, and if the knowledge gained was valuable in reducing overall suffering, then the study might be justified.[1] However, since the post–World War II trials of Nazi war criminals held in Nuremberg, Germany, standards for treatment of human research subjects have become widely accepted. One of the most basic principles of the Nuremberg Code is this, "The voluntary consent of the human subject is absolutely essential."[2] Consent must be informed and uncoerced. Implied in this principle is the belief that persons are autonomous, and this autonomy ought to be respected and protected even if this means that we cannot do certain types of research and cannot thereby discover valuable information. Based on the rule of voluntary consent and its respect for the autonomy of research subjects, the Tuskegee experiments were immoral, even if they produced valuable information.

This emphasis on personal autonomy and the idea that people ought not to be used as they were in the Tuskegee experiments are central tenets in the moral philosophy

Subjects in the infamous Tuskegee syphilis experiments.

National Archives and Records Administration.

of Immanuel Kant, which we examine in detail in this chapter. Kant also maintains that there are certain things we ought not do, even if these things would produce the greatest happiness for the greatest number.

DEONTOLOGY AND THE ETHICS OF DUTY

Kant's theory of ethics is best described as a **deontological theory**. The word *deontology* means "theory of duty" (the Greek word *deon* means "duty"). **Deontological ethics** focuses on duties, obligations, and rights. The term *deontological* was coined by the utilitarian philosopher Jeremy Bentham, who described it as "knowledge of what is right or proper."[3] Bentham thought that deontology points in the direction of the principle of utility. But contemporary philosophers use the term *deontological* to indicate a contrast with the utilitarian focus on the consequences of actions. Instead of focusing on consequences, deontological ethics focuses on duties and obligations: things we ought to do regardless of the consequences. One way of describing this is to say that deontological theories emphasize the *right* over the *good*, by which we mean that deontology focuses on right actions and right intentions, while downplaying the importance of the goods or benefits that are produced by these actions.

While utilitarian ethics focuses on producing the greatest happiness for the greatest number, deontological ethics focuses on what makes us worthy of happiness. For Kant, as for the Stoics and others who emphasize duty, we are worthy of happiness only when we do our duty. As Kant explained, morality "is not properly the doctrine of how we are to make ourselves happy but of how we are to become worthy of happiness."[4] For Kant, morality is not a "doctrine of happiness" or set of instructions on how to become happy. Rather, morality is the "rational condition of happiness."

There are a variety of deontological theories. Divine command ethics, as discussed in Chapter 2, is deontological in the sense that obedience to God's command is a duty that must be followed no matter what the consequences. The biblical story of Abraham and Isaac (in Chapter 22 of Genesis) provides an example of duty. Out of obedience to God's command, Abraham is willing to sacrifice his own son. In this story, religious duty must be done despite the consequences and the unhappiness that is produced.

This episode shows us one of the problems for divine command ethics—a problem that has been recognized since Socrates discussed it with Euthyphro in Plato's dialogue (see Chapter 2). How is morality related to God's commands? And how are we to know that it is, in fact, God who commands us and not the voice of our culture or our own selfish motives or even mental illness? The Abraham and Isaac episode famously prompted Kant to suggest that Abraham should have questioned God as follows: "That I ought not to kill my good son is quite certain. But that you, this apparition, are God—of that I am not certain, and never can be, not even if this voice rings down to me from heaven."[5] For Kant, the commands of ethics are clear, certain, and without exception—and they do not include the command to kill our own children. In response to this sort of criticism, the Danish philosopher Søren Kierkegaard suggested that the story of Abraham shows us that there may be religious duties that transcend the duties of ethics. Such a claim is rejected by Kant. For Kant, moral duties are universal and absolute; and we should use our knowledge of morality to criticize and interpret religious stories and ideas.

Another form of deontological ethics can be found in the ancient Greek and Roman philosophy of **Stoicism**. The Stoics emphasized doing your duty and playing your part as determined by the

The story of Abraham and Isaac is an example of how religious duties may conflict with ethical duties.

natural order of things. Rather than struggling against *external* circumstances that we cannot control—such as the things that happen to us and the actions of others—the Stoics argue that the key to morality and happiness is *internal*, a matter of how we orient our will and intentions. According to this view, duty is its own reward. Epictetus, a Stoic philosopher who died in 135 CE, explains, "As Zeus has ordained, so act: if you do not act so, you will feel the penalty, you will be punished. What will be the punishment? Nothing else than not having done your duty: you will lose the character of fidelity, modesty, propriety. Do not look for greater penalties than these."[6]

The typical image of a Stoic is of a sternly disciplined, courageous, and emotionally composed individual who acts solely for the sake of duty—and whose commitment to obedience and duty infuses every part of life. We often associate Stoic ethics with the kind of courageous and selfless obedience to duty that is typical of soldiers. This image of military service and duty was embodied in the Roman Stoic Emperor Marcus Aurelius, who describes the life of Stoic duty as follows: "It is thy duty to order thy life well in every single act; and if every act does its duty, as far as is possible, be content; and no one is able to hinder thee so that each act shall not do its duty."[7] He imagines someone objecting to the rigors of duty by claiming that some external circumstances stand in the way of the fulfillment of duty. But he replies, "Nothing will stand in the way of thy acting justly and soberly and considerately." As Marcus explains elsewhere, "it is thy business to do thy duty like a soldier in the assault on a town."[8] The basic idea of Stoicism is that we can control our own intentions and actions, even when we cannot control the consequences and external circumstances. From this standpoint, you fulfill your moral obligation by doing what you know is right, even if the external world makes that difficult.

Although Immanuel Kant admired the Stoics' emphasis on "strength of the soul,"[9] he also believed they underestimated the difficulty of being moral. One problem is that we are confused about moral duty—because we often confuse moral duties with other more practical concerns, including the concerns of happiness. To clarify this, Kant focused on the logical and rational structure of duty itself—apart from considerations of happiness, prudence, or the natural order of things.

While it is easy enough to state in general that there are duties and obligations that we ought to fulfill, it is more difficult to establish exactly what those duties and obligations are. Is patriotism an obligation—and does it include patriotism to an unjust or corrupt state? Is the duty to our parents and ancestors primary, as it is in the morality of Confucius? Do we have obligations of compassion and concern for all sentient beings, as many Buddhists argue? These questions remind us that deontological ethics might need to be supplemented with a broader theory of "the good," which tells us how the theory of duty should apply to personal, social, and political affairs. Indeed, this criticism of deontological ethics was noted by John Stuart Mill, who criticized Kant for defining a theory of duty that was so abstract that it could not rule out immoral actions.

As we turn to a discussion of Kant, bear this accusation in mind. Is Kant's conception of duty too abstract? Or does the Kantian theory help to specify our duties in sufficient detail to avoid this charge?

IMMANUEL KANT

Immanuel Kant (1724–1804) was a German philosopher who is now regarded as a central figure in the history of modern philosophy. Modern philosophy itself is sometimes divided into pre-Kantian and post-Kantian periods. In fact, some people regard him as the greatest modern philosopher. Although he is renowned for his moral philosophy, he wrote on a variety of matters including science, geography, beauty, and war and peace. He was a firm believer in the ideas of the Enlightenment (as discussed in Chapter 2), especially reason and freedom, and he also was a supporter of the American Revolution.

Two of the main questions that Kant believed philosophy should address are: "What can I know?" and "What ought I do?"[10] While Kant's theory of knowledge is important and influential, our concern here is his moral philosophy.

One way to begin your examination of Kant's moral theory is to think about how he would answer the question, *What gives an act moral worth?* It is not the consequences of the act, according to Kant, that matters most. Suppose, for example, that I try to do what is right by complimenting someone on her achievements. Through no fault of my own, my action ends up hurting that person because she misunderstands my efforts. According to Kant, because I intended and tried to do what I thought was right, I ought not to be blamed for things having turned out badly. The idea is that we generally ought not to be blamed or praised for what is not in our control. The consequences of our acts are not always in our control, and things do not always turn out as we want. However, Kant believed that our motives are in our control. We are responsible for our intention to do good or bad, and thus it is for this that we are held morally accountable.

Kant also objected to basing morality on the consequences of our actions for another reason. To make morality a matter of producing certain states of affairs, such as happy experiences, puts matters backward, he might say. On such a view, actions and even human beings could be thought of as merely having *use value*. We would be valued to the extent

A portrait of Immanuel Kant (1724–1804).

© Georgios Kollidas/Alamy

that we were instrumental in bringing about what itself was of greater value, namely, happy states or experiences. However, in Kant's view, we should not be used in this way for we are rational beings or *persons*. Persons have intrinsic or inherent value, according to Kant, not mere instrumental value. The belief that *people ought not to be used*, but ought to be regarded as having the highest intrinsic value, is central to Kant's ethics, as is having *a motive to do what is right*. As we shall see in the next two sections, Kant uses this second idea to answer the question: What gives an act moral worth?

What Is the Right Motive?

Kant believed that an act has moral worth only if it is done with a right intention or motive.[11] He referred to this as having a "good will." Kant writes that the only thing that is unconditionally good is a good will. Everything else needs a good will to make it good. Without a right intention, such things as intelligence, wit, and control of emotions can be bad and used for evil purposes. Having a right intention means doing what is right (or what one believes to be right) just because it is right. In Kant's words, it is to act "out of duty," out of a concern and respect for the moral law. Kant was not a relativist. He believed that there is a right and a wrong thing to do, whether or not we know or agree about it.

To explain his views on the importance of a right motive or intention, Kant provides the example of a shopkeeper who does the right thing, who charges her customers a fair price and charges the same to all. But what is her motive? Kant discusses three possible motives: (1) The shopkeeper's motive or reason for acting might be because it is a good business practice to charge the same to all. It is in her own best interest that she do this. Although not necessarily wrong, this motive is not praiseworthy. (2) The shopkeeper might charge a fair and equal price because she is sympathetic toward her customers and is naturally inclined to do them good. Kant said that this motive is also not the highest. We do not have high moral esteem or praise for people who simply do what they feel like doing, even if we believe they are doing the right thing. (3) If the shopkeeper did the right thing just because she believed it was right, however, then

this act would be based on the highest motive. We do have a special respect, or even a moral reverence, for people who act out of a will to do the right thing, especially when this comes at great cost to themselves. An act has moral worth only when it is motivated by concern for the moral law.

Now we do not always *know* whether our acts are motivated by self-interest, inclination, or pure respect for morality. Also, we often act from mixed motives. We are more certain that the motive is pure, however, when we do what is right even when it is not in our best interest (when it costs us dearly) and when we do not feel like doing the right thing. In these cases, we can know that we are motivated by concern to do the right thing because the other two motives are missing. Moreover, this ability to act for moral reasons, while resisting other inclinations, is one reason that human beings have a unique value and dignity. The person who says to himself, "I feel like being lazy (or mean or selfish), but I am going to try not to because it would not be right," is operating out of the motive of respect for morality itself. This ability to act for moral reasons or motives, Kant believes, is one part of what gives human beings dignity and worth.

What Is the Right Thing to Do?

For our action to have moral worth, according to Kant, we must not only act out of a right motivation but also do the right thing. Consider again the diagram that we used in the first chapter.

As noted earlier, Kant does not believe that morality is a function of producing good consequences. We may do what has good results, but if we do so for the wrong motive, then that act has no moral worth. However, it is not only the motive that counts for Kant. We must also do what is right. The act itself must be morally right. Both the act and the motive are morally relevant. In Kant's terms, we must act not only "out of duty" (have the right motive) but also "according to duty" or "as duty requires" (do what is right). How then are we to know what is the right thing to do? Once we know this, we can try to do it just because it is right.

To understand Kant's reasoning on this matter, we need to examine the difference between what he calls a **hypothetical imperative** and a **categorical imperative**. First of all, an imperative is simply a form of statement that tells us to do something, for example, "Stand up straight" and "Close the door" and also "You ought to close the door." Some, but only some, imperatives are moral imperatives. Other imperatives are hypothetical. For example, the statement "If I want to get there on time, I ought to leave early" does not embody a moral "ought" or a moral imperative. What I ought to do in that case is a function of what I happen to want—to get there on time—and of the means necessary to achieve this—leaving early. Moreover, I can avoid the obligation to leave early by changing my goals. I can decide that I do not need or want to get there on time. Then I need not leave early. These ends may be good or bad. Thus, the statement "If I want to harm someone, then I ought to use effective means" also expresses a hypothetical "ought." These "oughts" are avoidable, or, as Kant would say, contingent. They are contingent or dependent on what I happen to want or the desires I happen to have, such as to please others, to harm someone, to gain power, or to be punctual.

These "oughts" are also quite individualized. What I ought to do is contingent or dependent on my own individual goals or plans. These actions serve as means to whatever goals I happen to have (or whatever goals my particular community or society happens to approve). Other people ought to do different things than I because they have different goals and plans. For example, I ought to take introduction to sociology because I want to be a sociology major, while you ought to take a course on the philosophy of Kant because you have chosen to be a philosophy major. These are obligations only for those who have these goals or desires. Think of them in this form: "If (or because) I want X, then I ought to do Y." Whether I ought to do Y is totally contingent or dependent on my wanting X.

Moral obligation, on the other hand, is quite different in nature. Kant believed that we experience moral obligation as something quite demanding.

If there is something I morally ought to do, I ought to do it no matter what—whether or not I want to, and whether or not it fulfills my desires and goals or is approved by my society. Moral obligation is not contingent on what I or anyone happens to want or approve. Moral "oughts" are thus, in Kant's terminology, unconditional or necessary. Moreover, whereas hypothetical "oughts" relate to goals we each have as individuals, moral "oughts" stem from the ways in which we are alike as persons, for only persons are subject to morality. This is because persons are rational beings, and only persons can act from a reason or from principles. These "oughts" are thus not individualized but universal as they apply to all persons. Kant calls moral "oughts" *categorical imperatives* because they tell us what we ought to do no matter what, under all conditions, or categorically.

It is from the very nature of categorical or moral imperatives, their being unconditional and universally binding, that Kant derives his views about morality. In fact, he uses the term *the categorical imperative* to describe the basic moral principle by which we determine what we ought and ought not to do.

THE CATEGORICAL IMPERATIVE

The categorical imperative, Kant's basic moral principle, is comparable in importance for his moral philosophy to the principle of utility for utilitarians. It is Kant's test for right and wrong. Just as there are different ways to formulate the principle of utility, so also Kant had different formulations for his principle. Although at least four of them may be found in his writings, we will concentrate on just two and call them the first and second forms of the categorical imperative. The others, however, do add different elements to our understanding of his basic moral principle and will be mentioned briefly.

The First Form

Recall that moral obligation is categorical; that is, it is unconditional and applies to all persons as persons rather than to persons as individuals. It is in this sense universal. Moreover, because morality is not a matter of producing good consequences of any sort (be it happiness or knowledge or peace), the basic moral principle will be formal, without content. It will not include reference to any particular good. Knowing this, we are on the way to understanding the first form of the categorical imperative, which simply requires that we do only what we can accept or will that everyone do. Kant's own statement of it is basically the following:

Act only on that maxim that you can will as a universal law.

In other words, whatever I consider doing, it must be something that I can consistently will or accept that all others do. To will something universally is similar to willing it as a law, for a law by its very nature has a degree of universality. By *maxim*, Kant means a description of the action or policy that I will put to the test. This is expressed in the form of a rule or principle. For example, I might want to know whether "being late for class" or "giving all my money to the homeless" describes a morally permissible action. I need only formulate some maxim or rule and ask whether I could will that everyone follow that maxim. For example, I might ask whether I could will the universal maxim or general rule, "Whenever I have money to spare, I will give it to the homeless." However, this needs further clarification.[12]

How do I know what I can and cannot will as a universal practice? As a rational being, I can only will what is noncontradictory. What do we think of a person who says that it is both raining and not raining here now? It can be raining here and not there, or now and not earlier. But it is either raining here or it is not. It cannot be both. So also we say that a person who wants to "have his cake and eat it, too" is not being rational. "Make up your mind," we say. "If you eat it, it is gone."

How I know if I can rationally, without contradiction, will something for all can best be explained by using one of Kant's own examples. He asks us to consider whether it is morally permissible for me to "make a lying or false promise in order to extricate myself from some difficulty." Thus, I would consider the maxim, "Whenever I am in some difficulty that I can get out of only by making a lying or false promise, I will do so." To know whether this would be

morally acceptable, it must pass the test of the categorical imperative. If I were to use this test, I would ask whether I could will that sort of thing for all. I must ask whether I could will a general practice in which people who made promises—for example, to pay back some money—could make the promises without intending to keep them. If people who generally made such promises did so falsely, then others would know this and would not believe the promises. Consider whether you would lend money to a person if she said she would pay you back but you knew she was lying. The reasoning is thus: If I tried to will a general practice of false promise-making, I would find it impossible to do so because by willing that promises could be false, I would also will a situation in which it would be impossible to succeed in making a lying promise. Everyone would know that all promises were potential lies. No one could then make a promise, let alone a false promise, because no one would believe him or her. Part of being able to make a promise is to have it believed. The universal practice of false promise-making is self-contradictory and could not exist. If everyone made such lying promises, no one could!

Now consider the example at the beginning of this chapter: the Tuskegee syphilis experiments, in which people were used as medical test subjects without their full knowing consent. Using Kant's categorical imperative to test this, one would see that if it were a general practice for researchers to lie to their subjects in order to get them into their experiments, they would not be able to get people to participate. A general practice of deceiving potential research subjects would undermine the credibility of all researchers. The only way a particular researcher could lie would be if most other researchers told the truth. Only then could she get her prospective subjects to believe her. But this would be to make herself an exception to the universal rule. Like false promising, a universal practice in which researchers lied to their prospective subjects is self-contradictory and cannot be willed with consistency. Therefore, lying to prospective research subjects fails the test of the categorical imperative and is morally impermissible.

In some ways, Kant's basic moral principle, the categorical imperative, is a principle of fairness. I should not do what I am not able to will that everyone do. For me to succeed in making a lying promise, others must generally make truthful promises so that my lie will be believed. This would be to treat myself as an exception. But this is not fair. In some ways, the principle is similar to the so-called Golden Rule, which requires us only to do unto others what we would be willing for them to do unto us. However, it is not the same, for Kant's principle requires our not willing self-canceling or contradictory practices, whereas the Golden Rule requires that we appeal in the final analysis to what we would or would not like to have done to us. As you will see in the reading excerpt that follows, Kant explains in a footnote that the Golden Rule

> … cannot be a universal law, for it does not contain the principle of duties to oneself, nor of the duties of benevolence to others (for many a one would gladly consent that others should not benefit him, provided only that he might be excused from showing benevolence to them), nor finally that of duties of strict obligation to one another, for on this principle the criminal might argue against the judge who punishes him, and so on.[13]

To explain, the Golden Rule is only about what I or you like or don't like (what we would have others "do unto us"). But this fails to get us to the level of universal duty that is central to Kant's moral theory.

The Second Form

The first form of Kant's categorical imperative requires universalizing one's contemplated action or policy. In the second form, we are asked to consider what constitutes proper treatment of persons as persons. According to Kant, one key characteristic of persons is their ability to set their own goals. Persons are autonomous (from the Greek *auto*, meaning "self," and *nomos*, meaning "rule" or "law"). They are literally self-ruled, or at least capable of being self-ruled. As persons, we choose our own life plans, what we want to be, our friends, our college courses, and so forth. We have our own reasons for doing so. We believe that although our choices are influenced by our circumstances and by the advice and opinions of others, we knowingly allow ourselves to be so influenced, and thus these choices are still our own choices. In this way, persons are different from things. Things cannot choose what

they wish to do. We decide how we shall use things. We impose our own goals on things, using wood to build a house and a pen or computer to express our ideas. It is appropriate to use things for our ends, but it is not appropriate to use persons as though they were things purely at our disposal and without wills of their own. Kant's statement of this second form of the categorical imperative is as follows:

> Always treat humanity, whether in your own person or that of another, never simply as a means but always at the same time as an end.

This formulation tells us how we ought to treat ourselves as well as others, namely, as ends rather than merely as means. Kant believes that we should treat persons as having value in themselves and not just as having instrumental value. People are valuable, regardless of whether they are useful or loved or valued by others. We should not simply use others or let ourselves be used. Although I may in some sense use someone—for example, to paint my house—I may not *simply* use her. The goal of getting my house painted must be shared by the painter, who is also a person and not just an object to be used by me for my own ends. She must know what is involved in the project. I cannot lie to her to manipulate her into doing something to which she otherwise would not agree. And she must agree to paint the house voluntarily rather than be coerced into doing it. These and similar requirements are necessary for treating another person as an end rather than merely as a means to my ends or goals.

We can also use this second form of the categorical imperative to evaluate the examples we considered for the first form. The moral conclusions should be the same whether we use the first or second form. Kant believes that in lying to another person—for example, saying that we will pay back money when we have no intention of doing so—we would be attempting to manipulate another person against his will. (He is presumably unwilling to just give us the money.) This would violate the requirement not to use persons. Similarly, in the Tuskegee experiments, the deceptive researchers used the subjects as means to an end rather than as ends in themselves.

We noted that Kant provided more formulations of his categorical imperative than the two discussed here. In another of these formulations, Kant relies on his views about nature as a system of everything that we experience because it is organized according to laws. Thus, he says that we ought always to ask whether some action we are contemplating could become a universal law of nature. The effect of this version is to emphasize morality as universal and rational, for nature necessarily operates according to coherent laws. Other formulations of the categorical imperative stress autonomy. We are to ask whether we could consider ourselves as the author of the moral practice that we are about to accept. We are both subject to the moral law and its author because it flows from our own nature as a rational being. Another formulation amplifies what we have here called the second form of the categorical imperative. This formulation points out that our rationality makes us alike as persons, and together we form a community of persons. He calls the community of rational persons a **kingdom of ends**—that is, a kingdom in which all persons are authors as well as subjects of the moral law. Thus, we ask whether the action we are contemplating would be fitting for and promote such a community. These formulations of the categorical imperative involve other interesting elements of Kant's philosophy, but they also involve more than we can explore here.

EVALUATING KANT'S MORAL THEORY

There is much that is appealing in Kant's moral philosophy, particularly its central aspects—its focus on motives, its emphasis on fairness, its aim of consistency, and its basic idea of treating persons as autonomous and morally equal beings. Kant's deontological approach is quite different from that exemplified by utilitarianism, with its emphasis on the maximization of happiness and the production of good consequences. To more fully evaluate Kant's theory, consider the following aspects of his thought.

The Nature of Moral Obligation

One of the bases on which Kant's moral philosophy rests is his view about the nature of moral obligation. He believes that moral obligation is real and strictly binding. According to Kant, this is how we

generally think of moral obligation. If there is anything that we morally ought to do, then we simply ought to do it. Thus, this type of obligation is unlike that which flows from what we ought to do because of the particular goals that we each have as individuals. To evaluate this aspect of Kant's moral philosophy, you must ask yourself whether this is also what you think about the nature of moral obligation. This is important for Kant's moral philosophy because acting out of respect for the moral law is required for an action to have moral worth. Furthermore, being able to act out of such a regard for morality is also the source of human dignity, according to Kant.

The Application of the Categorical Imperative

Critics such as Mill (as noted previously) have pointed out problems with the universalizing form of the categorical imperative. For example, some have argued that when using the first form of the categorical imperative, there are many things that I could will as universal practices that would hardly seem to be moral obligations. I could will that everyone write their names on the top of their test papers. If everyone did that, it would not prevent anyone from doing so. There would be no contradiction involved if this were a universal practice. Nevertheless, this would not mean that people have a moral obligation to write their names on their test papers. A Kantian might respond that to write your name on your test paper is an example of a hypothetical, not a categorical, imperative. I write my name on my paper because I want to be given credit for it. If I can will it as a universal practice, I then know it is a morally permissible action. If I cannot will it universally, then it is impermissible or wrong. Thus, the categorical imperative is actually a negative test—in other words, a test for what we should not do, more than a test for what we ought to do. Whether or not this is a satisfactory response, you should know that this is just one of several problems associated with Kant's universalizing test.

Concern for the universality of moral rules is not unique to Kantian ethics. We saw in the previous chapter that rule utilitarianism is focused on the general utility of rules. Although Kantians and rule utilitarians are both interested in universalized rules, there is a difference in how Kantian and rule utilitarian reasoning proceeds. Rule utilitarians require that we consider what the *results* would be if some act we are contemplating were to be a universal practice. Reasoning in this way, we ask what would be the results or consequences of some general practice, such as making false promises, or whether one practice would have better results than another. Although in some sense Kant's theory requires that we consider the possible consequences when universalizing some action, the determinant of the action's morality is not whether its practice has good or bad consequences, but whether there would be anything contradictory in willing the practice as a universal law. Because we are rational beings, we must not will contradictory things.

The second form of the categorical imperative also has problems of application. In the concrete, it is not always easy to determine whether one is using a person—for example, what is coercion and what is simply influence, or what is deception and what is not. When I try to talk a friend into doing something for me, how do I know whether I am simply providing input for my friend's own decision-making or whether I am crossing the line and becoming coercive? Moreover, if I do not tell the whole truth or withhold information from another person, should this count as deception on my part? Although these are real problems for anyone who tries to apply Kant's views about deceit and coercion, they are not unique to his moral philosophy. Theories vary in the ease of their use or application. Difficulty of application is a problem for most, if not all, reasonable moral philosophies.

Duty

Some of the language and terminology found in Kant's moral theory can sound harsh to modern ears. Duty, obligation, law, and universality may not be the moral terms most commonly heard today. Yet if one considers what Kant meant by duty, the idea may not seem so strange to us. Kant was not advocating any particular moral code or set of duties held by any society or group. Rather, duty is whatever reason tells us is the right thing to do. However, Kant might acknowledge that there is a streak of *absolutism* in his philosophy. Absolutists think that morality consists of a set of exceptionless rules.

Kant does, at times, seem to favor absolutism. He provides examples in which it seems clear that he believes it is always wrong to make a false promise or to lie deliberately. There is even one example in which Kant himself suggests that if a killer comes to the door asking for a friend of yours inside whom he intends to kill, you must tell the truth. But Kant's moral theory provides only one exceptionless rule, and that is given in the categorical imperative. We are never permitted to do what we cannot will as a universal law or what violates the requirement to treat persons as ends in themselves. Even with these two tests in hand, it is not always clear just how they apply. Furthermore, they may not give adequate help in deciding what to do when they seem to produce contradictory duties, as in the conflict between telling the truth and preserving a life.

Moral Equality and Impartiality

One positive feature of Kant's moral theory is its emphasis on the moral equality of all persons, which is implied in his view that the nature of moral obligation is universally binding. We should not make exceptions for ourselves but do only what we can will for all. Moral obligation and morality itself flow from our nature as rational and autonomous persons. Morality is grounded in the ways in which we are alike as persons, rather than the ways in which we are different as individuals. These views might provide a source for those who want to argue for moral equality and equal moral rights. If we do not treat others as equal persons, we are disrespecting them. If we are not willing to make the same judgment for cases similar to our own, or if we are not willing to have the same rules apply to all, we can be accused of hypocrisy. When we criticize hypocrisy, we act in the spirit of Kant.

Another feature of Kant's moral philosophy is its spirit of impartiality. For an action to be morally permissible, we should be able to will it for all. However, persons do differ in significant ways. Among these are differences in gender, race, age, and talents. In what way does morality require that all persons be treated equally, and in what way does it perhaps require that different persons be treated differently?[14]

Some critics have wondered about Kant's stress on the nature of persons as rational and autonomous beings. It might be that human beings are not best conceived as rational autonomous beings, such as Kant describes. Kant seems to forget our emotions and our dependency relationships. (In Chapter 9, we examine a type of morality that stresses the emotional and personal ties we have to particular individuals.) Kant might reply to these critics that we often have no control over how we feel and thus our feelings should not be a key element of our moral lives. He might also argue that it is the common aspects of our existence as persons, and not the ways in which we are different and unique, that give us dignity and are the basis for the moral equality that we possess. In short, even if we are often not fully autonomous or rational, we ought to consider ourselves as autonomous and rational—and treat others as if they were autonomous and rational—for this is the source of human dignity.

PERFECT AND IMPERFECT DUTIES

In his attempt to explain his views, Kant provides us with several examples. We have already considered one of these: making a false promise. His conclusion is that we should not make a false or lying promise, both because we could not consistently will it for all and because it violates our obligation to treat persons as persons and not to use them only for our own purposes. Kant calls such duties **perfect duties** (they are sometimes described as *necessary* duties). As the term suggests, perfect duties are absolute. We can and should absolutely refrain from making false or lying promises. From the perspective of the first form of the categorical imperative, we have a perfect duty not to do those things that could not even exist and are inconceivable as universal practices. Using the second form of the categorical imperative, we have a perfect duty not to do what violates the requirement to treat persons as ends in themselves.

However, some duties are more flexible. Kant calls these duties **imperfect duties** (sometimes also called *meritorious* duties). Consider another example he provides: egoism. Ethical egoism, you will recall, is the view that we may rightly seek only our own interest and help others only to the extent that doing so also benefits us. Is this a morally acceptable philosophy of life? Using the first form of Kant's

categorical imperative to test the morality of this practice, we must ask whether we could will that everyone was an egoist. If I try to do this, I would need to will that I was an egoist as well as others, even in those situations when I needed others' help. In those situations, I must allow that they not help me when it is not in their own best interest. But being an egoist myself, I would also want them to help me. In effect, I would be willing contradictories; that they help me (I being an egoist) and that they not help me (they being egoists). Although Kant admits that a society of egoists could indeed exist, no rational person could will it, for a rational person does not will contradictories. We have an imperfect or meritorious duty, then, not to be egoists but to help people for their own good and not just for ours. However, just when to help others and how much to help them is a matter of some choice. There is a certain flexibility here. One implication of this view is that there is no absolute duty to give one's whole life to helping others. We, too, are persons and thus have moral rights and also can at least sometimes act for our own interests.

The same conclusion regarding the wrongness of egoism results from the application of the second form of the categorical imperative. If I were an egoist and concerned only about myself, I might argue that I was not thereby committed to using other people. I would simply leave them alone. But according to Kant, such an attitude and practice would still be inconsistent with the duty to treat others as persons. As persons, they also have interests and plans, and to recognize this I must at least sometimes and in some ways seek to promote their ends and goals. Thus, avoiding egoism appears to be an imperfect duty according to Kant's theory. The distinction between perfect and imperfect duties will have implications for handling conflicts among different duties. Perfect duties will take precedence over imperfect ones; we cannot help some by violating the rights of others.

VARIATIONS ON KANT AND DEONTOLOGY

Just as there are contemporary versions of and developments within the utilitarian tradition, there are also many contemporary versions of Kantian and deontological moral theory. One is found in the moral philosophy of W. D. Ross, who also held that there are things we ought and ought not do regardless of the consequences.[15] We discussed Ross in Chapter 3 in relation to pluralism. According to Ross, we have duties not only of beneficence but also to keep promises, pay our debts, and be good friends and parents and children. Contrary to Kant, Ross believed that we can know through moral intuition in any instance what we ought to do. Sometimes we are faced with a conflict of moral duties. It seems intuitive that we ought to be both loyal and honest, but we cannot be both. We have *prima facie* or conditional duties of loyalty and honesty. Ross is the source of the phrase *prima facie*, which is often used in ethical arguments. In such cases, according to Ross, we have to consider which duty is the stronger—that is, which has the greater balance of rightness over wrongness. In choosing honesty in some situations, however, one does not negate or forget that one also has a duty to be loyal. Obvious problems arise for such a theory. For example, how does one go about determining the amount of rightness or wrongness involved in some action? Don't people have different intuitions about the rightness or wrongness of any particular action? This is a problem for anyone who holds that intuition is the basis for morality.

One of the most noted contemporary versions of Kant's moral philosophy is found in the political philosophy of John Rawls. In *A Theory of Justice*, Rawls applies some aspects of Kantian principles to issues of social justice. According to Rawls, justice is fairness.[16] To know what is fair, we must put ourselves imaginatively in the position of a group of free and equal rational beings who are choosing principles of justice for their society. In thinking of persons as free and equal rational beings in order to develop principles of justice, Rawls is securely in the Kantian tradition of moral philosophy. Kant also stresses autonomy. It is this aspect of our nature that gives us our dignity as persons. Kant's categorical imperative also involves universalization. We must do only those things that we could will that everyone do. It is only a short move from these notions of autonomy and universalization to the Rawlsian

requirement to choose those principles of justice that we could accept no matter which position in society we happen to occupy. For details about Rawls's principles, see Chapter 14 on economic justice. Kantian and other versions of deontology continue to be influential. You will be able to better evaluate the Kantian theory as you see aspects of it applied to issues in Part Two of this text.

NOTES

1. At least this might be true from an act utilitarian point of view. A rule utilitarian might want to know whether the results of the general practice of not fully informing research participants would be such that the good achieved would not be worth it.
2. From *Trials of War Criminals before the Nuremberg Military Tribunals under Control Council Law No. 10, Vol. 2* (Washington, DC: U.S. Government Printing Office, 1949), 181–82.
3. Jeremy Bentham, *Deontology or the Science of Morality* (Edinburgh, William Tait, 1834), vol. 1, Chapter 2.
4. Immanuel Kant, *Critique of Practical Reason*, in *Practical Philosophy* (Cambridge: Cambridge University Press, 1999), 5: 130, p. 244.
5. Immanuel Kant, *The Conflict of the Faculties*, in *Religion and Rational Theology*, ed. A.W. Wood and G. di Giovanni (Cambridge: Cambridge University Press, 1996), 283.
6. Epictetus, *Discourses*, 3.7 (Internet Classics Archive: http://classics.mit.edu/Epictetus/discourses.3.three.html (accessed July 17, 2014).
7. Marcus Aurelius, *Meditations* (Internet Classics Archive: http://classics.mit.edu/Antoninus/meditations.html), bk. 8.
8. Aurelius, *Meditations*, bk. 7.
9. Kant, *Critique of Practical Reason* 5: 127, p. 242. Also see J. B. Schneewind, "Kant and Stoic Ethics," in *Essays on the History of Moral Philosophy* (Oxford University Press, 2009).
10. Immanuel Kant, *Critique of Pure Reason*, trans. Norman Kemp Smith (New York: St. Martin's, 1965), 635.
11. We will not distinguish here *motive* and *intention*, although the former usually signifies that out of which we act (an impetus or push) and the latter that for which we act (an aim or objective).
12. I thank Professor Joyce Mullan for suggestions regarding what Kant means by *maxim*.
13. Kant, *Fundamental Principles of the Metaphysics of Morals* trans. Abbott (Project Gutenberg: http://www.gutenberg.org/cache/epub/5682/pg5682.html), second section.
14. See also the criticism of Kantian theories of justice in the treatment of gender and justice in Susan Moller Okin, *Justice, Gender, and the Family* (New York: Basic Books, 1989), 3–22. See also Marilyn Friedman, "The Social Self and the Partiality Debates," in *Feminist Ethics*, ed. Claudia Card (Lawrence: University of Kansas Press, 1991).
15. W. D. Ross, *The Right and the Good* (Oxford: Oxford University Press, 1930).
16. John Rawls, *A Theory of Justice* (Cambridge, MA: Harvard University Press, 1971).

REVIEW EXERCISES

1. Give one of Kant's reasons for his opposition to locating an action's moral worth in its consequences.
2. When Kant refers to "a good will" or "good intention," does he mean wishing others well? Explain.
3. What does Kant mean by "acting out of duty"? How does the shopkeeper exemplify this?
4. What is the basic difference between a categorical and a hypothetical imperative? In the following examples, which are hypothetical and which are categorical imperatives? Explain your answers.
   a. If you want others to be honest with you, then you ought to be honest with them.
   b. Whether or not you want to pay your share, you ought to do so.
   c. Because everyone wants to be happy, we ought to consider everyone's interests equally.
   d. I ought not to cheat on this test if I do not want to get caught.
5. How does the character of moral obligation lead to Kant's basic moral principle, the categorical imperative?
6. Explain Kant's use of the first form of the categorical imperative to argue that it is wrong to make a false promise. (Make sure that you do not appeal to the bad consequences as the basis of judging it wrong.)
7. According to the second form of Kant's categorical imperative, would it be morally permissible for me to agree to be someone's slave? Explain.
8. What is the practical difference between a perfect and an imperfect duty?

7 Natural Law and Human Rights

DEA/VENERANDA BIBLIOTECA AMBROSIANA/De Agostini/Getty Images

Learning Outcomes

After reading this chapter, you should be able to:

- Understand the idea of natural law and how it relates to the idea of human rights.
- Understand the history of natural law ethics and the human rights tradition.
- Explain how natural law theory is related to the law of peoples and norms of international law.
- Identify the contributions to natural law theory made by key thinkers such as Cicero, Thomas Aquinas, and John Locke.
- Explain the importance of teleology for thinking about natural law.

- Explain differences between natural law theory and Kantian or utilitarian reasoning.
- Clarify how natural law arguments are grounded in claims about the essence of human nature.
- Provide an overview of the natural law argument against relativism.
- Defend your own thesis with regard to the value of natural law theory and the idea of human rights.

In 1776, Thomas Jefferson wrote in the Declaration of Independence, "We hold these truths to be self-evident, that all men are created equal, that they are endowed by their Creator with certain inalienable rights, that among these are life, liberty and the pursuit of happiness."[1] Jefferson had read the work of English philosopher John Locke, who had written in the second of his *Two Treatises of Government* that all human beings were of the same species, born with the same basic capacities.[2] Locke argues that because all humans have the same basic nature, they should be treated equally. This argument should sound familiar from our previous discussion of Kant and deontology. Kant does emphasize respect for human autonomy. But while Kant emphasize universal duties and the abstract demand that we respect persons as ends in themselves, Locke and Jefferson fill in this abstract idea with a list of natural human rights, including the right to life and liberty. Locke also thought that there was a natural right to own property, while Jefferson thought that there was a right to the pursuit of happiness. These **natural rights** are supposed to be grounded in self-evident truth. This self-evidence is found in "the Laws of Nature and Nature's God," as the first sentence of the Declaration of Independence puts it.

Discussions of human rights continue to be of interest today. We saw in Chapter 2 that the United Nations issued a Universal Declaration of Human Rights, which began by asserting "the inherent dignity and . . . the equal and inalienable rights of all members of the human family." These rights are said to be shared by all human beings, regardless of cultural, religious, or political differences. But in reality, respecting and upholding human rights is not always a simple task for societies and governments, including that of the United States.

For example, following the 2001 terrorist attacks on the World Trade Center and the Pentagon, and with the U.S. invasion of Afghanistan, questions arose about the legal status and treatment of individuals captured by the U.S. forces who were considered to be terrorists. In our discussion of utilitarianism in Chapter 5, we mentioned that the United States government endorsed the use of torture (referred to as "enhanced interrogation techniques") for these individuals. This would seem to be a violation of Article 5 of the UN Declaration of Human Rights, which states, "No one shall be subjected to torture or to cruel, inhuman or degrading treatment or punishment."

Furthermore, since 2004, many of these suspected terrorists have been transferred to a prison at Guantanamo Bay in Cuba, a U.S. naval base on the southeastern side of the island. (The United States still holds a lease to this land because of the 1903 Cuban–American Treaty.) It was thought that these individuals were members, supporters, or sympathizers of al Qaeda or the Taliban. It was said that these prisoners were not part of any army of any state and thus not prisoners of war but, rather, "enemy combatants" not covered by any of the protections of the Geneva Conventions. These individuals were not given the protections of U.S. laws. And they were denied such basic human rights as knowing the charges against them and being allowed to defend themselves in court. This treatment would seem to violate Article 6 of the UN Declaration, which states, "Everyone has the right to recognition everywhere as a person before the law."

In recent years—and after intense legal and humanitarian scrutiny of Guantanamo's detainment policies—many hundreds of the detainees have been sent back to their countries of origin. Some were finally allowed lawyers, although not of their own choosing. U.S. courts have also ruled that the detainees must be given trials in U.S. military, rather than civilian, courts. As of June 2013, 166 prisoners still remained in the Guantanamo detention facility, a number have died in custody.[3] Some may be brought to trial and some held indefinitely, either there or in maximum security prisons in the United States. Some of these prisoners went

Detainees in a holding area at Camp X-Ray at Guantanamo Bay, Cuba.

AP Photo/U.S. Navy/Shane T. McCoy

on a hunger strike in 2013 to protest their treatment. Prison officials force-fed them—by inserting feeding tubes up their noses. Critics argued that it was a violation of international law and a human rights violation to force-feed prisoners in this way.[4]

In this and many other contemporary situations, we may ask what is meant by "human rights"—and does every person possess such rights, even enemy combatants? This is one of the fundamental questions addressed in this chapter.

A related question is how the idea of rights applies in situations in which there is no legal or political system to enforce them. Is there a system of "natural law" that is more fundamental than the laws of any particular legal or political system? While the idea of natural law is an ancient one, the concept has been an object of renewed interest, especially now that we are aware that states can commit crimes against their own people, including war crimes and genocide. If there is something that we might call natural law, we would suppose that it would at least include a law against genocide.

The Nuremberg trials were trials of Nazi war criminals held in Nuremberg, Germany, from 1945 to 1949. There were thirteen trials in all. In the first trial, Nazi leaders were found guilty of violating international law by starting an aggressive war. Nine of them, including Hermann Goering and Rudolf Hess, were sentenced to death. In other trials, defendants were accused of committing atrocities against civilians. Nazi doctors who had conducted medical experiments on those imprisoned in the death camps were among those tried. Their experiments maimed and killed many people, all of whom were unwilling subjects. For example, experiments for the German air force were conducted to determine how fast people would die in very thin air. Other experiments tested the effects of freezing water on the human body. The defense contended that the military personnel, judges, and doctors were only following orders from their superiors in the Nazi regime. However, the prosecution argued successfully that even if the experimentation did not violate the defendants' own laws, they were still "crimes against humanity." The idea was that a law more basic than civil laws exists—a moral law—and these doctors and others should have known what this basic moral law required. (We discuss war crimes further in Chapter 19.)

The idea that the basic moral law can be known by human reason is a central tenet of natural law theory. Some treatments of human rights also use human nature as a basis. According to this view, human rights are those things that we can validly claim because they are essential for human beings to function well. These natural human rights are the same for all human beings, since on this theory all human beings share a common essence or human nature.

NATURAL LAW THEORY

The **natural law theory** is a theory of ethics that holds that there are moral laws found in nature and discernable by the use of reason. The way the term is used in discussions of ethics should not be confused with those other "laws of nature" that are the generalizations of natural science. The laws of natural science are *descriptive* laws. They describe how nature behaves. Gases, for example, expand with their containers when heat is applied. Boyle's law about the behavior of gases does not tell gases how they *ought* to behave. In fact, if gases were found to behave differently from what we had so far observed, then the laws would be changed to match this new information. Simply put, scientific laws are descriptive generalizations of fact.

Moral laws, on the other hand, are *prescriptive* laws. They tell us how we *ought* to behave. The natural law is the moral law written into nature itself. What we ought to do, according to this theory, is determined by considering certain aspects of nature. In particular, we ought to examine our nature as human beings to see what is essential for us to function well as members of our species. We look to certain aspects of our nature to know what is good and what we ought to do.

Civil law is also prescriptive. As an expression of the moral law, however, natural law is supposed to be more basic or higher than the laws of any particular society. Although laws of particular societies vary and change over time, the natural law is supposed to be universal and stable. In *Antigone,* an ancient Greek tragedy by Sophocles, the protagonist disobeys the king and buries her brother—thereby breaking the law of her monarchical society. She does so because she believes that she must follow a higher law, which requires that her brother be buried. In the play, Antigone loses her life for obeying this higher law. In the Nuremberg trials, prosecutors also argued that there was a higher law that all humans should recognize—one that takes precedence over national laws and customs.

People today sometimes appeal to this moral law in order to argue which civil laws ought to be instituted or changed. This is the basic idea behind the theory of civil disobedience as outlined and practiced by Henry David Thoreau, Mohandas K. Gandhi, and Martin Luther King Jr. (as discussed in Chapter 2). When Thoreau was imprisoned for not paying taxes that he thought were used for an unjust war, he defended his actions by appealing to a system of rights and wrongs that is superior to the civil law. In his famous essay, "Civil Disobedience," he writes, "Must the citizen ever for a moment, or in the least degree, resign his conscience to the legislator? Why has every man a conscience, then? I think that we should be men first, and subjects afterward. It is not desirable to cultivate a respect for the law, so much as for the right."[5]

HISTORICAL ORIGINS

The tradition of natural law ethics is a long one. Aristotle was the first to develop a complex ethical philosophy based on the view that certain actions are right or wrong because they are suited to or go against human nature (although one may find examples of this view in earlier writers). We discuss Aristotle in more detail in Chapter 8, "Virtue Ethics." Aristotle had a profound influence on the medieval Christian philosopher and Dominican friar Thomas Aquinas (1224–1274). Aquinas is often credited as a primary source for natural law ethics.

The natural law tradition has deep roots, however, in ideas found in a variety of other ancient Greek thinkers, especially the Stoics, who held that we have a duty to obey the basic laws of nature. (The Stoics were discussed in the previous chapter on deontological ethics.) The key moral principle for the Stoics was to "follow nature." This means that nature has a goal or *telos* for human beings, which we ought to pursue. They also believed that there are laws to which all people are subject, no matter what their local customs or conventions. Early Roman jurists believed that a common element existed in the codes of various peoples: a *jus gentium* or **"law of peoples."**

One of the most important of the Roman authors associated with the natural law tradition is Cicero. In his *Republic*, Cicero explained the natural law as follows:

> True law is right reason conformable to nature, universal, unchangeable, eternal, whose commands urge us to duty, and whose prohibitions restrain us from evil. Whether it enjoins or forbids, the good respect its injunctions, and the wicked treat them with indifference. This law cannot be contradicted by any other law, and is not liable either to derogation or abrogation. Neither the senate nor the people can give us any dispensation for not obeying this universal law of justice. It needs no other expositor and interpreter than our own conscience. It is not one thing at Rome, and another at Athens; one thing today, and another tomorrow; but in all times and nations this universal law must forever reign, eternal and imperishable. It is the sovereign master and emperor of all beings. God himself is its author, its promulgator, its enforcer. And he who does not obey it flies from himself, and does violence to the very nature of man. And by so

doing he will endure the severest penalties even if he avoid the other evils which are usually accounted punishments.[6]

Cicero's point is that the natural law transcends any time or place: it is eternal and imperishable, the same today and tomorrow, the same in Rome and in Athens. Moreover, Cicero maintains that the natural law comes from God himself. It is not surprising that Cicero and his ideas had a profound impact, for example, on Thomas Jefferson and the authors of the founding documents of the United States, including the Declaration of Independence and the U.S. Constitution.

During the medieval period, Greek and Roman philosophy died out in Western Europe, although these ideas were preserved in the East, especially in the work of Islamic scholars. However, medieval Islamic and Christian traditions tended to think that morality was primarily derived from scripture. Greek and Roman ideas eventually reentered European culture and were distilled and connected to Christianity by Aquinas. Aquinas's goal was to find a way to synthesize faith and reason, to connect the insights of reason with the commands of faith. While the natural law tradition is often connected to religion, it is not merely a version of divine command theory, since it holds that reason can discover the moral law independent of scripture.

Aquinas was a theologian who held that the natural law is part of the divine law or plan for the universe. The record of much of what he taught can be found in his work the *Summa Theologica*.[7] Aquinas maintains that "the natural law shares in the eternal law." He recognizes that this may make it seem that there is no need for human law. But Aquinas argues that particular human laws are a reflection of or incomplete manifestation of the divine law. Aquinas indicated his debt to Cicero by quoting him several times in his discussions of law and justice. For example, "Human law originally sprang from nature. Then things became customs because of their rational benefit. Then fear and reverence for law validated things that both sprang from nature and were approved by custom."[8] The point here is that human laws reflect both the natural law and the developed expression of these laws in the customs and positive laws made by humans.

A portrait of Thomas Aquinas (1225–1274).

Echoing the views of Aristotle, Aquinas held that the moral good consists in following the innate tendencies of our nature. We are by nature biological beings. Because we tend by nature to grow and mature, we ought to preserve our being and our health by avoiding undue risks and doing what will make us healthy. Furthermore, as sentient animals, we can know our world through the physical senses. We ought to use our senses of touch, taste, hearing, and sight; we ought to develop and make use of these senses to appreciate those aspects of existence that they reveal to us. We ought not to do things that injure these senses. Like many nonhuman animals, we reproduce our kind sexually through heterosexual intercourse. This is what nature means for us to do, according to this version of natural law theory. (See further discussion of this issue in Chapter 12 on sexual morality.)

Unique to persons are the specific capacities of knowing and choosing freely. Thus, we ought to treat ourselves and others as beings who are capable of understanding and free choice. Those things that help us pursue the truth, such as education and freedom of public expression, are good. Those things that hinder pursuit of the truth are bad. Deceit and lack of access to the sources of knowledge are morally objectionable simply because they prevent us from fulfilling our innate natural drive or orientation to know the way things are.[9] Moreover, whatever enhances our ability to choose freely is good. A certain amount of self-discipline, options from which to choose, and reflection on what we ought to choose are among the things that enhance freedom. To coerce people and to limit their possibilities of choosing freely are examples of what is inherently bad or wrong.

Finally, natural law theory argues that we ought to find ways to live well together, for this is a theory that emphasizes the interconnectedness of human beings in which no man—or woman—is an island. We are social creatures by nature. Thus, the essence of natural law theory is that we ought to further the inherent ends of human nature and not do what frustrates human fulfillment or flourishing. These ideas can be developed into a concern for social justice, including care for the poor and disabled, the right to decent work and living conditions, and even the right to health care.

After Aquinas and throughout the modern period of European history, the idea of natural law and natural right became more widespread and more secular. One of the important authors who developed ideas about the natural law was Hugo Grotius, a Dutch jurist who was working during the early part of the seventeenth century. Grotius explained the development of natural law from out of human nature as follows:

> For the mother of right, that is, of natural law, is human nature; for this would lead us to desire mutual society, even if it were not required for the supply of other wants; and the mother of civil laws, is obligation by mutual compact; and since mutual compact derives its force from natural law, nature may be said to be the grandmother of civil laws.[10]

Grotius is known as one of the founders of international law. His ideas about international law had a practical application, for example, in his discussion of the rules of war. Grotius maintained that there was a common law among nations, which was valid even in times of war. We will return to this topic in a later chapter where we will discuss the *just war theory*. Note that the idea of natural law may give us grounds to criticize the treatment of the prisoners at Guantanamo Bay, the case with which we began this chapter. If we think that all human beings have basic rights and that these rights exist even in time of war, then perhaps we ought to provide these rights to the prisoners at Guantanamo.

EVALUATING NATURAL LAW THEORY

Natural law theory has many appealing characteristics. Among them are its belief in the objectivity of moral values and the notion of the good as human flourishing. Various criticisms of the theory have also been advanced, including the following:

First, according to natural law theory, we are to determine what we ought to do by deciphering the moral law as it is written into nature—specifically, human nature. One problem that natural law theory must address concerns our ability to read nature. The moral law is supposedly knowable by human reason. However, throughout the history of philosophy, various thinkers have read nature differently. Aristotle, for example, thought that slavery could be justified in that it was in accord with nature.[11] Natural law arguments can also be used in support of gender inequality. Is it natural, for example, for fathers to rule within the family or men to rule over women? Today people might argue against slavery and gender inequality on natural law grounds that emphasize basic human equality. Defenders of the natural law theory may argue that those who defend slavery or gender oppression on a natural law basis are simply wrong in their interpretation of the natural law. Such a defense of natural law would maintain that slavery, racism, and sexism are wrong based on natural equality among the races and genders.

A further problem is that traditional natural law theory has picked out highly positive traits of human nature: the desire to know the truth, to choose the good, and to develop as healthy mature beings. Not all views of the essential characteristics of human nature have been so positive, however. Some philosophers have depicted human nature as deceitful, evil, and uncontrolled. This is why Hobbes argued that we need a strong government. Without it, he wrote, life in a state of nature would be "nasty, brutish, and short."[12] (We discussed Hobbes in Chapter 4.) A further problem is that if nature is taken in the broader sense—meaning *all* of nature—and if a natural law as a moral law were based on this, then the general approach might even endorse such theories as **social Darwinism**. This view holds that because the most fit organisms in nature are the ones that survive, so also the most fit should endure in human society and the weaker ought to perish. When combined with a belief in capitalism, social Darwinism justified, for example, arguments that it was only right and according to nature that wealthy industrialists at the end of the nineteenth century were disproportionally rich and powerful. It also implied that the poor were impoverished by the designs of nature and thus we ought not interfere with this situation.

Another question raised for natural law theory is the following: Can the way things are by nature provide the basis for knowing how they *ought* to be? On the face of it, this may not seem right. Just because something exists in a certain way does not necessarily mean that it is good. Floods, famine, and disease all exist, but that does not make them good. We saw in the introductory chapter to this book the problem of the naturalistic fallacy and Hume's law, indicating the problem of deriving an *ought* from an *is* (as discussed in Chapter 1). Evaluations cannot simply be derived from factual matters. Other moral philosophers have agreed. Henry Veatch, for example, worried that natural law and the related idea of natural rights were undermined by this problem: "the entire doctrine of natural rights and natural law would appear to rest on nothing less than a patent logical fallacy."[13]

In response to this objection, defenders of natural law might claim that what they are really focused on is a set of basic or intrinsic goods. Or they may deny, as Ralph McInerny has, that there is anything fallacious about deriving an ought from an is: "The concern not to infer value from fact, Ought from Is, is a symptom of false fastidiousness. Worse, it is to take at face value one of the most fundamental errors of modern moral thought."[14] According to McInerny, the value of things is connected to the purpose and function of those things. McInerny maintains that natural law makes best sense in a theistic framework, where the purpose of things is embedded in these things by God. Other authors have clarified that natural law is connected to a theory of basic goods that are known self-evidently: "they cannot be verified by experience or deduced from any more basic truths through a middle term. They are self-evident."[15] This idea of self-evident moral principles and basic goods fits with Jefferson's language in the Declaration: "We hold these truths to be self-evident. . . ."

A standard criticism of this idea would question whether any truths are self-evident in this way. And returning to Hume's problem of deriving an ought from an is, we can still ask (as G. E. Moore did) how we make the leap from fact to value. When we know something to be a fact, that things exist in a certain way, it still remains an open question whether this fact is good. One response for the natural law theory is to state that nature is teleological, that it has a certain directedness. The Thomistic approach grounds this directedness in God. But it is possible to develop this idea from a nontheistic point of view. In Aristotle's terms, we could say that things move or develop toward some natural goal, their final purpose. If we were going to defend natural law theory, we would have to be able to explain human nature in terms of its innate potentialities and the goals of human development. Yet from the time of the scientific revolution of the seventeenth century, such final purposes have become suspect. One could not always observe nature's directedness, and it came to be associated with discredited notions of nonobservable spirits directing things from within. If natural law theory does depend on there being purposes in nature, it must be able to explain where these purposes come from and how we can know what they are.

Consider one possible explanation of the source of whatever purposes there might be in nature. Christian philosophers have long maintained that nature manifests God's plan for the universe. For Aristotle, however, the universe is eternal; it always existed and was not created by God. His concept of God was that of a most perfect being toward which the universe is in some way directed. According to Aristotle, there is an order in nature, but it did not come from the mind of God. For Christian philosophers such as Augustine and Thomas Aquinas, however, the reason why nature

has the order that it does is because God put it there, so to speak. Because the universe was created after a divine plan, nature not only is intelligible but also exists for a purpose that was built into it. Some natural law theorists follow Aquinas on this, whereas others either follow Aristotle or abstain from judgments about the source of the order in nature. But can we conceive of an order in nature without a divine orderer? This depends on what we mean by order in nature. If it is taken in the sense of a plan, then this implies that it has an author. However, natural beings may simply develop in certain ways as a result of chance or evolutionary adaptation, while in reality there is no plan.

Evolutionary theory thus presents a challenge to natural law theory. If the way that things have come to be is the result of many chance variations, then there are no purposes, plans, or preordained functions in nature. The biological and anthropological sciences tend to undermine the idea that there is a universal human nature, since individuals and species vary and change over time. If we wanted to defend natural law theory in the context of contemporary biology, we would have to find natural bases and norms for behavior. One such Darwinian version of natural law has been defended by Larry Arnhart, who argues that human beings have a "natural moral sense" and that "modern Darwinian biology supports this understanding of the ethical and social nature of human beings by showing how it could have arisen by natural selection through evolutionary history."[16]

NATURAL RIGHTS

As we saw at the beginning of this chapter, the idea that moral requirements may be grounded in human nature is central to the theory of natural rights. John Locke provided a theory of natural rights that Thomas Jefferson drew on in the Declaration of Independence. According to Locke, certain things are essential for us as persons. Among these are life itself, as well as liberty and the ability to pursue those things that bring happiness. These are said to be rights not because they are granted by some state but because of the fact that they are important for us as human beings or persons. They are thus moral rights first, though they may need to be enforced by societal institutions and laws.

A central feature of the Declaration's statement of our inalienable rights is the idea that these rights are self-evidently true. These rights are supposed to be known by the light of reason with as much clarity as the truths of mathematics. One apparent problem for natural rights claims is that not everyone agrees about rights. We've already mentioned the problems of slavery and the unequal treatment of women. For centuries of U.S. history, it was not self-evidently true to a majority of citizens that Africans and women were entitled to equal rights. In response to this problem, defenders of natural rights will argue that experience and education are required to show us what is true. No one is born knowing the truths of mathematics or ethics—and people can be mistaken about these truths. We learn these things over time. Indeed, cultures and traditions develop (even the traditions of mathematics). John Finnis, for example, explains self-evident truth as follows: "The important thing about a self-evident proposition is that people (with the relevant experience and understanding of terms) *assent* to it without needing the proof of argument."[17] Thus, in this view, Jefferson might mean that people with relevant experience and understanding will agree that we have the inalienable rights he enumerates in the Declaration (although such agreement continues to be a problem in our diverse, pluralistic culture).

Throughout the eighteenth century, political philosophers often referred to the laws of nature in discussions of natural rights. For example, Voltaire wrote that morality has a universal source. It is the "natural law ... which nature teaches all men" what they should do.[18] The Declaration of Independence was influenced by the writings of jurists and philosophers who believed that a moral law is built into nature. Thus, in the first section it asserts that the colonists were called on "to assume among the powers of the earth, the separate and equal station, to which the Laws of Nature and of Nature's God entitle them."[19]

Today, various international codes of human rights, such as the United Nations' Universal Declaration of Human Rights and the Geneva Conventions' principles for the conduct of war, contain elements of a natural rights tradition. These attempt to specify rights that all people have simply by virtue of their being human, regardless of their country of origin, race, or religion.

EVALUATING NATURAL RIGHTS THEORY

A famous criticism of natural rights comes from the utilitarian philosopher Jeremy Bentham, "Natural rights is simple nonsense: natural and imprescriptible rights, rhetorical nonsense—nonsense upon stilts."[20] Bentham thought that there were no rights outside of the legal and political system. Bentham worried that the idea of natural rights was a perversion of language—since there were no "rights" in nature. Bentham also worried that when people made empty declarations about the "rights of man" (as happened during the French Revolution), this only invited destructive revolutions and anarchy. While Locke, Jefferson, and Hobbes used the idea of natural rights to argue that states were founded on an underlying social contract (which we also discussed in Chapter 4), Bentham thought that the social contract was also a fiction. According to Bentham, governments develop through a long history involving habit and force. And Bentham thought that the ethical goal was to make sure that the legal system pointed in the direction of general happiness—not to postulate rights, which could lead to revolution against the legal system.

One problem for a natural rights theory is that not everyone agrees on what human nature requires or which natural rights are central. In the UN's 1948 Universal Declaration of Human Rights, the list of rights includes welfare rights and rights to food, clothing, shelter, and basic security. Just what kinds of things can we validly claim as human rights? Freedom of speech? Freedom of assembly? Housing? Clean air? Friends? Work? Income? Many of these are listed in a range of treaties and other documents that nations have adopted. However, an account of human rights requires more than lists. A rationale for what constitutes a human right is necessary in order to determine which rights should be protected or promoted. This is also something that a natural rights theory should help provide. Some contemporary philosophers argue that the basic rights that society ought to protect are not welfare rights, such as rights to food, clothing, and shelter, but only liberty rights, such as the right not to be interfered with in our daily lives.[21] (See further discussion of negative and positive rights in the section on socialism in Chapter 14.) How are such differences to be settled?

As a further example of the problem of differences of opinion about the content of rights claims, consider the issue of equality for women (which we discuss further in Chapter 9). Does the concept of rights apply equally to men and to women? Women have historically not been given equal rights with men. In the United States, women were not all granted the right to vote until 1920, as some argued that they were by nature not fully rational or that they were closer in nature to animals than males! The women of Kuwait only gained the right to vote in 2005. Are our rights really self-evident, if people continue to disagree about them?

A theory of human rights should be connected to a theory of human nature, as discussed previously in relation to natural law. A significant problem arises, however, in terms of human beings who are not "natural" or "normal," and with regard to nonhuman animals. Do cognitively disabled humans or human fetuses have the same rights as adult human beings? Do nonhuman animals—especially those with advanced cognitive capacities, such as chimpanzees—have rights? These questions will return in our discussions of abortion and animal welfare in later chapters. But it is important to note here that considerations of rights raise complex questions about what sorts of creatures possess these rights. An account of rights that focuses on human nature will have to be careful to consider how human nature is expressed in fetuses and in disabled people. And if the concept of rights is to be restricted only to human beings, the defender of the concept of rights will have to explain the importance of the distinction between humans and our nonhuman relatives.

Finally, we should note that not all discussions of human rights are focused on human nature. John Stuart Mill argued that rights were related to general utility. "To have a right, then, is, I conceive, to have something which society ought to defend me in the possession of. If the objector goes on to ask, why it ought? I can give him no other reason than general utility."[22] For Mill, rights language provides a strong assertion of those values that promote the greatest happiness for the greatest number. Another example is found in the writings of Walter Lippmann, one of the most influential political commentators of the twentieth century, who held a rather utilitarian view that we ought to agree that there are certain rights because these provide the basis for a democratic society, and it is precisely such a society that works best. It is not that we can prove that such rights as freedom of speech or assembly exist; we simply accept them for pragmatic reasons because they provide the basis for democracy.[23]

The notion of rights can be and has been discussed in many different contexts. Among those treated in this book are issues of animal rights (Chapter 17), economic rights (Chapter 14), fetal rights (Chapter 11), women's rights (Chapter 9), equal rights and discrimination (Chapter 13), and war crimes and universal human rights (Chapter 19).

IS THERE A HUMAN NATURE?

Natural law and the idea of natural human rights presume that there is a common core to the human experience—that we are endowed with basic capacities, that we share common purposes, and that we value and enjoy a common set of intrinsic goods. In short, natural law and human rights rest upon an objective account of human nature. One way of putting this is to say that human nature is discovered by us through the use of reason—and that human nature is not created by us or constructed by society. Not all philosophers believe, however, that there is such a thing as human nature. In the twentieth century, existentialists such as Jean-Paul Sartre argued that there was no essential human nature. As Sartre put it, "existence precedes essence," which means that through the course of our lives we create our own nature or essence. More recent authors—who are often described as "postmodernists"—have made this argument in even stronger terms. Richard Rorty, whom we discussed in the chapter on relativism, put the criticism of human nature this way:

> There is nothing deep inside each of us, no common human nature, no built-in human solidarity, to use as a moral reference point. There is nothing to people except what has been socialized into them. . . . Simply by being human we do not have a common bond. For all we share with all other humans is the same thing we share with all other animals—the ability to feel pain.[24]

This skepticism about human nature might point toward a broader conception of what matters morally—toward solidarity with animals and toward inclusion of disabled humans. But from the standpoint of natural law, such a denial of a common human nature will look like the worst form of relativism. As Craig Boyd has argued in defense of natural law and against the sorts of criticism made by people like Sartre and Rorty, "Natural law requires, as a presupposition, that human beings have enduring, identifiable natures, which in turn requires some kind of realism."[25] As you reflect upon natural law ethics, one of the most fundamental questions is whether there is an enduring and identifiable human nature or whether the complexity and changeable history of the human experience undermines the very idea of a shared human nature.

NOTES

1. Thomas Jefferson, "The Declaration of Independence," in *Basic Writings of Thomas Jefferson*, ed. Philip S. Foner (New York: Wiley, 1944), 551.
2. John Locke, *Two Treatises of Government* (London, 1690), ed. Peter Laslett (Cambridge: Cambridge University Press, 1960).
3. "Justice Dept. Releases Recommended Fates for Guantánamo Detainees," *New York Times*, June 17, 2013, http://www.nytimes.com/2013/06/18/us/justice-dept-releases-recommended-fates-for-guantanamo-detainees.html?_r=0
4. "Is Force-Feeding Torture?" *New York Times*, May 31, 2013, http://www.nytimes.com/2013/06/01/opinion/nocera-is-force-feeding-torture.html
5. Henry David Thoreau, "Civil Disobedience," in *Miscellanies* (Boston: Houghton Mifflin, 1983), 136–37.
6. Cicero, *Republic*, in *Cicero's Tusculan Disputations. Also, Treatises on the Nature of the Gods, and on the Commonwealth*, bk. 3 at 22 (Project Gutenberg), http://www.gutenberg.org/files/14988/14988-h/14988-h.htm
7. Thomas Aquinas, *Summa Theologica*, in *Basic Writings of Saint Thomas Aquinas*, ed. Anton Pegis (New York: Random House, 1948).
8. Aquinas, *Summa Theologica*, Q.91 a.4. Aquinas is quoting Cicero's *Rhetoric*.
9. This is an incomplete presentation of the moral philosophy of Thomas Aquinas. We should also note that he was as much a theologian as a philosopher, if not more so. True and complete happiness, he believed, would be achieved only in knowledge or contemplation of God.
10. Hugo Grotius, *On the Rights of War and Peace* (Cambridge: Cambridge University Press, 1854), xxvii.
11. Aristotle, *Politics*, Chapters 5, 6.
12. Thomas Hobbes, *Leviathan*, ed. Michael Oakeshott (New York: Oxford University Press, 1962).
13. Henry Veatch, "Natural Law: Dead or Alive?" at Liberty Fund, http://oll.libertyfund.org/index.php?Itemid=259&id=168&option=com_content&task=view#anchor249499 (originally published 1978).
14. Ralph M. McInerny, *Ethica Thomistica* (Washington, DC: Catholic University of America Press, 1997), 56.
15. Germain Grisez, Joseph Boyle, and John Finnis, "Practical Principles, Moral Truth, and Ultimate Ends," *American Journal of Jurisprudence* 32 (1987): 106.
16. Larry Arnhart, *Darwinian Natural Right* (Albany: State University of New York Press, 1998), 7.
17. John Finnis, *Natural Law and Natural Rights* (Oxford: Oxford University Press, 2011), 31.
18. Voltaire, *Ouevres*, XXV, 39; XI, 443, quoted in Carl L. Becker, *The Heavenly City of the Eighteenth-Century Philosophers* (New Haven, CT: Yale University Press, 2003), 52; Becker's translation.
19. Thomas Jefferson, Declaration of Independence.
20. Jeremy Bentham, *Anarchical Fallacies*, in *The Works of Jeremy Bentham* (Edinburgh: William Tait, 1843), 501.
21. On negative or liberty rights, see, for example, the work of Robert Nozick, *State, Anarchy and Utopia* (New York: Basic Books, 1974). See further discussion on welfare and liberty rights in Chapter 14 of this book, "Economic Justice."
22. John Stuart Mill, *Utilitarianism*, in Mill, *On Liberty and Utilitarianism* (New York: Random House, 1993), 222.
23. The term *pragmatic* concerns what "works." Thus, to accept something on pragmatic grounds means to accept it because it works for us in some way. For Walter Lippmann's views, see *Essays in the Public Philosophy* (Boston: Little, Brown, 1955).
24. Richard Rorty, *Contingency, Irony, Solidarity* (Cambridge: Cambridge University Press, 1989), 175.
25. Craig Boyd, *A Shared Morality: A Narrative Defense of Natural Law Ethics* (Grand Rapids, MI: Brazos Press, 2007), 183.

REVIEW EXERCISES

1. Give a basic definition of natural law theory.
2. What is the difference between the scientific laws of nature and the natural law?
3. In what way is natural law theory teleological?
4. What specific natural or human species capacities are singled out by natural law theorists? How do these determine what we ought to do, according to the theory?
5. What is the difference between Aristotle and Aquinas on the theistic basis of natural law?
6. Explain one area of concern or criticism of natural law theory.
7. Describe the basis of rights according to natural rights theorists.
8. Give examples of what sorts of rights we are supposed to have according to natural law theory.
9. How do we know that we have natural rights?
10. Explain the criticism of natural law from the perspective of those who deny the idea of "human nature."

8 Virtue Ethics

Learning Outcomes

After reading this chapter, you should be able to:

- Understand how virtue ethics differs from other approaches to ethics.
- Describe some key virtues and how they are manifest in concrete situations.
- Explain how virtues are connected to an account of the functions or purposes of human life.
- Describe how *eudaimonia* functions in the theory of virtue.
- Identify some features of the diverse cultural approaches to virtue.
- Explain how the idea of the Golden Mean functions in virtue ethics.
- Provide an overview of Aristotle's moral philosophy.
- Defend your own thesis with regard to the value of virtue ethics.

© iStockphoto.com/Sebastiaan de Stigter

at Tillman was a successful NFL player. He played safety for the Arizona Cardinals, earning hundreds of thousands of dollars. After the September 11 attacks in 2001, Tillman turned down a $3.6 million contract offer and enlisted in the Army. He qualified to become an Army Ranger. His unit served in Iraq and in Afghanistan, where he was killed, by accident, by members of his own platoon during a firefight. Tillman's death prompted a number of controversies. The Army initially informed Tillman's family and the public that he had been killed by enemy fire, in an apparent effort to preserve the image of Tillman as a war hero. (Among other awards, he posthumously received the Army's Silver Star for Valor.) A subsequent book about Tillman claimed that Tillman was not a supporter of the Iraq war and was critical of President George W. Bush.[1] Nonetheless, Tillman remains a model of virtue and courage. Senator John McCain used Tillman's story to explain the virtues of citizenship and patriotism in his book *Character Is Destiny*.[2] What is remarkable about Tillman is his willingness to sacrifice a lucrative football career for life and death as an Army Ranger. He seemed to embody virtues—such as courage, loyalty, self-sacrifice, and patriotism—that are often mourned as deficient or absent in contemporary society. Do you agree with this assessment? What role do such virtues play in your own moral life?

When thinking about virtue, it is useful to think about the people you admire. Whether it is a relative, a coworker, a friend, or some celebrity, it is helpful to consider the traits that make those people good. We usually admire people who are courageous, kind, honest, generous, loyal, diligent, temperate, fair, modest, and hospitable. Such traits of character are traditionally known as *virtues*.

VIRTUES AND EVERYDAY LIFE

The theories that we have treated so far in this text are concerned with how we determine the right action to take or policy to establish. The focus on virtue takes a different approach to morality. Rather than asking what we ought to *do*, virtue ethics asks how we ought to *be*. Virtue ethics is concerned with those traits of character, habits, tendencies, and dispositions that make a person good. When some or all of the traits mentioned above are unusually well developed in a person, that person may be regarded as a hero or even as a saint. One version of virtue ethics is focused on thinking about saints and heroes as paradigms or exemplars of human excellence.

In a well-known article on the topic, Susan Wolf described a moral saint as, "a person whose every action is as good as possible, that is, who is as morally worthy as can be."[3] But Wolf goes on to argue that moral saints are not especially happy, since the demands of saintly perfection might include

Pat Tilman, during his NFL career.

John Cordes/Icon SMI/ZUMA/Corbis Wire/Corbis

self-sacrifice. At issue here is a definition of happiness. Virtue ethics tends to hold that happiness is something different from pleasure. Pat Tillman's life and death were not particularly pleasant—he suffered through Army Ranger training and then was killed at the age of 27. But perhaps there is something more important than pleasure. At any rate, even if it is difficult and unpleasant to become a hero or a saint, the virtue tradition maintains that people live better when they possess most or all of the virtues. People can also exhibit bad character traits. For example, they can be cowardly, dishonest, tactless, careless, boorish, stingy, vindictive, disloyal, lazy, or egotistical. Another word for these bad traits is *vice*. An ethics focused on virtue encourages us to develop the good traits and get rid of the bad ones, that is, to develop our virtues and eliminate our vices.

The ethical issues that are treated in the second half of this text are generally controversial social issues: the death penalty, abortion, and terrorism, for example. Virtue ethics seems more personal. It involves not so much asking which side of some social issue one should support as what kind of person one should be. Virtues can help us make good decisions in tough situations. But they also serve us on a daily basis. Virtues such as courage, loyalty, honesty, and fairness show up in our interactions with relatives, friends, and coworkers. We often think about virtues when we consider how our behavior serves as a good (or bad) model for our children, students, and colleagues.

Virtue ethics can be useful in thinking about the applied issues discussed in the second half of the text. Virtues depend, in part, on our roles and help us fulfill the requirements of our roles: so soldiers ought to be courageous and strong, while teachers ought to be patient and kind. Virtue ethics encourages us to consider the question of how a soldier's virtues might differ from those of a teacher. Some of the applied topics we will discuss have connections with questions about the virtues of various vocations and roles. In thinking about euthanasia and physician-assisted suicide, for example, issues arise regarding the proper virtues of health care providers. In thinking about the morality of abortion, we might think about proper virtues of parents and lawmakers, as well as doctors. In thinking about the morality of war, we consider the virtues we associate with military service.

There will be overlap among the virtues found in different vocations. But different roles require different character traits and habits. This reminds us that virtue ethics has a pluralistic aspect. There are many different virtues that can be emphasized and integrated in various ways in the life of an individual. Moreover, virtuous people tend to be responsive to the unique demands of various situations; they do the right thing, at the right time, in the right way, exhibiting a sort of "practical wisdom" that is sensitive to context. From the standpoint of utilitarianism or deontology, which wants clearly defined rules and principles for action, virtue ethics can seem imprecise and vague. But an asset of virtue ethics may be its sensitivity to context and its recognition of plurality in morals.

Although we probably do not use the term *virtuous* as frequently today as in times past, we still understand the essence of its meaning. A virtuous person is a morally good person, and virtues are good traits. Another word that is useful in understanding virtue is the word *excellence*. The virtues are those things that make us excellent; they allow us to manifest our highest potential. There is more than one thing that makes us excellent. Indeed, virtues are often described in the plural—as a list of qualities that lead to living well. Loyalty is a virtue, and so is honesty. A moral philosophy that concentrates on the notion of virtue is called a *virtue ethics*. For virtue ethics, the moral life is about developing good *character*. It is about determining the ideals for human life and trying to embody these ideals in one's own life. The virtues are ways in which we embody these ideals. If we consider honesty to be such an ideal, for example, then we ought to try to become honest persons.

ARISTOTLE

Aristotle was born in 384 BCE in Stagira in northern Greece. His father was a physician for King Philip of Macedonia. Around age seventeen, he went to study at Plato's Academy in Athens. Aristotle traveled for several years and then for two or three years was the tutor to Alexander, Philip's young son who later became known as Alexander the Great. In 335 BCE, Aristotle returned to Athens and organized his own school, called the Lyceum. There he taught and wrote almost until his death thirteen years later, in 322 BCE.[4] Aristotle is known not only for his moral theory but also for writings in logic, biology, physics, metaphysics, art, and politics. The basic notions of his moral theory can be found in his *Nicomachean Ethics*, named for his son Nicomachus.[5]

As noted in the previous chapter, Aristotle was one of the earliest writers to ground morality in nature, and specifically in *human* nature. His theory of ethics and morality also stressed the notion of virtue. For Aristotle, virtue was an excellence of some sort. Our word *virtue* originally came from the Latin *vir* and referred to strength or manliness.[6] In Aristotle's Greek, the term for virtue was *arete*, a word that can also be translated as "excellence."

According to Aristotle, there are two basic types of virtue (or excellence): intellectual virtues and moral virtues. Intellectual virtues are excellences of mind, such as the ability to understand and reason and judge well. Moral virtues, on the other hand, dispose us to act well. These virtues are learned by repetition. For instance, by practicing courage or honesty, we become more courageous and honest. Just as repetition in playing a musical instrument makes playing easier, so also repeated acts of honesty make it easier to be honest. The person who has the virtue of honesty finds it easier to be honest than the person who does not have the virtue. It has become habitual or second nature to him or her. The same thing applies to the opposite of virtue, namely, vice. The person who lies and lies again finds that lying is easier and telling the truth more difficult. One can have bad moral habits (vices) as well as good ones (virtues). Just like other bad habits, bad moral habits are difficult to change or break. And like other good habits, good moral habits take practice to develop.

Virtue as a Mean

Aristotle's philosophy outlines a variety of particular virtues including courage, temperance, justice, pride, and magnanimity. However, Aristotle also provides a unifying framework for understanding virtue in general, as a mean between extremes. This idea is occasionally known as the **Golden Mean** (and should not be confused with the Golden Rule, which we've discussed in previous chapters). By saying that virtue is a *mean*, we are using the word with reference to how it is used in mathematics, where the *mean* is in the middle, as the average. (The term *mean* here should also not be confused with the idea of using someone as a *means*, as we discussed in the chapter on Kant and deontology.)

To better understand the idea that virtue is a mean, take the following example. The virtue of courage can be understood as a mean or middle between the two extremes of deficiency and excess. Too little courage is cowardice, and too much is foolhardiness. When facing danger or challenges, we should have neither too much fear—which makes us unable to act—nor too little fear—which makes us take reckless or foolish risks. The virtue of courage is having just the right amount of fear, depending on what is appropriate for us as individuals and for the circumstances we face. So, too, the other virtues can be seen as means between extremes. Consider the following examples from Aristotle organized in the following table, with the virtuous mean listed in the middle between two vices.

Different authors have offered different lists of virtues and corresponding vices. For the Greek tradition, following Plato, there were four basic or **cardinal virtues**: prudence (or wisdom), justice, temperance, and courage. Questions arise about which traits count as virtues and how these virtues are related to corresponding vices. For example, we might want to count loyalty and honesty as virtues. If loyalty is a virtue, then is it also a middle between two extremes? Can there be such a thing as too little or too much loyalty? What about honesty? Too much honesty might be seen as undisciplined openness, and too little as deceitfulness. Would the right amount of honesty

be forthrightness? But not all virtues may be rightly thought of as means between extremes. For example, if justice is a virtue, then could there be such a thing as being too just? It is important to note that virtue ethics still maintains that some things are simply wrong and not amenable to explanation in virtue terminology. Murder, for example, is wrong; there is no right time for murder or right amount of murder.

Nature, Human Nature, and the Human Good

Aristotle was a close observer of nature. In fact, in his writings he mentions some 500 different kinds of animals.[7] He noticed that seeds of the same sort always grew to the same mature form. He opened developing eggs of various species and noticed that these organisms manifested a pattern in their development even before birth. Tadpoles, he might have said, always follow the same path and become frogs, not turtles. So also with other living things. Acorns always become oak trees, not elms. He concluded that there was an order in nature. It was as if natural beings such as plants and animals had a principle of order within them that directed them toward their goal—their mature final form. This view can be called a *teleological* view, from the Greek word for goal, *telos*, because of its emphasis on a goal embedded in natural things. It was from this conclusion that Aristotle developed his notion of the good. You might also notice that the idea of a natural goal, purpose, or function showed up in the discussion of natural law (in Chapter 7).

According to Aristotle, good things fulfill some purpose or end or goal. Thus, the good of the shipbuilder is to build ships. The good of the lyre player is to play well. The traits that allow for good shipbuilding or lyre-playing will be somewhat different. But good shipbuilders and good lyre players will share certain

	Deficit (Too Little)	Virtue (the Mean)	Excess (Too Much)
Fear	Foolhardiness	Courage	Cowardice
Giving	Illiberality	Liberality	Prodigality
Self-Regard	Humility	Pride	Vanity
Pleasures	(No Name Given)	Temperance	Profligacy

virtues such as intelligence and creativity. Aristotle asks whether there is anything that is the good of the human being—not as shipbuilder or lyre player, but simply as human. To answer this question, we must first think about what it is to be human. According to Aristotle, natural beings come in kinds or species. From their species flow their essential characteristics and certain key tendencies or capacities. A squirrel, for example, is a kind of animal that is, first of all, a living being. It develops from a young to a mature form. It is a mammal and therefore has other characteristics of mammals. It is bushy-tailed, can run along telephone wires, and gathers and stores nuts for its food. From the characteristics that define a squirrel, we also can know what a *good* squirrel is. A good specimen of a squirrel is one that is effective, successful, and functions well. It follows the pattern of development and growth it has by nature. A good squirrel does, in fact, have a bushy tail and good balance and knows how to find and store its food. It would be a bad example of a squirrel if it had no balance, couldn't find its food, or had no fur and was sickly. It would have been better for the squirrel if its inherent natural tendencies to grow and develop and live as a healthy squirrel had been realized.

Aristotle thought of human beings as natural beings with a specific human nature. Human beings have certain specific characteristics and abilities that we share as humans. Unlike squirrels and acorns, human beings can choose to act in the service of their good or act against it. But just what is their good? Aristotle recognized that a good eye is a healthy eye that sees well. A good horse is a well-functioning horse, one that is healthy and able to run and do what horses do. What about human beings? Is there something comparable for the human being as human? Is there some good for humans as humans?

Just as we can tell what the good squirrel is from its own characteristics and abilities as a squirrel, the same should be true for the human being. For human beings to function well or flourish, they should perfect their human capacities. If they do this, they will be functioning well as human beings. They will also be happy, for a being is happy to the extent that it is functioning well. Aristotle believed that the ultimate

good of humans is happiness, blessedness, or prosperity. The Greek word for this sort of happiness is **eudaimonia.** *Eudaimonia* is not to be confused with pleasure. Indeed, the virtues are often at odds with pleasure. A coward who is afraid of danger is reluctant to experience pain. And a courageous person may have to forgo pleasure and submit to pain—including the pain of being killed. Aristotle warned that pleasure can distract us from what is good. Thus, Aristotle's account of *eudaimonia* aims at a kind of happiness that is deeper and longer lasting than mere pleasure. The term *eudaimonia* gives us a clue about this. The *eu-* prefix means "good"; and *daimonia* is related to the Greek word for "spirit" or "soul." Thus, Aristotle's idea is that virtue produces the happiness of having a good soul or spirit, which fulfills essential human functions or purposes.

Aristotle is thus interested in the question of what our human functions or purposes might be. Human beings have much in common with lower forms of beings. We are living, for example, just as plants are. Thus, we take in material from outside us for nourishment, and we grow from an immature to a mature form. We have senses of sight and hearing and so forth, as do the higher animals. We are social animals as well, who must live in groups together with other human beings. Since human beings have various functions or purposes, there are various types of virtue. The virtues of social life, for example, help us fulfill our function as social beings. The moral or social virtues would include honesty, loyalty, and generosity.

But is there anything unique to humans, an essentially human function or purpose? Aristotle believed that it is our "rational element" that is peculiar to us. The good for humans, then, should consist in their functioning in a way consistent with and guided by this rational element. Our rational element has two different functions: one is to know, and the other is to guide choice and action. We must develop our ability to know the world and the truth. We must also choose wisely. In doing this, we will be functioning well specifically as humans. Thus, in addition to social or moral virtues, there are also intellectual virtues, which help us fulfill our function as intelligent animals. These virtues, according to Aristotle, include practical knowledge, scientific knowledge, and practical wisdom. It is not surprising that Aristotle—who was a philosopher and a student of Plato—thought that the intellectual virtues were more important than the other virtues, since they help us fulfill our uniquely human capacities.

CROSS-CULTURAL AND CONTEMPORARY VIRTUE ETHICS

Versions of virtue ethics can also be found in other traditions. The Confucian tradition in China is often described as a virtue tradition. This tradition traces its roots back to Confucius (551–479 BCE), a figure who plays a role in Chinese philosophy that is similar to the role played by Socrates in Greek philosophy—as founding character and touchstone for later authors who want to reflect upon virtue and wisdom. Unlike Socrates, however, who was something of a rough-mannered outsider to the elite social scene of Athens, Confucius was viewed as a model of courtly gentility and decorum. The Confucian tradition emphasizes two main virtues, *jen* (or *ren*) and *li*. *Jen* is often translated as "humaneness" or "compassion." *Li* is often translated as "propriety," "manners," or "culture." Confucian ethics aims toward a synthesis of the virtues oriented around compassion and propriety. In the *Analects* of Confucius, this is explained in various ways. Consider the following saying attributed to Confucius:

> A youth, when at home, should be filial, and, abroad, respectful to his elders. He should be earnest and truthful. He should overflow in love to all, and cultivate the friendship of the good. When he has time and opportunity, after the performance of these things, he should employ them in polite studies.[8]

Confucius advises young people to be polite and respectful, earnest and truthful, and to overflow with love. Similar advice holds for others who are at different stages of life's journey. Confucius also holds that there are specific virtues for those inhabiting different roles: for fathers, brothers, sons, and government officials. As is true of most of the other traditions of the ancient world, the primary focus here is on male roles; women's roles were defined in subordination to the male.

Other traditions emphasize different forms of virtue. Hinduism emphasizes five basic moral virtues

Statue of Confucius in Shanghai, China.

or *yamas*: nonviolence (*ahimsa*), truthfulness, honesty, chastity, and freedom from greed[9]. Hinduism also includes mental virtues to be perfected in meditation and yogic practice: calmness, self-control, self-settledness, forbearance, faith, and complete concentration, as well as the hunger for spiritual liberation.[10] Buddhism shares with Hinduism an emphasis on both intellectual and moral virtues. The "noble eight fold path" of Buddhism includes moral virtues such as right speech, right action, and right livelihood, as well as intellectual virtues of understanding and mindfulness.[11] Christian virtue ethics includes similar moral virtues, as well as what Thomas Aquinas called the "theological virtues." In the Christian tradition, the four cardinal moral virtues are prudence, justice, temperance, and fortitude, while the three theological virtues are faith, hope, and love. It is easy to see that there is overlap among these different traditions in terms of the virtues required for a good life, despite some clear differences. The common thread that links them as traditions of *virtue ethics* is the idea that habits and character traits matter, along with sustained philosophical reflection on the reasons that these habits and character traits matter.

Various contemporary moral philosophers have also stressed the importance of virtue.[12] Philippa Foot, for example, has developed a contemporary version of virtue ethics. She believes that the virtues are "in some general way, beneficial. Human beings do not get on well without them."[13] According to Foot, virtues provide benefits both to the virtuous person and to her community, just as vices harm both the self and the community. Think of courage, temperance, and wisdom, for example, and ask yourself how persons having these virtues might benefit others as well as themselves. Some virtues such as charity, however, seem to benefit mostly others. But this makes sense for social virtues, which help us fulfill our function as social beings. There is an open question, however, about which beneficial character traits are to be thought of as moral virtues and which are not. Wit or powers of concentration benefit us, but we would probably not consider them to be *moral* virtues.

Foot also asks whether virtue is best seen in the intention that guides an action or in the execution of an action. Think of generosity. Does the person who intends to be generous—but who cannot seem to do what helps others—really possess the virtue of generosity? Or rather is it the person who actually does help who has the virtue? Foot believes that virtue is also something we must choose to develop and work at personifying. Furthermore, following Aristotle, Foot argues that the virtues are *corrective*. They help us be and do things that are difficult for us. Courage, for example, helps us overcome natural fear. Temperance helps us control our desires. Since people differ in their natural inclinations, they also differ in what virtues would be most helpful for them to develop. Foot's view is just one example of how the notion of virtue continues to be discussed by moral philosophers.

EVALUATING VIRTUE ETHICS

One question that has been raised for virtue ethics concerns how we determine which traits are virtues, and whether they are so in all circumstances. Are there any universally valuable traits? Wherever friendship exists, loyalty would seem necessary, although the form it might take would vary according to time and place. So also would honesty seem necessary for human relations wherever they exist. We might also start with Aristotle's own list of virtues, which reflected what were considered the primary civic virtues of his day. But Aristotle's society included slavery and gender hierarchy. One wonders whether it makes sense to speak of virtuous slave-masters or whether the submissive traits of women in patriarchal cultures are really virtuous. Similar problems occur as we consider differences among civilizations. Are the virtues of Confucian culture the same (or better or worse) than the virtues of Muslim, Christian, or Hindu cultures?

Contemporary moral philosopher Alasdair MacIntyre believes that virtues depend at least partly on the practices of a culture or society. A warlike society will value heroic virtues, whereas a peaceful and prosperous society might think of generosity as a particularly important virtue.[14] However, these must also be virtues specific to human beings as humans, for otherwise one could not speak of "human excellences." But this is just the problem. What is it to live a full human life? Can one specify this apart from what it is to live such a life in a particular society or as a particular person? The problem here is not only how we know what excellences are human excellences but also whether there are any such traits that are ideal for all persons, despite differences in gender, social roles, and physical and mental capacity.

A further problem with regard to virtue is the question of the degree of effort and discipline required to be virtuous. Who manifests the virtue of courage the most—the person who, as Foot puts it, "wants to run away but does not or the one who does not even want to run away?"[15] We generally believe that we ought to be rewarded for our moral efforts, and thus the person who wants to run away but does not seems more praiseworthy. On the other hand, possession of the virtue of courage is supposed to make it easier to be brave. Part of Foot's own answer to this dilemma involves the distinction between those fears for which we are in some way responsible and those that we cannot help. Thus, the person who feels like running away because she has contributed by her own choices to being afraid is not the more virtuous person. Foot also addresses the question of whether someone who does something morally wrong—say, robs a bank or commits a murder—and does so courageously, demonstrates the virtue of courage.

We can also ask whether virtue ethics is really a distinct type of ethics. Consider two of the other theories we have discussed: utilitarianism and deontology. The concept of virtue is not foreign to Mill or Kant. However, for both of them it is secondary. Their moral theories tell us how we ought to decide what to *do*. Doing the right thing—and with Kant, for the right reason—is primary. However, if the development of certain habits of action or tendencies to act in a certain way will enable us to do good more easily, then they would surely be recognized by these philosophers as good. Utilitarians would encourage the development of those virtues that would be conducive to the maximization of happiness. If temperance in eating and drinking will help us avoid the suffering that can come from illness and drunkenness, then this virtue ought to be encouraged and developed in the young. So also with other virtues. According to a Kantian, we should develop habits and virtues that would make it more likely that we act fairly (according to universalizable maxims) and treat people as ends rather than simply as means.

When evaluating the virtue ethics tradition developed by Aristotle, we should also consider a more specific criticism of it introduced by Kant. Kant argues that Aristotle's notion of virtue as a mean between two vices—the Golden Mean—is simply false. Kant writes that, "it is incorrect to define any virtue or vice in terms of mere degree," which "proves the uselessness of the Aristotelian principles that virtue consists in the middle way between two vices."[16] Kant rejects the idea that there is a gradation of behaviors or dispositions from one extreme (or vice) to the other with virtue in the middle. Rather, for Kant, some things are praiseworthy and others are wrong, and do not vary by degrees on a continuum. Kant suggests that the Aristotelian idea of the Golden Mean simply confuses us and distracts us from thinking about why a given virtue is good. Bearing this argument in mind, it is worth considering whether the idea of virtue as a mean between vices really makes sense of the way we ordinarily understand virtues such as courage and vices like cowardice. Is this idea genuinely helpful to us in identifying the nature of virtue?

In virtue ethics, the primary goal is to be a good person. Now, a critic of virtue ethics might argue that *being* good is only a function of being *inclined* to do good. However, ethics appears to require not only a habitual inclination toward good deeds but also actually doing good. Is what matters the deed or the inclination to carry it out? If what really matters is the actions and deeds, then virtue is simply one aspect of an action-oriented moral philosophy such as consequentialism. However, virtue ethics does have a somewhat different emphasis. It is an ethics whose goal is to determine what is essential to being a well-functioning or flourishing human person. Virtue ethics stresses an ideal for humans or persons. As an ethics of ideals or excellences, it is an optimistic and positive type of ethics. One problem that virtue ethics may face is what to say about those of us who do not meet the ideal. If we fall short of the virtuous model, does this make us bad or vicious? As with all moral theories, many questions concerning virtue remain to engage and puzzle us.

NOTES

1. Jon Krakauer, *Where Men Win Glory* (New York: Doubleday, 2009).
2. John McCain, *Character Is Destiny* (New York: Random House, 2007).
3. Susan Wolf, "Moral Saints," *The Journal of Philosophy* 89, no. 8 (August 1982): 419.
4. W. T. Jones, *A History of Western Philosophy: The Classical Mind*, 2nd ed. (New York: Harcourt, Brace & World, 1969), 214–16.
5. This was asserted by the neo-Platonist Porphyry (ca. 232 CE). However, others believe that the work got its name because it was edited by Nicomachus. See Alasdair MacIntyre, *After Virtue* (Notre Dame, IN: Notre Dame University Press, 1984), 147.
6. Milton Gonsalves, *Fagothy's Right and Reason*, 9th ed. (Columbus, OH: Merrill, 1989), 201.
7. W. T. Jones, *A History of Western Philosophy*, 233.
8. Confucius, *Analects*, in *The Chinese Classics—Volume 1: Confucian Analects*, bk. 1, Chapter 6, trans. James Legge (Project Gutenberg), http://www.gutenberg.org/files/4094/4094-h/4094-h.htm
9. Sunil Sehgal, ed., *Encyclopedia of Hinduism* (New Delhi: Sarup and Sons, 1999), 2:364.

10. Vensus A. George, *Paths to the Divine: Ancient and Indian* (Washington, DC: CRVP Press, 2008), 205.
11. Peter Harvey, *Buddhism: Teachings, History and Practices* (Cambridge: Cambridge University Press, 1990), 68–69.
12. See, for example, the collection of articles in Christina Hoff Sommers, *Vice and Virtue in Everyday Life* (New York: Harcourt Brace Jovanovich, 1985).
13. Philippa Foot, *Virtues and Vices* (Oxford: Oxford University Press, 2002).
14. Alasdair MacIntyre, "The Virtue in Heroic Societies" and "The Virtues at Athens," in *After Virtue* (Notre Dame, IN: Notre Dame University Press, 1984), 121–45.
15. Foot, *Virtues and Vices,* 10.
16. Kant, "Doctrine of Virtue," in *Metaphysics of Morals*, trans. Mary Gregor (Cambridge: Cambridge University Press, 1996), § 10, 184–85.

REVIEW EXERCISES

1. What is the basic difference between virtue ethics and other types of ethics we have studied?
2. According to Aristotle, what is the difference between intellectual and moral virtue?
3. In what sense are virtues habits?
4. Give a list of some traits that have been thought to be virtues, according to Aristotle and other virtue theorists.
5. According to Aristotle, how is virtue a mean between extremes? Give some examples.
6. Explain the problem of determining whether virtues are human perfections or excellences, or socially valuable traits.
7. Explain the problem raised by Philippa Foot as to who most exemplifies the virtue of courage—the person who finds it difficult to be courageous or the person who finds it easy.

Feminist Thought and the Ethics of Care

Learning Outcomes

After reading this chapter, you should be able to:

- Understand the importance of feminist thought for ethical inquiry.
- Explain some of the problems confronting women around the world.
- Explain feminist criticisms of traditional views about ethics and moral development.
- Identify the arguments of key feminist authors, including Carol Gilligan, Nel Noddings, Sarah Ruddick, Martha Nussbaum, and Judith Butler.

- Describe the essential features of the ethics of care.
- Explain the difference between feminine ethics and feminist ethics.
- Distinguish the several versions or "waves" of feminism.
- Develop and defend your own ideas about the importance of feminist ethics and the ethics of care.

© IStockphoto/Thinkstock

In Pakistan in October 2012, a fifteen-year-old schoolgirl, Malala Yousafzai, was shot in the head by Taliban assassins as she waited for a bus. The Taliban targeted Malala because she had spoken out in defense of the right of girls to attend school. Malala recovered from her wounds and has gone on to become an international advocate for the rights of girls and women. Her case is an indication of the inequality and oppression that still afflict women throughout the world.

We like to imagine that violence against women is only a problem in other parts of the globe. But in the United States, there is still a significant amount of violence against women. According to data used by the White House in its "1 is 2 Many" campaign to reduce violence against women, one in five women will be sexually assaulted in college, one in nine teenage girls will be forced to have sex, and one in ten teens will be hurt on purpose by someone they are dating.[1] Some authors have also suggested that another insidious form of violence against women occurs through a cultural obsession with female beauty, which fuels the epidemic of eating disorders and the growing use of cosmetic surgery to "perfect" the female body.[2] Naomi Wolf links this to the rise of pornography; "the influence of pornography on women's sexual sense of self has now become so complete that it is almost impossible for younger women to distinguish the role pornography plays in creating their idea of how to be, look and move in sex from their own innate sense of sexual identity."[3] Some authors have argued that pornography is itself an example of violence against women, which in turn contributes to further violence against women.[4] It might be, however, that pornography is a celebration of sexuality, which empowers women.

Women holding signs in support of Malala Yousafzai in 2012 in Islamabad, Pakistan.

Pro-sex or sex-positive feminists such as Wendy McElroy argue that pornography benefits women both personally and politically. From McElroy's perspective, the point is to make sure that sex work is free of coercion and that it respects women by affording them the freedom to choose as individuals to participate or not.[5] This dispute reminds us that feminism, like other approaches to moral theory, is subject to diverse interpretations.

While the charge about the degrading and violent aspects of pornography has been made by Western feminists, a similar argument against the general sexual objectification of women comes from defenders of traditional roles for women and rules of modesty. While this argument has been made in a variety of cultural contexts, the most prominent current discussion involves rules governing the use of veiling in Muslim cultures. Defenders of the veil or *hijab* argue that modest dress protects women from being publicly harassed or molested, often quoting a passage from the Qur'an (33:59), which states that modest dress for women will ensure that they are not abused. Similar ideas are found in other cultures and religious traditions, including in some ultra orthodox Jewish communities. One example hit the headlines in 2011, as an eight-year-old girl was spat upon and cursed by some ultra orthodox men in Israel because she was not modestly dressed.[6] Critics argue that women should be free from molestation regardless of how they dress. From this perspective, the problem is not what women wear or how they behave but a male-dominated culture in which men seek to regulate and control women.

The problem of violence against women is a global issue. Nicholas Kristof and Sheryl WuDunn have chronicled the problem in their book (and documentary) *Half the Sky*. Across the world, rape and sex-slavery threaten the well-being of women. In some cases, women are denied access to medical care and resources simply because they are women. Female fetuses are aborted because of a cultural bias toward male offspring. Girls' genitals are mutilated in a practice of ritual "circumcision." And women are killed simply because they are women. Kristof and WuDunn conclude,

> It appears that more girls have been killed in the last fifty years, precisely because they were girls, than men were killed in all the battles of the twentieth century. More girls are killed in this routine "gendercide" in any one decade than people were slaughtered in all the genocides of the twentieth century.[7]

A significant problem is "honor killing." In some cultures, when a woman has done something that the culture considers shameful, the male members of the family feel justified in killing her. In some places, rape is "punished" by killing the woman who has been raped or by forcing the rape victim to marry her rapist. A CBS News report from April 2012 concluded that at least 5,000 women are killed every year because of "honor."[8] In Pakistan, in 2011, nearly 1,000 women were murdered in this way. Some cases occur within the United

© epa european pressphoto agency b.v./Alamy

States and Britain, including the murder in 2009 of Noor Almaleki by her own father in Peoria, Arizona, as reported on the CBS news program *48 Hours*.[9]

While the mainstream of Western culture now holds that women deserve to be treated equally, it is clear that we've still got a long way to go in terms of actualizing this idea internationally. Even within the United States there is room for progress. In 2012, the World Economic Forum ranked the United States twenty-second in the world in terms of gender equality, calculated by measuring a variety of factors indicating economic opportunity, educational attainment, health outcomes, and political empowerment of women (as compared to men).[10] On the one hand, women do seem to be outperforming men academically. According to a report from the White House in 2011 (based upon 2009 data), more women than men have earned college degrees; and more women than men have worked on advanced degrees.[11] And yet, that same report indicates that there is a remaining "pay gap" in the United States, with women earning only 75 percent as much as their male counterparts.

We might use the term *feminist* to describe those who are concerned about the well-being of women, while being critical of the unequal treatment and violence that afflict women. Feminist philosophers Sally Haslanger, Nancy Tuana, and Peg O'Connor define **feminism** as, "an intellectual commitment and a political movement that seeks justice for women and the end of sexism in all forms."[12] Feminism shows up in ethical theory as a critique of the traditional approach to ethics, which is primarily focused on values such as autonomy, impartiality, and neutrality. While it is useful to invoke these values in criticizing women's oppression, some feminists worry that these sorts of values are themselves morally problematic. This criticism argues that values such as autonomy, impartiality, and neutrality are patriarchal values, distinctively stressed by male-dominant cultures, which downplay the importance of concrete caring relationships. Such caring relationships are typical of the private sphere and family life—those parts of life that are viewed as being feminine (as opposed to the masculine and patriarchal public sphere).

Debate about sex or gender differences in moral perspectives and moral reasoning was sparked by the work of psychologist Carol Gilligan.[13] She interviewed both male and female subjects about various moral dilemmas and found that the females she interviewed had a different view than the males of what was morally required of them. They used a different moral language to explain themselves, and their reasoning involved a different moral logic. Gilligan concluded that males and females have different kinds of ethics. The ensuing debate, which will be discussed here, has focused on whether there is a distinctively feminine morality. One significant question is whether the idea that there is a female approach to ethics helps or hinders the cause of reducing violence against women, and whether it helps or hinders the effort to promote liberty and equality for women.

GENDER IN MORAL REASONING AND THE ETHICS OF CARE

In Carol Gilligan's studies, conducted in the 1970s, a hypothetical situation was posed to two eleven-year-old children, Jake and Amy.[14] A man's wife was extremely ill and in danger of dying. A certain drug might save her life, but the man could not afford it, in part because the druggist had set an unreasonably high price for it. The question was whether the man should steal the drug? Jake answered by trying to figure out the relative value of the woman's life and the druggist's right to his property. He concluded that the man should steal the drug because he calculated that the woman's life was worth more. Amy was not so sure. She wondered what would happen to both the man and his wife if he stole the drug. "If he stole the drug, he might save his wife then, but if he did, he might have to go to jail, and then his wife might get sicker again."[15] She said that if the husband and wife talked about this they might be able to think of some other way out of the dilemma.

One interesting thing about this case is the very different ways in which the two children tried to determine the right thing to do in this situation. The boy used a calculation in which he weighed and compared values from a neutral standpoint. The girl spoke about the possible effects of the proposed action on the two individuals and their relationship. Her method did not give the kind of definitive answer that is apparent in the boy's method. When researchers examined this and similar cases, they speculated that these differences in moral reasoning may be the result of sex or gender.[16]

Another representative example also seems to show a gender difference in moral reasoning.[17] In explaining how they would respond to a moral dilemma about maintaining one's moral principles in the light of peer or family pressure, two teen subjects responded quite differently. The case was one in which the religious views of each teen differed from those of their parents. The male said that he had a right to his own opinions, though he respected his parents' views. The female said that she was concerned about how her parents would react to her views. "I understand their fear of my new religious ideas." However, she added, "they really ought to listen to me and try to understand my beliefs."[18] Although the male and female subjects reached similar conclusions, they used different reasoning. They seemed to have two decidedly different orientations or perspectives. The male spoke in terms of an individual's right to his own opinions, while the female talked of the need for the particular people involved to talk with and come to understand one another. These and similar cases raise questions about whether a gender difference actually exists in the way people reason about moral matters.

Several contrasting pairs of terms are associated with or can be used to describe female and male ethical perspectives. These are listed in the following table:

Female Ethical Perspective	Male Ethical Perspective
Personal	Impersonal
Partial	Impartial
Private	Public
Natural	Contractual
Feeling	Reason
Compassionate	Fair
Concrete	Universal
Responsibility	Rights
Relationship	Individual
Solidarity	Autonomy

The various characteristics or values in this list may need explanation. First, consider the supposedly typical *female moral perspective*. The context for women's moral decision-making is said to be one of *relatedness*. Women are supposedly more concerned about particular people and their relations and how they will be affected by some action. On this view, women's morality is highly personal. They are partial to their particular loved ones and think that one's primary moral responsibility is to these people. It is the private and personal natural relations of family and friends that are the model for other relations. Women stress the concrete experiences of this or that event and are concerned about the real harm that might befall a particular person or persons. The primary moral obligation is to prevent harm and to help people. Women are able to empathize with others and are concerned about how they might feel if certain things were to happen to them. They believe that moral problems can be solved by talking about them and by trying to understand others' perspectives. Caring and compassion are key virtues. The primary moral obligation is not to turn away from those in need.

Nel Noddings's work *Caring: A Feminine Approach to Ethics and Moral Education* provides a good example and further description of the ethics of care.[19] Noddings has spent her career defending and explaining her ideas about **care ethics**. This approach includes an account of how caring relationships are important from the standpoint of evolution—as a mother's care for her children promotes their survival, and emotional and moral health. Indeed, Noddings maintains that we all have a natural desire to be cared for—and that we have the ability to provide care. This is true whether we are male or female, even though evolution and culture tend to make us think that care is more female than male. Noddings emphasizes that care is not a voluntary act of free and equal parties who enter into social contracts. Rather, we find ourselves already embedded in family and social contexts that create networks of care. These networks and relationships are not primarily governed by abstract rules; rather, they depend upon the needs and relations of the individuals. So, for Noddings, care is two-sided: it involves a complex interplay between the carer and the cared-for. For Noddings, caring means listening attentively and seeing lovingly. It involves what she describes as motivational displacement, where the needs of the other overwhelm us, as in a mother's physical reaction to the crying of her infant child. Noddings thinks that the deep connections of care are psychologically and morally important for human flourishing and that society would be better if it promoted caring relationships through education and institutional design.

The supposedly typical *male moral perspective* contrasts sharply with a feminine ethics of care, such as we find in the work of Noddings. In this view, men take a more universal and impartial standpoint in reasoning about what is morally good and bad. Men are more inclined to talk in terms of fairness, justice, and rights. They ask about the overall effects of some action and whether the good effects, when all are considered, outweigh the bad. It is as though they think moral decisions ought to be made impersonally or from some unbiased and detached point of view. The moral realm would then in many ways be similar to the public domain of law and contract. The law must not be biased and must treat everyone equally. Moral thinking, in this view, involves a type of universalism that recognizes the equal moral worth of all persons, both in themselves and before the law. People ought to keep their promises because this is the just thing to do and helps create a reliable social order. Morality is a matter of doing one's duty, keeping one's agreements, and respecting other people's rights. Impartiality and respectfulness are key virtues. The primary obligation is not to act unfairly.

What are we to make of the view that two very different sets of characteristics describe male and female morality? In suggesting a difference between men's and women's morality, Carol Gilligan was taking aim at one of the dominant points of view about moral development, namely, that of the psychologist Lawrence Kohlberg.[20] According to Kohlberg, the highest stage of moral development is the stage in which an adult can be governed not by social pressure but by personal moral principles and a sense of justice. Based on these principles, adults come to regard other people as moral equals and manifest an impartial and universal perspective. In his own research, Kohlberg found that women did

not often reach this stage of development. He thus judged them to be morally underdeveloped or morally deficient. Of course, his conclusions were not totally surprising because, as Gilligan notes, he had used an all-male sample in working out his theory.[21] After deriving his principles from male subjects, he then used them to judge both male and female moral development.

Gilligan and Kohlberg were not the first psychologists to believe a difference existed between men's and women's morality. Sigmund Freud held that women "show less sense of justice than men, that they are less ready to submit to the great exigencies of life, that they are more often influenced in their judgments by feelings of affection or hostility...."[22] According to Freud, women were morally inferior to men. Instead of being able to establish themselves as separate people living in society and adapting to its rules, girls remained in the home, attached to their mothers. Thus, girls developed a capacity for personal relations and intimacy while their male counterparts developed a sense of separateness and personal autonomy. The idea was that women base their morality on concerns about personal relations while men base their morality on rules that can reconcile the separate competing individuals in society.[23] Believing that a focus on personal relations rather than a sense of justice was a lesser form of morality, Freud and others thought that women were morally inferior to men.

Is There a Gender Difference in Morality?

Several questions ought to be asked about the theory that women and men exhibit a different type of moral perspective and moral reasoning. First, is this contention true? Is it an empirical fact that men and women manifest a different type of moral thinking? Second, if it is a fact, then how are we to explain it? What may be the source or cause of this difference? Third, if there is a difference, is one type of moral thinking higher or more developed or better than the other? We might also wonder whether the attempt to distinguish between male and female forms of moral experience serves the feminist goal of helping women or whether it simply reiterates traditional gender stereotypes.

To determine whether there is, in fact, a difference between the moral language and logic of males and females, we need to rely on empirical surveys and studies. What do people find who have examined this supposed phenomena? We have already described some of the earlier findings of Carol Gilligan. Her conclusions in more recent studies have varied somewhat.[24] For example, her later research finds some variation in moral reasoning among both men and women. According to these findings, while both men and women sometimes think in terms of a justice perspective, few men think in terms of a care perspective. Being able to take one perspective rather than the other, she wrote, is much like being able to see the following well-known line drawing figure as a rabbit or as a duck.

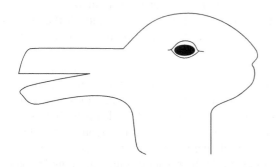

The perspective that one has affects how one sees the figure. If one has a justice perspective, one will see that "the *self* as moral agent stands as the figure against a ground of social relationships, judging the conflicting claims of self and others against a standard of equality or equal respect." If one has a care perspective, then one will see that "the *relationship* becomes the figure, defining self and others. Within the context of relationship, the self as a moral agent perceives and responds to the perception of need."[25] In these more recent studies, Gilligan used "educationally advantaged North American adolescents and adults" and found that two-thirds had one or the other orientation as their primary focus. Still she found sex differences in the results. "With one exception, all of the men who focused, focused on justice. The women divided, with roughly one-third focusing on justice and one-third on care" (the other third had a hybrid approach).[26] In this study, women did not always have the care perspective as their

focus—but without the women in the study, the care focus would have been almost absent.

Other theorists are not so sure about what the data show. For example, Catherine Greeno and Eleanor Maccoby believe that any difference between men's and women's morality can be accounted for by social status and experience rather than gender. Using other studies, they point out that in many cases, those who exhibit so-called feminine morality have been housewives and women who lack higher education. They found that career women showed types of moral reasoning similar to those of men.[27] The question of whether women do exhibit a unique type of moral language and logic will need to be decided by those who study the empirical data. And, of course, you can examine your own experience to see whether the males and females you know seem to reason differently when discussing moral issues.

The Source of Feminine Morality

At least three distinct types of explanation address a possible difference between masculine and feminine morality. One proposes differences in the psychosexual development of the two sexes, a second points to biological differences, and a third gives a social, cultural, or educational explanation.

We have already described something of the Freudian account of the effects of psychosexual development on male and female moral thinking. A few more points may be added. According to this view, males and females have different concepts of the self and their gender identities; this concept is influenced by their development in relation to their mothers and fathers. As they grow up, females develop a sense of being connected with their mothers, whereas males find themselves being different from their mothers. According to Nancy Chodorow, who amplifies Freud's theory, development of the self and one's sense of individuality depends on being able to separate oneself from others.[28] Thus males, who tend to separate themselves from their mothers, come to have a sense of self as independent, whereas females do not develop the sense of separate selves and rather see themselves as attached or connected to others. From this developmental situation, males and females supposedly develop different senses of morality—males a morality associated with separation and autonomy, and females a morality with relationships and interdependence. According to traditional views such as Kohlberg's (see earlier), mature moral thinking involves being able to be detached and see things from some impartial perspective. Judging from a care perspective means that one cannot judge dispassionately or without bias, and this was deemed to be a moral defect. However, as we have seen, this traditional view of care ethics has been criticized by feminists and others.

A second account of the source of differences in masculine and feminine morality is exemplified by the writings of Caroline Whitbeck, who locates it, at least in part, in women's and men's biology, that is, in the difference in their reproductive capacities and experiences. In pregnancy, labor, and childbirth, women experience certain feelings of dependency and contingency.[29] They do not have full control of their bodies. They experience weakness and pain. They feel themselves participating in "species life" at its most primitive level. Because of their own feelings during this time, they can sympathize more readily with the infant's or child's feelings of helplessness and dependency.

Some will claim that female caring and nurturing spring naturally from the intimate and sympathetic relation that mothers are supposed to have toward their children. A naturalistic explanation of this might maintain that there is some instinctive orientation toward nurturance in women that is ultimately a matter of biology and physiology. It might be, however, that culture and socialization also matter. Girls and women are taught to exhibit nurturing behaviors by a culture that expects them to be nurturers and caregivers. This points toward the idea that mothering is not only a biological phenomenon but also a social and cultural one. Although some women bear children, it is not necessary that they rear them. Still, because they do give birth to and nurse infants, women have generally come to be the primary child-rearers.

It is from the elements of so-called maternal practice that women's morality arises, according to this third view.[30] To Sara Ruddick, for example, maternal practice results in "maternal thinking," which is the "vocabulary and logic of connections" that arises

from women "acting in response to demands of their children."[31] She believes that maternal thinking is not simply a kind of feeling that comes naturally to women, but a purposeful way of thinking and acting. It involves finding ways to preserve, develop, and promote one's children. Infants are extremely vulnerable and will not survive if they do not have the basics of food, clothing, and shelter. Children must be safeguarded from the many dangers of life. They need help in growing—physically, socially, and morally. Particular virtues are required for a mother to be able to satisfy the needs of her children. Among those described by Ruddick are humility (for one cannot do everything), cheerfulness combined with realism, and love and affection. Mothers also need to guard against certain negative traits and feelings, for example, feelings of hopelessness and possessiveness. According to this view, it is because they spend much of their lives mothering that women develop a morality consistent with this experience. And cultural norms tend to reinforce the value of care and nurturance for women. We praise caregiving women and celebrate mothering, while wondering about the femininity of women who don't exemplify the maternal virtues. Maternal morality stresses relationships and the virtues that are necessary for mothering. One does not necessarily have to be a biological mother, however, both to engage in mothering and to develop maternal ethics, according to this viewpoint. Just because men and some women do not give birth does not mean that they cannot be parents and develop the outlook required for this practice. Until now, it has been a social phenomenon that maternal practice has been principally women's work.

Evaluating Gender-Specific Approaches to Morality

Many questions remain concerning these three explanations of gender differences in morality. Some are factual or empirical questions, for they ask whether something is or is not the case. Do women in fact think and act in the ways described above? Are they more likely to do so than men? Does giving birth or rearing children cause those involved in these practices to think in a certain way and to have a certain moral perspective? Much of what we say here is quite speculative in that we are making guesses that cannot strictly be proved to be true. Nevertheless, there is a great deal of appeal and suggestiveness in the theory of the ethics of care. In particular, we should compare this type of morality with more traditional theories such as utilitarianism and deontology to see how different the perspectives are as exemplified by the theories.

Whether one way of judging morally is *better* than the other is also an open question. As we have seen, there has been a tradition of thought that says that the so-called feminine morality—an ethics of care focused on particular relations—is a lower-level morality. When we consider the sources of this tradition, we find many reasons to criticize it. Perhaps, on the contrary, it is the ethics of care that provides a better moral orientation. For example, instead of judging war in terms of whether the overall benefits outweigh the costs, we may do well to think about the particular people involved—that every soldier, for example, is someone's daughter or son or sister or brother or mother or father. Or perhaps the two orientations are complementary. Perhaps a justice orientation is the minimum that morality requires. We could then build on this minimum and, for example, temper justice with care and mercy. On the other hand, the care orientation may be the more basic one, and justice concerns could then be brought in to determine how best to care.

If specific female and male virtues parallel these ethical orientations, then another question arises. Would it not be possible and good for both men and women to develop both sets of virtues? If these virtues are described in a positive way—say, caring and not subservience—would they not be traits that all should strive to possess? These traits might be simply different aspects of the human personality, rather than the male or female personality. They would then be human virtues and human perspectives rather than male or female virtues and perspectives. In this view, an ethics of fidelity and care and sympathy would be just as important for human flourishing as an ethics of duty and justice and acting on principle. While there would be certain moral virtues that all people should develop, other psychological traits could also vary according to temperament and choice. Individuals would be free to manifest, according to

their own personalities, any combination of positive moral characteristics. These sets of characteristics and virtues would synthesize in various ways both stereotypical masculine and feminine traits.

FEMINIST THOUGHT

Not all feminist writers are supportive of the ethics of care. While most would agree that one can describe a particular type of morality that exhibits the characteristics said to belong to an ethics of care, these writers question whether all aspects of such an ethics of care are good. For example, care ethics seems to be based on relations between unequals. The mother–child relation is such a relation. The dependency in the relation goes only one way. One does all (or most of) the giving, and the other all (or most of) the receiving. This may tend to reinforce or promote a one-sided morality of self-sacrifice and subjugation. It may reinforce the view that women ought to be the ones who sacrifice and help and support others, chiefly children and men.

Other criticisms include the worry that care ethics tends to rest upon stereotypes about female and male behavior, which tend to reinforce male dominance. If we think that men are impartial while women are not, this may lead us to think twice about assigning women to positions of authority where impartiality is required. Furthermore, the hard distinction between the genders is problematic. Some women are not all that caring; and some men are quite caring. The differences may be described in terms such as masculine and feminine— but in reality, this gendered terminology does not map accurately onto actual differences among diverse individuals. Furthermore, these supposed differences may only be cultural differences. It might be the case in Western cultures that women are more caring and men are more impartial. But this may not be true in other cultures. Michael Slote, a prominent defender of care ethics, notes that in African cultures, both men and women exhibit caring behaviors; he also argues that "there are very strong elements of care thinking in both Confucian and Buddhist thought." Slote concludes that this shows that "the ethics of care can and should be regarded as a potential overall human morality, rather than as something just about, or at most only relevant to, women."[32]

We defined feminism at the outset of this chapter (following Haslanger, Tuana, and O'Connor) as a movement that seeks justice for women and an end to sexism in all forms. The history of feminism includes both those who are primarily concerned with promoting women's equality with men, as well as those who wanted to raise the value of women's unique characteristics. However, the most well-known writers and activists of this movement have been those who have stressed women's rights and equality. Among the earliest examples is Mary Wollstonecraft, who wrote in *A Vindication of the Rights of Women* (1792)[33] that women were not by nature weak and emotional, but that their social situation had in many ways made them so. It was society that taught women negative moral traits such as cunning and vanity, she insisted. The suffragettes who sought political equality and the right to vote followed in her footsteps. Many years later, Simone de Beauvoir's work *The Second Sex* (1949) became a classic text for what has been called a "second wave" of feminists (the "first wave" being the nineteenth-century women's rights advocates).[34] According to de Beauvoir, women are a "second sex" because they are regarded always in terms of being an "other" to the primary male sex. In an existentialist vein, she stressed the need for women to be independent selves and free to establish their own goals and projects. Various other writers in the history of the women's movement stressed the importance of raising women's consciousness so that they might understand how women's experience is shaped by social and cultural norms. This involves helping women become aware of how certain social circumstances leave women with second-class status, while encouraging women to examine the various ways they have been oppressed and subordinated in their personal, professional, and political lives. The movement's aim was not only to raise consciousness but also to act politically to bring about the equality of women. Thus, for example, they sought the passage of the Equal Rights Amendment to the U.S. Constitution. Although the Equal Rights Amendment passed through both houses of the U.S. Congress in 1972, it failed to receive enough support in the states in order to be ratified. The original Congressional authorization expired in 1982. Since 1982, members of the U.S. Congress have continued to reintroduce the Equal Rights Amendment at each new session of the Congress.

The so-called "third wave" of feminism (developing since the 1990s) has been more aware of the problem of diversity in dealing with women's issues. This includes the range of women's experiences in diverse cultures. Women's issues will be different in Pakistan, in Israel, and in the United States, depending upon religious, cultural, and even generational differences. Women in the Western world who are concerned with liberty and equality for women in the rest of the world have been more aware of the need to listen to women and appreciate their unique cultural situations. One prominent feminist who has been working on international women's issues is the philosopher Martha Nussbaum (whose work we touched upon in Chapter 3). Nussbaum reminds us that cultures are dynamic and internally complex. Nonetheless, Nussbaum thinks that it is still important to clarify abstract moral principles, provided that they are grounded in empirical reality. She explains that although feminist philosophy has often been "skeptical of universal moral normative approaches," feminism can make universal claims that "need not be insensitive to difference or imperialistic."[35] Nussbaum's own work dealing with gender issues in India exemplifies the approach she champions; criticism must be grounded in local practices and based upon the needs and interests of the women whose lives are characterized by the specifics of the local context.

Other recent feminist discussions point toward a further critique of abstract moral principles. These discussions are often concerned with the sheer complexity of gender terms and sexuality. One prominent author associated with third-wave feminism is Judith Butler, whose work is influenced by poststructuralist philosophy and what is often called *queer theory*—which is an approach that aims to deconstruct traditional norms for thinking about gender and sexuality. In her most influential book, *Gender Trouble*, Butler discusses such figures as hermaphrodites and drag queens in order to elucidate the ways in which gender norms are socially constructed and "performed," in an attempt to liberate gender and sexuality from strict social conventions.

Many of these forms of feminist moral thought may be said to advance a ***feminist ethics,*** distinguishable

Feminist philosopher and queer theorist Judith Butler.

AP photo/dapd/Thomas Lohnes

from an ethics of care (sometimes called *feminine ethics,* because of its focus on feminine virtues).[36] Writers who explore feminist ethics often focus on analyzing the causes of women's subordination and oppression, and systematic violence against women. Feminist ethicists are also engaged in strategies for eliminating this violence and oppression. In this, they have an explicitly political orientation.

The political activist side of feminism may be directed at local and national issues, such as the Equal Rights Amendment mentioned previously. It might also have a global focus. At the international level, women have worked together to raise the status of women around the world and seek ways to better the conditions under which they live. International conferences have brought women together from all nations to discuss their problems and lend each other support. One initiative is the effort to provide small loans to women in impoverished areas (so-called microfinancing) so that women can stabilize their financial and family lives. Other focuses of activism include reproductive health, preventing violence against women, and educating women in an effort to equalize literacy rates and life prospects. Of course, such international and cross-cultural work requires sensitivity and awareness of the problems of cultural relativism and religious diversity.

Among the causes of women's oppression, some feminists point out, has been philosophy itself.

Traditional moral philosophy has not been favorable to women. It has tended to support the view that women should develop "women's virtues," such as modesty, humility, and subservience—which are often to the detriment of women. For example, Aristotle seems to have held that women are inferior to men not only because of certain biological phenomena having to do with heat in the body but also because they lack certain elements of rationality. According to Aristotle, free adult males could rule over slaves, women, and children because of the weakness in their "deliberative" faculties. In the case of women, while they have such a faculty, Aristotle claims it is "without authority."[37] In *Emile,* Jean-Jacques Rousseau's work on the education of the young, the French philosopher advances a quite different type of ideal education for the protagonist Emile than for Emile's wife-to-be, Sophie. Because morality is different for men and women, the young of each sex ought to be trained in different virtues, according to Rousseau. Emile is to be trained in virtues such as justice and fortitude, while Sophie is to be taught to be docile and patient.[38] With this history of male-dominant moral philosophy in mind, it is easy to see why some feminists may be reluctant to affirm traditional notions about feminine virtues, since these are associated with a long history of the subordination of women.

Even contemporary moral philosophers have not given women and women's concerns their due, according to many feminist writers. They have not been interested in matters of the home and domesticity. They have tended to ignore issues such as the "feminization of poverty," the use of reproductive technologies, sexual harassment, and violence against and sexual abuse of women. It is mainly with women writing on these topics in contemporary ethics that they have gained some respectability as topics of genuine philosophical interest. So also have the issues of female oppression and subordination become topics of wider philosophical interest.

EVALUATION OF FEMINIST THOUGHT AND THE ETHICS OF CARE

We have already pointed out some questions that have been raised about the ethics of care. As we have seen, some writers point out that care does not always come naturally to women, and not all women are good mothers or good nurturers. Moreover, men may also exhibit these characteristics, and some cultures emphasize care as a primary value for both men and women. However, supporters of the ethics of care may reply that their main concern is not the gender issue as much as the need to advance care in opposition to more traditional values such as impartiality and universality.

In addition, many critics of care ethics contend that the promotion of so-called feminine traits may not be of benefit to women and may reinforce women's subservient position in society. Defenders of care ethics might respond that it is not such "feminine" virtues as obedience, self-sacrifice, silence, and service that define an ethics of care. Rather, such an ethics tells us from what perspective we are to judge morally, namely, from the perspective of specific persons in relation to each other, susceptible to particular harms and benefits.

Can an ethics of care free itself from the negative associations of traditional femininity? Can feminist ethicists support an ethics of care while also seeking to promote women's equality? It is clear, at least, that women cannot be restricted to traditionally subservient roles if they are to be treated equally and fairly in both the public realm and the realm of the home and family.

What these discussions have also suggested is that we can no longer maintain that one ethics exists for the home and the private realm (an ethics of care and relationships) and another ethics for work or the public realm (an ethics of justice and fairness and impartiality). "Neither the realm of domestic, personal life, nor that of non domestic, economic and political life, can be understood or interpreted in isolation from the other," writes feminist political philosopher Susan Moller Okin.[39] These two realms not only overlap, Okin argues, but also can and should exemplify the values and virtues of each other. Elements of altruism and concern for particular, concrete individuals have a place in the political as well as the domestic realms. Furthermore, when feminists say that "the personal is political," they mean that "what happens in the personal life, particularly in relations between the sexes, is not immune from the dynamic of *power*, which has typically been seen as a distinguishing feature of the political."[40] These relations should thus also be restrained by considerations of fairness and justice.

One further question arises about the ethics of care. While such an ethics describes an ideal context for ethical decision-making, it does not tell us how we are to determine what will help or harm particular individuals. It does not in itself say what constitutes benefit or harm. It gives no rules for what we are to do in cases of conflict of interest, even among those to whom we are partial, or what to do when we cannot benefit all. It seems to give little definitive help for knowing what to do in cases where we must harm some to benefit others. Supporters of care ethics may respond that by setting the context for ethical decision-making, an ethics of care has already done something valuable, for it thus provides a balance to the otherwise one-sided traditional ethics of the impersonal and universal. Perhaps this is a valuable minimum achievement. Or perhaps care ethics, with its emphasis on human connectedness, has an even more central role to play in today's ethical and political discussions. As Gilligan notes,

> By rendering a care perspective more coherent and making its terms explicit, moral theory may facilitate women's ability to speak about their experiences and perceptions and may foster the ability of others to listen and to understand. At the same time, the evidence of care focus in women's moral thinking suggests that the study of women's development may provide a natural history of moral development in which care is ascendant, revealing the ways in which creating and sustaining responsive connection with others becomes or remains a central moral concern.[41]

NOTES

1. The White House, "1 is 2 Many," http://www.whitehouse.gov/1is2many
2. Naomi Wolf, *The Beauty Myth: How Images of Beauty Are Used against Women* (New York: Harper Perennial, 2002); Cressida J. Heyes and Meredith Jones, *Cosmetic Surgery: A Feminist Primer* (New York: Ashgate, 2009).
3. Naomi Wolf, *The Beauty Myth*, 5.
4. Most prominently, Andrea Dworkin, *Pornography: Men Possessing Women* (New York: Perigree Books, 1981).
5. Wendy McElroy, *XXX: A Woman's Right to Pornography* (New York: St. Martin's Press, 1995).
6. "Israeli Girl, 8, at Center of Tension over Religious Extremism," *New York Times*, December 27, 2011.
7. Nicholas D. Kristof and Sheryl WuDunn, *Half the Sky: Turning Oppression into Opportunity for Women Worldwide* (New York: Vintage, 2010), xvii.

8. http://www.cbsnews.com/8301-504083_162-57409395-504083/honor-killing-under-growing-scrutiny-in-the-u.s/

9. CBS, *48 Hours*, September 1, 2012.

10. World Economic Forum, *The Global Gender Gap Index 2012* (October 2012), http://www3.weforum.org/docs/GGGR12/MainChapter_GGGR12.pdf

11. The White House, *Women in America: Indicators of Social and Economic Well-Being* (March 2011), http://www.whitehouse.gov/sites/default/files/rss_viewer/Women_in_America.pdf

12. Sally Haslanger, Nancy Tuana, and Peg O'Connor, "Topics in Feminism," *Stanford Encyclopedia of Philosophy* (2011), http://plato.stanford.edu/entries/feminism-topics/

13. Carol Gilligan, "Concepts of the Self and of Morality," *Harvard Educational Review* (November 1977): 481–517.

14. This is a summary of a question that was posed by researchers for Lawrence Kohlberg. In Carol Gilligan, *In a Different Voice* (Cambridge, MA: Harvard University Press, 1982), 28, 173.

15. Ibid.

16. We use the term *sex* to refer to the biological male or female. The term *gender* includes psychological feminine and masculine traits as well as social roles assigned to the two sexes.

17. From Carol Gilligan, "Moral Orientation and Moral Development," in *Women and Moral Theory*, eds. Eva Kittay and Diana Meyers (Totowa, NJ: Rowman & Littlefield, 1987), 23.

18. Ibid.

19. Nel Noddings, *Caring: A Feminine Approach to Ethics and Moral Education* (Berkeley: University of California Press, 1984).

20. Lawrence Kohlberg, *The Psychology of Moral Development* (San Francisco: Harper & Row, 1984).

21. Gilligan, "Moral Orientation and Moral Development," 22.

22. Cited in Gilligan, "Moral Orientation and Moral Development."

23. See also Nancy Chodorow, *The Reproduction of Mothering* (Berkeley: University of California Press, 1978).

24. See, for example, Gilligan, "Adolescent Development Reconsidered," in *Mapping the Moral Domain*, eds. Carol Gilligan, Janie Victoria Ward, and Jill McLean Taylor (Cambridge, MA: Harvard University Press, 1988).

25. Gilligan, "Moral Orientation and Moral Development," 22–23. Emphasis added.

26. Ibid., 25.

27. Catherine G. Greeno and Eleanor E. Maccoby, "How Different Is the Different Voice?" in "On *In a Different Voice*: An Interdisciplinary Forum," *Signs: Journal of Women in Culture and Society* 11, no. 2 (Winter 1986): 211–20.

28. Nancy Chodorow, *The Reproduction of Mothering* (Berkeley: University of California Press, 1978).

29. See, for example, Caroline Whitbeck, "The Maternal Instinct," in *Mothering: Essays in Feminist Theory*, ed. Joyce Treblicot (Totowa, NJ: Rowman & Allanheld, 1984).

30. See, for example, Sara Ruddick, *Maternal Thinking: Toward a Politics of Peace* (Boston: Beacon, 1989).

31. Ibid., 214.

32. Michael Slote, *The Ethics of Care and Empathy* (New York: Routledge, 2007), p. 9, footnote no. 7.

33. Mary Wollstonecraft, *A Vindication of the Rights of Women*, ed. Miriam Brody (London: Penguin, 1988). Originally published in 1792.

34. Simone de Beauvoir, *The Second Sex*, trans. H. M. Parshley (New York: Knopf, 1953). Originally published in 1949.

35. Martha C. Nussbaum, *Women and Human Development: The Capabilities Approach* (Cambridge: Cambridge University Press, 2001), 7.

36. This terminology is from Rosemary Tong's *Feminine and Feminist Ethics* (Belmont, CA: Wadsworth, 1993). As a source of this terminology, Tong also cites Betty A. Sichel, "Different Strains and Strands: Feminist Contributions to Ethical Theory," *Newsletter on Feminism* 90, no. 2 (Winter 1991): 90; and Susan Sherwin, *No Longer Patient: Feminist Ethics and Health Care* (Philadelphia: Temple University Press, 1992), 42.

37. Aristotle, *Politics*, as quoted in "Theories of Sex Difference," by Caroline Whitbeck in *Women and Moral Theory*, 35.

38. Jean-Jacques Rousseau, *Emile*, trans. Allan Bloom (New York: Basic Books, 1979). Also see Nancy Tuana, *Woman and the History of Philosophy* (New York: Paragon House, 1992).

39. Susan Moller Okin, "Gender, the Public and the Private," in *Political Theory Today*, ed. David Held (Stanford, CA: Stanford University Press, 1991), 77.

40. Ibid.

41. Gilligan, "Moral Orientation and Moral Development," 32.

REVIEW EXERCISES

1. Identify and explain the supposed differences between male and female ethical perspectives.

2. Contrast the research findings of Carol Gilligan and Lawrence Kohlberg on male and female moral development.

3. According to Freud, why were women supposed to be morally deficient?

4. What are the basic features of the ethics of care?

5. How does Gilligan's duck and rabbit example help explain the difference between the two moral perspectives?

6. Describe the psychosexual development explanation of female and male moral perspectives.

7. Summarize Caroline Whitbeck's biological explanation of the difference between female and male moral perspectives.

8. How has the difference been explained in terms of "maternal thinking"?

9. Describe the basic issues involved in trying to decide whether one type of moral perspective is better than another.

10. Describe some of the history and characteristics of feminist thought, including the so called "waves" of feminism.

Euthanasia

Hemera/Thinkstock

Learning Outcomes

After reading this chapter, you should be able to:

- Describe the differences among the various forms of euthanasia: active, passive, voluntary, nonvoluntary, involuntary.
- Understand disputes over criteria for determining death.
- Explain key cases and examples of euthanasia and other end-of-life decisions.
- Explain the importance of advance directives and living wills, as well as

- the difference between ordinary and extraordinary medical interventions.
- Evaluate moral arguments about suicide and killing, including both consequentialist and non-consequentialist arguments.
- Differentiate between killing and letting die.
- Understand and apply the principle of double effect.
- Defend your own ideas about the ethics of euthanasia.

In May 2013, Vermont became the fourth state in the United States to permit physician-assisted suicide, joining Washington, Montana, and Oregon—although legal challenges remain in Montana, and the courts are still working out the details.[1] According to physician-assisted suicide laws in Oregon—which has become the model for such laws—a patient who has fewer than six months to live, according to the judgment of two independent doctors, may receive a prescription for a lethal dose of a drug to be taken orally. The patient must be competent; must have a clear and continuing request, made orally and in writing; and must be able to take the drug without assistance. Voters in several states, including Michigan, Maine, Massachusetts, and California, have previously rejected physician-assisted suicide initiatives. But in 2013, there was a wave of states considering the legalization of physician-assisted suicide.[2] In Europe, active euthanasia—where instead of simply prescribing lethal medication, the doctor administers the lethal injection—is legal in the Netherlands, Belgium, Luxembourg, and Switzerland. Active euthanasia is not legal in the United States.

According to data published by the state of Oregon in January 2013, a slowly growing number of patients in Oregon obtain lethal prescriptions and take them. In the fifteen years that assisted suicide has been legal in Oregon, 1,050 people have obtained lethal prescriptions, and 673 patients have died as a result of these prescriptions.[3] In 2012, there were 77 such cases: 67.5 percent of these assisted suicides were 65 years old or older, with a median age of 69. Most were white (97.4 percent), well educated (42.9 percent had at least a baccalaureate degree), and had cancer (75.9 percent). In 2012, there was one case in which an individual ingested the lethal drug but regained consciousness and later died of the underlying illness.

In the Netherlands, euthanasia has been legal since 2002, when the Termination of Life on Request and Assisted Suicide (Review Procedures) Act took effect. The law in the Netherlands stipulates that physicians must exercise "due care" in assisting in suicide or when terminating life on request. According to the law, "due care" means that the physician

› holds the conviction that the request by the patient was voluntary and well considered.
› holds the conviction that the patient's suffering was lasting and unbearable.
› has informed the patient about the situation he was in and about his prospects.
› holds the conviction, along with the patient, that there was no other reasonable solution for the situation he was in.
› has consulted at least one other, independent, physician who has seen the patient and has given his written opinion on the requirements of due care.
› has terminated a life or assisted in a suicide with due care.[4]

This law applies only to adults; euthanasia for children is not legally permitted. However, there are some doctors who have argued in favor of euthanasia for infants when they suffer from "unbearable and hopeless pain" and when their parents agree in consultation with doctors.[5] A protocol has been proposed for dealing with infant euthanasia that is known as the Groningen Protocol. Although infant euthanasia remains a legal gray area in the Netherlands, adult euthanasia is regulated, and detailed records of the practice exist. The government was notified in 2011 that 196 individuals were assisted with suicide and 3,446 were actively euthanized—with 53 other cases involving a combination of assisted suicide and active euthanasia.[6] Most of these cases (2,797) involved patients with cancer. The report indicates that the number of cases increased by 18 percent over 2010, when there were 3,136 notifications.

In Belgium, a euthanasia law became effective on January 1, 2002. The Belgian law differs somewhat from the Dutch law in two ways. First, it allows **advance directives**—documents by which patients dictate health care decisions in advance of treatment in case they are incapacitated. Second, it promotes

"the development of palliative care."[7] (**Palliative care** is focused on pain management and alleviating the symptoms of disease.) Euthanasia may seem like a radical remedy for pain management—but the idea is that the euthanasia discussion helps focus attention on patient autonomy and solutions for pain management.

European opinion and law about euthanasia remain divided. With its own history of Nazis gassing some 100,000 people who were deemed physically or mentally handicapped, Germany has criticized Dutch approval of the practice as a dangerous breaching of a dike.[8] Still, 80 percent of Dutch citizens support the law as the best way to allow people to control their own lives. Assisted suicide is also legal in Switzerland, and people from countries where it is illegal often go to Switzerland to commit suicide, a controversial practice that has been described as "suicide tourism." An episode of PBS's *Frontline* in March 2010 featured the story of Craig Ewert, an American who was diagnosed with ALS (Lou Gehrig's Disease) and who traveled to Switzerland to end his life. Ewert explained, "If I go through with it, I die, as I must at some point. If I don't go through with it, my choice is essentially to suffer and to inflict suffering on my family and then die—possibly in a way that is considerably more stressful and painful than this way. So I've got death, and I've got suffering and death. You know, this makes a whole lot of sense to me."[9]

Several questions suggest themselves regarding this matter. One is about the terminology we are supposed to use with regard to these sorts of cases. The title of this chapter is **euthanasia**, which is a word meaning "good death" (the Greek root *eu-* means good; the Greek root *thanatos* means death). Death is usually not considered to be a good thing. But is there such a thing as a good death? Is a good death one that comes suddenly or after some time to think about and prepare for it? Is it one that takes place at home and in familiar surroundings or one that occurs in a medical facility? Is it one that we know is coming and over which we have control or one that comes on us without notice? What about our obligations to our family and loved ones? And what about the physician's obligations; is it to "do no harm" and defend life, to fulfill patient requests for help in dying, or to allow death in order to prevent suffering? Under what conditions should euthanasia be permitted—for consenting adults, for the disabled who cannot provide consent, for children and infants? And what methods of euthanasia are appropriate?

Euthanasia has been a controversial topic for decades. The discussion of euthanasia involves issues of patient rights, life and death, the proper function of doctors, the ethics of suicide, and the overlap between law and morality. This chapter addresses each of these issues.

EUTHANASIA FOR INFANTS AND THE DISABLED

Death is usually thought of as a bad thing. But could it be that in some cases death is a mercy? Consider the case of an infant, Sanne, who was born with a severe form of Hallopeau-Siemens syndrome.[10] The disease caused the infant's skin to blister and peel, leaving painful scar tissue in its place. The prognosis was for a life of suffering until the child would eventually die of skin cancer before reaching her teenage years. The hospital refused to allow the infant to be euthanized, and Sanne eventually died of pneumonia. In such a case, would it be more humane to actively end the infant's life?

Modern medicine has made great strides in the treatment of newborn and premature infants. According to one recent study in the United Kingdom, "overall survival among those born between 22 and 25 weeks rose from 40 percent in 1995 to 53 percent in 2006."[11] However, while newborn survival is better, premature infants still tend to struggle with complications and disability. That same study also noted, "the proportion of such infants who experience severe disability as a result has not changed. That stood at 18 percent in 1995 and was 19 percent in 2006." In the United States, according to the Centers for Disease Control and Prevention,

> Each year, preterm birth affects nearly 500,000 babies—that's 1 of every 8 infants born in the United States. Preterm birth is the birth of an infant prior to 37 weeks gestation. It is the most frequent cause of infant death, the leading cause of long-term neurological disabilities in children, and costs the U.S. health care system more than $26 billion each year.[12]

One obvious remedy for this situation is finding ways to decrease preterm birth through better prenatal care. Another remedy would be expanding social resources to support preterm infants and their families, especially those with severe disabilities.

Despite the progress in care for preterm infants, some seriously ill newborns do not fare well. Some have severe defects and cannot survive for long, while others will live but with serious impairments. Thus, improvements in medicine that have enabled us to save the lives of newborns have also given us new life-and-death decisions to make.

One issue to consider here is the patient's quality of life. Parents who consider letting severely disabled infants die struggle with questions about the quality of life their child is likely to have. A further utilitarian consideration might also focus on the impact that expensive and possibly futile health care might have on the rest of the family. An influential utilitarian philosopher, Peter Singer, has argued that it is possible to imagine killing a disabled newborn and "replacing" it with another healthy baby in a subsequent pregnancy to achieve a net outcome of happiness. Singer notes that we allow women to abort disabled fetuses, and he sees very little difference between abortion and euthanasia for infants. Singer argues that, "killing a disabled infant is not morally equivalent to killing a person. Very often it is not wrong at all."[13] One of Singer's points is that disabled infants lack the sort of mental capacity that would give them moral status as "persons" who have a right to life. We will return to the issue of moral status in the chapter on abortion.

Singer's approach has prompted criticism and protest. Some donors—including former presidential candidate Steve Forbes—threatened to withdraw funding from Princeton University when Princeton hired Singer to teach ethics.[14] Disability rights advocates have been especially critical of Singer. Harriet McBryde Johnson argues that Singer is advocating genocide against the disabled. She explains that the problem is Singer's "unexamined assumption that disabled people are inherently 'worse off,' that we 'suffer,' that we have lesser 'prospects of a happy life.' Because of this all-too-common prejudice, and his rare courage in taking it to its logical conclusion, catastrophe looms."[15]

Those who advocate euthanasia for infants often focus on the question of the well-being of the infant, arguing that the lives of some disabled infants are miserable and hopeless. As indicated above, in the Netherlands there is a quasi-legal protocol for considering active euthanasia for newborns—the Groningen Protocol. That protocol focuses on infants with a hopeless prognosis and extremely poor quality of life. This latter designation specifically includes "severe cases of spina bifida," a birth defect in which the spinal column does not fully close in development; the most serious cases result in death or, if treated, may leave the person with "muscle weakness or paralysis below the area of the spine where the incomplete closure (or cleft) occurs, loss of sensation below the cleft, and loss of bowel and bladder control."[16] In some cases, spinal fluid builds up and can cause learning problems. In cases such as this, it is not clear whether medical assistance is in the infant's best interest. However, people have survived spina bifida and been able to enjoy life and contribute to their communities.[17] The question of quality of life and disability points toward a variety of issues including the kinds of functions that we view as normal and healthy. It also points toward reflection on how we view suffering, caregiving, and dependency. The care-ethics standpoint (which we discussed in Chapter 9) acknowledges the importance of caregiving and dependency. Indeed, we are all dependent for the first few years of life; and there will be moments of dependency in our future; in illness and old age. What value do we place upon care and dependency? Other approaches to ethics—including especially the Kantian approach—emphasize autonomy. As we shall see, autonomy is a central question for discussions of end of life care, assisted suicide, and euthanasia.

One significant problem here is whether we can accurately predict or judge the quality of an individual's life. Several authors have pointed out that it is difficult for those of us with normal function to judge the quality of life of the disabled. Those in the disability rights movement will also argue, as Tom Shakespeare does, that judgments about quality of life depend on social context; in nurturing societies, with ample resources to support people with different abilities, some "impairments" may not be "disabling."[18] Shakespeare emphasizes that the primary focus should be on providing adequate health care—and not so much on the question of euthanasia.

Even with better health care and social supports, there do seem to be truly hopeless cases, such as that of the infant Sanne, mentioned previously. Even skeptics about making such quality-of-life judgments, such as John Robertson—a professor of law and ethics—admit that there may be obvious cases, "a deformed, retarded, institutionalized child, or one with incessant unmanageable pain, where continued life is itself torture. But these cases are few."[19] In many other cases, it is not clear what counts as suffering or hopelessness. Down syndrome (also called trisomy 21) is a genetic anomaly that causes mental retardation and sometimes physical problems as well. In a well-known case in the bioethics literature discussed by philosopher James Rachels, the child had a repairable but life-threatening blockage between the stomach and the small intestines.[20] The parents refused permission for surgery to repair the problem, and the doctors followed their wishes and let the infant die. Critics protested that this surgery was simple and effective, and the infant, although developmentally disabled, could have led a generally happy life.

Choosing not to treat in such cases has been interpreted as not using what would be considered ordinary means of life support—ordinary because the benefits to the patient would outweigh any burdens. Such cases have been criticized for their "buck-passing"—that is, shifting responsibility for the death to nature, as though in this situation but not elsewhere in medicine we should "let nature take its course."[21]

Two different moral questions can be raised about such cases. The first asks: who would be the best to decide whether to provide or deny certain treatments? The second asks: what are the reasons to provide or deny care? Some people insist that the primary decision makers should be the parents because they are not only the most likely to have the infant's best interests at heart but also the ones most likely to provide care for the child. Needless to say, we can imagine situations in which the parents would not be the most objective judges. They might be fearful, disappointed about the child's health conditions, or in disagreement about the best course of action. A 1983 presidential commission that was established to review medical ethics problems concluded that parents ought to make decisions for their seriously ill newborns, except in cases of decision-making incapacity, an unresolvable difference between parents, or a choice that is clearly not in the infant's best interests. (According to this commission, if a treatment is futile, it is not advised.) While the commission gives priority to parental decision-making, it also sets forth a more general and objective standard for surrogate decision-making,

> Permanent handicaps justify a decision not to provide life-sustaining treatment only when they are so severe that continued existence would not be a net benefit to the infant. Though inevitably somewhat subjective and imprecise in actual application, the concept of "benefit" excludes honoring idiosyncratic views that might be allowed if a person were deciding about his or her own treatment. Rather, net benefit is absent only if the burdens imposed on the patient by the disability or its treatment would lead a competent decision maker to choose to forgo the treatment. As in all surrogate decision making, the surrogate is obligated to try to evaluate benefits and burdens from the infant's own perspective.[22]

CRITERIA FOR DEATH

This last claim points toward the problem of trying to adopt the standpoint of one who is suffering and whose death we are contemplating. This issue came up in the past decade in the controversial case of Terri Schiavo, a severely brain-damaged woman who was allowed to die in 2005 after more than a decade of being kept alive by a feeding tube. Schiavo was twenty-six years old when she suffered a cardiac arrest on the morning of February 25, 1990. Her husband, Michael Schiavo, called 911. Emergency personnel arrived and resuscitated her. However, Schiavo's brain had been deprived of oxygen for some time, and she remained in a **persistent vegetative state (or PVS)** for the next fifteen years. A persistent vegetative state is often defined as one of "unconscious wakefulness" that lasts for more than a few weeks. A person in this state has lost all cerebral

cortex function but retains a basic level of brain stem function. In contrast, someone who is not totally brain dead but who is in a coma is unconscious but "asleep." His or her brain stem functions poorly, and thus this person does not live as long as someone in a persistent vegetative state.[23]

Schiavo's case was contentious because of the difficulty in determining what was in Terri's best interests and what she would have wanted for herself. The legal dispute involved the question of whether Schiavo's parents could prevent her husband—who had been appointed her legal guardian—from removing her feeding tube. Her husband claimed Terri would not want to be kept alive artificially with minimal chance of recovery, and in fact had expressed such wishes orally before her cardiac arrest. Her parents disagreed, claiming that Terri's Catholic faith prohibited this sort of euthanasia. Over the ensuing years, Terri's parents repeatedly challenged Michael Schiavo's guardianship in court and were repeatedly denied—with Terri's feeding tube being removed and reinserted on multiple occasions. The legal battle surrounding Terri's care would eventually involve the Florida legislature and courts, as well as the U.S. Congress, which passed controversial legislation in 2005 to intervene in the case. Ultimately, Schiavo's case was fast-tracked to the U.S. Supreme Court. The court refused to intervene and Schiavo's tube was removed.

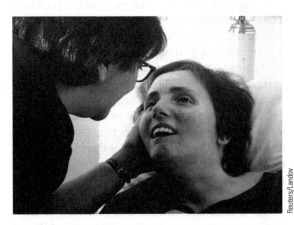

This photograph of Terri Schiavo was used to support the argument for keeping her on life support.

Terri Schiavo died on March 31, 2005, at age 41. An autopsy later revealed that her brain had shrunk to half its normal size, and thus that she had not been conscious or aware. Some had claimed over the years that Terri seemed to follow their motions and to respond to their voices. However, we know from her autopsy as well as earlier brain scans that she had no conscious function and that these were autonomic or reflexive responses. Even though her body might have continued its basic functions for decades, the medical evidence strongly suggests that Schiavo's consciousness permanently ceased in 1990.

The Schiavo case points to one of the problems of thinking about death and euthanasia. When does "death" occur?

Years ago, the *New York Times* reported on the case of a judge who was presiding over a similarly disputed medical situation. The dispute concerned whether a woman's respirator could be disconnected. The judge was reported to have said, "This lady is dead, and has been dead, and they are keeping her alive artificially."[24] Did the judge believe that the woman was alive or dead? She could not be both. He said that she was dead but also that she was being kept alive by machines. If the woman was really dead, then machines might have been keeping some of her bodily functions going, but could not have been keeping her *alive.* Perhaps the judge meant that, given her condition, she should be allowed to die. If so, then he should not have said she was dead. It is clear that we confuse questions about whether someone is dead or ought to be considered dead with other questions about whether it is permissible to do things that might hasten death.

We need not believe that an individual is dead in order to think it justifiable to disconnect her from a respirator and let her die. In fact, only if someone is not dead can we then sensibly ask whether we may let her die. It seems useful here to consider *how* we do determine whether someone is dead so as to distinguish this issue from other issues more properly related to euthanasia.

Throughout history, people have used various means to determine whether a human being is dead, and those means were a function of what they believed to be essential aspects of life. For example, if spirit was

thought of as essential and was equated with a kind of thin air or breath, then the presence or absence of this "life breath" would indicate whether a person was living. When heart function was regarded as the key element of life, and the heart was thought to be like a furnace, then people would feel the body to see if it was warm in order to know whether the person was still living. Even today, with our better understanding of the function of the heart, other organs, and organ systems, we have great difficulty with this issue. One reason for this is that we now can use various machines to perform certain bodily functions such as respiration and blood circulation. Sometimes this is a temporary measure, such as during a surgery. However, in other cases, the person may have lost significant brain function. In this latter sort of case, it is important to know whether the person is to be considered alive or dead.

Determining a precise condition and test for death became even more problematic in the past half-century, with the advent of heart transplants. Surgeons could not take a heart for transplant from someone who was considered living, only from someone who had been declared dead. Was an individual whose heart function was being artificially maintained but who had no brain function considered living or dead? We still wonder about this today. As transplantation science and life-support technologies were developing in the 1960s and 1970s, some courts had difficulty in figuring out how to apply brain death criteria. In some cases defendants who were accused of murder attempted to argue that since the victim's heart was still beating after an initial assault, the assailant did not actually kill the victim—but that a subsequent transplant procedure or removal from life-support did. Since the 1980s the courts have clarified that brain death is the appropriate criteria for use in such cases.[25]

In 1968, an ad hoc committee of the Harvard Medical School was set up to establish criteria for determining when a person should be declared dead. This committee determined that someone should be considered dead if she or he has permanently lost all detectable brain function. This meant that if there was some nonconscious brain function, for example, or if the condition was temporary, then the individual would not be considered dead. Thus, various tests of reflexes and responsiveness were required to determine whether an individual had sustained a permanent and total loss of all brain function.[26] This condition is now known as **whole brain death** and is the primary criterion used for the legal determination of death. This is true even when other secondary criteria or tests, such as loss of pulse, are used.

Whole brain death is distinguished from other conditions such as persistent vegetative states. In PVS, the individual has lost all cerebral cortex function but has retained some good brain stem function. Many nonconscious functions that are based in that area of the brain—respiratory and heart rate, facial reflexes and muscle control, and gag reflex and swallowing abilities—continue. Yet the individual in a permanent or persistent vegetative state has lost all conscious function. One reason for this condition is that the rate of oxygen used by the cerebral cortex is much higher than that of the brain stem, so these cells die much more quickly if deprived of oxygen for some time. The result is that the individual in this state will never regain consciousness but can often breathe naturally and needs no artificial aid to maintain circulation. Such an individual does not feel pain because he or she cannot interpret it as such. Because the gag reflex is good, individuals in this condition can clear their airways and thus may live for many years. They go through wake and sleep cycles in which they have their eyes open and then closed.

If we use whole brain death criteria to determine whether someone is dead, then neither a person in a persistent vegetative state nor a person in a coma is dead. In these cases, euthanasia questions about whether to let them die can be raised. On the other hand, if someone is dead by whole brain death criteria, then disconnecting equipment is not any form of euthanasia. We cannot let someone die who is already dead.

TYPES OF EUTHANASIA

If you were approached by a pollster who asked whether you supported euthanasia, you would do well first to ask what she meant and to what kind of euthanasia she was referring. It is important to distinguish what is called passive euthanasia from what is called active euthanasia. **Passive euthanasia** refers to withholding or withdrawing treatment and letting

a patient die. Thus, passive euthanasia can also be described as "letting die" or "allowing to die." Sometimes this is referred to as "letting nature take its course." This might include either withdrawing care (as in removing a feeding tube) or withholding care (as in not prescribing antibiotics to cure an infection). **Active euthanasia** refers to more active intervention that aims to bring about the death of a person—a lethal injection, for example. **Physician-assisted suicide** is yet another thing—as the physician merely prescribes the lethal medication without administering it herself. A further set of concepts focuses on whether euthanasia is given to those who request it and consent to it or not. **Voluntary euthanasia** implies that the patient consents. **Nonvoluntary euthanasia** describes euthanasia for those who are unable to give consent (infants or those with severe brain damage). **Involuntary euthanasia** implies that the killing is done in violation of the patient's will. There is no moral justification for involuntary euthanasia, which can also be called murder.

Passive euthanasia: Stopping (or not starting) some treatment, which allows the person to die. The person's condition causes his or her death.

Active euthanasia: Doing something such as administering a lethal drug or using other means that cause the person's death.

Voluntary euthanasia: Causing death with the patient's consent, knowingly and freely given.

Involuntary euthanasia: Causing death in violation of the patient's consent.

Nonvoluntary euthanasia: Causing the death of a patient who is unable to consent.

Physician-assisted suicide: Suicide that results from a physician's prescription of lethal medication.

Active and Passive Euthanasia

Passive euthanasia is now a common practice and is not prohibited by law. Often patients will decide in advance whether they want to be allowed to die from the progress of a fatal disease or from medical complications after surgery. Since the 1990s, with the passage of the Patient Self-Determination Act (PSDA) and through related case law, it has been acknowledged that patients have a right to refuse treatment. In these cases, the decision is made voluntarily. More controversial cases occur when the patient has not consented in advance and is unable to provide consent (or, as in the Schiavo case, there is a dispute about what the patient would have wanted). In such cases, next of kin are consulted in order to decide what the patient would have wanted in terms of treatment.

Legal precedents dealing with passive euthanasia were established in the cases of Karen Quinlan and Nancy Cruzan.[27] In Quinlan's case, the issue was whether a respirator that was keeping her alive could be disconnected. For some still unknown reason (some say it was a combination of prescription drugs and alcohol), she had gone into a coma in 1975. When doctors assured her parents that she would not recover, they sought permission to retain legal guardianship (since by then she was twenty-one years old) and have her respirator disconnected. After several court hearings and final approval by the Supreme Court of the state of New Jersey, the Quinlans were finally permitted to disconnect her respirator. Although they expected she would die shortly after her respirator was removed, she continued to live in this comatose state for ten more years. One basic reason given by the court for its opinion in this case was that Quinlan did not lose her right of privacy by becoming incompetent and that her guardians could thus refuse unwanted and useless interventions by others to keep her alive. None of the various state interests or social concerns that might override this right were found to be relevant in her case.

Nancy Cruzan was twenty-five years old in 1983 when an accident left her in a persistent vegetative state until her death eight years later. In her case, the issue brought to the courts was whether a feeding tube that was providing her with food and water could be withdrawn. This case eventually reached the U.S. Supreme Court, which ruled that such lifesaving procedures could be withdrawn or withheld, but only if there was "clear and convincing evidence" that Cruzan would have wanted that herself. Eventually,

such evidence was brought forward. Her feeding tube was removed and she was allowed to die.

In contrast to the cases described above, active euthanasia involves taking a step that directly brings about a person's death. In the past, it used to be called "mercy killing." Drugs are the most common means. Rather than letting a person die, these means are used to actually kill the person. This is generally regarded as much more problematic.

In the United States, active euthanasia is legally prohibited. However, as we've noted, in the Netherlands and elsewhere, active euthanasia is permitted. The Netherlands has a historical tradition of tolerance and freedom going back centuries, as evidenced by its provision of refuge for religious minorities and such controversial philosophers as Descartes and Spinoza.[28] The Netherlands also allows for legalized prostitution and drug usage. Legalized active euthanasia in the Netherlands is not without its critics—some of whom worry that active euthanasia is the first step on a slippery slope toward killing people who do not want to be killed. Critics also worry that this practice opens the door to killing those who feel they have become a financial burden on their families or who merely fear future suffering. One example of this occurred in 2012, when twin brothers Marc and Eddy Verbessem requested euthanasia in Belgium.[29] The twins were born deaf. They feared that they were going blind and suffered from other medical problems. They decided that rather than become incapacitated and dependent, and unable to see each other, they would rather die. In December 2012, their lives were ended at a hospital in Brussels. This case was unique, not only because it was a "double euthanasia" but also because the 45-year-old brothers were not terminally ill.

Voluntary, Nonvoluntary, and Involuntary Euthanasia

The laws in Belgium and the Netherlands require that the patient request euthanasia. These laws primarily focus on regulating *voluntary* euthanasia. Euthanasia laws—even in the United States—do allow for *nonvoluntary* passive euthanasia, which occurs, for example, when a feeding tube is removed from a patient in a persistent vegetative state.

Clearly, someone like Terri Schiavo could not voluntarily request to be allowed to die, which makes her death a case of nonvoluntary passive euthanasia. There is some fear, however, that the legalization of euthanasia might create a slippery slope from voluntary euthanasia toward involuntary euthanasia—that is, toward letting people die or actively killing them against their will.

In 2012, Senator Rick Santorum, who was campaigning for president, stoked the fear of involuntary euthanasia by claiming that "half of the people who are euthanized—ten percent of all deaths in the Netherlands—half of those people are euthanized involuntarily at hospitals because they are older and sick."[30] It would be frightening if 10 percent of deaths and half of all euthanasia cases were involuntary. It turns out, however, that the data are not so frightening; and Santorum's alarmism was widely repudiated. The *New England Journal of Medicine* published an investigation of Dutch euthanasia practices in 2007, which indicated that only 0.4 percent of deaths "were the result of the ending of life without an explicit request by the patient."[31] This indicates that these were cases of nonvoluntary euthanasia, not involuntary euthanasia. We might still worry that even one involuntary case is too many. But it appears that the worry about a slippery slope is exaggerated.

Of course, one reason we might worry about a slippery slope toward involuntary euthanasia involves the high cost of heath care at the end of life. Some people can benefit from the death of a patient: family members who worry about losing an inheritance or paying for medical bills, and insurance companies who have related financial concerns. (Also in the case of young patients, there is concern about pressures with regard to organ donation.) It is possible to imagine a utilitarian argument that attempts to justify involuntary euthanasia. However, most serious discussions of euthanasia will insist that patient consent remains essential. Indeed, one might also argue that euthanasia should be for the sake of the one dying—and not for the sake of others (insurance companies, organ recipients, or heirs and family members).

In some circumstances, others must make decisions for a patient because the patient is incapable of doing so. This is true of infants and small children, and patients in comas or permanent vegetative states. It is also true of people who are only minimally competent, as in cases of senility or certain psychiatric disorders. Deciding who is sufficiently competent to make decisions for themselves is clear in many but not all cases. What should we say, for example, of the mental competence of an eighty-year-old man who refuses an effective surgery that would save his life and at the same time says he does not want to die? Is such a person being rational?

Advance Directives   In some cases, when a patient is not able to express his or her wishes, we can attempt to infer what the person would want. We can rely, for example, on past personality or statements the person has made. Perhaps the person commented to friends or relatives as to what he or she would want in specific medical situations.

In other cases, a person might have left a written expression of his or her wishes in an advance medical directive. One form of advance directive is a **living will**. The living will may specify that one does not want extraordinary measures used to prolong life if one is dying and unable to communicate. However, such a specification leaves it up to the physician—who may be a stranger—to determine what is extraordinary. Another directive is called a **durable power of attorney**. In this case, the patient appoints someone close to her who knows what she wants under certain conditions if she is dying and unable to communicate. Patients are generally advised to have one or two alternate appointees for durable powers of attorney.

The person with durable power of attorney need not be a lawyer but serves as the patient's legal representative to make medical decisions for her in the event of incapacitation. The form for durable power of attorney also provides for individualized expressions in writing about what a patient would want done or not done under certain conditions. The appointed person will also be the only one able to give permission for "do not resuscitate" (DNR) orders, or orders not to revive the patient under certain conditions. DNR orders can be controversial, particularly in cases in which a patient's family requests that physicians take all possible measures to save the patient. This causes conflict, especially if the physician believes that resuscitation attempts will be futile or even make the patient worse off.[32] At the very least, however, these directives have moral force as expressions of patients' wishes. They also have legal force in those states that have recognized them.[33] There is some dispute about whether advance directives are effective. One study published in 2010 maintains that advance directives are usually followed.[34] However, an editorial accompanying that study in the *New England Journal of Medicine* indicates that there are important limitations—including the impossibility of imagining all health care options in advance and the fact that our preferences may change.[35]

Living wills and durable powers of attorney can, if enforced, give people some added control over what happens to them in their last days. To further ensure this, Congress passed the Patient Self-Determination Act, which went into effect in December of 1991. This act requires that health care institutions that participate in the Medicare and Medicaid programs have written policies for providing individuals in their care with information about and access to advance directives such as living wills.

Physician-Assisted Suicide

In 2010, there were 38,364 suicides in the United States, which is approximately 1.6 percent of all deaths. Of those suicides, 5,994 people were older than 65 (and 4,600 were between the ages of 15 and 24); 30,277 males committed suicide compared to only 8,087 females. It is estimated that there are twenty-five nonfatal attempts for every actual suicide.[36]

There are a number of ethical issues related to suicide. Immanuel Kant famously condemned suicide in the *Fundamental Principles of the Metaphysic of Morals* (for discussion of Kant's ethics see Chapter 6). He held that it violated the categorical imperative, since the maxim of suicide was not universalizable. If the maxim of suicide were universalized, we'd end up saying that everyone should kill themselves, which Kant rejects as an impossible law of nature. Furthermore, if one commits suicide

out of a self-interested motive (say to avoid misfortune), then there is a contradiction. Self-interest—what Kant calls self-love—contradicts itself when it leads to the killing of the self. Kant also held that suicide was disrespectful of personhood, in violation of the second form of the categorical imperative. The problem is that if a person destroys himself in order to escape painful circumstances, he uses his own life as a means to an end. Western religious traditions also tend to condemn suicide. Catholic moral teachings are, for example, radically pro-life, which means that they are opposed to suicide, euthanasia, and abortion. From this standpoint, suicide is wrong because it is anti-life and violates the dignity and worth of the human person. Pope John Paul II claims, for example, that suicide is immoral because it is a "rejection of God's absolute sovereignty over life and death."[37]

Just as questions can be raised about whether suicide is ever morally acceptable, so also can questions be raised about whether it is morally permissible for physicians (or others for that matter) to help someone commit suicide. Physician-assisted suicide also poses problems for doctors who take the Hippocratic Oath to "do no harm." In some ways, it looks like active euthanasia. Whereas in passive euthanasia, the doctor refrains from trying to do what saves or prolongs life, in active euthanasia the doctor acts to bring about the death by some cause or means. However, the causation by the doctor in physician-assisted suicide (i.e., the prescription of potentially lethal medication) is not immediate or direct, but rather takes place through the action of the patient.

One well-known advocate and practitioner of physician-assisted suicide was Dr. Jack Kevorkian. For several years, he helped people who wanted to die by providing them with the means to kill themselves. His first method was a "suicide machine" that consisted of a metal pole to which bottles of three solutions were attached. First, a simple saline solution flowed through an intravenous needle that had been inserted into the patient's vein. The patient then flipped a switch that started a flow of an anesthetic, thiopental, which caused the patient to become unconscious. After sixty seconds, a solution of potassium chloride followed, causing death within minutes by heart seizure. In a later version of the machine, carbon monoxide was used. When a patient pushed a control switch, carbon monoxide flowed through a tube to a bag placed over the patient's head.[38]

For eight years, starting in 1990, Kevorkian assisted more than 100 suicides, almost all of them in Michigan. To prevent these incidents from taking place in their state, Michigan legislators passed a law in 1993 against assisting a suicide. However, the law was struck down in the courts. Kevorkian was brought to trial in three separate cases, but juries found him not guilty in each case. However, in November 1998, he himself administered a lethal injection to a fifty-two-year-old man who was suffering from Lou Gehrig's disease. He also provided the news media with a videotape of the injection and death. It was aired on CBS's *60 Minutes* on November 22, 1998. This was no longer a case of suicide, and after a brief trial, on April 13, 1999, Kevorkian was convicted of second-degree murder and sentenced to serve a 10- to 25-year prison term in a Michigan prison. He was paroled in 2007 and died in 2011.

Many families of people he helped to die speak highly of Dr. Kevorkian. In addition, Dr. Kevorkian's patients can be seen pleading to be allowed to die in the videotapes he made of them before their deaths. His critics have a different view, however. They say that at least some of the people who wanted to die might not have done so if they had received better medical care—if their pain were adequately treated, for example. Some of the people were not terminally ill. One was in the early stages of Alzheimer's disease, and another had multiple sclerosis. The primary physician of another patient who claimed to have multiple sclerosis said the patient showed no evidence of this or any other disease; the patient had a history of depression, however. Another patient was determined by the medical examiner to have no trace of an earlier diagnosed cancer.[39] In still another case, a woman had what has come to be called "chronic fatigue syndrome" and a history of abuse by her husband.

Some critics have pointed out that Kevorkian's patients were predominantly women, who may have been worried about the impact of their diseases on others as much as the difficulty of the diseases themselves. In fact, according to data on suicide in the United States from 2010, three times as many women as men attempt suicide, though men succeed more often than do women.[40] Some suggest that women's suicide attempts are more of a cry for help than an actual desire to die. The choice of assisted suicide may also appear to women as a requirement of feminine virtues of care and service toward the family (as discussed in Chapter 9). However, the data on assisted suicide in Oregon, for example, do not indicate a gender gap in assisted suicide; in 2012, 39 men and 38 women were assisted in committing suicide—and such a 50–50 gender split is common for the past decade of record keeping on the issue.[41]

The American Medical Association continues to oppose physician-assisted suicide. The Hippocratic Oath contains the following claim: "I will neither give a deadly drug to anybody if asked for it, nor will I make a suggestion to this effect." This statement goes on to say that a physician should not provide abortion to women. Indeed, many people see a connection between the ethics of abortion and the ethics of euthanasia and suicide. They argue that a consistently pro-life position is opposed to all of these things (along with the death penalty and war, in most cases). But the medical profession does not have the same problem with abortion as it does with physician-assisted suicide. The American Medical Association continues to reject physician-assisted suicide as unethical. The organization's position on physician-assisted suicide states,

> It is understandable, though tragic, that some patients in extreme duress—such as those suffering from a terminal, painful, debilitating illness—may come to decide that death is preferable to life. However, allowing physicians to participate in assisted suicide would cause more harm than good. Physician-assisted suicide is fundamentally incompatible with the physician's role as healer, would be difficult or impossible to control, and would pose serious societal risks.[42]

Legal scholars and philosophers have long seen a connection between the ethics of euthanasia and abortion. Some of the arguments that have been used to support physician-assisted suicide make use of the passive euthanasia decisions discussed above (Quinlan and Cruzan), as well as the legal reasoning that has been used to defend abortion. When cases involving physician-assisted suicide reached the Supreme Court in 1997, a group of well-known philosophers made arguments in favor of the practice in an amicus curiae known as "The Philosopher's Brief." (The group included many prominent philosophers, including Judith Jarvis Thomson, Robert Nozick, Thomas Nagel, and John Rawls.) These philosophers conclude,

> Certain decisions are momentous in their impact on the character of a person's life—decisions about religious faith, political and moral allegiance, marriage, procreation, and death, for example. Such deeply personal decisions pose controversial questions about how and why human life has value. In a free society, individuals must be allowed to make those decisions for themselves, out of their own faith, conscience, and convictions.[43]

Despite such arguments, the U.S. Supreme Court decided in 1997 that there is no constitutional right to assisted suicide. However, individual states have not been prohibited from allowing the practice, and in 2006, the court struck down an attempt by the Bush administration to invalidate the Oregon Death with Dignity Law through the use of federal drug laws. This opened the door to the legalization of physician-assisted suicide in other states, as noted previously.

Pain Medication and Palliative Sedation

A different practice that may be confused with active euthanasia but ought to be distinguished from it is giving pain medication to gravely ill and dying patients. In some cases, the amount of pain medication given can also be a contributing factor in bringing about death. This is known as **terminal sedation** or **palliative sedation**. To call it terminal sedation implies that the use of sedation aims at the termination of life; to call it palliative sedation implies that the sedation is intended as palliative (relieving or soothing) care. Palliative sedation can also hasten death when it is combined with other

practices, such as cutting off food and water or withdrawing other medications. Various forms of palliative care, pain management, and passive euthanasia are now standard practices in hospice care (a *hospice* is a nursing facility that provides care for the dying). However, the intentional use of pain medication to end life remains controversial.[44] One notorious case involved the possibility that terminal sedation was used to end the lives of patients after Hurricane Katrina in New Orleans.[45]

Physicians are often hesitant to administer sufficient pain medication to severely ill patients because they fear that the medication will actually cause their deaths. They fear that this would be considered comparable to mercy killing (or active euthanasia), which is legally impermissible. (The fact that they might cause addiction in their patients is another reason why some doctors hesitate to give narcotics for pain relief. This seems hardly a reasonable objection, especially if the patient is dying!) The **principle of double effect** may help justify physicians' use of terminal sedation. According to the principle of double effect, it is morally wrong to intend to do something bad as a means to an end; it is acceptable, however, to do something morally permissible for the purpose of achieving some good, while knowing that it also may have a bad secondary effect.

The following diagram may be used to help understand the essence of this principle. It shows a morally permissible act with two effects: one intended main effect and one unintended side effect.

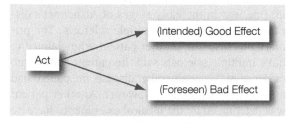

According to the principle of double effect, it may be morally permissible to administer a drug with the intention of relieving pain (a good effect), even though we know or foresee that our action also may have a bad effect (weakening the person and risking his death). Certain conditions must be met, however, for this to be permissible. First, the act itself must be morally permissible. One cannot do what is wrong to bring about a good end. Second, the person who acts must intend to bring about the good end rather than the harmful result. Third, the good results must outweigh the bad ones.

The idea behind the double effect principle is that there is a moral difference between intending to kill someone and intending to relieve pain. There is a moral difference between intending that someone die by means of one's actions (giving a drug overdose) and foreseeing that they will die because of one's actions (giving medication to relieve pain). Doing the latter is not, strictly speaking, active euthanasia. Active euthanasia would be the intentional giving of a drug with the purpose of bringing about a person's death. The difference is seen in the case of the conscientious dentist who foresees that she might cause her patient pain and the sadistic dentist who seeks to produce pain in her patient.

The principle of double effect continues to be an object of debate.[46] In real-world medical situations, it may be difficult to assess people's intentions—whether, for example, a patient requests an increased dose of pain medication just to relieve pain or actually bring about his own death. People may also have mixed or hidden motives for their actions. Nevertheless, trying to satisfy the principle of double effect can be useful for doctors, allowing them to give their patients sufficient pain medication without fear of being prosecuted for homicide. This principle may also help those who want patients to have good pain relief but are morally opposed to active euthanasia.

Advances in the treatment of pain may increasingly separate the questions of palliative and terminal sedation. New developments in pain control may make it possible to treat pain without causing death, thereby keeping this issue separate from that of active euthanasia—although pain management at the end of life remains a complicated and delicate task. Doctors and nurses are also increasingly aware of the need for a comprehensive approach to pain management. Nonetheless, it remains important to distinguish between pain management and the intention to end life. The American Nurses Association explains,

> While nurses should make every effort to provide aggressive pain control and symptom relief for patients at the end of life, it is never ethically permissible for a nurse to act by omission or commission, including, but not limited to medication administration, with the intention of ending a patient's life.[47]

Ordinary and Extraordinary Measures

Philosophers have sometimes labeled those measures that are ineffective or excessively burdensome as *extraordinary*. They are often called *heroic* in the medical setting, in the sense that such extraordinary measures can be burdensome and go above and beyond what is likely to benefit the patient. A person's hospital medical chart might have the phrase *no heroics* on it, indicating that no such measures are to be used. There are other cases in which what is refused would actually be effective for curing or ameliorating a life-threatening condition. These measures are called *ordinary*—not because they are common but because they promise reasonable hope of benefit. With ordinary measures, the chances that the treatment will help are good, and the expected results are also good. And yet decisions are sometimes made not to use these measures and to instead let the person die.

Critics have complained that the idea of what is heroic or extraordinary is vague. One difficulty with determining whether a treatment would be considered ordinary or extraordinary is in making an objective evaluation of the benefits and burdens. It would be easier to do this if there were such a thing as an objective minimum standard for a patient's quality of life. Any measure that would not restore a person to at least that standard could then be considered extraordinary. However, if we were to set this standard very high, using it might also wrongly imply that the lives of disabled persons are of little or no benefit to them.

What would be considered an ordinary measure in the case of one person may be considered extraordinary in the case of another; a measure may effectively treat one person's condition, but another person would die shortly even if the measure were used (a blood transfusion, for example). Furthermore, the terminology can be misleading because many of the medical tools that used to be considered experimental and risky (such as antibiotics and respirators) are now common and largely beneficial. In many cases, such tools are now considered ordinary, whereas they once could have been considered extraordinary.

The basic difference between ordinary and extraordinary measures of life support, then, is as follows:

Ordinary measures: Measures or treatments with reasonable hope of benefit, or the benefits outweigh the burdens to the patient

Extraordinary measures: Measures or treatments with no reasonable hope of benefit, or the burdens outweigh the benefits to the patient

One question that arises in relation to ordinary and extraordinary measures is how to view the withholding or withdrawing of artificial nutrition, as in the Terri Schiavo case discussed previously. It is instructive to remember that Schiavo's family was Catholic and that Catholic theology provides much of the intellectual basis for the distinctions between ordinary and extraordinary measures. Although we introduced the definitions above in the context of euthanasia, the key to the difference between ordinary and extraordinary is whether any medical measure that is withheld or withdrawn offers "a reasonable hope of benefit."[48] Although the U.S. Catholic medical guidelines assert that "a person may forgo extraordinary or disproportionate means of preserving life ... there should be a presumption in favor of providing nutrition and hydration to all patients, including patients who require medically assisted nutrition and hydration, as long as this is of sufficient benefit to outweigh the burdens involved to the patient."[49] In other words, in some cases this form of medical intervention would be deemed of insufficient benefit to a patient, for example, if it did not promise to return him or her to a conscious state. In Schiavo's case, Terri's parents argued that the potential benefits of artificial nutrition outweighed the burdens; her husband and the medical community concluded that no benefits (such as restored consciousness) were possible.

Combining the Types of Euthanasia

We have noted the differences between various types of euthanasia: voluntary and nonvoluntary (we will ignore involuntary euthanasia, assuming it to be immoral), active and passive, and (if passive) the withholding of ordinary and extraordinary measures. Combining the types of euthanasia gives six forms, as illustrated below.

There are three types of voluntary euthanasia.

1. Voluntary active euthanasia: The person who is dying says, "Give me the fatal dose."
2. Voluntary passive euthanasia, withholding ordinary measures: The person says, "Don't use lifesaving or life-prolonging medical measures even though the likely results of using them would be good and the costs or burdens minimal, because I want to die."
3. Voluntary passive euthanasia, withholding extraordinary measures: The person says, "Don't use those medical measures because the chances of benefit in terms of saving or extending my life would be small, the burdens too great, or both."

Likewise, there are three types of nonvoluntary euthanasia.

4. Nonvoluntary active euthanasia: Others decide to give the person a fatal drug overdose.
5. Nonvoluntary passive euthanasia, withholding ordinary measures: Others decide not to use lifesaving or life-prolonging medical measures even though the likely results of using them would be good and the costs or burdens minimal.
6. Nonvoluntary passive euthanasia, withholding extraordinary measures: Others decide not to use those medical measures because the chances of benefit—saving or extending life—are small, the burdens are too great, or both.

So far, we have attempted only to classify types of euthanasia. Our purpose has been to describe the various possible types so that we will then be better able to make appropriate distinctions in our moral judgments about these cases.

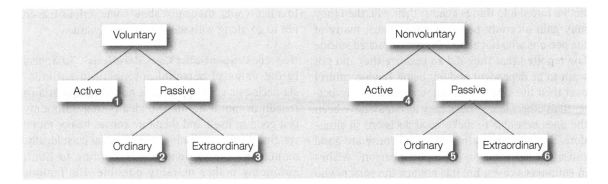

MAKING MORAL JUDGMENTS ABOUT EUTHANASIA

Before we consider the moral arguments about euthanasia, we should first distinguish moral judgments from assertions about what the law should or should not be on this matter. Although we may sometimes have moral reasons for what we say the law should or should not do, the two areas are distinct. There are many things that are moral matters that ought not to be legislated or made subject to law and legal punishment. Not everything that is immoral ought to be illegal. For example, lying, while arguably a moral issue, is only sometimes subject to the law. In our thinking about euthanasia, it would be well to keep this distinction in mind. On the one hand, in some cases we might say that a person acted badly, though understandably, in giving up too easily on life. Yet we also may believe that the law should not force some action here if the person knows what he or she is doing, and the person's action does not seriously harm others. On the other hand, a person's request to end his or her life might be reasonable given his or her circumstances, but there might also be social reasons why the law should not permit it. These reasons might be related to the possible harmful effects of some practice on other persons or on the practice of medicine. Just because some action (for example, euthanasia) might be morally permissible does not necessarily mean that it ought to be legally permissible.

One way to get a handle on what to think about the morality of euthanasia is to look at its various types. We can then ask ourselves whether euthanasia of a certain type is morally justifiable. One way to help us answer these questions is to use the distinction introduced earlier between consequentialist theories (such as utilitarianism) and non-consequentialist theories (such as Kant's moral theory or natural law theory). If you think that it is the consequences rather than the nature of actions themselves that matter morally, then you can focus on those considerations. If, instead, you think that we should judge whether some action is right or wrong in itself for some reason, then you can focus on those considerations.

The Moral Significance of Voluntariness

Today, an individual's right over his or her own life is highly valued. And yet the commonsense moral view is that there are limits to this right. It is limited, for example, when it conflicts with the interests or rights of others. Under what conditions and for what reasons should a person's own wishes prevail in euthanasia matters? How important is voluntary consent?

Consequentialist Considerations From your study of utilitarianism, you know that one major method of deciding moral right and wrong appeals to the consequences of our actions (act utilitarianism) or practices (rule utilitarianism). From this perspective, voluntariness matters morally only to the extent that it affects human happiness and welfare. Respecting people's own choices about how they will die surely would have some beneficial consequences. For example, when people know that they will be allowed to make decisions about their own lives and not be forced into things against their will, then they may gain a certain peace of mind. Thus, many of the persons who have used Oregon's assisted suicide law reported that they did so because they did not want to be dependent and felt better having control over their lives. Moreover, knowing themselves better than others knew them, they also may have been the ones best able to make good decisions in situations that primarily affected them. These are good consequentialist reasons to respect a person's wishes in euthanasia cases. But it is not just the person who is dying who will be affected by the decision. Thus, it can be argued that the effects on others—on their feelings, for example—are also relevant to the moral decision-making.

However, individual decisions are not always wise and do not always work for the greatest benefit of the person making them, or for that of others. For example, critics of euthanasia worry that people who are ill or disabled might refuse certain lifesaving treatments because they lack money or do not know about services and supports available to them. On consequentialist grounds, we should do what, in fact, is most likely to bring about the greatest happiness, not only for ourselves but also for all those affected by our actions. It does not in itself matter who makes the judgment. But it does matter insofar as one person rather than another is more likely to make a better judgment—one that would have better consequences overall, including consequences to the individual.

Moreover, from the perspective of rule utilitarian thinking, we ought to consider which policies and practices would maximize happiness. (It is here that morality comes closer to concerns about what the law should be.) Would a policy that universally follows individual requests about dying be most likely to maximize happiness? Or would a policy that gives no special weight to individual desires, but that directs us to do whatever some panel decides, be more likely to have the best outcome? Or would some moderate policy be best, such as one that gives special but not absolute weight to what a person wants? An example of such a policy might be one in which the burden of proof for denying what a person wishes is placed on those who would deny it.

In other words, they must show some serious reason not to go along with what the person wants.

Non-consequentialist Considerations   To appeal to the value of personal autonomy in euthanasia decisions is to appeal to a non-consequentialist reason or moral norm. The idea is that autonomy is a good in itself and therefore carries heavy moral weight. We like to think of ourselves, at least ideally, as masters of our own fate. According to Kant, autonomy makes morality possible. His famous phrase "an ought implies a can" indicates that if and only if we can or are free to act in certain ways can we be commanded to do so. According to a Kantian deontological position, persons are unique in being able to choose freely, and this capacity for choice ought to be respected.

However, in many euthanasia cases a person's mental competence and thus autonomy is compromised by fear, lack of understanding, dependency, and hopelessness. Illness and dependency can make a person more subject to undue influence or coercion. Moreover, patients with terminal illnesses can become depressed and despondent. One study of terminally ill patients who consider suicide concluded, "Depression and hopelessness are the strongest predictors of desire for hastened death."[50] It might make sense for people with terminal illness to be depressed and to feel hopeless. But it might also be that it is possible to treat the depression along with pain in order to provide patients with more autonomy as they confront the end of life.

The issues of depression, dependency, and hopelessness point toward some of the problems for thinking about the importance of autonomy. **Autonomy** literally means self-rule. But how often are we fully clear about who we are and what we want to be? Is the self whose decisions are to be respected the current self or one's ideal or authentic self? In cases of dementia or mental illness, should the person's current wishes outweigh the wishes the person expressed before he became demented or mentally ill? These issues of selfhood and personal identity are crucial to euthanasia arguments that focus on autonomy and personal decision-making. It is also the case that they take us beyond ethics itself into philosophical notions of the self and freedom as well as into empirical psychology.

Note also here that although we have concentrated on pointing out the kinds of things that would be morally relevant from both consequentialist and non-consequentialist points of view, the issues also may be analyzed from the perspective of an ethics of care. One would suppose that from this perspective both matters that relate to benefits and harms and those that relate to a person's autonomy would be relevant.

Active versus Passive Euthanasia

The distinction between active and passive euthanasia is a conceptual distinction, a matter of classification. Giving a patient a lethal drug to end her life is classified as active euthanasia. Stopping or not starting some life-lengthening treatment, knowing that a patient will die, is classified as passive euthanasia. For example, either not starting a respirator or disconnecting it is generally considered passive euthanasia because it is a matter of not providing life-prolonging aid for the person. In this case, the person's illness or weakness is the cause of her death if she dies. That passive euthanasia does not directly cause a patient's death tells us nothing about whether the practice is justified or unjustified.

Let us pose the moral question about active and passive euthanasia like this: Is there any moral difference between them? Is active euthanasia more morally problematic than passive euthanasia? Or are they on a moral par such that if passive euthanasia is morally permissible in a particular case, then so is active euthanasia? Is physician-assisted suicide (in which a physician only provides the means of death to the person) any more or less problematic than cases in which the physician actually administers the drug or uses other means to bring about death?

Consequentialist Concerns   Again, if we take the perspective of the consequentialist or act utilitarian, for example, we should be concerned about our actions only in terms of their consequences. The means by which the results come about do not matter in themselves. They matter only if they make a difference in the result. Generally, then, if a person's death is the *best outcome* in a difficult situation, it

would not matter whether it came about through the administration of a lethal drug dose or from the discontinuance of some lifesaving treatment. Now, if one or the other means did make a difference in a person's experience (as when a person is relieved or pained more by one method than another), then this would count in favor of or against that method.

If we take the perspective of a rule utilitarian, we should be concerned about the consequences of practices and policies. We should want to know which of the various practices or policies would have the best results overall. Which would be the best policy: one that allows those who are involved to choose active euthanasia, one that requires active euthanasia in certain cases, one that permits it only in rare cases, or one that prohibits it and attaches legal penalties to it? Which policy would make more people happy and fewer people unhappy? One that prohibited active euthanasia would frustrate those who wished to use it, but it would prevent some abuses that might follow if it were permitted. Essential to this perspective are predictions about how a policy would work. Some people are concerned in particular about the effects of physician participation in the practice of euthanasia. It may have the positive results of being under the control of a profession known for its ethical concerns. Or it may have negative effects such as the lessening of patient trust in physicians. The disability advocacy group called Not Dead Yet has voiced its concerns about physician-assisted suicide and the plight of the disabled.[51] Its members argue that legalized physician-assisted suicide may make people more inclined to think the lives of the disabled are not worth living and that there might be pressure on them to commit suicide. Instead of legalizing assisted suicide, critics argue, we should emphasize universal access to health care, better pain management, and better social work to deal with the concerns of the aged and disabled.

Even those who support physician-assisted suicide and in some cases active euthanasia worry about whether these practices would be open to abuse. The argument that there would be abuse has been given various names, depending on the particular metaphor of choice: the "domino effect," "slippery slope," "wedge," or "camel's nose" argument. The idea is that if we permit active euthanasia in a few reasonable cases, then we may approve it in more and more cases until we were approving it in cases in which it was clearly unreasonable. In other words, if we permit euthanasia when a person is soon dying, in unrelievable pain, and has requested that his life be ended, then we will eventually permit it when a person is not dying or has not requested to be killed. Evidence about involuntary euthanasia in the Netherlands, as cited above, may or may not be relevant in the United States or elsewhere. But we may still ask: Would we slide down the slope to involuntary euthanasia or other morally unacceptable results? Is there something about us that would cause us to slide? Would we be so weak of mind that we could not see the difference between these cases? Would we be weak of will, not wanting to care for people whose care is costly and burdensome? This is an empirical and predictive matter. To know the force of the argument, we would need to show evidence about the likelihood of sliding down such a slippery slope.

Non-consequentialist Concerns   Many arguments and concerns about active and passive euthanasia are not based on appeals to good or bad results or consequences. Arguments about the right to die or to make one's own decisions about dying are non-consequentialist arguments. On the one hand, some people argue that respecting personal autonomy is so important that it should override any concerns about bad results. Thus, we might conclude that people ought to be allowed to end their lives when they choose as an expression of their autonomy, and that this choice should be respected regardless of the consequences to others or even mistakes about their own cases.

On the other hand, some people believe that there is a significant moral difference between killing another person or killing themselves and letting a person die. Killing people, except in self-defense, is morally wrong, according to this view. Just why it is thought wrong is another matter. Some people rely on reasons like those advanced by natural law, citing the innate drive toward living as a good in itself, however compromised—a good that should not be suppressed. Kant uses reasoning similar to this in his argument against suicide. He argues that making a case for

ending life based on a concern for life is inherently contradictory and a violation of the categorical imperative. Some people use religious reasons to argue against any form of suicide, such as the belief that life-and-death decisions are for God and not ourselves to make. Some people use reasons that rely on concerns about the gravity of ending a life directly and intentionally, and claim that in doing so we ally ourselves with what is at best a necessary evil.

We each need to consider what role consequentialist and non-consequentialist or deontological reasons play in our own views about the morality of active and passive euthanasia. If consequentialist arguments (either egoistic or utilitarian) have primacy, then one's argument for or against active euthanasia will depend on empirical judgments about the predicted consequences. If deontological reasons have primacy, then these reasons must be evaluated. Is the principle of respecting patient autonomy more important, for example, than prohibitions against killing? This text does not intend to answer these questions for the student, but it does assume that a good start can be made in answering them if one is able to know whether an argument is based on egoistic, utilitarian, or deontological considerations.

NOTES

1. "Vermont Passes Law Allowing Doctor-Assisted Suicide," Reuters, May 21, 2013, accessed July 16, 2013, http://www.reuters.com/article/2013/05/21/usa-vermont-assistedsuicide-idUSL2N0E11FD20130521

2. Susan Haigh, "Assisted Suicide on Legal Agenda in Several States," *Yahoo! News*, February 8, 2013, accessed February 11, 2013, http://news.yahoo.com/assisted-suicide-legal-agenda-several-states-084111046.html

3. Oregon Public Health Division, *Oregon's Death with Dignity Act—2012* (January 14, 2013), accessed February 11, 2013, http://public.health.oregon.gov/ProviderPartnerResources/EvaluationResearch/DeathwithDignityAct/Documents/year15.pdf

4. *Termination of Life on Request and Assisted Suicide (Review Procedures) Act* in *Death and Dying: A Reader*, ed. Thomas A. Shannon (Rowman & Littlefield, 2004), 122.

5. Eduard Verhagen and Pieter J. J. Sauer, "The Groningen Protocol—Euthanasia in Severely Ill Newborns," *New England Journal of Medicine* 352 (March 10, 2005): 959–62.

6. Regional Euthanasia Review Committees, *Annual Report 2011* (August 2012), accessed February 11, 2013, http://www.euthanasiecommissie.nl/Images/RTE.JV2011.ENGELS.DEF_tcm52-33587.PDF

7. Richard H. Nicholson, "Death Is the Remedy?" *Hastings Center Report* 32, no. 1 (January–February 2002): 9.

8. *New York Times*, April 12, 2001, A6.
9. "The Suicide Tourist," PBS's *Frontline*, March 2, 2010, http://www.pbs.org/wgbh/pages/frontline/suicidetourist/
10. Jim Holt, "Euthanasia for Babies?" *New York Times Magazine*, July 10, 2005, accessed February 13, 2013, http://travel.nytimes.com/2005/07/10/magazine/10WWLN.html?pagewanted=all
11. Denis Campbell, "Premature Babies Study Shows Survival Rates on Rise," *Guardian*, December 4, 2012, accessed February 13, 2013, http://www.guardian.co.uk/society/2012/dec/05/survival-rates-premature-babies-rise
12. "Preterm Birth," Centers for Disease Control and Prevention, accessed February 13, 2013, http://www.cdc.gov/reproductivehealth/maternalinfanthealth/PretermBirth.htm
13. Peter Singer, *Practical Ethics*, 3rd ed. (Cambridge: Cambridge University Press, 2011), 167.
14. Debra Galant, "Peter Singer Settles In, and Princeton Looks Deeper; Furor over the Philosopher Fades Though Some Discomfort Lingers," *New York Times*, March 5, 2000, accessed February 13, 2013, http://www.nytimes.com/2000/03/05/nyregion/peter-singer-settles-princeton-looks-deeper-furor-over-philosopher-fades-though.html?pagewanted=all&src=pm
15. Harriet McBryde Johnson, "Unspeakable Conversations," *New York Times Magazine*, February 16, 2003, accessed February 13, 2013, http://www.nytimes.com/2003/02/16/magazine/unspeakable-conversations.html?pagewanted=all&src=pm
16. Spina bifida fact sheet, National Dissemination Center for Children with Disabilities, accessed March 21, 2013, http://nichcy.org/disability/specific/spinabifida
17. John Schwartz, "When Torment Is Baby's Destiny, Euthanasia Is Defended," *New York Times*, March 10, 2005, A3.
18. Tom Shakespeare, *Disability Rights and Wrongs* (New York: Routledge, 2006), Chapter 8.
19. John A. Robertson, "Involuntary Euthanasia of Defective Newborns: A Legal Analysis," *Stanford Law Review* 27, no. 2 (January 1975): 255.
20. James Rachels, "Active and Passive Euthanasia" The New England Journal of Medicine 292, no. 2 (January 9, 1975).
21. From a comment made by a reviewer of this text, Robert P. Tucker of Florida Southern College, who has had hospital experience in this regard.
22. *The President's Commission Report*, reprinted in *Source Book of Bioethics*, ed. Albert R. Jonsen, Robert M. Veatch, and LeRoy Walters (Washington, DC: Georgetown University Press, 1998), 192–93. For a perspective from a disabled person, see Harriett McBryde Johnson, "Unspeakable Conversations," *New York Times Magazine*, February 16, 2003. I thank Jennifer MacKinnon for this reference.
23. Two types of cases are to be distinguished from both persistent vegetative state and coma. One is called *locked-in syndrome*, in which a person may be conscious but unable to respond. The other is *dementia*, or senility, in which the content of consciousness is impaired, as in Alzheimer's disease. Neither the person in a persistent vegetative state or coma nor the person with locked-in syndrome or dementia is considered dead by whole brain death criteria. We may say the person's life has a diminished value, but he or she is not legally dead. However, some people argue that because the ability to think is what makes us persons, when someone loses this ability, as in the case of PVS, we ought to consider the person dead. Newborns with little or no upper brain or brain function also then and for the same reason could be considered dead. However, these are living, breathing beings, and it would be difficult to think of them as dead in the sense that we would bury them as they are. Rather than declare them dead, as some people have argued, others believe that it would be more practical and reasonable to judge these cases in terms of the kind of life they are living and to ask whether it would be morally permissible to bring about their deaths or allow them to die.
24. "Life-Support Ended, A Woman Dies," *New York Times*, December 5, 1976.
25. Robert Miller, *Problems in Health Care Law* 9th ed. (Sudbury, MA: Jones and Bartlett Publishers), 768 ff.
26. Ad Hoc Committee of the Harvard Medical School to Examine the Definition of Brain Death, "A Definition of Irreversible Coma," *Journal of the American Medical Association* 205 (1968): 377.
27. See *In re Quinlan*, 70 N.J. 10, 335 A. 2d 647 (1976); and *Cruzan v. Director, Missouri Department of Health*, United States Supreme Court, 110 S. Ct. 2841 (1990).
28. Herbert Hendin, "The Dutch Experience," *Issues in Law & Medicine* 17, no. 3 (Spring 2002): 223–47.
29. Bruno Waterfield, "Euthanasia Twins 'Had Nothing to Live For,'" *Telegraph*, January 14, 2013, accessed February 11, 2013, http://www.telegraph.co.uk/news/worldnews/europe/belgium/9801251/Euthanasia-twins-had-nothing-to-live-for.html
30. "Euthanasia in the Netherlands: Rick Santorum's Bogus Statistics," *Washington Post*, February 22, 2012, accessed March 18, 2013, http://www.washingtonpost.com/blogs/fact-checker/post/euthanasia-in-the-netherlands-rick-santorums-bogus-statistics/2012/02/21/gIQAJaRbSR_blog.html
31. "End-of-Life Practices in the Netherlands under the Euthanasia Act," *New England Journal of Medicine* (May 10, 2007), accessed March 18, 2013, quotation from "Results" section at http://www.nejm.org/doi/full/10.1056/NEJMsa071143
32. "The Last Word on the Last Breath" *New York Times*, October 10, 2006, http://www.nytimes.com/2006/10/10/health/10dnr.html?pagewanted=all
33. However, what is requested in these documents may or may not be followed, depending on the circumstances and on what is requested. Medical staff may decide not to stop life-saving treatments for a person who is not otherwise dying, even if she has stated this in writing. Staff members also may decide not to do certain things that they consider not medically appropriate or not legally permissible, even though these things have been requested in writing.
34. Maria J. Silveira, Scott Y. H. Kim, and Kenneth M. Langa, "Advance Directives and Outcomes of Surrogate Decision Making before Death," *New England Journal of Medicine* 362 (2010): 1211–18.
35. Muriel R. Gillick, "Reversing the Code Status of Advance Directives?" *New England Journal of Medicine* 362 (2010): 1239–40.
36. John L. McIntosh and Christopher W. Drapeau (for the America Association of Suicidology), *U.S.A. Suicide: 2010 Official Final Data*, accessed February 11, 2013, http://www.suicidology.org/c/document_library/get_file?folderId=262&name=DLFE-636.pdf

37. Pope John Paul II, *Evangelium Vitae* (1995), para. 66, accessed March 18, 2013, http://www.vatican.va/holy_father/john_paul_ii/encyclicals/documents/hf_jp-ii_enc_25031995_evangelium-vitae_en.html

38. *New York Times*, December 4, 1990, describes the first publicized case in which Dr. Kevorkian's "suicide machine" was used, and the other two cases can be found, for example, in the *San Francisco Chronicle*, October 29, 1991.

39. Stephanie Gutmann, "Death and the Maiden," *The New Republic*, June 24, 1996, 20–28.

40. McIntosh and Drapeau, "U.S.A. Suicide: 2010," http://www.suicidology.org/c/document_library/get_file?folderId=262&name=DLFE-636.pdf

41. Oregon Public Health Division, *Oregon's Death with Dignity Act—2012* (January 14, 2013), accessed March 18, 2013, http://public.health.oregon.gov/ProviderPartnerResources/EvaluationResearch/DeathwithDignityAct/Documents/year15.pdf

42. "Opinion 2.211—Physician-Assisted Suicide," American Medical Association, issued June 1994, accessed February 11, 2013, https://www.ama-assn.org/ama/pub/physician-resources/medical-ethics/code-medical-ethics/opinion2211.page

43. "Assisted Suicide: The Philosophers' Brief," *New York Review of Books*, March 27, 1997.

44. See "When Is Sedation Really Euthanasia?" *Time*, March 21, 2008; and Molly L. Olsen, Keith M. Swetz, and Paul S. Mueller, "Ethical Decision Making with End-of-Life Care: Palliative Sedation and Withholding or Withdrawing Life-Sustaining Treatments," *Mayo Clinic Proceedings* 85, no. 10 (October 2010): 949–54.

45. Denise Grady, "Medical and Ethical Questions Raised on Deaths of Critically Ill Patients," *New York Times*, July 20, 2006, accessed February 11, 2013, http://www.nytimes.com/2006/07/20/health/20ethics.html?_r=0

46. See, for example, Warren S. Quinn, "Actions, Intentions, and Consequences: The Doctrine of Double Effect," *Philosophy and Public Affairs* 18, no. 4 (Fall 1989): 334–51.

47. American Nurses Association, *Position Statement*, "Registered Nurses' Roles and Responsibilities in Providing Expert Care and Counseling at the End of Life" (2010), accessed March 18, 2013, http://www.nursingworld.org/MainMenuCategories/EthicsStandards/Ethics-Position-Statements/etpain14426.pdf

48. Directives 56 and 57 of the *Ethical and Religious Directives for Catholic Health Care Services*, approved by the U.S. bishops in 1995 and approved by the Vatican. See James Keenan, S. J., "A 400-Year-Old Logic," *Boston College Magazine*, Spring 2005: 41–42.

49. Ibid.

50. William Breitbart, Barry Rosenfeld, Hayley Pessin, Monique Kaim, Julie Funesti-Esch, Michele Galietta, Christian J. Nelson, and Robert Brescia, "Depression, Hopelessness, and Desire for Hastened Death in Terminally Ill Patients with Cancer," *Journal of the American Medical Association* 284, no. 22 (2000): 2907–11.

51. Not Dead Yet, http://www.notdeadyet.org/

REVIEW EXERCISES

1. What is the difference between "whole brain death" and "persistent vegetative state"?

2. If a person has whole brain death, then what kind of euthanasia is possible? Explain.

3. What is the difference between active and passive euthanasia? Is physician-assisted suicide more like active or passive euthanasia? How so?

4. Where do advance directives such as living wills and durable powers of attorney fit into the distinction between voluntary and nonvoluntary euthanasia?

5. What is the difference between ordinary and extraordinary measures of life support? If some measure of life support were common and inexpensive, would this necessarily make it an ordinary means of life support? Explain.

6. Label the following as examples of voluntary or nonvoluntary and active or passive euthanasia; if passive, are the measures described more likely to be considered ordinary or extraordinary measures of life support?

   a. A person who is dying asks to be given a fatal drug dose to bring about his death.

   b. A dying patient asks that no more chemotherapy be administered because it is doing nothing but prolonging her time until death, which is inevitable in a short time anyway.

   c. Parents of a newborn whose condition involves moderate retardation refuse permission for a simple surgery that would repair a physical anomaly inconsistent with continued life, and they let the infant die.

   d. A husband gives his wife a lethal overdose of her pain medicine because he does not want to see her suffer anymore.

   e. Doctors decide not to try to start an artificial feeding mechanism for their patient because they believe that it will be futile, that is, ineffective given the condition of their patient.

7. List the consequentialist concerns that could be given in arguing about whether the actions proposed in three of the scenarios in Question 6 are justified.

8. What non-consequentialist concerns could be given in arguing about these same three scenarios?

DISCUSSION CASES

1. **Respirator Removal**. Jim is an active person. He is a lawyer by profession. When he was forty-four years old, a routine physical revealed that he had a tumor on his right lung. After surgery to remove that lung, he returned to a normal life. However, four years later, a cancerous tumor is found in his other lung. He knows he has only months to live. Then comes the last hospitalization. He is on a respirator. It is extremely uncomfortable for him, and he is frustrated by not being able to talk because of the tubes. After some thought, he decides that he does not want to live out his last few weeks like this and asks to have the respirator removed. Because he is no longer able to breathe on his own, he knows this means he will die shortly after it is removed.

   Do Jim or the doctors who remove the respirator and then watch Jim die as a result do anything wrong? Why or why not? Would there be any difference between this case and that of a person such as Terri Schiavo, who was in a persistent vegetative state, was not able to express her current wishes, and had left no written request? Would there be a difference in cases such as hers between removing a respirator (which she was not using) and removing a feeding tube? How would you tell whether a respirator or a feeding tube would be considered an ordinary or extraordinary means of life support? What would be the significance of these labels in each case?

2. **Pill Overdose**. Mary Jones has a severe case of cerebral palsy. She has spent twenty-eight years of life trying to cope with the varying disabilities it caused. She can get around somewhat in her motorized wheelchair. An aide feeds her and takes care of her small apartment. She went to junior college and earned a degree in sociology. She also has a mechanism whereby she can type on a computer. However, she has lately become weary with life. She sees no improvement ahead and wants to die. She has been receiving pain pills from her doctor. Now she asks for several weeks' worth of prescriptions so that she will not have to return for more so often. Her doctor suspects that she might be suicidal.

Should Mary Jones's doctor continue giving her the pills? Why or why not? Would she be assisting in Mary's suicide if she did? Should Mary have a right to end her life if she chooses? Why or why not? Should her physician actually be able to administer some death-causing drug and not just provide the pills? Why or why not?

3. **Teen Euthanasia**. Thirteen-year-old Samantha is in the last stages of cancer. She says she doesn't want any further treatment because she thinks that it is not going to make her well. Her parents want the doctors to try a new experimental therapy for which there is some hope. If they cannot convince Samantha to undergo this experimental procedure, should the doctors sedate Samantha and go ahead with it anyway, or should they do what she asks and let her die? Do you think that the doctors should be allowed to end her life with a fatal dose of a drug if that is what she wishes, even though her parents object and they are still her legal guardians?

4. **Baby John Doe**. Sarah and Mike's baby boy was born with a defect called spina bifida, which involves an opening in the spine. In his case, it is of the more severe kind in which the spinal cord also protrudes through the hole. The opening is moderately high in the spine, and thus they are told that his neurological control below that level will be affected. He will have no bowel and bladder control and will not be able to walk unassisted. The cerebral spinal fluid has already started to back up into the cavity surrounding his brain, and his head is swelling. Doctors advise that they could have a shunt put in place to drain this fluid and prevent pressure on the brain. They could also have the spinal opening repaired. If they do not do so, however, the baby will probably die from an infection. Sarah and Mike are afraid of raising such a child and worry that he would have an extremely difficult life. In a few cases, however, children with this anomaly who do not have the surgery do not die, and then they are worse off than if the operation were performed. What should Sarah and Mike do? Why?

11 Abortion

Carolina Biological/Visuals Unlimited/Corbis

Learning Outcomes

After reading this chapter, you should be able to:

- Describe different stages of fetal development and various forms of abortion.
- Understand disputes about the morality of abortion.
- Explain key cases and moral issues relating to abortion, including women's rights, sex-selective abortion, parental consent laws, and laws requiring the use of ultrasound technology.

- Evaluate moral arguments about abortion, including both consequentialist and non-consequentialist arguments.
- Differentiate among various ways of approaching the moral status of the fetus.
- Understand and apply moral concepts to a variety of issues related to abortion, including fetal abnormality, rape, and birth control.
- Defend your own ideas about the ethics of abortion.

Abortion has been legal in the United States since 1973, when the U.S. Supreme Court's *Roe v. Wade* decision prohibited states from banning the procedure before the last three months of pregnancy. Rooted in the concept of a woman's "right to privacy," the *Roe* decision was often seen as the culmination of a growing societal concern for women's equality and autonomy. In fact, in the 1970s, many people assumed that the abortion issue was settled and that Americans would never return to the days of "back alley" abortions—the illegal and unsafe procedures that had become notorious in states prohibiting abortion. But far from settling the abortion issue, the years since *Roe v. Wade* have witnessed the growth of a vehement political and religious movement opposed to abortion and a countermovement in support of women's reproductive rights. Today, Americans continue to carry on a highly emotional and sometimes violent debate over the morality and legality of abortion.

In 2013, for example, many Americans celebrated the fortieth anniversary of *Roe v. Wade*, and polls indicated that as many as 70 percent of Americans opposed overturning the decision.[1] At the same time, a number of state governments have taken action in recent years to restrict abortion access and to establish the "personhood" and legal rights of the preterm fetus. In Arkansas, for example, legislators overrode a gubernatorial veto to pass a "heartbeat" bill, which prohibits abortion after a fetal heartbeat is detected (at around twelve weeks into a pregnancy).[2] Following Arkansas's lead, North Dakota enacted a similar law in March 2013, banning almost all abortions after six weeks of pregnancy.[3] The North Dakota State Senate also passed an amendment to the state constitution that, if approved by voters, would guarantee the "inalienable right to life of every human being at every stage of development,"[4] including newly fertilized eggs. (Voters in Mississippi rejected a similar measure in 2011, after concerns were raised that the law could be interpreted to prohibit **in vitro fertilization** and certain forms of birth control.)

All of these new state laws appear to violate the legal framework for abortion that was established in Supreme Court decisions such as *Roe v. Wade* and *Casey v. Planned Parenthood* (1992)—which prohibits states from banning abortion before the point of fetal viability. (A fetus's ability to survive outside the womb is generally considered to begin late in the second trimester of pregnancy.) But even if these new abortion restrictions are declared unconstitutional, they exemplify the fierce opposition to abortion that exists in many parts of the country.

Such opposition is particularly apparent in the nongovernmental arena, where abortion opponents employ a range of strategies. Take, for example, "crisis pregnancy centers," which often advertise on billboards, suggesting that "pregnant and scared" women should visit their offices for help. Visitors quickly discover that rather than offering medical services (such as abortion), these centers are focused on counseling women *against* terminating their pregnancies—presenting them with baby booties, congratulatory "you're a mom!" cards, and tiny rubber fetuses. Such centers, which are generally funded by Christian charities, have been criticized for providing inaccurate information about links between abortion and breast cancer, infertility, and suicide.[5] While pro-choice groups argue that these centers take advantage of women at emotionally difficult moments, abortion opponents see them as laudable outposts in a grassroots battle against legalized mass murder.

The high-stakes abortion issue—which abortion opponents frequently compare to slavery and the Holocaust—has, unfortunately, also produced its share of violence. Since 1993, at least eight people associated with abortion clinics—including doctors, clinic staff, a security guard, and a clinic escort—have been murdered by antiabortionists. In 2009, for instance, a Kansas physician named George Tiller was shot and killed in his church during a service. He was known to perform late-term abortions and had been the subject of previous threats and assassination attempts. Scott Roeder, a vehement antiabortion activist, was arrested for the murder and declared he had acted to prevent more babies from being killed.[6] Another militant abortion opponent, Eric Rudolph, was sentenced to life in prison for the 1998 bombing of an Alabama women's health care clinic that also performed abortions. This bomb killed an off-duty police officer and seriously

Pro-choice and pro-life protesters confront each other at a demonstration.

injured and blinded the director of nursing at the clinic. (Rudolph was also responsible for using bombs to target another abortion clinic, a gay club, and the 1996 Olympics.) At his latest sentencing, Rudolph continued to insist that he was justified in attacking those involved in abortion, which he considers murder.

In contrast to these violent incidents, many abortion opponents disagree with the tactics of the movement's more militant individuals and groups. They believe that these tactics and the murders of physicians have hurt their cause. They preach nonviolence and urge respect for all persons, including the unborn.[7] Nevertheless, many also believe that they are justified in applying intense pressure on individuals involved in abortions, whom they view as murderers. Activists have distributed "Wanted" posters, featuring photos of abortion providers along with their names, addresses, telephone numbers—and sometimes even information about their children and other family members. Abortion opponents also demonstrate outside family planning clinics that provide abortions and forcefully try to persuade female visitors not to go inside. Supporters of abortion rights have responded by seeking legal injunctions to keep protesters from blocking clinic entrances and by engaging volunteers to escort patients through the protests.

As these examples demonstrate, abortion is an issue about which people have extremely strong opinions. Expressions of these opinions are often highly emotionally charged. For those opposed to abortion, the practice constitutes nothing less than the murder of more than a million innocent children each year in the United States. For abortion rights supporters, the practice is a crucial component in women's ability to control their own bodies and exercise their rights to autonomy and equality under the law. Abortion touches on some of the most intimate and powerful aspects of our lives as women and men and as mothers and fathers. Many people's views about abortion are based on religious beliefs, but this is not always the case.

To complicate matters further, there may be a difference between what we think about the morality of abortion and what we think about the law regulating abortion. In fact, one could hold that the law ought to allow abortion and still believe that abortion is

morally objectionable. In addition, the language that is used in the debate over abortion often begs important questions: "pro-life" and "pro-choice" labels do not tell us what counts as "life" or whether there are moral limits to our choices. In this chapter, we try to avoid labels and analyze the issues and arguments in such a way as to help us focus more clearly on the alternative views and the reasons behind them.

What we say about the morality of abortion depends on several issues. Some are strictly ethical matters and involve basic ethical perspectives, such as the nature and basis of moral rights. Others are factual matters, such as what happens at different stages of fetal development and what the likely consequences are of certain actions given particular social conditions. Others still are conceptual matters, such as the meaning of terms such as *abortion* or *personhood* or even *human*. We begin our analysis with certain factual matters about the stages of fetal development and contemporary methods of abortion.

STAGES OF FETAL DEVELOPMENT

The scientific stages of fetal development are important for our analysis because many ethical discussions about abortion take into account such factors as the fetus's heartbeat, its ability to feel pain, and its ability to survive outside the womb. The scientific labels given to the different stages of fetal development do not, in themselves, help us reach ethical conclusions. But they provide a standard framework for any discussion of human development. In fact, the terms used to describe human fetal development are used throughout the biological sciences and pertain to most if not all vertebrates.

Conception occurs when an egg is fertilized by a sperm. This produces a *zygote*—which simply means "joining together"—a single cell that begins to divide and move through the fallopian tube. When the ball of cells reaches the uterus seven to ten days after fertilization, it is called a *blastocyst*. (A *blastula* is a fluid-filled cavity surrounded by a single layer of cells.) From the second to eighth week of gestation, the developing organism is called an *embryo*, as is any mammal at this early stage of primitive tissue and organ development. From then until birth, it is called a *fetus,* which means "young unborn." It is common in philosophical discussions of abortion to use the term *fetus* for all stages of prenatal development, but use of this term does not imply anything about value or status. We can single out the following stages of fetal development (times are approximate):

> **Day 1:** Fertilization—An ovum, or egg (twenty-three chromosomes), is penetrated by sperm (twenty-three chromosomes), and one cell is formed that contains forty-six chromosomes.
> **Days 2–3:** The fertilized ovum passes through the fallopian tube as cell division increases.
> **Days 7–10:** The blastocyst reaches the uterus; it has now become a "ball of cells."
> **Week 2:** The developing embryo becomes embedded in the uterine wall.
> **Weeks 2–8:** Organ systems such as the brain, spinal cord, heart, and digestive tube—and certain structural features such as arm and leg buds—begin and then continue to develop. (The photo that opens this chapter is of an embryo 40 days after conception.)
> **Weeks 12–16:** *Quickening* occurs, which means that the mother can begin to feel the fetus's movements; the fetus is approximately 5½ inches long.
> **Weeks 20–26:** Fetal brain development makes it possible that fetuses could feel pain. While there is controversy about exactly when this level of brain development takes place, the consensus is that neuronal activity and neural pathways are not sufficiently established to allow for the experience of pain prior to twenty weeks.[8]
> **Weeks 20–28:** The process of **viability** takes place, and the fetus is able to live apart from its mother, depending on its size and lung development.
> **Week 40:** Birth.

All changes during fetal development occur gradually. Even conception takes some time as the sperm penetrates the egg and together they come to form one cell. Any of these stages may or may not be morally relevant, as we shall consider shortly.

METHODS OF ABORTION

The historical record suggests that humans have had access to various methods of abortion for millennia. As early as 1550 BCE, the Egyptians recommended inserting pieces of papyrus into the cervix to stimulate an abortion.[9] Plato recognized that midwives could cause a miscarriage with "drugs and incantations," and in the *Republic* he indicates that abortion and infanticide might be useful methods of creating eugenic outcomes.[10] The **Hippocratic Oath** of the fourth century BCE forbids giving a woman a pessary (a vaginal suppository) to produce abortion.[11] Ancient methods of inducing abortion included shaking women and inserting foreign objects into the vagina in the hope of causing infection. The first law forbidding abortion was promulgated by the Roman Emperor Caracalla in 211 CE; Christian authors at the time, such as Tertullian, also condemned abortion.[12]

When we speak of abortion today, we mean induced abortion performed by trained doctors. This is to be distinguished from spontaneous abortion, or what we generally call *miscarriage*. Among current methods of inducing abortion are the following:

> **Morning-after pill:** This chemical compound, which the Food and Drug Administration refers to as Plan B, is considered by some to be related to abortion because it prevents the blastocyst from embedding in the uterine wall. The intrauterine device—IUD—and some contraceptive pills operate in a similar way, causing the fertilized egg to be expelled by making the uterine wall inhospitable. Since August 2006, the Plan B pill has been available over the counter for customers eighteen years of age and older. Not everyone agrees that the use of Plan B and the IUD count as abortion, since they *prevent* pregnancy rather than terminate it.
> **RU486 (mifepristone):** This prescription drug used in combination with other prostaglandin drugs such as misoprostol induces uterine contractions and expulsion of the embryo. It must be used within sixty-three days of a missed menstrual period. Although there has been some concern about its safety, since the drug was approved for use in the United States millions of women have safely used it to end their pregnancies.[13]
> **Uterine or vacuum aspiration:** In this procedure, the cervix (the opening of the uterus) is

dilated, and the uterine contents are removed by suction tube.

> **Dilation and curettage (D&C):** This procedure also dilates the cervix so that the uterus can be scraped with a spoon-shaped curette. This method is similar to the vacuum method except that it is performed somewhat later and requires that the fetus be dismembered and then removed.
> **Saline solution:** A solution of salt and water is used to replace amniotic fluid and thus effect a miscarriage.
> **Prostaglandin drugs:** These pharmaceuticals induce early labor and may be used in combination with RU-486, as mentioned previously.
> **Hysterotomy:** This uncommon procedure is similar to a cesarean section but is used for later-term abortions.
> **Dilation and extraction (D&X) or intact D&X or "partial birth abortion":** In this uncommon second- and third-trimester procedure, forceps are used to deliver the torso of the fetus, its skull is punctured and the cranial contents suctioned out, and then delivery is completed.

In recent years, there have been around one million abortions performed annually in the United States, with the abortion rate slowly declining from a high in the 1980s. According to the Guttmacher Institute, each year two out of every hundred women aged fifteen to forty-four have an abortion. Half have had at least one previous abortion. Eighteen percent of women obtaining abortions are teenagers younger than twenty. Women in their twenties account for more than 50 percent of abortions.[14] African American women are five times as likely as white women to have an abortion, and Hispanic women are twice as likely as whites to have the procedure.[15] One cause of this higher rate may be cuts to family planning funding in recent years, resulting in, among other things, reduced contraceptive use, especially among poor women.[16] *New York Times* columnist Nicholas Kristof argues, "The cost of birth control is one reason poor women are more than three times as likely to end up pregnant unintentionally as middle-class women."[17] Indeed, 42 percent of women who have abortions have incomes below

the federal poverty line. In terms of claimed religious affiliation, 37 percent are Protestant and 28 percent are Catholic.[18] A 2004 study reported that among the reasons that women cite for choosing an abortion are the following:

> Having a child would dramatically change their lives, their ability to continue with school or work, or their ability to care for others (74 percent).
> They could not afford children (73 percent).
> They did not want to become single mothers (48 percent).
> They were finished having children (38 percent).
> Health problems of either fetus or mother (12 percent).[19]

Around the world, abortion is permitted without restriction as to reason in fifty-six countries (39 percent of the world's population) and is completely illegal in thirty-two countries, with no exception for rape or to save the life of the woman (6 percent of the world's population).[20] Thirty-six countries allow abortion only to save the life of the mother or in exceptional cases, such as when the woman has been raped or there is fetal impairment (21 percent of the world's population).[21] There are more than 40 million abortions performed each year around the world. Of these, 21.6 million are deemed unsafe—the vast majority in countries where abortion is illegal or highly restricted. According to the World Health Organization, "deaths due to unsafe abortion remain close to 13 percent of all maternal deaths," with forty-seven thousand women dying each year from complications of unsafe abortions.[22]

In China, abortion is used as a means of population control in tandem with a general policy of encouraging one child per family. In some cases, women have been forced to have abortions when they cannot pay the fine for having more than one child.[23] This has resulted in a strange demographic phenomenon because of Chinese parents' preferences for boys (who are expected to financially support their parents in old age). According to a study published in 2009, the ratio of boys to girls in China is now 120 to 100. (Among families' second births—which are often permitted only if the first child is a girl—the ratio is 143 to 100.[24]) This means that for children under twenty, there are thirty-two million more boys than girls. Since the widespread availability of ultrasound scanners in the 1990s, many potential parents have chosen to terminate their pregnancies if the fetus is female. This practice is less prevalent in larger cities, where women have a higher status.[25]

Similar problems occur in India, where the ratio of boys to girls is 1,000 to 914.[26] And a recent report indicates that immigrant communities in Europe and the United Kingdom also practice **sex-selective abortion.**[27] This practice—in which parents choose to terminate a pregnancy based solely on the fetus's sex—is illegal in Canada, the UK, France, and Germany. There is currently no such restriction on a national level in the United States, although American lawmakers have considered bills that would ban the practice (for example, the Prenatal Nondiscrimination Act).[28] More recently, North Dakota enacted a law outlawing both sex-selective abortion and abortions based upon genetic abnormalities in the fetus. Like many of the other recent state-level abortion bills, the ultimate constitutional status of this bill remains unclear.

ABORTION AND THE LAW

Much of the contemporary debate about abortion is concerned with whether the law ought to permit abortion and, if so, what, if any, legal regulations ought to be placed on it. The relationship between morality and the law is often ignored in these debates. Sometimes, it is assumed that if abortion is immoral, it ought to be illegal just for that reason, or if it is morally permissible, it therefore ought to be legally permissible. As noted in the previous chapter on euthanasia, this equivalence between morality and the law is questionable. We can think of actions that are possibly immoral but that we would not want to be legally prohibited. For example, I may wrongly waste my talents, but I would not want the law to force me to develop and use them. However, many of our laws, such as civil rights laws, are grounded in moral reasons. The profound questions about what the law should and should not do are bound up with an entire philosophy of law. Because this is an ethics text, we will not be able to explore such questions here. Nevertheless, as we review the

constitutional and legislative status of abortion (primarily in the United States), we should pay close attention to the moral reasons claimed for various positions in the debate and the appeals made to rights and other moral values.

It may be surprising to discover that abortion was not always prohibited or condemned by many of the authorities that are now most emphatically opposed to it, including the Roman Catholic Church. Following the teachings of Augustine and Aquinas, the Church held that the fetus was not human until sometime after conception when the matter was suitable for the reception of a human soul.[29] The Church fathers held, for example, that the soul did not enter the fetus until forty days of gestation for males and eighty or ninety days for females, a calculation that they based upon ideas found in Aristotle and in the Bible—a point that was noted in a footnote to the *Roe v. Wade* decision.[30] It was not until 1869 that Pope Pius IX decreed that the embryo's soul was present from conception, declaring abortion to be a sin.[31] Indeed, for much of Western history and in British Common Law, abortion before the quickening of the fetus (at twelve to sixteen weeks) was legal and not considered immoral.[32] Nor was it always illegal in the United States before the 1970s. As U.S. Supreme Court Justice Blackmun notes in the *Roe v. Wade* opinion, "At the time of the adoption of our Constitution, and throughout the major portion of the 19th century, abortion was viewed with less disfavor than under most American statutes currently in effect."[33]

In the first half of the twentieth century, most U.S. states passed laws regulating or making abortion illegal, except in certain cases such as a pregnancy resulting from rape or incest or when the pregnant woman's life or health was threatened. However, women continued to have abortions illegally and under dangerous conditions. (The most notorious of these "back alley" abortion methods involved the use of a coat hanger to scrape the uterine lining, which became a symbol used by the movement to legalize abortion.) In the early 1970s, a pregnant woman from Texas, who was given the fictitious name Jane Roe, challenged the state's abortion law, which allowed the procedure only to save the life of the mother. This case, which became known as *Roe v. Wade*, made its way to the U.S. Supreme Court, which ruled in favor of Jane Roe in 1973. In the majority opinion, the court concluded that no state may ban abortion before the time of fetal viability based on a fundamental "right to privacy" grounded in the Constitution, chiefly in the liberty and due process clauses of the Fourteenth Amendment. The term *privacy* here does not refer to matters that must be kept secret or to what goes on in one's own home, but to a basic liberty, a freedom from restraint in decisions about how to live and enjoy one's life.[34]

However, the court noted that the state did have some interest in protecting maternal health as well as what it called the "potential life" of the fetus. (Note that the phrase is not especially illuminating because most people do not deny that the fetus is actually alive.) In the case of maternal health, this interest becomes "compelling" only after the first *trimester* (or third month) of pregnancy and allows for some degree of health-related regulation. In the case of the fetus's "potential life," the right to privacy was said not to be absolute but limited, due to state or social interests that become compelling at the point of fetal viability. The ruling was thus based on the trimester formula and concluded that

1. from approximately the end of the first trimester, state laws could regulate the medical safety of abortion procedures;
2. before the time of viability, about the end of the second trimester (the sixth month), the abortion decision should be left up to the pregnant woman and her doctor; and
3. from the time of viability on, states could prohibit abortion except in those cases in which the continued pregnancy would endanger the life or health of the pregnant woman.[35]

While the trimester formula is considered to be a rough guide to the legal status of abortion, the U.S. Supreme Court has handed down several other abortion-related decisions that have altered this original formulation. Most important, in *Casey v. Planned Parenthood* (1992), the court rejected the trimester formula and simply maintained that states could not ban abortion before the point of viability. (Advances in medical science had already shifted the point at which fetal viability was possible.) It also reiterated the state's compelling interest in protecting life after the point of viability. Nonetheless, the court affirmed the basic decision in *Roe v. Wade*. Citing the importance of a legal precedent on which citizens have come to depend and the absence of significant factual or legal developments, the court again ruled in favor of a constitutional right to privacy and abortion. The majority opinion also commented on the essential relationship of abortion rights to the "capacity of women to act in society and to make reproductive decisions" and upheld those rights as a matter of liberty and "personal autonomy." While the court concluded that states could impose such restrictions as twenty-four-hour waiting periods and parental or state consent requirements (for minors seeking abortions), they must not place an *undue burden* on women in the exercise of their constitutional right to privacy. This means that state laws may not create "substantial obstacles" for women who seek to have abortions, such as the requirement that they first get consent from their spouses—a regulation the court rejected.[36]

Since 1992, many abortion-related legal decisions have involved the *undue burden* standard. In 2007, in *Gonzalez v. Carhart*, the U.S. Supreme Court upheld, by a vote of five to four, a federal law banning so-called "partial birth abortion" or "intact dilation and extraction." It held that this law did not impose "an undue burden on women's exercise of their right to end a pregnancy." The majority opinion concluded that there were alternatives to this procedure and that the law enacted by Congress reflected the government's "legitimate, substantial interest in preserving and promoting fetal life."[37] The decision raised controversy, however, because the law it upheld allowed exceptions to protect a woman's life but not her health. Some physicians and other critics of the measure argued that the procedure is "often the safest to use late in the pregnancy because it minimizes the chances of injury to the uterus" and was thus deemed appropriate for certain cases by the American College of Obstetricians and Gynecologists.[38] Other critics have challenged parental consent laws as placing an undue burden on minors seeking abortions (especially in cases of incest) and pointed to the court's ruling in *Planned Parenthood of Kansas City v. Ashcroft* (1983) that such laws must offer a "judicial alternative" whereby a judge can overrule parental refusals.[39]

As we noted at the beginning of this chapter, the past decade has witnessed an increasing number of legal efforts to restrict abortion based on a number of different criteria. In 2010, for example, the governor of Nebraska signed into law a statute "banning most abortions 20 weeks after conception or later on the theory that a fetus by that stage in pregnancy has the capacity to feel pain."[40] An increasing number of state legislatures and referenda (in North Dakota, Mississippi, Virginia, and Colorado) have also sought to establish full legal "personhood" beginning at conception. Other states are in the process of enacting fetal "heartbeat" laws, some of which (in Virginia and Michigan) would require that women seeking abortions undergo transvaginal ultrasounds to detect fetal heartbeat. This last requirement has generated a particularly intense controversy. Antiabortion advocates support the requirement based on their belief that if a woman views the fetus on an ultrasound she will mostly likely decide against abortion, while women's rights advocates have called state-mandated transvaginal ultrasounds a form of "medical rape."[41] Meanwhile, the evidence appears to show that there is very little correlation between ultrasound viewing and women's choice to abort.[42]

Questions have also been raised about the new "feticide" laws now enacted in more than half of U.S. states. These are laws that make it a crime to cause harm to a fetus. Thus someone who attacks a pregnant woman and kills the fetus that she wanted to carry to term can be found guilty of murder or manslaughter. States differ in how they classify the crime, whether as "feticide" or under general manslaughter or murder laws. It may seem contradictory that the woman can end a fetus's life through abortion but a third party who kills the fetus she wanted may be guilty of murder. Some have said that the difference is between one who exercises a "reproductive choice" and another person who does not. Further questions are raised by state laws that seek to protect fetal life from harmful actions of the pregnant woman herself, such as ingesting drugs or alcohol. She could be punished if her fetus is born harmed but not if she aborts the fetus.

And in some jurisdictions, the state can commit a pregnant woman who has drug or alcohol problems with the goal of defending the health of the unborn child. A law in Wisconsin, for example, states that "unborn children have certain basic needs which must be provided for, including the need to develop physically to their potential and the need to be free from physical harm due to the habitual lack of self-control of their expectant mothers in the use of alcohol beverages, controlled substances or controlled substance analogs, exhibited to a severe degree."[43] Should a state be able to prevent a mother from continuing drug use during pregnancy by having her committed against her will to a rehab facility? Many abortion rights supporters see such policies as withholding from women the rights of autonomy and personal liberty that are granted to men. Those who condemn abortion, on the other hand, typically support these measures.

In recent years, abortion opponents have worked to find other legal ways to restrict access to abortion. Consider what happened in Wichita, Kansas, after Dr. George Tiller was murdered. His clinic, the state's only abortion clinic outside of Kansas City, closed after his death in 2009. In 2013, a former employee was attempting to reopen the clinic but faced legal challenges and local lobbying efforts, including attempts to change zoning and taxation rules.[44] Throughout the country, abortion providers and clinics are facing similar legal challenges and restrictions, effectively blocking access to abortion in large portions of many states. For example, laws in Mississippi and Tennessee require doctors to have admitting privileges at local hospitals, which frequently refuse them to avoid controversy. In Virginia, a new law requires abortion clinics to adhere to architectural standards that apply to hospitals. A recent *Time* magazine article noted that in 2011 alone, ninety-two abortion-restricting provisions passed state legislatures. And in North Dakota, South Dakota, Mississippi, and Arkansas, there is just one abortion provider left in each state. As the *Time* article concluded, "getting an abortion in America is, in some places, harder today than at any point since it became a constitutionally protected right 40 years ago."[45]

Recent Supreme Court decisions on abortion have not been unanimous. This indicates the difficulty of balancing concerns for the various moral values involved. In doing so, however, these decisions have made neither side in the abortion debate particularly happy. On the one hand, they stress the values of privacy, liberty, and equal opportunity; on the other hand, they conclude that some recognition ought to be given to the origins of human life. Because these are moral values reflected in the law, some of the issues surrounding the morality of abortion will be relevant to what we think the law should or should not do. In what follows, however, we will concentrate on the underlying moral issues that typically frame the abortion debate.

ABORTION: THE MORAL QUESTION

Although many people have argued that abortion is a private decision that ought not be a matter of law, it is much more difficult to make the case that abortion is not a moral matter at all. After all, abortion involves questions about rights, happiness, and well-being, as well as the status and value of human life. If these things are morally relevant, then abortion is a moral matter. This is not to say that abortion is good, bad, or neutral, but simply that it is morally important.

The moral status of abortion also may have relevance for how we approach fetal research. For example, promising studies have shown that embryonic stem cells (taken from human blastocysts) as well as tissue from aborted fetuses might be used for treatments for diseases such as Parkinson's disease and to regenerate damaged organs and tissues. These issues are discussed further in Chapter 18.

Rather than outlining so-called conservative, liberal, and moderate views on abortion, we will avoid these political labels and attempt to look at the issue from a fresh, philosophically grounded perspective. We will consider two types of arguments both for and against abortion: (1) arguments for which the moral status of the fetus is irrelevant, and (2) arguments for which it is relevant. One might suppose that all arguments regarding abortion hinge on the moral status of the fetus, but this is not the case. As we will see, when we use the phrase "moral status of the fetus," we refer to questions about whether the fetus is a human being or a person and whether the fetus has inherent value or any rights, including a right to life. We look first at arguments that do not

concern themselves with these questions. As you examine these arguments, you may find that one or another seems more valid or reasonable to you.

ARGUMENTS THAT DO NOT DEPEND ON THE MORAL STATUS OF THE FETUS

First, we will consider arguments for which the moral status of the fetus is irrelevant. These arguments are typically either based on utilitarian reasoning or on claims about the rights of persons.

Utilitarian Reasoning

Many arguments that focus on something other than the moral status of the fetus are consequentialist in nature and broadly utilitarian. Arguments for abortion often cite the bad consequences that may result from a continued pregnancy—for example, the loss of a job or other opportunities for the pregnant woman, the suffering of the future child, the burden of caring for the child under difficult circumstances, and so on. Some utilitarian arguments against abortion also cite the loss of potential happiness and future social contributions of the being who is aborted.

According to act utilitarian reasoning, each case or action stands on its own, so to speak. Its own consequences determine whether it is good or bad, better or worse than other alternatives. Act utilitarians believe that the people making the abortion decision must consider the likely consequences of the alternative actions—in other words, having or not having an abortion (as well as such considerations as where and when these events might occur). Among the kinds of consequences to consider are health risks and benefits, positive or negative mental or psychological consequences, and financial and social results of the alternative choices. For example, a pregnant woman should consider questions such as these: What would be the effect on her of having the child versus ending the pregnancy? What are the consequences to any others affected? Would the child, if born, be likely to have a happy or unhappy life, and how would one determine this? How would an abortion or the child's birth affect her family, other children, the father, the grandparents, and so on?

Notice that the issue of whether the fetus (in the sense we are using it here) is a person or a human being is not among the things to consider when arguing from this type of consequentialist perspective. Abortion at a later stage of pregnancy might have different effects on people than at an earlier stage, and it might also have different effects on the fetus in terms of whether it might experience pain. It is the effects on the mother, the fetus, the potential child, and others that count in utilitarian thinking, not the moral status of the fetus (what kind of value it has) or its **ontological status** (i.e., what kind of being we say it is). Also notice that on utilitarian or consequentialist grounds, abortion sometimes would be permissible (the morally right thing to do) and sometimes not; it would depend on the consequences of the various sorts noted earlier. Moral judgments about abortion will be better or worse, according to this view, depending on the adequacy of the prediction of consequences.

Critics of utilitarian reasoning generally object to its seeming disregard of rights. They may point out that if we do not take the right to life seriously, then utilitarian reasoning may condone the taking of any life if the overall consequences of doing so are good. A utilitarian may respond by appealing to the idea of rule utilitarianism. A rule utilitarian must consider which practice regarding abortion would be best. Would the rule "No one should have an abortion" be likely to maximize happiness? Would the rule "No one should have an abortion unless the pregnancy threatens the mother's health or well-being" have better consequences overall? What about a rule that says "Persons who are in situations *x, y,* or *z* should be allowed to have abortions"? How would easy access to abortion affect our regard for the very young? How would the practice of abortion when the fetus has certain abnormalities affect our treatment of the physically or mentally disabled in general? How would a restrictive abortion policy affect women's health as well as their ability to participate as equal human beings, enjoying jobs and other opportunities? Whichever practice or rule is likely to have the better net result—that is, more good consequences and fewer bad ones—is the best practice or rule to follow.

In any case, some critics of the utilitarian approach would argue that the moral status of the fetus, such as whether it is the kind of being that has a right to life, is in fact essential to moral decisions about abortion. Others would insist that we address the matter of the rights of the pregnant woman (or others) and the problem of conflicts of rights.

Some Rights Arguments

Some arguments about abortion do consider the rights of persons but still maintain that the moral status of the fetus is irrelevant. It is irrelevant in the sense that whether or not we think of the fetus as a person with full moral rights is not crucial for decisions about the morality of abortion. A well-known article on abortion by Judith Jarvis Thomson presents such an argument. She does assume for the purpose of argument that the fetus is a person from early on in pregnancy. But her conclusion is that abortion is still justified, even if the fetus is a person with a right to life (and she assumes it is also permissible if the fetus is not a person).[46] This is why the argument does not turn on what we say about the moral status of the fetus.

The question Thomson poses is whether the pregnant woman has an obligation to sustain the life of the fetus by providing it with the use of her body. To have us think about this, she asks us to consider an imaginary scenario. Suppose, she says, that you wake up one morning and find yourself attached through various medical tubes and devices to a famous violinist. You find out that during the night you have been kidnapped and "hooked up" to this violinist by a group of classical music enthusiasts. The violinist has severe kidney problems, and the only way that his life can be saved is through being so attached to another person—so that the other person's kidneys will do the work of purifying his blood for some fixed period of months, until his own kidneys have recovered. The question Thomson poses is this: Would you be morally permitted or justified in "unplugging" the violinist, even though doing so would result in his death? Thomson argues that you would be justified, in particular because you have not consented to devote your body and your time to saving the violinist's life. She goes on to argue that this example has an analogy to abortion, most obviously in cases of pregnancy due to rape.

However, Thomson means her argument to apply more widely, and she uses other analogies to help make her point. One would only have a responsibility to save the violinist (or nurture the fetus) if one had agreed to do so. The consent that Thomson has in mind is a deliberate and planned choice. She argues that although it would be generous of you to save the life of the violinist (or the fetus), you are not obligated to do so. Her point is that no one has a right to use your body, even to save his own life, unless you give him that right. Such views are consistent with a position that insists that women are persons and have the same right to bodily integrity as men do. As persons they ought not to be used against their will for whatever purposes by others, even noble purposes such as the nurturing of children. Critics of this argument point out that it may apply at most to abortion in cases of rape, for in some other cases one might be said to implicitly consent to a pregnancy if one did what one knew might result in it. One response to this is that we do not always consider a person to have consented to chance consequences of their actions. Thomson argues that in the end it is the woman's right to choose whether to allow her body to be used or not—in the case of rape or in other cases of accidental pregnancy.

These rights-based and utilitarian arguments are examples of positions on abortion that do not depend on what we say about the moral status of the fetus, but other arguments hold this issue to be crucial. Some arguments for the moral permissibility of abortion as well as some against it rely in crucial ways on what is said about the fetus. We next consider some of these arguments.

ARGUMENTS THAT DEPEND ON THE MORAL STATUS OF THE FETUS

Abortion arguments that emphasize the moral status of the fetus are concerned with a broad range of ethical issues. They ask such questions as: Is the fetus a human being? A person? Alive? Let us for the moment focus not on these terms and what they might mean, but on an even more fundamental question, namely, what kind of value or moral status does the developing fetus have? Does it have a different moral status in various stages of development? If so, when does the status change, and why? (Further questions may include how to weigh its

value or rights in comparison to other values or the rights of others.) At bottom, these questions point toward the ontological and moral status of the fetus. **Ontology** means "theory of being," so the ontological question asks what sort of being the fetus is (whether it is merely a part of its mother or whether it is a unique and distinct being and so on). The ontological question is connected to the moral question of the moral status of the being. What we want to know is both what kind of a being the fetus is and what sort of value that kind of being has.

To begin to answer these questions, we will examine an initial approach to the value of the fetus and call it "Method I," to distinguish it from a broader approach we will term "Method II." Briefly put, Method I focuses on the characteristics of the fetus and asks when it has characteristics sufficiently significant to classify it as a person, who is worthy of our moral concern. Method II asks a more general question. It asks us to think about what kind of beings of any sort, human or nonhuman, have some special moral status or rights, such as a right to life.

Method I

In using this method, we focus on fetal development and ask three things about each potentially significant stage: (1) *What* is present? (2) *When* is this present (at what stage)? and (3) *Why* is this significant—in other words, why does this confer a special moral status, if it does? By "special moral status," we might mean various things. Among the most important would be a status such that the fetus would be thought to have something like a right to life. If this were the case, then abortion would become morally problematic.[47]

In the following sections, we will apply Method I to the various stages of fetal development and see what the arguments would look like. In each case, we will consider the arguments for the position and then some criticisms of these arguments.

Conception or Fertilization Conception, or the stage at which the sperm penetrates and fertilizes the ovum, is the time at which many opponents of abortion say that the fetus has full moral status. The reason usually given for this claim is that at conception the fetus receives its full genetic makeup, from the combination of sperm and egg.[48] The argument for taking this stage as morally significant appears to be based on an ontological argument that goes something like this: If the being that is born at the end of a pregnancy is a human being or person, and if there is no substantial change in its constitution from its initial form, then it is the same being all the way through the stages of development. Otherwise, we would be implying that different beings are succeeding one another during this process.

Critics of this position often point out that although fetal development is continuous, the bare genetic material present at conception is not enough to constitute a person at that point. In this early stage, the cells are *totipotent*, which means they can become skin cells or heart cells or many other types of cells.[49] There is no structure or differentiation at this point of development, nothing that resembles a person in this initial form. The fertilized egg is not even clearly an individual. Consider, for example, what happens in the case of identical twinning. Before implantation, identical twins are formed by the splitting of cells in the early embryo. Each resulting twin has the same genetic makeup. Now what are we to think of the original embryo? Suppose we assume that its conception created an individual being or person and we name him John. The twins that develop from the original embryo and are later born we name Jim and Joe. But what happened to John, if there was a John? Jim and Joe are two new individuals, genetically alike as twins, but also two different people. Is there a little of John in each of them? Or does the fact that there are two individuals after twinning mean that there was not any individual there before that time—that John never existed? Those who support conception as the crucial time at which we have a being with full moral status and rights must explain how there can be an individual at conception, at least in the case of identical twinning.

Brain Development Another possible stage at which a fetus might attain new moral status is that point at which the brain is sufficiently developed. The idea is reasonable given that the human brain is the locus of consciousness, language, and communication, and it is what makes us crucially different from other animals. Moreover, we now use the cessation of brain function as the determinant of death. Why should we not use the beginning of brain function as the beginning of an individual's life? We can detect brain activity between the sixth and eighth weeks of fetal development, which makes that point the significant time period for this argument.

Critics of the argument point out that brain activity develops gradually, and we cannot identify any single point during fetal development that presents an entirely unique or qualitative change in brain activity. Of course, this may be only a practical problem. We might be satisfied with an approximation rather than a determinate time. Other questions about the type of brain function also might be raised. At six to eight weeks, the brain is quite simple; only much later do those parts develop that are the basis of conscious function. Early in pregnancy, the brain is arguably not significantly different from other animal brains in structure or function. And as mentioned previously, most experts maintain that neuronal development is not advanced enough to speak of the fetus as feeling pain until somewhere between twenty and twenty-six weeks of development.

Quickening Usually, the pregnant woman can feel the fetus kick or move in approximately the fourth month of fetal development. This is what is meant by *quickening*. In prescientific eras, people believed that there was no fetal movement before this time—and if this were so, it would then constitute a persuasive reason to consider this stage as crucial. While contemporary science can detect movement before this stage, one might still focus on quickening as the start of self-initiated movement in the fetus, arising from a new level of brain development. This would constitute a better reason for identifying quickening as the beginning of a new moral status or right to life because the fetus would now be moving about on its own. As we saw previously, for much of Western history, civil and religious authorities prohibited abortion only after this stage.

Critics of this position may make the same argument about quickening as was made with regard to brain development, namely, that there is no dramatic break in the development of the fetus's ability to move. Moreover, they might also point out that other animals and even plants move on their own, and this does not give them special moral status or a right to life. Furthermore, those who argue for animal rights usually do so because of their *sentience*—that is, their ability to feel pleasure and pain—and not their ability to move.

Viability Viability is possible at approximately the twenty-fourth week of fetal development and means that the fetus is at least potentially capable of existing apart from the mother. Its organs and organ systems are sufficiently developed that it may have the capacity to function on its own. The last of these systems to be functionally complete is the respiratory system, which often causes fatal problems for fetuses delivered before six months. During previous stages of fetal development, the fetus "breathes" amniotic fluid. Before twenty-three or twenty-four weeks of gestation, "capillaries have not yet moved close enough to the air sacs to carry gases to and from the lung."[50] A lubricant, called surfactant, can be administered to assist the lungs' capacity to breathe air, but even then the chance of survival is slim.

As we can see, one practical problem with using viability as a moral criterion is its variability. When *Roe v. Wade* took effect, the point of viability for a premature infant was considered to be approximately twenty-six weeks; the estimation has since been shortened by a couple of weeks. At twenty-three or twenty-four weeks, a "micropreemie" weighs slightly less than a pound. Its viability is also a function of this weight and the mother's socioeconomic status; if she's poor, then the chances are that her nutrition is poor, which has negative effects on the fetus. The degree of prematurity at different stages of pregnancy also varies by sex and race: girls are approximately one week ahead of boys in development, and blacks are approximately one week ahead of whites.[51]

Why is the stage of viability singled out as the stage at which the fetus may take on a new moral status? Some answer that it is the potential for life independent of the mother that forms the basis of the new status. However, if the fetus were delivered at this stage and left on its own, no infant would be able to survive. Perhaps the notion of separate existence is a better basis for viability as a moral criterion. The idea would be that the fetus is more clearly distinct from the mother at this point in pregnancy. Or perhaps the notion of completeness is what is intended. Although the fetus is not fully formed at viability because much development takes place after birth, the argument might be made that the viable fetus is sufficiently complete, enabling us to think of it as an entirely new being.

Critics of the viability criterion may point again to the gradual nature of development and the seeming arbitrariness of picking out one stage of completeness as crucially different from the others. They also can point out that even if it were delivered at the point of viability, the fetus would still be dependent on others (and on an array of sophisticated medical technologies) for its survival. They can also question the whole notion of making moral status a function of independence. We are all dependent on one another, and those who are more independent (e.g., because they can live apart from others) have no greater value than those who are more dependent. Even someone dependent on medical machines is not for this reason less human, they might argue. Furthermore, a viable unborn fetus is still, in fact, dependent on its mother and does not have an existence separate from her. Birth, on these terms, would be a better stage to pick than viability, these critics might argue, if it is separateness and independence that are crucial.

Each point in fetal development may provide a reasonable basis for concluding something about the moral status of the fetus. However, as we can clearly see, none are problem free. In any case, the whole idea of grounding moral status and rights on the possession of certain characteristics also may be called into question. Instead, we may want to consider a more general approach to this problem by looking at a second method.

Method II

If the status of the fetus is crucial to arguments about the morality of abortion, then we may want to compare those arguments with more general arguments made with regard to beings other than human fetuses. Why, for example, do we believe that people generally have rights? Are we significantly different from other animals such that we have unique moral status simply because we are human beings? Or is the crucial determinant of that special moral status the ability to reason or imagine or use language or something else? If so, then if there are other intelligent beings in the universe, would they have the same moral status as we do, even if they are not members of our species? And what of human beings who do not have the capacity for reasoning and imagination and communication?

Take for example, the case of a newborn with anencephaly—that is, without a developed upper brain and thus no chance of consciousness or thought. In fact, such an infant does not usually live for long. But it is a human being biologically and not a member of some other species. Or take the case of a person in a permanent vegetative state. There is no doubt that the person is still human in the biological sense, but does this person lack human rights because he or she lacks some mental qualities that are the basis for rights?

Finally, perhaps it is not actual ability to think or communicate but the *potential* for the development of such characteristics that grounds special moral worth and rights. A normal fetus would have this potentiality whereas a two-year-old dog would not. Of course, this depends on the level or type of thinking that is seen to be crucial because dogs do have some type of mental capacity and some ability to communicate.

Distinguishing among the different criteria discussed above, we might arrive at something like the following positions. Each gives an answer to this question: What kind of beings have special moral status, which may include something like a right to life?[52]

Being Human   According to one point of view, it is being human that counts—being a member of the human species. Now, using this criterion, we might note that human fetuses are members of the human species and conclude that they have equal moral status with all other human beings. The argument for this position might include something about the moral advance we make when we recognize that all humans have equal moral worth. This has not always been the case, for example when children

or women were treated more like property than as human beings with equal and full moral status, or when African American slaves were deemed in the U.S. Constitution to be three-fifths of a person.

Critics of this position may point out that unfertilized eggs and sperm, not to mention organs such as gallbladders and appendices, are also biologically human. But no one argues that they deserve equal moral status with human persons. Questions can also be raised about why only members of the human species are included here. If some other species of being were sufficiently like us in the relevant respects, then should they not be considered to have the same worth as members of our own species? In considering this possibility, we may be better able to decide whether it is membership in a species or something else that grounds moral worth. (See further discussion in Chapter 17.)

Being Like Human Beings   Suppose that moral status (or personhood) depends on being a member of any species whose members have certain significant characteristics like human beings. But what characteristics are significant enough to ground high moral value and status, including rights? For example, consider the abilities to communicate, reason, and plan. Depending on how high a level of communicating, reasoning, and planning is required, perhaps other animals would qualify for the high moral status envisioned. Some chimpanzees and gorillas, for instance, appear to be able to communicate through sign language. If there are beings elsewhere in the universe who are members of a different species but who can communicate, reason, and plan, then according to this criterion they too would have the same moral worth as humans. If a lower level of ability were used, then members of other animal species would also qualify. It is important to aim for some kind of consistency here in thinking about the moral standing of fetuses and nonhuman animals. It is useful to clarify our thinking about animals by considering what we think about fetuses and vice versa. We might also want to test our intuitions by considering what we think about cognitively disabled humans or those with brain injuries. But those who want to emphasize species-belonging as the primary criterion for personhood will not be persuaded by arguments that focus on cognitive capacities.

These first two criteria are alike in that it is membership in a species that is the determinant of one's moral status. If any humans have this status, then they all do. If chimpanzees or Martians have this status, then all members of their species also have this status. It does not matter what the individual member of the species is like or what individual capacities she or he possesses. On the other hand, perhaps it is not what species you belong to but what individual characteristics you possess that forms the basis of the special moral status. If this were the case, then there would be at least three other possible positions about the basis of this moral status. These are as follows:

Potentiality *Potentiality* literally means "power." According to this criterion, all beings that have the power to develop certain key characteristics have full moral worth. Thus if a particular fetus had the potential for developing the requisite mental capacities, then this fetus would have full moral status. However, any fetus or other human being that does not have this potential (anencephalic infants or those in a permanent vegetative state, for example) does not have this status.

Some critics of abortion argue that abortion is wrong because it prevents a being (the fetus) from actualizing its potential. One version of this argument has been articulated by the philosopher Don Marquis. Marquis argues that it is seriously wrong to kill children and infants because we presume that children and infants have "futures of value."[53] According to Marquis, abortion is wrong for a similar reason, which is that it deprives the fetus from obtaining the future good it would have if it were left alone and allowed to be born. Marquis concludes, "The future of a standard fetus includes a set of experiences, projects, activities, and such which are identical with the futures of adult human beings and are identical with the futures of young children."[54] To kill the fetus is to deprive the fetus of those goods that it potentially could have enjoyed.

Yet how important is potential and what, in fact, is it? If a fetus is aborted and it is unaware that it even had the potential to develop into a person with a future of value, how has it been deprived of anything? Is it possible to deprive you of something if you are not aware or conscious? Potentiality appears to be vague and undefined. Suppose that one had the potential to become a famous star or hold high political office. Would one then deserve the same respect and powers of an actual star or legislator? Consider the following fictitious story described by philosopher Michael Tooley.[55] Suppose that we have a kitten that will grow into a mature cat if left alone. We also have a serum that if injected into the kitten will make it grow into a human being. Tooley suggests that there is no reason to allow the kitten to develop into a human being, since although it has the potential to develop into a human being (after being injected by this magic serum), it is not yet actually a human being. Tooley concludes, "If it is seriously wrong to kill something, the reason cannot be that the thing will later acquire properties that in themselves provide something with a right to life.... if it is wrong to kill a human fetus, it cannot be because of its potentialities."[56] Tooley's point is that those potentialities are merely that—potentialities—and so are not yet actual.

Taking Tooley's story a bit further, we might wonder if there is an obligation to inject the kitten with the serum since the serum possesses the potentiality to cause the kitten to develop into a human being. But the same argument applies. This points toward a consideration of contraception. Is contraception wrong because it somehow prevents the potentiality contained in the sperm and egg from actualizing itself? Marquis responds to this question by maintaining that there is a qualitative difference between contraception and abortion. Prior to fertilization, there is no actual thing—only a net of probabilities. We don't know, for example, which of the millions of sperm will fertilize the egg. And so no definite subject is deprived of its potentiality through contraception. But, according to Marquis, once the fetus is developing in the womb, there is a definite set of potentialities that now are worthy of moral consideration.

Actuality At the other end of the spectrum is the view according to which simple "potentiality" for developing certain characteristics counts for nothing (or at least does not give one the kind of moral status about which we are concerned). Only the actual possession of the requisite characteristics is sufficient for full moral status. Again, it makes a significant difference to one's position here whether the characteristics are high level or low level. For example, if a rather high level of reasoning is required before an individual has the requisite moral status, then newborns probably would not be included, as well as many others. The claim that even newborns lack the high-level capacities relevant to full moral status is defended by the philosopher Mary Anne Warren.[57] According to this view, although the fetus, newborn infant, and extremely young child are human beings biologically, they are not yet persons or beings with the requisite moral status. They are not yet members of the moral community. There may be good reasons to treat them well and with respect, but it is not because they are persons with rights.

Evolving Value   Finally, let us consider a position that is intermediate between the last two positions. Its underlying idea is that potential counts but not as much as actual possession of the significant characteristics. Furthermore, as the potential is gradually realized, the moral status of the being also grows. This position also could be described in terms of competing interests and claims. The stronger the claim, the more it should prevail.

In applying this criterion to fetal development, the conclusion would be that the early-term fetus has less moral value or moral status than the late-term fetus. Such an approach would parallel the idea, found in the law, that the state can regulate late-term abortions but not early-term abortion. Less of a claim or interest on the part of others is needed to override the early-term fetus's claim to consideration. Moderately serious interests of the pregnant woman or of society could override the interests or claims of the early-term fetus, but it would take more serious interests to override the claims of the late-term fetus. In the end, according to this view, when potentiality is sufficiently actualized, the fetus or infant has as much right as any other person.

We might note a variant view held by some feminists. Most feminists support a woman's legal right to abortion, but not all are happy with the rationale for it provided in *Roe v. Wade*.[58] For example, some worry that the "right to privacy" could be interpreted in ways that are detrimental to women. If this right is taken to imply that everything done in the privacy of one's home is out of the law's reach, then this might seem to suggest that the subordination or abuse of women and children is merely "domestic" and not a matter of public concern.

Some feminists also have misgivings about denying the moral status of the fetus, viewing the focus on moral status and individual rights as the product of a male-dominant worldview. Such a worldview is taken to approach individuals as distinct atomic beings who are separated from one another and whose conflicts are best described as conflicts of rights. Feminists such as Catharine A. MacKinnon point out that, from the standpoint of women, things may be more complicated:

> So long as it gestates in utero, the fetus is defined by its relation to the pregnant woman. More than a body part but less than a person, where it is, is largely what it is. From the standpoint of the pregnant woman, it is both me and not me. It "is" the pregnant woman in the sense that it is in her and of her and is hers more than anyone's. It "is not" her in the sense that she is not all that is there. In a legal system that views the individual as a unitary self, and that self as a bundle of rights, it is no wonder that the pregnant woman has eluded legal grasp, and her fetus with her.[59]

This approach recognizes that abortion is morally problematic precisely because of the ontological and moral question of motherhood—which is a circumstance in which one being gives birth to another. According to this approach, the loss of an early form of human life is a significant loss which is indicated by the seriousness with which most women treat miscarriages. However, this is not to imply that the fetus has full moral status and rights.

Another approach along these lines is associated with the work of philosopher Rosalind Hursthouse, who uses **virtue ethics** to consider the topic of abortion. Hursthouse is critical of those who have abortions for frivolous reasons, but she argues that there may be a number of virtuous reasons that a woman could choose to have an abortion.[60] One reason might be that the mother is concerned for the well-being of her other children when an unexpected pregnancy occurs. Or perhaps a mother wants to prevent possible suffering for a fetus that would suffer from severe disability.

If the fetus does not have the requisite moral status, then abortion is probably morally permissible. If it is considered to be a person, then abortion is morally problematic. If the fetus is said to have a somewhat in-between status, then the conclusion about abortion may be mixed or vary depending on stages of development or other factors. Again, these are positions that put the whole weight of the moral judgment about abortion on what status the fetus does or does not have.

As the utilitarian and rights-based arguments exemplified, however, there are other considerations about what counts in thinking about the morality of abortion. We might be concerned, for example, as Hursthouse is, about whether a mother aborts for serious reasons or whether she does so for frivolous reasons. Along these lines, some will argue that abortion should not be used as birth control. But such a claim holds weight only if we believe that there is something wrong with abortion to begin with, perhaps because of a claim about the moral status of the fetus. Finally, remember that not everything that we consider immoral can (or should) be made illegal. Thus even if abortion were in some case thought to be immoral, one would need to give further reasons about the purpose of law to conclude that it also ought to be illegal. At the same time, we must ask if the only reason to make something illegal is if it is immoral. There may be cases when we want to permit people the liberty to choose for themselves about morally controversial issues. This seems to be the status quo for the moment in the United States, where even some of those who think that abortion is morally wrong agree that women should be permitted to make decisions about abortion based upon their own conception of morality. This conclusion points toward a broader conversation about the importance of liberty, tolerance, and individual conscience.

NOTES

1. See http://firstread.nbcnews.
   com/_news/2013/01/21/16626932-nbcwsj-poll-majority-for-first-time-want-abortion-to-be-legal?lite

2. "Arkansas Adopts a Ban on Abortions after 12 Weeks," *New York Times*, March 6, 2013.

3. "Bill in North Dakota Bans Abortion after Heartbeat Is Found," *New York Times*, March 15, 2013.

4. ND 4009, 2013–2014, 63rd Legislative Assembly, North Dakota Senate Concurrent Resolution 4009, http://legiscan.com/ND/bill/4009/2013

5. In fact, the National Cancer Institute, in a 2003 study, found no increased risk of breast cancer associated with abortion. Other studies note that "fewer than 0.3% of patients experience a complication serious enough to require hospitalization." Abortion, rather, is said to be "one of the most common surgical procedures" and especially in the first trimester is "extremely safe." (*Time*, February 26, 2007, 28).

6. David Barstow, "An Abortion Battle, Fought to the Death," *New York Times*, July 25, 2009, accessed April 23, 2013, http://www.nytimes.com/2009/07/26/us/26tiller.html?pagewanted=all&_r=0

7. Based on a report in the *New York Times*, March 7, 1993, B3, and March 11, 1993, A1. Also see Jennifer Gonnerman, "The Terrorist Campaign against Abortion," *Village Voice*, November 3–9, 1998, www.villagevoice.com/features/9845/abortion.shtml

8. Bonnie Steinbock, *Life Before Birth: The Moral and Legal Status of Embryos and Fetuses, Second Edition* (Oxford: Oxford University Press, 2011), 46–50. Also see American Congress of Obstetricians and Gynecologists, *ACOG Statement on HR 3803* (June 18, 2012), accessed April 23, 2013, http://www.acog.org/∼/media/Departments/Government%20Relations%20and%20Outreach/20120618DCAborStmnt.pdf?dmc=1&ts=20120915T2120559712

9. Joyce Salisbury, *Women in the Ancient World* (Santa Barbara, CA: ABC-CLIO, 2001), 1.

10. Plato, "Theatetus," 149d and Plato, "Republic," 461c both in *Plato: Collected Dialogues*, ed. Edith Hamilton and Huntington Cairns (Princeton: Bollingen, 1961).

11. Hippocrates, "The Oath" (Internet Classics Archive: http://classics.mit.edu//Hippocrates/hippooath.html)

12. Salisbury, *Women in the Ancient World*, 2.

13. "Facts about Mifepristone (RU-486)," National Abortion Federation, accessed April 23, 2013, http://www.prochoice.org/about_abortion/facts/facts_mifepristone.html

14. "Facts on Induced Abortion in the United States," Guttmacher Institute, August 2011, accessed February 15, 2013, http://www.guttmacher.org/pubs/fb_induced_abortion.html

15. "Abortion and Women of Color: The Bigger Picture," *Guttmacher Policy Review* 11, no. 3 (Summer 2008), accessed April 23, 2013, http://www.guttmacher.org/pubs/gpr/11/3/gpr110302.html

16. *New York Times*, May 5, 2006, A19.

17. Nicholas D. Kristof, "Beyond Pelvic Politics," *New York Times*, February 11, 2012, accessed April 23, 2013, http://www.nytimes.com/2012/02/12/opinion/sunday/kristof-beyond-pelvic-politics.html

18. "Facts on Induced Abortion in the United States," Guttmacher Institute, http://www.guttmacher.org/pubs/fb_induced_abortion.html

19. "Reasons U.S. Women Have Abortions: Quantitative and Qualitative Perspectives," *Perspectives on Sexual and Reproductive Health* 37: 3 (September 2005), accessed July 27, 2013, http://www.guttmacher.org/pubs/journals/3711005.pdf

20. Guttmacher Institute, *Abortion Worldwide: A Decade of Progress* (2009), accessed February 15, 2013, http://www.guttmacher.org/pubs/Abortion-Worldwide.pdf

21. Sushelela Singh et al., *Abortion Worldwide: A Decade of Uneven Progress* (New York: Guttmacher Institute, 2009), accessed July 27, 2013, http://www.guttmacher.org/pubs/Abortion-Worldwide.pdf

22. "Expanding Access to Medical Abortion in Developing Countries," World Health Organization, accessed February 15, 2013, http://www.who.int/reproductivehealth/topics/unsafe_abortion/en/index.html; also see http://www.who.int/reproductivehealth/topics/unsafe_abortion/magnitude/en/index.html

23. Frank Langfitt, "After a Forced Abortion, a Roaring Debate in China," NPR's *All Things Considered*, July 5, 2012, accessed February 15, 2013, http://www.npr.org/2012/07/05/156211106/after-a-forced-abortion-a-roaring-debate-in-china

24. Wei Xing Zhu, Li Lu, and Therese Hesketh, "China's Excess Males, Sex Selective Abortion, and One Child Policy: Analysis of Data from 2005 National Intercensus Survey," *British Medical Journal* (April 9, 2009): 388, accessed February 15, 2013, http://dx.doi.org/10.1136/bmj.b1211

25. Stanley K. Henshaw, Sushelela Singh, and Taylor Haas, "Recent Trends in Abortion Rates Worldwide," *Family Planning Perspectives* 25, no. 1 (March 1999).

26. Sneha Barol, "A Problem-and-Solution Mismatch: Son Preference and Sex-Selective Abortion Bans," *Guttmacher Policy Review* 15, no. 2 (Spring 2012), accessed February 15, 2013, http://www.guttmacher.org/pubs/gpr/15/2/gpr150218.html

27. Rowena Mason, "The Abortion of Unwanted Girls Taking Place in the UK," *Telegraph*, January 10, 2013, accessed February 15, 2013, http://www.telegraph.co.uk/news/uknews/crime/9794577/The-abortion-of-unwanted-girls-taking-place-in-the-UK.html

28. Ed O'Keefe, "Bill Banning 'Sex-Selective Abortions' Fails in the House," *Washington Post*, May 31, 2012, accessed February 15, 2013, http://www.washingtonpost.com/blogs/2chambers/post/bill-banning-sex-selective-abortions-fails-in-the-house/2012/05/31/gJQAgCYn4U_blog.html

29. See John Noonan, *The Morality of Abortion* (Cambridge, MA: Harvard University Press, 1970), 18ff.

30. Associate Justice Harry A. Blackmun, majority opinion in *Roe v. Wade*, 410 U.S. 113 (1973), footnote 22.

31. Dorothy E. McBride, *Abortion in the United States: A Reference Book* (Santa Barbara, CA: ABC-CLIO, 2008), 7.

32. "Historical Attitudes to Abortion," BBC Ethics Guide, accessed April 4, 2013, http://www.bbc.co.uk/ethics/abortion/legal/history_1.shtml

33. Associate Justice Harry A. Blackmun, majority opinion in *Roe v. Wade*, 410 U.S. 113 (1973).

34. See comments about this interpretation in Ronald Dworkin, "Feminists and Abortion," *New York Review of Books*, no. 11 (June 10, 1993): 27–29.

35. Blackmun, *Roe v. Wade*.

36. Justices O'Connor, Kennedy, and Souter, majority opinion in Planned Parenthood of Southeastern *Pennsylvania v. Casey*, 505 U.S. 833 (1992).

37. *Gonzalez v. Carhart*, 550 U.S. 124 (2007).

38. David Stout, "Supreme Court Upholds Ban on Abortion Procedure," *New York Times*, April 18, 2007, http://www.nytimes.com/2007/04/18/us/18cnd-scotus.html?_r=0

39. *Planned Parenthood Assn. v. Ashcroft*, 462 U.S. 476 (1983).

40. *New York Times*, April 14, 2010, A15.

41. Kathy Lohr, "Virginia Governor Backs Down from Ultrasound Bill," NPR's *All Things Considered*, February 23, 2012, accessed April 4, 2013, http://www.npr.org/2012/02/23/147297375/virginia-governor-backs-down-from-ultrasound-bill

42. "Ongoing Study Shows Ultrasounds Do Not Have Direct Impact on Abortion Decision," *American Independent*, February 6, 2012, accessed March 8, 2013, http://american-independent.com/210411/ongoing-study-shows-ultrasounds-do-not-have-direct-impact-on-abortion-decision

43. WIS. STAT. § 48.193 (2003); see Erin N. Linder, "Punishing Prenatal Alcohol Abuse: The Problems Inherent in Utilizing Civil Commitment to Address Addiction," *University of Illinois Law Review* 2005, no. 3.

44. "Four Years Later, Slain Abortion Doctor's Aide Steps into the Void," *New York Times*, February 13, 2013, accessed February 15, 2013, http://www.nytimes.com/2013/02/14/us/kansas-abortion-practice-set-to-replace-tiller-clinic.html

45. "What Choice?" *Time*, January 14, 2013.

46. Judith Jarvis Thomson, "A Defense of Abortion," *Philosophy and Public Affairs* 1, no. 1 (Fall 1971): 47–66.

47. Note that if the fetus had no right to life, then this would not automatically make abortion problem free. See the comments in the last paragraph under "Method II."

48. In the prescientific era, many people held that the egg provided the entire substance and the sperm only gave it a charge or impetus to grow, or that the sperm was "the little man" and only needed a place to grow and obtain nourishment, which the egg provided! We now know about the contribution of both sperm and ovum to the zygote.

49. This issue has recently arisen with developments in stem cell research and cloning.

50. Sheryl Gay Stolberg, "Definition of Fetal Viability Is Focus of Debate in Senate," *New York Times*, May 15, 1997, A13.

51. Ibid.

52. Compare this discussion with similar discussions in Chapters and on the environment and animal rights. In particular, note the possible distinction between having moral value and having rights.

53. Don Marquis, "Why Abortion Is Immoral," *Journal of Philosophy* 86, no. 4 (1989):191.

54. Marquis, "Why Abortion Is Immoral," 192.

55. This is taken from Michael Tooley's "Abortion and Infanticide," *Philosophy and Public Affairs* 2, no. 1 (1972):37–65.

56. Tooley, "Abortion and Infanticide," 62.

57. Mary Anne Warren in "On the Moral and Legal Status of Abortion," *Monist* 57, no. 1 (January 1973):43–61.

58. See the summary of these views in Dworkin, "Feminists and Abortion," op. cit.

59. Catharine A. MacKinnon, *Women's Lives—Men's Laws* (Cambridge, MA: Harvard University Press, 2005), 140.

60. See Rosalind Hursthouse, "Virtue Theory and Abortion," *Philosophy and Public Affairs* 20:3 (1991).

1. Outline the various stages of fetal development.
2. Explain the conclusions of *Roe v. Wade* and *Planned Parenthood v. Casey*.
3. Give a utilitarian argument for abortion. Give one against abortion. Are these act or rule utilitarian arguments? Explain.
4. Describe how Thomson uses the violinist analogy to make an argument about the moral permissibility of abortion.
5. Use Method I to make one argument for and one against abortion.
6. Which of the positions under Method II does each of the following statements exemplify?
   a. Because this fetus has all the potential to develop the abilities of a person, it has all the rights of a person.

b. Only when a being can think and communicate does it have full moral status. Because a fetus does not have these abilities, it has neither moral rights nor claims.
c. If a fetus is a human being, then it has full moral status and rights.
d. Its capacity to feel pain gives a being full moral status. The fetus has this capacity beginning in the fifth or sixth month, and so abortion is not morally justifiable beyond that stage.
e. Early-term fetuses do not have as much moral significance as later-term fetuses because their potential is not as fully realized as it is later.

1. **Abortion for Sex Selection.** The sex of a child can now be determined before birth. In the waiting room of a local women's clinic, June has started a conversation with another woman, Ann. She finds out that each woman is there for an amniocentesis to determine the sex of her fetus. June reveals that she wants to know the sex because her husband and his family really want a boy. Because they plan to have only one child, they plan to end this pregnancy if it is a girl and try again. Ann tells her that her reason is different. She is a genetic carrier of a particular kind of muscular dystrophy. Duchenne muscular dystrophy is a sex-linked disease that is inherited through the mother. Only males develop the disease, and each male child has a 50 percent chance of having it. The disease causes muscle weakness and often some mental retardation. It also causes death through respiratory failure, usually in early adulthood. Ann does not want to risk having such a child, and this abnormality cannot yet be determined through prenatal testing. Thus if the prenatal diagnosis reveals that her fetus is male, she plans to end this pregnancy.

   Is Ann justified in her plan to abort a male fetus? Is June justified? Should there be laws regulating sex-selective abortion?

2. **Father's Consent to Abortion.** Jim and Sue have been planning to have a child for two years.

Finally, she becomes pregnant. However, their marriage has been a rough one, and by the time she is in her third month of pregnancy they have decided to divorce. At this point, both parents are ambivalent about the pregnancy. They had both wanted the child, but now things are different. Sue finally decides that she does not want to raise a child alone and does not want to raise Jim's child. She wants to get on with her life. However, Jim has long wanted a child, and he argues that the developing fetus is partly his own because he has provided half of its genetic makeup. He does not want Sue to end the pregnancy. He wants to keep and raise the child.

   Do you think that Jim has any moral rights in this case or should the decision be strictly Sue's? Why or why not?

3. **Parental Consent to Abortion.** Judy is a high school sophomore and fifteen years old. She recently became sexually active with her boyfriend. She does not want to tell him that she is now pregnant, and she does not feel that she can talk to her parents. They have been quite strict with her and would condemn her recent behavior. They also oppose abortion. Judy would like simply to end this pregnancy and start over with her life. However, minors in her state must get parental consent for an abortion; it is viewed as a medical procedure like any

other, and parents must consent to other medical procedures for their children.

What should Judy do? Do you agree that states should require parental consent for abortion for minors? Why or why not?

4. **Pregnant Woman Detained.** In 1995, a woman who was pregnant and refused to discontinue her use of cocaine was reported by her obstetrician to child-abuse authorities.[1] They obtained an order from the juvenile court to take custody of the unborn child, which in this case involved detaining the mother against her will. The court maintained that in order to protect the fetus, it had to detain the mother. The mother gave birth while in a drug treatment center. She sued the state for detaining her illegally. The case was settled after the child was born, with the court finding that the state acted wrongly in taking protective custody of the fetus while it was still in the womb. As a result of these sorts of cases, state legislatures have passed laws, such as the Wisconsin law mentioned above, that define fetuses more clearly as children deserving protection.[2]

If the fetus is regarded as a child who is being abused, then is it reasonable, in your view, to detain the mother? If the fetus is thus viewed as a person, should it have access to other rights and privileges? Would it also be reasonable for a pregnant woman to be able to use a carpool lane by counting her fetus as a second person in the car? If a pregnant woman is killed, resulting in the death of the fetus, does that count as one murder or two?

NOTES

12 Sexual Morality

Learning Outcomes

After reading this chapter, you should be able to:

- Understand the complexity of categorizing and evaluating sexual activity.
- Summarize disputes about gay marriage and other topics in sexual ethics.
- Explain key cases and examples, including recent developments in sexual ethics.
- Explain the importance of autonomy and consent in thinking about the morality of rape and sexual assault.

- Evaluate moral arguments about sexual ethics including both consequentialist and non-consequentialist arguments.
- Understand and criticize natural law approaches to sexual morality.
- Defend your own ideas about sexual ethics.

Eyecandy Images/Thinkstock

In 2004, Kris Perry and Sandy Stier were married in the city of San Francisco, where homosexual marriages were legal at that time. Six months later, the California Supreme Court invalidated their marriage and similar marriages. Less than four years later, in May of 2008, the state Supreme Court overturned California's ban on gay marriage. The court held that restrictions on marriage were unconstitutional, arguing that "an individual's sexual orientation—like a person's race or gender—does not constitute a legitimate basis upon which to deny or withhold legal rights."[1] But by November of 2008, the voters of California approved a referendum (Proposition 8) banning gay marriage and defining marriage as the union of a man and a woman. Kris Perry and Sandy Stier then sued the state of California. A gay couple from Los Angeles, Paul Katami, and Jeffrey Zarrillo, also joined the lawsuit. The lawsuit claimed that the Fourteenth Amendment right to equal protection under the law prohibits the state of California from defining marriage as the union of a man and a woman. Their lawsuit, which became known as *Hollingsworth v. Perry*, made it to the U.S. Supreme Court in the spring of 2013. In June of 2013, the Court issued a ruling that opened the door to legal homosexual marriages in California. Kris and Sandy were finally married on June 28, 2013.

Through this tumultuous period, Kris Perry and Sandy Stier have raised four boys—two from Stier's previous heterosexual marriage and two more of their own.[2] According to Perry, the couple was looking forward to being done with the legal challenge. She said that they had been waiting "a very long time to be married and to celebrate that with our children and our parents."[3] One of their sons, Spencer Perry, explained, "When Proposition 8 doesn't allow parents like mine to marry, it says that our family, that my brothers, that my mothers, shouldn't belong, that we don't get to be the same as my friends' families."[4]

In his second inaugural speech in 2012, President Barack Obama said that the journey toward liberty and equality would not be complete "until our gay brothers and sisters are treated like anyone else under the law." Under President Obama, homosexuals have gained more equality. As of 2011, for example, homosexuals have been allowed to openly serve in the military; in 2013, the Pentagon extended medical and other benefits to the partners of gay soldiers.[5] Obama continued, in his inaugural address, to explain the importance of equality: "for if we are truly created equal, then surely the love we commit to one another must be equal as well." Weeks later, Obama's legal team argued in defense of gay marriage in a legal brief delivered to the U.S. Supreme Court as it considered gay marriage in *Hollingsworth v. Perry*.

As of October of 2013, gay marriage was legal in fourteen states: California, Connecticut, Delaware, Iowa, Maine, Maryland, Massachusetts, Minnesota, New Hampshire, New Jersey, New York, Rhode Island, Vermont, and Washington (as well as in the District of Columbia). The evolution of Americans' perspectives on same-sex marriage has also helped produce a constitutional challenge to the federal Defense of Marriage Act, which was passed in 1996 and signed into law by President Bill Clinton. The Supreme Court heard the challenge to the Defense of Marriage Act at the same time that it considered *Hollingsworth v. Perry*. The Act is intended to "define and protect the institution of marriage" and defines marriage as follows: "The word 'marriage' means only a legal union between one man and one woman as husband and wife, and the word 'spouse' refers only to a person of the opposite sex who is a husband or a wife."[6] The law stipulates that states do not have to recognize marriages between homosexual couples or provide these couples with the federal benefits accorded to couples in heterosexual marriages. There are some 1,100 benefits that do not extend to same-sex partners, including eligibility to file joint income taxes, to inherit Social Security benefits, and to defer estate taxes by passing property on to surviving spouses.[7] In June 2013, the Supreme Court ruled, in *United States v. Windsor*, that part of the Defense of Marriage Act was unconstitutional. The Court concluded, "DOMA instructs all federal officials, and indeed all persons with whom same-sex couples interact, including their own children, that their marriage is less worthy than the marriages of others." The Court ruled that by "treating those persons as living in marriages less respected than others" the law violated citizens due process rights.[8]

While the United States has been debating the issue, other countries have legalized gay marriage: the Netherlands, Belgium, Canada, Spain, South Africa, Norway, Sweden, Argentina, Iceland, and Portugal. In late 2012, the Mexican Supreme Court struck down a law that banned same-sex marriage in the state of Oaxaca. And France legalized gay marriage in April 2013. While the legal tides appear to be rapidly turning in favor of gay marriage in some parts of the world, homosexuality and legal recognition of homosexual relationships are fiercely contested in the United States and elsewhere. It has only been since 2003 that the Supreme Court (in its decision in *Lawrence v. Texas*) declared that laws against sodomy are unconstitutional—*sodomy* is usually taken to include any form of homosexual sex, as well as oral and anal sex between heterosexual couples.

Some may think that the gay marriage issue is merely a matter of civil rights, more properly discussed in the chapter that follows on equality and discrimination. They might point out that interracial marriage was once viewed as a "moral" issue while today it is viewed almost exclusively as a question of civil rights. But underlying many of the arguments against gay marriage is a moral claim about the proper form of sexual relationships. Supreme Court Justice Antonin Scalia explained this in his dissent in the *Lawrence v. Texas* decision: "Many Americans do not want persons who openly engage in homosexual conduct as partners in their business, as scoutmasters for their children, as teachers in their children's schools, or as boarders in their home. They view this as protecting themselves and their families from a lifestyle that they believe to be immoral and destructive."[9] The claim that homosexuality is immoral and destructive points beyond the question of civil rights toward a deeper moral analysis.

We should recall that the legal questions and moral questions are different—as we noted in Chapter 11's discussion of abortion. One could be morally opposed to a given behavior and still think that there should be a legal right for individuals to decide to engage in that behavior. Nonetheless, there is an organized movement that opposes the legalization of gay marriage, often spearheaded by conservative religious groups. The Mormon Church, for example, worked hard to pass Proposition 8, the California referendum that banned gay marriage—although as a result of backlash against its position on gay marriage, the Church has apparently softened its efforts to oppose same-sex unions.[10] Arguments against gay marriage made by these groups are often grounded in claims about sexual ethics that appeal to religious and natural law arguments about sex and marriage. The archbishop of San Francisco, Salvatore Cordileone (who is also chairman of the U.S. Conference of Catholic Bishops Subcommittee for the Promotion and Defense of Marriage), made this clear in his response to the legalization of gay marriage in Rhode Island in 2013. Archbishop Cordileone said, "The meaning of marriage cannot be redefined, because its meaning lies in our very nature. Therefore, regardless of what law is enacted, marriage remains the union of one man and one woman—by the very design of nature, it cannot be otherwise."[11]

The enduring stigma of homosexuality means that it is difficult to obtain reliable numbers on the percentage of the population that is homosexual. A recent Centers for Disease Control and Prevention study, for example, found that among adult women, 3.9 percent identify as bisexual, and 1.2 percent identify as homosexual; among men, 1.2 percent identify as bisexual, and 1.8 percent identify as homosexual.[12] However, such survey data are often contested and variable, in part due to respondents' reluctance to self-identify as homosexual. The numbers of those who self-identify as homosexual may vary from state to state; and differences in homosexual demographics and self-identification depend upon location—whether in small rural towns or in big cities. That homosexuals are reluctant to self-identify should not be surprising since they are still subject to high rates of bullying, harassment, and physical assault. As we'll discuss in more detail in the next chapter,

the FBI reports that **hate crimes** against homosexuals account for more than 20 percent of reported hate crimes (in 2011 that included more than 1,500 hate crimes based upon sexual orientation).[13]

This brief discussion of homosexuality and gay marriage shows us that sexual relationships are the subject of intense moral and political scrutiny.

CURRENT ISSUES

The issue of homosexuality and gay marriage is one example of the range of ethical issues that can be raised with regard to sexuality and family relationships. Most would agree that rape is wrong—because it violates the autonomy of the victim. But what about sexual acts that are freely consented to: masturbation, anal or oral sex, sex with multiple partners, and so on—are those actions somehow intrinsically wrong, or should consenting adults be permitted to do whatever they want with their own bodies? A related question is whether the law should regulate these practices, or whether the law should leave individuals alone to pursue their own sexual gratification and sexual relationships.

It is clear that there are a variety of ways that human beings engage in sexual activity. Recent CDC data on sexuality offer some striking details about sexuality in the United States.[14] For example, the average age at which boys and girls first have intercourse is 17 years old. More than 80 percent of adults report that they have engaged in oral sex. With regard to same-sex sexual activity, the percentage of males between 15 and 44 who have had oral or anal sex with another male is 5.2 percent. Females in the same age range report same-sex experiences at a rate of 12.5 percent.[15]

Other interesting conclusions from the CDC include the following:

> 7.6 percent of females 18–24 years of age who have had sex before age 20 report that their first intercourse was not voluntary

> 2.9 percent of all women 15–44 years of age have had four or more male partners in the past 12 months

> 6 percent of all men 15–44 years of age have had four or more female partners in the past 12 months

> Median number of female sexual partners in lifetime, for men 25–44 years of age: 6.1
> Percent of men 15–44 years of age who have had 15 or more female sexual partners: 21.6
> Median number of male sexual partners in lifetime, for women 25–44 years of age: 3.6
> Percent of women 15–44 years of age who have had 15 or more male sexual partners: 9.0

All of this sexual activity is not without its risks. In the period from 2006 to 2010, 3.3 percent of people ages 15 to 44 reported receiving treatment for a sexually transmitted disease other than HIV within the past 12 months: 2.6 percent of men and 4.1 percent of women.[16] The Centers for Disease Control and Prevention concluded in its 2012 report on HIV surveillance, "HIV continues to have a devastating toll on Americans, particularly men who have sex with men (MSM) and racial/ethnic minorities."[17] While the population of men who have sex with men is likely well under 10 percent of the total male population, this population accounts for 62 percent of all HIV diagnoses. African Americans represent only 12 percent of the U.S. population, but 47 percent of HIV diagnoses occur among African Americans. "At the end of 2010, there were an estimated 872,990 persons in the U.S. living with diagnosed HIV infection."[18] HIV is also a problem globally. As of 2011, according to World Health Organization statistics, 34 million people worldwide are living with HIV: 30.7 million adults and 3.3 million children. Each year 2.5 million new people are infected with the disease. And 1.7 million people die from AIDS each year—including 230,000 children.[19]

Sexually transmitted diseases raise a number of ethical issues. Lying or concealing one's STD status from sexual partners is generally considered to be a violation of moral standards, although ethicists disagree about when in a romantic relationship this information must be disclosed. One could also argue that risky sexual behavior is not only dangerous for the individuals involved but also for society. From a utilitarian perspective that is concerned with public health—including the costs of sexually transmitted diseases—it is important to work to reduce the incidence of such diseases. One conservative strategy is

to minimize casual sexual encounters and encourage monogamous sex within the confines of marriage. A more liberal strategy is to find ways to increase usage of condoms, especially among sex workers, homosexual men, African Americans, and others who are at an increased risk of contracting and transmitting disease.

In addition to its impact on physical health, sexuality can also affect emotional and psychological health. A 2007 study that explored teens' post-sex emotions found that many first-time experiences resulted in guilt or feeling manipulated, with girls more often reporting this than boys. Of the teens who had engaged in oral sex, 41 percent "said they felt bad about themselves later" and "nearly 20 percent felt guilty, and 25 percent felt used," while the figures were 42 percent and 38 percent for sexual intercourse.[20] It's not just teens who report mixed feelings about sexual experiences and their outcomes. The CDC found that 13.8 percent of all pregnancies were "unwanted at the time of conception."[21] But the good news is that teen pregnancy rates have been declining in recent years. In 2011, teen birth rates fell to an historic low of only 31.3 per 1,000 women. That rate represents a 49 percent drop from the high teen birth rate of 61.8 per 1,000 in 1991.[22]

One solution to unwanted pregnancy and sexually transmitted disease is better sex education. But in the United States, sex education is a contested area. Some want to promote abstinence and discourage sexual activity among teenagers and outside of marriage. Others maintain that the key is to teach sexual health, including information about condoms—which prevent STDs—and other forms of birth control. Studies do not clearly indicate whether any single approach to sex education has any significant impact on the subsequent sexual behavior of students.[23] But some studies do indicate that comprehensive sex education may help reduce teen pregnancies without increasing levels of sexual intercourse or sexually transmitted disease.[24] Sexual education curricula pose ethical challenges. Proponents of comprehensive sex education want to empower students to make informed choices about sexuality, without imposing moral values on students. But proponents of abstinence-only sex education maintain that teenagers are too young to be engaging in sexual acts, which they believe should take place only within marriages. Defenders of abstinence-only sex education also worry that when sexual practices are discussed with children, this discussion can stimulate unhealthy interest in having sex. Opponents of abstinence-only sex education complain that abstinence programs sneak religious ideas about marriage and sexuality into the classroom, while proponents of abstinence maintain that their primary concern is student health.[25]

While teen pregnancy has declined, the overall rate of births outside of marriage is rising. More than half of births to women under age 30 occur outside of marriage.[26] In addition, the incidence of *cohabitation,* or living with one's partner before marriage, has increased dramatically in recent years, nearly tripling between 1990 and 2000.[27] As of May 2009, there were more than five million cohabiting couples in the United States. Further, "the majority of cohabitants either break up or marry within five years."[28] This rise in cohabitation comes at a time when Americans are delaying marriage until later in life. Those who marry after age twenty-five are less likely to divorce than those who marry in their teens. It is often assumed that cohabiting couples who marry are more likely to divorce than those who did not live together before marriage, and there is some evidence for this.[29] "Couples who live together before they get married are less likely to stay married," a recent study has found.[30] However, this may also be because of the type of people who cohabitate, being more liberal and less religious, for example. If they are engaged or committed or their relationship is based on love, then they are no less likely to later divorce.[31]

Almost everywhere in the world, different sexual standards apply to men and to women. In many traditional societies, women's sexuality is viewed as unclean or sinful and in need of control or suppression. In some Arab countries, women are not allowed to appear in public without special clothing to preserve their "modesty" or without the presence of a male relative. Many religious traditions, including Orthodox Judaism, prohibit men from coming into contact with women while they are menstruating and require rituals to "cleanse" women after menstruation.

A particularly extreme example of societal control of women's sexuality is that of **female genital mutilation** (FGM), or so-called female circumcision. Although many countries have outlawed it, the practice persists in more than twenty-eight African countries and several countries in Asia and the Middle East, as well as some immigrant communities in the West.[32] According to the World Health Organization, 140 million girls and women are living with the consequences of FGM, while more than three million girls have this done to them every year (that's more than eight thousand girls per day).[33] FGM can involve different degrees of severity—from excision of the skin surrounding the clitoris, to removal of all or part of the clitoris and some of the surrounding tissues, to stitching the labia together so that only a small opening remains. Among the cultural and parental reasons given for these practices are to enable families to exercise control over reproduction, to keep women virgins until marriage, and to reduce or eliminate female sexual pleasure.[34] The procedure is usually done without even a local anesthetic and often performed with unclean and crude instruments. If the labia have been stitched together, a reverse cutting is frequently necessary before intercourse can take place—this subsequent procedure can also be quite painful. In addition, FGM can cause problems in childbirth.[35] In fact, the more extensive forms of this procedure raise "by more than 50 percent the likelihood that the woman or her baby will die."[36] The World Health Organization explains, "the FGM procedure that seals or narrows a vaginal opening needs to be cut open later to allow for sexual intercourse and childbirth. Sometimes it is stitched again several times, including after childbirth, hence the woman goes through repeated opening and closing procedures, further increasing both immediate and long-term risks."[37]

The 1996 U.S. Federal Criminalization of Female Genital Mutilation Act prohibited this practice for women under eighteen years of age. Human rights groups have lobbied internationally for an end to this practice, which in some countries is "routinely forced on girls as young as four or five years old, and ... sustained through social coercion."[38] In Africa, between 60 and 90 percent of all women and girls in certain countries undergo the procedure, even in countries where it is illegal. Many Muslim critics argue that there is no basis for this practice in the Qur'an; in fact, they note that this holy book commands parents to protect their children from harm and regards people's anatomy as part of God's creation.[39] Despite the fact that FGM is already illegal in this country, the practice persists in some immigrant communities, and parents have been known to take their daughters to other countries for this procedure. In early 2013, President Obama signed the Transport for Female Genital Mutilation Act, which amended the 1996 law by making it a crime to take girls from the United States to foreign countries for the purpose of mutilating their genitals. This followed closely a United Nations General Assembly resolution that called for a global ban against the practice of FGM. According to the UN Women website, "the FGM resolution urges countries to condemn all harmful practices that affect women and girls, in particular female genital mutilations, and to take all necessary measures, including enforcing legislation, awareness-raising and allocating sufficient resources to protect women and girls from this form of violence."[40]

A central idea in the move to eliminate female genital mutilation is the idea that women as well as men have a right to benefit from sexual pleasure and that individuals have a right to control their own anatomy. According to the World Health Organization, one significant motivation behind the practice appears to be the desire to control female sexuality. One common theme in cultures that practice FGM is an effort to minimize women's sexual urges, which would "thereby increase their ability to remain a virgin prior to marriage, and to remain faithful and not too demanding within marriage."[41] The issue of controlling female sexuality is obviously connected to feminist concerns (as discussed in Chapter 9).

Attempts to exercise control over female sexuality is also closely connected to the problem of rape. At one point, rape was rationalized as being the result of uncontrollable male lust. But starting in the 1970s, feminists such as Susan Brownmiller began pushing society to recognize that rape is "not a crime of irrational, impulsive, uncontrollable lust, but is a deliberate, hostile, violent act of degradation and possession on the part of a would-be conqueror."[42] While it is important to recognize that rape is a crime of violence and domination, it also has an unmistakably sexual element. Reliable statistics on the incidence of rape are difficult to establish. One reason is underreporting. Another reason is the incidence of acquaintance rape. Two-thirds of rapes are committed by someone known to the victim.[43] One form of this is so-called "date rape," a form of sexual assault that is particularly prevalent among young adults of college age. While there are problems with regard to the way that data on rape and sexual assault are collected, one estimate, from the Rape, Abuse & Incest National Network, is that every two minutes someone in the United States is sexually assaulted. In raw numbers, that means that more than two hundred thousand people are sexually assaulted in the United States every year. These numbers remain high despite the fact that sexual assault has fallen by more than 60 percent in recent years.[44] Rape is clearly wrong according to many different ethical standards. In most places it is illegal. But in many parts of the world, women are still blamed (to varying degrees) for being victims of rape. As we mentioned in our discussion of honor crimes in Chapter 9, in some cultures rape victims are forced to marry their rapists or are even killed by family members for bringing shame on the family.

Rape can happen within the family. In most cases, incest is a form of rape because it involves minors who cannot consent to sexual acts. And since the 1970s, European countries and individual states in the United States have recognized that women can be raped by their husbands. It wasn't until 1993 that all states in the United States criminalized spousal rape.[45] But married women in other parts of the world are not protected by marital rape laws. There is no law against raping a wife in India, China, Afghanistan, Pakistan, or Saudi Arabia.[46]

Another issue of profound moral concern is **sex trafficking**, which generally involves women and girls being coerced into the sex trade both in the United States and abroad. Sex trafficking is a subset of human trafficking, which involves the transport and captivity of individuals across international borders for a variety of illegal purposes. According to a 2012 report by the United Nations Office on Drugs and Crime, "trafficking for the purpose of sexual exploitation accounts for 58 percent of all trafficking cases detected globally."[47] The FBI states that, "human sex trafficking is the most common form of modern-day slavery. Estimates place the number of domestic and international victims in the millions, mostly females and children enslaved in the commercial sex industry for little or no money."[48] The report continues,

> The average age at which girls first become victims of prostitution is 12 to 14. It is not only the girls on the streets who are affected; boys and transgender youth enter into prostitution between the ages of 11 and 13 on average.… These women and young girls are sold to traffickers, locked up in rooms or brothels for weeks or months, drugged, terrorized, and raped repeatedly. These continual abuses make it easier for the traffickers to control their victims. The captives are so afraid and intimidated that they rarely speak out against their traffickers, even when faced with an opportunity to escape.

The bleak and brutal reality of the sex trade throws a moral wrench in the arguments of those who would defend consensual prostitution as a victimless crime. (It also raises questions about pornography, some of which clearly involves victims of sex trafficking.) It might be that some sex transactions are consensual and mutually beneficial both for the prostitute and for the customer. But in many cases, there is coercion and exploitation. One proposal to solve this problem is to legalize prostitution to encourage healthy and noncoercive sexual exchanges. In the state of Nevada, some counties allow highly regulated brothels to operate legally. And in some countries, such as the Netherlands, prostitution is itself legal. In other countries, such as Thailand and Belgium, prostitution is nominally illegal—but in practice it is tolerated. It remains an open question whether legal sex trades prevent or reduce sex crimes and abuse.

Sex trafficking, rape, and FGM clearly raise serious moral issues about human autonomy, agency, and rights to bodily integrity. Some ethicists would argue that it is these ethical standards that should be the focus of what we call "sexual morality"—rather than any judgments we make about the sexual preferences and practices between consenting adults. They would further argue that we make too much of the morality of sexual behavior and often talk about it as the only moral issue. When we hear expressions such as "Doesn't he have any morals?" or "She has loose morals," the speakers are often referring to the person's sexual morals. But many other moral issues are arguably more important than sexual behavior between consenting adults.

Some people may even be inclined to say that one's sexual behavior is not a moral matter at all. Is it not a private matter and too personal and individual to be a moral matter? To hold that it is not a moral matter, however, would seem to imply that our sexual lives are morally insignificant. Or it might imply that something has to be public or universal in order to have moral significance. However, most of us would not want to hold that personal matters cannot be moral matters. Furthermore, consider that sexual behavior lends itself to valuable experiences—those of personal relations, pleasure, fruitfulness and descendants, and self-esteem and enhancement. It also involves unusual opportunities for cruelty, deceit, unfairness, and selfishness. Because these are moral matters, sexual behavior must itself have moral significance.

CONCEPTUAL PROBLEMS: WHAT IS AND IS NOT SEXUAL

Discussions of sexual morality are likely to benefit from a more intensive analysis of sexuality itself. Just what are we talking about when we speak of sexual pleasure, sexual desire, or sexual activity? Consider the meaning of the qualifier *sexual*. Suppose we said that behavior is sexual when it involves "pleasurable bodily contact with another." Will this do? This definition is quite broad. It includes passionate caresses and kisses as well as sexual intercourse. But it would not include activity that does not involve another individual, such as masturbation or looking at pornography. It would also exclude erotic dancing, phone sex, and "sexting" because these activities do not involve physical contact with another. So the definition seems to be too narrow.

However, this definition is also too broad. It covers too much. Not all kisses or caresses are sexual, even though they are physical and can be pleasurable. And the contact sport of football is supposedly pleasurable for those who play it, but presumably not in a sexual way. It seems reasonable to think of sexual pleasure as pleasure that involves our so-called erogenous zones—those areas of the body that are sexually sensitive. Could we then say that sexuality is necessarily bodily in nature? To answer this question, try the following thought experiment. Suppose we did not have bodies—in other words, suppose we were ghosts or spirits of some sort. Would we then be sexual beings? Could we experience sexual desire, for example? If we did, it would surely be different from that which we now experience. Moreover, it is not just that our own bodily existence seems required for us to experience sexual desire, but sexual desire for another would seem most properly to be for the embodied other. It cannot be simply the body of another that is desirable—or dead bodies generally would be sexually stimulating. It is an embodied person who is the normal object of sexual desire. This is not to say that bodily touching is necessary, as is clear from the fact that dancing can be sexy and phone sex can be heated. Finally, if the body is so important for sexuality, we also can wonder whether there are any significant differences between male and female sexuality in addition to, and based on, genital and reproductive differences.

Let us also note one more conceptual puzzle. Many people refer to sexual intercourse as *making love*. Some people argue that sexual intercourse should be accompanied by or be an expression of love, while others do not believe that this is necessary. Perhaps we would do best to consult the poets about the meaning of love. But let us briefly consider what you would regard as the difference between being in love (or falling in love) and loving someone. To *be in love* seems to suggest passivity. Similarly, to *fall in love* seems to be something that happens to a person. Supposedly, one has little control over one's feelings and even some thoughts in such a state. One cannot get the other person out of one's mind. We say one is *head over heels in love* or *madly in love*; one has *fallen passionately in love*. Yet compare these notions to those of *loving someone*. This is not necessarily a sexual feeling, and we often say we love our relatives and friends. Many people would say that to genuinely love someone in this way is to be actively directed to that person's

good. We want the best for him or her. In his essay on friendship in *The Nicomachean Ethics*, Aristotle wrote that true friendship is different from that which is based on the usefulness of the friend or the pleasure one obtains from being with the friend. The true friend cares about his friend for the friend's own sake. According to Aristotle, "Those who wish well to their friends for their sake are most truly friends."[49] This kind of friendship is less common, he believed, though more lasting. For Aristotle and the Greeks of his time, true friendship was more or less reserved for men. One contribution an ethics of care makes to this discussion is the importance to all of friendship and loving care. Moreover, we need not be in love with someone to love them. We can love our friends, or parents, or children, and yet we are not in love with them. So when considering what sex has to do with love, we would do well to consider the kind of love that is intended. We might also do well to ponder what happens when sexual feelings are joined with friendship.

RELEVANT FACTUAL MATTERS

In addition to conceptual clarification, certain factual matters may also be relevant to what we say about matters of sexual morality. For example, would it not be morally significant to know the effects of celibacy or of restraining sexual urges? It is well known that Freud thought that if we repressed our sexual desires we would become either neurotic or artists! Art, he argues, provides an emotionally expressive outlet for repressed sexual feelings. Freudian theory about both sexual repression and the basis of art still has supporters—Camille Paglia, for example, is a social critic and theorist of sexuality who credits Freud with inventing "modern sex analysis."[50] It also has not gone unchallenged. Knowing what the likely effects of sexual promiscuity would be, both psychologically and physically, might also be useful for thinking about sexual morality. Does separating sex and bodily pleasure from other aspects of oneself have any effect on one's ability to have a psychologically healthy and fulfilling sexual experience? Furthermore, factual matters such as the likelihood of contracting a disease such as AIDS would be important for what we say about the moral character of some sexual encounters. Our conclusions about many factual or empirical matters would seem to influence greatly what we say about sexual morality—that is, the morality of sex, just like the morality of other human activities, is at least sometimes determined by the benefits and harms that result from it.

SEXUAL MORALITY AND ETHICAL THEORIES

Factual matters may be relevant only if we are judging the morality of actions on the basis of their consequences. If instead we adopt a non-consequentialist moral theory such as Kant's, then our concerns will not be about the consequences of sexual behavior but about whether we are cherishing or using people, for example, or being fair or unfair. If we adopt a natural law position, our concerns will again be significantly different, or at least based on different reasons. We will want to know whether certain sexual behavior fits or is befitting of human nature.

In fact, the moral theory that we hold will even determine how we pose the moral questions about sex. For example, if we are guided by a consequentialist moral theory such as utilitarianism, then we will be likely to pose moral questions in terms of good or bad, better or worse outcomes of sexual behavior. If we are governed by deontological principles, then our questions will more likely be in terms of right or wrong, justifiable or unjustifiable sexual behavior. And if we judge from a natural law basis, then we will want to know whether a particular sexual behavior is natural or unnatural, proper or improper, or even perverted. Let us consider each of these three ways of posing moral questions about sexual matters and see some of the probable considerations appropriate to each type of reasoning.

Consequentialist or Utilitarian Considerations

If we were to take a consequentialist point of view— say, that of an act utilitarian—we would judge our actions or make our decisions about how to behave sexually one at a time. In each case, we would consider our alternatives and their likely consequences for all who would be affected by them. In each case, we would consider who would benefit or suffer as well as the type of benefit or suffering. In sexual relations, we would probably want to consider

physical, psychological, and social consequences. Considerations such as these are necessary for arguments that are consequentialist in nature. According to this perspective, the sexual practice or relation that has better consequences than other possibilities is the preferred one. Any practice in which the bad consequences outweigh the good consequences would be morally problematic.

Among the negative consequences to be avoided are physical harms, including sexually transmitted diseases. Psychic harms are no less real. There is the embarrassment caused by sexual rejection or the trauma of rape. Also to be considered are possible feelings of disappointment and foolishness for having false hopes or of being deceived or used. Pregnancy, although regarded in some circumstances as a good or a benefit, may in other circumstances be unwanted and involve significant suffering. Some people might include as a negative consequence the effects on the family of certain sexual practices. Incest could create harms and dysfunction within the family. And adultery is generally seen to undermine marriages, although some couples in "open marriages" (with a mutual agreement to have sexual partners outside of the marriage) would disagree. Opponents of gay marriage go further, arguing that if homosexuals were allowed to marry it would undermine the institution of marriage. By contrast, many maintain that there is no evidence that gay marriage would have any impact whatsoever on straight marriages. And same-sex couples (such as Kris Perry and Sandy Stier) claim the right to marry in order to strengthen and benefit their families. In consequentialist reasoning, all of the consequences count, and short-term benefit or pleasure may be outweighed by long-term suffering or pain. However, the pain caused to one person also can be outweighed by the pleasure given to another or others, which is a major problem for this type of moral theory.

Many positive consequences or benefits also may come from sexual relations or activity. First of all, there is sexual pleasure itself. Furthermore, we may benefit both physically and psychologically from having this outlet for sexual urges and desires. It is relaxing. It enables us to appreciate other sensual things and to be more passionate and perhaps even more compassionate. It may enhance our perceptions of the world. Colors can be brighter and individual differences more noticeable. For many people, intimate sexual relations supposedly improve personal relations by breaking down barriers. However, many would argue that this is likely to be so only where a good relationship already exists between the persons involved.

What about sex in the context of marriage and children? The future happiness or unhappiness of potential children must play a role in consequentialist considerations. The increased availability of contraception now makes it easier to control these consequences, so offspring that result from sexual relations are presumably (but not necessarily) more likely to be wanted and well cared for. Abortion and its consequences also may play a role in determining whether a particular sexual relation is good from this perspective.

Finally, consequentialist thinking has room for judging not only what is good and bad, or better and worse, but also what is best and worst. On utilitarian grounds, the most pleasurable and most productive of overall happiness is the best. If one cannot have the ideal best, however, then one should choose the best that is available, provided that this choice does not negatively affect one's ability to have the best or cause problems in other aspects of one's life. It is consistent with a consequentialist perspective to judge sexual behavior not in terms of what we must avoid to do right but in terms of what we should hope and aim for as the best. Nevertheless, in classical utilitarianism, the ideal is always to be thought of in terms of happiness or pleasure.

It is important to note in this regard that although the utilitarian philosopher John Stuart Mill was a proponent of liberty, he was also a defender of sexual equality. This helps explain why Mill was opposed to prostitution.

> Of all modes of sexual indulgence, consistent with the personal freedom and safety of women, I regard prostitution as the very worst; not only on account of the wretched women whose whole existence it sacrifices, but because no other is anything like so corrupting to the men. In no other is there the same total absence of even a temporary gleam of affection and tenderness; in no other is the woman to the man so completely a mere thing used simply as a means, for a purpose which to herself must be disgusting.[51]

Mill's point is that appropriate sexual relations should be mutual and equal. To use another as a means for sexual gratification may produce pleasure. But from a utilitarian perspective, this produces more unhappiness on balance, since it corrupts the men involved and degrades the women.

A rival utilitarian argument was made by Jeremy Bentham. Bentham held that although prostitution was shameful, it was better to legalize it than to make it illegal. Bentham thought that illegal prostitution increased the corrupting effect of prostitution on the prostitute, driving prostitutes to excessive use of "intoxicating liquors, that they may find in them a momentary oblivion of their misery," which also renders them "insensible to the restraint of shame."[52] A utilitarian might argue in a similar way that if prostitution were legalized and regulated, it might provide happiness for both the women and men involved. The customers would obtain sexual pleasure, the prostitutes would be able to capitalize on the transaction, state regulation would ensure healthy and safe sex, and the state could tax the transaction. But opponents of this idea, such as Carol Pateman, argue that there is something wrong with the idea that men could pay to use women's bodies in this way.[53]

Non-consequentialist or Deontological Considerations

The idea that it is simply wrong to use another person's body for sexual pleasure is a deontological one. Discussions of what is corrupting and degrading also point toward non-consequentialist concerns. Non-consequentialist moral theories, such as that of Kant, would direct us to judge sexual actions as well as other actions quite differently from consequentialist theories. Although the Golden Rule is not strictly the same thing as the categorical imperative, there are similarities between these two moral principles. According to both, as a person in a sexual relation, I should do only what would seem acceptable no matter whose shoes I were in or from whose perspective I judged. In the case of a couple, each person should consider what the sexual relation would look like from the other's point of view, and each should proceed only if a contemplated action or relation is also acceptable from that other viewpoint. This looks like a position regarding sexual relations according to which anything is permissible sexually as long as it is agreed to by the participants.

In one interpretation of Kantian sexual ethics—which focuses on respect for persons—consent and autonomy are the key factors to be considered. However, it is important to note that Kant's own views of sexual ethics are not exclusively focused on consent. Instead, he brings in considerations of the function and natural purpose of sex. In fact, he views the purpose of sexuality as the preservation of the species and condemns homosexuality, masturbation, and sex with animals on these grounds.[54]

We will turn to the natural law argument in the next section. But let's first further examine the Kantian emphasis on consent and respect for autonomy. The primary concern would be whether mutual consent to any given sexual act is real. For example, we would want to know whether the participants are fully informed and aware of what is involved. Lying would certainly be morally objectionable. So also would other forms of deceit and failure to inform. Not telling someone that one is married or that one has a communicable disease could also be forms of objectionable deceit, in particular when this information, if known, would make a difference to the other person's willingness to participate.

In addition, any sexual relation would have to be freely entered into. Any form of coercion would be morally objectionable on Kantian grounds. This is one of the strongest reasons for prohibiting sex with children, namely, that they cannot fully consent to it. They have neither the experience nor understanding of it, and they are not independent enough to resist pressure or coercion. As with deceit, what counts as coercion is not always easy to say, both in general and in any concrete case. Certainly, physically forcing a person to engage in sexual intercourse against his or her will is coercion. We call it rape. However, some forms of "persuasion" may also be coercive. Threats to do what is harmful are coercive. For example, threatening to demote an employee or deny him

a promotion if he does not engage in a sexual relation can be coercive. But more subtle forms of coercion also exist, including implied threats to withhold one's affection from the other or to break off a relationship. Perhaps even some offers or bribes are coercive, especially when what is promised is not only desirable but also something that one does not have and cannot get along without. Saying "I know that you are starving, and I will feed you if you have sex with me" is surely coercive.

Natural Law Considerations

Natural law theories (as described in Chapter 7) hold that morality is grounded in human nature. That is good which furthers human nature or is fitting for it, and that is bad or morally objectionable which frustrates or violates or is inconsistent with human nature. How would such a theory be used to make moral judgments about sexual behavior? Obviously, the key is the description of human nature.

In any use of human nature as a basis for determining what is good, a key issue will be describing that nature. To see how crucial this is, suppose that we examine a version of natural law theory that stresses the biological aspects of human nature. How would this require us to think about sexual morality? It would probably require us to note that an essential aspect of human nature is the orientation of the genital and reproductive system toward reproducing young. The very nature of heterosexual sexual intercourse (unless changed by accident or human intervention by sterilization or contraception) is to release male sperm into a female vagina and uterus. The sperm naturally tend to seek and penetrate an egg, fertilizing it and forming with the egg the beginning of a fetus, which develops naturally into a young member of the species. On this version of natural law theory, that which interferes with or seeks deliberately to frustrate this natural purpose of sexual intercourse as oriented toward reproduction would be morally objectionable. Thus contraception, masturbation, and homosexual sexual relations would be contrary to nature. Further arguments would be needed for natural law theories that claim that sexual relations should take place only in marriage. These arguments would possibly have to do with the relation of sex and commitment, with the biological relation of the child to the parents, and with the necessary or best setting for the raising of children.

We could also envision other nature-focused arguments about sexual morality that are based on somewhat different notions of human nature. For example, we could argue that the natural purpose of sexual relations is pleasure because nature has so constructed the nerve components of the genital system. Furthermore, the intimacy and naturally uniting aspect of sexual intercourse may provide a basis for arguing that this is its natural tendency—to unite people, to express their unity, or to bring them closer together. This account of the function of sex would not necessarily rule out homosexual relations.

To believe that there is such a thing as sexual behavior that is consistent with human nature— or natural—also implies that there can be sexual behavior that is inconsistent with human nature or unnatural. Sometimes the term *perverted* has been used synonymously with *unnatural*. Thus in the context of a discussion or analysis of natural law views about sexual morality, we also can consider the question of whether there is such a thing as sexual perversion. This is not to say that notions of sexual perversion are limited to natural law theory, however. *Perversion* literally means "turned against" or "away from" something—usually away from some norm. Perverted sexual behavior would then be sexual behavior that departs from some norm for such behavior. "That's not normal," we say. By norm here we mean not just the usual type of behavior, for this depends on what in fact people do. Rather, by norm or normal we mean what coincides with a moral standard.

To consider whether there is a natural type of sexual behavior or desire, we might compare it with another appetite, namely, the appetite of hunger, whose natural object we might say is food. If a person were to eat pictures of food instead of food, this would generally be considered abnormal. Would we also say that a person who was satisfied with pictures of a sexually attractive person and used them as a substitute for a real person was in some sense abnormal or acting abnormally? This depends on whether there is such a thing as a normal sex drive

and what its natural object would be. People have used the notion of normal sex drive and desire to say that things such as shoe fetishism (being sexually excited by shoes) and desire for sex with animals or dead bodies are abnormal. One suggestion is that the object of normal sexual desire is another individual, and the desire is not just for the other but for the other's mutual and embodied response.

These notions of perverted versus normal sexual desire and behavior can belong in some loose way to a tradition that considers human nature as a moral norm. Like the utilitarian and Kantian moral traditions, natural law theory has its own way of judging sexual and other types of behavior. These three ways of judging sexual behavior are not necessarily incompatible with one another, however. We might find that some forms of sexual behavior are not only ill-fitted for human nature but also involve using another as a thing rather than treating her or him as a person, and that such behavior also has bad consequences. Or we may find that what is most fitting for human nature is also what has the best consequences and treats persons with the respect that is due them. The

Tori (left) and Kate Kuykendall with their five-month-old daughter, Zadie, celebrate their civil marriage ceremony in West Hollywood, California.

more difficult cases will be those in which no harm comes to persons from a sexual relation, but they have nevertheless been used. No less difficult will be cases in which knowing consent is present but it is for activities that seem ill-fitted for human nature or do not promise happiness, pleasure, or other benefits.

GAY MARRIAGE

We can further explore the moral theories we have just discussed by attempting to apply them to the issue with which we began this chapter: gay marriage. When making moral judgments about homosexuality and gay marriage, the same considerations can be used as for sexual morality generally: consequentialist and non-consequentialist considerations, as well as naturalness. Some issues are conceptual, such as what is meant by *homosexual* as opposed to *heterosexual* and *bisexual*. And there is a deep and contested empirical question of whether one's gender or sexual identity is a naturally given fact of life or whether it is a matter of individual choice. Some opponents of gay marriage will claim that sexuality is a matter of choice and that individuals simply ought to choose traditional heterosexual relationships. In opposition to this, some proponents of gay marriage will claim that individuals should be free to choose to marry whomever they want. Other defenders of gay marriage will argue that since homosexual attraction is not a matter of choice but, rather, a natural disposition over which individuals have no control, homosexuals should be free to engage in relationships that are natural and rewarding for them.

From a consequentialist point of view, there is nothing in the nature of sex itself that requires that it be heterosexual or for reproductive purposes. In this view, the sexual activity that produces the most happiness for the people involved is the best, regardless of the gender of the parties involved and whether or not they intend to produce children. Some have argued against gay marriage and homosexuality in general on the grounds that such relationships and sexual behavior produce more bad consequences than good ones—that they undermine the traditional family, de-couple marriage from reproduction, and deprive children of a stable family environment. As with many other controversial topics, the empirical evidence supporting

such consequentialist claims is disputed. One widely discussed recent study by sociologist Mark Regnerus has been cited by conservatives who claim that it shows that children raised by homosexual couples fare poorly.[55] This study was cited by the U.S. Conference of Catholic Bishops in its friend-of-the-court brief filed in the *Hollingsworth v. Perry* case. The bishops appealed to the Regnerus study in arguing that heterosexual marriages created the "optimal environment" for raising children.[56] On the other side, sociologists have criticized the Regnerus study's conclusions as well as its source of funding (the study was supported by funding from conservative, "family values" sources).[57] The American Sociological Association concluded, in its friend-of-the-court brief for the *Hollingsworth v. Perry* case, that the "scholarly consensus is clear: children of same-sex parents fare just as well as children of opposite-sex parents."[58]

While it is true that traditional heterosexual marriage has declined as a social value—with more divorce and more people cohabitating outside of marriage—there is no evidence that gay marriage is the cause of these phenomena. Rather, the general decline in marriage is better described in terms of a variety of causal factors, including the decline of religious traditionalism, changing sexual mores, the liberation of women, and larger economic forces.[59] Proponents of gay marriage have also pointed out that if the true moral purpose of marriage is reproduction, then we should ban infertile heterosexual couples from marrying, as well as older couples and couples who desire to remain childless.

The social context may also make a difference to consequentialist viewpoints on homosexuality. Social acceptability or stigma will make a difference in whether people can be happy in certain kinds of relationships. Greater social acceptance of homosexuality—along with legalization of gay marriage—might produce more happiness for homosexuals. Moreover, if gay marriage were legalized throughout the country, then the full benefits of marriage would be extended to homosexuals, including benefits for married couples that are obtained through tax policy, insurance coverage, and inheritance law.

Non-consequentialist considerations also apply to discussions about homosexuality and gay marriage.

One of the most common non-consequentialist arguments against homosexual sex is that it is unnatural, that it goes against nature. Many gay men and lesbians respond to such arguments by emphasizing that their same-sex attractions are profoundly "natural" and were present from childhood. They also point to the occurence of same gender sexual behavior in the natural world.

According to traditional natural law theory, although we differ individually in many ways, people share a common human nature. I may have individual inclinations or things may be natural to me that are not natural to you, simply because of our differing talents, physical and psychological traits, and other unique characteristics. Natural law theory tells us that certain things are right or wrong not because they further or frustrate our individual inclinations but because they promote or work against our species' inclinations and aspects of our common human nature. Arguments about homosexuality that appeal to traditional natural law theory may need to determine whether homosexuality is consistent with common human nature or simply present in some individual natures.

Thus the argument that gay men or lesbian women find relating sexually to members of their own sex "natural" to them as individuals may or may not work as part of a natural law argument that supports that behavior. However, if one takes a broader view of sexuality in its passionate, emotional, and social aspects, then one could make a reasonable argument based on natural law that homosexuality is but one expression of a common human sexuality. Historically, natural law arguments have not gone this way. But this is not to say that such an argument could not be reasonably put forth.

Natural law arguments against homosexuality and same-sex marriage have often traditionally been grounded in religious viewpoints on sexuality and the sanctity of heterosexual marriage. For example, many Christians and Jews who denounce homosexuality do so on the basis of Old Testament Bible verses such as Deuteronomy 23:17–18, Leviticus 18:22, and Leviticus 20:13. The apostle Paul also condemns it in the New Testament: 1 Corinthians 6:9–10 and Timothy 1:9–10 and in Romans 1:26–27.[60] One problem for such scripturally based arguments is that these sacred texts are based upon ancient social mores, which include values that we might find objectionable today such as the subordination of women. The Old Testament appears to permit polygamy. And the New Testament prohibits divorce. If we reject gay marriage on biblical grounds, should we also reject divorce and permit polygamy? Some religions (Islam, for example, and Mormonism at one point in its history) do permit polygamous marriage, which is now illegal in the United States and other Western countries. (It is an open question of whether it is more natural for men to be polygamous or monogamous.) An explicitly religious foundation for marriage also runs afoul of secular principles (as discussed in Chapter 2), which aim to keep the legal system neutral with regard to religion.

As noted earlier, arguments about homosexuality and gay marriage may be more properly framed as civil rights issues rather than moral issues per se. It may be helpful to put this issue in a larger context. For example, African Americans in the United States were not allowed to marry until after the Civil War, and mixed race couples could not do so everywhere in the United States until a Supreme Court decision in 1967. Since the early 2000s, various countries around the world and states in the United States have come to permit same-sex marriage. More widely available are so-called **civil unions** or domestic partnerships that grant many of the same legal benefits as married couples have.

While proponents of civil unions may think that this solves the question without extending the concept of marriage in a way that includes gay marriages, the current debate about gay marriage points beyond the legal issue of how domestic partners might share social benefits. The larger question is whether homosexual relationships deserve to be considered as the same kind of loving and sexual relationship as heterosexual relationships. The Defense of Marriage Act of 1996, which we mentioned at the outset of this chapter, was described in a report to Congress as focused on the *moral* question of homosexuality: "Civil laws that permit only heterosexual marriage reflect and honor a collective moral judgment about human sexuality. This judgment entails both moral disapproval of homosexuality, moral conviction that heterosexuality better comports with traditional (especially Judeo-Christian) morality."[61] The 2013 Supreme Court ruling overturning the Defense of Marriage Act rejects this institutional expression of moral disapproval of homosexuality.

Laws that address issues of civil rights, whether in this area or others, are often grounded in questions of morality. Nevertheless, morality is a distinct realm, and we may ask whether certain actions or practices are morally good or bad apart from whether they ought to be regulated by law. So, in the realm of sexual matters, we can ask about the morality of certain actions or practices. Questions about sexual morality are obviously quite personal. Nevertheless, because this is one of the major drives and aspects of a fulfilling human life, it is important to think about what may be best and worst, and what may be right and wrong in these matters.

NOTES

1. *In re Marriage Cases*, May 15, 2008, p. 7, accessed March 1, 2003, http://www.courts.ca.gov/documents/S147999.pdf
2. Mark Sherman, "AP Interview: Lesbian Couple in Gay Marriage Case," AP, March 24, 2013, accessed April 25, 2013, http://bigstory.ap.org/article/ap-interview-lesbian-couple-gay-marriage-case
3. Miranda Leitsinger, "Couples Leading Prop. 8 Fight," NBC News, accessed April, 25, 2013, http://usnews.nbcnews.com/_news/2013/03/21/17405046-couples-leading-prop-8-fight-we-are-very-excited-to-have-the-end-in-sight?lite
4. "Prop. 8: Gay Plaintiffs See End to 'Dark Wall of Discrimination,'" *Los Angeles Times*, February 7, 2012, accessed April 25, 2013, http://latimesblogs.latimes.com/lanow/2012/02/prop-8-gay-marriage-discrimination.html
5. Thom Shanker, "Partners of Gays in Service Are Granted Some Benefits," *New York Times*, February 11, 2013, accessed March 1, 2013, http://www.nytimes.com/2013/02/12/us/partners-of-gay-military-personnel-are-granted-benefits.html
6. Defense of Marriage Act, accessed March 1, 2013, http://www.gpo.gov/fdsys/pkg/BILLS-104hr3396enr/pdf/BILLS-104hr3396enr.pdf
7. Lindsay Wise, "In Federal Gay-Marriage Case, More Than 1,100 Benefits at Stake," McClatchy News, March 27, 2013, accessed April 25, 2013, http://www.mcclatchydc.com/2013/03/27/187120/in-federal-gay-marriage-case-more.html#storylink=cpy
8. *United States v. Windsor* 570 U.S. 12 (2013), p. 25–26.
9. Justice A. Scalia dissent, *Lawrence v. Texas* (02-102) 539 U.S. 558 (2003).
10. Stephanie Mencimer, "Mormon Church Abandons Its Crusade against Gay Marriage," *Mother Jones*, April 12, 2013, accessed May 13, 2013, http://www.motherjones.com/politics/2013/04/prop-8-mormons-gay-marriage-shift
11. U.S. Conference of Catholic Bishops, May 3, 2013, accessed May 13, 2013, http://usccb.org/news/2013/13-084.cfm
12. "National Survey of Family Growth" (2005–2010), Centers for Disease Control and Prevention, accessed March 1, 2013, http://www.cdc.gov/nchs/nsfg.htm
13. "Hate Crime Statistics, 2011," FBI, accessed March 21, 2013, http://www.fbi.gov/about-us/cjis/ucr/hate-crime/2011/narratives/incidents-and-offenses
14. "National Survey of Family Growth" (2005–2010), Centers for Disease Control and Prevention, http://www.cdc.gov/nchs/nsfg.htm
15. Anjani Chandra et al., National Health Statistics Reports, *Sexual Behavior, Sexual Attraction, and Sexual Identity in the United States: Data from the 2006–2008 National Survey of Family Growth*, March 3, 2011, www.cdc.gov/nchs/data/nhsr/nhsr036.pdf
16. "Key Statistics from the National Survey of Family Growth," Centers for Disease Control and Prevention, accessed April 25, 2013, http://www.cdc.gov/nchs/nsfg/abc_list_s.htm
17. "2011 HIV Surveillance Report," Centers for Disease Control and Prevention, accessed March 1, 2013, http://www.cdc.gov/hiv/ehap/resources/direct/022813/index.htm
18. "HIV/AIDS," Centers for Disease Control and Prevention, February 28, 2013, accessed April 29, 2013, http://www.cdc.gov/hiv/dhap/eHAP/direct/022813.html
19. "Global Summary of the AIDS Epidemic," 2011, accessed March 1, 2013, http://www.who.int/hiv/data/2012_epi_core_en.png
20. Ilene Lelchuk, "UCSF Explores Teens' Post-Sex Emotions," *San Francisco Chronicle*, February 15, 2007, accessed April 26, 2013, http://www.sfgate.com/bayarea/article/SAN-FRANCISCO-UCSF-explores-teens-post-sex-2617439.php
21. "Key Statistics from the National Survey of Family Growth," Centers for Disease Control and Prevention, http://www.cdc.gov/nchs/nsfg/abc_list_u.htm
22. Brady E. Hamilton, Donna L. Hoyert, Joyce A. Martin, Donna M. Strobino, and Bernard Guyer, "Annual Summary of Vital Statistics: 2010–2011," *Pediatrics* (published online February 11, 2013), accessed July 27, 2013, http://pediatrics.aappublications.org/content/early/2013/02/05/peds.2012-3769.abstract
23. "Under Obama Administration, Abstinence-Only Education Finds Surprising New Foothold," *Washington Post*, May 8, 2012, accessed March 1, 2013, http://www.washingtonpost.com/blogs/wonkblog/post/under-obama-administration-abstinence-only-education-finds-surprising-new-foothold/2012/05/08/gIQA8fcwAU_blog.html; also see *Impacts of Four Title V, Section 510 Abstinence Education Program*, Mathematica Policy Research for Department of Health and Human Services (April 2007), accessed April 26, 2013, http://www.mathematica-mpr.com/publications/pdfs/impactabstinence.pdf
24. "Sex Ed Can Help Prevent Teen Pregnancy," *Washington Post*, March 24, 2008, accessed March 1, 2013, http://www.washingtonpost.com/wp-dyn/content/article/2008/03/24/AR2008032401515.html
25. For abstinence sex education, see National Abstinence Education Association, http://www.abstinenceassociation.org/

index.html; for comprehensive sex education, see Advocates for Youth, http://www.advocatesforyouth.org/index.php

26. Jason DeParle and Sabrina Tavernise, "For Women Under 30, Most Births Occur Outside Marriage," *New York Times*, February 17, 2012, accessed April 26, 2013, http://www.nytimes.com/2012/02/18/us/for-women-under-30-most-births-occur-outside-marriage.html?pagewanted=all

27. Dennie Hughes, "Is It So Wrong to Live Together?" *USA Weekend*, January 16–18, 2004, 12.

28. *Time*, May 25, 2009, 57–58.

29. David Whitman, "Was It Good for Us?" *U.S. News & World Report* 122, no. 19 (May 19, 1997):56.

30. *New York Times,* March 3, 2010, A14.

31. Hughes, op. cit.

32. "Violence against Women," Amnesty International, accessed April 26, 2013, http://www.amnestyusa.org/our-work/issues/women-s-rights/violence-against-women/violence-against-women-information

33. "Female Genital Mutilation Fact Sheet," World Health Organization, updated February 2013, accessed April 26, 2013, http://www.who.int/mediacentre/factsheets/fs241/en/

34. James Ciment, "Senegal Outlaws Female Genital Mutilation," *British Medical Journal* 3 (February 6, 1999): 348; and Joel E. Frader et al., "Female Genital Mutilation," *Pediatrics* 102 (July 1998):153.

35. Ibid.

36. Elizabeth Rosenthal, "Genital Cutting Raises by 50% Likelihood Mothers or Their Newborns Will Die, Study Finds," *New York Times,* June 2, 2006, A10, accessed May 12, 2013, http://www.nytimes.com/2006/06/02/world/africa/02mutilation.html?_r=0

37. "Female Genital Mutilation Fact Sheet," World Health Organization, http://www.who.int/mediacentre/factsheets/fs241/en/

38. Xiaorong Li, "Tolerating the Intolerable: The Case of Female Genital Mutilation," *Philosophy and Public Policy Quarterly* 21, no. 1 (Winter 2001):4.

39. Ibid., 6.

40. "United Nations Bans Female Genital Mutilation," UN Women, December 20, 2012, accessed March 1, 2013, http://www.unwomen.org/2012/12/united-nations-bans-female-genital-mutilation/

41. "Female Genital Mutilation and Other Harmful Practices," World Health Organization, accessed April 26, 2013, http://www.who.int/reproductivehealth/topics/fgm/fgm-sexuality/en/

42. Susan Brownmiller, *Against Our Will: Men, Women, and Rape* (New York: Ballantine Books, 1993, originally published in 1975), 391.

43. "The Offenders," Rape, Abuse, & Incest National Network, accessed July 27, 2013, http://www.rainn.org/get-information/statistics/sexual-assault-offenders

44. "How Often Does Sexual Assault Occur?" Rape, Abuse & Incest National Network (2010 data), accessed March 1, 2013, http://www.rainn.org/get-information/statistics/frequency-of-sexual-assault

45. "Marital Rape," Rape, Abuse & Incest National Network, accessed April 26, 2013, http://www.rainn.org/public-policy/sexual-assault-issues/marital-rape

46. Preetika Rana, "Why India Still Allows Marital Rape," *Wall Street Journal*, March 26, 2013, accessed April 26, 2013, http://blogs.wsj.com/indiarealtime/2013/03/26/why-india-allows-men-to-rape-their-wives/

47. UNODC, "Global Report on Trafficking in Persons" (2012), p. 7, accessed March 1, 2013, http://www.unodc.org/documents/data-and-analysis/glotip/Trafficking_in_Persons_2012_web.pdf

48. Amanda Walker-Rodriguez and Rodney Hill, "Human Sex Trafficking," FBI, March 2011, accessed March 1, 2103, http://www.fbi.gov/stats-services/publications/law-enforcement-bulletin/march_2011/human_sex_trafficking

49. Aristotle, *The Nicomachean Ethics,* bk. 8, Chapter 4.

50. Camille Paglia, *Sex, Art, and American Culture* (New York: Vintage Books, 1992), 113.

51. John Stuart Mill, "Letter to Lord Amberly," February 2, 1870, in *The Collected Works of John Stuart Mill*, vol. 17, ed. Francis E. Mineka and Dwight N. Lindley (Toronto: University of Toronto Press, London: Routledge and Kegan Paul, 1972), 1525.

52. Jeremy Bentham, *Principles of Penal Law* in *Works of Jeremy Bentham* (Edinburgh: W. Tait, 1838), vol. 1, pt. 2, 546.

53. Carol Pateman, "What's Wrong with Prostitution?" Chapter 7 in *The Sexual Contract* (Stanford, CA: Stanford University Press, 1988).

54. Kant, *Lectures on Ethics* (Indianapolis, IN: Hackett Publishing, 1981), 169–71.

55. Mark Regnerus, "How Different Are the Adult Children of Parents Who Have Same-Sex Relationships? Findings from the New Family Structures Study," *Social Science Research* 41 (2012):752.

56. "Brief Amicus Curiae of the United States Conference of Catholic Bishops in Support of Petitioners and Supporting Reversal"—re *Hollingsworth v. Perry*, January 29, 2013, accessed April 26, 2013, http://www.usccb.org/about/general-counsel/amicus-briefs/upload/hollingsworth-v-perry.pdf

57. "Controversial Gay-Parenting Study Is Severely Flawed, Journal's Audit Finds," *Chronicle of Higher Education* (July 26, 2012).

58. "Brief of Amicus Curiae American Sociological Association in Support of Respondent Kristin M. Perry and Respondent Edith Schlain Windsor"—re *Hollingsworth v. Perry*, accessed April 26, 2013, http://www.asanet.org/documents/ASA/pdfs/12-144_307_Amicus_%20(C_%20Gottlieb)_ASA_Same-Sex_Marriage.pdf

59. Derek Thompson, "The Decline of Marriage and the Rise of Unwed Mothers: An Economic Mystery," *Atlantic* March 18, 2013, accessed April 26, 2013, http://www.theatlantic.com/business/archive/2013/03/the-decline-of-marriage-and-the-rise-of-unwed-mothers-an-economic-mystery/274111/

60. See Andrew Fiala, *What Would Jesus Really Do?* (Lanham, MD: Rowman & Littlefield, 2007), Chapter 9.

61. *Defense of Marriage Act*, accessed April 26, 2013, http://www.gpo.gov/fdsys/pkg/CRPT-104hrpt664/pdf/CRPT-104hrpt664.pdf

REVIEW EXERCISES

1. Distinguish conceptual from factual matters with regard to sexual morality. What is the difference between them?

2. What are some factual matters that would be relevant for consequentialist arguments regarding sexual behavior?

3. According to a Kantian type of morality, we ought to treat persons as persons. Deceit and coercion violate this requirement. In this view, what kinds of things regarding sexual morality would be morally objectionable?

4. How would a natural law theory be used to judge sexual behavior? Explain.

5. What is meant by the term *perversion*? How would this notion be used to determine whether there was something called "sexual perversion?"

6. How do arguments about homosexuality and gay marriage connect to claims about other forms of nonmarital sex, adultery, and even marital sex among sterile couples?

7. Is the move toward the legalization of gay marriage in some countries and states in the United States a good thing or a bad thing? Justify your response with specific references to the moral theories discussed in this chapter.

DISCUSSION CASES

1. **Date Rape.** Early one Sunday morning, Dalia opens her dorm room door and finds her friend Amy standing there, her eyes red from crying. Inside Dalia's room, Amy begins talking about what happened to her the night before. She had been at a large party in another dorm, drinking beer and dancing with a group of friends, until the party started winding down around 2:00 a.m. Then a guy she'd been flirting with invited her back to his room down the hall from the party. She said goodbye to her friends and went with him. In his room, they had another beer and started making out. Amy tells Dalia that everything was fine until the guy pushed her down hard onto his bed and began pulling off her clothes. "It happened so fast," Amy said. "I was in shock and was scared because all of a sudden he was acting so rough. I just sort of let it happen, but it was awful." Amy begins to cry. "Did you tell him to stop?" Dalia asks. "I didn't say anything," Amy says. "But inside, I was screaming 'no.' I just lay there completely still until it was over."

"Are you saying he raped you?" Dalia asks. "I don't know," Amy says. "Maybe."

Do you think what happened to Amy was rape? Why or why not? What do you think is required for true consent to a sexual encounter?

2. **Defining Marriage.** Maria is opposed to the idea of gay marriage. In a recent conversation in the school cafeteria, Maria argues, "If homosexuals are allowed to marry, then why not allow polygamy or other kinds of marriages?" Richard is gay. He

responds, "That's ridiculous. All we're asking is that our relationships be respected by society and the law. Nobody is asking to legalize polygamy. Even the Mormons have given up on polygamy." Maria replies, "I know the Mormon Church no longer officially approves of it. But there are still Mormons who live in polygamous families. Haven't you seen it on TV shows like *Sister Wives* on TLC and *Big Love* on HBO? What if some of those folks—or Muslims who live in the U.S.—want to legalize polygamy?" Richard thinks about it for a minute and then replies, "I still think you are comparing apples and oranges. Gay marriage is not at all like polygamous marriage. I'm talking about marriage between two and only two committed partners, not marriage of multiple partners. You can legalize the one without legalizing the other. You think that there's a slippery slope here. But I deny it." Maria responds, "How can you draw the line once you open the door to nontraditional marriage?"

Is there a slippery slope here? Should we open marriage up to a variety of other arrangements? Is it possible to draw a clear line in this case? Please justify your response with specific reference to the philosophical concepts discussed in the chapter.

3. **Prostitution.** David's friends are arranging his bachelor party. They are making plans to go as a group to Las Vegas for one last weekend "out with the boys." One of David's friends, Steven, suggests that they pool their money and treat David to a night in one of Nevada's legal brothels. Another friend, Tom,

is opposed to the idea. Tom says that prostitution is wrong. Tom thinks prostitution exploits women. Tom also thinks that David's fiancée, Monica, would be hurt if she ever found out about it. But Steven argues that prostitution is legal in Nevada and the women make good money doing what they do. Steven also says that David has already told him that he wants to go to a strip club as part of the bachelor party. "There's not much difference between a strip club and a brothel," Steven says. Tom responds, "But one is fantasy and the other is reality." Steven shakes his head. "It's all sex, man," he adds. Tom thinks about that for a moment. Then he says, "You know, maybe we shouldn't go to the strip club either. Monica wouldn't like it." Steven replies, "Well, this is David's party. And it all depends on what we tell Monica. Remember, what happens in Vegas stays in Vegas!"

Whose side are you on? Is there something wrong with prostitution? Is there a difference between visiting a strip club and visiting a prostitute? Would it make a difference if David and his friends were honest with Monica about their plans?

13

Equality and Discrimination

Learning Outcomes

After reading this chapter you, should be able to:

- Understand the role of discrimination in contemporary societies.
- Think critically about the idea of race and racism.
- Explain the idea of institutional racism.
- Describe and evaluate the principle of equality.

- Analyze how consequentialist and non-consequentialist reasoning applies in discussions of discrimination and affirmative action.
- Understand the development of civil rights law in the United States.
- Defend a thesis about the ethics of racial profiling and affirmative action.

© Patrick Poendl/Shutterstock.com

In 2011, Antonio Montejano was detained for two days in the Los Angeles county jail on an immigration hold. Montejano had been stopped by the police on suspicion of shoplifting a $10 bottle of perfume. The shoplifting charge was dropped, but the police suspected him of being an illegal immigrant and held him on those grounds. He was incarcerated for four nights, until authorities confirmed that Montejano is in fact a U.S. citizen. Apparently, Montejano had triggered a positive identification in Homeland Security databases because he had been mistakenly deported in 1996. Montejano argues that he has been singled out for such treatment because "I look Mexican, 100 percent."[1] In a 2011 interview, Montejano said that he feared his eight-year-old son would suffer a similar fate. "Even though he is an American citizen—just like me—he too could be detained for immigration purposes because of the color of his skin—just like me."[2] Montejano's unlawful detention occurred as part of the Secure Communities initiative of the Immigration and Customs Enforcement (ICE). In response to complaints, ICE maintains that it is making efforts to reduce "the risk of discrimination or racial profiling."[3] ICE acknowledges that discrimination and profiling are wrong, but these practices remain a source of contention in political and even philosophical circles. Some ask if is it always wrong to use profiling if that helps us catch bad guys and deport illegal aliens. And why, exactly, is it wrong to discriminate? To think seriously about these sorts of cases, we will have to define discrimination and profiling. We also need to understand the importance of the moral idea of equality.

DISCRIMINATION

A very basic definition of discrimination tells us that to discriminate is to distinguish between things, usually in ways that imply a judgment about what is better or worse.

We say, for example, that someone has discriminating taste, which implies that she makes good judgments about what is good or bad (say with regard to food, wine, art, or music). As we shall see in the discussion of war (in Chapter 19), discrimination is viewed as a good thing in the ethics of war; we want soldiers and armies to discriminate between those who can legitimately be killed (soldiers) and those who ought not be killed (civilians). But in this chapter we are primarily concerned with *unjust* discrimination. In this negative sense, **discrimination** is unjustified differential treatment, especially on the basis of characteristics such as race, ethnicity, gender, sexual orientation, or religion. The goal of eliminating unjustified discrimination is an established policy of our legal system, with a variety of civil rights laws focused on preventing and finding remedies for it. The Civil Rights Act of 1964 explicitly states that its goal is to "provide relief from discrimination" and to "prevent discrimination" in public and federally funded programs and institutions.[4] This idea has led to the development of explicit equal opportunity clauses that show up in policy statements and contracts for a variety of institutions. The Equal Employment Opportunity Commission (EEOC) explains its own antidiscrimination policy as follows:

> EEOC employees are protected by federal laws prohibiting discrimination on the basis of race, religion, color, sex (including pregnancy and gender identity), national origin, age, disability, family medical history, or genetic information. Moreover, consistent with Presidential Executive Orders and other laws designed to protect federal employees, we must vigilantly prevent discrimination based on sexual orientation, parental status, marital status, political affiliation, military service, or any other non-merit based factor.[5]

This statement provides an extensive list of factors that should not be considered as relevant to employment. Indeed, as the statement's conclusion implies, the only relevant consideration should be "merit."

Racial Discrimination

While each of the potentially discriminatory factors listed above is worthy of further consideration, in this section we'll look more closely at the issue of *racial* discrimination as a paradigmatic example of the problem of discrimination. One might think, given the fact that the United States has elected an African American president, that racism is behind us. But while some imagine that we are entering a post-racial era, evidence suggests that we continue to deal with racism. A poll conducted by the Associated Press in October 2012 found that 51 percent of Americans were willing to express explicitly antiblack attitudes. This is up from 48 percent four years ago.[6] Discriminatory stereotypes about other racial and ethnic groups show up in other ways. Asians, for example, are often viewed as a "model minority." But this stereotype implicitly condemns other minorities. And it ignores much. Viewing Asians as a "model minority" creates a stereotype that does not necessarily comport with the diverse range of people who are counted as "Asian."[7] Moreover, the "positive" stereotype of Asians as hardworking and brainy has created disadvantages for some Asians. One worry is that elite universities are trying to find ways to limit the number of Asians they admit.[8] Racial stereotypes—whether positive or negative—are based upon generalizations about groups. These generalizations treat different people in groups as if they were all alike. And they may foster divisive competition among groups and their members.

Race and Racialism One significant philosophical problem in discussions of racial discrimination is the very idea of race, a category that attempts to identify similarities among diverse individuals. Racial differences are often held to be natural biological differences. Racial distinctions have been drawn based upon such factors as appearance, blood group, geographic location, and gene frequency. It is difficult, however, to clearly define the sorts of biological differences that might create racial identity. It is also difficult to narrow down the number of races of human beings. Depending on which characteristics and criteria are employed, anthropologists have classified the human species into anywhere from six to eighty races.[9] Thus any strictly biological definition of race is seriously flawed. One problem is that human populations have rarely been isolated in ways that would limit genetic intermingling. Indeed, even if we were able to isolate populations in this way, there would be substantial overlap among the supposedly different races; and individuals within a given racial or ethnic group show substantial genetic variation. Another problem with genetic accounts of race is that human populations across the globe do not vary that much from one another genetically. As one important study concludes, "the major stereotypes, all based on skin color, hair color and form, and facial traits, reflect superficial differences that are not confirmed by deeper analysis with more reliable genetic traits and whose origin dates from recent evolution mostly under the effect of climate and perhaps sexual selection."[10]

While we should be wary of reductive biological accounts of racial differences—especially those racial categories that are used to unjustly discriminate—we might want to consider a genetic basis of race for benevolent purposes. Genetic variations do have implications for human health. Different ethnic and racial groups may have different susceptibilities to disease. Thus it is important to understand how medical treatments affect different racial types. Some scientific studies, for instance, have been designed to "catalogue and compare the genetics of people with African, Asian, and European ancestry."[11] It would be beneficial to understand how these differences affect susceptibility to diseases such as sickle-cell anemia, diabetes, and hypertension. One international project—the Haplotype (or HapMap) Project—seeks to determine why certain groups suffer differential rates of high blood pressure and heart attacks, for example, by finding genetic variants or mutations that may be involved in these conditions. Such information might help scientists design tailor-made drugs or treatments for people in these groups.[12]

Nevertheless, the conceptual and scientific basis for race remains highly contested. The philosopher Kwame Anthony Appiah, for example, maintains that the idea of firm and essential differences among the races is false[13]. Appiah uses the term *racialism* to describe the problematic notion that there are firm distinctions among races. Appiah argues that the superficial characteristics that people use to distinguish among the races are merely skin deep and not tied to a deeper essential difference. Another problem

for racialist views is that there is a long history of people marrying, having children, and raising families across so-called racial divides. In many cases, it is difficult for people to decide how they might identify themselves based upon old-fashioned racial categories. President Obama is a case in point; his mother was white and his father was Kenyan, but he identifies himself as an African American. Critics of **racialism** generally agree that race is a *social construct*. That is to say, racial categories are ideas made up for social purposes, which are not clearly grounded in hard and fast natural distinctions. The ethical question is whether those categories are used to make *unjust* discriminatory judgments, which are typically described as racist.

Racism It is generally understood that **racism** involves making race a significant factor in the judgment and treatment of persons. Racism sets people of one race apart from people of other races, leading to demarcations between "us" and "them" and the construction of unequal or hierarchical social conditions. Racism involves not only making distinctions and grouping people but also denigration. It involves beliefs that all persons of a certain race are inferior to persons of other races in some way. Racism appears to be unjust to individuals not just because such generalizations are typically false but also because individuals do not choose their own parents or racial heritage and cannot change their external appearance. Similarly, racists or racial supremacists who celebrate their own race take credit for something over which they have no control.

There is nothing inherently wrong with noting our physical differences. In the abstract, it would seem that believing that someone is shorter than another or less strong is not necessarily objectionable, especially if the belief is true. However, what makes racism wrong is that it involves making false judgments about people and their worth. It also involves power and oppression, for those groups that are devalued by racism are also likely to be treated accordingly, even by those who don't think of themselves as racist.

Racism is not exactly the same as prejudice. *Prejudice* is making judgments or forming beliefs before knowing the truth about something or someone. These prejudgments might accidentally be correct beliefs. However, the negative connotation of the term *prejudice* indicates that these beliefs or judgments are formed without adequate information and are also mistaken. Moreover, prejudice in this context also may be a matter of judging an individual on the basis of stereotypical characteristics of a group to which he or she belongs. There is often a problem here of false or hasty generalization (when we make judgments about all members of a group based upon a few we've encountered). Racism, although different from prejudice, may follow from prejudiced beliefs. Racism appears especially objectionable when it leads to unequal treatment and harmful behavior.

Structural Racism   Racism is usually thought of in terms of the attitudes and behaviors of individuals. It is possible, however, for racism and other forms of oppression to occur at the level of institutions and social structures.[14] **Structural** or **institutional racism** occurs when social structures and institutions are set up in ways that are oppressive or produce unequal outcomes. It is more difficult to see institutional or structural oppression because we often take social structures for granted. Moreover, nonbiased individuals may be working within a system that produces racially biased outcomes. These individuals may not be racist themselves—even if the system or institution produces undeserved unequal outcomes.

Consider this issue in the context of education. Education is often thought of as the great equalizer and the hope of the less fortunate. However, educational outcomes are often strikingly unequal in the United States. Poorer schools in urban, minority neighborhoods typically have lower standardized test scores and lower graduation rates than affluent, largely white schools in the suburbs. The problem is not typically that teachers or administrators are racist. Rather, the problem may be that present (and past) institutions have been set up in ways that reinforce disparate outcomes.

These outcomes include a dropout rate for African American college students that is substantially higher than for white students. The six-year college graduation rates by race—as calculated in 2011—were white students (62 percent), Hispanic students (50 percent), and black and American Indian/Alaska Native students (39 percent each).[15] Black and Hispanic youth also drop out of high school at a higher rate than white youth. In 2010, the high school dropout rates were white (5.1 percent), Hispanic (8.0 percent), and black (15.1 percent).[16] These racially disparate outcomes are most likely not caused by racist teachers. Rather, they are the result of a variety of social structures.

One of these structures may be social class and income level. If we look at employment statistics, for example, we find racial disparities. In 2010, with the economy in recession, the black unemployment rate stood at 16 percent, Hispanic unemployment at 12.5 percent, Asian unemployment at 7.5 percent, and white unemployment at 8.7 percent.[17] According to 2011 data, white Americans have, on average, twenty-two times more wealth than blacks and fifteen times more wealth than Hispanics.[18] Such economic disparities have clear impacts on education. According to a special report by the *New York Times* in 2012, "Low-income students with above-average scores on eighth grade tests have a college graduation rate of 26 percent—lower than more affluent students with worse test scores. Thirty years ago, there was a 31 percentage point difference in the share of affluent and poor students who earned a college degree. Now the gap is 45 points."[19] It is difficult to disentangle the differences between race, class, and education in this sort of data. This is a reminder that there are a variety of social categories (including gender, religion, sexual orientation, etc.) that should concern us when we are thinking about equality and discrimination. Different people have access to different opportunities based upon racial, class, gender, and other differences.

One area in which such differences occur is standardized testing. Consider the correlation between ethnicity, race, and SAT scores. White students earned on average (in 2012) 527 on the verbal section, 536 on the mathematics section, and 515 on the writing section.[20] Black students earned 428 (verbal), 428 (math), and 417 (writing). Similar disparities exist for Hispanic and Native American students. Critics of the SAT say this and other standardized tests are culturally biased and rely on references and associations tied to a particular class or cultural background. Children of those who are fortunate enough to have good incomes and access to good schools will have an advantage over other children. They can afford to take expensive SAT preparation courses, for example. This has led one critic to claim, "The SAT is increasingly a wealth test, and it provides the highest scores for those who have the most opportunity in society."[21] This is not necessarily the fault of any of the parents or children involved. Rather, it is a feature of the structure of our institutions, which leaves us with unequal outcomes. Those who seek to remedy institutional and structural disparities remind us that these institutions could be organized differently. We could devote greater funds to schools in minority neighborhoods so that students from those schools will have more opportunities to succeed later in life. Or colleges and universities could offer greater financial aid and other forms of assistance to poor students. Further, we could encourage employers to take positive steps (**"affirmative action"**) to recruit and train poor and minority applicants.

Another potential source of institutional racism may be racial stereotyping that occurs in the media. A 2008 analysis by Travis Dixon, an expert on stereotypes in the media, concludes, "African Americans typically occupy roles as poor people, loud politicians, and criminals on network news."[22] There is evidence that these stereotypical depictions can taint people's judgments about individual African Americans. Dixon conducted a related study, in which he examined how attitudes about crime and race correspond to media viewing habits. He concludes that "exposure to Blacks' overrepresentation as criminals on local news programming was positively related to the perception of Blacks as violent."[23] Critics of structural racism argue that things could be different; news organizations could de-emphasize race in their coverage of crime stories and focus instead on economic issues, for example. Those who are concerned with structural racism will argue that structural and institutional changes must be made to remedy the unequal outcomes that occur in society. It is not enough for individuals to overcome racist attitudes; the institutions must be changed, and proactive remedies must be employed to respond to racially disparate outcomes. One example of this is affirmative action, which we discuss in more detail below.

Other Forms of Discrimination   We have considered racism as one example of unjustified discrimination. Similar issues come up in consideration of other forms of discrimination. Consider gender discrimination, which we discussed in more detail in Chapter 9. At the end of that chapter, we noted that some philosophers, such as Judith Butler, argue that gender is a social construction—an argument that can be seen as similar to Appiah's claim that race is a social construction. Feminists also speak of structural or institutional gender discrimination, which occurs when institutions are set up in ways that unjustifiably harm women. For example, while the average income of women compared to that of men has improved over the years, in 2011 women still earned only 77 percent of what men earned.[24] This wage gap also has a racial element, with Hispanic and black women earning the least. One interpretation of the gender wage gap is that it is structural or institutional. Those who do so-called women's work—traditionally teaching, nursing, food service, and so on—have historically been underpaid. As women move into less traditionally female jobs, perhaps the pay gap will be reduced. However, there is substantial evidence that women continue to make less than their male counterparts in various professions; for example, women who work as physicians, real estate agents, and stockbrokers make less than 70 percent of what their male counterparts make.[25]

Other forms of discrimination exist. Forty-three million Americans have one or more physical or mental disabilities. Substantial legal efforts have been made to remove barriers and expand opportunities for such individuals, most notably the Americans with Disabilities Act (ADA) of 1990. But disabled individuals are still disadvantaged in many areas. Although fewer disabled people are trapped in their homes or institutionalized, stereotypes and stigma remain. And social institutions are sometimes set up in ways that create structural and institutional impediments for the disabled. For example, many private businesses still provide no alternatives to steps and staircases for customers in wheelchairs. The architects and planners who designed buildings with such features were not necessarily bigoted against the disabled, but they did not consider how their designs caused systematic hardship. The ADA requires that new construction and remodeling include ramps, if necessary, to give disabled people greater access.

Age can also be grounds for unjust discrimination and stereotyping. Older workers are subjected to arbitrary age limits in employment, as, for example, when age alone rather than judgments of individual job performance is used to dismiss someone. Discrimination also occurs against lesbian, gay, bisexual, and transgendered (LGBT) people, a topic we discussed in Chapter 12 with regard to sexual morality and gay marriage. Religious minorities can also be discriminated against, most notoriously in the treatment of Jews throughout Europe, which culminated in the Nazi Holocaust of the 1930s and 1940s. The ideal of equal treatment and equal respect for all people regardless of race, ethnicity, sex, sexual orientation, national origin, and religion is an important goal, one that contemporary societies are still working to achieve.

THE PRINCIPLE OF EQUALITY

Racism, sexism, and other forms of discrimination are unfair and unjust. As we have seen, the racist, sexist, or homophobic individual treats people of a particular race, gender, or sexual orientation poorly simply because of these characteristics.

Yet perhaps we still have not gotten to the root of what is wrong with racism or sexism. Suppose that our views about members of a group are not based on prejudice but on an objective factual assessment of that group. For example, if men differ from women in significant ways—and surely they do— then is this not a sufficient reason to treat them differently? A moral principle can be used to help us think about this issue. The **principle of equality** is the idea that we should treat equal things in equal ways and that we may treat different things in unequal ways. In analyzing this principle, we will be able to clarify whether or why discrimination is morally objectionable. The principle of equality can be formulated in various ways. Consider the following formulation:

It is unjust to treat people differently in ways that deny to some of them significant social benefits unless we can show that there is a difference between them that is relevant to the differential treatment.

To better understand the meaning of this principle, we can break it down into several different concerns.

Justice

The principle of equality is a principle of justice. It tells us that certain actions or practices that treat people unequally are unjust. Consider, for instance, our symbol of justice, as represented by the image reproduced at the start of this chapter. (A similar statue stands outside the U.S. Supreme Court building in Washington, D.C.) Justice is depicted as blindfolded and holding a scale in one hand. The idea here is that justice is blind—in other words, it is not biased. It does not favor one person over another on the basis of irrelevant characteristics. The same laws are supposed to apply to all. The scale suggests that justice need not involve strict equality but must be proportional. It requires that treatment of persons be according to what is due them on some grounds. Therefore, it requires that there be valid reasons for differential treatment.

Social Benefits and Harms

We are not required to justify treating people differently from others in every case. For example, I may give personal favors to my friends or family and not to others without having to give a reason. However, sometimes social policies and practices treat people differently in ways that harm some and benefit others. This harm can be obvious or it can be subtle. In addition, there is a difference between *primary* discrimination and *secondary* discrimination.[26] In primary discrimination, a person is singled out and directly penalized simply because he or she is a member of a particular group, as when denied school admissions or promotions just because of this characteristic. In secondary discrimination, criteria for benefit or harm are used that do not directly apply to members of particular groups and only indirectly affect them. Thus, the policy "last hired, first fired" is often likely to have a discriminatory effect. Such a policy may seem harmless but can actually have a harmful effect on certain groups—particularly if these groups, such as women or blacks, have traditionally been excluded from a particular profession. The principle of equality directs us to consider the ways that social benefits and harms are distributed.

Proof and Reality of Difference

The principle of equality states that we must show or prove that certain differences exist if we are to justify treating people differently. The principle can be stronger or weaker depending on the kind of proof of differences required by it. It is not acceptable to treat people differently on the basis of differences that we only think or suspect exist. Scientific studies of sex differences, for example, must be provided to show that certain sex differences actually exist, if we are to allow for differential treatment based on sex.

The principle of equality requires that we show or prove that actual differences exist between the people whom we would treat differently. Many sex differences are obvious, and others that are not obvious have been confirmed by empirical studies—such as differences in metabolic rate, strength and size, hearing acuity, shoulder structure, and disease susceptibility. However, it is unlikely that these differences would be relevant for any differential social treatment. More relevant would be differences such as certain types of intellectual ability, aggressiveness, or nurturing capacity.

We might look to scientific studies of sex differences to help us determine whether any such possibly relevant sex differences exist. For example, women have been found to do better on tests that measure verbal speed, and men have been found to do better at being able to imagine what an object would look like if it were rotated in three-dimensional space. Recent discoveries have shown that men and women use different parts of their brains to do the same tasks. For example, to recognize whether nonsense words rhyme, men use a tiny area in the front left side of the brain, whereas women use a comparable section of the right side.[27] Whether such differences have a wider significance for different types of intelligence is a matter of intense debate. So also are the studies of aggressiveness. Testosterone has been shown to increase size and strength, but whether it also makes males more aggressive than females is disputed. This dispute arises not only because of the difficulties we have in tracing physical causation but also because of our uncertainty about just what we mean by aggressiveness.

Most studies that examine supposed male and female differences also look at males and females after they have been socialized. Thus it is not surprising that they do find differences. Suppose that a study found that little girls play with dolls and make block houses while little boys prefer trucks and use the blocks to build imaginary adventure settings. Would this necessarily mean that some innate difference causes this? If there were such differences and if they were innate, then this may be relevant to how we would structure education and some other aspects of society. We might prefer women for the job of nurse or early child care provider, for example. We might provide women, but not men, with paid child care leave. However, if we cannot prove that these or any such characteristics come from nature rather than nurture, then we should be more careful about differential treatment. We should consider whether our social institutions perpetuate socially induced differences.

Relevant Differences

The principle of equality requires more than proving that innate or real differences exist between groups of people before we are justified in treating them differently. It also requires that the differences be relevant. For example, if it could be shown that women are by nature better at bricklaying than men, then this would be a "real" difference between them. Although we might then be justified in preferring women for bricklaying jobs, we would not be justified in using this difference to prefer women for the job of airline pilot. On the other hand, if men and women think differently and if certain jobs require these particular thinking skills, then according to the principle of equality we may well prefer those individuals with these skills for the jobs. We might also prefer different people for bona fide reasons, such as hiring men to model male swimsuits and women to model female swimsuits. What counts as a bona fide reason will depend on the context.

The relevance of a talent, characteristic, or skill to a job is not an easy matter to determine. For example, is upper body strength an essential skill for the job of firefighter or police officer? Try debating this one with a friend. In answering this question, it would be useful to determine what kinds of things firefighters usually have to do, what their equipment is like, and so forth. Similarly, with the job of police officer, we might ask how much physical strength is required and how important are other physical or psychological skills or traits. And is being an African American, Asian American, or female an essential qualification for a position as university teacher of courses in black studies, Asian studies, or women's studies? It may not be an essential qualification, but some people argue that one's identity does help qualify a person because she or he is more likely to understand the issues and problems with which such courses deal. Nevertheless, this view has not gone unchallenged.

In addition to determining which characteristics or skills are relevant to a particular position, we must be able to assess adequately whether particular persons possess these characteristics or skills. Designing such assessments presents a difficulty, as prejudice may play a role in designing or evaluating them. For instance, how do we know whether someone works well with people or has sufficient knowledge of the issues that ought to be treated in a women's studies course? This raises a broader issue. Should we always test or judge people as individuals, or is it ever permissible to judge an individual as a member of a particular group?

Challenges to the Principle

One significant problem for the principle of equality stems from the fact that those group differences that are both real and relevant to differential treatment are often, if not always, *average* differences. In other words, a characteristic may be typical of a group of people, but it may not belong to every member of the group. Consider height. Men are typically taller than women. Nevertheless, some women are taller than some men. Even if women were typically more nurturing than men, it would still be possible that some men would be more nurturing than

some women. Thus it would seem that we ought to consider what characteristics an individual has rather than what is typical of the group to which he or she belongs. This would only seem to be fair or just. But social life does occasionally require that we deal with individuals as members of groups, especially when making policies from a utilitarian perspective that aims to produce the greatest happiness for the greatest number of people. Critics will object, however, that individuals rather than groups ought to be the focal point of moral concern. Such an objection might be a Kantian one that holds that we ought to respect persons as ends in themselves and that to consider individuals merely as members of a group is an affront to their dignity.

Are we ever justified in treating someone differently because of her membership in a particular demographic and because of that group's typical characteristics—even if she does not possess them? We do this in some cases and presumably think it is just. Consider our treatment of people as members of an age group, say, for purposes of driving or voting. We have rules that require that a person must be at least fifteen years old to obtain a driver's permit or license. Of course it is true that some individuals who are fourteen would be better drivers than some individuals who are eighteen. Yet we judge them on the basis of a group characteristic rather than their individual abilities. Similarly, in the United States, we require that people be eighteen years of age before they can vote. However, some people who are younger than eighteen would be more intelligent voters than some who are older than eighteen.

Social policies about voting and driving are based on generalizations about age cohorts. Those who agree to the policies resulting from these generalizations most likely do so for utilitarian reasons; these policies tend to produce good outcomes for most of us. If a fourteen-year-old is well qualified to drive, then she has only to wait a year or two, depending on the laws in her state. This causes no great harm to her. Nor is any judgment made about her natural abilities. Even those fifteen and older have to take a test on which they are judged as individuals and not just as members of a group. Furthermore, suppose that we tried to judge people as individuals for the purposes of voting. We would need to develop a test of "intelligent voting ability." Can you imagine what political and social dynamite this testing would be? The cost to our democracy of instituting such a policy would be too great, whereas the cost to the individual of being judged as a member of an age group and having to wait a couple of years to vote is comparatively small. Thus this practice does not seem unduly unfair.

However, if real and relevant sex differences existed, and if we treated all members of one sex alike on the basis of some typical group characteristic rather than on the basis of their characteristics as individuals, then this would involve both significant costs and significant unfairness. It would be of great social cost to society not to consider applicants or candidates because of their sex; these individuals might otherwise make great contributions to society. In addition, those who are denied consideration could rightly complain that it was unfair to deny them a chance at a position for which they qualified, something that would also affect them their whole lives.

One significant recent example is the decision to allow women to serve in combat roles in the American military. Prior to this decision, the military careers of women were limited because of a "brass ceiling": high-level military jobs tend to go to soldiers with combat experience. Proponents of combat roles for women argue that now individual women will have the opportunity to be judged on merit and ability and not merely on their membership in a group. As former Army Capt. Tanya L. Domi concludes, "With this momentous shift, America once again reaffirms its core values of equality and respect—values predicated upon a person's capabilities and demonstrated competence, not an immutable characteristic like gender. This is good for our military, and our country too."[28]

Another challenge to the principle of equality, or to its application, can be found in the debates over *preferential treatment* programs. Past discrimination may be a relevant difference between groups of people, which might justify differential treatment in order to remedy differences that have resulted from past injustice. Preferential treatments would be designed to benefit those who are members of groups that have been discriminated against in the past. The idea here is that being a member of a group is a sufficient reason to treat someone in a special way. Would we need to show that every member of that group was in some way harmed or affected by past discrimination? Some individual members of particular groups would not obviously have been harmed by past discrimination. However, we should also be aware of the complicated ways in which group or community membership affects a person and the subtle ways in which she might thus be harmed.

A different problem for the principle concerns the problem of managing natural and cultural differences. Recall that over the past centuries, women have sought equality with men in the workplace, in education, and in public life generally. At the same time, they remain the primary child care providers in most families, which places them at an inevitable disadvantage in terms of advancement in many professions. As a result, some feminists have argued that the liberal notion of equality can be detrimental to women because it fails to take gender-specific circumstances into account. Perhaps differences between males and females in such areas as parental responsibilities would be relevant to the justness of requirements for professional advancement. Perhaps women should be treated differently in ways that allow them to fulfill the responsibilities of breastfeeding and child care. Other feminists point out that if men took an equal share of child care, such differential treatment would not be required, except with regard to such things as pregnancy and childbirth.

Issues of multiculturalism also could be raised with regard to the principle of equality. Americans live in a complex society in which there are many forms of cultural expression and heritage. To what extent should individuals' distinct cultural backgrounds and traditions be acknowledged and encouraged? Sometimes, respect for such cultural practices would lead to the condoning of gender inequality and discrimination.[29] The challenge raised here is a variety of the paradox of toleration (which we discussed in Chapter 2). Do those groups that deny the principle of equality deserve to be treated equally? Do groups who do not treat their own members equally deserve to be treated equally? The challenges to the principle of equality that we've mentioned here indicate that while the principle of equality is an important one, it is not always clear how it is to be applied in practice.

CURRENT ISSUES AND THE LAW

Civil rights laws enacted in the United States and other Western countries have proved to be powerful tools for reducing racial injustice and promoting equal treatment of citizens. When we speak of *civil rights*, we are referring primarily to rights that are granted by the government—they are rights of civil or political society, so-called rights of citizenship. Civil rights can be contrasted with the idea of natural rights or human rights, which we discussed in Chapter 7. Some may think that civil rights and human rights are synonymous. To understand the difference between civil rights and human rights, you might consider whether citizens should have different rights than noncitizens. Most civil societies do recognize a difference between the rights of citizens and the natural rights possessed by noncitizens. Civil rights are sometimes thought of as applications of or means for the protection of more basic human rights. As Thomas Paine explained, "every civil right grows out of a natural right; or in other words, is a natural right exchanged."[30] Thus the right to vote may be understood as the result of certain democratic social and political arrangements. Such a right is ultimately based on some other claim about natural rights, such as the right to liberty or self-governance. In the United States, civil rights are thought to rest upon constitutional bases, such as the rights enumerated in the Bill of Rights (the first ten amendments to the Constitution, which were ratified in 1791).

From the founding of the United States onward, there were deep and often violent conflicts about which members of society should be granted civil rights—most notably with regard to the issue of slavery. African slaves had become an integral part of the American colonies' culture and economy long before the nation's independence from Britain. By the time the founding documents were written, slavery was so ingrained in America, particularly in the South, that its presence was officially affirmed in Article I of the Constitution. (Slaves were to be counted as three-fifths of a person for purposes of taxation and representation.) Thus from the start, America's concept of civil rights for all "men"

explicitly excluded several categories of people living in America (women were also excluded from many of these civil rights, including the right to vote).

In the nineteenth century, grassroots movements to abolish slavery developed in America, particularly among Northern religious constituencies. As the abolitionist movement gained political traction, a stark regional conflict arose between North and South, a struggle that culminated in the Civil War. In 1868, after the Civil War ended slavery in the United States, the Fourteenth Amendment to the Constitution was ratified. This amendment declares that no state may "deny to any person within its jurisdiction the equal protection of the law." The Fourteenth Amendment guaranteed full citizenship rights to adult males who were born or naturalized in the United States. (It was not until 1920 that women secured voting rights, with the ratification of the Nineteenth Amendment.) Although the Fourteenth Amendment established formal equality for males, the United States remained racially segregated after its passage due to a combination of laws known as "Jim Crow." The Jim Crow system in the American South included laws that restricted voting rights and others that kept blacks segregated from whites. A challenge to Jim Crow was mounted by Homer Plessy, a black man who sat in a white-only railroad car. After he was arrested, he sued in a case that made it to the U.S. Supreme Court. The Court ruled in *Plessy v. Ferguson* (1896) that it was acceptable for states to create a segregated system based on the idea of "separate but equal." But the "equality" affirmed by this ruling was in name only; accommodations and services for African Americans were invariably below the quality of those provided for white Americans. This legal system of segregation and discrimination continued largely unchallenged until the U.S. Supreme Court ruling *Brown v. Board of Education* (1954) overturned the idea that "separate but equal" schooling was justifiable. In 1955, Rosa Parks challenged the segregated bus system in Montgomery, Alabama, by sitting in a bus seat reserved for whites. This prompted a bus boycott in Montgomery led by a young Baptist minister named Martin Luther King Jr.

The 1960s ushered in a host of significant civil rights legislation. In an executive order in 1961,

President John F. Kennedy instituted affirmative action in government hiring and in governmental contracts with the goal of encouraging "by positive measures" equal opportunity for all qualified persons.[31] These new hiring procedures increased the number of African Americans in the employ of the federal government.[32] In 1965, President Lyndon B. Johnson issued enforcement procedures such as goals and timetables for hiring women and underrepresented minorities. The Equal Pay Act of 1963 required that male and female employees receive equal pay for substantially equal work. The landmark Civil Rights Act of 1964 prohibited a range of discriminatory practices by private employers, employment agencies, and unions; it also prohibited, among other things, discriminatory voter registration requirements. In 1965, the Voting Rights Act prohibited states from creating restrictions on voting that would "abridge the right of any citizen to vote based on race or color."

While the 1960s saw a broad expansion of civil rights protections, more recent decades have witnessed a narrowing of their scope and legal foundations. Take, for instance, affirmative action laws. In the 1978 *Bakke v. U.C. Davis Medical School* decision, the Supreme Court forbade the use of racial quotas in school admissions but allowed some consideration of race in admissions decisions. This decision was challenged by the 1995 decision *Adarand v. Pena*, which held that any race-conscious federal program must serve a "compelling state interest" and must be "narrowly tailored" to achieve its goal. However, in 2003, a less rigid standard for acceptance of a race-conscious program was used by the court in its decision regarding the affirmative action practices of the University of Michigan. In *Grutter v. Bollinger*, the court upheld the university's law school policy, which considers an applicant's race as one factor among others such as test scores, talent, and grade-point average in admissions. The court rejected the undergraduate school's more mechanical practice of automatically giving extra points to applicants with specific racial backgrounds. The court also gave added support to earlier rulings that there was a "compelling state interest" in racial diversity in education.[33] In an affirmative action case involving an employer, the 1979 *Weber v. Kaiser Aluminum* decision, the court permitted a company to remedy its past discriminatory practices by using race as a criterion for admission to special training programs. These programs were aimed at ensuring that a percentage of black persons equal to that in the local labor force could rise to managerial positions in the company.

In the 1990s, two significant pieces of civil rights legislation were passed: the Americans with Disabilities Act of 1990, which prohibited discrimination based upon disability and was discussed previously, and the Civil Rights Act of 1991. The latter required that businesses using employment practices with a discriminatory impact (even if unintentional) must show that the practices are business necessities; otherwise, these businesses must reform their practices to eliminate this impact.[34] Hiring quotas were forbidden except when required by court order for rectifying wrongful past or present discrimination. Sexual harassment was also noted as a form of discrimination.

Many of the most recent advances in civil rights law have involved issues of sex, gender, and sexual harassment. Today, two forms of sexual harassment are generally recognized. One promises employment rewards for sexual favors, and the other creates a "hostile work environment." Sexual harassment also includes harassment based on sexual orientation or gender identity; discrimination based on these categories is also illegal in some, but not all, areas in the United States. A case decided by the Equal Employment Opportunity Commission in 2012 (*Macy v. Department of Justice*) established that Title VII of the Civil Rights Act of 1964 extends to protect transgendered persons against discrimination.[35] Other recent developments include the passage in 2009 of the Lilly Ledbetter Fair Pay Act, which guarantees an employee's right to fair compensation without discrimination.[36] The law is named after a supervisor at a Goodyear tire plant who experienced systematic pay discrimination based on gender for nearly two decades.

These are just a few of the highlights of the past 150 years of civil rights laws. A more thorough discussion might involve laws and court decisions that concern housing, lending, and the busing of school students, as well as laws that have been designed to prevent discrimination on the basis of religion, age, and other characteristics.

Profiling

One basic issue that arises in the context of civil rights law is the problem of profiling. Profiling happens when law enforcement agencies treat individuals as suspects simply because of their race, ethnicity, religion, or other traits.

Profiling has sometimes been endorsed by law enforcement agencies as a useful tool for identifying criminals. But critics complain that profiling leads to unjustified harassment. African Americans, for example, have for decades reported being stopped by traffic police simply because they were African Americans—for the supposed crime of "driving while black."[37] One analysis offered this data from traffic stops in Missouri in 2007:

> Blacks were 78 percent more likely than whites to be searched. Hispanics were 118 percent more likely than whites to be searched. Compared to searches of white drivers, contraband was found 25 percent less often among black drivers and 38 percent less often among Hispanic drivers.[38]

Police stopped black and Hispanic drivers more often but found contraband at a lower rate among these drivers. This makes one wonder whether profiling of this sort is really effective.

Profiling is often connected to drug enforcement practices, such as the federal Drug Enforcement Administration's Operation Pipeline drug interdiction project. According to critics, in the 1980s and 1990s police agencies involved in Operation Pipeline used **racial profiling** in their effort to stop drug traffickers on the highways.[39] U.S. courts have tended to rule that racial profiling is illegal—under the Constitution's Fourth Amendment protection against unreasonable searches and seizures and the Fourteenth Amendment requirement of equal protection under the law. But the practice continues. In 2010, the ACLU and the NAACP filed a lawsuit against the state of Maryland, alleging that the state police practiced racial profiling and demanding that the state turn over internal documents—a request that was affirmed by the Maryland Supreme Court in 2013. Similar issues

have arisen in New York City, where a widespread policy of "stop-and-frisk" policing has been criticized as relying heavily on racial profiling. According to ABC News, "While black and Hispanic residents make up only 23 percent and 29 percent of the city's population respectively, 84 percent of recorded stops are young men of color and only around 6 percent of stops lead to an arrest."[40]

Other recent events have raised concerns about profiling. In 2010, the governor of Arizona, Jan Brewer, signed into law Senate Bill 1070, which gave local police extensive power to enforce federal immigration law. The law was intended to discourage illegal immigration, and its stated goal is to "discourage and deter the unlawful entry and presence of aliens and economic activity by persons unlawfully present in the United States."[41] The law authorized local police officers to stop people if they have a "reasonable suspicion" of their being unauthorized immigrants.[42] Police could demand that they show proof of citizenship without there being any indication of criminal activity. Other states, such as Alabama, Georgia, Indiana, South Carolina, and Utah, have modeled immigration laws on the Arizona law. However, the Arizona law was soon legally contested, and parts of the law were overturned by the U.S. Supreme Court in 2012. Nevertheless, the court allowed law enforcement to act on "reasonable suspicion" that a person is an unauthorized immigrant, a standard that critics say encourages profiling and discrimination. They argue that racial and ethnic characteristics are the only possible basis for a "reasonable suspicion" that a person is in the United States illegally. Some immigration advocates call such legal measures "Juan Crow" laws—recalling the Jim Crow laws of the twentieth century, which discriminated against African Americans.[43] They cite cases of harassment and wrongful detention such as that of Antonio Montejano, whom we discussed at the outset of this chapter.

A different type of profiling involves suspicions based on a person's religion. Since the September 11 terrorist attacks, there have been a number of cases in which American Muslims have been harassed and profiled. For example, consider the 2006 case of six imams (Muslim religious leaders) detained at the Minneapolis–Saint Paul airport while trying to return

U.S. Immigration and Customs Enforcement officers arrest a suspected illegal immigrant during an early morning operation in Silver Spring, Maryland.

from an Islamic conference. Several passengers and a gate agent complained that the imams' behavior was suspicious. They said the imams had knelt and prayed loudly at the boarding gate and made anti-American comments. When the imams boarded their U.S. Airways flight, they sat in different places throughout the plane, and a couple of them asked for seat belt extenders with heavy buckles on the ends. In response to the reports of fellow passengers, security personnel asked the six imams to leave the plane before takeoff. When they refused, the police were called, and they were handcuffed and taken off the plane. After hours of questioning, they were allowed to take another flight.[44] The imams later said they had not acted suspiciously or even prayed loudly and that their only "crime" was being identifiable as Muslims. They sued the airline, the police authorities, and the passengers who had reported them to authorities, claiming that they had been discriminated against. Their lawsuit was settled in 2009 for an undisclosed amount. A similar case occurred in 2009 when a Muslim family from Alexandria, Virginia, was ordered off an AirTran flight

and detained after other passengers overheard them discussing the safest place to sit on a plane. Despite the absence of evidence that the family meant any harm, the airline refused to let them purchase new tickets. After the story became public, AirTran apologized and offered to refund the cost of the family's replacement tickets on another airline.[45]

While many people condemn such incidents as unjustified discrimination, popular author Sam Harris has argued that security officials should use profiling at airports. He argues that it is a waste of security resources to try to be fair and randomly screen people, including grandmothers, who pose no threat. Harris calls the effort to avoid profiling "the tyranny of fairness." Harris writes, "Some semblance of fairness makes sense and, needless to say, everyone's bags should be screened, if only because it is possible to put a bomb in someone else's luggage. But the TSA has a finite amount of attention; Every moment spent frisking the Mormon Tabernacle Choir subtracts from the scrutiny paid to more likely threats."[46] Arguments of this sort are often subject to criticism from civil rights advocates. Not only does profiling unfairly generalize about group members but it also can have negative consequences. Not all terrorists are Muslims; terrorists can also be Christians or Jews or atheists. Furthermore, profiling Muslims may generate resentment and provoke backlash.

One of the problems of profiling is that it tends to focus on obvious and overt signs of racial, ethnic, or religious belonging and then involves sweeping generalizations about the behaviors of individuals who appear to fit those categories. Whether a policy counts as profiling and whether it always implies discrimination is a matter of some debate. For example, when decisions to stop motorists are made primarily or solely on the basis of race, this is surely discriminatory. However, in other cases in which race is just one of many factors in selecting targets of investigation, the question of discrimination is not so clear. This is the difference between "hard" and "soft" profiling. In the former case, race is the only factor used to single out someone, whereas in the latter it is just one of many factors. An example of the latter might be "questioning or detaining a person because of the confluence of a variety of factors—age (young), dress (hooded sweatshirt, baggy pants, etc.), time (late evening), geography (the person is walking through the 'wrong' neighborhood)—that include race (black)."[47] Sometimes it may be hard to tell what kind of profiling an example involves. Consider a New Jersey highway patrolman who pulls over a black driver in a Nissan Pathfinder because the police have intelligence that Jamaican drug rings favor this car as a means for their marijuana trade in the Northeast.[48] Is this an example of unjust discrimination or a reasonable procedure?

Hate Crimes

A more obvious expression of discrimination and bias can be found in hate crimes, which are defined as crimes accompanied or motivated by bias. The attack on the Sikh temple in Oak Creek, Wisconsin, in August 2012 was a sadly typical case. A white supremacist, motivated by racial hatred, opened fire at a Sikh temple, killing six.

The FBI defines a hate crime as a "criminal offense against a person or property motivated in whole or in part by an offender's bias against a race, religion, disability, ethnic origin or sexual orientation."[49] The legal focus on crimes that are motivated by bias became an issue in the 1980s, as Washington and Oregon passed legislation identifying this category of crime.[50] By 2009, the U.S. Congress passed the "Matthew Shepard and James Byrd Jr. Hate Crimes Prevention Act." The two individuals named in this legislation were murdered by offenders who targeted them because of bias. Matthew Shepard was brutally beaten, tied to a fence, and left to die in 1998 in Laramie, Wyoming, where he was a university student. Shepard's assailants targeted him because he was gay. However, Wyoming did not have a hate crime law at the time. James Byrd Jr. was a black man who was murdered in 1998 in Jasper, Texas, by three white men who beat him, urinated on him, tied a chain around his legs, and dragged him behind their truck until his arm and head were severed when his body hit a culvert. The murderers were white supremacists. Byrd's murder prompted the Texas legislature to pass hate crime legislation in 2001.

As a result of the federal Hate Crime Statistics Act of 1990, the Department of Justice keeps extensive data on hate crimes.[51] Recent data indicate that more than 6,200 hate crimes were reported in 2011, involving more than 7,600 victims.[52] Of those crimes,

> 46.9 percent were racially motivated.
> 20.8 percent resulted from sexual-orientation bias.
> 19.8 percent were motivated by religious bias.
> 11.6 percent stemmed from ethnicity/national origin bias.
> less than 1 percent (0.9) were prompted by disability bias.

While hate crimes occur in a variety of ways, they often focus on humiliating the victim. Consider, for example, a hate crime that occurred in Ohio in 2011 among the Amish. Some Amish men attacked other Amish people, holding them down and cutting off the women's hair and the men's beards. The beards and hair were a symbol of faith. The crime was motivated by religious reasons. And so it was prosecuted as a hate crime.[53]

Just as there are special, more severe penalties for killing police officers, federal and state laws sometimes impose more severe penalties for crimes motivated by hatred. Critics of these policies respond that to do this is to punish people for the views they hold, and that no matter how objectionable hate crimes might be, such laws constitute a violation of free speech. The FBI makes it clear, however, that its hate crime prosecutions are focused on crimes such as murders, arsons, and assaults that are *accompanied by* bias—and not in prosecuting bias itself, which is protected by the First Amendment. As we have seen in other chapters, equality and nondiscrimination are ethical values that must be balanced against other values such as the free speech and privacy rights of individuals.

AFFIRMATIVE ACTION AND PREFERENTIAL TREATMENT

One recurrent question in discussions of equality and discrimination is whether it is ever justified to treat people in unequal ways as a remedy for past discrimination. This question is most frequently raised with regard to programs of affirmative action and preferential treatment. Affirmative action plans try to take active ("affirmative") steps to remedy past inequality. One way to do this is to give preferential consideration or treatment to members of groups that have been discriminated against in the past.

As noted previously, there are still stark disparities in American society, which many say are the legacy of past injustices. Some of these disparities will be outlined in economic terms in Chapter 14. And in Chapter 15 we discuss racial disparities in the **criminal justice** system. In terms of the general demographic of the United States, whites make up 78.1 percent of the population, blacks make up 13.1 percent, Hispanics make up 16.7 percent, and Asian and Pacific Islanders make up 5.2 percent.[54] But consider that only thirteen African Americans have ever been a CEO of a Fortune 500 company.[55] Despite this, we are making progress toward more diversity and equality. The 113th Congress (resulting from the November 2012 elections) has the following makeup (out of 535 members): 98 women, 43 African Americans, 31 Latinos, 12 Asian Americans and Pacific Islanders, 7 gay and bisexual members, as well as a first-ever Buddhist senator and the first Hindu member of the House of Representatives.[56]

Affirmative action comes in many forms. The idea suggested by the term is that to remedy certain injustices we need to do more than follow the negative requirement "Don't discriminate" or "Stop discriminating." The basic argument given for doing something more is usually that merely ceasing discrimination will not or has not worked. Psychological reasons may be cited, for example, that discrimination and prejudice are so ingrained in people that they cannot help discriminating and do not even recognize when they are being discriminatory or prejudiced. To illustrate this dynamic, the philosopher Robert Fullinwider asks us to imagine that we have been transported to a land of giants, where everything is made for folks their size. They might fail to see why smaller people like us might have difficulties, assuming instead that we are just inferior or incompetent.[57] Social and political reasons for affirmative action can also be given, such as evidence of structural or institutional racism (as we discussed previously). The only way to change things, the argument goes, is to do something more positive, which would change established patterns of discrimination.

But what are we to do? There are many possibilities. One is to make a greater positive effort to find qualified persons from underrepresented groups. Thus, in hiring, a company might place ads in minority newspapers. In college admissions, counselors might recruit more actively among disadvantaged minority groups. Once the pool is enlarged, then all in the pool are judged by the same criteria, and no special preferences are given on the basis of race or sex.

Other versions of affirmative action involve what have come to be known as *preferences*. In this approach, preference is given to minority group members or women who are as well qualified as other candidates—their membership in a disadvantaged group simply gives them an edge. Preference also may be given to underrepresented group members who are somewhat less well qualified than other applicants. In either case, it is clear that determining equality of qualifications is in itself a problem. One reason for this is that applicants are usually better qualified for some aspects of a given position and less well qualified for others. Another is the difficulty of deciding just what qualifications are necessary or important for a given position. Although those who support and those who oppose preferences often imply that determining requirements for a position is easy, it is not at all that simple.

Other forms of affirmative action also exist. For example, companies or institutions may establish goals and quotas to be achieved for increasing minority or female representation. *Goals* are usually thought of as ideals that we aim for but that we are not absolutely required to reach. Goals can be formulated in terms of percentages or numbers. *Quotas*, in contrast, are usually fixed percentages or numbers that an institution intends to actually reach. Thus a university or professional school might set aside a fixed number of slots for its incoming first-year class for certain minority group members. The institution would fill these positions even if this meant admitting people with lesser overall scores or points in the assessment system.

In past decades an effort was made to increase the representation of minority groups on college campuses. These efforts have been successful enough to prompt a backlash against race-based admissions processes. In its 1996 decision in *Hopwood v. Texas*, a three-judge panel of the U.S. Court of Appeals for the Fifth Circuit struck down an affirmative action program at the University of Texas law school. This program had accepted lower scores on the Law School Admission Test (LSAT) for black and Hispanic applicants. In a parallel development, Proposition 209 in California outlawed racial preferences in the public sector, and in 1995 the board of regents of the University of California (UC) system voted to ban race considerations in admissions. As we saw previously, the U.S. Supreme Court upheld the University of Michigan's graduate admissions program, in which race was one of several factors, but found unconstitutional the university's undergraduate admissions program, which gave a fixed number of additional points to minority applicants.

The *Hopwood* decision and others like it had negative impacts on minority enrollments in colleges and universities. In Texas, black college enrollment fell by 28 percent in the two years following *Hopwood*.[58] In California, between 1995 (when Prop. 209 passed) and 1998, minority enrollments at UC Berkeley and UCLA dropped by more than 50 percent. The numbers of minority students continue to be low and fail to reflect California's rapidly changing demography.[59] Other analyses indicate that while these policies may have an adverse effect on minority enrollment at elite universities, this problem is not as pronounced for less selective schools. Moreover, there is some data to suggest that minority graduation rates are increasing.[60] Nonetheless, there is still concern about finding ways to increase minority enrollments. Some states have attempted to find other ways to help generate a diverse student body. In Texas, the legislature guaranteed a place in Texas's public universities to the top 10 percent of graduates from Texas high schools. The idea of this approach was to ensure that students from minority-serving high schools had a better chance at college admissions.

Most recently, the Supreme Court considered affirmative action in *Fisher v. University of Texas at Austin*, in which the plaintiff challenged the University of Texas's affirmative action policy. The plaintiff claimed that the state had achieved a sufficient level of diversity in the university and thus that the university no longer had a need to give extra consideration to applicants based upon race. It is a factual question as to whether affirmative action has been effective or not. The moral question of whether affirmative action is justified is another matter. At any rate, the Supreme Court's decision in *Fisher* was not decisive—they returned the case to the lower courts—and the moral and legal debate about affirmative action is ongoing.

In any discussion of affirmative action, it is important to specify exactly what kind of practice one favors or opposes. Let us examine the arguments for and against the various types of affirmative action in terms of the reasons given to support them. As in other chapters, these arguments can be divided into consequentialist and non-consequentialist approaches.

Consequentialist Considerations

Arguments both for and against various affirmative action programs have relied on consequentialist considerations for their justification. These considerations are broadly utilitarian in nature. The question is whether affirmative action programs do more good than harm or more harm than good. People who argue in favor of these programs urge the following sorts of considerations: These programs benefit us all. We live in a multiracial society and benefit from mutual respect and harmony. We all bring diverse backgrounds to our employment and educational institutions, and we all benefit from the contributions of people who have a variety of diverse perspectives. Our law schools should reflect the full diversity of our society to help ensure all people have access to adequate representation and protection under the law. Others argue that affirmative action is one way to break the vicious cycle of discrimination and inequality. Past discrimination has put women and some minority group members at a continuing disadvantage. Unless something is done, they will never be able to compete on an equal basis. Low family income leads to poorer education for children, which leads to lower-paying jobs, which leads to low family income, and so on. Children need role models to look up to. They need to know that certain types of achievement and participation are possible for them. Otherwise, they will lack hope and opportunities to pursue success. Without affirmative action programs, supporters argue, things are not likely to change. Discrimination and its long-term effects are so entrenched that drastic measures are needed to overcome them.

Those who argue against affirmative action on consequentialist grounds usually maintain that the programs do not work or that they do more harm than good. They cite statistics to show that these programs have benefited middle-class African Americans, for example, but not the lower class. As Stephen Carter argues, "The most disadvantaged black people are not in a position to benefit from preferential admission."[61] Critics such as Carter suggest that unless affirmative action admissions programs are accompanied by other aid, both financial and tutorial, they are often useless or wasted. Some critics point out that lawsuits filed under the 1964 Civil Rights Act have done more than affirmative action to increase the percentage of blacks in various white-collar positions.[62] Other consequentialist critics argue that there is a stigma attached to those

who have been admitted or hired through affirmative action programs and that this can be debilitating for those so chosen. Some black neoconservatives even argue that quotas and racially weighted tests "have psychologically handicapped blacks by making them dependent on racial-preference programs rather than their own hard work."[63]

Those who oppose affirmative action programs also cite the increased racial tension that they believe results from these programs—in effect, a white male backlash against women and members of minority groups. Some of the same writers who support affirmative action for underrepresented minority groups and women have also made a case for giving special attention to economically disadvantaged students in college and university admissions.[64] They point out that elite universities have only a minuscule percentage of admissions from lower-income families, even when they have sizable minority enrollments. These thinkers argue that such class-based affirmative action is not only justified for reasons of fairness but also serves the purpose of increasing class diversity.

The key to evaluating these consequentialist arguments both for and against affirmative action is to examine the validity of their assessments and predictions. What, in fact, have affirmative action programs achieved? Have they achieved little because they benefit those who least need it and might have succeeded without them, or have they actually brought more disadvantaged students into the system and employees into better and higher-paying jobs, thus helping break a vicious cycle? Have affirmative action programs benefited society by increasing diversity in the workforce and in various communities, or have they led only to increased racial tensions? These are difficult matters to assess. Here is another place where ethical judgments depend on empirical information drawn from the various sciences or other disciplines. The consequentialist argument for affirmative action programs will succeed if it can be shown that there is no better way to achieve the good the programs are designed to achieve and that the good done by these affirmative action programs outweighs any harm they cause. The consequentialist argument against affirmative action programs will succeed if it can be shown that there are better ways to achieve the same good ends or that the harm they create outweighs the good they help achieve.

Non-consequentialist Considerations

Not all arguments about affirmative action programs are based on appeals to consequences. Some arguments appeal to deontological considerations. For instance, some people argue for affirmative action programs on the grounds that they provide *compensatory justice*, a way of compensating for past wrongs done to members of certain groups. People have been harmed and wronged by past discrimination, and we now need to make up for that by benefiting them, by giving them preferential treatment. However, it can be difficult to assess how preferential treatment can right a past wrong. We may think of it as undoing the past harm done. But we find that it is often difficult to undo the harm. How does one really prevent or erase results such as the loss of self-esteem and confidence in the minority child who asks, "Mom, am I as good as that white kid?" or in the little girl who says, "I can't do that; I'm a girl"? This interpretation of making compensation then becomes a matter of producing good consequences or eliminating bad ones. It is a matter of trying to change the results of past wrongs. Thus if we are to compensate for non-consequentialist reasons, then it must involve a different sense of righting a wrong— a sense of justice being done in itself, whether or not it makes any difference in the outcome.

Some non-consequentialist critics also argue against affirmative action on grounds of its injustice. They appeal to the principle of equality, arguing that race and sex are irrelevant characteristics that should not be recognized by government policy. Just as it was wrong in the past to use these characteristics to deny people equal chances, so it is also wrong in the present, even if it is used this time to their advantage. Race and sex are not differences that should count in treating people differently, they argue. Preferences for some also mean denial of benefits to others. For this reason, preferential treatment programs have sometimes been labeled *reverse discrimination*. Moreover, opponents of affirmative action criticize the use of compensatory justice arguments. In a valid

application of compensatory justice, they argue, only those wronged should be compensated, and only those responsible for the wrong should be made to pay. They object to affirmative action programs that compensate people based on group membership and without establishing whether they themselves have been harmed by past discriminatory practices. Those who lose out in affirmative action programs, they argue, may not have ever been guilty of discrimination or may not have wronged anyone.

Consider the case of a group of white firefighters in New Haven, Connecticut, that went to the U.S. Supreme Court in 2009. That city administered a test to its firefighters to determine who would be promoted. When no black firefighters passed the test, the city simply dropped all of the results. Those white firefighters who had passed the test complained of reverse discrimination. By a 5-4 ruling, the Court agreed with them.[65]

The arguments for affirmative action based on considerations of justice will succeed only if those persons who make them also can make a case for the justice of the programs. They must show that such programs do in fact compensate those who have been wronged, even if they have been affected by discrimination in ways that are not immediately obvious. Supporters may also argue that those who lose out as a result of preferences are not badly harmed—they have other opportunities and are not demeaned by their loss. And though they have not intentionally wronged anyone, they have likely benefited from structures of discrimination.

Those who oppose affirmative action based on considerations of justice will succeed if they can effectively apply the principle of equality to their arguments. They may argue, for example, that affirmative action singles out some groups for special treatment in a way that is inconsistent with the idea of equality. But if they rely primarily on the harms done by continuing to use race or sex as grounds for differential treatment, then they will be appealing to a consequentialist consideration and must be judged on that basis.

This chapter has dealt with a range of issues collected together under the general rubric of equality and discrimination: racial profiling, racism, hate crimes, and affirmative action. The guiding principle is that we should treat people fairly and equally. While there is disagreement about how the principle of equality applies in these cases and about its moral basis, there is widespread agreement that equality matters.

NOTES

1. Julia Preston, "Immigration Crackdown Also Snares Americans," *New York Times*, December 13, 2011, accessed April 11, 2013, http://www.nytimes.com/2011/12/14/us/measures-to-capture-illegal-aliens-nab-citizens.html?pagewanted=all

2. "Law Enforcement, Gov't Officials, Victims Speak Out," ACLU, press release, November 30, 2011, accessed April 11, 2013, http://www.aclu.org/immigrants-rights/end-secure-communities-now; also see "Immigration Enforcement Snares Citizens in L.A. County," *Los Angeles Times*, December 15, 2011, accessed April 11, 2013, http://articles.latimes.com/2011/dec/15/local/la-me-1215-detained-citizens-20111214

3. "Secure Communities: Get the Facts," U.S. Immigration and Customs Enforcement, accessed April 11, 2013, http://www.ice.gov/secure_communities/get-the-facts.htm

4. Preamble to the Civil Rights Act of 1964, accessed April 11, 2013, http://www.ourdocuments.gov/doc.php?flash=true&doc=97&page=transcript

5. EEO Policy Statement, U.S. Equal Employment Opportunity Commission, January 31, 2011, accessed April 11, 2013, http://www.eeoc.gov/eeoc/internal/eeo_policy_statement.cfm

6. "Racial Prejudice in US Worsened during Obama's First Term, Study Shows," *Guardian*, October 27, 2012, accessed March 24, 2013, http://www.guardian.co.uk/world/2012/oct/27/racial-prejudice-worsened-obama

7. See Julianne Hing, "Asian Americans Respond to Pew: We're Not Your Model Minority," *Colorlines*, June 21, 2012, accessed April 30, 2013, http://colorlines.com/archives/2012/06/pew_asian_american_study.html; also see, "The Rise of Asian Americans," Pew Center Report, June 19, 2012, accessed April 30, 2013, http://www.pewsocialtrends.org/2012/06/19/the-rise-of-asian-americans/

8. Carolyn Chen, "Asians: Too Smart for Their Own Good?" *New York Times*, December 19, 2012, accessed April 30, 2013, http://www.nytimes.com/2012/12/20/opinion/asians-too-smart-for-their-own-good.html?_r=0; also see "Fears of an Asian Quota in the Ivy League," *New York Times*, December 19, 2012, accessed April 30, 2013, http://www.nytimes.com/roomfordebate/2012/12/19/fears-of-an-asian-quota-in-the-ivy-league/?ref=opinion

9. R. C. Lewontin, "Race: Temporary Views on Human Variation," *Encyclopedia Americana*, http://ea.grolier.com; also see R. C. Lewontin, *Human Diversity* (New York: W. H. Freeman, 1982).

10. Luigi Luca Cavalli-Sforza, Paolo Menozzi, and Alberto Piazza, *History and Geography of Human Genes* (Princeton, NJ: Princeton University Press, 1994), 19.

11. Carolyn Abraham, "Race," *Globe and Mail*, June 18, 2005, F1, F8.

12. See International HapMap Project, www.hapmap.org

13. Kwame Anthony Appiah, "Racisms" in *Anatomy of Racism*, ed. David Theo Goldberg (Minneapolis, MN: University of Minnesota Press, 1990), pp. 3-17.

14. See Sally Haslanger, "Oppressions: Racial and Other," in *Racism in Mind* (Ithaca, NY: Cornell University Press, 2004).

15. U.S. Department of Education, National Center for Education Statistics, 2012, *The Condition of Education 2011* (NCES 2012-045), accessed March 22, 2013, http://nces.ed.gov/fastfacts/display.asp?id=40

16. U.S. Department of Education, National Center for Education Statistics, 2012, *The Condition of Education 2012* (NCES 2012-045), accessed March 22, 2013, http://nces.ed.gov/fastfacts/display.asp?id=16

17. Bureau of Labor Statistics, U.S. Department of Labor, "Unemployment Rates by Race and Ethnicity, 2010," accessed March 22, 2013, http://www.bls.gov/opub/ted/2011/ted_20111005.htm

18. Tami Luhby, "Worsening Wealth Inequality by Race," *CNN Money*, June 21, 2012, accessed March 23, 2013, http://money.cnn.com/2012/06/21/news/economy/wealth-gap-race/index.htm

19. "Affluent Students Have an Advantage and the Gap Is Widening," *New York Times*, December 22, 2012, accessed March 22, 2013, http://www.nytimes.com/interactive/2012/12/22/education/Affluent-Students-Have-an-Advantage-and-the-Gap-Is-Widening.html?_r=0

20. Scott Jaschik, "SAT Scores Drop Again," *Inside Higher Ed*, September 25, 2012, accessed March 22, 2013, http://www.insidehighered.com/news/2012/09/25/sat-scores-are-down-and-racial-gaps-remain

21. Scott Jaschik, "SAT Scores Down Again, Wealth Up Again," *Inside Higher Ed*, August 29, 2007, accessed April 30, 2013, http://www.insidehighered.com/news/2007/08/29/sat#ixzz2Rzt6hJJ3

22. Travis L. Dixon, "Network News and Racial Beliefs: Exploring the Connection between National Television News Exposure and Stereotypical Perceptions of African Americans," *Journal of Communication* 58 (2008): 321–37.

23. Travis L. Dixon, "Crime News and Racialized Beliefs: Understanding the Relationship between Local News Viewing and Perceptions of African Americans and Crime," *Journal of Communication* 58 (2008): 106–25.

24. "The Simple Truth about the Pay Gap" (2013), AAUW, accessed March 22, 2013, http://www.aauw.org/resource/the-simple-truth-about-the-gender-pay-gap/

25. Lam Thuy Vo, "The Jobs with the Biggest (and Smallest) Pay Gaps between Men and Women," NPR Planet Money, accessed April 22, 2013, http://www.npr.org/blogs/money/2012/02/05/171196714/the-jobs-with-the-biggest-and-smallest-pay-gaps-between-men-and-women

26. See Mary Anne Warren, "Secondary Sexism and Quota Hiring," *Philosophy and Public Affairs* 6, no. 3 (Spring 1977): 240–61.

27. Gina Kolata, "Men and Women Use Brain Differently, Study Discovers," *New York Times*, February 16, 1995, A8.

28. Tanya L. Domi, "Women in Combat: Policy Catches Up with Reality," *New York Times*, February 8, 2013, accessed May 1, 2013, http://www.nytimes.com/2013/02/09/opinion/women-in-combat-policy-catches-up-with-reality.html?_r=0

29. Susan Moller Okin, *Is Multiculturalism Bad for Women?*, ed. Joshua Cohen, Matthew Howard, and Martha C. Nussbaum (Princeton, NJ: Princeton University Press, 2000).

30. Thomas Paine, *"Rights of Man"* in *Thomas Paine: Collected Writings* (New York: Library of America, 1955, reprinted 2012), 465.

31. Executive Order 10925 (1961), accessed May 13, 2013, http://www.eeoc.gov/eeoc/history/35th/thelaw/eo-10925.html

32. Bruce P. Lapenson, *Affirmative Action and the Meanings of Merit* (Lanham, MD: University Press of America, 2009), 3.

33. Linda Greenhouse, "University of Michigan Ruling Endorses the Value of Campus Diversity," *New York Times*, June 24, 2003, A1, A25.

34. This aspect of the bill confirmed the "disparate impact" notion of the 1971 U.S. Supreme Court ruling in *Griggs v. Duke Power Company*, which required companies to revise their business practices that perpetuated past discrimination. This was weakened by the Court's 1989 ruling in *Wards Cove Packing Co. v. Antonio*, which, among other things, put the burden of proof on the employee to show that the company did not have a good reason for some discriminatory business practice.

35. Equal Opportunity Employment Commission, accessed May 2, 2013, http://www.eeoc.gov/federal/otherprotections.cfm

36. http://www.lillyledbetter.com/

37. David A. Harris, "Driving While Black: Racial Profiling on Our Nation's Highways," ACLU, June 7, 1999, accessed March 21, 2013, http://www.aclu.org/racial-justice/driving-while-black-racial-profiling-our-nations-highways

38. Donald Tomaskovic-Devey and Patricia Warren, "Explaining and Eliminating Racial Profiling," *American Sociological Association Contexts* (Spring 2009), accessed March 21, 2013, http://contexts.org/articles/spring-2009/explaining-and-eliminating-racial-profiling/

39. Harris, "Driving While Black."

40. Bill Weir and Nick Capote, "NYPD's Controversial Stop-and-Frisk Policy: Racial Profiling or 'Proactive Policing'?" ABC's *Nightline*, May 1, 2013, accessed May 2, 2013, http://abcnews.go.com/US/nypds-controversial-stop-frisk-policy-racial-profiling-proactive/story?id=19084229#.UYLbtSvEo_s

41. SB 1070, accessed March 21, 2013, http://www.azleg.gov/legtext/49leg/2r/bills/sb1070s.pdf

42. Ibid.

43. Diane McWhorter, "The Strange Career of Juan Crow," *New York Times*, June 16, 2012, accessed March 21, 2013, http://www.nytimes.com/2012/06/17/opinion/sunday/no-sweet-home-alabama.html

44. Libby Sander, "6 Imams Removed from Flight for Behavior Deemed Suspicious," *New York Times*, November 22, 2006, accessed April 23, 2013, http://www.nytimes.com/2006/11/22/us/22muslim.html?bl&ex=1164517200&en=24531ca1fa7314e1&ei=5087%0A

45. Amy Gardner, "9 Muslim Passengers Removed from Jet," *Washington Post*, January 2, 2009, accessed April 11, 2013, http://www.washingtonpost.com/wp-dyn/content/article/2009/01/01/AR2009010101932.html?hpid=topnews; also see Amy Gardner and Spencer S. Hsu, "Airline Apologizes for Booting 9 Muslim Passengers from Flight," *Washington Post*, January 3, 2009, accessed April 23, 2013, http://www.washingtonpost.com/wp-dyn/content/article/2009/01/02/AR2009010201695.html

46. Sam Harris, "In Defense of Profiling," Sam Harris Blog, April 2012, accessed March 19, 2013, http://www.samharris.org/blog/item/in-defense-of-profiling

47. Randall Kennedy, "Suspect Policy," *New Republic*, September 13 and 20, 1999, 35.

48. Heather MacDonald, "The Myth of Racial Profiling," *City Journal* 11, no. 2 (Spring 2001), http://www.city-journal.org/html/11_2_the_myth.html

49. "Hate Crime—Overview," FBI, accessed March 21, 2013, http://www.fbi.gov/about-us/investigate/civilrights/hate_crimes/overview

50. "Hate Crime," National Institute of Justice, accessed May 2, 2013, http://www.nij.gov/topics/crime/hate-crime/

51. Brian Levin, "The Long Arc of Justice: Race, Violence and the Emergence of Hate Crime Law," in *Hate Crimes*, ed. Barbara Perry (Westport, CT: Greenwood Publishing, 2008), 1:8.

52. "Hate Crime Statistics, 2011," FBI, accessed March 21, 2013, http://www.fbi.gov/about-us/cjis/ucr/hate-crime/2011/narratives/incidents-and-offenses

53. "Amish Beard Cutting Case," FBI, February 8, 2013, accessed March 21, 2013, http://www.fbi.gov/news/stories/2013/february/16-sentenced-in-amish-beard-cutting-case

54. U.S. Census Bureau, QuickFacts 2011, accessed March 24, 2013, http://quickfacts.census.gov/qfd/states/00000.html

55. "African American CEO's of Fortune 500 Companies," *Black Entrepreneur*, April 7, 2012, accessed May 2, 2013, http://www.blackentrepreneurprofile.com/fortune-500-ceos/

56. Jim Acosta, "Meet the 113th Congress: More Diverse Than Ever," CNN, January 3, 2013, accessed May 2, 2013, http://inamerica.blogs.cnn.com/2013/01/03/meet-the-113th-congress-more-diverse-than-ever/

57. Robert K. Fullinwider, "Affirmative Action and Fairness," *Report from the Institute for Philosophy and Public Policy* 11, no. 1 (Winter 1991): 10–13.

58. John F. Kain, Daniel M. O'Brien, and Paul A. Jargowsky, *Hopwood and the Top 10 Percent Law: How They Have Affected the College Enrollment Decisions of Texas High School Graduates*, Report for the Texas Schools Project at the University of Texas at Dallas, March 25, 2005, accessed May 2, 2013, http://www.utdallas.edu/research/tsp-erc/pdf/wp_kain_2005_hopwood_top_10_percent.pdf.pdf

59. "Despite Diversity Efforts, UC Minority Enrollment Down Since Prop. 209," California Watch, February 24, 2013, accessed May 2, 2013, http://californiawatch.org/dailyreport/despite-diversity-efforts-uc-minority-enrollment-down-prop-209-15031

60. Peter Arcidiacono, Esteban Aucejo, Patrick Coate, and V. Joseph Hotz, "The Effects of Proposition 209 on College Enrollment and Graduation Rates in California" (working paper, December 2011), accessed May 2, 2013, http://public.econ.duke.edu/~psarcidi/prop209.pdf

61. Stephen Carter, *Reflections of an Affirmative Action Baby* (New York: Basic Books, 1991).

62. Professor Jonathan Leonard, cited in the *San Francisco Examiner*, September 29, 1991.

63. *Time*, May 27, 1991, 23.

64. Amy Argetsinger, "Princeton's Former President Challenges 'Bastions of Privilege,'" *San Francisco Chronicle*, April 17, 2004, A5.

65. *Ricci v. DeStefano*, 557 U.S. ___ (2009).

1. Summarize the history of civil rights law, including recent affirmative action decisions. Have we made progress in actualizing the principle of equality in the law? Why or why not?

2. Should racial, gender, or other differences ever be relevant to making decisions about qualified candidates for jobs or educational opportunities? Please support your answer with reference to concepts discussed in the chapter.

3. Explain the principle of equality. How is this principle related to other moral principles we've discussed in other chapters?

4. Evaluate the ethics of racial profiling and hate crime legislation. Are these useful legal tools?

5. What is "affirmative action," and why does it have this name? Explain different types of affirmative action. Which of them involve or may involve giving preferential treatment?

6. Summarize the consequentialist arguments for and against affirmative action.

7. Summarize the non-consequentialist arguments for and against affirmative action.

1. **Women in Combat.** Denise and Edward are debating the new plan to allow women to officially serve in combat in the military. Denise is opposed to the idea. She says, "I think that fighting is men's work. Men are stronger and they are more aggressive. They're just better at fighting. Plus, it just seems better to leave women behind the lines to care for the wounded and take care of logistics." Edward can't believe that Denise is saying this. "You're kidding, right? I thought you were a feminist, in favor of equality for women. I mean, if men are asked to fight and die for their country, it's only fair to ask women to do that too." Denise says, "Yes, I know that equality matters. But in this case, there are some big differences between men and women—especially their upper body strength—that are relevant to what kinds of jobs they should have." Edward responds, "But not all men are stronger or more aggressive than all women. There are lots of women who are stronger than me." "Yes," Denise answers. "But we need a general policy that creates the best fighting unit. I'm worried that allowing women into combat will have bad results." Edward shakes his head. "I doubt it," he says. "And besides, it's only fair to give women a chance to prove themselves in combat."

   Which side are you on? Should women be allowed into combat? Why or why not?

2. **Campus Diversity.** During the past couple of decades, colleges and universities have tried to increase their numbers of minority students by various forms of affirmative action. At Campus X, this has led to controversy and discord. Some students criticize as unfair the policy of accepting students with lower SAT and other scores just because of their race or minority status. Others believe that the diversity that results from such policies is good for everyone because it is reflected in the broader society and a university should prepare people to participate in our diverse culture. Still, there is some question even among members of this group as to how well different ethnic groups relate on campus. Furthermore, a different type of problem has recently surfaced. Because Asian Americans are represented on campus in numbers greater than their percentage of the population, Campus X may restrict the percentage of Asians they will accept even when their scores are higher than others. Campus X is also considering eliminating its affirmative action program entirely, which alarms some students. They point to declining numbers of minorities at certain medical and law schools that have done away with their affirmative action programs.

   Do you think that diversity ought to be a goal of campus admissions? Or do you believe that only academic qualifications ought to count? Do you think limiting the university enrollment of overrepresented groups (such as Asians and whites) based on their percentage of the overall population would be justified? Why?

3. **Profiling.** Daniel and Ezra were both recently stopped and frisked by the cops while walking down the street in New York City. Daniel is African

American. Ezra is an immigrant from Israel. Daniel feels like the "stop-and-frisk" policy is blatantly racist. "The cops just target people of color, looking for an excuse to hassle us," he says. "I've got no reason to fear the police. I've done nothing wrong. But it makes me mad." Ezra is a bit more sympathetic to stop-and-frisk policing. In Israel, people's bags are searched when they go to the corner store. Ezra says, "I'm not worried about it. The cops know something about who is likely to commit a crime. They're not searching old ladies. That would be a waste of time. There are bad guys out there. And I want the cops to catch them. If I fit the profile somewhat, it's worth the hassle. It actually makes me feel safer to know that they are targeting their searches." Daniel replies, "Yeah, but this is America, not the Middle East!"

Is it racist and discriminatory to target certain people for searches? Would it make you feel safer to know that the police were targeting people in this way? Should equal treatment be sacrificed in the name of public safety?

Blend Images/Thinkstock

14 Economic Justice

Learning Outcomes

After reading this chapter, you should be able to:

- Understand current facts with regard to economic inequality.
- Explain the concept of social justice from both utilitarian and deontological points of view.
- Describe why charity might be considered supererogatory.
- Identify differences between capitalism and socialism.

- Explain libertarian and liberal ideas about distributive justice.
- Describe the difference between procedural and end-state ideas about justice.
- Recount John Rawls's theory of justice.
- Defend a thesis about economic justice.

In the Fall of 2011 people took to the streets in massive numbers across the globe, protesting economic inequality. The protests, which began under the name "Occupy Wall Street," grew out of frustration with practices in the financial sector that contributed to the global recession that began in 2007. Occupy encampments were set up in cities across the country, as protesters showed up with tents and sleeping bags in city parks, outside of city halls, and in public places from San Francisco to Washington, D.C. The movement identified itself with the slogan, "We are the 99 percent," which was meant to highlight the economic gap between the vast majority of people (the 99 percent) and the wealthiest (top 1 percent). In the United States in 2010, for example, the top 1 percent owned 35 percent of all wealth in the nation, which made those in the top 1 percent 288 times richer than the median American household.[1] One of the explanations for the growing wealth disparity is that while incomes have increased for the wealthy, they are also paying less in taxes. Since the 1970s, tax rates on the rich have fallen dramatically in the United States. In 2013, the top 1 percent—those earning more than $1.4 million—paid an effective tax rate of 35.5 percent; this was a slight increase from the previous decade.[2] But in 1960 that same group, the top 1 percent of earners, would have paid an effective tax rate of more than 50 percent.[3] The Occupy Movement and the global recession that began in 2007 brought the issue of economic justice into the forefront of people's consciousness, with many arguing that government had a greater role to play in ensuring economic fairness and a basic level of security for all members of society.

The Occupy Movement arose in contrast to the Tea Party—a conservative grassroots movement concerned about rising national debt and government overreach in areas such as health care and taxation. Rather than focusing on inequality, the Tea Party emphasized

THIS PROTEST IS ABOUT
1% OF AMERICA
STEALING FROM

99%

MEANING YOU

Marjorie Kamys Cotera/Bob Daemmrich Photography/Alamy

Protester at an Occupy Austin demonstration in Austin, Texas.

the importance of liberty and the free market and viewed government as a threat to both. Those who support this approach might argue, for example, that as a matter of equality and fairness, tax rates should be the same for the poor and the wealthy.

The growth of the Tea Party and Occupy Movements reflects a serious debate in the United States and beyond about the state of the economy, the morality of capitalism, and the problem of economic justice. In classrooms, in the media, and around dinner tables, Americans can still be heard having conversations much like the following debate between Betty (a business major) and Phil (a philosophy major).

Betty: I think that people have a right to make and keep as much money as they can as long as they do not infringe on others' rights. We shouldn't be taxing the rich to give to the poor.

Phil: Is it fair that some people are born with a silver spoon in their mouths and others are not?

Society should ensure that everyone has an equal opportunity to succeed. Right now it seems like the deck is stacked against the working and middle classes, which are 99 percent of the population.

Betty: But how could we guarantee that the poor will not waste what we give them? In any case, it is just not right to take the money of those who have worked hard for it and redistribute it. The top 1 percent earned their money and deserve to keep it.

Phil: Have they really earned it? A lot of rich people inherit money and other benefits from their parents, including access to good schools, connections, and other opportunities. Even if they didn't, they probably benefited from public goods paid for by taxes, such as interstate highways, the Internet, and public schools.

Betty: In any case, if we take away what people have earned, whether they deserve it or not, they will have no incentive to work. Profits are what make the economy of a nation grow.

Phil: And why is that so? Are you saying that the only reason people work is for their own self-interest? And do you really think self-interest alone can produce a just society, as Adam Smith and his "invisible hand" would have it? Capitalism sometimes creates inequalities that are unjust; governments should correct for this.

Betty: A just society doesn't mean that everyone has to have equal amounts of wealth. If justice is fairness, as some of your philosophers say, it is only fair and therefore just that people get out of the system what they put into it. And, besides, there are other values. We value freedom, too, don't we? People ought to be free to work and keep what they earn.

Phil: Freedom? What freedom is there for the little guy when the economy collapses as a result of the greed and corruption of the corporate elites? It's the little guy whose house is taken away in foreclosure and loses his job. While most people's real wages have stagnated for decades, the incomes of the top 1 percent have continued to increase.

Betty: Well, that's the way capitalism works. People take risks with their money, buying houses or investing in businesses. Sometimes they lose big bucks, the market turns downward—maybe they lose a house or a business. But in the long run, this shock to the system increases productivity, as people have to respond creatively to the demands of the market.

Phil: But it's not a level playing field; not everyone can afford to take risks with their money. Unrestrained capitalism helps rich people get richer but gives poor people few opportunities to get ahead. While your 1 percent is responding "creatively" to the market crash, the 99 percent is just trying to pay for their kids' college education or save for retirement.

Betty: You sound like a socialist. But you can't be serious about thinking that the government should control large sectors of the economy, as they do in Cuba, or that we should be taxed to the hilt like they are in Europe.

Phil: Well, the average worker does pretty well in Europe and has to pay far less for things like health care and retirement. From a utilitarian perspective, some degree of socialism isn't so bad.

Betty: But socialism limits the freedom of the individual. It is disrespectful of the right of individuals to earn as much as they can.

Phil: At least we can agree on one thing, that something ought to be done about corporate misdeeds. We need good ethics to prevail in the corporate boardroom.

Betty: Agreed. Corruption doesn't produce good outcomes in the long run. If there is not sufficient transparency in corporate business practices, then investors will not be able to make wise decisions and inefficiency will harm the system.

The issues touched on in this conversation belong to a group of issues that fall under the topic of *economic justice*. This includes other issues as well. For example, do people have a right to a job and good wages? Is welfare aid to the poor a matter of charity or justice? Is it fair to tax the rich more heavily than the middle class? And what should the role of the government be in terms of controlling the economy and regulating business practices?

ECONOMIC INEQUALITY

In the United States, 46.2 million people—15 percent of the population—live in poverty. For children under age eighteen, the poverty rate is higher: 21.9 percent of children (more than one in five) live in poverty.[4] According to the Census Bureau, these numbers have remained about the same for several years. The poverty threshold varies according to family size. But, for example, in 2011 the poverty threshold for a family of five was $27,517. The median household income in the United States between 2007 and 2011 was $52,762.[5] The richest American, Bill Gates, has a net worth of $67 billion.[6]

These statistics point toward the problem of income inequality. In March 2007, Alan Greenspan, the former chairman of the Federal Reserve, noted, "Income inequality is where the capitalist system is most vulnerable. You can't have the capitalist system if an increasing number of people think it is unjust."[7] By the end of 2007, the global economy was afflicted by a financial crisis that stemmed, in part, from the bursting of a speculative housing bubble. Large numbers of people lost their homes, and still more lost home equity. The banking and financial sector experienced a massive shock. Many wondered about the causes of this catastrophe. Some blamed banks for making bad loans. Others blamed the financial industry for creating exotic financial instruments, which allowed some investors to profit at the expense of homeowners and others. And some blamed unscrupulous financiers such as Bernie Madoff, who ran an elaborate Ponzi scheme—a pyramid scheme that takes money from new investors and uses it to pay previous investors in an ever-growing cycle of debt. Eventually the crisis caused several important financial firms to collapse. Lehman Brothers—the fourth largest investment bank in the country—declared bankruptcy. The U.S. government stepped in and bailed out several other large banking and financial concerns, insurance companies, and auto manufacturers.

As a result of the economic meltdown, cities suffered, with some, including Stockton and San Bernardino in California, collapsing into bankruptcy. States suffered economic problems as tax revenues fell. As they struggled to respond, the states borrowed and cut—laying off state workers and accumulating debt. At the same time, the federal government struggled to balance its books. By early 2013, the national debt was above $16 trillion. The rising debt has prompted intense political squabbling and last-minute budget deals, as politicians and economists struggle to find some way to manage the economy. Worse debt obligations have wreaked havoc in other countries—Greece, Italy, Spain, and other European countries have faced economic turmoil as a private and public debt crisis swept through Europe. In these countries, pensions have vanished and unemployment rates have hovered around 20 percent for several years.

Meanwhile, the richest among us are doing very well, especially in the United States. One 2013 study found that since 2009, incomes for the bottom 99 percent of Americans have fallen by 0.4 percent, while incomes of the top 1 percent have risen by 11.2 percent.[8] In 2012, the net worth of the richest 1 percent was more than the net worth of the bottom 95 percent combined. The four hundred wealthiest individuals on the *Forbes* 400 list had more wealth than the bottom 150 million Americans combined.[9] Another measure of economic disparity is the difference between the amount of money the average worker makes and the compensation of corporate CEOs. Between 1979 and 2011, CEO compensation rose 725 percent, but worker pay rose only 5.7 percent during that same time period.[10] According to 2011 data compiled by PayScale.com, the ratio of CEO wages to median worker wages was 213:1 for the top fifty companies on the Fortune 500 list.[11] The PayScale.com data show that at Walmart, for example, the CEO earned $16,270,000, while the median worker was paid $22,700 (for a ratio of 717:1). At Verizon, the CEO earned $36,750,000, while the median worker was paid $60,000 (for a ratio of 613:1). According to *Forbes*, CEOs of the biggest five hundred companies got a collective pay raise of 16 percent in 2011. The total pay for those five hundred CEOs added up to $5.2 billion, which averages out to $10.5 million per CEO.[12]

These disparities in wealth might not matter all that much if it were possible for each of us to do better through hard work and natural talent. Modern social life is no longer bound by traditional class distinctions, and there are no legal barriers to social and economic advancement. However, in reality, social mobility is not as easy as we might think. One analysis concludes that roughly half of Americans remain in the same social strata into which they are born. And movement from bottom to top is difficult. If you were born in the bottom 20 percent, you have a 5 percent chance of making it into the top 20 percent; and those who were born into the top 20 percent have a similar one in twenty chance of falling into the bottom 20 percent.[13]

Other interesting facts help describe economic inequality. In the previous chapter, we noted that white Americans have twenty-two times more wealth than blacks and fifteen times more wealth than Hispanics.[14] We also discussed the difference between male and female income; in 2011, women still earned only 77 percent of what men earned.[15] But economic prospects for women are improving. According to a report from *Time* magazine in 2012, a growing number of women outearn their husbands.[16] Women are also doing better in terms of educational attainment, which may factor into improved economic prospects in the future.[17] Some have pointed out that the gender income gap may be in part a result of the fact that more women leave work to care for children and elderly parents, and they are more likely to work part time. It should be noted, though, that women experience a variety of social and economic pressures that men do not—including the gender pay gap—that may push them to put caregiving ahead of their careers. Even after factoring out differences between men and women in educational attainment, work experience, occupation, career interruptions, part-time status, and overtime worked, the gender wage gap is still between 4.8 and 7.1 percent.[18] (This remaining gap is attributable to simple gender discrimination.)

One explanation of general income inequality is that it reflects differences in employees' value to their employers. So in this theory, if a woman (or a man) takes time off to raise a family, she or he will earn less as a result of missing out on training and experience that would have occurred during the absence. But does a similar argument work to explain the gross disparities in income between CEOs and average workers or between the top 1 percent and the rest of us? Are CEOs justified in earning seven hundred times more than the average worker? One justification of those sorts of disparities would focus on the skills, intelligence, effort, and experience of CEOs and other top earners. Maybe the CEO is simply a seven hundred times better worker than the average employee. Another justification of wage disparities focuses on the need to allow the free market to determine compensation—people should be free to negotiate and earn whatever the market will pay them.

A critic might point in another direction, toward the sorts of burdens faced by those on the low end of the economic pyramid. Is it fair that the poor and unemployed have reduced opportunities and decreased life prospects? One problem for the unemployed is that even if they are willing to work, they often cannot find a job. The problem for the working poor is that even though they do work, they cannot earn a decent living. One factor to consider is the issue of the difference between the minimum wage and a living wage. The **minimum wage** is the minimum hourly wage an employer can pay its employees, a standard that is set by federal and state governments. In the United States in 2013, the federal minimum wage was set at $7.25 per hour (in some states it is higher, for example, it is $8.00 per hour in California). By contrast, a **living wage** is calculated based upon the cost of living in a given region, factoring in things like rent, food, transportation, and child care. Living wage calculations vary from place to place. In New York City, the living wage is calculated at $12.75 an hour for a single adult; for an adult with one child, the living wage is calculated at $24.69. In Los Angeles, California, the living wage for a single adult is calculated at $11.37; for an adult with one child, the living wage is $23.53. In a small town like Green Bay, Wisconsin, the living wage is $9.03 for a single adult and $19.65 for an adult with one child.[19] In each of these cases, the living wage is above the legal minimum wage. And in each of these places, a working mother with one child would be unable to provide for herself and her child by working at a minimum wage job. This helps explain why one in five American children is living in poverty. According to the U.S. Census Bureau, 26.2 percent of all children live with only one of their parents (49.2 percent of black children live with only one parent)—and 28.3 percent of single parents have incomes below the poverty line.[20] The question of fairness and justice arises here: is it fair

to impoverished children that, through no fault of their own, they grow up in poverty?

Poverty, Education, and Health Care

And why does poverty matter? One reason is that income disparities lead to disparate outcomes in terms of life prospects. The poor suffer from a variety of problems, many of which also become problems for society as a whole. One significant problem is the educational achievement gap between poor and wealthier children. Children from poor families do worse in school. The gap in standardized test scores between affluent and low-income students has grown by 40 percent since the 1960s. A similar income gap shows up in terms of college completion—with fewer poor kids completing college. This has a lifelong impact, as college completion is correlated with better prospects for future income.[21]

Income inequities are matched by inequities in health care. Although genes and lifestyle certainly play their roles in a person's health, poverty does as well. Poor people are more likely to be obese and to suffer from diabetes and heart disease than those who are economically better off. Low-income families also tend to be uninsured and to defer preventive medical and dental care. Children in low-income families are more prone to asthma, lead poisoning, anemia, and other ailments that create cognitive and behavioral problems. They are more likely to live in neighborhoods that are unsafe. They are more likely to lack access to books and computers.

One recent study concludes, "poverty, low levels of education, poor social support and other social factors contribute about as many deaths in the United States as such familiar causes as heart attacks, strokes and lung cancer."[22] Such health disparities between the rich and poor are even starker outside the developed world (we will look at the issue of global poverty in more detail in Chapter 20).

One pressing issue in the United States is the high cost of health care and health insurance. A family's savings can be wiped out by a major health problem if the family lacks health insurance. A recent Harvard study found that seven hundred thousand Americans go bankrupt every year due to medical bills. (Medical bankruptcy is unheard of in almost all other developed nations.)[23] One of the goals of the Affordable Care Act, passed in 2010, was to expand health insurance coverage to many of the tens of millions of uninsured, mostly low-income Americans. One of the mechanisms to accomplish this is to expand Medicaid to allow the working poor to obtain coverage through the program. The Affordable Care Act includes coverage for preventive care such as blood pressure, diabetes, and cholesterol tests. It also covers prenatal care and well visits and checkups for children. And it covers routine health care for women, including mammograms.[24] Another of the goals of the Affordable Care Act was to address health care inequities related to income level and employment—those in lower-income jobs tend to lack health care benefits while people in high-paying jobs tend to be offered generous health care benefits. While there is more to be said about how the Affordable Care Act is going to be implemented, the overarching goal of the Act is to make health care more accessible. By 2022, the law will provide health insurance to thirty-three million Americans who would otherwise be uninsured.[25] Defenders of the law argue that it is providing access to the basic good of health care.

Opponents of the Act criticize it as "socialized medicine." They argue that the government should not heavily regulate, much less provide, health insurance because this interferes with the free market. According to the conservative Heritage Foundation, which opposes the Affordable Care Act and is calling for its repeal, the solution is "market-based health care that gives people better choices and allows them to take account of the price and value of health care."[26]

The conservative approach is premised on the idea that government should stay out of the health care business, allowing individuals to make their own choices about insurance coverage. From this perspective, health care, like other businesses, should be left alone so that free markets might work to regulate prices and basic services. In this view, health care is a commodity like others to be bought and sold in an open market, where the laws of supply and demand would operate freely. Some unfortunate people may end up with bad outcomes in such a system—losing their savings to pay for health care or being denied health care—but this is part of the risk of a free-market society. Some conservatives even suggest that emergency medical care (currently guaranteed by law in the United States regardless of one's ability to pay) should also be subject to market forces, allowing hospitals to turn away indigent or uninsured dying patients.

The conservative idea is that the market will provide the best outcome for the greater number of people. Some conservatives also worry that government regulation of health care may result in "rationing," with the government denying coverage for certain expensive treatments. But liberals will reply that the market also "rations" health care in other ways, namely, by price and ability to pay.[27] Furthermore, liberals will argue that health care is a basic right that should be guaranteed by the government and not subject to market forces. From this perspective, health care is not simply a commodity to be bought and sold; rather, justice requires that individuals be provided with basic health care—even if they cannot afford it. While other nations do stipulate that health care is a basic right, in the United States there is no civil right to health care (see previous chapter for a discussion of civil rights).[28] The Constitution does not guarantee a right to health care. However, some will argue that there is a basic human right to health care, as well as a right to a living wage, a right to education, and so on.

CONCEPTIONS OF SOCIAL JUSTICE

As we saw in the previous section, there is a fundamental dispute between those who focus on the fairness of social institutions in terms of their outcomes and those who advocate the importance of individual choice and the free market. The first concern—for the impact that social arrangements have on people—is often called **social justice** (as distinguished, for example, from criminal justice). The idea of social justice has roots in the natural law tradition of Thomas Aquinas, as developed by the Catholic tradition (which we discussed in Chapter 7). Thomas Massaro, a Jesuit scholar of social justice, explains that the notion of social justice boils down to "the goal of achieving a right ordering of society. A just social order is one that ensures that all people have fair and equitable opportunities to live decent lives free of inordinate burdens and deprivation."[29] Social justice is often focused on distributions of goods among people in society, with an emphasis on minimizing inequalities across social classes.

While the social justice idea has roots in Christian natural law ethics, it can also be grounded in utilitarianism. John Stuart Mill, for example, was particularly interested in the question of economic justice. Mill thought that the vast majority of workers were "slaves to toil in which they have no interest, and therefore feel no interest—drudging from early morning till late at night for bare necessaries, and with all the intellectual and moral deficiencies which that implies."[30] As a utilitarian, Mill was interested in finding ways to alleviate drudgery and poverty, while producing the greatest happiness for the greatest number.

Mill was, we should also note, opposed to slavery, which was legal in the United States during most of his life. Not only did he reject the notion that whites should have despotic power over blacks, but he also rejected the idea that individuals should be reduced to mere working machines. He saw no value in "work for work's sake" and he thought that human happiness required leisure. Mill concluded, "To reduce very greatly the quantity of work required to carry on existence, is as needful as to distribute it more equally."[31] He also thought that the economy was unjust insofar as it did not connect hard work with profit. From Mill's perspective, the problem is that the rich are born into wealth and leisure, while the poor are born into a life of poverty and hard work. This runs counter to the idea that there should be a connection between success and merit. As Mill explains, "The very idea of distributive justice, or of any proportionality between success and merit, or between success and exertion, is in the present state of society so manifestly chimerical as to be relegated to the regions of romance."[32] Mill means that there is no justice in an economy in which those who work hard remain poor, while the rich don't work. Mill wanted to find a way to help the poor without producing dependence upon that help. As he explained it, the goal is to "give the greatest amount of needful help, with the smallest encouragement to undue reliance on it."[33] From the utilitarian standpoint, the challenge is to figure out how best to regulate the economy in a way that produces encouragement for hard work, while also preventing the impoverished, unemployed, and working poor from falling through the cracks.

Concern for social justice is sometimes connected with claims about the value of equality itself, as well as with claims about the value of human rights, human dignity, and solidarity among people. There are disagreements about the exact definition of these terms, even among those who are concerned with social justice. For example, equality may be defined as *substantial equality*, meaning that individuals should have exactly the same access to and amount of substantial goods. Or equality can be defined as *equality of opportunity*, meaning that individuals should have an equal chance to obtain goods. In either case, the pursuit of equality can lead to a conflict with other values, such as liberty. For example, to ensure equality, we may have to violate the liberty of those who possess certain goods so that we might redistribute those goods among others (as we do to some extent in a system of taxation that redistributes private property for social welfare purposes). Some conceptions of justice do emphasize liberty as the central value, as Mill himself did in his work *On Liberty*. The trick, for a utilitarian like Mill, is to find a way to balance liberty and the need for distributive or social justice.

The deontological theory of Immanuel Kant provides another source for thinking about human dignity and respect for autonomy. Kant is opposed to using individuals as a means to an end, and some would argue that to take a part of someone's income through taxation and redistribute it to others is a form of using that person as a means. But Kant also thought that charity and beneficence were important values. According to Kant's Categorical Imperative (which we discussed in Chapter 6), those who don't want to help the needy end up contradicting themselves, since they would expect others to help them if they were in need. In his *Lectures on Ethics*, Kant indicates that one reason to give to the needy is out of a sense that the social structure is unjust:

> In giving to an unfortunate man we do not give him a gratuity but only help to return to him that of which the general injustice of our system has deprived him. For if none of us drew to himself a greater share of the world's wealth than his neighbor, there would be no rich and no poor. Even charity therefore is an act of

duty imposed upon us by the rights of others and the debt we owe to them.[34]

Accounts of justice that emphasize liberty are often grounded in a natural law approach to ethics with roots in the work of John Locke. Locke's emphasis on a natural right to property is a fundamental starting point for those who want to defend a free-market economy. Other philosophers who focus on liberty connect their ideas to those of Ayn Rand (whom we mentioned in our discussion of egoism in Chapter 4). Tibor Machan, a contemporary libertarian author who builds upon Rand's ideas, stresses the idea that individual human beings "possess free will and need to guide their own lives to achieve excellence or to flourish."[35] Machan contrasts his theory of justice with other views of justice that require fairness, order, harmony, or social welfare. From Machan's libertarian point of view, the economy should be left alone so that individuals are free to create, trade, and earn whatever nature and the market allow them to. From this standpoint, charity is acceptable—but as the free choice of an individual to help others in need and not as an obligation of justice.

We can see from the philosophies of social justice discussed previously that we should distinguish justice from certain other moral notions. For example, justice is not the same as charity. It is one thing to say that a community, like a family, should help its poorer members when they are in need, out of concern for their welfare. But is helping people in need ever a matter of justice? If we say that it is, then we imply that it is not morally optional. Justice is often defined as giving people what is rightly due. Charity gives above and beyond the requirements of justice. Ethicists use the term **supererogatory** to describe actions that go above and beyond the call of duty. The word *supererogatory* comes from Latin roots, which can be translated to mean "paying more than is due" or "payment in addition." There is nothing unjust about giving charity. But we usually think that charity is not required by justice, it is supererogatory. Furthermore, justice is not the only relevant moral issue in economic matters. Efficiency and liberty are also moral values that play a role in discussions on ethics and economics. When we say that a particular economic system is *efficient*, we generally mean that it produces a maximum amount of

desired goods and services, or the most value for the least cost. Thus, some people say that a pure free-market economy is a good economic system, based on the claim that it is the most efficient, the one best able to create wealth. But it is quite another question whether such a system is also a *just* system or if it enhances liberty. If we could have the most efficient and perhaps even the most just economic system in the world, then would it be worth it if we were not also free to make our own decisions about many things, including how to earn a living?

Sorting out the relationship among these values is one of the primary goals of social justice philosophies. Such philosophies are often primarily concerned with the issue of **distributive justice**, which involves how the benefits and burdens of society are allocated—for example, who and how many people have what percentage of the goods or wealth in a society. Thus suppose that in some society, 5 percent of the people possessed 90 percent of the wealth, and the other 95 percent of the people possessed only 10 percent of the wealth. Asking whether this arrangement would be just is raising a question of distributive justice. Now how would we go about answering this question? It does seem that this particular distribution of wealth is quite unbalanced. But must a distribution be equal for it to be just? To answer this question, we can examine two quite different ways of approaching distributive justice. One is what we can call a *process view*, and the other is an *end-state view*.

Process Distributive Justice

According to some philosophers, any economic distribution (or any system that allows a particular economic distribution) is just if the process by which it comes about is itself just. Some call this **procedural justice**. For example, if the wealthiest 5 percent of the people got their 90 percent of the wealth fairly—they competed for jobs, they were honest, they did not take what was not theirs—then what they earned would be rightly theirs. In contrast, if the wealthy obtained their wealth through force or fraud, then their having such wealth would be unfair because they took it unfairly. Indeed, we might suspect that because talent is more evenly distributed, there is something suspicious about this uneven distribution of wealth. But there would be nothing unfair or unjust about the uneven distribution in itself. Some people are wealthy because of good luck and inheritance, and others are poor because of bad economic luck. However, in this view, those with money they get through luck or inheritance are not being unjust in keeping it even when others are poor.

End-State Distributive Justice

Other philosophers believe that the process by which people attain wealth is not the only consideration relevant to determining the justice of an economic distribution. They believe that we also should look at the way things turn out, the end state, or the resulting distribution of wealth in a society, and ask about its fairness. Suppose that, through inheritance, a small minority of lucky people came to possess 95 percent of society's wealth. Would it be fair for them to have so much wealth when others in the society are extremely poor? How would we usually judge whether such an arrangement is fair? We would look to see if there is some good reason why the wealthy are wealthy. Did they work hard for it? Did they make important social contributions? These might be nonarbitrary or good reasons for the wealthy to possess their wealth rightly or justly. However, if they are wealthy while others are poor because they, unlike the others, were born of a certain favored race or sex or eye color or height, then we might be inclined to say that it is not fair for them to have more. What reasons, then, justify differences in wealth?

Several different views exist on this issue. Radical egalitarians deny that there is any good reason why some people should possess greater wealth than others. Their reasons for this view vary. They might stress that human beings are essentially alike as human and that this is more important than any differentiating factors about them, including their talents and what they do with them. They might argue that society is an agreement for the mutual advancement of all and should treat each of its members as free and equal citizens. Or they might use religious or semireligious reasons, such as the idea that the Earth is given to all of us equally and thus we each have an equal right to the goods derived from it. Even egalitarians, however, must decide what it is that they believe

should be equal. Should there be equality of wealth and income or equality of satisfaction and welfare, for example? These are not the same. Some people have little wealth or income but nevertheless are quite satisfied, while others who have great wealth or income are quite dissatisfied. Some have champagne tastes, and others are satisfied with beer!

On the other hand, at least some basic differences between people should make a difference in what distribution of goods is thought to be just. For example, some people simply have different needs than others. People are not identical physically, and some of us need more food and different kinds of health care than others. Karl Marx's phrase, "To each according to his need" captures something of this variant of egalitarianism.[36] Nevertheless, why only this particular differentiating factor—need—should justify differences in wealth is puzzling. In fact, we generally would tend to pick out others as well—differences in merit, achievement, effort, or contribution.

Suppose, for example, that Jim uses his talent and education and produces a new electronic device that allows people to transfer their thoughts to a computer directly. This device would alleviate the need to type or write the thoughts—at least, initially. Surely, people would value this device, and Jim would probably make a great deal of money from his invention. Would not Jim have a right to or *merit* this money? Would it not be fair that he has this money and others who did not come up with such a device have less? It would seem so. But let us think about why. Is it because Jim has an innate or *native talent* that others do not have? Then through no fault of their own, those who happen to lack the talent would have less. It is a matter of arbitrary luck that Jim was born with this talent and thus became wealthy.

But perhaps Jim's wealth stems not only from his talent but also from his use of it. He put a great deal of *effort* into cultivating his talent. He studied electronics and brain anatomy and spent years working on the invention in his garage. His own effort, time, and study were his own contribution. Would this be a good reason to say that he deserved the wealth that he earned from it? This might seem reasonable, if we did not also know that his motivation and work ethic might also have been in some ways gifts of his circumstances and family upbringing. Furthermore, effort alone would not seem to be a good reason for monetary reward, or else John, who takes three weeks to make a pair of shoes, should be paid more than Jeff, who can make equally good ones in three hours. Similarly, a student would not be justified in demanding an A simply because she spent a lot of time and effort studying for a test—when her performance actually merited a B.

Finally, perhaps Jim should have the rewards of his invention because of the nature of his *contribution*, because of the product he made and its value to people. Again, this argument seems at first reasonable, and yet there are also fairness problems here. Suppose that he had produced this invention before computers became affordable for most consumers. The invention would be wonderful but not valued by people because they could not use it. Or suppose that others at the same time produced similar inventions. Then this happenstance would also lessen the value of the product and its monetary reward. Jim could rightly say that it was unfair that he did not reap a great reward from his invention just because he happened to be born at the wrong time or finished his invention a little late. This may be just bad luck. But is it also unfair? Furthermore, it is often difficult to know how to value particular contributions to a jointly produced product or result. How do we measure and compare the value of the contributions of the person with the idea, the investors, the product developers, and so forth, so that we can know what portion of the profits are rightly due them? Marxists are well known for their claim that the people who own the factories or have put up the money for a venture profit from the workers' labor unfairly or out of proportion to their own contributions.

This mention of Marx and Marxism reminds us that there is no consensus about what counts as a fair distribution of wealth. Revolutions and wars have been fought in the name of various ideas of economic justice.

Equal Opportunity

Another viewpoint on distributive justice does not fit easily into either the process or end-state categories. In this view, the key to whether an unequal distribution

of wealth in a society is just is whether people have a fair chance to attain positions of greater income or wealth. That is, equality of wealth is not required, only equal opportunity to attain it. (We discussed equal opportunity in connection to civil rights and nondiscrimination in the previous chapter.) We might see the notion of equal opportunity as symbolized by the Statue of Liberty in New York Harbor. The statue sits on Liberty Island, where, historically, new immigrants to the United States were processed. It represents the idea that in the United States all people have a chance to make a good life for themselves provided they work hard. But just what is involved in the notion of equal opportunity, and is it a realizable goal or ideal? Literally, it involves both opportunities and some sort of equality of chances to attain them. An *opportunity* is a chance to attain some benefit or goods. People have equal chances to attain these goods first of all when there are no barriers to prevent them from attaining them. Opportunities can still be said to be equal if barriers exist as long as they affect everyone equally. Clearly, if racism, sexism, or other forms of prejudice prevent some people from having the same chances as others to attain valued goals or positions in a society, then there is not equal opportunity. For example, if women have twice the family responsibilities as men, then do they really have an equal opportunity to compete professionally? Our discussion of the gender pay gap previously shows how opportunities that are supposed to be equal by law or policy may, in fact, be rendered unequal by social practices.

According to James Fishkin, an expert on political theory, if there is equal opportunity in my society, "I should not be able to enter a hospital ward of healthy newborn babies and, on the basis of class, race, sex, or other arbitrary native characteristics, predict the eventual positions in society of those children."[37] However, knowing what we do about families and education and the real-life prospects of children, we know how difficult this ideal would be to realize. In reality, children do not start life with equal chances. Advantaged families give many educational, motivational, and experiential benefits to their children that disadvantaged families cannot, and this makes their opportunities effectively unequal. Schooling greatly affects equal opportunity, and money spent for a school—teachers, facilities, and books—can make a big difference in the kind of education provided. However, funding per pupil on schooling in the United States varies considerably according to locale.[38] And affluent parents can supplement public schooling with private tutors, educational summer camps, music lessons, and other educational opportunities. Is it fair that some kids have these opportunities while others do not?

One version of equal opportunity is the *starting-gate theory*, which assumes that if people had equal starts in life, then they would have equal chances. The philosopher Bernard Williams provides a famous example of such a theory. In his imaginary society, a class of skillful warriors has for generations held all of the highest positions and passed them on to their offspring. At some point, the warriors decide to let all people compete for membership in their class. The children of the warrior class are much stronger and better nourished than the other children who, not surprisingly, fail to gain entrance to the warrior class. Would these other children have had effective equality of opportunity to gain entrance to the warrior class and its benefits? Even if the competition was formally fair, the outside children were handicapped and had no real chance of winning. But how could initial starting points then be equalized? Perhaps by providing special aids or help to the other children to prepare them for the competition. Applying this example to our real-world situation would mean that a society should give special aid to the children of disadvantaged families if it wants to ensure equal opportunity.[39] However critics may suggest that, to do this effectively would require serious infringements on family autonomy. For it would mean not only helping disadvantaged children but also preventing wealthier parents from giving special advantages to their children. Moreover, people have different natural talents and abilities, and those who have abilities that are more socially valued will likely have greater opportunities. Does this mean, then, that the idea of equal opportunity is unrealizable? It may only mean that our efforts to increase equality of opportunity must be balanced with the pursuit of other values such as family autonomy and efficiency.

Still, some philosophers have other questions about the ideal of equal opportunity. They argue that the whole emphasis on equality is misplaced and distracts us from what is really important. The philosopher Harry Frankfurt claims that rather than focusing on the fact that some have more than others, it would be better to focus on whether people have enough. We care not that one billionaire makes a few million more than another, but rather that everyone should have sufficient means to pursue their aspirations. Frankfurt calls his position the "doctrine of sufficiency," in contrast to theories that make equality in itself the primary goal.[40]

Although the doctrine of equal opportunity is appealing because it implies equal rewards for equal performance and doors open to all, some thinkers object to the notion of meritocracy on which it is based. According to John Schaar, the equal opportunity ideal is based on notions of a natural aristocracy.[41] Those of us who do not have the natural talent of an Einstein, a Steve Jobs, or a LeBron James will not have the same chances to succeed and prosper as those who do have such talents. We can enter the race, but we delude ourselves if we think that we have a real chance to win it. Schaar believes that stress on equal opportunity thus contributes to the gap between rich and poor. He also argues that emphasis on equal opportunity threatens the foundations of equality and democracy. Based, as it is, on the notion of a marketplace in which we, as atomic individuals, compete against our fellows, it threatens human solidarity. It does so even more if it is accompanied by a tendency to think that those who win are in some way more valuable as persons.[42]

Other philosophers argue that justice demands that people should not be penalized for things over which they have no control. Thus, it would seem unjust or unfair for people to suffer who, through no fault of their own, cannot compete or cannot compete well in the market, for example, the physically or mentally ill, or the physically or mentally handicapped.[43] Here we return to the idea that matters of luck may be seen as morally arbitrary and should not be reflected in a just distribution of society's benefits and burdens.

POLITICAL AND ECONOMIC THEORIES

Within discussions of economic justice, people often make use of specific economic and political terms and theories—including *libertarianism, capitalism, socialism, liberalism,* and *communitarianism.* To more fully understand the central issues of economic justice, it will be helpful to take a closer look at these terms and theories, to distinguish them from each other and to determine how each relates to different conceptions of justice. Some of the theories—capitalism and socialism, for example—can be differentiated from one another not only by basic definitions but also by the different emphases they place on the values of liberty, efficiency, and justice. They are further differentiated by how they favor or disfavor process or end-state views of distributive justice. A brief discussion of each will help elucidate these values and views of distributive justice.

Libertarianism

Libertarianism is a political theory about both the role of government and the importance of liberty in human life. Libertarians such as Tibor Machan (whom we mentioned previously) and Ayn Rand (see Chapter 4) believe that we are free when we are not constrained or restrained by other people. Sometimes, this type of liberty is referred to as a basic right to noninterference. Thus if you stand in the doorway and block my exit, you are violating my liberty to go where I wish. However, if I fall and break my leg and am unable to leave, then my **liberty rights** are violated by no one. The doorway is open and unblocked, and I am free to go out. I cannot go out simply because of my injury.

According to **libertarianism**, government has a minimal function that is primarily administrative. It should provide an orderly civic space in which people can go about their business. It does have an obligation to ensure that people's liberty rights are not violated, that people do not block doorways (or freeways, for that matter). However, government has no obligation to see that my broken leg is repaired so that I can walk where I please. In particular, it has no business taxing you to pay for my leg repair or any other good that I (or you) might like to have or even need. Such needs can be addressed by charities, but they are not matters of social justice or obligation.

Libertarians would be more likely to support a process view of distributive justice than an end-state view. Any economic arrangement would be just so long as it resulted from a fair process of competition, and so long as people did not take what is not theirs or get their wealth by fraudulent or coercive means. Libertarians do not believe, however, that governments should be concerned with end-state considerations. They should not try to even out any imbalance between rich and poor that might result from a fair process. They should not be involved in any redistribution of wealth. This includes potential redistributions from social insurance arrangements such as Social Security, Medicare, and Medicaid.

The work of Robert Nozick illustrates many aspects of the libertarian theory. For example, he argues in his 1974 book *Anarchy, State, and Utopia* that people ought to be free to exchange or transfer to others what they have acquired by just means. Nozick's theory of justice is not focused on end-states. He refers to end-state concerns as "patterned" or "current time-slice principles of justice." For Nozick, the goal should not be to establish a pattern of distribution, since that pattern would hold good only for a limited slice of time. If individuals were free to trade and create, then the pattern would be disrupted. To ensure that the distributive pattern would continue to hold, the state would have to employ coercive measures to enforce the ideal pattern. Those coercive measures would violate the liberty of individuals to create, to trade, and to acquire surpluses that create inequalities. Following other libertarians, Nozick thinks of taxation of earnings to achieve even desirable public goods as "on a par with forced labor." You can reflect further on these views as you study this selection.

Ultimately, libertarianism is a theory about the importance of liberty, of rights to noninterference by others, and of the proper role of government. Libertarians also have generally supported capitalist free-market economies, so brief comments about this type of economic system and its supporting values are appropriate here.

Capitalism

Capitalism is an economic system in which individuals or business corporations (not the government or community) own and control much or most of the country's capital. *Capital* is the wealth or raw materials, factories, and other means that are used to produce more wealth. Capitalism is also usually associated with a free-enterprise system, an economic system that allows people freedom to set prices and determine production, and to make their own choices about how to earn and spend their incomes. A more extreme version of free enterprise is often called a **laissez-faire** economic system. *Laissez-faire* means "leave alone" or "let be"; in laissez-faire capitalism, the government is supposed to leave the economy and markets alone, without regulation or other interference. It generally assumes that people are motivated by profit and engage in competition, and that value is a function of supply and demand. Proponents of laissez-faire capitalism take a range of positions—with some arguing that the government should keep its hands entirely off the economy and others accepting various minimal forms of governmental regulation.

Certain philosophical values and beliefs also undergird capitalism. Among these can be a libertarian philosophy that stresses the importance of liberty and limited government. Certain beliefs about the nature of human motivation also are often implicit, for example, that people are motivated by rational self-interest. Some people argue that capitalism and a free-market economy constitute the best economic system because it is the most efficient one, producing greater wealth for more people than any other system. People produce more and better, they say, when there is something in it for them or their families, or when what they are working for is their own profit. Moreover, producers will usually make only what consumers want, and they know what consumers want by what they are willing to buy. So if people make mousetraps and mind-reading computers that consumers want, they will be rewarded by people buying their products. Exemplifying this outlook is economist Milton Friedman, who maintained that the one and only "social responsibility" of a business is "to use its resources and engage in activities designed to increase profits."[44] Friedman warned that it was "subversive" to claim that corporations have any other form of responsibility than profit making. "Few

trends could so thoroughly undermine the very foundations of our free society as the acceptance by corporate officials of a social responsibility other than to make as much money for their stockholders as possible."[45] Libertarians and other supporters of capitalism stress process views of justice. They generally agree that people deserve what they earn through natural talent and hard work.

Socialism

Socialism is an economic system, a political movement, and a social theory. Socialists tend to hold that the economy should be deliberately structured so that the results benefit most people. This way of describing socialism suggests its overlap with utilitarianism. Indeed, it is not surprising that John Stuart Mill was sympathetic to socialism (as might be inferred from some of Mill's comments discussed previously).[46] In contemporary societies, socialism often involves some degree of public management and ownership of goods and services such as education, health care, utilities, or (more rarely) industry and natural resources.

Communism, which can be considered an extreme version of socialism, calls for public ownership of all means of production, radical equality, and the abolition of social classes. Communism is most closely associated with the ideas of the philosopher Karl Marx, who called for a revolution of the working class (what he called *the proletariat*) against the ruling upper class of capitalists (what he called *the bourgeoisie*).

Socialists criticize capitalism for its unpredictable business cycles, which often produce unemployment and poverty. They argue that it inevitably generates conflicts between workers and the owners of the means of production. Rather than allow the few to profit, often at the expense of the many, socialism holds that government should engage in planning and adjust production to the needs of all of the people. Justice is stressed over efficiency, but central planning is thought to contribute to efficiency as well as justice. Socialism generally is concerned with end-state justice and is egalitarian in orientation, while making allowances for obvious differences among people in terms of their different needs. Socialism can also be seen to emphasize the value of a certain form of liberty. But in contrast to libertarianism, socialism holds that it is not just external constraints, such as laws, that can limit people's liberty. Socialists tend to think that liberty actually requires freedom from such "internal" constraints as lack of food, education, or health care. Socialists believe that government has an obligation to address these needs.

As with all labels, the term socialism simplifies. Thus, there are also different kinds or levels of socialism. Some are highly centralized and rely on a command economy, where the state determines prices and wages. Others stress the need for government to cushion the economy in times of recession, for example, by manipulating interest rates and monetary policy. Most contemporary societies are, in fact, hybrids of socialism and capitalism. For example, in the United States most K–12 education is socialized, along with police and fire services and such programs as Medicare and Social Security. In various European countries, such services as health insurance, health care, and higher education may be publicly managed or provided.

One key distinction between a libertarian and a socialist conception of justice is that the former recognizes only negative rights and the latter stresses positive rights. **Negative rights** are rights not to be harmed in some way. Because libertarians take liberty as a primary value, they stress the negative right of people not to have their liberty restricted by others. These are rights of noninterference. In the economic arena, libertarians support economic liberties that create wealth, and they believe that people should be able to dispose of their wealth as they choose. For the libertarian, government's role is to protect negative rights, not positive rights. Contrary to this view, socialists believe that government should not only protect people's negative rights not to be interfered with but also attend to their positive rights to basic necessities. Consequently, a right to life must not only involve a right not to be killed but also a right to what is necessary to live, namely, food, clothing, and shelter. **Positive rights** to be helped or benefited are sometimes called "**welfare rights.**" Those who favor such a concept of rights may ask what a right to life would amount to if one did not have the means to live. Positive economic rights are often defined as rights to basic economic subsistence. Those who favor positive rights would allow for a variety of ways to provide for them, from direct public grants to incentives of various sorts.

None of these systems is problem free. Socialism, at least in recent times, often has not lived up to the ideals of its supporters. Central planning systems have often failed as societies become more complex and participate in international economic systems. Communist societies have tended to become authoritarian, in part because it is difficult to get universal voluntary consent to centrally controlled plans for production and other policies. Basic necessities may be provided for all, but their quality has often turned out to be low.

Capitalism and a free-market economy also are open to moral criticism. Many people, through no fault of their own, cannot or do not compete well and fall through the cracks. Unemployment is a natural part of the system, but it is also debilitating for the unemployed worker. When unemployment is high and labor markets are tight, as they have been in recent years, employers can make ever-increasing demands on their employees, knowing that they can always be replaced by someone who will be grateful for a job. While this means that recessions and high unemployment help to increase productivity, the cost of increased productivity is felt in the lives of laborers. As productivity increases, those at the top profit, while those at the bottom suffer. As the economy has worked to recover from the "Great Recession," corporate profits have soared, while unemployment has remained high.[47] From a social justice standpoint, what matters most is the dignity and well-being of working people, not the profits of those at the top of the corporate ladder.

Libertarianism has been criticized for failing to notice that society provides the means by which individuals seek their own good, for example, by means of transportation and communication. It often fails to notice that state action is needed to protect liberty rights and rights to security, property, and litigation. It has also been criticized for rejecting popular social welfare programs such as publicly funded compulsory primary education.[48] Libertarians have been accused of ignoring the effects that individuals' initial life circumstances have on their fair chances to compete for society's goods.

Let us consider whether a hybrid political and economic system might be better, one that combines aspects of libertarianism, capitalism, and socialism. The most accurate term for such a system is *modern liberalism,* even though the term *liberalism* has meant many things to many people. One reason for using this name is that it is typically applied to the views of one philosopher whose work exemplified it and whose philosophy we shall also discuss here: John Rawls.

Modern Liberalism

Suppose we were to attempt to combine the positive elements of libertarianism, capitalism, and socialism. What would we pull from each? Liberty, or the ability to be free from unjust constraint by others, the primary value stressed by libertarianism, would be one value to preserve. However, we may want to support a fuller notion of liberty that also recognizes the power of internal constraints. We also might want to recognize both positive and negative rights and hold that government ought to play some role in supporting the former as well as the latter. Stress on this combination of elements characterizes modern liberalism.

In a draft version of the American Declaration of Independence, Thomas Jefferson wrote of the inalienable rights to life, liberty, and happiness, and concluded that, "in order to *secure these ends* governments are instituted among men." In Jefferson's final draft, the phrase is "in order to *secure these rights* governments are instituted among men."[49] In some ways, these two accounts of the purpose of government parallel the two major approaches to determining when a distribution of wealth is just: the end-state view with its stress on positive rights ("to secure these ends") and the process view with its stress on negative rights of noninterference ("to secure these rights"). Liberalism features a mixture of these two conceptions of rights.

Modern liberalism also generally seeks to promote an economic system that is efficient as well as just. Thus it usually allows capitalist incentives and inequalities of wealth. However, since it values positive as well as negative rights, modern liberalism is also concerned about the least advantaged members of the society. In this view, companies and corporations are generally regarded as guests in society, because government allows their creation and protects them from certain liabilities, with the understanding that they will contribute to the good of all. Accordingly, they are thought to owe something in return to the community—as a matter of justice—and have responsibilities beyond their own best interest. Modern liberalism also points out that the economic productivity and efficiency of a society depend on human development and communication and transportation systems. Thus public investment in education, health, roads, technology, and research and development provides a crucial foundation for the private economy.[50]

John Rawls's Theory of Justice

The most widely discussed work of political philosophy of the past four decades is John Rawls's 1971 book, *A Theory of Justice*, which lays out a moral justification for a modern liberal state.[51] According to Rawls, justice is the first virtue of social institutions, just as truth is the first virtue of scientific systems. It is most important for scientific systems to be true or well supported. They may be elegant or interesting or in line with our other beliefs, but that is not the primary requirement for their acceptance. Something similar would be the case for social and economic institutions with regard to justice. We would want them to be efficient, but what is the point of efficiency if the overall society is unjust? Among the fundamental questions Rawls raises are: what is justice, and how do we know whether an economic system is just? Rawls sought to develop a set of principles or guidelines that we could apply to our institutions, enabling us to judge whether they are just or unjust. To do so, he uses a famous thought experiment, which he calls the *original position,* designed to produce basic principles of justice.

Rawls asks us to consider what rational individuals would agree upon if they came together to form a society for their mutual benefit. Rawls argues that the principles these rational individuals would select to guide their society can be taken as basic principles of justice, provided that the decision procedure was genuinely fair. In other words, we must first ensure that these individuals are so situated that they can choose fairly. We can then ask what principles of justice they would be likely to accept.

But what makes a choice or a choice situation fair, and what would make it unfair? One obvious answer is that a fair decision should be free from *bias*; it should prevent individuals from being able to "rig the system" in their favor or "stack the deck" to benefit people like them. The way to avoid bias is for people to ignore or forget their own particular situation so that their judgments might be free from bias. To eliminate such bias, then, Rawls argues that people in the original position must not be able to know biasing information about themselves. They must not know their age, sex, race, talents, education, social and economic status, religion, political views, and so on. A truly fair choice can thus be made only from behind what he calls a *veil of ignorance.*

With this basic requirement of fairness established, we can then try to determine what principles of justice our would-be citizens might select. Rawls takes pains to emphasize that we need not think of these people as altruistic or selfless. Indeed, they are assumed to want what most people want of the basic goods of life. And they want the means to be able to pursue their own conceptions of a good life (whatever those may be), free from unnecessary interference. Based on these simple motives, and assuming that our citizens make a rational choice (rather than one out of spite or envy), then what basic principles would they select? Rawls argues that we can determine that they would choose two fundamental principles in particular. The first has to do with their political liberties, and the second concerns economic arrangements:

1. Each person is to have an equal right to the most extensive total system of equal basic liberties compatible with a similar system of liberty for all.
2. Social and economic inequalities are to be arranged so that they are:
   a. to the greatest benefit of the least advantaged ..., and
   b. attached to offices and positions open to all under conditions of fair equality of opportunity.[52]

Much of *A Theory of Justice* is devoted to explaining why individuals would in fact choose these two principles for their society, if they didn't know their identities or position in that society. But the basic reasoning for each principle is fairly simple. Rawls believes that such individuals, seeking liberty to pursue their own conceptions of the good life (but not knowing what they are), would require that there be *equality of liberties*—that is, they would not be willing to be the people who had less freedom than others. They would want as much say about matters in their society that affect them as any other people, no matter what their personal characteristics or conceptions of life happen to be. This reflects the importance of liberty to all people as people, no matter who they are.

When it comes to society's goods, however, Rawls argues that the would-be citizens would accept a society with *unequal shares* of wealth and other goods, provided certain conditions were met. They would accept that some would be richer and some poorer, provided that the not-so-rich are better off than they otherwise would be if all had equal amounts of wealth. Since each individual could turn out to be the poorest member of the society, this principle makes sense as a kind of insurance against the worst outcome.

You can test yourself to see if your choices coincide with Rawls's claim for the acceptance of unequal shares. The table below shows the average yearly income at three different wealth levels (high, medium, and low) in three societies (A, B, and C). Assume that you have no information about which income group you will end up in, or about your relative odds of ending up in one rather than another. Under these circumstances, to which society would you want to belong?

Wealth Levels	Society A	Society B	Society C
High income	$200,000	$70,000	$20,000
Medium income	$70,000	$40,000	$20,000
Low income	$15,000	$30,000	$20,000

If you chose Society A—perhaps because you think it would be great to earn $200,000 a year—then you are taking an irrational risk, according to Rawls. For you do not know (under the **veil of ignorance**) what your chances are of being in any of the three positions in the society. You do not know, for example, whether your chances of being in the highest income group are near zero or whether your chances of being in the lowest income group are greater than 50 percent. Your best bet, when you do not know what your chances are, is to choose Society B. In this society, no matter what group you are in, you will do better than you would in any position in completely egalitarian Society C. And even if you were in the lowest income group in Society B, you would be better off than you would be in the lowest groups of either A or C. Choosing Society B for these reasons is often called a *maximin* strategy; in choosing under conditions of uncertainty, you select that option with the best worst or minimum position.

The maximin approach has clear relevance to Rawls's principles of justice and his argument that they would be selected in the original position. Remember that to avoid bias, people in the original position must choose principles for their society in ignorance of the basic facts about who they are. They do not know the economic or social position they will occupy—and they know that they might end up in the group that is worst off. Thus Rawls argues that rational self-interest will demand that they look out for the bottom position in society. If economic inequalities (some people being richer than others) would produce a better situation for the worst off than equal shares would, then it would be selected as a principle. For it ensures the best possible life for the individuals in the lowest group, which they know could be themselves. This is the rationale for the first part of Rawls's second principle of justice, which says that economic inequalities should be arranged to the benefit of the least advantaged.

Rawls also provides a corollary argument for his "maximin" principle, one that does not depend on the idea of the original position. Here he examines "accidents of natural and social circumstance," the random facts of where one is born and what capacities one is born with—which he says are neither just nor unjust, but *morally arbitrary*. If some are born into unfortunate circumstances, it is through no fault of their own but merely because of the arbitrary circumstances of

their birth. Similarly, "No one deserves his greater natural capacity nor merits a more favorable starting place in society."[53] While society cannot eliminate these different starting places, a just society should not blindly accept such morally arbitrary facts—as does the warrior aristocracy imagined by Bernard Williams described previously. Rawls maintains that in a just society, those who have been favored by nature may be permitted to gain from their good fortune "only on terms that improve the situation of those who have lost out."[54] Again, the idea is that economic inequalities can be allowed by justice, but only if these inequalities work to the benefit of society's least fortunate members.

The second part of Rawls's second principle concerns equal opportunity. If inequality of income and wealth are to be considered just, then society's institutions must provide an equal opportunity for those with the relevant interests, talents, and ambition to attain positions of wealth, power, and prestige. For Rawls, social class distinctions should not prevent social mobility. As he explains, the point is not merely to guarantee *formal* equality and nondiscrimination, but to guarantee that everyone should have a fair chance at gaining access to social goods. "The expectations of those with the same abilities and aspirations should not be affected by their social class."[55] Rawls's primary concern is to limit the impact of social class. But the idea of fair equality of opportunity can also apply to racial and gender disparities (such as we discussed in the previous chapter).

Rawls's two principles would most likely be accepted by people who are brought up in modern democratic and liberal societies. But modern democratic societies are also pluralistic—that is, their people will have many different and irreconcilable sets of moral and religious beliefs. Rawls admits, in his later work, that pluralism is a problem.[56] He acknowledges that in modern societies people have sharply different moral and religious views; there is irremediable and irreducible pluralism. Thus the only way that citizens can agree is by thinking of themselves as persons who want whatever persons in general would want and who do not bias the rules of society in their own favor based on their particular characteristics. But such an approach may not satisfy all those with diverse points of view on culture, religion, economics, and justice; libertarians and communists, for example, may not agree with the procedures Rawls uses to derive his basic principles of justice. This substantial problem points back toward the issues of pluralism and relativism, which we discussed in Chapters 2 and 3.

Communitarianism

The issue of pluralism reminds us that there are other possible views of economic justice. Some might defend traditional class structures based upon religious or cultural claims about caste. Others might argue in favor of radical egalitarianism that requires a kind of communal pooling of assets. And others may maintain, as egoists do, that in the dog-eat-dog world of economics, it is every man for himself.

While Rawls's version of economic liberalism is based on the notion of rational beings applying a maximin strategy to the problem of economic justice, not everyone agrees with this strategy. One line of substantial criticism of Rawls's notion of rationality and his vision of economic justice has been offered by communitarian philosophers. Communitarians generally reject Rawls's idea that justice should be understood as a maximin strategy developed from within the original position. They also think that liberals like Rawls smuggle in claims about rationality and about social justice when they make claims about how rational persons would think about justice. Some communitarian writers object to what they believe are the individualistic elements in Rawls's theory. For example, Rawls asks us to imagine thinking about social justice as individuals under a veil of ignorance, rather than as members of families, who have substantial obligations to the welfare of our family members.

Communitarians in general tend to believe that people are by nature social and naturally belong to communities. They often invoke Aristotle and Aquinas as sources, who each claimed that human beings are naturally social beings. Communitarians do not generally accept the idea that individuals are rational choosers who could consistently apply the maximin theory of rationality that Rawls advocates. They stress the importance of belonging to families, cities, nations, religious communities, neighborhood associations, political parties, and groups supporting particular causes. The communitarian view of social justice may depend upon the views of the groups to which they belong, as a matter of tradition and culture. But in general, communitarian ideas emphasize concrete social relations instead of abstract principles of distributive justice. One explanation can be found in the "Responsive Communitarian Platform," which asserts, "At the heart of the communitarian understanding of social justice is the idea of reciprocity: each member of the community owes something to all the rest and the community owes something to each of its members. Justice requires responsible individuals in a responsive community."[57]

There is some connection between communitarian ideas of social justice and the ideas of care ethics (as discussed in Chapter 9). But the communitarian approach is more focused on economic issues, including the problem of economic inequality. Amitai Etzioni, one of the authors of the aforementioned "Responsive Communitarian Platform" and an important proponent of **communitarianism**, explains that inequality creates a serious social problem. "If some members of a community are increasingly distanced from the standard of living of most other members, they will lose contact with the rest of the community. The more those in charge of private and public institutions lead lives of hyperaffluence … the less in touch they are with other community members."[58]

Rawls might permit economic inequalities so long as they benefit the least advantaged and so long as there is fair opportunity for advancement. Nozick and the libertarians would not see economic inequality as a problem, so long as it results from a free marketplace in which individual talent and ambition were rewarded. But the communitarian critique worries that the fabric of community becomes frayed when there is too much inequality.

A problem for communitarianism is that it can sometimes seem to resemble a kind of cultural relativism that claims that the values of any community are as good as the values of any other. Some communitarian authors do appear to affirm a version of cultural relativism. However, Etzioni focuses on basic features of human communities and human functions, such as the need for solidarity and a sense of connection within a community. The idea of basic human function is also central to the work of Amartya Sen, a Nobel Prize–winning economist. Sen rejects relativism, but he is also critical of Rawls's abstract approach to distributive justice. Sen's idea is that concerns about economic equality should focus on human functions and capabilities—what people can actually do with their resources—and not merely on the abstract idea of income equality.[59] (Sen's account is connected with Martha Nussbaum's ideas about human capabilities as discussed in Chapter 3.) The point of this sort of criticism is that there are a variety of concerns that we ought to attend to when thinking about equality including family structure, age, ability (or disability), gender roles, cultural practices, traditions, and so on. A concern for equality requires us to account for the complexity of human life in all of its richness.

This chapter has considered the complicated issues of economic justice, social justice, and political philosophy. One basic question of this chapter is whether one should egoistically pursue one's own self interest and maximize profit or whether there are ethical constraints to profit, such as a worry about inequality or equality of opportunity. There is much more to be said about the limits of political power and the proper relation between the state and the economy. To better evaluate the theories we've examined here, we would also need further empirical study of the efficiency of various forms of economic organization. And there are vexing psychological and sociological problems that remain to be considered, such as how best to help those in poverty and the unemployed without disempowering or denigrating them. These issues remind us that questions of justice also need to be informed by practical information from empirical fields of study.

NOTES

1. Economic Policy Institute, "Inequality" (fact sheet based on 2010 data), *The State of Working America, 12th Edition*, accessed March 24, 2013, http://stateofworkingamerica.org/fact-sheets/inequality-facts

2. "Wealthy's Tax Bill Will Hit 30-Year High in 2013," CNBC, March 4, 2013, accessed May 4, 2013, http://www.cnbc.com/id/100518058

3. *Economic Report of the President* (Washington, DC: Government Printing Office, 2010), 154, accessed May 4, 2013, http://www.whitehouse.gov/sites/default/files/microsites/economic-report-president.pdf

4. U.S. Census Bureau, accessed March 23 2013, https://www.census.gov/hhes/www/poverty/about/overview/index.html

5. U.S. Census Bureau, accessed March 23, 2013, http://quickfacts.census.gov/qfd/states/00000.html

6. "The World's Billionaires," *Forbes*, March 2013, accessed April 9, 2013, http://www.forbes.com/profile/bill-gates/

7. Martin Crutsinger, "Greenspan Talk Doesn't Roil Markets," *Washington Post*, March 13, 2007, accessed March 23, 2013, http://www.washingtonpost.com/wp-dyn/content/article/2007/03/13/AR2007031300744.html

8. Emmanuel Saez, "Striking It Richer: The Evolution of Top Incomes in the United States" (updated with 2011 estimates), January 23, 2013, accessed March 23, 2013, http://elsa.berkeley.edu/~saez/saez-UStopincomes-2011.pdf; summarized at Bill Moyers.com, accessed March 23, 2013, http://billmoyers.com/2013/02/22/in-this-recovery-the-rich-get-richer/

9. Chuck Collins, *99 to 1: How Wealth Inequality Is Wrecking the World and What We Can Do about It* (San Francisco: Berrett-Koehler, 2012), 3.

10. Lawrence Mishel and Natalie Sabadish, "CEO Pay and the Top 1%: How Executive Compensation and Financial-Sector Pay Have Fueled Income Inequality," Economic Policy Institute, May 2, 2012, accessed May 4, 2013, http://www.epi.org/publication/ib331-ceo-pay-top-1-percent/

11. "CEO Pay in Perspective," PayScale, accessed March 23 2013, http://www.payscale.com/ceo-income

12. "America's Highest Paid CEOs" *Forbes*, April 4, 2012, accessed March 23, 2013, http://www.forbes.com/sites/scottdecarlo/2012/04/04/americas-highest-paid-ceos/

13. Eric Zuesse, "Why Social Mobility in the United States Is a Total Myth," *Business Insider*, March 18, 2013, accessed May 4, 2013, http://www.businessinsider.com/social-mobility-is-a-myth-in-the-us-2013-3#ixzz2SGsOOa4I

14. Tami Luhby, "Worsening Wealth Inequality by Race," *CNN Money*, June 21, 2012, accessed March 23, 2013, http://money.cnn.com/2012/06/21/news/economy/wealth-gap-race/index.htm

15. "The Simple Truth about the Pay Gap" (2013), AAUW, accessed March, 22, 2013, http://www.aauw.org/resource/the-simple-truth-about-the-gender-pay-gap/

16. Liza Mundy, "Women, Money, and Power," *Time*, March 26, 2012, accessed March 23, 2013, http://www.time.com/time/magazine/article/0,9171,2109140,00.html

17. "Women Make Significant Gains in the Workplace and Educational Attainment, but Lag in Pay," Pew Research Center, March 8, 2013, accessed May 6, 2013, http://www.pewresearch.org/daily-number/women-make-significant-gains-in-the-workplace-and-educational-attainment-but-lag-in-pay/

18. *An Analysis of Reasons for the Disparity in Wages between Men and Women*, report prepared for U.S. Department of Labor (January 2009), accessed March 23, 2013, http://www.consad.com/content/reports/Genderpercent20Wagepercent20Gappercent20Finalpercent20Report.pdf

19. See the Living Wage Calculator, accessed March 24, 2013, http://livingwage.mit.edu/

20. U.S. Census Bureau, *Custodial Mothers and Fathers and Their Child Support: 2009* (December 2011), accessed March 24, 2013, http://www.census.gov/prod/2011pubs/p60-240.pdf

21. Sabrina Tavernise, "Education Gap Grows between Rich and Poor, Studies Say," *New York Times*, February 9, 2012, accessed March 23, 2013, http://www.nytimes.com/2012/02/10/education/education-gap-grows-between-rich-and-poor-studies-show.html?pagewanted=all&_r=0

22. "Death by Poverty," accessed March 23, 2010, http://www.mailman.columbia.edu/academic-departments/epidemiology/research-service/death-poverty; this conclusion is based on data from Sandro Galea, Melissa Tracy, Katherine J. Hoggatt, Charles DiMaggio, and Adam Karpati, "Estimated Deaths Attributable to Social Factors in the United States," *American Journal of Public Health* 11, no. 8 (2011), 1456–65.

23. David Himmelstein et al., "MarketWatch: Illness and Injury as Contributors to Bankruptcy," *Health Affairs* Web Exclusive, February 2, 2005, W5–62. As cited in T. R. Reid, *The Healing of America: A Global Quest for Better, Cheaper, and Fairer Health Care* (New York: Penguin, 2009).

24. "How Does the Health Care Law Protect Me?," HealthCare.gov, accessed March 24, 2013, http://www.healthcare.gov/law/features/rights/preventive-care/index.html

25. Ezra Klein, "11 Facts about the Affordable Care Act," *Washington Post*, June 24, 2012, accessed May 6, 2013, http://www.washingtonpost.com/blogs/wonkblog/wp/2012/06/24/11-facts-about-the-affordable-care-act/

26. Nina Owcharenko, "Repealing Obamacare and Getting Health Care Right," The Heritage Foundation, November 9, 2010, accessed March 24, 2013, http://www.heritage.org/research/reports/2010/11/repealing-obamacare-and-getting-health-care-right

27. Beatrix Hoffman, *Health Care for Some: Rights and Rationing in the United States Since 1930* (Chicago: University of Chicago Press, 2012).

28. Ibid.

29. Thomas Massaro, *Living Justice: Catholic Social Teaching in Action*, 2nd classroom ed., (Lanham, MD: Rowman & Littlefield, 2011), 2.

30. John Stuart Mill, *Principles of Political Economy with some of their Applications to Social Philosophy,* ed. William J. Ashley (originally published 1909; from Library of Economics and Liberty), bk. 2, Chapter 13, sec. 2, accessed March 24, 2013, http://www.econlib.org/library/Mill/mlP26.html

31. John Stuart Mill, "The Negro Question" (1850) in *The Collected Works of John Stuart Mill, Volume XXI - Essays on Equality, Law, and Education*, ed. John M. Robson (Toronto: University of Toronto Press, London: Routledge and Kegan Paul, 1984), accessed March 24, 2013, http://oll.libertyfund.org/title/255/21657

32. John Stuart Mill, *"Chapters on Socialism"* (1879) in *The Collected Works of John Stuart Mill, Volume V - Essays on Economics and Society Part II*, ed. John M. Robson (Toronto: University of Toronto Press, London: Routledge and Kegan Paul, 1967), accessed March 24, 2013, http://oll.libertyfund.org/title/232/16747

33. John Stuart Mill, *Principles of Political Economy*, bk. 5, Chapter 11, sec. 44.

34. Immanuel Kant, *Lectures on Ethics* (Indianapolis, IN: Hackett, 1981), 194.

35. Tibor R. Machan, "Libertarian Justie: A Natural Rights Approach" in Tibor R. Machan, ed., *Liberty and Justice* (Stanford, CA: Hoover Institution Press, 2006), 111.

36. We associate the saying "From each according to his ability, to each according to his need" with Karl Marx, but it actually originated with the "early French socialists of the Utopian school, and was officially adopted by German socialists in the Gotha Program of 1875." Nicholas Rescher, *Distributive Justice* (Indianapolis, IN: Bobbs-Merrill, 1966), 73–83.

37. James Fishkin, *Justice, Equal Opportunity, and the Family* (New Haven, CT: Yale University Press, 1983), 4.

38. See "D.C. Leads Nation as U.S. per Pupil Tops $10,600, Census Bureau Reports," U.S. Census Bureau, June 21, 2012, accessed March 24, 2013, http://www.census.gov/newsroom/releases/archives/finance_insurance_real_estate/cb12-113.html; or "California School District Spending and Test Scores," California Watch, June 2, 2011, accessed May 6, 2013, http://schoolspending.apps.cironline.org/

39. Bernard Williams, "The Idea of Equality," in *Philosophy, Politics and Society* (second series), ed. Peter Laslett and W. G. Runciman (Oxford: Basil Blackwell, 1962), 110–31.

40. Harry Frankfurt, "Equality as a Moral Ideal," *Ethics* 98 (1987): 21–43.

41. John H. Schaar, "Equality of Opportunity, and Beyond," in *NOMO SIX: Equality*, ed. J. Chapman and R. Pennock (New York: Atherton Press, 1967).

42. Ibid.

43. See Thomas Nagel, "Justice," in *What Does It All Mean: A Very Short Introduction to Philosophy* (New York: Oxford University Press, 1987), 76–86.

44. Milton Friedman, *Capitalism and Freedom* (Chicago: University of Chicago Press, 1982), 133.

45. Ibid.

46. Stephen Nathanson, "John Stuart Mill on Economic Justice and the Alleviation of Poverty," *Journal of Social Philosophy* 43, no. 2 (Summer 2012), 161–76.

47. Nelson D. Schwartz, "Recovery in U.S. Is Lifting Profits, but Not Adding Jobs," *New York Times*, March 3, 2013, accessed May 6, 2013, http://www.nytimes.com/2013/03/04/business/economy/corporate-profits-soar-as-worker-income-limps.html?pagewanted=all

48. Stephen Holmes, "Welfare and the Liberal Conscience," *Report from the Institute for Philosophy and Public Policy* 15, no. 1 (Winter 1995): 1–6.

49. Morton White, *The Philosophy of the American Revolution* (New York: Oxford University Press, 1978), 161. Italics added by White and editors.

50. Robert B. Reich, "The Other Surplus Option," *New York Times*, July 11, 1999, A23.

51. John Rawls, *A Theory of Justice* (Cambridge, MA: Harvard University Press, 1971).

52. Ibid., 302.

53. Ibid., 100–03.

54. Ibid.

55. Ibid., 73.

56. John Rawls, *Political Liberalism* (New York: Columbia University Press, 1993).

57. Amitai Etzioni and Rothschild Volmert, in *The Communitarian Reader: Beyond the Essentials* (Lanham, MD: Rowman & Littlefield, 2004), 21.

58. Amitai Etzioni, *Next: The Road to the Good Society* (New York: Basic Books, 2001), 101.

59. Amartya Sen, *Development as Freedom* (Oxford: Oxford University Press, 1999).

REVIEW EXERCISES

1. Consider the morality of the sorts of economic inequalities discussed in this chapter; are they justifiable?
2. What is the difference between a process view of distributive justice and an end-state view?
3. Discuss the meaning and problems associated with using the end-state view criteria of merit, achievement, effort, and contribution.
4. What is the literal meaning of *equal opportunity*? What criterion does James Fishkin use for judging whether it exists? What is Bernard Williams's "starting-gate theory" of equal opportunity?

5. Describe some problems raised by philosophers Frankfurt and Schaar regarding equal opportunity.
6. Summarize the libertarian position on liberty and the role of government.
7. What are the basic differences between capitalism and socialism as social and economic theories?
8. What is Rawls's *original position,* and what role does it play in his derivation of principles of justice?
9. What is Rawls's "maximin" principle, and how is it related to his second principle of justice?
10. How does communitarianism differ from liberalism?

DISCUSSION CASES

1. **The Homeless.** Joe was laid off two years ago from the auto repair company where he had worked for fifteen years. For the first year he tried to get another job. He read the want ads and left applications at local employment agencies. After that, he gave up. He had little savings and soon had no money for rent. He has been homeless now for a year. He will not live in the shelters because they are crowded, noisy, and unsafe. As time goes by, he has less and less chance of getting back to where he was before. When he can, he drinks to forget the past and escape from the present. Other people he meets on the streets are developmentally disabled or psychologically disturbed. He realizes that the city offers some things to try to help people like him, but there is little money and the number of homeless people seems to be growing. Does society have any responsibility to do anything for people like Joe? Why or why not? What ethical principles might be relevant to this situation?

2. **Rights to Keep What One Earns.** Gene and his coworkers have been talking over lunch about how their taxes have continued to rise. Some complain that the harder they work, the less they are making. Others are upset because their taxes are going to pay for things that they do not believe the government should support with our tax dollars—the arts, for example. "Why should we support museums or arts programs in public schools when we don't use these services?" they ask. They argue these should be matters for charity. They also complain that they work hard but that their income is being used to take care of others who could work but do not.

   Are they right? Why or why not?

3. **Inequality.** Stephanie and Peyton are working the midnight shift at a fast-food restaurant, where they make slightly above the national minimum wage. Business is slow, and they begin discussing income inequality after a Mercedes SUV full of college-aged kids comes through the drive-thru for burgers and shakes. Stephanie believes that the growing disparity between the rich and the poor is wrong: "It's just not fair that people like us are poor and often out of work, while millionaires and their kids are living large." Peyton is not so sure. "Well, millionaires work hard for their money. They deserve to enjoy the fruit of their labors." Stephanie says, "But we work hard too. I could work forever at this minimum wage job and never get ahead. Most rich people start out with an advantage, go to a good college, and then get richer. And that's not fair." Peyton responds, "It may not be fair, but capitalism is the only system that works, and everyone deserves a chance to get rich. Would you prefer a communist system where nobody has that chance?" Stephanie shrugs. "Maybe not communism," she replies. "But I say we should tax the rich more heavily and use that money to reduce the burden on the poor and unemployed." Peyton shakes his head, "Do that and you'll ruin our country."

   Whose side are you on? Do you agree with Stephanie or with Peyton? Is there a third alternative? Explain your answer with specific concepts discussed in this chapter.

Punishment and the Death Penalty

Stockphoto/Thinkstock

15

Learning Outcomes

After reading this chapter, you should be able to:

- Cite incarceration rates and execution practices in the United States and elsewhere.
- Understand the problem of racial disparities in the punishment system.
- Explain and apply key terms such as *deterrence, prevention, retributive justice,* and *restorative justice.*
- Evaluate moral arguments about punishment and the death penalty.

- Apply consequentialist and non-consequentialist arguments to the issue of punishment.
- Differentiate between legal punishment and other forms of punishment.
- Understand and apply ideas about the death penalty described by Mill and Kant.
- Defend your own ideas about punishment and the death penalty.

The Boston Marathon bombing in April 2013 is a reminder of the devastating impact that violent crime can have on contemporary societies. The bombing killed three and injured 264 others. Two brothers, apparently motivated by Islamic fundamentalist beliefs and opposed to the U.S. foreign policy, were accused of the crime. One brother, Tamerlan Tsarnaev, was killed in a shootout with the police, while the other, Dzhokhar Tsarnaev, was captured alive. In the weeks after his capture, a poll conducted by the *Washington Post* found that 70 percent of those surveyed believed that Tsarnaev should be given the death penalty.[1] In Massachusetts, however, the death penalty is not a legal punishment. For that reason, some argued that Tsarnaev should be prosecuted by the federal government because federal prosecution can result in the death penalty. (Still others argued that Tsarnaev should be held as an enemy combatant and tried in military court—a topic that is further addressed in the discussion on terrorism in Chapter 19.) More and more states are moving to abolish the death penalty. But would the death penalty be justifiable in cases of mass murder and terrorism?

While horrific crimes such as the Boston Marathon bombing can make us feel insecure, the good news is that crime is down in the United States. The murder rate has fallen from 8 per 100,000 in 1995 to 5 per 100,000 today.[2] In New York City, the home of more than eight million people, there have even been days in recent years when no one at all has been murdered.[3] Some American cities still have significant crime problems, but nationwide there is a general downward trend in violent crime. There is also a trend toward less violent forms of punishment. Although American authorities did use torture on suspects in the "war on terrorism" following September 11, the Supreme

Court has restricted the use of the death penalty (for example, it has forbidden the practice when the convicted is mentally retarded or a minor at the time the crime was committed), and some states have abolished capital punishment altogether. As of 2014, eighteen states have eliminated capital punishment, including Maryland which abolished it in 2013.

So why is crime down? Experts debate the reasons for this. It may have something to do with economics and opportunities. Or it may have something to do with our massive prison system and the huge numbers of people incarcerated in it. It may have to do with the epidemiology of drug addiction. Or it may have to do with aggressive policing—for example, the use of "stop-and-frisk" techniques. On the other hand, it may have to do with more engaged community policing and grassroots neighborhood activism. Perhaps it has to do with the success of social welfare programs, which provide hope, opportunities, and alternatives to crime and violence. At least one expert, economist Steven Levitt, has claimed that the decline in crime may have something to do with the legalization of abortion, which prevents the birth of unwanted children.[4] A more recent theory is that the decrease in crime may be a result of decreasing levels of lead in the atmosphere. According to this view, the lead produced by old-fashioned leaded gasoline—which causes neurological and behavioral problems—may have produced the rise in violence and deviance that peaked in the 1990s.[5]

Not all the news is good, however, and we still hear stories of horrible violence across the United States. School shootings, kidnappings, rapes, and other violent crimes fill the front pages of newspapers. In late 2012, a school shooting in Newtown, Connecticut, claimed the lives of twenty children and six adults. In early 2013, a man in Alabama shot a school bus driver and kidnapped a five-year-old boy, taking him to an underground bunker and keeping him there for seven days. Also in early 2013, a heavily armed former police officer went on a rampage in Los Angeles, killing several people and targeting police and their families in an event that terrorized Southern California. In each of these cases, the perpetrators wound up dead—either killing themselves or being killed by police. If these men

had been taken alive, would it have been appropriate to sentence them to death? We tend to assume that police, in the heat of the moment, are entitled to kill dangerous criminals, without a trial, in order to protect themselves or the general public. But can that justification of lethal violence be extended to a justification of the death penalty, which is carried out after a legal trial and subsequent appeals, long after the original crime occurred?

Standard justifications for the death penalty include utilitarian claims about the deterrent effect of capital punishment, along with deontological claims about the demand for retributive justice and retaliation. This chapter will consider justifications for punishment such as these. But moral questions abound with regard to punishment. How do we determine appropriate sentences for criminals, converting such disparate crimes as shoplifting, selling drugs, and murder into the common currency of months and years in prison? And while some argue against the death penalty in favor of life imprisonment without the possibility of parole, we may wonder whether it remains useful to keep seventy-year-olds in prison for crimes committed half a century ago. We might also wonder why taxpayer dollars should be used to keep people in prison, feeding and housing them for decades, while the victims of crime have to fend for themselves and pay their bills just like anyone else. Other moral questions might focus on the conditions in prison—for example, whether it is cruel to use solitary confinement in supermax facilities as a way to control the worst criminals. We might also be concerned about the impact of prison or the death penalty on the families and communities of those who are imprisoned or executed. Further, we may consider whether there are ways to rehabilitate criminals and restore communities that are broken by crime.

THE NATURE OF LEGAL PUNISHMENT

To know what to think about the ethics of prison and the death penalty, we need to first examine some of the reasons that have been given for the practice of legal punishment. What we want to examine here is not *any* sort of punishment, only legal punishment. Eight-year-old Jimmy's parents can punish him with no TV for a week for a failing grade, and I can punish myself for a caloric indulgence by spending twice as much time at the gym—but these punishments are not legal. What legal punishment does have in common with parental and self-punishment is that it is designed to "hurt"; if something is gladly accepted or enjoyed, then it is not really punishment. The most visible form of legal criminal punishment is imprisonment. Other forms include fines and court-mandated community service.

However, legal punishment is distinct from other forms of punishment in several respects. Legal punishment must follow legal rules of some sort. It is authorized by a legal entity and follows a set of rules that establish who is to be punished, how, and by how much. Lynching is not a legal punishment since it is carried out by a mob and not by a constituted authority. Furthermore, to be punished within the legal system you must first commit the crime or be suspected of it. Whatever we say about the justification of detaining people before they commit (or we think they will commit) a crime, it is not punishment. Punishment of any sort presumes someone has done something to merit the penalty. In the case of legal punishment, it is a penalty for doing what the law forbids. Criminal law, by its very nature, must have some sanction, some threat attached to breaking it, or else it loses its force. Without such force, it may be a request, but it is not law.

Thus we can say that legal punishment is the state's infliction of harm or pain on those who break the law, according to a set of legally established rules. But is such a practice justified? What gives a society the right to inflict the pain of punishment on any of its members? In asking this, we are asking a moral and not just a legal question. Is legal punishment of any sort morally justifiable? If so, why?

Traditional approaches to the justification of punishment focus on **deterrence** and prevention, or the idea of **retribution** and just deserts. When we say a punishment *deters*, we mean that it prevents other crimes in the future. When we speak of *retribution*, we mean making wrongdoers somehow pay for the crimes they have committed. But it is important to note that an alternative to these approaches can be found in the ideas of rehabilitation, crime prevention, and restorative justice. These approaches aim to transform the social situation in ways that minimize the need for punishment. While restorative justice is an important idea, it is not exactly "punishment," but rather an alternative to punishment. The traditional justifications for punishment focus either on utilitarian concerns about preventing and deterring crime, or on natural law or deontological ideas about the need for just retribution. We will turn to utilitarian arguments first.

THE DETERRENCE ARGUMENT

One answer to the question of whether legal punishment is morally justifiable is, "Yes, if (and only if) the punishment could be fashioned to prevent or deter crime." The general idea involved in this first rationale for legal punishment is related to both the nature of law and its purpose. For a criminal law to be a law and not just a request, sanctions must be attached to it. It must have force behind it. Further, law has many possible purposes, and one purpose is to prevent people from harming others. Since our laws presumably are directed to achieving some good, penalties for breaking these laws should help ensure that the good intended by the laws will be achieved. Of course, not all laws are good laws. However, the idea is that we want not only to have good laws but also to have them enforced in ways that make them effective.

The purpose of legal punishment, according to this reasoning, is to prevent people from breaking the law, deter them from doing so, or both. As such, this is a forward-looking, consequentialist rationale. In terms of prevention, crime is prevented when would-be or actual criminals are arrested and held somewhere so that they cannot do social damage. We also can prevent crime by other means such as increased street lighting, more police officers, and so on. In terms of deterrence, we deter crime by holding out a punishment as a threat, which persuades would-be criminals not to break the law. If a punishment works as a deterrent, then it works in a particular way through the would-be lawbreaker's thinking and decision-making processes. One considers the possibility of being punished for doing some contemplated action and concludes that the gain achieved from the act is not worth the price to be paid, namely, the punishment. Then one acts accordingly.

If deterrence works as described above, we can readily identify certain circumstances in which it is not likely to succeed in preventing crime. Deterrence is not likely to prevent crimes of passion, for instance, in which people are overcome by strong emotions. They are not in the mood to calculate the risks and benefits of what they're about to do and are unlikely to stop themselves from continuing to act as they will. The threat of punishment is also not likely to work in cases in which people *do* calculate the risks and the benefits and decide the benefits are greater than the risks. These would be cases in which the risks of being caught and punished are perceived as small, and the reward or benefit is perceived as great. The benefit could be financial, status-oriented, or even the reward of having done what one believed to be right as in acts of civil disobedience or in support of any cause, whether actually good or bad. Although punishment does not deter in some cases, in others, presumably, it does. A system of legal punishment is worthwhile if it works for the great majority, even if not for all, and if bad consequences do not outweigh good ones.

The deterrence rationale for legal punishment raises a more general issue about any utilitarian perspective on punishment, which relies on weighing costs and benefits. Punishment, in this view, is *externally related* to lawbreaking. In other words, it is not essential. If something else works better than punishment, then that other means ought to be used, either as a substitution for punishment or in addition to it. Some people argue that punishment itself does not work, but might only be effective when combined with rehabilitation, psychological counseling, and perhaps even job training or placement. However, if a punishment system is not working, then, in this view, it is not morally justifiable, for the whole idea is not to punish for punishment's sake but to achieve the goal of law enforcement. On utilitarian grounds, pain is never good in itself. Thus if punishment involves suffering, it must be justified. The suffering must be outweighed by the good to be achieved by it.

One problem is that if deterrence is the sole ground of legal punishment, we might seem to be justified in using extreme measures to achieve the desired deterrent effect—if these measures work better than less extreme ones. Suppose that a community has a particularly vexing problem with graffiti. To get rid of the problem, suppose the community decides to institute a program in which it randomly picks up members of particular gangs believed to be responsible for the graffiti and punishes these individuals with floggings in the public square. Or suppose that cutting off their hands would work better! We would surely have serious moral objections to this program. One objection would be that these particular individuals may not themselves have been responsible for the graffiti; they were just picked because of their gang affiliation. Another objection would be that the punishment seems out of proportion to the offense. However, on deterrence grounds, there would be nothing essentially wrong with such punishments. It would not be necessary that the individual herself be guilty or that the punishment fit the crime. What would be crucial for the deterrence argument would be whether this punishment worked or worked better than alternative forms.

Another version of the deterrence argument that we might evaluate has to do with how deterrence is supposed to work. According to this view, legal punishment is part of a system of social moral education. A society has a particular set of values, and one way to instill those values in its members from their youth is to establish punishments for those who undermine them. If private property is valued, then society should punish those who damage or take others' property. These punishments would act as deterrents, helping individuals to internalize social values and giving them internal prohibitions against violating those values. Key to evaluating this view is determining whether punishment actually works in this fashion. What does punishment teach us? Does it help us internalize values, and does it motivate us? The way the system is administered also can send a message, and in some cases, it might be the wrong message. For example, if legal punishment is not applied fairly or equally, what might people learn?

THE RETRIBUTIVIST ARGUMENT

The second primary rationale for legal punishment is retribution. In the retributivist view, legal punishment is intended to make those who are responsible for a crime pay for it. As such, it is a backward-looking argument because it is based on past actions. This idea can be understood from a natural law or deontological perspective. The natural law approach maintains that it is only fair or right for a criminal to pay for what he has damaged, and as Locke suggests in his *Second Treatise on Government* (discussed in Chapter 7), there is a natural right to repayment. A retributivist might say that when someone harms another, it is only just or fair that he suffer similarly or proportionately to the harm or pain he caused the other person. Or we might say that he deserves to suffer because he made his victim suffer; the punishment is deserved as fair recompense. In this view, punishment is *internally related* to the wrongful conduct. In a sense, the punishment "fits the crime." One cannot say, from the retributivist standpoint, that if something else works better than punishment, then that is what ought to be done. The concern here is not what works but, rather, what is right. Indeed, retributivists might also maintain that punishment is required as a matter of duty; from a deontological standpoint we ought to punish people who do wrong because they *deserve* to be punished. From this perspective, it would be wrong not to punish someone, since failing to punish them would give them less than what they deserve.

This approach is based on a somewhat abstract notion of justice. We punish to right a wrong or restore some original state, or to reset the scales of justice. However, in many cases we cannot really undo the suffering of the victim by making the perpetrator suffer. One can pay back stolen money or return stolen property. But even in these cases, there are other harms that cannot be undone, such as the victim's lost sense of privacy or security. Thus the erasing, undoing, or righting of the wrong is of some other abstract or metaphysical type. It may be difficult to explain, but supporters of this rationale for punishment believe that we do have some intuitive sense of what we mean when we say "justice was done."

According to the retributivist view, payment must be made in some way that is equivalent to the crime or harm done. Philosophers distinguish two senses of equivalency: an *egalitarian* sense and a *proportional* sense. With egalitarian equivalency, one is required to pay back something identical or almost identical to

what was taken. If you make someone suffer for two days, then you should suffer for two days. It would also mean that if you caused someone's arm to be amputated, then your arm should be cut off as well. This version of retributivism is often given the label *lex talionis*. Translated, it means the "law of the talon" (as among birds of prey). We also call egalitarian equivalency the "law of the jungle" or taking "an eye for an eye."

Proportional equivalency holds that what is required by punishment is not something more or less identical to the harm done or pain caused, but something proportional. In this version, we can think of harms or wrongs as matters of degree, namely, of bad, worse, and worst. Punishments are also scaled from the minimal to the most severe. In this view, punishment must be proportional to the degree of the seriousness of the crime.

Obviously, there are serious problems, both practical and moral, with the *lex talionis* version of the retributivist view. In some cases—for example, in the case of multiple murders—it is not possible to deliver something equal to the harm done, for one cannot kill the murderer more than once. We would presumably also have some moral problems with torturing a torturer or raping a rapist.

We should notice that the retributivist justification of legal punishment responds to two major problems with the deterrence argument, namely that deterrence-focused punishments need not punish actual criminals nor be proportional to crimes. By contrast, if retributivist punishments are to be just, they must fit both the perpetrator and the crimes.

First, only those who are responsible for a crime should be punished: guilt must be proved, and we should not single out likely suspects or representatives of a group to make examples of them or use them to intimidate other group members, as in our graffiti example. It is also important that the punishment fit the person in terms of the degree of his responsibility. This requirement would address concerns we have about differentiating between criminals and their accomplices and also about the mental state of a criminal. Diminished mental capacity, mitigating circumstances, and duress—which lessen a person's responsibility—are significant elements of the U.S. criminal punishment system.

Second, it is essential in the retributivist view that the punishment fit the crime. Defacing property is not a major wrong or harm and thus should not be punished with amputation of the perpetrator's hand, however well that might work to deter graffiti. Thus this view requires that we have a sense of what is more or less serious among crimes and also among punishments so that they can be well matched.

It is because the punishment should fit the crime that many people argue against the "three-strikes" laws that several states have passed. These laws mandate life imprisonment for anyone with two previous convictions for serious crimes who is then found guilty of a third felony. In California in 2012, voters overturned the state's three-strikes law. Opponents had noted that in some cases the third "strike" was merely petty theft—a felony charge for anyone who had already served a prison sentence for theft. A life sentence looks quite out of proportion to such infractions. On the other side, however, consequentialists might support three-strikes laws, arguing that it is better for all of us when people who have a history of lawbreaking are removed from society and prevented from continuing in such behavior.

As with the deterrence argument, one might raise objections against the retributivist argument. We have already referred to one: that punishing the perpetrator does not concretely undo the wrong done to the victim. Those who defend retributivism would have to explain in what sense the balance is restored or the wrong righted by punishment. However, the retributivist would not have any problem with those who point out that a particular form of punishment does not work. According to a retributivist, this is not the primary reason to punish. Someone should be punished as a way of achieving satisfaction or restitution, even if it does the perpetrator or others no good.

A more common objection to the retributivist view is that it amounts to condoning revenge. To know whether or not this is true, we would have to clarify what we mean by *revenge*. Suppose we mean that particular people—say a victim or her family—will get a sense of satisfaction in seeing the wrongdoer punished. This sense of satisfaction is merely contingent and psychological—a matter of feelings. We may

not want a system of legal punishment to be used to satisfy merely personal feelings of vengeance or resentment. But the retributivist view is not about our feelings. Indeed, if we have a duty to punish on retributivist grounds, we ought to carry out the punishment, even if we do not feel inclined to do so (perhaps because we are squeamish about carrying out a particular punishment). Retributive justice requires that justice be done, whether or not people feel good about it. However, some may question whether any type of justice exists that is not a matter of providing emotional satisfaction to victims or others who are enraged by a wrong done to them.

Finally, we can wonder whether the retributivist view provides a good basis for a system of legal punishment. Is the primary purpose of such a system to see that justice is done? Do we not have a system of legal punishment to ensure social order and safety? If so, then it would seem that the deterrence argument is the best reason for having any system of legal punishment.

One solution to the problem of whether to use deterrence or retribution to justify legal punishment is to use both.[6] In designing such a hybrid system, we could retain consequentialist reasons for having a legal punishment system, and consider first what works best to deter and prevent crimes. However, we could also use retributivist standards to determine who is punished (only those who are guilty and only to the extent that they are guilty) and by how much (the punishment fitting the crime). In fashioning the punishment system, however, there may be times when we need to determine which rationale takes precedence. For example, in setting requirements for conviction of guilt, we may need to know how bad it is to punish an innocent person. We may decide to give precedence to the retributivist rationale and then make the requirements for conviction of guilt very strenuous, requiring unanimous jury verdicts and guilt beyond a reasonable doubt. In so doing, we also let some guilty people go free and thus run the risk of lessening the deterrent effect of the punishment system. Or we may decide to give precedence to the deterrence rationale. We thus may weaken the requirements for conviction so that we may catch and punish a greater number of guilty people. In doing so, however, we run the risk of also punishing a greater number of innocent persons.

PUNISHMENT AND RESPONSIBILITY

A key element of our legal punishment system and practice is the link between punishment and responsibility. The retributivist believes responsibility is essential for punishment, and thus it is unjust to punish those who are not responsible for a crime. This concept can also can be supported on deterrence grounds; it probably would work better to punish only those who are responsible for crimes, since this focuses punishment in a way that encourages obedience to the law.

Our legal system allows for defenses that appeal to the question of responsibility. For example, under the defense of *duress*, we would probably say a person was not responsible if she were forced to commit a crime, either physically forced or under threat to life. She may have committed the crime, but that is not enough to prove she was responsible. (We do not have a system of strict liability, in which the only issue is whether or not you actually did or caused something.)

One of the most problematic defenses in our criminal justice system may well be the insanity defense. It involves a plea and a finding of "not guilty by reason of insanity," or something similar such as "mental defect." Another verdict available in some jurisdictions is that the defendant is "guilty but mentally ill." The difference between these two ways of conceiving crime, guilt, and mental illness is significant. Is someone *guilty but mentally ill* or are they *not guilty* because of their mental illness? This points toward a deep question about responsibility and guilt. We presume that someone ought to know the difference between right and wrong in order to be held responsible for their actions, and that a responsible person has the capacity to control his own behavior. There have been a variety of standards for describing responsibility and guilt and their connection with mental competence. One significant event in the evolution of these standards in the United States was the trial of John Hinckley Jr., who shot President Ronald Reagan and two other individuals in 1981. Hinckley was found not guilty by reason of insanity and confined to a hospital. In response, there was a backlash against the insanity defense, with some states—Idaho, Montana, and Utah—abolishing it altogether. States that retain some version of the insanity defense have different standards for determining mental illness. One common standard has roots in nineteenth-century England, with the *M'Naughton Rule* (1843). According to this rule, people are not responsible for their actions if they did not know what they were doing or did not know that it was wrong. This is often referred to as the "right from wrong test." Since that time, other attempts have been made to list the conditions under which people should not be held responsible for their actions. One example is the "irresistible impulse test." The idea underlying this test for insanity is that sometimes persons are not able to control their conduct and thus act through no fault of their own. The moral question of responsibility and guilt rests upon our capacity to understand right from wrong and the ability to control our own behavior.

Common criticisms of the insanity defense concern our ability to determine whether someone is mentally insane or incompetent. Can't someone feign this? How do psychiatrists or other experts determine whether a person knows what she is doing? Even if we could diagnose these conditions with absolute certainty, a more basic question would still remain, namely, would the conditions diminish or take away responsibility? If so, then would punishment be appropriate? In the extreme case in which a person has a serious brain condition that prevents normal mental function, we assume that this would excuse him from full responsibility. He may, however, be dangerous, and this may be another reason to detain as well as treat him.

Some people have criticized the entire notion of mental illness, especially as it is used in criminal proceedings. For example, it may result in indeterminate sentences for minor crimes because one must remain in custody in a criminal mental institution until sane. One longtime critic of the penal system, Thomas Szasz, holds that we have sometimes used the diagnosis of mental illness to categorize and stigmatize people who are simply different.[7] He finds this diagnosis often to be a dangerous form of social control. Another significant concern here is indefinite civil commitment for sex offenders. In some states in the United States, sexual predators who continue to report having violent sexual thoughts can be detained indefinitely out of suspicion that they will commit a crime.[8] But does it make sense to confine people for their thoughts when they have not yet committed a crime?

Some of us tend to look at heinous crimes and say, "No sane person could have done that!" Or we might say that a certain crime was "sick." We use the horror of the crime, its serious wrongness, to conclude that the person committing it must be mentally diseased. One problem with this conclusion is that it implies that the person is not responsible, since mental competence is a requirement for criminal liability. Are we then implying that people who do evil things are not responsible for what they do? If so, then perhaps they should not be punished. The connection between punishment and responsibility is not only central to our system of legal punishment but is also an important element of the morality of legal punishment.

Underlying this discussion of responsibility is a metaphysical account of free will. We hold people responsible for things that they freely choose to do. But, of course, there are deep questions here. Are we really free? Or are our actions determined by genetics, by social context, and by the laws of physics? If our actions are entirely determined, then we are not entirely responsible for what we do (in the sense that we could not have done otherwise). If we are not free, then it would seem that punishment as such (at least in the retributive sense of giving someone what was due them) would never be appropriate. Our legal system normally assumes that we have free will and treats criminals accordingly. But social context and physiological factors can mitigate responsibility and guilt.

Advocates of rehabilitation and alternatives to punishment often focus on the issue of social context, arguing that instead of seeking retribution, we should work to change the social conditions that cause crime. From a consequentialist perspective, if drug-treatment programs or job-training programs in prison would help reduce crime, then those programs would be morally recommended. From a non-consequentialist perspective, there might also be grounds for promoting such programs. One might want to consider whether persons ought to be given a second chance in light of the fact that, given certain circumstances, they might not have been fully responsible for their crimes. On the other hand, those who argue from a consequentialist perspective might point out that in certain kinds of cases—say, with sexual predators—there is not much likelihood of reform. Similarly, from a non-consequentialist perspective, some might argue that given the severity of certain crimes, persons deserve the strictest and most severe punishment, not a second chance.

PRISONS

In the past half-century, the incarceration rate in the United States has increased by a factor of seven.[9] According to the U.S. Bureau of Justice Statistics, adult correctional authorities supervised about 6,977,700 offenders at year-end 2011. At the same time, about 2.9 percent of adults in the United States (or 1 in every 34 adults) were under some form of correctional supervision (including probation and alternatives to incarceration).[10] (In more recent years, there has been a slow decline in incarceration rates due in part to budget pressures on state governments.)

In this chapter's opening, we mentioned that U.S. crime rates have fallen in recent years. Although it is difficult to establish any single reason that crime is down, one fact may be that more people are in prison. If deterrence is one of the primary purposes of punishment, we might conclude that the prison system is doing a good job. However, the U.S. incarceration system has generated serious charges of injustice and inefficiency. One concern is the cost and extent of the American prison system. Another worry is racial and other disparities in rates of incarceration. Still others argue that rehabilitation or restorative justice could provide a more effective and humane alternative to prison.

The number of people incarcerated in the United States dwarfs that of other countries, amounting to about 25 percent of the world's entire prison population.[11] The Sentencing Project lists the U.S. prison population rate at 716 per 100,000. The next highest rates are in Rwanda at 595, Russia at 568, Brazil at 253, Spain at 159, Australia at 133, and China at 122.[12] In the United States there are racial disparities in rates of incarceration, as will be discussed further below. The rate of incarceration per 100,000 white males is 478. For Latino males it is 1,238, and for black males it is 3,023.[13]

There are various reasons for the high rate of incarceration in the United States. The causes most often cited are mandatory sentences for drug crimes, an increase in the number of so-called three-strikes violations, and truth-in-sentencing laws that lessen the number of prisoners released early.[14] Also mentioned are democratically elected judges, as they may "yield to populist demands for tough justice."[15] There is also the issue of gun ownership and the easy availability of guns. Some claim that gun ownership could decrease crime by empowering citizens to defend themselves, while others claim that the high number of guns available in the United States exacerbates the problem of crime. While some see high incarceration rates as a justifiable response to the threat of violent crime, critics argue that the prison system reinforces a legacy of racial and class division in the United States.

Although many prisoners are incarcerated for having committed violent crimes, more than half are nonviolent, mostly drug-related, offenders. Moreover, it is estimated that some 16 percent of the prison population suffers from mental illness.[16] A report on prisons from 2006 warned that the experience of prisoners is too often marked by "rape, gang violence, abuse by officers, infectious disease, and never-ending solitary confinement."[17] In 2013, Human Rights Watch concluded that the American prison system was suffering from problems caused by "massive overincarceration" resulting from harsh sentencing practices that were "contrary to international law." Problems include a growing population of elderly prisoners, the incarceration of children in adult facilities, and the use of solitary confinement.[18]

The average annual cost to incarcerate an inmate in the United States is about $31,000.[19] In some states—New York, Washington, and Connecticut—the cost is $50,000 to $60,000 per inmate. When multiplied by the nearly seven million inmates in the United States, the total annual cost of our prison system is staggering. Out of all states, California has the highest overall expenditure on prisons. With a prison population of more than 167,000 and a cost per inmate of $47,421, the total annual cost in California is more than $7.9 billion. In 2011, the amount of money California spent on prisons exceeded the amount it spent on higher education.[20] This prompted former Gov. Arnold Schwarzenegger to opine, "the priorities have become out of whack over the years.... What does it say about any state that focuses more on prison uniforms than on caps and gowns?"[21] The comparison serves as a reminder that budget priorities reflect ethical judgments. Are we spending too much on prisons? And is this spending working? We noted that crime is down. But recidivism rates for ex-cons remain high—around 65 percent.[22] Such seemingly conflicting facts further complicate cost-benefit analyses of the U.S. prison system.

Race

Other ethical concerns arise from the stark racial disparities in the criminal justice system. As we have seen, black and Hispanic males are imprisoned at dramatically higher rates than white non-Hispanic males. As the U.S. Bureau of Justice Statistics reports: "[A]bout 0.5 percent of all white males, more than 3.0 percent of all black males, and 1.2 percent of all Hispanic males were imprisoned in 2011. Between 6.6 percent and 7.5 percent of all black males ages 25 to 39 were imprisoned in 2011." The report continues, "Among persons ages 20 to 24, black males were imprisoned at about 7 times [the rate] of white males."[23] One issue here is that a disproportionate number of blacks and Hispanics are sentenced to prison on drug charges.[24] Furthermore, while all high school dropouts are at greater risk for being in prison, "by the time they reach their mid-thirties, a full 60 percent of black high-school dropouts are now prisoners or ex-cons."[25]

There are political implications to the racial disparities in incarceration rates. For example, given that many states do not allow ex-felons to vote and that a high percentage of blacks vote Democratic, conviction and incarceration rates can have an impact on election outcomes. According to one estimate, and using conservative figures on voting, if ex-felons had been able to vote in the 2000 presidential election, Al Gore would have carried the state of Florida by 30,000 votes and, thus, would have won the Electoral College and the presidency.[26] Prison also tends to produce social stigma and disadvantage for ex-convicts and their families. Michelle Alexander, a civil rights advocate and law professor, suggests that these social costs have a racial complexion that has contributed to the creation of a new "Jim Crow" system. Alexander explains, "the criminalization and demonization of black men has turned the black community against itself, unraveling community and family relationships, decimating networks of support, and intensifying the shame and self-hate experienced by the current pariah caste."[27]

Racial disparities in imprisonment are also linked to disparities in social class. Affluent people get better lawyers, while poor people are more likely to take a plea bargain, resulting in incarceration.[28] Some sociologists have noted that incarceration fosters social stratification, with imprisonment helping to define the experience of those in the so-called "underclass." Incarceration disrupts families. And it pushes convicts out of the labor market, depresses their wages, and undermines their long-term life prospects.[29] Although it is illegal to discriminate against ex-convicts, employers remain wary of hiring those with prison records.[30] From a perspective that takes equality and social justice concerns seriously (as discussed, for example, in Chapter 13), racial disparities in incarceration are a cause for further reflection.

Restoration and Rehabilitation

These sorts of issues have led some authors—such as Angela Davis—to argue that the current system of mass incarceration ought to be abolished. Davis is concerned with the way that racial, gender, and economic inequities show up in the prison system. She suggests that the prison system ought to be replaced with a system that is focused on principles of reparation, restoration, and rehabilitation, rather than on principles of retributive justice.

Related ideas have been defended by the U.S. Conference of Catholic Bishops, which maintains that the human dignity of crime victims and perpetrators should both be respected. The bishops note that "the status quo is not really working—victims are often ignored, offenders are often not rehabilitated, and many communities have lost their sense of security."[31] While not advocating for the abolition of prisons, the bishops emphasize "responsibility, rehabilitation, and restoration." They conclude,

> We respect the humanity and promote the human dignity of both victims and offenders. We believe society must protect its citizens from violence and crime and hold accountable those who break the law. These same principles lead us to advocate for rehabilitation and treatment for offenders, for, like victims, their lives reflect that same dignity. Both victims and perpetrators of crime are children of God.[32]

Such perspectives draw on the idea of **restorative justice**, which seeks to heal the wounds caused by crime, while finding a way to allow criminals to take responsibility, make amends, and restore the community that they have broken. Proponents of restorative justice admit that it is not appropriate for all crimes, especially in situations where offenders are unable or unwilling to take responsibility or make amends. But proponents argue that restorative justice can produce better outcomes for both victims and offenders, while also reducing recidivism.[33] Interest has been growing in restorative justice programs as ways of dealing with bullying and other forms of misbehavior in schools. Restorative justice programs have been developed for school systems in cities such as in Oakland, California, in which the goal is to build community and defuse conflict among students whose lives are impacted by violence.[34]

Restorative justice points toward a broader conception of social justice that aims to alter social conditions so that crime is prevented and its harms are minimized. The move toward restorative justice and away from prisons is often connected with religious groups that have a historical commitment to pacifism, such as the Quakers and the Mennonites.[35] Key values in this approach include mercy and forgiveness, as well as justice.[36]

The most famous example of restorative justice is the "truth and reconciliation" process that occurred in the 1990s in South Africa. South Africa had suffered for decades under the racist system of apartheid that bred violence and resentment. The truth and reconciliation process allowed offenders to apply for amnesty from prosecution in exchange for honest testimony and public scrutiny. In the six-year period during which the Truth and Reconciliation Committee did its work, 22,000 victim statements were taken and 7,000 perpetrators applied for amnesty; 849 people were granted amnesty, while thousands of others were not.[37] The process was itself contentious, but it is generally regarded as a successful model. Archbishop Desmond Tutu explained in his foreword to the South African Truth and Reconciliation Committee report, "We believe, however, that there is another kind of justice—a restorative justice which is concerned not so much with punishment as with correcting imbalances, restoring broken relationships—with healing, harmony and reconciliation."[38] While rehabilitation and restorative justice sound like noble ideas, they appear to run counter to the demand for retributive justice. And from a utilitarian perspective, one might wonder whether those ideas are useful for deterring and preventing crime.

THE DEATH PENALTY

One of the most contentious issues for any philosophical conception of legal punishment—whether focused on retribution, deterrence, or some other value—is capital punishment. While the vast majority of developed nations (the United States being a notable exception) have abolished the death penalty, this most extreme form of punishment raises profound moral questions about the nature of punishment itself. Retributivists might be seen to favor capital punishment for murderers as an application of *lex talionis*, but it is hard to see how the death of another person "makes up for" the loss of the victim. Consequentialists may argue that the death penalty deters people from committing murder, but scholars continue to debate the actual deterrent effect of the death penalty.

The outrage, harm, and injustice of murder seem to call for the harshest of punishments, which may be why murder remains one of the only crimes punishable by death (at least in some states within the United States). We should note, however, that advocates of restorative justice are often opposed to the death penalty. The U.S. Conference of Catholic Bishops also rejects the death penalty as part of a broader theological and philosophical commitment to a "culture of life." But retributivist advocates of the death penalty argue that for murder, the only

acceptable punishment is death. The murder victim cannot be restored to life, and it also seems unlikely that the murderer can make amends for her crime in the same way that a thief can. Moreover, for some unrepentant predatory criminals—such as those who continue to murder while in prison—execution may be viewed as the only solution. Although the death penalty was once widely used for a variety of crimes, most people now view the death penalty as an extraordinary sort of punishment that requires extra justification. For example, ethicist Lloyd Steffen argues on natural law grounds, in his 2012 book *Ethics and Experience*, that we ought to preserve life and not kill people, and that the state ordinarily ought not kill its own citizens.[39] Thus he maintains that the death penalty requires special justification and that it may no longer be justifiable in contemporary social and political circumstances.

Legal Issues

According to Amnesty International, ninety-seven countries have abolished the death penalty, including almost all industrialized democracies. And approximately 90 percent of the world's countries no longer carry out executions.[40] The global leader in death sentences is China, where the number of suspected executions annually is in the thousands (but data on Chinese executions are not officially published by the Chinese government). After China, the largest numbers of executions in 2011 (according to official reports) occurred in Iran (360), Saudi Arabia (82), Iraq (68), the United States (43), and Yemen (41). Bucking the international trend toward abolition of the death penalty, two countries resumed executions in 2011: Afghanistan and the United Arab Emirates.[41]

Capital punishment has a long history in the United States, but by the 1960s a majority of Americans had come to oppose it.[42] In 1972, the U.S. Supreme Court case *Furman v. Georgia* ushered in a brief moratorium on the death penalty, as the court found that its imposition had become too "arbitrary and capricious" and thus violated the Constitution's ban on cruel and unusual punishment. That ruling also invalidated the use of the death penalty as punishment for the crime of rape. By 1976, however, the country's mood had again begun to change, and states had established less

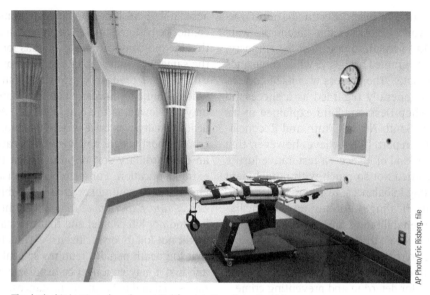

The lethal injection chamber at California's San Quentin Prison.

arbitrary sentencing guidelines. That year, the high court ruled in *Gregg v. Georgia* that the death penalty does not violate the Eighth Amendment's ban on cruel and unusual punishment. The court argued that the death penalty is justifiable on both retributivist and deterrence grounds. The court concluded that the death penalty could be "an expression of the community's belief that certain crimes are themselves so grievous an affront to humanity that the only adequate response may be the penalty of death."[43] The court acknowledged that there was no conclusive empirical evidence about the deterrent effect of the death penalty—but the court also held that it was reasonable to suspect that it might deter. Public support for the death penalty has varied in the decades since. According to the Pew Center for the People and the Press, "In 1996, 78 percent favored capital punishment for people convicted of murder. Support for the death penalty subsequently declined, falling to 66 percent in 2001 and 62 percent in late 2005. Since then, support has mostly remained in the low-to-mid-60s, though it dipped slightly (to 58 percent) in October 2011."[44]

Currently, eighteen states and the District of Columbia do not have the death penalty, and several states have only recently abolished it: New Jersey

and New York in 2007, New Mexico in 2009, Illinois in 2011, and Connecticut in 2012. In 2013, Maryland's legislature voted to abolish the death penalty. In 2012, however, voters in California rejected a referendum (Proposition 34) that would have abolished the death penalty. As of early 2013, there have been 1,325 executions in the United States since the death penalty was reinstated in 1976.[45] The largest number of executions have occurred in Texas (with 493 executions as of early 2013), Virginia (with 110), and Oklahoma (with 103).[46]

Exonerations

One issue of grave concern is whether the U.S. justice system can ensure that people are never wrongfully executed for crimes they did not commit. Indeed, many opponents of the death penalty believe the United States has already executed innocent people. How could this happen? Explanations range from the sinister to the banal: "revelations of withheld evidence, mistaken eyewitness identification, questionable forensic practices, prosecutorial misconduct, and simple error."[47] Defendants, especially those who have to rely upon court-appointed public defenders, are often represented by overworked and underprepared lawyers—with some even cited for dozing off during their clients' trials. Since 1973, more than 140 convicts on death row in the United States have been exonerated, with two death row inmates being exonerated in 2012.[48] According to the Innocence Project, a national organization that works to exonerate the wrongly convicted, there have been 302 people who were proved innocent of a variety of crimes since 1989 by the use of DNA technology, including 18 people on death row.[49] Among those exonerated, the average prison time served is 13.6 years, and the total years served is more than 4,000.[50]

Such revelations of innocence have raised doubts about the death penalty for some political leaders who once supported it. In January 2000, the governor of Illinois, George Ryan, ordered that all executions in his state be halted—after Northwestern University journalism students reviewed cases and proved the innocence of several inmates, including one who was within forty-eight hours of his scheduled execution. "Until I can be sure with moral certainty," Ryan said, "that no innocent man or woman is facing a lethal injection, no one will meet that fate."[51] Because of these concerns and after a review of the cases, Ryan—in one of his last acts as governor in 2003—pardoned four inmates and commuted the death sentences of the remaining 167 on death row. Illinois officially abolished the death penalty in 2011.

Racial Bias and Fairness

Another issue that raises concerns about the death penalty is the evidence of racial bias in death penalty sentencing. A number of sources including Amnesty International have indicated that there is racial bias in the death penalty system.[52] The Death Penalty Information Center (an anti–death penalty organization) has collected a number of empirical studies that show racial bias in the death penalty in a number of states. For example, in many states blacks are more likely to receive a death sentence than whites, especially when the murder victim is white.[53]

Not surprisingly, then, there are significant racial disparities in the number of prisoners executed. Since 1976, the race of the executed is 56 percent white, 35 percent black, 7 percent Hispanic, and 2 percent other; and 41 percent of the death row

population is black.[54] Compare that to the general population, which is 64 percent non-Hispanic white, 13 percent black, and 16 percent Hispanic.[55] Most interesting, perhaps, is the fact that cases resulting in death sentences for interracial murders are quite skewed. Nineteen whites have been executed for murdering a black victim, but 257 blacks have been executed for killing a white victim.[56] There are also racial issues in the makeup of juries. According to a 2003 report from Amnesty International, "At least one in five of the African Americans executed since 1977 had been convicted by all white juries, in cases which displayed a pattern of prosecutors dismissing prospective black jurors during jury selection."[57]

Other issues related to the death penalty have recently gained public attention, for example, whether mentally retarded persons or juveniles should be executed. In June 2002, in *Atkins v. Virginia*, the U.S. Supreme Court ruled that mentally retarded defendants should not be subject to the death penalty. Obviously, one practical problem is how to determine when someone is retarded and what degree of mental retardation should exempt a person from the death penalty. In Georgia, for example, the defense has to determine beyond a reasonable doubt that a convict is mentally retarded. This standard is quite strict, requiring substantial proof of disability. Consider the case of Warren Lee Hill, a convicted Georgia murderer with an IQ of 70. (Those with IQs below 70 are generally regarded to be intellectually disabled.) Hill was scheduled to be executed in February 2013, but the execution was stayed hours before it was scheduled to allow courts to review the issue of Hill's mental capacity. Through 2013, Hill's execution was subject to ongoing legal challenges.[58]

Related to the question of mental capacity is the issue of executing juveniles. In March 2005, the U.S. Supreme Court ruled (in *Roper v. Simmons*) that it was cruel and unusual punishment, forbidden by the Constitution, to execute those who were under age eighteen when they committed their crimes. (A growing body of biological and psychological evidence suggests that adolescents "lack mature judgment and a full appreciation of the consequences of their actions."[59]) Until this ruling, the United States had been the only remaining country in the world that executed juveniles, as Justice Kennedy explained in the court's majority decision.

Racial disparities in executions, as well as executions of juveniles and the mentally disabled, raise serious questions about the fairness of the death penalty and its application. These cases remind us that concepts such as criminal responsibility and appropriate punishment are complex and highly disputed issues, and are all the more so when the punishment being considered is death.

Costs

Death penalty cases are expensive, both in terms of court costs and prison costs. While costs vary from state to state, one analysis from the Death Penalty Information Center concludes that, "for a single trial, the state may pay $1 million more than for a non-death penalty trial. But only one in every three capital trials results in a death sentence, so the true cost of that death sentence is $3 million. Further down the road, only one in ten of the death sentences handed down may result in an execution. Hence the cost to the state to reach that one execution is $30 million."[60]

The costs of death row itself are also inordinate. The California Innocence Project estimates that it costs $175,000 per year to house a death row inmate, compared to about $47,000 per year for an inmate not on death row. This means that $177 million per year is spent housing the more than 700 inmates on death row in California.[61] This is especially stunning considering that only thirteen California inmates have been executed since 1978. Opponents of the death penalty often cite the high cost as an argument against capital punishment. Proponents argue that costs could be controlled by speeding up the trial and appeals process. But a central reason for the lengthy trials and appeals is to ensure that innocent people are not executed.

The controversies surrounding the death penalty point to deeper philosophical questions about its justification. The same two arguments regarding legal punishment—deterrence and retribution—generally are used in arguments about the death penalty. We will return now to these rationales and see what considerations would be relevant to arguments for and against the death penalty.

Deterrence Considerations

Utilitarian philosopher John Stuart Mill defended the death penalty by arguing that it was the least cruel punishment that works to deter murder.[62] Mill pointed out that there were punishments worse than death—torture, for example. However, Mill argued, people fear death, even though a quick and painless death is not nearly as bad as a life of torture. For a utilitarian such as Mill, the death penalty works to minimize pain (for the convict), while promoting the greatest happiness (by deterring murder).

But is the death penalty a deterrent? Does it prevent people from committing certain capital crimes? Consider first the issue of prevention. One would think that at least there is certainty here. If you execute someone, then that person will not commit any future crime—including murders—because he will be dead. However, on a stricter interpretation of the term *prevent,* this may not necessarily be so.[63] When we execute a convicted murderer, do we really prevent that person from committing any further murders? The answer is, "Maybe." If that person would have committed another murder, then we have prevented him from doing so. If that person would not have committed another murder, then we would not have prevented him from doing so. In general, by executing all convicted murderers we would, strictly speaking, have prevented some of them (those who would have killed again) but not others (those who would not have killed again) from doing so. How many murders would we have prevented? It is difficult to tell. Those who support the death penalty may insist that it will have been worth it, no matter how small the number of murders prevented, because the people executed are convicted murderers anyway.

By contrast, what do we make of arguments for the death penalty that claim it deters those who have not already committed murder? If the death penalty deters would-be murderers from committing their crimes, then it is worth it, according to this rationale. Granted, it will not deter those who kill out of passion or those who determine the crime is worth the risk of punishment, but presumably it would deter others. How can we determine if the death penalty really is an effective deterrent? First, we can consider our intuitions about the value of our own lives—that we would not do what would result in our own death. Threats of being executed would deter us, and thus, we think, they also would deter others. More likely, however, reasons other than fear of the death penalty restrain most of us from committing murder.

We might also gauge the death penalty's deterrent effect by examining empirical evidence. For example, we could compare two jurisdictions, say, two states. One has the death penalty, and one does not. If we find that in the state with the death penalty there are fewer murders than in the state without the death penalty, can we assume that the death penalty has made the difference and is thus a deterrent? Not necessarily. Perhaps it was something else about the state with the death penalty that accounted for the lesser incidence of murder. For example, the lower homicide rate could be the result of good economic conditions or a culture that has strong families or religious institutions. Something similar could be true of the state with a higher incidence of homicide. The cause in this case could be high unemployment, high rates of drug and alcohol abuse, and other social problems. So, also, if there were a change in one jurisdiction from no death penalty to death penalty (or the opposite), and the statistics regarding homicides also changed, then we might conclude that the causal factor was the change in the death penalty status. But again this is not necessarily so. For example, the murder rate in Canada actually declined after that country abolished the death penalty in 1976.[64] Other studies have found no correlation between having, instituting, or abolishing the death penalty and the rate of homicide.[65] For example, statistics show that states without the death penalty and with similar demographic profiles do not differ in homicide rates from states with the death penalty. Moreover, since 1976, homicide rates in states that instituted the death penalty have not declined more than in states that did not institute the death penalty. And homicide rates in states with the death penalty have been found to be higher than states without it.[66] But some studies still maintain that executions have a deterrent effect. A 2007 article in the *Wall Street Journal* claimed that "Capital Punishment Works." The authors charted execution rates and murder rates

for the twenty-six-year period from 1979 through 2004. The data indicate that as execution rates increase, murder rates decline. They conclude, "each execution carried out is correlated with about 74 fewer murders the following year."[67] These results—and others like them from recent studies—have been criticized by economists and statisticians who maintain that any deterrent effect, if there is one, is "too fragile to be certain."[68] One problem is that there are very few executions and these occur in a few states. It is difficult to draw general conclusions about a causal relation between execution rates and murder rates from the sorts of correlations mentioned here. The National Academy of Sciences concluded in 2012, "research to date on the effect of capital punishment on homicide is not informative about whether capital punishment decreases, increases, or has no effect on homicide rates."[69]

To make a good argument for the death penalty on utilitarian grounds, a proponent would have to show that it works to deter crime. In addition, the proponent may have to show that the death penalty works better than alternatives—for example, life in prison without the possibility of parole or community-based crime prevention efforts. If we have the death penalty and it does not provide an effective deterrent, then we will have executed people for no good purpose. If we do not have the death penalty and it would have been an effective deterrent, then we risk the lives of innocent victims who otherwise would have been saved. Because this is the worse alternative, some argue, we ought to retain the death penalty. But because the deterrence argument broadly construed is a consequentialist argument, using it also should require thinking more generally of costs and benefits. Here the higher cost of execution could be compared to the lower cost of life imprisonment.

On Retributivist Grounds

Immanuel Kant defended the death penalty on retributivist grounds. He argues, "undeserved evil which any one commits on another, is to be regarded as perpetrated on himself."[70] This principle has obvious connections with Kant's idea that the categorical imperative requires that we view our maxims as universal moral laws (as discussed in Chapter 6).

Kant advocates a type of retaliation, which demands like for like or life for life. Kant maintains that the death penalty is justified because it treats a murderer as a rational being, giving him what he deserves according to this basic principle of retributive justice. Kant also maintains that we should respect the human dignity of a prisoner awaiting execution and not torture or abuse him.

As we have already noted, according to the retributivist argument for legal punishment, we ought to punish people to make them pay for the wrong or harm they have done. Those who argue for the death penalty on retributivist grounds must show that it is a fitting punishment and the only or most fitting punishment for certain crimes and criminals. This is not necessarily an argument based on revenge—that the punishment of the wrongdoer gives others satisfaction. It appeals rather to a sense of justice and an abstract righting of wrongs done. Again, there are two different versions of the retributive principle: egalitarian (or *lex talionis*) and proportional. The egalitarian version says that the punishment should equal the crime. An argument for the death penalty would attempt to show that the only fitting punishment for someone who takes a life is that her own life be taken in return. In this view, the value of a life is not equivalent to anything else, thus even life in prison is not sufficient payment for taking a life, though it would also seem that the only crime deserving of the death penalty would be murder. Note that homicide is not the only crime for which we have assigned the death penalty. We have also done so for treason and, at times, for rape. Moreover, only some types of murder are thought by proponents of the death penalty to call for this form of punishment. And as noted in the critique of the *lex talionis* view previously, strict equality of punishment would be not only impractical in some cases but also morally problematic.

Perhaps a more acceptable argument could be made on grounds of proportionality. In this view, death is the only fitting punishment for certain crimes. These are worse than all others and should receive the worst or most severe punishment. Surely, some say, death is a worse punishment than life in prison. However, others argue that spending one's life in prison is worse. This form of the retributivist principle would not require that the worst crimes receive the worst possible punishment. It only requires that, of the range of acceptable punishments, the worst crimes receive the top punishment on the list. Death by prolonged torture might be the worst punishment, but we probably would not put that at the top of our list. So, also, the death penalty could be—but need not be—included on that list.

Using the retributivist rationale, one would need to determine the most serious crimes. Can these be specified and a good reason given as to why they are the worst crimes? Multiple murders would be worse than single ones, presumably. Murder with torture or of certain people also might be found to be among the worst crimes. What about treason? What about huge monetary swindles that cost thousands of people their life savings? We rate degrees of murder, distinguishing murder in the first degree from murder in the second degree. The first is worse because the person not only deliberately intended to kill the victim but also did so out of malice. These crimes are distinguished from manslaughter (both voluntary and involuntary), which is also killing. The idea supposedly is that the kind of personal and moral involvement makes a difference. The more the person planned with intention and deliberateness, the more truly the person owned the act. The more malicious crime is also thought to be worse. Critics of the death penalty sometimes argue that such rational distinctions are perhaps impossible to make in practice. However, unless it is impossible in principle or by its very nature, supporters could continue to try to refine the current distinctions.

Mercy and Restorative Justice

Opponents of the death penalty often argue against it on deterrent grounds, maintaining that if it does not work to deter crime (or if some other punishment works better), it causes unnecessary and unjustifiable pain. Utilitarian philosopher Jeremy Bentham opposed the death penalty, for example, by arguing that life imprisonment would work better. Others argue against the death penalty while acknowledging the retributivist argument in favor of capital punishment. Philosopher Jeffrey Reiman maintains that the death penalty represents a sort of maximal amount of retribution that can be justified. We can execute a murderer, for example, but we cannot kill his family. Reiman further suggests that there are circumstances in which it is morally permissible to give criminals less than the maximum punishment, so long as we attend to the needs and interests of the victims of crime.[71] In other words, we could execute murderers, but there may be good reasons for not doing so. Among the reasons for not executing may be upholding other values, such as mercy. Along these lines, Pope John Paul II argued that while the death penalty could be justified in cases where it was absolutely necessary to protect society, in a world with a modern prison system, the death penalty was no longer necessary.[72] The U.S. Conference of Catholic Bishops explains that while the death penalty can be justified, there is a higher road that involves the value of mercy.[73]

Indeed, the relatively greater value of mercy is often a central claim for religious opponents of the death penalty. Such opposition to capital punishment is often connected with a broader commitment to nonviolence and pacifism (see Chapter 19), one that sees little purpose in responding to violence with violence. "An eye for an eye leaves the whole world blind" is a sentiment that is frequently attributed to Mohandas Gandhi. In the Christian tradition, the value of mercy is connected to other values such as forgiveness and compassion.[74] The Catholic Church is opposed to the death penalty on these grounds, holding that mercy is an important value and that the death penalty is simply not the best way for murder victims to find closure.[75]

The idea of finding closure is connected with arguments in favor of restorative justice. While it is certainly not possible to restore a murder victim to life, it may be possible to imagine responses to murder that do not involve the desire for retribution. Consider, for example, the response to a 2006 school shooting in an Amish community in Nickel Mines, Pennsylvania. (Ten Amish children were shot and five killed by a local milk truck driver who was not Amish.) The community gathered together after these murders and offered forgiveness to the murderer (who had committed suicide) and his family.[76] Afterward, the mother of the murderer recalled how the Amish community's forgiving attitude helped her heal and recover from the horror of knowing that her son was

a mass murderer.[77] Another example comes from Tallahassee, Florida. Ann Grosmaire, a nineteen-year-old college student, was shot and killed by her boyfriend, Conor McBride, in 2010. Despite their grief and the horrific nature of the crime, the Grosmaire family reached out to Conor's family. Citing their Christian faith and a belief that Ann would want them to forgive Conor, the Grosmaires worked with the prosecutor to implement a version of restorative justice. A conference was held in which Conor confessed his crime to Ann's family, and Ann's family explained the depth of the loss that they had experienced. Conor was eventually sentenced to twenty years in prison. Kate Grosmaire, Ann's mother, later explained that forgiveness had a positive effect on her. "Forgiveness for me was self-preservation," she said. But she also noted that forgiveness is a difficult and ongoing process, "Forgiving Conor doesn't change the fact that Ann is not with us. My daughter was shot, and she died. I walk by her empty bedroom at least twice a day."[78] While proponents of restorative justice argue that the message of forgiveness and mercy provides an important addition to discussions of the death penalty, retributivists will argue that mercy and forgiveness give people less than what they deserve.

Humane Executions

Other concerns with regard to the death penalty are often about the nature of political power. Should the state have the power to kill people? As mentioned previously, most Western nations no longer have a death penalty. One reason may be that liberal-democratic polities want to limit the power of the state. Others may argue, as Reiman suggests, that killing is uncivilized, brutalizing, degrading, barbarous, and dehumanizing. This sort of argument may be grounded in a kind of visceral repugnance about the act of killing. But it also appeals to the constitutional prohibition on cruel and unusual punishment. Is the death penalty inherently cruel or inhumane? Or is it possible to humanely execute criminals?

Contemporary methods of execution can sometimes appear to cause suffering. Depending on the form of execution, the one put to death may gasp for air, strain, or shake uncontrollably. With some methods, the eyes bulge, the blood vessels expand, and sometimes more than one try is needed to complete the job. In 1999, for example, 344-pound Allen Lee Davis was executed in Florida's electric chair. The execution caused blood to appear on Davis's face and shirt, which some believed demonstrated that he had suffered greatly. Others said it was simply a nosebleed.[79] Nevertheless, in 2000, the Florida legislature voted to use lethal injections instead of the electric chair in future executions.[80]

Just as the electric chair was thought to be more humane than earlier execution methods when Thomas Edison invented it in 1888, so now death by lethal injection has generally taken the place of electrocution and other earlier methods. The last death by gas chamber was in 1999 in Arizona, the last death by hanging in 1996 in Delaware. In June 2010, Ronnie Lee Gardner was executed by firing squad in Utah but this was at his own request. Though there has been a move toward lethal injections as other methods of execution have been criticized, one of the current debates regarding the death penalty is whether lethal injection itself is humane.

Three chemicals are used in a lethal injection, which is administered via an IV. First, an ultrashort-acting barbiturate, usually sodium thiopental, is given. This causes the inmate to become unconscious. Next, a muscle relaxant, either pancuronium bromide or a similar drug, is given to cause paralysis of the muscles, including those responsible for breathing. Finally, potassium chloride, which causes cardiac arrest, is given. If all goes as expected, the inmate loses consciousness and does not experience any pain as death takes place. The entire process can take as little as ten minutes or much longer. Some of the delay is caused by the difficulty the technicians sometimes have in finding an acceptable vein to use. There have been cases of drug users, for example, whose veins were not in good condition or who had to help the technician find a good vein. It is also possible that the condemned person may remain conscious or partially conscious and experience acute pain or the feeling of suffocation but cannot communicate this because of the inability to move caused by the second chemical. Technicians can be more or less capable of giving the drugs correctly and in sufficient quantity. Doctors would be more capable but

are prohibited by their code of ethics from taking part in executions in this way.[81] There have been at least forty-three cases of botched executions recorded since 1976. These include instances in which IVs were not administered properly, prolonging the execution process; those in which the initial administration of gas or electricity failed to kill; and those in which the bodies of the condemned caught fire during electrocutions.[82] In recent years, several states suspended lethal injection out of the concern that the practice was not humane.[83] Meanwhile, American prisons have had difficulty obtaining lethal drugs since European manufacturers oppose their use in executions and have refused to sell them to American prisons.[84] Clearly, both opponents and supporters of the death penalty may find evidence for their positions in the various descriptions of lethal injection as a more or less humane method of execution.

The concern about lethal injection is related to a range of questions about the meaning of the death penalty and what it symbolizes. For example, some who favor more violent forms of execution argue that those who spill blood must have their own blood spilled. In this view, a firing squad may be more appropriate than lethal injection. Nevertheless, Americans tend to view beheading, such as happens in Saudi Arabia and elsewhere, as a barbaric way to execute a criminal. Consider, further, the question of whether a condemned prisoner should have the right to choose his own means of execution. Is it morally appropriate to give a criminal that choice? As noted, the Utah execution by firing squad in 2010 was selected by the condemned man himself; not long ago, a convicted murderer in Oregon asked to be hanged.[85] A further question in terms of the symbolic value of executions is whether they should be held in public or videotaped for purposes of information and instruction. We might consider the potential deterrent power of public executions. But we may also think that executions are no longer held in public for good reasons. Is it because we are ashamed of them? Do we think it is cruel or inhumane to display an executed person's body in public as a warning to others? Or are we simply trying to keep the proceedings dignified, while avoiding the use of the executed criminal's death as a means (in a way that

Kant would find immoral)? When we ask questions such as these, our views on the death penalty and our reasons for supporting or opposing it will be put to the test, which is probably not a bad thing.

NOTES

1. Jon Cohen, "Most Want Death Penalty for Dzhokhar Tsarnaev if He Is Convicted of Boston Bombing," *Washington Post*, May 1, 2013, accessed May 9, 2013, http://articles.washingtonpost.com/2013-05-01/world/38940946_1_death-penalty-whites-35-percent

2. "Intentional Homicide, Count and Rate per 100,000 Population (1995–2011)," United Nations Office on Drugs and Crime, accessed February 1, 2013, http://www.unodc.org/unodc/en/data-and-analysis/homicide.html

3. Chris Francescani, "Violent Crime Takes a Holiday in New York City," Reuters, November 28, 2012, accessed February 15, 2012, http://www.reuters.com/article/2012/11/28/us-usa-newyork-crime-idUSBRE8AR18S20121128

4. Steven D. Levitt, "Understanding Why Crime Fell in the 1990s: Four Factors That Explain the Decline and Six That Do Not," *Journal of Economic Perspectives* 18, no. 1 (2004): 163–90.

5. Kevin Drum, "America's Real Criminal Element: Lead," *Mother Jones*, January/February 2013, accessed February 15, 2013, http://www.motherjones.com/environment/2013/01/lead-crime-link-gasoline

6. See Richard Brandt, *Ethical Theory* (Englewood Cliffs, NJ: Prentice Hall, 1959).

7. Thomas Szasz, *The Myth of Mental Illness* (New York: Harper & Row, 1961).

8. "The Science of Sex Abuse" *New Yorker*, January 14, 2013.

9. Todd R. Clear, Michael D. Reisig, and George F. Cole, eds., *American Corrections* (Stamford, CT: Cengage Learning, 2012), Chapter 18.

10. "Correctional Populations in the United States, 2011," Bureau of Justice Statistics, November 29, 2012, accessed March 24, 2013, http://bjs.gov/index.cfm?ty=pbdetail&iid=4537

11. "The Cost of a Nation of Incarceration," CBS News, April 22, 2012, accessed February 15, 2013, http://www.cbsnews.com/8301-3445_162-57418495/the-cost-of-a-nation-of-incarceration/

12. The Sentencing Project, *Trends in U.S. Corrections*, accessed March 24, 2013, http://sentencingproject.org/doc/publications/inc_Trends_in_Corrections_Fact_sheet.pdf; also see International Centre for Prison Studies, accessed March 24, 2013, http://www.prisonstudies.org/info/worldbrief/wpb_stats.php?area=all&category=wb_poprate

13. The Sentencing Project, *Trends in U.S. Corrections*, http://sentencingproject.org/doc/publications/inc_Trends_in_Corrections_Fact_sheet.pdf

14. Jim Webb, "Why We Must Fix Our Prisons," *San Francisco Chronicle*, March 29, 2009, 4; also see Associated Press, "Nation's Inmate Population Increased 2.3 Percent Last Year," *New York Times*, April 25, 2005, A14.

15. "U.S. Inmate Count Far Exceeds Those of Other Nations," *New York Times*, April 23, 2008, A1, A14.

16. "The American Prison Nightmare," *New York Review of Books*, April 12, 2007, 33, 36.

17. John J. Gibbons and Nicholas de B. Katzenbach, *Confronting Confinement* (New York: Vera Institute of Justice, 2006), iii.

18. "US: Injustices Filling the Prisons," Human Rights Watch, January 31, 2013, accessed June 3, 2013, http://www.hrw.org/news/2013/01/31/us-injustices-filling-prisons

19. Vera Institute of Justice, *The Price of Prisons* (January 2012, updated July 20, 2012), http://www.vera.org/sites/default/files/resources/downloads/Price_of_Prisons_updated_version_072512.pdf

20. "Winners and Losers: Corrections and Higher Education in California," *California Common Sense,* September 2012, accessed February 15, 2013, http://www.cacs.org/ca/article/44

21. Jennifer Steinhauer, "Schwarzenegger Seeks Shift from Prisons to Schools," *New York Times,* January 6, 2010, accessed May 13, 2013, http://www.nytimes.com/2010/01/07/us/07calif.html

22. "Recidivism," Bureau of Justice Statistics, accessed February 15, 2013, http://bjs.ojp.usdoj.gov/index.cfm?ty=tp&tid=17

23. Bureau of Justice Statistics, *Prisoners in 2011* (December 2012), p. 8, accessed April 9, 2013, http://www.bjs.gov/content/pub/pdf/p11.pdf

24. Jim Webb, "Why We Must Fix Our Prisons," *San Francisco Chronicle*, March 29, 2009, 5.

25. "The American Prison Nightmare," *New York Review of Books*, April 12, 2007, 33, 36.

26. Ibid.

27. Michelle Alexander, *The New Jim Crow: Mass Incarceration in the Age of Colorblindness* (New York: The New Press, 2010), 17.

28. John H. Langbein interview, *Frontline*, PBS, January 16, 2004, accessed February 15, 2013, http://www.pbs.org/wgbh/pages/frontline/shows/plea/interviews/langbein.html

29. Sara Wakefield and Christopher Uggen, "Incarceration and Stratification," *Annual Review of Sociology* 36 (2010), 387–406.

30. Stan Alcorn, "'Check Yes Or No': The Hurdles of Job Hunting with a Criminal Past," NPR's *All Things Considered*, January 31, 2013, accessed February 15, 2013, http://www.npr.org/2013/01/31/170766202/-check-yes-or-no-the-hurdles-of-employment-with-criminal-past

31. "Responsibility, Rehabilitation, and Restoration: A Catholic Perspective on Crime and Criminal Justice" (2000), U.S. Conference of Catholic Bishops, accessed February 15, 2013, http://old.usccb.org/sdwp/criminal.shtml#introduction

32. Ibid.

33. Hennessey Haynes, "Reoffending and Restorative Justice," in *Handbook of Restorative Justice*, eds. Gerry Johnstone and Daniel Van Ness (London: Willan Publishing, 2007), 432 ff.

34. Patricia Leigh Brown, "Opening Up, Students Transform a Vicious Circle," *New York Times*, April 4, 2013, accessed May 9, 2013, http://www.nytimes.com/2013/04/04/education/restorative-justice-programs-take-root-in-schools.html?pagewanted=all

35. See Laura Magnani and Harmon L. Wray, *Beyond Prisons: A New Interfaith Paradigm for Our Failed Prison System* (Minneapolis, MN: Fortress Press, 2006).

36. See Trudy Conway, David McCarthy, and Vicki Schieber, eds., *Where Justice and Mercy Meet* (Collegeville, MN: Liturgical Press, 2013).

37. Lyn S. Graybill, *Truth and Reconciliation in South Africa* (London: Lynne Rienner Publishing, 2002), 8; "Truth and Reconciliation Commission (TRC)," South African History Online, accessed May 9, 2013, http://www.sahistory.org.za/topic/truth-and-reconciliation-commission-trc

38. *Truth and Reconciliation Commission of South Africa Report* (1998), para. 36, p. 9, accessed February 15, 2013, http://www.justice.gov.za/trc/report/finalreport/Volumepercent201.pdf

39. Lloyd Steffen, *Ethics and Experience* (Lanhan, MD: Rowman and Littlefield, 2012).

40. "Abolitionist and Retentionist Countries," Amnesty International, accessed February 15, 2013, http://www.amnesty.org/en/death-penalty/abolitionist-and-retentionist-countries

41. Amnesty International, *Death Sentences and Executions 2011* (2012), accessed February 15, 2013, http://www.amnesty.org/en/library/asset/ACT50/001/2012/en/241a8301-05b4-41c0-bfd9-2fe72899cda4/act500012012en.pdf

42. "Introduction to the Death Penalty," Death Penalty Information Center, http://www.deathpenaltyinfo.org/part-i-history-death-penalty#susp

43. *Gregg v. Georgia,* 428 U.S. 153 (1976) at III.c.

44. "Continued Majority Support for Death Penalty," Pew Center, January 6, 2012, accessed February 15, 2013, http://www.people-press.org/2012/01/06/continued-majority-support-for-death-penalty/

45. "Execution List 2013," Death Penalty Information Center, accessed April 9, 2013, http://www.deathpenaltyinfo.org/execution-list-2013

46. "Number of Executions by State and Region Since 1976," Death Penalty Information Center, accessed April 9, 2013, http://www.deathpenaltyinfo.org/number-executions-state-and-region-1976

47. Mike Farrell, "Death Penalty Thrives in Climate of Fear," *San Francisco Chronicle*, February 24, 2002, D3.

48. "Innocence and the Death Penalty," Death Penalty Information Center, accessed February 15, 2013, http://www.deathpenaltyinfo.org/innocence-and-death-penalty

49. Innocence Project, accessed February 22, 2013, http://www.innocenceproject.org/Content/Facts_on_PostConviction_DNA_Exonerations.php

50. Ibid.

51. Margaret Carlson, "Death, Be Not Proud," *Time*, February 21, 2000, 38.

52. "Death Penalty and Race," Amnesty International, accessed March 27, 2013, http://www.amnestyusa.org/our-work/issues/death-penalty/us-death-penalty-facts/death-penalty-and-race

53. "Research on the Death Penalty," Death Penalty Information Center, accessed May 13, 2013, http://www.deathpenaltyinfo.org/research-death-penalty

54. "Race of Death Row Inmates Executed Since 1976," Death Penalty Information Center, accessed February 15, 2013, www.deathpenaltyinfo.org/race-death-row-inmates-executed-1976

55. U.S. Census Bureau QuickFacts 2011, accessed May 13, 2013, http://quickfacts.census.gov/qfd/states/00000.html

56. "Race of Death Row Inmates Executed Since 1976," Death Penalty Information Center, www.deathpenaltyinfo.org/race-death-row-inmates-executed-1976

57. Amnesty International, *Death by Discrimination: The Continuing Role of Race in Capital Cases* (April 2003), p. 2, accessed April 9, 2013, http://www.amnesty.org/en/library/asset/AMR51/046/2003/en/bd8584ef-d712-11dd-b0cc-1f0860013475/amr510462003en.pdf

58. Lincoln Caplan, "Disgracing 'the Quintessential System of Justice,'" *New York Times*, April 26, 2013, accessed May 13, 2013, http://takingnote.blogs.nytimes.com/2013/04/26/disgracing-the-quintessential-system-of-justice/

59. See, for example, Claudia Wallis, "Too Young to Die," *Time*, March 14, 2005, 40.

60. Death Penalty Information Center, *Smart on Crime: Reconsidering the Death Penalty in a Time of Economic Crisis* (2009), accessed February 15, 2013, http://www.deathpenaltyinfo.org/documents/CostsRptFinal.pdf

61. Jeff Chinn, "Death Penalty Infographic," December 18, 2012, accessed February 15, 2013, http://californiainnocenceproject.org/blog/2012/12/18/death-penalty-infographic/

62. John Stuart Mill, "Speech in Defense of Capital Punishment," vol. 28 in *The Collected Works of John Stuart Mill*, eds. John M. Robson and Bruce L. Kinzer (Toronto: University of Toronto Press, 1988), 305–10.

63. See Hugo Bedau, "Capital Punishment and Retributive Justice," in *Matters of Life and Death*, ed. Tom Regan (New York: Random House, 1980), 148–82.

64. It dropped from 3.09 people per 100,000 residents in 1975 to 2.74 per 100,000 in 1983. "Amnesty International and the Death Penalty," Amnesty International USA, *Newsletter* (Spring 1987).

65. See Hugo Bedau, *The Death Penalty in America* (Chicago: Aldine, 1967), in particular Chapter 6, "The Question of Deterrence."

66. "What's New," Death Penalty Information Center, www.deathpenaltyinfo.org; Raymond Bonner and Ford Fessenden, "States with No Death Penalty Share Lower Homicide Rates, *New York Times*, September 22, 2000, www.truthinjustice.org/922death.htm

67. Roy D. Adler and Michael Summers, "Capital Punishment Works," *Wall Street Journal*, November 2, 2007.

68. Gebhard Kirchgassner, "Econometric Estimates of Deterrence of the Death Penalty: Facts or Ideology?," *Kyklos* 64, no. 3 (August 2011), 468–69.

69. Daniel S. Nagin and John V. Pepper, eds., *Deterrence and the Death Penalty* (Washington, DC: National Academies Press, 2012), 2.

70. Immanuel Kant, *The Philosophy of Law* (Edinburgh: T&T Clark, 1887), Part. 2, Sec. 49.E.

71. Jeffrey Reiman, "Justice, Civilization, and the Death Penalty," *Philosophy and Public Affairs* 14 (1985), 119–34.

72. Pope John Paul II, *Evangelium Vitae*, Para. 56.

73. U.S. Conference of Catholic Bishops, *A Culture of Life and the Penalty of Death* (2005), accessed May 13, 2013, http://www.usccb.org/issues-and-action/human-life-and-dignity/death-penalty-capital-punishment/upload/penaltyofdeath.pdf

74. See Andrew Fiala, *What Would Jesus Really Do?* (Lanham, MD: Rowman & Littlefield, 2006), especially Chapter 8.

75. Vicki Schieber, Trudy D. Conway, and David Matzko McCarthy, *Where Justice and Mercy Meet: Catholic Opposition to the Death Penalty* (Collegeville, MN: Liturgical Press, 2013).

76. Donald Kraybill, Steven Nolt, and David Weaver-Zercher, *Amish Grace* (San Francisco, CA: John Wiley and Sons/Jossey-Boss, 2007). See Andrew Fiala, "Radical Forgiveness and Human Justice," *Heythrop Journal* 53, no. 3 (May 2012), 494–506.

77. Lauren McLane, "Mother of Nickel Mines Shooter Says Amish Faith and Forgiveness Helped Her Heal," *York Daily Record*, December 12, 2012, accessed May 13, 2013, http://www.ydr.com/local/ci_22158578/mother-nickel-mines-shooter-forgives

78. Paul Tullis, "Can Forgiveness Play a Role in Criminal Justice?," *New York Times,* January 4, 2013, accessed June 3, 2013, http://www.nytimes.com/2013/01/06/magazine/can-forgiveness-play-a-role-in-criminal-justice.html?pagewanted=all

79. "Uproar over Bloody Electrocution," *San Francisco Chronicle*, July 9, 1999, A7; "An Execution Causes Bleeding," *New York Times*, July 8, 1999, A10.

80. *New York Times*, January 7, 2000, A14.

81. See Adam Liptak, "Critics Say Execution Drug May Hide Suffering," *New York Times*, October 7, 2003, A1, A18.

82. "Some Examples of Post-Furman Botched Executions," Death Penalty Information Center, accessed May 27, 2013, http://www.deathpenaltyinfo.org/some-examples-post-furman-botched-executions

83. "Drugs for Lethal Injection Aren't Reliable, Study Finds," *New York Times*, April 24, 2007, accessed May 13, 2013, http://www.nytimes.com/2007/04/24/us/24injection.html?_r=0

84. Makiko Kitamura and Adi Narayan, "Europe Pushes to Keep Lethal Injection Drugs from U.S. Prisons," *Bloomberg Business Week*, February 7, 2013, accessed February 15, 2013, http://www.businessweek.com/articles/2013-02-07/europe-pushes-to-keep-lethal-injection-drugs-from-u-dot-s-dot-prisons

85. Thanks to Wendy Lee-Lampshire of Bloomsburg University, for sharing this fact.

REVIEW EXERCISES

1. What essential characteristics of legal punishment distinguish it from other types of punishment?

2. What is the difference between the mechanisms of deterrence and prevention? Given their meanings, does the death penalty prevent murders? Deter would-be killers? How?

3. If legal punishment works as a deterrent, then how does it work? For whom would it work? For whom would it likely not work?

4. How do the retributivist arguments differ from the deterrence arguments?

5. Explain the idea of restorative justice and the possibility of alternatives to incarceration.

6. What is the *lex talionis* view of punishment? How does it differ from the proportional view?

7. Discuss the arguments for and against the identification of retributivism with revenge.

8. Why is the notion of responsibility critical to the retributivist view of legal punishment? How does the insanity defense fit in here?

9. Discuss the use of deterrence arguments for the death penalty. Also summarize opponents' criticisms of these arguments.

10. Discuss the use of retributivist arguments for the death penalty. Also summarize opponents' criticisms of these arguments.

11. Discuss the idea that even if the death penalty can be justified, the current system of execution may not live up to the standards of the theory of justified execution.

DISCUSSION CASES

1. **Imprisonment.** Steven's mother was imprisoned for drug possession with intent to distribute when Steven was just a baby. Steven grew up visiting his mother in prison. Steven has since become politically active and has been advocating on campus for alternatives to incarceration. Steven asks an acquaintance from his philosophy class, Janelle, to sign a petition that aims to provide more state funding for rehabilitation and drug treatment. Janelle is opposed to this. She says, "I have no sympathy for criminals. They get what they deserve." Steven replies, "But consider my mom's case. She's not really a bad person. She had a drug addiction problem and she sold drugs to support her own habit. Her addiction could have been treated by rehab. But she ended up in prison, which meant pretty hard times for me and my sisters." "Well, she should have thought about that before she committed the

crime," Janelle says. "If we start letting the drug dealers out of prison, all hell will break loose." Steven responds, "Well, growing up with a mom in prison was pretty much hell for me. And now that she's out of prison, she's having a hard time getting a job and an apartment. She feels like it's harder than ever to make ends meet, and I worry she's going to turn back to drugs or even dealing. How did her imprisonment help her or society?"

Whose side are you on? Is prison an appropriate punishment for nonviolent drug crimes? Does it matter whether a criminal has a family that is impacted by imprisonment? Why or why not?

2. **Doctors and Execution.** Dr. Kaur has been asked to serve as a consultant for the state as it is revising its protocol for use of lethal injection in executions. Dr. Kaur is not personally opposed to the death penalty, but he knows that the American Medical Association and other doctors' groups object to the involvement of doctors in executions. These organizations argue that doctors take an oath to preserve life and thus should not be accessories to the taking of life. But Dr. Kaur thinks it is important to find humane ways to execute people. And he figures that it would be better if doctors, who understand how the lethal injection protocol works, were involved in the process. He agrees to work with the state as it reviews and revises its lethal injection protocol.

Is Dr. Kaur doing the right thing? Should doctors be involved in finding humane ways to execute convicted criminals? Why or why not?

3. **Death Penalty Cases.** Suppose you are a member of a congressional committee that is determining the type of crime that can be punishable by death. What kinds of cases, if any, would you put on the list? The killing and sexual assault of a minor? War crimes? Killings of police officers or public figures? Multiple murderers? Mob hits or other cases in which someone gives an order to kill but does not carry it out himself? Others? What about the premeditated killing of a physically abusive spouse?

Why would you pick out just those crimes on your list as appropriately punishable by death or as the worst crimes? What ethical values can you cite to justify your choices?

Environmental Ethics

16

© iStockphoto.com/maakenzi

Learning Outcomes

After reading this chapter, you should be able to:

- Understand current environmental challenges, including pollution, climate change, and wilderness preservation.
- Explain the difference between anthropocentric and ecocentric or biocentric ideas about environmental ethics.
- Clarify the difference between intrinsic value and instrumental value.

- Explain how cost–benefit analysis applies in thinking about environmental issues.
- Understand the idea of environmental justice.
- Explain the idea of Leopold's "land ethic."
- Outline basic differences between ecofeminism and deep ecology.
- Defend a thesis with regard to environmental issues and the value of nonhuman nature.

On May 31, 2013, the widest tornado ever recorded on the planet (measuring 2.6 miles across) tore a 16.2-mile path across Oklahoma near El Reno, outside of Oklahoma City. Wind speeds reached 295 miles per hour, and the storm was rated an EF-5, the highest possible rating on the Enhanced Fujita scale. Eighteen people were killed.[1] This storm came barely a week after another EF-5 tornado hit Oklahoma, striking Moore and its surrounding areas, flattening entire neighborhoods and killing twenty-four. Oklahoma is in the area of the United States known as "Tornado Alley," where tornadoes most frequently occur. But even in this tornado-prone area, two EF-5s back-to-back was unusual. In addition to record-strength tornadoes, the United States has also been hit with especially damaging hurricanes in recent years. In 2005, Hurricane Katrina killed more than 1,800 people and caused massive damage along the coast of the Gulf of Mexico. It was the most expensive storm in U.S. history, with devastating destruction of infrastructure as well as long-term damage to jobs and the economy. In 2012, Hurricane Sandy hit the East Coast, killing 285 people and causing billions of dollars of damage; it was the country's second most expensive storm in history.

Some worry that storms such as these are warning signs, harbingers of our changing climate. Others dispute the idea that climate change could be blamed for particular tornadoes or hurricanes. But behind that dispute is the fact that natural disasters can quickly destroy lives. And this points toward the question of the value of nature and our place within it. Is the natural world something to be revered and cherished? Or is Mother Nature to be feared and dominated? And what sort of impact should human beings have on the environment?

These sorts of questions must be confronted as the human population continues to expand. Earth's human population is currently above seven billion. The human population is expected to increase by two billion—up to a population of nine billion—by 2050. At the same time, standards of living are increasing, which creates greater demand for energy, more pollution, and related environmental impacts. The Organisation for Economic Co-operation and Development concluded in a 2012 report that if we continue developing at the current pace, there will be serious and irreversible environmental impacts that could "endanger two centuries of rising living standards." Among the issues indicated as problems in the report are climate change, loss of biodiversity, water pollution and depletion, and high urban air pollution.[2]

The air pollution problem is particularly severe in developing countries. Poor air quality reportedly contributed to 1.2 million premature deaths in China in 2010.[3] In Beijing and other cities, the air is often so thick with smog that it is difficult to see the tops of skyscrapers. Even in the United States air pollution remains a problem. California's Central Valley has some of the worst air pollution in the country. It also has a high number of children with asthma and other respiratory problems. Studies in the Central Valley show that air pollution rates are correlated with asthma attacks, heart attacks, and emergency room visits for pneumonia and bronchitis.[4]

We can see from just these few examples that our environment affects us greatly. Some may argue that this is not really an ethical issue, since it is not clear that we have ethical obligations to something as abstract as "the environment." Others will argue that we do have obligations to the environment, as well as to animal species (we will discuss obligations to animals in more detail in the next chapter). Regardless, most would agree that we ought to be concerned about the negative impacts that environmental problems cause for people, especially the vulnerable poor who are often most adversely affected by pollution and by natural disasters. We may also have obligations to future generations: to leave a livable world to our children and grandchildren.

THE ENVIRONMENT AND ITS VALUE

To answer the question of whether we have moral obligations with regard to the environment, we should first define our terms. The word *environment* comes from *environs*, which means "in circuit" or "turning around in" in Old French.[5] From this comes

House along the Jersey Shore partially swept away by the wall of water created by Hurricane Sandy in 2012.

the common meaning of environment as surroundings; note its spatial meaning as an area. However, we have also come to use the term to refer to what goes on in that space—that is, the climate and other factors that act on living organisms or individuals inhabiting the space. We can think of the environment as a systematic collection of materials with various physical and chemical interactions. Or we can think of it in a more organic way, giving attention to the many ways in which individual life forms are interdependent in their very nature. From the latter viewpoint, we cannot even think of an individual as an isolated atomic thing because its environment is a fundamental part of itself. From this point of view, the environment stands in relation to the beings within it—not externally, but internally.

What does it mean for people to "value" the environment? Certainly, most people realize the important effects that their environment has on them. Those things that produce benefit are good or of positive value, and those that cause harm are bad or of negative value. Most of the time it is a mixture of both. Growth is generally good, and poison is bad. But where does this goodness and badness, or positive or negative value, come from? Is it there in the poison or in growth? This is a considerably difficult metaphysical and moral problem. Does a thing have value in the same sense that it has hair or weight? This does not seem to be so because a thing's value does not seem to be something it possesses. When we value something, we have a positive response toward it. One way to explain this is to think that the value of things is a matter of our preferences or desires. But we also want to know whether we *should* prefer or desire them. Is there something about the things that we value, some attributes that they have, for example, that are the legitimate basis for our valuing them? In answering this sort of question, we should bear in mind our earlier discussions (in the first half of this book) of the objectivity of values and the relation between the facts of nature and value judgments. Is it possible to derive an "ought" with regard to the environment? Is there a natural state of affairs that we ought to value? Or are our environmental values merely tastes or preferences?

One distinction about value plays a particularly significant role in **environmental ethics**: that

between intrinsic and instrumental values. Things have **intrinsic value** or worth (sometimes referred to as **inherent value**) when they have value or worth in themselves. We value things that have intrinsic value for their own sake and not for what we can get or do with them. Something has **instrumental value** if it is valued because of its usefulness for some other purpose and for someone. Some environmentalists believe that trees, for example, have only instrumental and not intrinsic value. They think that trees are valuable because of their usefulness to us. Other environmentalists believe that plants and ecosystems have value in themselves.

Another term sometimes used in discussions about environmental ethics is *prima facie value*. (As we saw in our discussion of W. D. Ross's concept of *prima facie duties* in Chapter 3, *prima facie* means "at first glance" or "at first sight.") Something has prima facie value if it has the kind of value that can be overcome by other interests or values. For example, we might think that a rainforest has some sort of prima facie value but that if the local population needed more land on which to cultivate food, people might be justified in cutting some of the trees to make room for crops.

These considerations about the nature of value and distinctions between different kinds of value play a key role in judging ethical matters that relate to the environment. This is exemplified by two quite different perspectives in environmental ethics. One is *anthropocentrism*, and the other is *ecocentrism* or *biocentrism*.

ANTHROPOCENTRISM

The terms **anthropocentrism** and **anthropocentric** refer to a human-centered perspective. A perspective is anthropocentric if it holds that humans alone have intrinsic worth or value. According to the anthropocentric perspective, things are good to the extent that they promote the interests of human beings. Thus, for example, some people believe that animals are valuable only insofar as they promote the interests of humans or are useful to us in one or more of a variety of ways. (More discussion of this is found in the following chapter on animal ethics.) For example, animals provide nutritional, medical, protective, emotional, and aesthetic benefits for us. Those people who hold an anthropocentric view also may believe that it is bad to cause animals needless pain, but if this is necessary to ensure some important human good, then it is justified. We do obtain useful products from the natural world. For example, taxol is a drug synthesized from the bark of the Pacific yew tree and is useful in treating ovarian and breast cancers. In the most basic and general sense, nature provides us with our food, shelter, and clothing.

According to an anthropocentric perspective, the environment or nature has no value in itself. Instead, its value is measured by how it affects human beings. Wilderness areas are instrumentally valuable to us as sources of recreation and relaxation, and they provide natural resources to meet our physical needs, such as lumber for housing and fuel. Estuaries, grasslands, and ancient forests also purify our air and clean our water. Sometimes anthropocentric values conflict. For instance, we cannot both preserve old growth forests for their beauty or historical interest and yet also use them for lumber. Therefore, we need to think about the relative value of aesthetic experiences and historical appreciation as compared with cheaper housing, lumbering jobs, and the impact of lumbering on erosion, climate change, forest fire risks, and so on. Consider the value of 2,000-year-old sequoia trees. Touching one of these giants today is in some way touching the beginning of the Common Era. We can imagine all of the major events in history that have occurred in the life of this tree, and in doing so gain a greater appreciation of the reality of those events and their connection to us and the world as we experience it. How would the value of this experience compare with the value of the tree's wood on the lumber market? Cost–benefit analyses present one method for making such comparisons.

Cost–Benefit Analysis

Because many environmental issues appeal to diverse values and involve competing interests, we can use a technique known as *cost–benefit analysis* to help us think about how to approach any given environmental problem. If we have a choice between various actions or policies, then we need to assess and compare the various harms (or costs) and benefits that each entails in order to know which is the better action or policy. Using this method, we should choose the option that has the greater net balance of *benefits* over harms (or *costs*). This is connected to utilitarian reasoning. For example, suppose we are considering whether to hold industrial polluters to stricter emissions standards. If emissions were reduced, acid rain and global warming would be curtailed—important benefits. However, this would also create increased costs for the polluting companies, their employees, and those who buy their products or use their services. We should consider whether the benefits would be worth those costs. We would also need to assess the relative costs and benefits of alternative policies designed to address the acid rain and global warming.

Involved in such analyses are two distinct elements. One is an assessment or description of these factual matters as far as they can be known. What exactly are the likely effects of doing this or that? The other is evaluation, or the establishment of relative values. In cost–benefit analyses, the value is generally defined in anthropocentric terms. But we still need to clarify which values matter most—clean air, economic development, etc. In addition, if we have a fixed amount of money or resources to expend on an environmental project, then we know that this money or these resources will not be available for projects elsewhere. Thus, every expenditure will have a certain *opportunity cost*. In being willing to pay for the environmental project, we will have some sense of its importance in comparison with other things that we will not then be able to do or have. However, if we value something else just as much or more than cleaner air or water, for example, then we will not be willing to pay for the cleaner air or water.

In making such evaluations, we may know what monetary costs will be added to a particular forest product, such as lumber, if limits on logging were enacted. However, we are less sure about how we should value the 2,000-year-old tree. How do we measure the historical appreciation or the aesthetic value of the tree (or the animals that live in the tree)? How do we measure the recreational value of the wilderness? What is beauty or the life of a tree worth? The value of these "intangibles" is difficult to measure because measuring implies that we use a standard means of evaluation. Only if we have such a standard can we compare, say, the value of a breathtaking view to that of a dam about to be built on the site. Sometimes we use monetary valuations, even for such intangibles as human lives or life years. For example, in insurance and other contexts, people attempt to give some measure to the value of a life.[6] Doing so is sometimes necessary, but it is obviously also problematic.

Environmental Justice

Another concern from the anthropocentric perspective is how environmental costs are distributed. This is connected to the issues of social justice and economic justice (as discussed in Chapter 14). One central and difficult issue is the question of how our activities will affect future generations. Do we have an obligation to leave them a clean environment? It is difficult to figure out what justice requires for future generations. But the more pressing issue is the distribution of benefits and harms for actual persons living in the present.

Environmental justice is a mainstream idea, which the EPA defines as "the fair treatment and meaningful involvement of all people regardless of race, color, national origin, or income with respect to the development, implementation, and enforcement of environmental laws, regulations, and policies."[7] It may seem odd that we would need to emphasize that environmental issues should contain an element of social justice and equity. But in reality, it is often the poor and disenfranchised who end up suffering most from environmental degradation. Consider, for example, the fact that affluent nations with established and efficient infrastructure will be able to respond to the changing climate in ways that poorer nations will not. Poor people tend to live closer to polluted lands and toxic waste dumps because more affluent people can move away and can use their resources to fight against pollution in their areas. This is not only a concern within the United States, where poor people suffer most from the effects of pollution, but it is also a concern across the globe. Environmental regulations are often nonexistent or are loosely enforced in developing countries.

One notorious case that frequently comes up in discussions of environmental justice is the gas leak at the Union Carbide plant in Bhopal, India, in 1984. More than 3,000 people died within the first days of the poisonous gas leak. The final death toll is estimated to be at least 15,000, with the health of more than 600,000 people affected.[8] Amnesty International puts the death toll higher: 22,000 killed with at least 150,000 still battling diseases of the lungs or liver that are attributed to the toxic waste.[9] In addition to the human casualties, the disaster left behind polluted land and water, which is still not cleaned up. The local managers responsible for the disaster received minor fines and punishments after being found guilty of criminal negligence in the case. However, the former chairman of Union Carbide, Warren Anderson, never received any punishment. In 2012, an American court dismissed a lawsuit filed by Bhopal residents against Anderson and Dow Chemical, which owns Union Carbide. The dismissal protected Anderson and the company from claims for environmental remediation at the disaster site.[10] This case is remarkable because of the numbers affected, the relatively minor punishments meted out to responsible parties, and because it pushes our understanding of what counts as "the environment." Often we think of environmentalism as focused on wild natural settings. But the air and water of urban landscapes are also part of the environment. The Bhopal case reminds us that pollution can cause death and that it is often poor people who suffer the most from the impacts of industrial accidents.[11]

There are a variety of issues that come under the rubric of environmental justice including where waste dumps are located, whether farm workers and farming communities are properly protected from the effects of fertilizers and pesticides, how uranium is mined, how hunting and fishing is regulated and enforced, who pays for environmental remediation efforts, and who guarantees that polluters are punished. These concerns are connected to other social justice concerns and are entirely anthropocentric. This has led some to complain that the focus on environmental justice is a distraction from the larger concern for the value of ecosystems in themselves, apart from human interests. One scholar of environmentalism, Kevin DeLuca, laments this anthropocentric focus, concluding, "Abandoning wilderness-centered environmentalism is a disastrous error. The finest moments of environmentalism often involve humans exceeding self-concern and caring for wilderness and other species because of their intrinsic being."[12] This view points us toward the ecocentric or biocentric approach to environmental ethics.

ECOCENTRISM

According to the anthropocentric perspective, environmental concerns ought to be directed to the betterment of people, who alone have intrinsic value. In contrast with this view is one that is generally called an **ecocentric** (or **biocentric**) perspective, which holds that it is not just humans who have intrinsic worth or value, but also such things as plants, animals, and ecosystems. There are variations within this perspective, with some theorists holding that individual life forms have such intrinsic worth and others stressing that it is whole systems or ecosystems that have such value. In this view, ethical questions related to the environment involve determining what is in the best interests of these life forms, or what furthers or contributes to (or is a satisfactory fit with) some ecosystem.

Ecocentrists are critical of anthropocentrists. Why, they ask, do only humans have intrinsic value while everything else has merely instrumental value for us? Some fault the Judeo-Christian tradition for this view. In particular, they single out the biblical mandate to "subdue" the earth and "have dominion over the fish of the sea and over the birds of the air and every living thing that moves upon the Earth" as being responsible for this instrumentalist view of nature and other living things.[13] Others argue that anthropocentrism is a reductionist perspective. All of nature, according to this view, is reduced to the level of "thing-hood." The seventeenth-century French philosopher René Descartes is sometimes cited as a source of this reductionist point of view because of his belief that the essential element of humanity is the ability to think ("I think, therefore I am," etc.) and his belief that animals are mere biological machines.[14] Early evolutionary accounts also sometimes depicted humans as the pinnacle of evolution or the highest or last link in some great chain of being. We can ask ourselves whether we place too high a value on human beings and their powers of reason and intelligence. Ecocentrists criticize the view that we ought to seek to understand nature so that we can have power over it because it implies that our primary relation to nature is one of domination.

Ecocentrists hold that we ought rather to regard nature with admiration and respect because nature and natural beings have intrinsic value. Let us return to our example of the 2,000-year-old sequoia tree. You may have seen pictures of trees large enough for tunnels to be cut through, allowing cars to pass. In the 1880s, such a tunnel was cut through a giant sequoia near Wawona, California, on the south end of what is now Yosemite National Park. Tourists enjoyed driving through the tunnel. However, some people claimed that this was a mutilation of and an insult to this majestic tree. They said that the tree itself had a kind of integrity, intrinsic value, and dignity that should not be invaded lightly. Another way to put it would be to say that the tree itself had moral standing.[15] What we do to the tree itself matters morally, they insisted.

On what account could trees be thought to have this kind of moral standing? All organisms, it might be argued, are self-maintaining systems.[16] Because they are organized systems or integrated living wholes, organisms are thought to have intrinsic value and even moral standing. The value may be only prima facie, but nevertheless they have their own value in themselves and are not just to be valued in terms of their usefulness to people. According to this perspective, the giant sequoias of Wawona should not merely be thought of in terms of their tourist value.

Further, there are things that can be good and bad for the trees themselves. The tunnel in the Wawona tree, for example, eventually weakened the tree, and it fell during a snowstorm in 1968. Although trees are not **moral agents**—beings who act responsibly for moral reasons—they may still be thought of as moral patients. A **moral patient** is any being for which what we do to it matters in itself. A moral patient is any being toward whom we can have *direct duties* rather than simply *indirect duties*. If a tree is a moral patient, then we ought to behave in a certain way toward the tree for its sake and not just indirectly for the sake of how it will eventually affect us. Ecocentrists may argue that there are things that are in the best interests of trees, even if the trees take no conscious interest in them.

In addition to those ecocentrists who argue that all life forms have intrinsic value, there are others who stress the value of ecosystems. An *ecosystem* is an integrated system of interacting and interdependent parts within a circumscribed locale. They are loosely structured wholes. The boundary changes and some members come and go. Sometimes there is competition within the whole—as in the relation between predators and prey in a given habitat. Sometimes there is *symbiosis*, with each part living in cooperative community with the other parts—as in the relationship between flowers and the bees that pollinate them. The need to survive pushes various creatures to be creative in their struggle for an adaptive fit. There is a unity to the whole, but it is loose and decentralized. Why is this unity to be thought of as having value in itself?

One answer is provided by the environmental philosopher Aldo Leopold. In the 1940s, he wrote in his famous essay "The Land Ethic" that we should think about the land as "a fountain of energy flowing through a circuit of soils, plants, and animals."[17] Look at any environment supporting life on our planet and you will find a *system* of life—intricately interwoven and interdependent elements that function as a whole. Such a system is organized in the form of a *biotic pyramid*, with myriad smaller organisms at the bottom and gradually fewer and more complex organisms at the top. Plants depend on the earth, insects depend on the plants, and other animals depend on the insects. Leopold did not think it amiss to speak about the whole system as being healthy or unhealthy. If the soil is washed away or abnormally flooded, then the whole system suffers or is sick. In this system, individual organisms feed off one another. Some elements come and others go. It is the whole that continues. Leopold also believed that a particular type of ethics follows from this view of nature—a biocentric or ecocentric ethics. He believed that "a thing is right when it tends to preserve the integrity, stability, and beauty of the biotic community. It is wrong when it tends to do otherwise."[18] The system has a certain *integrity* because it is a unity of interdependent elements that combine to make a whole with a unique character. It has a certain *stability*, not in that it does not change, but that it changes only gradually. Finally, it has a particular *beauty*. Here beauty is a matter of harmony, well-ordered form, or unity in diversity.[19] When envisioned on a larger scale, the entire Earth system may then be regarded as one system with a certain integrity, stability, and beauty. Morality becomes a matter of preserving this system or doing only what befits it.

The kind of regard for nature that is manifest in biocentric views is not limited to contemporary philosophers. Native American views on nature provide a fertile source of biocentric thinking. For example, Eagle Man, an Oglala Sioux writer, emphasizes the unity of all living things. All come from tiny seeds and so all are brothers and sisters. The seeds come from Mother Earth and depend on her for sustenance. We owe her respect, for she comes from the "Great Spirit Above."[20] Also, certain forms of European and American Romanticism imbue nature with spiritual value. The transcendentalists Ralph Waldo Emerson and Henry David Thoreau fall into this category. Transcendentalism was a movement of romantic idealism that arose in the United States in the mid-nineteenth century. Rather than regarding nature as foreign or alien, Emerson and Thoreau thought of it as a friend or kindred spirit. Acting on such a viewpoint, Thoreau retreated to Walden Pond to live life to its fullest and commune with nature. He wanted to know its moods and changes and all its phenomena. Although Thoreau and Emerson read the "lessons" of nature, they also read Eastern texts and were influenced by the history of Western philosophy. Some have characterized aspects of their nature theory as idealism, the view that all is ideas or spirit; others characterize it as pantheism, the doctrine that holds that God is present in the whole of nature. The transcendentalists influenced John Muir, the founder of the Sierra Club. Muir held a similar view of the majesty, sacredness, and spiritual value of nature.[21] Muir transformed his love of nature into practical action, successfully petitioning Congress for passage of a national parks bill that established Yosemite and Sequoia national parks.

Romantic and idealistic ideas provide a stark contrast to anthropocentric views of a reductionist type. However, they also raise many questions. For example, we can ask the transcendentalist how nature can be spirit or god in more than a metaphorical sense. And we can ask proponents of views such as Aldo Leopold's the following question: Why is it that nature is good? Nature can be cruel, at least from the point of view of certain animals and even from our own viewpoint as we suffer the damaging results of typhoons or volcanic eruptions. And, more abstractly, on what basis can we argue that whatever exists is good?

Deep Ecology

Another variant of ecocentrism is the **deep ecology** movement. Members of this movement wish to distinguish themselves from mainstream environmentalism, which they call "shallow ecology" and criticize as fundamentally anthropocentric. The term *deep ecology* was first used by Arne Naess, a Norwegian philosopher and environmentalist.[22] Deep ecologists take a holistic view of nature and believe that we should look more deeply to find the root causes of environmental degradation. The idea is that our environmental problems are deeply rooted in the Western psyche, and radical changes of viewpoint are necessary if we are to solve these problems. Western reductionism, individualism, and consumerism are said to be the causes of our environmental problems. The solution is to rethink and reformulate certain metaphysical beliefs about whether all reality is reducible to atoms in motion. It is also to rethink what it is to be an individual. Are individuals separate and independent beings? Or are they interrelated parts of a whole?

According to deep ecologists, solving our environmental problems requires a change in our views about what is a good quality of life. The good life, deep ecologists assert, is not one that stresses the possession of things and the search for satisfaction of wants and desires. Instead, a good life is one that is lived simply, in communion with one's local ecosystem. Arne Naess lived his message. He retreated to a cabin in the mountains of Norway, which he built with his own hands. He lived a modest life until his death at age ninety-six in 2009.

In addition to describing the need for radical changes in our basic outlook on life, the deep ecologist platform also holds that any intrusion into nature to change it requires justification. If we intervene to change nature, then we must show that a vital need of ours is at stake.[23] We should be cautious in our actions because the results of our actions may be far-reaching and harmful. And we should view nature *as it is* as good and right and well balanced. Deep ecology also includes the belief that the flourishing of nonhuman life requires a "substantial decrease in the human population."[24] George Sessions argues that "humanity must drastically scale down its industrial activities on Earth, change its consumption lifestyles, stabilize" and "reduce the size of the human population by humane means."[25]

Some critics maintain that deep ecologists are misanthropic because of their interest in reducing the human population, or suggest that they are advocating totalitarian methods for achieving a reduction in human population. Some go so far as to malign deep ecology as "eco-fascism," equating it with fascist plans to create an ecological utopia through population control. Others worry that there may be implicit eugenic and imperialistic agendas when affluent Americans and Europeans advocate population control. Deep ecologists would reply, however, that they recognize that population reduction can be achieved only through humane methods such as the empowerment of women and making contraception available.

The members of the deep ecology movement have been quite politically active. Their creed contains the belief that people are responsible for Earth. Beliefs such as this often provide a basis for the tactics of groups such as Earth First! Some radicals advocate direct action to protect the environment including various forms of "ecosabotage"—for example, spiking trees to prevent logging and cutting power lines.[26] It is important to note that Arne Naess himself was interested in nonviolence. He wrote extensively about Gandhi's nonviolent methods, and he conceived his commitment to the environment in conjunction with Gandhian ideas about the interconnectedness of life. And he employed nonviolent methods in his own protests—such as chaining himself to a boulder to protest a project aimed at building a dam on a river.

Critics of deep ecology describe aggressive forms of environmental protest as "ecoterrorism."[27] Of course, there are important distinctions to be made between nonviolent protest, civil disobedience, and more violent forms of protest. Nonetheless, deep ecologists maintain that the stakes are high and that action should be taken to change the status quo—even if this action is only at the level of personal lifestyle choices. On a philosophical level, the view that all incursions into nature can be justified only by our vital needs seems to run counter to our intuitions. The implication here is that we must not build a golf course or a house patio because these would change the earth and its vegetation, and the need to play golf or sit on a patio is hardly vital. Do natural things have as much value as people and their interests? The view that nature itself has a "good of its own" or that the whole system has value in itself raises complex metaphysical and psychological questions. However we may feel about these issues, deep ecologists provide a valuable service by calling our attention to the possible deep philosophical roots and causes of some of our environmental problems.

Ecofeminism

Another variant of ecological ethics is called *ecofeminism* or *ecological feminism*.[28] It may be seen as part of a broader movement that locates the source of environmental problems not in metaphysics or worldviews, as deep ecologists do, but in social practices. *Social ecology*, as this wider movement is called, holds that we should look to particular social patterns and structures to discover what is wrong with our relationship to the environment. Ecofeminists believe that the problem lies in a male-centered view of nature—that is, one of human domination over nature. According to Karen Warren, a philosopher and environmental activist, **ecofeminism** is "the position that there are important connections … between the domination of women and the domination of nature, an understanding of which is crucial to both feminism and environmental ethics."[29] Note here that deep ecologists and ecofeminists do not necessarily agree. The deep ecologists may criticize ecofeminists for concentrating insufficiently on the environment, and ecofeminists may accuse deep ecologists of the very

male-centered view that they believe is the source of our environmental problems.[30]

A variety of ecofeminist views are espoused by diverse groups of feminists.[31] One version celebrates the ways that women differ from men. This view is espoused by those who hold that women—because of their female experience or nature—tend to value organic, non-oppressive relationships. They stress caring and emotion, and they seek to replace conflict and assertion of rights with cooperation and community. This idea has obvious connections with the work of those interested in the feminist ethics of care (as discussed in Chapter 9). From this perspective, a feminine ethic should guide our relationship to nature. Rather than use nature in an instrumentalist fashion, they urge, we should cooperate with nature. We should manifest a caring and benevolent regard for nature, just as we do for other human beings. One version of this view would have us think of nature itself as in some way divine. Rather than think of God as a distant creator who transcends nature, these religiously oriented ecofeminists think of God as a being *within* nature. Some also refer to this God as "Mother Nature" or "Gaia," after the name of a Greek goddess.[32]

Another version of ecofeminism rejects the dualism often found in the Western philosophical tradition. They hold that this tradition promotes the devaluing and domination of both women and nature. Rather than divide reality into contrasting elements—the active and passive, the rational and emotional, the dominant and subservient—they encourage us to recognize the diversity within nature and among people. They would similarly support a variety of ways of relating to nature. Thus, they believe that even though science that proceeds from a male-oriented desire to control nature has made advances and continues to do so, its very orientation causes it to miss important aspects of nature. If instead we also have a feeling for nature and a listening attitude, then we might be better able to know what actually is there. They also believe that we humans should see ourselves as part of the community of nature, not as distinct, non-natural beings functioning in a world that is thought to be alien to us. Some versions of ecofeminism emphasize the way that women understand their bodies and their reproductive power, maintaining that women have a closer relationship with the body and thus with the natural world. Others view feminine categories as socially constructed, albeit in a way that emphasizes the female connection with nature (and the male as liberated from and thus able to dominate nature).

It is sometimes difficult to know just what, in particular, are the practical upshots of ecocentrism, ecological feminism, and deep ecology. We noted previously that Naess and the deep ecologists emphasize living simply and in connection with the local environment. Ecofeminists might add that a sense of justice and equality also requires that we attend to the ways in which environmental destruction impacts women and the way that male-dominant gender roles tend to reinforce exploitation and domination of nature. Ecofeminism and deep ecology both pose a serious challenge to the status quo and its anthropocentric and dominating approach to the natural world.

Ethical anthropocentrists will advocate wise and judicious use of nature, one that does not destroy the very nature that we value and on which we depend. But nonanthropocentrists maintain that we must care for and about nature for its own sake and not just in terms of what it can do for us. This debate is about the very place of human beings within the natural world.

CURRENT ISSUES

We can now take these anthropocentric and ecocentric theories and examine how they might apply to environmental issues confronting us today. We will consider the following problems: climate change, ozone depletion, waste disposal and pollution, and wilderness preservation. We will also consider international environmental conventions as a possible means of addressing global environmental issues. And finally we will consider the vexing problem of sustainable development and a problem known as "the tragedy of the commons."

Climate Change

The great majority of scientists now agree that our modern industrial society has created a potentially deadly phenomenon known as the *greenhouse effect*, *global warming*, or *climate change*. There is no denying that the global climate is changing, as the level of carbon dioxide in the atmosphere has increased during the past century. In the spring of 2013, the concentration of carbon dioxide (CO_2) in the atmosphere was measured at a new high of 400 parts per million (or ppm). This level of CO_2 concentration had not been seen on Earth since the Pliocene epoch, 2.5 million years ago, when Earth was three degrees Centigrade warmer than it is today and when sea levels were five meters higher.[33] Coastlines are crumbling as the climate changes and sea levels rise.[34] There is substantial, albeit complicated, evidence that storms are increasing in severity as a result of climate change heating up the oceans.[35] And there is no question that the Arctic ice cap is melting, with ever-larger swaths of ice disappearing during the summer months. In the summer of 2012, the seasonal Arctic melt reached a new low, with the ice covering only about 24 percent of the Arctic Ocean. In the 1970s, coverage during this season was around 50 percent.[36] In the winter of 2013, NASA indicated that the winter maximum (the maximum extent of Arctic sea ice) was the fifth lowest sea-ice maximum measured in the past thirty-five years. According to NASA, "some models predict that the Arctic Ocean could be ice-free in the summer in just a few decades."[37] Melting Arctic ice is not only a *sign* of climate change; it is also a *contributor* to the process. The white Arctic ice reflects the sun, so the more ice there is, the more heat is reflected without being absorbed by the ocean. As the ice melts, however, the dark blue water of the ocean absorbs the solar rays no longer being reflected by the ice, which in turn warms the nearby air. The warmer air melts more ice, and so on, creating a feedback loop.

The Arctic ice cap is not the only significant melting process associated with climate change. The ice that covers Greenland, the biggest land mass of the Arctic region, has also been melting at an alarming rate and slipping into the sea. In 2012, there was a rapid melting event that caused 97 percent of the Greenland ice sheet to shed water. If Greenland's 680,000 cubic miles of ice melted, it would raise sea levels by up to 20 feet.[38] While most experts think it is unlikely that this massive rise in sea levels will happen for several hundred years, some experts believe that sea levels could rise by up to three feet by 2100.[39] The U.S. Environmental Protection Agency (EPA) predicts that by 2100, global temperatures will rise from 2°F to 11.5°F and sea levels will rise about two feet.[40] Climate change has also caused the oceans to become more acidic as carbon dioxide is absorbed into the oceans. This process has already had negative impacts on delicate marine life, such as the oysters of the Pacific Northwest: oyster shells don't form properly in more acidic water.[41] There will be adverse impacts on fish and corals as the oceans become more acidic.

Melting Arctic ice may also change patterns of ocean currents that have been stable for the past 10,000 years. The Gulf Stream, for example, pulls warm water north from near the equator and into the north Atlantic, where some of it evaporates; as the water evaporates, the ocean becomes saltier and heavier and the denser water sinks, cooling and starting a return path to the south. Changing temperatures could alter this process. Shifts in the Gulf Stream could cause weather and climatic changes in Europe and North America, although scientists disagree about what these impacts might be. Some warn that Europe would cool if the Gulf Stream shifted, and others think this is unlikely.[42] While this dispute is an indication of the difficulty of making predictions about climate change, the vast majority of scientists agree that the atmosphere and the oceans are changing.[43]

Climate change may produce hundreds of millions of environmental refugees, which is an environmental justice concern. Those refugees may be displaced by rising tides, storm damage, and changes in agricultural production.[44] Residents of low-lying islands—such as Kirbati, the Maldives, and the Seychelles—and low, flood-prone countries—such as Bangladesh—may be dislocated as sea levels rise and river floods become harder to control.[45]

Some skeptics dispute whether the changes are entirely man-made, but the vast majority of experts believe that one of the major causes of climate change is the burning of fossil fuels, which are the primary energy source for modern societies. The resulting gases—carbon dioxide, methane, fluorocarbons, and nitrous oxide, among others—are released into the atmosphere. There, these gases combine with water vapor and prevent the sun's infrared rays from radiating back into space. The trapped solar radiation contributes to increased air temperature. In this way, the gases function much as do the glass panes of a greenhouse. Newly released gases will remain in the atmosphere for thirty to a hundred years; since greenhouse gas emissions continue to rise, their buildup in the atmosphere is expected to increase over time. Automobile exhaust, along with industrial power plants and agricultural operations, produces most of the gases that lead to climate change. Deforestation also contributes to the warming because there are fewer trees and other plant life to absorb carbon dioxide before it reaches the atmosphere.

According to the EPA, carbon dioxide accounts for 84 percent of U.S. greenhouse gas emissions.[46] Carbon dioxide (CO_2) is emitted when fossil fuels are burned to produce electricity or to fuel cars and other forms of transportation. CO_2 is also produced as a by-product of industrial processes and, along with methane, as a result of animal agriculture. According to the United Nations, "emissions due to human activities have grown since pre-industrial times, with an increase of 70 percent between 1970 and 2004." The United Nations also states, "climate scientists have determined that temperature increases should be limited to 2°C—to avoid causing irreversible damage to our planet. To achieve this, global emissions need to peak by 2015 and decline thereafter reaching a reduction of 50 per cent by 2050."[47] The nations of the world agreed to attempt to limit global temperature increase to 2°C in 2009 at a global summit in Copenhagen. To meet that goal, it was agreed that carbon dioxide levels in the atmosphere must be kept to 350 parts per million. However, in 2012 and 2013, mean CO_2 levels were around 395 parts per million, according to the National Oceanic and Atmospheric Administration. And as we've seen, on some days in 2013, the level has been as high as 400 parts per million.[48] This makes it unlikely that global temperature increase will be limited to 2°C.

Although the bulk of greenhouse gases emitted since the start of the Industrial Revolution have come from Europe, the United States, and other developed regions, recent increases in carbon dioxide levels are often attributed to growth in the developing world, especially in China.[49] According to the EPA (based upon 2008 data), the main CO_2 producers as a share of the world's total CO_2 emitted are China (23 percent), the United States (19 percent), and the European Union (13 percent).[50]

Climate changes have occurred throughout Earth's history, and while they have usually been gradual, that has not always been the case. Sixty-five million years ago, the dinosaurs are thought to have been wiped out by a dramatic and rapid change in climate caused by a giant meteorite that hit Earth near Mexico's Yucatán Peninsula. The meteorite may have put so much dust into the air that it blocked much of the sun's light, causing temperatures to drop and plants to die—which in turn brought about the demise of the dinosaurs. Within the time span of human existence, climate changes have usually occurred over several generations, allowing people to adapt. If these changes occur rapidly, however, such adaptation becomes more difficult. Food supplies, for example, could be severely stressed. Reduced land fertility could also pose a threat to international security. If crop yields decrease and water shortages increase, peoples and nations suffering severe shortages may resort to violence. These people may migrate to urban slums, causing overcrowding, widespread poverty, and infrastructure breakdown.[51] All the issues listed above are anthropocentric concerns—they are focused on how climate change may impact human beings. These issues might also be supplemented with a more ecocentric focus on the species and ecosystems that may be disrupted by climate change.

How do we know that present-day global warming is not just a part of a natural pattern? Scientists have determined that recent temperatures and the increased levels of carbon dioxide in the atmosphere are dramatically greater than anything that has occurred in the past. Scientists have drilled deep into the ice and brought up cylindrical *ice cores* that have markings similar to the rings inside of trees. They can read the age of the ice cores and analyze the chemicals and air bubbles in them to determine the average temperature of each year, as well as the carbon dioxide levels during each year. Samples as old as six hundred thousand years have been obtained, and from these samples scientists know that the temperature and greenhouse gases have increased with unprecedented speed in the past decades. From this they can also predict how temperatures will continue to rise unless emissions are controlled.[52]

Scientists still disagree, however, on how much Earth will warm, how quickly it will happen, and how different regions will be affected. However, evidence is now accumulating for the acceleration of this effect in the form of receding glaciers, rising sea levels, and the spreading of plant and animal species farther north and to higher altitudes that were previously too cold to support such life. Some European butterfly and bird species have moved their habitats northward of their previous ranges. Unfortunately, some studies show that not all species are able to keep pace with rapidly changing climate zones. During the past twenty years, some butterfly species have failed to keep pace with changing climate zones by a magnitude of approximately 85 miles; some birds are now living 130 miles from their natural climate range.[53] When we consider the problem of animals unable to adapt quickly enough to the planet's changing climate zones, should we focus on the intrinsic value of butterflies and birds, or should we focus on what this may portend for human beings as global temperatures continue to rise?

Further evidence of accelerated global warming can be seen in the melting of mountain glaciers.[54] While some ecocentrists may argue that mountain glaciers have a kind of intrinsic value, the loss will also have a practical impact on human communities that depend upon glaciers for their water supply. The melting of mountain glaciers can also produce more severe flooding during the rainy season, along with less regular flows of water during the rest of the year.[55]

Some people may benefit from climate change—say, those living in northern latitudes. But it is most likely that changing crop yields and lost coastlines will have negative impacts on billions of human beings. Returning us to the concerns of environmental justice, it is important to note that those who are historically most responsible for climate-changing emissions are the least likely to be harmed. Affluent people living in developed countries will be able to adapt and respond to climate change, while poor people in developing countries are most likely to be harmed. Moreover, the cost to future generations must also be considered. How much we worry about the impact on our descendants will depend on the expected severity of the effects. Those who calculate the costs and benefits must also factor in the uncertainties that are involved.

What can be done about global warming? And is it too late? Scientists generally believe that we may still have time to prevent radical climate change. But they tend to agree that we need to reduce the emission of greenhouse gases now. James Hansen, the former head of the NASA Goddard Institute for Space Studies, has sounded a significant alarm. According to Hansen, if we continue to exploit fossil fuel reserves, the climate will be radically altered:

> Concentrations of carbon dioxide in the atmosphere eventually would reach levels higher than in the Pliocene era, more than 2.5 million years ago, when sea level was at least 50 feet higher than it is now. That level of heat-trapping gases would assure that the disintegration of the ice sheets would accelerate out of control. Sea levels would rise and destroy coastal cities. Global temperatures would become intolerable. Twenty to fifty percent of the planet's species would be driven to extinction. Civilization would be at risk.[56]

Hansen's argument is ultimately anthropocentric: he means *human* civilization is at risk. Because Hansen views the risk as so great and the consequences so dire, he opposes new fossil fuel projects that would ultimately lead to more CO_2 emissions—including the development of tar sands in Canada and new pipelines to transport crude oil. From Hansen's perspective, remaining fossil fuel reserves should stay buried in the ground, no matter how profitable or useful they may prove in the short term.

Among the means of reducing greenhouse gases are better mileage standards for cars and expanded public transportation options. Other methods include alternative sources of power, such as wind, solar, and nuclear. European countries have taken the lead in this effort. Germany, for example, has made a commitment to abandon fossil fuels by 2050 and in recent years has made great strides toward replacing its fossil fuel infrastructure with renewable energy sources.[57] According to Stanford professor Mark Z. Jacobsen, "It's absolutely not true that we need natural gas,

coal, or oil—we think it's a myth.... You could power America with renewables from a technical and economic standpoint. The biggest obstacles are social and political—what you need is the will to do it."[58] Opponents of alternative energy sources argue that the economic costs would be prohibitive and would place great burdens on taxpayers. Whether or not this is true, the position points to a different set of values and a different assessment of costs and benefits.

Instead of, or in addition to, greater fuel efficiency standards and alternative energy sources, some suggest imposing a carbon tax on people and companies that burn fossil fuels. This tax could be used, for example, to reimburse or give tax credits to homeowners who use solar cells or energy-efficient appliances; the tax could also be used to fund research into possible means of capturing carbon dioxide and preventing it from being released into the atmosphere. A small tax could yield some $50 billion for such purposes. Former Vice President Al Gore even proposes that such a tax be used in place of payroll taxes for Social Security and Medicare.[59]

Other proposed solutions to climate change involve so-called "geo-engineering" projects. These technological solutions include proposals to remove carbon from the atmosphere and store it underground, as well as proposals to protect Earth from the sun—either by building shades in space or by stimulating volcanoes to produce ash, which would reflect sunlight. These geo-engineering solutions aim to fix the problem without addressing the underlying issues of consumption and pollution. From the standpoint of deep ecology, such an approach looks like another example of human hubris. But proponents of geo-engineering argue that it is too late to halt climate change by returning to the sort of simple, eco-friendly living espoused by deep ecologists. Furthermore, as the climate continues to change, environmental justice concerns will point in the direction of plans to mitigate the damage that climate change will create for vulnerable human populations.

Ozone Depletion

A second environmental problem—and one about which activists and scientists have been concerned for decades—is ozone depletion. In the 1970s scientists detected holes or breaks in the layer of ozone at the upper reaches of the stratosphere. This layer of ozone protects Earth from the damaging effects of excessive ultraviolet radiation from the sun, which can cause skin cancer and cataracts. The holes in the ozone layer were determined to be caused by chlorine-bearing pollutants such as the chlorofluorocarbons, which were widely used in fire extinguishers and as refrigerants, cleaning agents, and spray propellants. Climate change is also a factor in ozone depletion, as the heating of the lower atmosphere has an impact on ozone in the upper atmosphere.

Like global warming, ozone depletion negatively impacts both humans and wildlife. For example, fish in waters around Great Britain "are suffering sunburn and blisters caused by the thinning ozone layer," and such effects threaten some fish species with extinction.[60] And the ozone hole over the South Pole has affected the circulation of ocean waters in the Southern Ocean.[61] This will cause further changes in ocean temperatures, which will impact global climate. The good news is that the international community worked together to ban the use of the chlorofluorocarbons (CFCs). The Montreal Protocol (1987) called for many developed countries to phase out their use by 1996. This is a hopeful sign of international cooperation. However, given current rates of depletion and the amount of CFCs in the atmosphere, it may take fifty years for the ozone layer to repair itself.[62]

From a cost–benefit perspective, we should ask whether the cost to us of decreasing or eliminating the causes of ozone depletion is worth the savings in human lives. Here again we come up against the issue of how to value human life. The greater its value, the more surely we ought to stop using these chemicals, and the harder we ought to work to find alternatives. The issue of ozone depletion may be viewed as one example of the way that international cooperation based on cost–benefit analysis can work to solve some environmental problems.

Waste Disposal and Pollution

Another issue of environmental concern is waste disposal and pollution. Like global warming and ozone depletion, the negative impacts of these problems on humans and animals are far-reaching. Humans produce tons of garbage each year that must be put somewhere. Just how much garbage is there? According to the EPA, "In 2010, Americans generated about 250 million tons of trash and recycled and composted over 85 million tons of this material, equivalent to a 34.1 percent recycling rate. On average, we recycled and composted 1.51 pounds of our individual waste generation of 4.43 pounds per person per day."[63] While the United States has the world's highest rate of per capita garbage production, China is quickly catching up. According to the World Bank, China has the fastest growing rate of waste production.[64]

Typical American trash includes a variety of disposable items. According to the Clean Air Council, every year Americans use one billion shopping bags, which create tons of landfill waste. Less than 1 percent of plastic bags are recycled each year.[65] The problem with plastic shopping bags is that they do not biodegrade, or break down, in landfills. Instead, they break into small pieces, which contaminate the soil and water. Cities across the country have considered banning plastic bags or imposing a use tax on them. In 2013, the California State Assembly considered a statewide ban on such bags, which was defeated. Proponents of the ban argued that the plastic bags make up a majority of marine debris and cost millions to dispose of. But critics pointed out that paper bags are not really that much better—since they take up more space in landfills.[66] Many say the preferred option is reusable cloth bags; however, some maintain that reusable cloth shopping bags are unsanitary and spread disease, citing a study that showed that foodborne illness increased in San Francisco after the city banned plastic bags in 2007.[67]

We also generate a lot of garbage through the use of disposable cups and food service items. The Clean Air Council reports that the average American office worker uses about 500 disposable cups every year.[68] Americans use one billion Starbucks cups per year.[69] Starbucks has worked to find ways to make sure that those cups are recyclable and has recently introduced reusable cups as an alternative. But garbage generated by fast-food restaurants still remains a common feature of urban litter.[70]

So-called e-waste is also becoming a major problem. This includes outdated cellphones, computers, TVs, and printers. Approximately 20 to 50 million tons of this waste is discarded globally per year, with projected e-waste of 40 to 70 million tons by 2015.[71] Such items contain huge amounts of toxins: beryllium, cadmium, chromium, lead, mercury, and so on. Some electronics companies are working hard to find less harmful ways to deal with electronic waste. But too often there are environmental justice issues involved, as electronic waste is commonly sent to countries in Africa and Asia, where it is dumped, often at the expense of local populations and pollution of the local environment.[72] One recent study indicates that people living near an electronic waste dump in China face elevated cancer risks, as a result of exposure to hazardous chemicals. Residents were melting down scavenged electronic products in their homes and backyards in order to extract precious metals concealed within those products, with health hazards resulting from exposure to toxic fumes produced during this process.[73]

One obvious solution to the e-waste problem is recycling. Indeed, the solution to the problem of waste disposal in general is recycling. For example, recycled bottles and cans can be turned into reusable metal and glass, as well as roads, bike parts, and even carpets.[74] Americans use more than eighty billion aluminum beverage cans every year, recycling over sixty billion of them.[75] The energy used to recycle aluminum is 95 percent less than the cost of manufacturing cans from virgin materials. Recycling one aluminum can saves enough energy to keep a 100-watt bulb burning for nearly four hours.[76]

Recycling, in fact, is tackling a wide variety of problems related to waste disposal and pollution. One promising idea is to find ways to convert food and plant waste into fuel. Organic material converted to fuel is known as *biomass fuel* or *biofuel*. Methane gas can be collected from landfills. And plants can be converted directly into usable forms of energy— such as corn that is converted into ethanol. Biomass fuels can be produced in ways that contribute to pollution and to climate change, but when done right— using waste products, rather than growing plants only for fuel consumption—they could hold one of the keys to a sustainable future. One promising idea is to use switchgrass—a common grass native to North America—to produce biofuels in the form of pellets that can be burned in stoves or in the form of ethanol, which can run combustion engines.[77]

While the use of recycling and the development of biomass fuels offer solutions to the problem of waste and pollution, these approaches remain firmly within the anthropocentric approach that emphasizes minimizing costs and maximizing benefits for human beings. A simpler solution, and one that is espoused by advocates of ecocentrism, would be to cut down on consumption in general. From this perspective, it is not enough to recycle or to drive a biofuel vehicle— since recycling itself uses resources and energy and the biofuel vehicle still contributes its share of pollution. A more ecocentric approach would encourage people to ask, for example, whether it is necessary to use aluminum cans at all (not just whether it is necessary to recycle them) or whether it is possible to cut down on driving. The anthropocentric approach is not necessarily opposed to cutting down on consumption; however, it is in favor of finding ways to maximize our ability to consume while minimizing the ecological impact of consumption.

Wilderness Preservation

The use and preservation of the planet's wild and undeveloped areas is an issue of enduring ethical concern. According to the University of Montana's Wilderness.net information site, the United States now has 758 designated wilderness areas, encompassing 109,510,858 acres in forty-four states and Puerto Rico. That means that about 5 percent of the United States is protected as wilderness—an area that is slightly larger than the state of California. Much of this wilderness is in Alaska. Within the lower forty-eight states, about 2.7 percent of land is preserved as wilderness—an area about the size of Minnesota.[78] If these wilderness areas were not set aside and protected, their natural resources—including oil reserves, minerals, and forests—would almost certainly be developed. But we also value these wilderness areas for our own recreation, including fishing and hunting, as well as for the habitats they provide to various animal species.

One example of the controversy over protecting wilderness is the question of drilling for oil in Alaska's

Arctic National Wildlife Refuge. The refuge is the last part of Alaska's Arctic coastline not open for oil production; its **ecosystem** includes a number of birds and animals in a tundra area. We might have an ecocentric concern for protecting this fragile ecosystem. Opponents of oil development in the refuge argue that such development would hurt the ecosystem. It might also have a negative impact on the humans who hunt the animals that live there. By contrast, those who argue in favor of drilling point out that the refuge contains large oil deposits that could benefit the economy. As the price of gasoline and other petroleum products goes up, we are looking for new, unexplored oil reserves—the refuge is just such a site, they argue. Advocates of drilling maintain that efforts to protect sensitive wilderness areas are preventing necessary economic development.[79] Opponents argue that oil development would create unacceptable environmental costs, accelerating climate change and harming animals and natural ecosystems.

Related issues include the construction of oil pipelines and the use of *fracking*, a process for oil and gas extraction that uses hydraulic fracturing (or "fracking") of subterranean rock formations to release gas and oil. The procedure allows extractors to reach reserves that are inaccessible through other drilling technologies. Opponents of fracking argue that the chemicals used in the process are hazardous, and that these chemicals can migrate and contaminate groundwater. Opponents have also argued that fracking can cause earthquakes, even in seismically stable regions. Defenders of the process argue that such risks are negligible and that the benefits of recovering more fossil fuels outweigh the risks.

The means of extraction isn't the only controversial issue related to oil and gas development. Also a subject of intense debate is the way these resources are transported to market. One contentious prospective project is the Keystone XL Pipeline, which aims to deliver petroleum products from Alberta, Canada, to the United States. The pipeline would carry 830,000 barrels of petroleum daily from the tar sands of Alberta to the Gulf Coast. The route for the proposed pipeline has been changed to avoid sensitive environmental areas, such as the Sand Hills of Nebraska, but environmentalists argue that these modifications are insufficient. Furthermore, environmentalists are opposed to the development of petroleum products from the tar sands of Alberta because of the large-scale destruction of forests and other ecosystems involved in the process. They argue that instead of producing more fossil fuels in wild places, the burning of which contributes to climate change, we should be investing in alternative energy sources.[80] The National Wildlife Federation, for example, says, "Tar sands oil is one of the dirtiest, costliest, and most destructive fuels in the world. Unlike conventional crude oil, unrefined tar sands is hard to extract, and in order to mine this resource, oil companies are digging up tens of thousands of acres of pristine forest in Alberta, Canada, and leaving behind a toxic wasteland."[81] But on the other hand, the demand for oil continues to rise: the development of tar sand deposits and fracking are driven by the market demand for petroleum products. Alberta's oil reserves are the third largest on Earth, with current production of about 1.6 million barrels per day.[82] If we want to continue driving gasoline-fueled cars the way we do, we'll need that oil.

Forests and wilderness areas are valuable for many reasons. They can provide beneficial new technologies—such as cures for diseases derived from wild species of plants and animals. Forests also provide habitats for wildlife, including threatened species. They provide us with leisure and relaxation, and with recreational opportunities such as whitewater rafting, fishing, hiking, and skiing. They also provide aesthetic and religious experiences, and a chance to commune with the wider world of nature. But the question remains: Are we preserving wilderness for its own sake—or should wilderness areas be viewed as resource reserves, which ought to be developed when and how humans need them?

International Environmental Conventions

Because of widespread concerns about these and other environmental issues, many international meetings and conventions have been held over the past several decades. One example is Earth Summit, the U.N. Conference on Environment and Development, which was held in Rio de Janeiro, Brazil, in 1992. Its focus was the interrelation between environmental issues and sustainable development.

At its conclusion, the conference issued, among other documents, a Framework Convention on Climate Change, a Convention on Biological Diversity, and a Statement of Forest Principles. The Framework Convention on Climate Change went into force in March 1994 and had as its primary objective "stabilization of greenhouse gas concentrations in the atmosphere." The United States, along with many other nations, signed this agreement—updated in Kyoto, Japan, in 1997, under an agreement known as the Kyoto Protocol. Key provisions of the protocol included mandatory restrictions on greenhouse gas emissions to "at least 5 percent below levels measured in 1990" by the year 2012.[83] The protocol also allowed the thirty-five industrialized countries that were covered by it to "earn credits toward their treaty targets by investing in emissions cleanups outside their borders," a so-called *cap-and-trade* system.[84] Developing countries such as India and China were exempt from the controls so as to give them a better chance to catch up economically with the more developed nations. Although the United States helped develop this agreement, Congress refused to pass it and President George W. Bush pulled out of the agreement when he took office in 2001, holding that it was flawed and would hurt the U.S. economy. (Even though the United States did not ratify the treaty, the mayors of more than five hundred U.S. cities pledged to meet its targets.[85]) The Kyoto Protocol was ratified by 141 other nations and took effect on February 16, 2005.

Despite its broad international acceptance, the Kyoto Protocol has not achieved its goals because some developed countries have not met their lowered emissions targets. And from its inception, a significant problem for the Kyoto Protocol was the exemption for developing countries. China, for example, has become an emissions titan; since the Kyoto Protocol was signed, China's emissions have nearly tripled and India's have doubled.[86] While some European countries have reduced their emissions in recent years, these reductions may be attributable to the global economic downturn and not necessarily connected with a deliberate shift in emissions strategies. The United States, which under the agreement was supposed to reduce its emissions 7 percent below 1990 levels by 2012, had, as of 2011, increased emissions

by 8 percent since 1990, according to the EPA.[87] In 2011, Canada officially rejected the Kyoto Protocol, arguing that it was not working to impose limits on the two largest producers of greenhouse gases, the United States and China, and that there was no way to meet the Kyoto targets without serious economic dislocation in Canada.[88] Nevertheless, international negotiations to reduce greenhouse gas emissions continue. The most recent round of climate talks is aiming to create a new international agreement by 2015.

In addition to the negotiation of the Kyoto Protocol, various other global summits and meetings have been held in the twenty years since the original Earth Summit in Rio de Janeiro. The most recent was the Rio+20 Earth Summit, held in Rio de Janeiro in 2012. Global leaders, such as the UN Secretary General Ban Ki-moon and U.S. Secretary of State Hillary Clinton, declared the Rio+20 meeting a success for clarifying global aspirations for a sustainable future.[89] But environmentalists decried the meeting. The executive director of Greenpeace, Kumi Naidoo, criticized its lack of binding agreements and described it as a meeting full of "empty rhetoric and greenwash from world leaders."[90]

Such conflicts indicate the nature of the divide between those who want radical action to fix environmental problems and those who advocate a more cautious approach, such as politicians and business leaders. At issue here is a substantial difference of opinion about fundamental values. On the one hand, people value the success of short-term business ventures. But on the other hand, long-term environmental sustainability is also important to human well-being—not to mention the well-being of animals, plants, and ecosystems. What is the extent of our obligation to curb emissions and preserve forests and other wilderness areas, especially in light of the fact that these efforts often have a negative effect on other human interests such as the ability of many people to make a living?

Global Justice and the Tragedy of the Commons

The preservation of the environment is a global issue. Although many problems are specific to certain areas of the world, others such as global warming are shared in common. As we have noted, poor people in developing countries may be the most negatively impacted by climate change. However, just as in the developed world, many in developing countries are more concerned with economic growth and development than they are with the environment. In fact, some people in poor nations even view the environmentalist movement as an example of Western elitism. Only wealthy Westerners, they suggest, can afford to preserve, unchanged, an environment or wilderness that the poor need to use and change in order to survive. From this perspective, poor people who are struggling to survive should not be asked to curtail their own development while citizens of affluent nations enjoy goods unobtainable in the poorer countries.

The concern for environmental justice, which we discussed previously, will tell us that we ought to consider social justice concerns as we deal with environmental issues. Is it fair that those in affluent nations are able to live comfortable lives, while generating a disproportionately large share of waste and pollution? Most environmentalists agree that a sustainable solution to current environmental crises will have to deal with remaining social inequalities across the globe. As we've seen, international agreements regulating greenhouse gases contain variances that attempt to accommodate the inequalities between developed and developing countries.

While alternative fuels, recycling, and other environmentally friendly technologies seem to offer promising solutions to our environmental problems, they do not address the problem of inequality and egoistic rationality. Those in the poorer parts of the world want to have the goods that those in the affluent nations have. And those in affluent countries do not want to give up their current standard of living. However, there are not enough resources available for everyone to enjoy the standard of living of an average American. One solution is to find ways for those in developing regions to raise living standards in ways that create minimal impact on the environment; economic growth that is environmentally sustainable is referred to as *sustainable development*. But those in the affluent countries cannot reasonably expect poorer nations to do their part for the environment while the affluent countries fail to control their own growth and consumption. It might be necessary, in the name of global environmental justice, for affluent countries to radically scale back their level of consumption. Paul and Anne Ehrlich, influential demographers who have been warning about overpopulation for decades, warn: "if we fail to bring population growth and over-consumption under control, then we will inhabit a planet where life becomes increasingly untenable."[91] The problem is not only that the human population has exceeded seven billion but also that everyone wants to consume as much as the average American.

Who has a right to consume the world's resources? Issues surrounding resource consumption and allocation may make it impossible to create a stable system of global environmental justice. One concern is based upon claims about property rights and capitalism. According to this perspective, landowners have a natural right to develop the resources they possess. To maintain that certain landowners (or countries) should not develop their land or resources appears to be a violation of basic property rights. Furthermore, there is no guarantee that common areas not owned by anyone—the so-called "commons"—will be adequately protected. The oceans and the atmosphere are vast commons. Since they belong to no one, they are easy prey for exploitation and they are also used as vast sinks into which we flush our waste. The American ecologist Garrett Hardin warns that self-interested individuals will tend to take advantage of unprotected common areas, according to a concept that he calls "the tragedy of the commons." Hardin also points out the ethical challenge of global environmental justice in his discussion of what he calls "life-boat ethics." According to Hardin, we should imagine that we are each floating in an isolated lifeboat, competing with one another to survive. Our lifeboats have a limited carrying capacity, so our obligation is to take care of ourselves first—to manage our own resources. Hardin's perspective leaves us with a world of isolated nation-states, each struggling to survive as the growing human population continues to strain the earth's limited resources. Moreover, Hardin's tragic conclusion is that if this is the way we conceive the world, we may not be able to fend off the collapse of the commons, since each of us will try to exploit what's left for our own benefit.[92] This is a form of the prisoner's dilemma that results from egoism (as discussed in Chapter 4): as each pursues his own self-interest in a world of self-interested people, we may soon end up with unwanted outcomes.[93] From this perspective, which is firmly anthropocentric and even egocentric, the most rational short-term strategy may be to find ways to exploit the environment and enrich oneself before the true impact of the environmental crisis is upon us, to build up our reserves so that we can ride out the coming environmental storm.

This sort of short-term and self-interested reasoning is criticized by both anthropocentric and ecocentric environmentalists. Ecocentrists maintain that we have an obligation to the ecosystem not to overexploit it. Anthropocentrists point out that we have a humanitarian obligation to help others who are suffering, as well as an obligation to future generations to make sure we don't destroy the commons and overexploit the ecosystem. Both note that short-term self-interest can lead to disastrous consequences, as evidenced by "collapsed" or failed societies such as the Rapa Nui on Easter Island and the Maya in the Yucatán.[94] In each case, unsustainable growth led to the downfall of an entire civilization. Societies that collapse do so because they are unable to restrain their own development and unable to focus on the long-term sustainability of their practices. It may be that this is simply part of the natural cycle of life. Organisms grow, reproduce, and consume until they outstrip their resource base. When the resource base is overexploited, the population dies back. But the stakes are quite high now that environmental impacts have created truly global problems. And those who suffer the most from environmental degradation will be the most vulnerable among us. An environmental justice perspective will tell us that we have an obligation to protect those vulnerable people.

We have seen in this chapter that there are a variety of environmental problems confronting us today: from urban pollution to climate change. Some may view these problems from an anthropocentric perspective, focused on cost–benefit analysis or a concern for environmental justice. Others will point toward a deeper set of ecocentric concerns

that emphasize the intrinsic value of wilderness and natural systems. The ethical issues to be considered here are complex, as are the causes and possible solutions to environmental challenges.

NOTES

1. Jason Samenow, "Deadly El Reno, Okla. Tornado Was Widest Ever Measured on Earth, Had Nearly 300 MPH Winds," *Washington Post*, June 4, 2013, http://www.washingtonpost.com/blogs/capital-weather-gang/wp/2013/06/04/deadly-el-reno-okla-tornado-was-widest-ever-measured-on-earth-had-nearly-300-mph-winds/
2. Organisation for Economic Co-operation and Development, *OECD Environmental Outlook to 2050: The Consequences of Inaction*, accessed April 2, 2013, http://www.oecd.org/environment/indicators-modelling-outlooks/49846090.pdf
3. "Air Pollution Linked to 1.2 Million Premature Deaths in China," *New York Times*, April 1, 2013, accessed April 2, 2013, http://www.nytimes.com/2013/04/02/world/asia/air-pollution-linked-to-1-2-million-deaths-in-china.html
4. Central Valley Health Policy Institute, *The Impacts of Short-Term Changes in Air Quality on Emergency Room and Hospital Use in California's San Joaquin Valley*, accessed April 2, 2013, http://www.fresnostate.edu/chhs/cvhpi/documents/snapshot.pdf
5. Ernest Weekley, *An Etymological Dictionary of Modern English* (New York: Dover, 1967), 516, 518.
6. Safety regulation needs to make use of such monetary equivalencies, for how else do we decide how safe is safe enough? There is no such thing as perfect safety, for that would mean no risk. Thus, we end up judging that we ought to pay so much to make things just so much safer but no more. The implication is that the increased life years or value of the lives to be saved by stricter regulation is of so much but no more than this much value. See Barbara MacKinnon, "Pricing Human Life," *Science, Technology and Human Values* (Spring 1986): 29–39.
7. "Environmental Justice," U.S. EPA, accessed April 5, 2013, http://www.epa.gov/environmentaljustice/
8. Andrew North, "Legacy of Bhopal Disaster Poisons Olympics," BBC News, accessed April 5, 2013, http://www.bbc.co.uk/news/world-asia-18254334
9. "28 Years Later, Women in Bhopal Still Waiting for Justice," Amnesty International, December 3, 2012, accessed April 5, 2013, http://www.amnesty.org/en/news/28-years-later-women-bhopal-still-waiting-justice-2012-12-03
10. Bob Van Voris and Patricia Hurtado, "Union Carbide Wins Dismissal of Suit over Bhopal Plant," Bloomberg, June 27, 2012, accessed April 5, 2013, http://www.bloomberg.com/news/2012-06-27/union-carbide-wins-dismissal-of-suit-over-bhopal-plant.html
11. See Kristin Shrader-Frechette, *Environmental Justice: Creating Equity, Reclaiming Democracy* (Oxford: Oxford University Press, 2002), 10.
12. Kevin DeLuca, "A Wilderness Environmentalism Manifesto: Contesting the Infinite Self-Absorption of Humans," in *Environmental Justice and Environmentalism: The Social Justice Challenge to the Environmental Movement*, eds.

Ronald D. Sandler and Phaedra C. Pezzullo (Cambridge, MA: MIT Press, 2007), 49.

13. Genesis 1:26–29. Others will cite St. Francis of Assisi as an example of the Christian with a respectful regard for nature.

14. René Descartes, *Meditations on First Philosophy*. However, it might be pointed out that for Descartes this was not so much a metaphysical point as an epistemological one; that is, he was concerned with finding some sure starting point for knowledge and found at least that he was sure that he was thinking even when he was doubting the existence of everything else.

15. See Christopher Stone, *Do Trees Have Standing? Toward Legal Rights for Natural Objects* (Los Altos, CA: William Kaufmann, 1974).

16. Holmes Rolston III, *Environmental Ethics: Duties to and Values in the Natural World* (Philadelphia: Temple University Press, 1988), 97.

17. Aldo Leopold, "The Land Ethic," in *Sand County Almanac* (New York: Oxford University Press, 1949).

18. Ibid., 262.

19. See John Hospers, *Understanding the Arts* (Englewood Cliffs, NJ: Prentice Hall, 1982).

20. Ed McGaa, Eagle Man, "We Are All Related," in *Mother Earth Spirituality: Native American Paths to Healing Ourselves and Our World* (San Francisco: Harper & Row, 1990), 203–09.

21. See Stephen R. Fox, *The American Conservation Movement: John Muir and His Legacy* (Madison, WI: University of Wisconsin Press, 1981), 5.

22. Arne Naess, *Ecology, Community, and Lifestyle*, trans. David Rothenberg (Cambridge: Cambridge University Press, 1989).

23. Paul Taylor, *Respect for Nature* (Princeton, NJ: Princeton University Press, 1986).

24. Naess, *Ecology, Community, and Lifestyle*, op. cit.

25. George Sessions, ed., *Deep Ecology for the 21st Century: Readings on the Philosophy and Practice of the New Environmentalism* (Boston: Shambhala Publications, 1995), xxi.

26. On the tactics of ecosabotage, see Bill Devall, *Simple in Means, Rich in Ends: Practicing Deep Ecology* (Layton, UT: Gibbs Smith, 1988).

27. See Michael Martin, "Ecosabotage and Civil Disobedience," *Environmental Ethics* 12 (Winter 1990): 291–310.

28. According to Joseph des Jardins, the term *ecofeminism* was first used by Françoise d'Eaubonne in 1974 in her work *Le Feminisme ou la Mort* (Paris: Pierre Horay, 1974). See des Jardins, *Environmental Ethics*, op. cit., 249.

29. Karen J. Warren, "The Power and Promise of Ecological Feminism," *Environmental Ethics* 9 (Spring 1987): 3–20.

30. I thank an anonymous reviewer for this point.

31. See the distinctions made by Allison Jaggar between liberal (egalitarian) feminism, Marxist feminism, socialist feminism, and radical feminism. *Feminist Politics and Human Nature* (Totowa, NJ: Rowman & Allanheld, 1983).

32. See Carol Christ, *Laughter of Aphrodite: Reflections on a Journey to the Goddess* (San Francisco: Harper & Row, 1987).

33. David Biello, "400 PPM: Carbon Dioxide in the Atmosphere Reaches Prehistoric Levels," *Scientific American*, May 9, 2013, accessed June 6, 2013, http://blogs.scientificamerican.com/observations/2013/05/09/400-ppm-carbon-dioxide-in-the-atmosphere-reaches-prehistoric-levels/

34. Elizabeth Rosenthal, "As the Climate Changes, Bits of England's Coast Crumble," *New York Times*, May 4, 2007, A4, accessed July 5, 2013.

35. John McQuaid, "Hurricanes and Climate Change," Nova, accessed July 5, 2013, http://www.pbs.org/wgbh/nova/earth/hurricanes-climate.html

36. Justin Gillis, "Ending Its Summer Melt, Arctic Sea Ice Sets a New Low That Leads to Warnings," *New York Times*, accessed April 2, 2013, http://www.nytimes.com/2012/09/20/science/earth/arctic-sea-ice-stops-melting-but-new-record-low-is-set.html

37. "2013 Wintertime Arctic Sea Ice Maximum Fifth Lowest on Record," NASA, April 3, 2013, accessed April 3, 2013, http://www.nasa.gov/topics/earth/features/arctic-seaicemax-2013.html

38. "Ice Is Flowing Slower on Greenland Than Many Feared," Climate Central, May 3, 2012, http://www.climatecentral.org/news/ice-is-flowing-slower-on-greenland-than-many-feared-study-says/

39. John Roach, "'Horrible' Sea Level Rise of More Than 3 Feet Plausible by 2100, Experts Say," NBC News, January 6, 2013, accessed April 3, 2013, http://science.nbcnews.com/_news/2013/01/06/16369939-horrible-sea-level-rise-of-more-than-3-feet-plausible-by-2100-experts-say?lite

40. "Future Climate Change," U.S. EPA, accessed April 3, 2013, http://www.epa.gov/climatechange/science/future.html

41. "How Climate Change Threatens the Seas," *USA Today*, March 28, 2013, accessed April 3, 2013, http://www.usatoday.com/story/news/nation/2013/03/27/climate-change-seas/2024759/

42. "New Simulations Question the Gulf Stream's Role in Tempering Europe's Winters," *Scientific American*, February 11, 2013, accessed June 6, 2013, http://www.scientificamerican.com/article.cfm?id=new-simulations-question-gulf-stream-role-tempering-europes-winters&page=2

43. Al Gore, *An Inconvenient Truth* (New York: Rodale, 2006), 148–51.

44. Gore, op. cit., 194–209; Andrew Revkin, "Climate Panel Reaches Consensus on the Need to Reduce Harmful Emissions," *New York Times*, May 4, 2007, A6; Tim Appenzeller, "The Big Thaw," *National Geographic*, June 2007.

45. Randy Astaiza, "11 Islands That Will Vanish When Sea Levels Rise," *Business Insider*, October 12, 2012, accessed June 6, 2013, http://www.businessinsider.com/islands-threatened-by-climate-change-2012-10?op=1#ixzz2VU4tcYVu

46. "Overview of Greenhouse Gases," U.S. EPA, accessed April 3, 2013, http://www.epa.gov/climatechange/ghgemissions/gases/co2.html

47. "Gateway to the United Nations Systems Work on Climate Change," accessed April 3, 2013, http://www.un.org/wcm/content/site/climatechange/pages/gateway/the-science

48. "Recent Global CO2," National Oceanographic and Atmospheric Administration, accessed April 3, 2013, http://www.esrl.noaa.gov/gmd/ccgg/trends/global.html

49. "U.S. Scientists Report Big Jump in Heat-Trapping CO2," AP News, March 5, 2013, accessed April 3, 2013, http://bigstory.ap.org/article/us-scientists-report-big-jump-heat-trapping-co2

50. "Global Greenhouse Gas Emissions Data," U.S. EPA, accessed April 3, 2013, http://www.epa.gov/climatechange/ghgemissions/global.html#four

51. Thomas Homer-Dixon, "Terror in the Weather Forecast," *New York Times*, April 24, 2007, A25; Celia W. Dugger, "Need for Water Could Double in 50 Years, U.N. Study Finds," *New York Times*, August 22, 2006, A12; Jane Kay, "Report Predicts Climate Calamity," *San Francisco Chronicle*, May 7, 2007, A1.

52. Gore, op. cit., 60–67.

53. "Butterflies and Birds Unable to Keep Pace with Climate Change in Europe," *Science Daily*, January 18, 2012, accessed April 3, 2013, http://www.sciencedaily.com/releases/2012/01/120118111742.htm

54. Gore, op. cit., 42–59; Appenzeller, 60.

55. United Nations Environment Programme, *High Mountain Glaciers and Climate Change* (2010), accessed April 3, 2013, http://www.unep.org/pdf/himalayareport_screen.pdf

56. James Hansen, "Game Over for the Climate," *New York Times*, May 9, 2012, accessed April 3, 2013, http://www.nytimes.com/2012/05/10/opinion/game-over-for-the-climate.html

57. Elisabeth Ponsot, "Will Germany Banish Fossil Fuels Before the US?," *Mother Jones*, January 23, 2013, accessed June 10, 2013, http://www.motherjones.com/environment/2013/01/video-germany-will-banish-fossil-fuels-renewable-energy

58. Quoted in "Life after Oil and Gas," *New York Times*, March 23, 2013, accessed April 3, 2013, http://www.nytimes.com/2013/03/24/sunday-review/life-after-oil-and-gas.html?ref=opinion

59. Michael Riordan, "Time for a Carbon Tax?," *San Francisco Chronicle*, March 23, 2007, B11.

60. "Study: Fish Suffer Ozone Hole Sunburn," *San Francisco Sunday Examiner and Chronicle*, November 12, 2000, A20.

61. "Ozone Thinning Has Changed Ocean Circulation," *Science Daily*, January 31, 2013, accessed April 3, 2013, http://www.sciencedaily.com/releases/2013/01/130131144106.htm

62. "Ozone Depletion," *National Geographic*, accessed June 11, 2013, http://environment.nationalgeographic.com/environment/global-warming/ozone-depletion-overview/

63. "Municipal Solid Waste," U.S. EPA, accessed April 3, 2013, http://www.epa.gov/epawaste/nonhaz/municipal/index.htm

64. Sarah Zhang, "Charts: What Your Trash Reveals about the World Economy," *Mother Jones*, July 16, 2012, accessed April 3, 2013, http://www.motherjones.com/environment/2012/07/trash-charts-world-bank-report-economy; based upon World Bank report, *What a Waste* (March 1, 2012).

65. "Waste and Recycling Facts," Clean Air Council, accessed April 3, 2013, http://www.cleanair.org/Waste/wasteFacts.html#_edn1

66. "Are Paper Bags Really That Much Better Than Plastic?" KQED, June 5, 2013, accessed June 11, 2013, http://blogs.kqed.org/newsfix/2013/06/05/paper-bags-vs-plastic/

67. Jonathan Klick and Joshua D. Wright, "Grocery Bag Bans and Foodborne Illness" (University of Pennsylvania, Institute for Law & Economics research paper no. 13-2, November 2, 2012), accessed June 11, 2013, http://ssrn.com/abstract=2196481 or http://dx.doi.org/10.2139/ssrn.2196481

68. "Waste and Recycling Facts," Clean Air Council, http://www.cleanair.org/Waste/wasteFacts.html#_edn1

69. Leslie Kaufman, "Where Does That Starbucks Cup Go?" *New York Times*, November 30, 2010, accessed April 3, 2013, http://green.blogs.nytimes.com/2010/11/30/what-next-after-tossing-a-starbucks-cup/

70. Clean Water Council, *Taking Out the Trash* (2011), accessed April 3, 2013, http://www.cleanwateraction.org/files/publications/ca/TakingOuthteTrash%20monitoring%20results.pdf

71. "E-waste Management Workshop," United Nations Environment Programme, accessed June 11, 2013, http://www.unep.org/ietc/wastemanagementworkshopontakebacksystem/tabid/79437/default.aspx

72. "Ghana: Digital Dumping Ground," PBS's *Frontline*, January 23, 2009, accessed April 3, 2013, http://www.pbs.org/frontlineworld/stories/ghana804/video/video_index.html

73. "Residents Near Chinese E-Waste Site Face Greater Cancer Risk," *Science Daily*, January 22, 2013, accessed April 3, 2013, http://www.sciencedaily.com/releases/2013/01/130123101615.htm

74. *Sierra Club Magazine*, November–December 2005, 42–47.

75. "Aluminum Recycling Facts," accessed June 10, 2013, http://www.recycling-revolution.com/recycling-facts.html; and "What We Really Save by Recycling," Earth 911.com, accessed April 4, 2013, http://earth911.com/news/2012/10/17/how-much-energy-water-saved-by-recycling/

76. "What We Really Save by Recycling," Earth 911.com, http://earth911.com/news/2012/10/17/how-much-energy-water-saved-by-recycling/

77. "Biomass Energy and Cellulosic Ethanol," National Resources Defense Council, accessed June 11, 2013, http://www.nrdc.org/energy/renewables/biomass.asp

78. "Creation and Growth of the National Wilderness Preservation System," Wilderness.net, accessed April 4, 2013, http://www.wilderness.net/index.cfm?fuse=nwps&sec=fastfacts

79. See "Making the Case for ANWR Development," Arctic National Wildlife Refuge, accessed April 4, 2013, http://www.anwr.org/case.htm

80. See "When to Say No," *New York Times*, March 10, 2013, accessed April 4, 2013, http://www.nytimes.com/2013/03/11/opinion/when-to-say-no-to-the-keystone-xl.html?smid=pl-share&_r=0

81. "Tar Sands," National Wildlife Federation, accessed April 4, 2013, http://www.nwf.org/What-We-Do/Energy-and-Climate/Drilling-and-Mining/Tar-Sands.aspx

82. "Alberta's Oil Sands," Alberta Government, accessed April 4, 2013, http://oilsands.alberta.ca/resource.html

83. Larry Rohter and Andrew C. Revkin, "Cheers, and Concern, for New Climate Pact," *New York Times*, December 13, 2004, A6.

84. Ibid.

85. "U.S. Conference of Mayors Climate Protection Agreement," accessed April 4, 2013, http://www.usmayors.org/climateprotection/agreement.htm

86. Quirin Schiermeier, "The Kyoto Protocol: Hot Air," *Nature*, November 28, 2012, accessed April 4, 2013, http://www.nature.com/news/the-kyoto-protocol-hot-air-1.11882

87. U.S. EPA, *Trends in Greenhouse Gas Emissions*, accessed April 4, 2013, http://www.epa.gov/climatechange/Downloads/ghgemissions/US-GHG-Inventory-2011-Chapter-2-Trends.pdf

88. Ian Austen, "Canada Announces Exit from Kyoto Climate Treaty," *New York Times*, December 12, 2011, accessed April

4, 2013, http://www.nytimes.com/2011/12/13/science/earth/canada-leaving-kyoto-protocol-on-climate-change.html

89. Jonathan Watts and Liz Ford, "Rio+20 Earth Summit: Campaigners Decry Final Document," *Guardian*, June 22, 2012, accessed April 4, 2013, http://www.guardian.co.uk/environment/2012/jun/23/rio-20-earth-summit-document

90. "Greenpeace Press Statement: Rio+20 Earth Summit—A Failure of Epic Proportions," Greenpeace.org, June 22, 2012, accessed April 4, 2013, http://www.greenpeace.org/international/en/press/releases/Greenpeace-Press-Statement-Rio20-Earth-Summit-a-failure-of-epic-proportions/

91. Paul and Anne Ehrlich, "Too Many People, Too Much Consumption," *Environment 360*, August 4, 2008, accessed

June 11, 2013, http://e360.yale.edu/feature/too_many_people_too_much_consumption/2041/

92. Garrett Hardin, "The Tragedy of the Commons," *Science* 162 (1968): 1243–248; also see Garrett Hardin, "Lifeboat Ethics: The Case against Helping the Poor," *Psychology Today*, September 1974.

93. See Andrew Fiala, "Nero's Fiddle: On Hope and Despair and the Ecological Crisis," *Ethics and the Environment* 15, no. 1 (Spring 2010).

94. Jared Diamond, *Collapse* (New York: Viking Press, 2005).

REVIEW EXERCISES

1. Why is the notion of *value* problematic when discussing environmental ethics?
2. What are the differences among intrinsic, instrumental, and prima facie values? Give an example of each.
3. What is anthropocentrism? How is it different from ecocentrism?
4. How do cost–benefit analyses function in environmental arguments? Give an example of an environmental problem today and how a cost–benefit analysis could be used to analyze it.
5. Explain how the concept of environmental justice can be used to provide a critical analysis of the impact of pollution.
6. Describe two different types of ecocentrism.
7. What is Aldo Leopold's basic principle for determining what is right and wrong in environmental matters?
8. What is deep ecology? According to this view, what are the root causes of our environmental problems?
9. Summarize the different ecofeminist views described in this chapter.
10. What is the problem of the tragedy of the commons, and how is it connected to capitalism and the idea of property rights?

DISCUSSION CASES

1. **Climate Change.** Carla and Greg are debating climate change. Carla believes that climate change is nothing to worry about. "Even if the scientists could ever really establish that burning fossil fuels causes climate change, there's no need to worry. Scientists will find ways to fix the problem. And we can always move to higher ground or just move north, where it's cooler." Greg laughs out loud. "Ha! That's easy for you to say," Greg replies. "Americans will probably be able to survive the changing climate. But people in other parts of the world are really going to suffer. And anyway, it's not just about the humans. We should also be concerned about the value of natural things like glaciers and forests." Carla shakes her head. "I don't really get you environmentalists. First you say that poor people will suffer. Then you say that glaciers and forests will suffer. But aren't people

more important than glaciers? And if we had to melt all the glaciers to provide drinking water for poor people, wouldn't that be the right thing to do?"

Whom do you agree with here? Explain your answer with reference to philosophical concepts such as anthropocentrism and ecocentrism.

2. **Preserving the Trees.** XYZ Timber Company has been logging forests in the Pacific Northwest for decades. It has done moderately well in replanting areas it has logged, but it has also been logging in areas where some trees are hundreds of years old. Now the company plans to build roads into a similar area of the forest and cut down similarly ancient trees. An environmental group, "Trees First," is determined to prevent this. Its members have blocked the roads that have been put in by the timber company and have also engaged in the

practice known as *tree spiking*—in which iron spikes are driven into trees to discourage the use of power saws. Loggers are outraged, because tree spiking can make logging extremely dangerous. When a saw hits these spikes, it becomes uncontrollable, and loggers can be seriously injured. Forest rangers have been marking trees found to be spiked and have noted that some spikes are not visible and will present a hidden danger for years to come. People from Trees First insist that this is the only way to prevent the shortsighted destruction of old-growth forests. They argue that XYZ Timber Company has too much political power and has ignored public protests against their logging practices. The only way to get the company's attention, they say, is to put their employees at risk.

What is your assessment of the actions of the XZY Timber Company and the actions of Trees First? Is it ever justifiable to use extreme protest methods such as tree spiking that put lives at risk? Why or why not?

3. **Sustainable Development.** The people of the Amazon River basin, who live in rural poverty, have begun burning and clearing large sections of the forest. They are doing so to create farmland in order to earn a living for themselves and their families. But the burning and deforestation destroy ecosystems of rare plants and animals and contribute to global warming. As a result, representatives from environmental groups in the United States and other wealthy countries have traveled to the region seeking to persuade the locals to cease this practice and pursue a more sustainable livelihood based on ecotourism. The people of the Amazon River basin are offended by these proposals. They point out that North Americans already have destroyed much of their own forests and become prosperous. "Who are you to criticize us?" they ask. "It is a luxury to worry about what the weather will be like a hundred years from now. We have to worry about what we will eat tomorrow."

Whose position do you find more persuasive here—the environmentalists or the people of the Amazon River basin? How would you balance global concerns about deforestation and global warming against the subsistence needs of cultures in environmentally sensitive areas?

iStockphoto/Thinkstock

17 Animal Ethics

Learning Outcomes

After reading this chapter, you should be able to:

- Understand current issues in animal ethics including hunting, vegetarianism, animal research, and endangered species protection.

- Explain the difference between a concern for animal welfare and a concern for animal rights.

- Define *speciesism* and articulate criticisms of this idea.

- Explain the idea of "equal consideration" and what that might mean for animal ethics.

- Understand anthropocentric and non-anthropocentric criticisms of animal cruelty.

- Explain Peter Singer's notion of animal liberation and how the idea might apply in thinking about animal research or industrial farming.

- Defend a thesis with regard to animal ethics.

Gray wolves were once hunted to the brink of extinction in the United States. By 1970, only two states—Alaska and Minnesota—still had viable gray wolf populations. During the 1970s, various subspecies of gray wolf were given protection from hunting under the Endangered Species Act. For some subspecies—the Texas wolf, for example—it was too late. The Texas wolf and other subspecies have disappeared forever. By 1978, all gray wolf subspecies in the lower forty-eight states were protected against hunting.[1] In 1995, wolves captured in Canada were reintroduced to the western United States, in an effort to regenerate the U.S. wolf population. Western ranchers feared that these wolves would prey upon their livestock, and in some places they were permitted to shoot wolves that had killed their sheep or cattle. By 2009, the population of wolves had grown large enough that the U.S. Fish and Wildlife Service removed the gray wolf from the list of endangered species. This move prompted some states to legalize wolf hunting. Controversially, this included wolf hunting near Yellowstone National Park—a practice that raised objections because the national parks are supposed to protect animals from hunting. In 2012, wolf hunting was allowed in Wyoming, and by 2013 there had been wolf hunts in Wisconsin, Minnesota, Idaho, Wyoming, and Montana. The wolf hunts (or "harvests") of 2012–13 resulted in more than 1,000 wolves killed.[2]

Opponents of wolf hunts criticize the language used to describe these hunts, complaining that it is a euphemism to use the word "harvest" to describe such killing. This points to the question of whether a wolf is a creature with a right to life or something more like a crop to be managed and harvested. Some view wolves as noble symbols of a vanishing wilderness. Others see them as animals very similar to the dogs we keep as pets. Still others view wolves as dangerous predators that pose a risk to sheep and other herd animals. Such perspectives reflect different answers to the question: What is the value of a wolf—or any other animal?

Is there a humane way to kill a wolf or another nonhuman animal? During the wolf harvest, the animals can be shot or trapped. Animal welfare advocates have been especially critical of using leg traps to kill wolves. One anti-trapping group, Foot-loose Montana, argues that trapping is cruel because it causes excessive suffering and is not in line with the "fair chase" ethos of hunting.[3] Leg traps are intended to hold the wolf until the hunter arrives to finally kill it. Trappers insist that they check their traps often and kill the animals quickly. But some animals are caught in traps for long periods of time. Some die of hypothermia. Others chew off their own legs or are attacked by other predators. Another problem with trapping is that it is indiscriminate. A 2012 report about a trapping program employed by the Wildlife Services in California indicated that traps in California have killed 50,000 unintended animals since 2000, including protected species such as bald eagles and more than one thousand dogs.[4]

A further question is whether trapping lives up to the standards of "fair chase." The idea of **fair chase** in hunting ethics is that the animal should stand some chance and the hunter requires some skill and good luck. According to one definition, fair chase involves a balance between the hunter and the hunted animal "that allows hunters to occasionally succeed, while animals generally avoid being taken."[5] The concept of fair chase might be used to criticize the practice of "rigged" hunting, in which companies obtain "trophy" animals and confine them in certain ways so that hunters have a much better chance at a kill. Such companies often buy their animals from dubious suppliers, including exotic animal auctions, and their hunts have been known to include "zebras, camels, ostriches, kangaroos, and lion cubs."[6] Other problematic forms of hunting include the use of bait to attract animals to be shot. The practice of baiting bears, for example, is banned in eighteen of the twenty-eight states in which bear hunting is legal. The former governor of

Minnesota, Jesse Ventura, once said of bear baiting, "that ain't sport, that's an assassination."[7] The state of Alaska, however, allows and even promotes bear baiting, publishing a bear baiters "code of ethics."[8]

Also controversial is the practice of hunting wolves and other animals from helicopters or small planes, such as occurs in Alaska. According to one report, aerial wolf hunts in Alaska kill several hundred wolves every winter.[9] This practice is not only a matter of sport hunting but also a way of balancing predator and prey populations—which is the only legal reason for such hunts under federal law. Critics of airborne hunting consider it cruel and inhumane because the plane or helicopter is used to chase animals across the snow until they are exhausted and because shots fired from the air rarely result in a clean kill.[10] In 2008, when the former governor of Alaska, Sarah Palin, was a candidate for vice president of the United States, aerial wolf hunting in Alaska became a political issue, since Governor Palin had championed the program of shooting wolves from the air.

The debate over wolf hunting and controversial hunting practices points toward several complex ethical questions. Should we be concerned for the welfare of wild animals? Do such animals have a right to live their lives free from human interference? Is it acceptable to "harvest" them, so long as we kill them humanely? Is hunting part of an ancient predator–prey dynamic that defines the rest of the natural world, or do humans have greater moral responsibilities than other animals. How and why should human beings care about the well-being of individual animals or animal species, or about ecosystems that include both predators and prey animals?

These sorts of questions point toward fundamental issues concerning the ontological and moral status of animals. They also point toward fundamental questions about being human and the extent to which we are similar to and different from nonhuman animals. Human beings are animals, after all. But we are also the only animals that raise questions about the morality of killing other animals. Does this make us superior to nonhuman animals; or does it give us a greater responsibility? Anthropocentric (or human-centered) answers to these questions will maintain that humans are superior or that human concerns matter most. Non-anthropocentric answers will reject such claims, maintaining that we also ought to consider things from a standpoint that takes the interests and welfare of nonhuman animals seriously. The distinction between anthropocentric and non-anthropocentric approaches showed up in our discussion of environmental ethics (in Chapter 16). It returns here with a specific focus on the value of nonhuman animals.

CURRENT ISSUES
Moral Vegetarianism

There are a variety of concrete issues that arise in discussing animals and their welfare. Perhaps the most obvious issue is whether we ought to raise and kill animals for food. The discussion of hunting overlaps with discussions of eating animals. Although wolves are not hunted for their meat, harvesting wolves is intended to protect domesticated animals such as cattle and sheep and to protect wild herds of elk, caribou, moose, and deer, which are hunted for their meat. This raises the interesting question about which animals we eat and which animals we don't, and evokes the philosophical issue of cultural relativism (as discussed in Chapter 3). Some cultures eat dogs; others don't. Some cultures eat pigs; others don't. Do these differences reflect moral truths of some kind, or mere cultural conventions and taboos?

There are some cultures and individuals that don't eat animals at all. The ancient Greek philosopher Pythagoras and his followers were vegetarians, as are some Hindus, Buddhists, and Jains in varying degrees. The nineteenth-century Russian novelist Leo Tolstoy was a vegetarian. Tolstoy maintained that those who are "really and seriously seeking to live a good life" will abstain from animal food because "its use is simply immoral, as it involves the performance of an act which is contrary to moral feeling—killing."[11] Tolstoy's ideas had an influence on Mohandas Gandhi (discussed in Chapter 2), whose **vegetarianism** was also connected to his Hindu religion and culture. In his autobiography, Gandhi describes witnessing a ceremonial sacrifice of a lamb. When a friend explained to him that a sheep does not feel anything while being slaughtered, Gandhi replied that if the sheep could speak, it would tell a different tale. Gandhi concludes,

> To my mind the life of a lamb is no less precious than that of a human being. I should be unwilling to take the life of a lamb for the sake of the human body. I hold that, the more helpless a creature, the more entitled it is to protection by man from the cruelty of man.[12]

There are degrees of vegetarianism. All vegetarians avoid eating animals, although some may eat eggs, dairy products, or even fish. Vegans avoid consuming both animals and animal products, including eggs, dairy, and in some cases honey. Some people observe vegetarian diets for health reasons—because of a food allergy or in an effort to follow a high-fiber, low-fat diet. But many vegetarians avoid eating animals for ethical reasons. The deep ethical question is whether there are good moral reasons to avoid meat and animal products or whether the consumption of animals is morally justified.

Most meat eaters think that there is nothing wrong with consuming animals and animal products. Meat eating is deeply rooted in custom and tradition. One traditional idea holds that animals are given to us by God for our use. A related idea maintains that there is a hierarchy of beings, with humans at the top, and this entitles us to use the animals below us. Others may assume that animals do not feel pain when they are slaughtered, or that animals are not moral "persons" because they do not have the sort of consciousness that would give them an interest in living. (You might want to compare such positions to Mary Anne Warren's account of the moral status of fetuses in Chapter 11.) Another argument holds that vegetarianism is supererogatory: that it might be admirable to abstain from eating animals but that there is no duty to do so.[13] Still others argue that the morality of eating meat depends upon the way the meat is raised—whether it is produced on industrial farms or whether it is produced in a "cruelty-free" manner (including free-range or cage-free animals). This issue has even shown up on state ballots: in California in 2008, voters approved the Prevention of Farm Animal Cruelty Act, which aimed to prevent cruelty in the treatment of veal calves, pigs, and chickens. Similar laws have been established in several other states and in the European Union.

A strictly utilitarian account of animal ethics would be focused on whether causing animal suffering can be justified by some account of the greater good. If we are primarily focused on human good, we might say that animal suffering is outweighed by the human interest in nutritious and delicious meat and other animal products. Another utilitarian argument might point out that by growing animals for food and clothing, we produce animals that otherwise would never have been born—so even though these animals are used and killed, they enjoy pleasures while alive that they would not have enjoyed if not for animal agriculture. Unless their lives involve a greater amount of pain than pleasure, we may have done these animals a favor by raising them.

But critics of industrialized agriculture will argue that "factory farms" produce animals that live miserable lives and are then killed for human purposes. While such farms are not intentionally cruel, they employ practices that would certainly appear to be cruel if viewed from the perspective of the animals. Animals are branded, force-fed, and confined, frequently without enough space to exercise or even turn around. They are kept in close proximity to other animals, which makes them susceptible to infectious diseases—and prompts industrial farms to pump them full of antibiotics. Industrialized agriculture also uses breeding technologies, including genetic engineering and cloning, which aim to maximize meat production. These processes create animals that are, for example, bred to be large and that are then fed so much that they eventually cannot stand up. Chickens packed into close quarters often have their beaks and claws removed to prevent injury to themselves and other chickens. And some animals—veal cattle and geese raised for foie gras—are kept in cages that prevent almost all movement and force-fed in ways that negatively impact their health. Tasty veal comes from anemic calves; and tasty foie gras comes from diseased goose liver.

Animals are crowded into trucks and transported for slaughter in ways that often result in significant stress, with thousands of animals dying on the way.[14] In the slaughterhouses, there are assembly-line processes by which animals are stunned and killed. Some animals are severely injured before they are slaughtered. Animal welfare advocates have posted videos of "downer cattle" (cattle who can't or won't walk under their own power to the slaughterhouse) who are dragged or forklifted into the killing line. Federal law requires that mammals be stunned before killing. But in some cases, there may be a problem in properly stunning the animals. Peter Singer and Jim Mason conclude, "it is probable that anyone who eats meat will, unknowingly, from time to time be eating meat that comes from an animal who died an agonizing death."[15] There are legal and ethical standards that regulate the meat production industry. But the industrial meat production process is focused on speed and efficiency. This is necessary because of the great demand for meat among the general public. In the United States in 2010, the meat industry processed 92 billion pounds of meat, produced from 8.6 billion chickens, 34.3 million cattle, 242 million turkeys, 2.5 million sheep and lambs, and 110.4 million hogs.[16]

The appetite for meat is growing worldwide, with global meat production tripling between 1980 and 2002, and meat production expected to double again by 2050.[17] There will likely be substantial environmental costs from more extensive meat production. But defenders of industrial agriculture argue that if we want to feed a human population of seven billion and counting, we need intensified agricultural procedures. Indeed, if the demand for meat continues to grow, we will need to develop even more efficient and productive ways of raising animals for meat: the global population cannot be fed on meat from free-range farms.

Vegetarian critics of factory farming and the growing appetite for meat argue that there are nutritious and delicious alternatives to meat. They also point out that animal agriculture is hard on the environment. The animals that we consume eat grains, require fresh water, and produce waste. Vegetarians argue that it would be more efficient and less wasteful to feed the growing human population if we ate lower on the food chain. This would leave a smaller ecological footprint and make more grain and other food available to fight human hunger around the world.[18]

Vegetarianism is also connected with other political and moral ideas. Some feminists argue that meat eating is connected to male dominance and the oppression of women; other feminists argue that the idea

Chicks being processed on a conveyor belt in an industrial agriculture operation.

iStockphoto.com/Joan Vicent Cant Roig

of care ethics should encompass care for animals.[19] Vegetarians often cite medical studies that indicate eating meat is not necessary for human health. This is especially true in much of the developed world, where nutritious alternatives are easily found in the typical supermarket. If meat eating is not necessary for human health, then meat becomes a luxury good. And we may then ask whether it is morally justified to cause animal suffering in support of a human indulgence. On the other hand, however, many will argue that human interests matter more than animal interests and that eating meat is easily justified by appealing to basic human interests.

Animal Experimentation

Another issue is the use of animals in scientific and industrial research. Some **animal rights** advocates claim that it is cruel and unnecessary to use animals in scientific and industrial research. Defenders of animal experimentation argue that most of the gains we have made in terms of modern medicine and in safety for modern industrial products are the results of experiments performed on animals.

Animal research has a long history. In the third century BCE in Alexandria, Egypt, animals were used to study bodily functions.[20] Aristotle cut open animals to learn about their structure and development.

The Roman physician Galen used certain animals to show that veins do not carry air but blood. And in 1622, William Harvey used animals to exhibit the circulation of the blood. Animals were used in 1846 to show the effects of anesthesia and in 1878 to demonstrate the relationship between bacteria and disease.[21]

In the twentieth century, research with animals made many advances in medicine possible, from cures for infectious diseases and the development of immunization techniques and antibiotics to the development of surgical procedures. For example, in 1921 an Ontario doctor and his assistant severed the connection between the pancreases and digestive systems of dogs in order to find the substance that controlled diabetes. In so doing, they isolated insulin and thus opened the possibility for treating the millions of people who have that disease.[22] In the development of a polio vaccine, hundreds of primates were killed, but as a result of these experiments, polio is now almost eradicated in the developed world. In 1952, there were fifty-eight thousand cases of this crippling disease in the United States, and in 1984 there were just four. There are now few reported cases.[23] AIDS researchers have used monkeys to test vaccines against HIV, and animal research has been an important part of the study of human paralysis. In 2000, "researchers at the University of Massachusetts Medical School [took] immature cells from the spinal cords of adult rats, induced them to grow, and then implanted them in the gap of the severed spinal cords of paralyzed rats."[24] The rats soon were able to move, stand, and walk. This research has given hope to the three hundred thousand to five hundred thousand people in the United States and more around the world who suffer from spinal-cord damage. It is part of a growing field of tissue engineering in which scientists grow living tissue to replace damaged parts of the human body (see further discussion of biotechnologies such as this in Chapter 18).

Today, laboratory researchers are using leopard frogs to test the pain-killing capacity of morphine, codeine, and Demerol. Japanese medaka fish are being used as a model to determine the cancer-causing properties of substances that are released into rivers and lakes. And research using the giant Israeli scorpion has found a way to use the scorpion venom

to treat brain tumors called gliomas.[25] Other promising research creates genetically modified animals to use as drug-producing machines. For example, scientists have spliced human genes into the DNA of goats, sheep, and pigs. These mammals then secrete therapeutic proteins in their milk. These products can be used to treat hemophilia and cystic fibrosis.[26]

Opposition to animal research dates back to at least the nineteenth century. *Antivivisectionists* campaigned against dissecting live animals and other common practices that inflicted pain on animals. In 1876, the British Parliament passed the first animal welfare act, the Cruelty to Animals Act. A few states in the United States passed anticruelty laws in the nineteenth and early twentieth centuries, but it was not until 1966 that the United States instituted a federal law regulating animal research. The Animal Welfare Act (AWA) of 1966 came about, in part, in response to a national outcry over a family dog, Pepper, who had become a stray and ended up being euthanized in a hospital after being subjected to a laboratory experiment. The AWA set minimum standards for handling cats, dogs, nonhuman primates, rabbits, hamsters, and guinea pigs. It also sought to regulate the use of dogs and cats so that pets like Pepper did not end up in lab experiments.[27] In a 1976 amendment, Congress exempted rats, mice, birds, horses, and farm animals from the protections of the AWA because of problems with enforcement and funding.[28] Such exclusions were reinforced in 2002, in an amendment to the annual farm bill, and subsequent efforts to revoke it have failed in Congress. So while the Animal Welfare Act requires careful treatment of some animals used in research, such as dogs, it does not cover the vast majority of laboratory animals. It is estimated that 95 percent of animals used in laboratory research are mice, rats, and birds, all of which the AWA does not cover.[29] The Animal Legal Defense Fund argues that these animals deserve protection: "Modern science has established that birds, mice, and rats are sentient: capable of experiencing pain, fear, distress, and joy. Recent studies show mice feel pain individually and for others. Yet current AWA exclusions mean researchers are not obligated to consider any alternatives to the unnecessary suffering of these animals."[30]

The Humane Society estimates that some twenty-five million animals in total are used in animal experiments each year in the United States.[31] Opponents of animal research argue that this is too much cruelty in the name of research. Groups like People for the Ethical Treatment of Animals (PETA), the American Society for the Prevention of Cruelty to Animals (ASPCA), and the Humane Society continue to question the need for animal research and argue that alternatives are being neglected. Johns Hopkins University's Center for Alternatives to Animal Testing maintains that "the best science is humane science."[32]

The AWA requires laboratories to report the number of animals used. On university campuses, animal use is monitored by Institutional Animal Care and Use Committees (IACUCs). If you do scientific research involving animals as a student, you may have to learn how to prepare a protocol for approval by an IACUC. According to the U.S. Department of Agriculture, which also monitors the use of animals in research, in 2010 there were more than 21,000 cats, nearly 65,000 dogs, and over 71,000 primates being used in animal research in the United States.[33] One particularly controversial type of medical research involves chimpanzees, an intelligent species of ape that is a close relative of human beings. In 2013, the National Institutes of Health announced that it was going to end chimpanzee research, in part as a result of ethical concerns.[34] The NIH has some 450 chimps, which it plans to maintain in retirement from research. This move was applauded by the Humane Society as well as PETA.

A basic question here is whether we are justified in using nonhuman animals for research that may benefit human beings (and that may also benefit animals, as in veterinary research). A utilitarian approach that focused only on human interests and concerns would claim that if human beings benefit, then such research is justified. A broader utilitarian position that takes animal suffering into account would explore the question of whether the benefits of animal research outweigh the harms of such research upon the animals involved.

While opponents of animal research criticize the large numbers of animals used in research, defenders of animal research point out that these numbers are best interpreted in comparison with other uses of animals. The advocacy group Speaking of Research defends the use of animals in research as follows:

> Scientists in the US use approximately 26 million animals in research, of which only around 1 million are not rats/mice/birds/fish. We use fewer animals in research than the number of ducks eaten per year in this country. We consume over 1,800 times the number of pigs than the number used in research. We eat over 340 chickens for each animal used in a research facility, and almost 9,000 chickens for every animal used in research covered by the Animal Welfare Act. For every animal used in research, it is estimated that 14 more are killed on our roads.[35]

One important moral question is whether the use of animals is really *necessary* to facilitate the medical advances of the past two centuries. Even if it was once necessary, is the use of animals still necessary in today's medical research, given dramatic technological advances? Animal rights activists argue that other sources of information can now be used, including population studies or epidemiology, monitoring of human patients, noninvasive medical imaging devices, autopsies, tissue and cell cultures, in vitro tests, and computer models. Activists also argue that the use of animals as experimental subjects has sometimes actually delayed the use of effective treatment. One example cited in this regard is the development of penicillin for the treatment of bacterial infections. When Alexander Fleming tested penicillin on infected rabbits, it proved ineffective and thus he put it aside for a decade, not knowing that rabbits, unlike humans, excrete penicillin in their urine.[36]

Further, activists argue that those who hold we can use animals in experimentation are inconsistent because they claim both that animals are sufficiently different from humans to be ethically used in experiments, and that they are sufficiently like humans to make the experimental results apply to us. Proponents of animal research answer this criticism by pointing out that mice, although quite different from humans, make very good models for the study of human health simply because we share so many genes with them.[37] Furthermore, they contend, cell culture and computer studies are insufficient. If we moved directly from these cell or computer studies to the use of these drugs or treatments in humans, we would put patients at risk. Take the case of the drug thalidomide, an antinausea drug that was insufficiently tested on animals and ended up causing more than ten thousand babies to be born with birth defects when it was prescribed to pregnant women in the 1950s.

Whether using animals is necessary for various medical advances or whether other kinds of studies can be substituted is an empirical matter. However, most likely some animal research is redundant or simply unnecessary and other methods could serve just as well or better. For example, longitudinal human epidemiological studies provide better and more reliable data than many animal studies—even though human epidemiological studies are harder and more costly to conduct.

A primary ethical concern about the use of nonhuman animals in research involves the extent to which pain is inflicted on these experimental subjects. Sometimes pain is a necessary part of the experiment, such as in pain studies in which the purpose is to find better ways to relieve pain in humans. Those who oppose animal research cite other examples of cruelty to animal subjects. It is not only the physical pain of the experiments they point to, but also psychological pains, such as those that stem from being caged for long periods of time. This is especially true, they argue, for intelligent social animals.

There are at least three positions on the use of nonhuman animals in research. One opposes all use of animals. At the other end of the spectrum is the position that nonhuman animals have no rights or moral standing and thus can be used as we choose. In the middle is the belief that animals have some moral status and thus we should place limits and restrictions on research that is conducted using theses creatures. But even many who support animal rights agree that the use of animals in experimentation can sometimes be ethically justified. In this view, animal research may be justified if it does, in fact, help us develop significant medical advances, if it provides information that cannot be obtained in any other way, and if experiments are conducted with as little discomfort for the animals as possible.

The ethical status of animal experiments for other less vital purposes, such as cosmetics development, is an even more controversial issue.

Endangered Species

International efforts to protect animals often aim to prevent animals from going extinct or losing their natural habitats. International conferences such as the United Nations Convention on International Trade in Endangered Species, held in November 2002, in Santiago, Chile, try to address these problems. Among the issues discussed in Santiago was whether certain African nations should be allowed to sell elephant ivory, which they had stockpiled in the decades before elephants became a legally protected species. The United States prohibits imports of ivory through laws that include the African Elephant Conservation Act of 1989. But ivory remains in demand in various parts of the world, fueled by the illegal hunting, or *poaching*, of elephants. According to a 2013 report from the *Los Angeles Times*, "At least 25,000 African elephants were slaughtered last year [2012] by criminal gangs eager to market the lucrative ivory from their tusks. The poachers' take has risen to alarming levels over the last six years, with about one in 17 wild elephants being felled in 2012, by some estimates. That is a pace that confronts some herds with extinction as elephant births are again being outpaced by the illegal kills." Elephant populations have fallen from 5 million a century ago to fewer than 420,000 today.[38]

In the United States, the protection of wild animals is handled by a patchwork of laws and agencies. For example, the Marine Mammal Protection Act of 1972 "establishe[d] a moratorium on the taking and importation of marine mammals, including parts and products." The Department of the Interior is charged with enforcing the management and protection of sea otters, walruses, polar bears, dugong, and manatees. The 1973 Endangered Species Act protects species threatened with extinction and which the secretaries of the interior or commerce place on a list of endangered species. As we saw at the outset of this chapter, this has been a successful endeavor in the case of the gray wolf, which has increased to a self-sustaining population in the United States.

But the news is not good for other species. In the United States, 623 animal species are listed as either endangered or threatened. This includes 85 mammalian species, such as bears, foxes, manatees, ocelots, otters, panthers, rats, and whales.[39] The International Union for Conservation of Nature (IUCN) produces a "red list" of animal and plant species that are endangered around the world. In its 2012 update, the IUCN reported, "of the 63,837 species assessed, 19,817 are threatened with extinction, including 41 percent of amphibians, 33 percent of reef building corals, 25 percent of mammals, 13 percent of birds, and 30 percent of conifers."[40] Some species, such as the Sumatran rhino, are on the verge of extinction—with only 100 living specimens left in 2012.[41] On the other hand, there has been some good news. After many years of conservation efforts, the mountain gorillas in Eastern Africa are making a comeback, with a 26 percent increase in population, according to a 2010 census.[42]

Some of the successes are due to the fact that there are more protected areas in the world, including wildlife refuges and reserves. Destruction of animal habitat may be the most potent threat to animal species. Although animals can often adapt to gradual changes in their environment, rapid change often makes such adjustment impossible. Many human activities—such as cutting down trees, damming rivers, mining, drilling, and pipeline building—can cause such rapid change. Another cause of species loss is the introduction by humans of non-native species into an environment, thus upsetting a delicate ecological balance. Overexploitation of animal populations is also a source of extinction. Many species of sharks, for example, are being fished into extinction by fishermen—who only want their fins for the Asian delicacy shark-fin soup, although the Chinese government has recently taken action to limit consumption of shark-fin soup.[43] The commercial fishing industry threatens not only the species it harvests for food but also other species caught as "by-catch." Whales, dolphins, and other marine mammals are also threatened by commercial fishing operations. Marine mammals caught in gill nets drown, trapped under water, unable to reach the surface to breathe. According to a 2011 report, "At least 300,000 whales and dolphins a year end up dead in fishing nets alone, as so-called by-catch."[44] Accidental entrapment in fishing nets intended to catch other fish could be remedied by the use of other fishing technologies.

Some point out that species go extinct naturally without human intervention. Through the course of evolution, the species that have been lost have been replaced at a higher rate than they have disappeared, which helps explain the wondrous diversity of our planet's species. But the rate of replacement may no longer be able to keep up because of the accelerated pace of species loss. Those who are concerned about the global ecosystem worry about this loss of biodiversity—both because they value different species for their own sake as having intrinsic value (as we discussed in Chapter 16) and because they see biodiversity as good for the larger ecosystem and thus good for human beings.

While some hold that individual animals have rights or a particular moral status, others believe it is animal species that we ought to protect, not individual animals. It may seem obvious that we have good anthropocentric reasons for preserving animal as well as plant species. We have aesthetic interests in a variety of different life forms. Naturalists, hikers, hunters, and bird watchers know the thrill of being able to observe rare species. The diversity and strangeness of nature are themselves objects of wonder. We also have nutritional and health interests in preserving species. Some species may now seem to have no value for humans, but examples such as the medaka fish and the giant Israeli scorpion, discussed previously, should remind us how important seemingly "minor" species can prove to be for human needs. Loss of species leaves us genetically poorer and more ignorant about the natural systems to which we belong. Animals tell us about ourselves, our history, and how natural systems work or could work. "Destroying species is like tearing pages out of an unread book, written in a language humans hardly know how to read, about the place where they live," writes environmental ethicist Holmes Rolston.[45] If we destroy the mouse lemur, for example, we destroy the modern animal that is closest to the primates from which our own human line evolved.[46]

However, when we ask whether animal species have *moral standing* or *intrinsic value* or even *rights*, we run into puzzling issues. An animal species is not an individual. It is a collection and in itself cannot have the kind of interests or desires that may be the basis for the moral standing or rights of individual animals. Thus, according to philosopher Nicholas Rescher, "moral obligation is … always interest-oriented. But only individuals can be said to have interests; one only has moral obligations to particular individuals or particular groups thereof."[47] If we can have duties to a group of individuals and a species is a group, then we may have duties to species. Still, this does not imply that the species has rights.

Some people challenge the notion of species itself and question whether a species is identical with the individuals that make it up. Consider just what we might mean by a *species*. Is it not a concept constructed by humans as a way of grouping and comparing organisms? Charles Darwin wrote, "I look at the term species, as one arbitrarily given for the sake of convenience to a set of individuals closely resembling each other."[48] If a species is but a class or category of things, then it does not actually exist as an individual thing. If it does not exist, then how could it be said to have interests or rights? However, consider the following possibility, suggested by Holmes Rolston: "A species is a living historical form (Latin *species*), propagated in individual organisms, that flows dynamically over generations."[49] As such, species are units of evolution that exist in time and space. According to Rolston, "a species is a coherent, ongoing form of life expressed in organisms, encoded in gene flow, and shaped by the environment."[50] If we think of species in this way, it may be intelligible to speak of our having duties to an animal species, as forms of life that span millions of years through their genetic legacies. Our duties then would be to a dynamic continuum, a living environmental process, and extinction would be wrong because it ends a "lifeline" or a "unique story." Or, finally, as Rolston writes, "A duty to a species is more like being responsible to a cause than to a person. It is commitment to an *idea*."[51] Although Rolston's explanation of the nature of species and his arguments for the view that we have duties to them are often metaphorical ("story," "lifeline"), his reasoning is nevertheless intriguing. It also raises metaphysical and ontological questions: What kinds of beings exist or have worth?

Those who support animal rights as the rights of individual animals to certain treatment do not always agree in concrete cases with those who believe that it is species that ought to be protected. Suppose, for example, that a certain population of deer is threatened because its numbers have outstripped the food supply and the deer are starving to death. In some such cases, wildlife officials have sought to thin herds by euthanizing animals or allowing for limited hunting. It is thought to be for the sake of the herd that these animals are killed. Those who seek to protect species of animals may endorse such "thinning" if it does, in fact, help preserve the species. But animal rights activists might criticize such an approach and argue that ways should be found to save each of the deer. The animal rights scholar Tom Regan has referred to such holistic claims about animals and ecosystems as a sort of "environmental fascism."[52] By using this phrase, Regan means to connect the idea of controlling animal populations to the policies of fascist governments such as Nazi Germany. If individual animals are thought to have rights, then it would be wrong to cull them for the well-being of the whole.

APPROACHES TO ANIMAL ETHICS

The ethical questions raised by animals are all around us. The moral question of which animals we eat (or do not eat) is something we confront three times a day as we make choices about food. We also likely consume products tested on animals every day. We may occasionally go to zoos, circuses, and rodeos. Some of us own pets or raise domesticated animals. Our lives are intertwined with the lives of animals, both wild and domesticated. The U.S. legal system contains extensive regulations for animal care and to prevent cruelty to animals, and we generally see ourselves as caring about their proper treatment. However, most Americans do not often reflect on the moral status of animals. We are often unclear about the underlying reasons for what we see as acceptable or unacceptable ways of treating them.

One way to get a clearer sense of these reasons is to consider the different ways in which we might value animals. Some people, for example, find pleasure in animals as pets or companions. Others have an economic interest in them, raising and selling them as commodities. Animals are sources of food and clothing. We benefit from them when they are used in experiments to test the safety and effectiveness of drugs, detergents, and cosmetics. Some people enjoy fishing and hunting. Even ecotourism depends upon animals, as people travel to appreciate and photograph animals in their natural habitats. Animals are also sources of pleasure and wonder because of their variety, beauty, and strength.

This suggests the wide range of reasons that animals may be viewed as having value. The most obvious is that animals satisfy human needs: they feed us, clothe us, work for us, and allow some of us to make money. A perspective that focuses on human need and satisfaction is *anthropocentric* (a term we encountered in Chapter 16, when we discussed environmental ethics). It is possible to develop a theory of animal welfare from within anthropocentric concerns. Many farmers, horse racers, and pet owners say they get more out of their animals when they treat them well. Thus, concern for the health and welfare of animals allows us to profit from them. In this view, there is more profit in humane animal treatment than in cruel treatment (although critics of modern industrial farming may disagree). Those who manage herds of wildlife and those who raise and kill animals for human consumption view animals as members of species and as commodities to be managed and controlled.

A further anthropocentric position is that learning to care for animals and treat them well is a natural and normal part of human experience—that humans developed among other animals and in specific relations to them. From a virtue ethics standpoint, one could argue that there are important virtues developed in properly relating to animals. The ethics of hunting mentioned above may be described in virtue ethics terms: that virtuous hunters allow for fair chase, kill in moderation, and kill cleanly and without cruelty. A similar idea can be found in the writing of Immanuel Kant. Kant did not think that animals had any value in themselves, since nonhuman animals are not rational beings. But Kant thought that cruelty to animals was a breeding ground for callousness and indifference to suffering, which tended to make

human beings treat each other more cruelly.[53] From this perspective, moral duties to animals are only indirect: the treatment of animals matters in terms of its impact or potential impact on other humans. We might also recall here that animals are often considered to be property—and that damaging another person's pets or livestock is frequently viewed as a property crime.

A different approach to animal ethics focuses on non-anthropocentric accounts of the value of animals. Such approaches ask about what is in the interest of the animals themselves, apart from human interests. One non-anthropocentric approach focuses on nonhuman animals as *sentient* creatures, which means that they can feel pleasure and pain just as we do. Indeed, many animals, especially the primates that are genetically closest to us, display striking similarities to human beings in their emotions, communication, relationships, and social groups. In this view, we may be obliged to ask whether we are ever justified in causing them physical or psychological suffering, or killing them. A second approach focuses on nonhuman animals as individuals who have interests and rights. Those who focus on animal sentience and welfare tend to operate with a framework that can be defined in consequentialist or utilitarian terms, while those who focus on animal rights more typically appeal to non-consequentialist or deontological theories of value. From the sentience/welfare perspective, we may have to balance the interests of different sentient beings according to some version of the utilitarian calculus: perhaps some nonhuman animals could be killed or used in a cruelty-free fashion for the well-being of a greater number of human animals. But from the animal rights perspective, there is a positive duty to respect the rights of animals—and, more controversially, there may be an active duty to prevent them from being harmed.

Sentience, Equal Consideration, and Animal Welfare

According to some philosophers, **sentience** is the key to the ethical status of animals. If animals have the capacity to feel and sense, then it makes sense to talk about their welfare or well-being, and we should take their sentience into account. This tradition dates back at least to the utilitarian Jeremy Bentham, who wrote that to know the ethical status of animals, we need only ask if they can suffer.[54] Besides feeling pleasure and pain, many animals, especially highly social mammals, seem to experience other types of emotions, such as fear, grief, and anger. While philosopher René Descartes thought that animals were mere machines devoid of an inner sense or consciousness, the welfare approach views animals as sentient, suffering beings. The assumption of sentience is one of the reasons we have laws that protect animals from cruelty. What counts as cruelty, however, is disputed. Whether caging certain animals, for example, is cruel is a matter about which many people disagree.

People also disagree about the reasons why we ought not to be cruel to animals. Some believe—as Kant did—that animal cruelty is wrong because of the effect of cruelty on those who are cruel. They argue that if one is cruel to a sentient animal, then one is more likely to be cruel to people as well. We might also note that those who witness cruelty to animals may be affected by it. They may themselves suffer at seeing an animal suffer, as Gandhi reported previously, after seeing a lamb slaughtered.

However, unless one believes that human suffering is the only suffering that can be bad, then the most obvious reason not to be cruel to animals is that the suffering of the animals is bad for *them*. Whether or not something is cruel to an animal might be determined by the extent of the pain and the purpose for which it is caused. We might speak of some veterinary medical procedures as causing "necessary" pain to heal a sick animal; cruel farming practices might be said to cause animals "unnecessary" pain. Not all pain is bad, even for humans. Pain often tells us of some health problem that can be fixed. The badness of suffering also may be only prima facie bad. The suffering may be worth it—that is, overcome by the good end to be achieved by it. Doing difficult things is sometimes painful, but we think it is sometimes worth the pain. In these cases, we experience not only the pain but also the benefit. In the case of animals, however, they often experience the pain of, say, an experiment performed on them without understanding it or enjoying its potential benefit. Is this ever justified?

In discussions of animal sentience, we also have to ask whether animals have different capacities to feel pain. Nonhuman animals with more developed and complex nervous systems and brains will likely have more capacity to feel pain as well as pleasure of various sorts. To fully decide this question, we would need to think carefully about the physiology of various animals. It might be, for example, that because horses have thick skin, being kicked with spurs does not pain a horse the way it would pain a human.

One significant point of emphasis for the discussion of sentient animals and their welfare is the question of what sorts of experiences are normal and good for animals. The pain of childbirth in humans, for example, is frequently considered part of a productive and joyful activity. But defenders of **animal welfare** will argue that much of the pain and suffering animals are subjected to—especially in intensive animal agriculture—is not productive of any benefit for the animals. Indeed, some argue that the process of intensive animal agriculture as a whole is wrong because it continuously violates the normal functioning of the animals. This happens, for example, when animals are kept confined in small spaces, packed together in intensive feeding operations, and when their bodies are altered. Previously, we discussed practices such as those in which chickens' beaks are cropped, horns are removed from cattle, veal calves are confined and fed a diet that makes them anemic, and geese are force-fed a diet that sickens them in order to produce foie gras. These operations do not respect what philosopher Martha Nussbaum calls "the dignity of the species." Nussbaum claims that sentient animals should be given the opportunity to live according to the natural dignity of their species. Nussbaum concludes: "No sentient animal should be cut off from the chance for a flourishing life, a life with the type of dignity relevant to that species ... all sentient animals should enjoy certain positive opportunities to flourish."[55] Of course, there is an open and complex question about what it means for an animal to flourish. Should domesticated cats and dogs be allowed to reproduce unchecked; in other words, does spaying and neutering prevent them from flourishing? If we don't spay and neuter our pets, how will we deal with overpopulation?

Further, should animals be allowed to roam freely, or is it permissible to confine them? And so on. What counts as living according to the natural dignity of a species remains open to debate.

In the wild, it is a fact of life that animals feed on and cause pain to one another. Predation prevails. Carnivores kill for food. The fawn is eaten by the cougar. Natural processes such as floods, fires, droughts, and volcanic eruptions also contribute to animal suffering and death. If animal suffering is important, then are we ethically obligated to lessen it in cases where we could do so? For example, in 1986 the Hubbard Glacier in Alaska began to move, and in a few weeks it had sealed off a fjord. As freshwater runoff poured into the enclosed water, its salinity decreased, threatening the lives of porpoises and harbor seals that were trapped inside by the closure. Some people wanted to rescue the animals, while others held that this was a natural event that should be allowed to run its course.[56]

We tend to think that we have a greater obligation not to *cause* pain or harm than we do to *relieve* it. In special cases, however, we may have a duty to relieve pain or prevent the harm. A lifeguard may have an obligation to rescue a drowning swimmer that the ordinary bystander does not. A parent has more obligation to prevent harm to his or her child than a stranger does. In the case of nonhuman animals, do we have similar obligations to prevent harms? Do we feel constrained to prevent the pain and deaths of animals in the wild? In general, it would seem that although we may choose to do so out of sympathy, we may not be obligated to do so. At least the obligation to prevent the harm seems less stringent than the obligation not to cause a similar harm. But if there is this moral difference between preventing and causing harm, then while we may be justified in *allowing* animals in the wild to die or suffer pain, it does not follow that we are justified in *causing* similar pains or harms to them. Just because nature is cruel does not necessarily give us the right to be so.

The animal welfare focus is most closely associated with the work of the influential ethicist Peter Singer, as articulated in his 1975 book, *Animal Liberation.* Singer maintains that since animals are sentient, their interests should be given equal consideration to those of humans. Singer does not mean that animals should be treated as exactly equal to humans but, rather, that animal interests should be taken into account. Animals may have different interests than we do, but that does not mean that their interests may be ignored. Philosopher David De Grazia has explained the idea of equal consideration as follows: "equal consideration, whether for humans or animals, means in some way giving equal moral weight to the relevantly similar interests of different individuals."[57] De Grazia goes on to explain that if we don't consider relevantly similar interests equally, we are guilty of creating a differential hierarchy of moral status that is elitist and resembles caste systems or aristocracies.

Singer rejects such an elitist or hierarchical account of animal interests as the result of a self-interested and arbitrary way of drawing moral lines. Singer maintains that not giving equal consideration to the interests of animals is **speciesism**, an objectionable attitude similar to racism or sexism. Speciesism is objectionable because it involves treating animals badly simply because they are members of a different species and giving preference to members of our own species simply because we are human beings.[58] But on what grounds is this objectionable? According to Singer, having interests is connected to the ability to feel pleasure and pain, because the pleasure is derived from the satisfaction of an interest. Thus, from Singer's standpoint, animal interests should be considered because there is no non-speciesist way to draw the line between animal interests and human interests. Both humans and animals seek pleasure and avoid pain; valuing human pleasure over animal pleasure, for example, is arbitrary and unjustifiable. (Animals are different from plants in this regard. Plants have things that are *in their interest* even though they do not *have interests*.) Singer concludes that among animals that have relevantly similar interests, these interests should be given equal consideration. Not everyone accepts this idea, of course. Philosopher, Bonnie Steinbock, for example, argues that it is appropriate to give preference to the interests of humans. Her argument focuses on specific mental capacities that human beings have, which she views as superior to the mere sentience of nonhuman animals. She writes, "certain capacities, which seem to be unique to human beings, entitle their possessors to a privileged position in the moral community."[59] Among those capacities may be the ability to think about morality and to act on moral responsibility—which seems to involve more than the bare ability to experience pleasure and pain and to have interests.

Animal Rights

It is one thing to say that the suffering of a nonhuman animal is a bad thing in itself. It is another to say that nonhuman animals have a *right* not to be caused to suffer or feel pain. To consider the question of animal rights, we need to first review our discussions about what a right is and what it means to have a right. A *right* is generally defined as a strong and *legitimate claim* that can be made by a claimant against someone. Rights claims are often grounded in ideas about what is natural or fitting, as we saw in our discussion on natural law and natural rights in Chapter 7. Thus, if I claim a right to freedom of speech, I am asserting my legitimate claim against anyone who would prevent me from speaking out, and I am claiming that there is something about me as a human being that makes my freedom of speech essential. A person can claim a right to have or be given something (a positive right) as well as a right not to be prevented from doing something (a negative right). Legal rights are claims that the law recognizes and enforces. However, we also hold that there are moral rights—in other words, things we can rightly claim even if the law does not enforce the claim.

Just who can legitimately claim a moral right to something, and on what grounds? One might think that to be the kind of being who can have rights, one must be able to claim them and understand them. If this were so, then the cat who has left money in a will would not have a right to it because the cat does not understand that it has such a right and could not claim that its rights have been violated if the money is withheld. But if the capacity to understand or claim a right is the only thing that matters, then we might have to conclude that human infants have no rights—to inherit money or be protected from abuse and neglect—because they cannot understand or

claim them. But we generally think that infants have a right to care from their parents even if they do not understand this right and cannot claim it. We make similar claims for the rights of the developmentally disabled, who are also often unable to claim or understand their rights. One might think that only **moral agents**—those beings who can make and act upon moral judgments—have rights. According to this view, only if one is a full member of the moral community with duties and responsibilities does one have rights. On the other hand, it is not unreasonable to think that this is too stringent a requirement. Perhaps it is sufficient for one to be a moral patient in order to be the type of being who can have rights. A **moral patient** is an object of moral concern, the kind of being who matters morally. Moral patients have rights but they do not have correlated responsibilities. Thus, children have rights but are not considered to be full moral agents; we ought not to harm them, but they are viewed as less than fully responsible. As we considered in the previous chapter, it might be that some trees can be thought to be moral patients; if so, they could be said to have rights. If this does not seem to be correct, then what other reasons can be given for why a being might have rights?

We could argue that it is just because they can feel pain that sentient beings have a *right not to suffer*, or at least not to suffer needlessly. This would mean that others have a *duty* with regard to this claim. However, we may have duties not to cause pain needlessly to animals even if they have no *right* not to be treated in ways that cause them pain. We have many duties to do or not do this or that, and those duties are not directly a matter of respecting anyone's rights. For example, I may have a duty not to purchase and then destroy a famous and architecturally important building—but not because the building has a right to exist. Thus, from the fact that we have duties to animals—not to make them suffer needlessly, for example—we cannot necessarily conclude that they have rights. If we want to argue for this view, then we would need to make a clearer connection between duties and rights or to show why some particular duties also imply rights. Not all duties are a function of rights, as I might have a duty to develop my talents even though no one has a right that I do so. However, having a right seems to entail that someone has a duty to protect that right.

As we have seen, some philosophers have pointed to the fact that animals have *interests* as a basis for asserting that they have rights. To have an interest in something is usually thought to require consciousness of that thing as well as desire for it. A being that has a capacity for conscious desire is a being that can have rights, according to this position. Thus, the philosopher Joel Feinberg says that it is because nonhuman animals have "conscious wishes, desires, and hopes; ... urges and impulses" that they are the kind of beings who can have rights.[60] It is these psychological capacities that make animals capable of having rights to certain treatment, according to this view. Similarly, Tom Regan argues that nonhuman animals have rights just as we do because they are what he calls the "subject of a life."[61] The idea is similar to Feinberg's in that it is the fact that animals have an inner life, which includes conscious desires and wants, that is the basis for their status as rights possessors. Nonhuman animals differ among themselves in their capacity to have these various psychological experiences, and it probably parallels the development and complexity of their nervous systems. A dog may be able to experience fear, but most probably the flea on its ear does not. In more ambiguous cases, however, drawing such distinctions may prove difficult in practice, when we would have to determine the character of a particular animal's inner life. The more serious challenge for such views is to support the more basic claim that inner psychic states are a moral foundation for rights.

We noted previously that Peter Singer maintains that because the interests of animals are similar to ours, they ought to be given equal weight. This does not mean, in his view, that animals have a *right* to whatever we have a right to. It would make no sense to say that a pig or horse has a right to vote, because it has no interest in voting nor does it have the capacity to vote. However, according to Singer, it would make sense to say that we ought to give equal consideration to the pig's suffering. Pigs ought not be made to suffer needlessly to satisfy human whims. But Singer is reluctant to say that animals have rights. As a utilitarian, Singer avoids speaking of rights (you might recall from Chapter 7 that the utilitarian Jeremy Bentham described rights as "nonsense upon stilts"). This can lead to some confusion. Singer has explained, for example, that the "animal rights movement" has no need of the concept of rights.[62] The point here is that the phrase "animal rights" is sometimes used in popular parlance as an umbrella term that encompasses a variety of philosophical perspectives, including both utilitarian and non-consequentialist positions.

Others argue that animals need not be treated as equal to humans and that their interests ought not to be given equal weight with ours. It is because of the difference in species' *abilities* and *potentialities* that animals are a lesser form of being, according to these views. This does not mean, however, that animals' interests ought to be disregarded. It may mean that peripheral or minor interests of human beings should not override more serious interests of animals. It is one thing to say that animals may be used if necessary for experiments that will save the lives of human beings and quite another to say that they may be harmed for the testing of cosmetics or clothing that is not important for human life. Whether this position would provide a sufficient basis for vegetarianism might then depend on the importance of animal protein to human health, for example, and whether animals could be raised humanely for food.

NOTES

1. Peter Steinhart, *The Company of Wolves* (New York: Random House, 1996), chap. 7.
2. Combining numbers from the following sources: "Wolf Hunting and Trapping," Wisconsin Department of Natural Resources (DNR), accessed April 5, 2013, http://dnr.wi.gov/topic/hunt/wolf.html; "Wolf Hunting," Minnesota DNR, accessed April 5, 2013, http://www.dnr.state.mn.us/hunting/wolf/index.html; "More than 550 Wolves Taken by Hunters and Trappers in Rockies," *Los Angeles Times*, March 6, 2013, accessed April 5, 2013, http://articles.latimes.com/2013/mar/06/nation/la-na-nn-wolves-idaho-montana-hunt-trap-20130305; "Wolf Harvest," Idaho Fish & Game, accessed April 5, 2013, http://fishandgame.idaho.gov/public/hunt/?getPage=121
3. "Top Ten Reasons to Oppose Public Lands Trapping," Footloose Montana, accessed April 5, 2013, http://www.footloosemontana.org/the-issue-2/top-ten-reasons/
4. "The Killing Agency: Wildlife Services' Brutal Methods Leave a Trail of Animal Death," *Sacramento Bee*, April 29, 2012, accessed April 5, 2013, http://www.sacbee.com/2012/

04/28/4450678/the-killing-agency-wildlife-services.html
#storylink=cpy#storylink=cpy

5. Jim Posewitz, *Beyond Fair Chase* (Guilford, CT: Globe Pequot, 1994), 57.

6. Wayne Pacelle, "Stacking the Hunt," *New York Times*, December 9, 2003, A29.

7. "Fact Sheet on Bear Baiting," Humane Society, November 2, 2009 accessed April 5, 2013, http://www.humanesociety .org/issues/bear_hunting/facts/bear_baiting_fact_sheet.html

8. "Online Bear Baiting Clinic: Ethics and Responsibilities," Alaska Department of Fish and Game, accessed April 5, 2013, http://www.adfg.alaska.gov/index.cfm?adfg= bearbaiting.ethics

9. "Palin and the Wolves," *Daily Beast*, April 9, 2009, accessed April 5, 2013, http://www.thedailybeast.com/newsweek/ 2009/04/09/palin-and-the-wolves.html

10. Defenders of Wildlife, *Aerial Hunting FAQs*, accessed April 5, 2013, http://www.defenders.org/sites/default/files/ publications/aerial_hunting_q_and_a.pdf

11. Leo Tolstoy, "The First Step," in *Cultural Encyclopedia of Vegetarianism*, ed. Margaret Puskar-Pasewicz (Santa Barbara, CA: ABC-CLIO), 248.

12. Mohandas K. Gandhi, *An Autobiography: The Story of My Experiments With Truth* (Boston: Beacon Press, 1993), 235.

13. Michael Martin, "A Critique of Moral Vegetarianism," *Reason Papers* No. 3 (Fall 1976) 13–43.

14. See Erik Marcus, *Meat Market: Animals Ethics, and Money* (Boston: Brio Press, 2005), 33.

15. See Peter Singer and Jim Mason, *The Ethics of What We Eat: Why Our Food Choices Matter* (New York: Rodale, 2006), 67–68.

16. "The United States Meat Industry at a Glance," American Meat Institute, accessed April 5, 2013, http://www.meatami .com/ht/d/sp/i/47465/pid/47465

17. United Nations, *Livestock in a Changing Landscape* (April 2008), accessed April 5, 2013, http://unesdoc.unesco.org/ images/0015/001591/159194e.pdf

18. See James Rachels, "Vegetarianism and 'the Other Weight Problem,'" in *World Hunger and Moral Obligation,* eds. William Aiken and Hugh LaFollette (Englewood Cliffs, NJ: Prentice Hall, 1977).

19. See Carol J. Adams, *The Sexual Politics of Meat: A Feminist-Vegetarian Critical Theory* (New York: Continuum, 1990) or Josephine Donovan and Carol J. Adams, eds., *The Feminist Care Tradition in Animal Ethics: A Reader* (New York: Columbia University Press, 2007).

20. Jerod M. Loeb, William R. Hendee, Steven J. Smith, and M. Roy Schwarz, "Human vs. Animal Rights: In Defense of Animal Research," *Journal of the American Medical Association* 262, no. 19 (November 17, 1989), 2716–20.

21. Ibid.

22. John F. Lauerman, "Animal Research," *Harvard Magazine* (January–February 1999), 49–57.

23. Ibid.; see also http://apps.who.int/immunization_monitoring/ globalsummary/timeseries/tsincidencepolio.html

24. Holcomb B. Noble, "Rat Studies Raise Hope of Conquering Paralysis," *New York Times*, January 25, 2000, D7.

25. "Radioactive Scorpion Venom for Fighting Cancer," *Science Daily*, June 27, 2006, accessed April 5, 2013, http://www .sciencedaily.com/releases/2006/06/060627174755.htm

26. Tom Abate, "Biotech Firms Transforming Animals into Drug-Producing Machines," *San Francisco Chronicle*, January 25, 2000, B1.

27. "Legislative History of the Animal Welfare Act," U.S. Department of Agriculture, March 26, 2012, accessed June 18, 2013, http://www.nal.usda.gov/awic/pubs/AWA2007/ intro.shtml

28. Lauerman, "Animal Research," op. cit., 51.

29. "Rats, Mice, and Birds Deserve Protection under the Animal Welfare Act," PETA, accessed April 5, 2013, http://www .peta.org/features/unc-awa.aspx

30. "Animal Legal Defense Fund Urges Support of House Bill to Restore Animal Welfare Act," ALDF, December 20, 2012, accessed April 5, 2013, http://aldf.org/article.php?id=2280

31. "Biomedical Research," Humane Society, accessed April 5, 2013, http://www.humanesociety.org/issues/ biomedical_research/

32. Center for Alternatives to Animal Testing, accessed April 5, 2013, http://caat.jhsph.edu/

33. *Annual Report Animal Usage by Fiscal Year* (2010), U.S. Department of Agriculture, accessed April 5, 2013, http:// www.aphis.usda.gov/animal_welfare/efoia/downloads/ 2010_Animals_Used_In_Research.pdf

34. James Gorman, "Agency Moves to Retire Most Research Chimps," *New York Times*, January 22, 2013, accessed April 5, 2013, http://www.nytimes.com/2013/01/23/science/ nih-moves-to-retire-most-chimps-used-in-research.html?_r=0

35. "US Statistics," Speaking of Research, accessed April 5, 2013, http://speakingofresearch.com/facts/statistics/

36. See "Historical Breakthroughs Attributed to Animals," Americans for Medical Advancement, http://www .curedisease.com/historical-breakthroughs.html

37. Lauerman, "Animal Research." op. cit.

38. Carol J. Williams, "Thriving Illicit Ivory Trade Decimating African Elephant Herds," *Los Angeles Times*, March 13, 2013, accessed April 5, 2013, http://www.latimes.com/ news/world/worldnow/la-fg-wn-endangered-species-ivory-20130305,0,5204939.story

39. "Summary of Listed Species Listed Populations and Recovery Plans," U.S. Fish and Wildlife Service, accessed June 21, 2013, http://ecos.fws.gov/tess_public/pub/boxScore.jsp

40. "Securing the Web of Life," International Union for Conservation of Nature (IUCN), June 2012, accessed April 5, 2013, http://www.iucnredlist.org/news/securing-the-web-of-life

41. "Last Chance for the Sumatran Rhino," IUCN, April 4, 2013, accessed April 5, 2013, http://www.iucn.org/?12741/ Last-chance-for-the-Sumatran-rhino

42. "Mountain Gorilla Census Results: Population Increases by 26.3%," Gorilla.CD, December 15, 2010, accessed April 5, 2013, http://gorillacd.org/2010/12/15/ mountain-gorilla-census-results-population-increases-by-263/

43. "Fishing Is Pushing Sharks Closer to Extinction," *Washington Post*, March 1, 2013, accessed April 5, 2013, http:// articles.washingtonpost.com/2013-03-01/national/ 37365646_1_fin-soup-shark-species-juliet-eilperin

44. "Whales & Dolphins Need More Protected Areas," IUCN, September 5, 2011, accessed April 5, 2013, http://www .iucn.org/?8179/Whales–dolphins-need-more-protected-areas

45. Holmes Rolston III, *Environmental Ethics* (Philadelphia: Temple University Press, 1988), 129.

46. Ibid.
47. Nicholas Rescher, "Why Save Endangered Species?" in *Unpopular Essays on Technological Progress* (Pittsburgh: University of Pittsburgh Press, 1980), 83. A similar point is made by Tom Regan, *The Case for Animal Rights* (Berkeley: University of California Press, 1983), 359, and Joel Feinberg, "Rights of Animals and Unborn Generations," in Tom Regan and Peter Singer (Eds.), *Animal Rights and Human Obligations* (Englewood Cliffs, NJ: Prentice Hall, 1976), 55–56.
48. Charles Darwin, *The Origin of Species* (Baltimore: Penguin, 1968), 108.
49. Holmes Rolston III, op. cit., 135.
50. Ibid., 136.
51. Ibid., 145.
52. Tom Regan, *The Case for Animal Rights* (Berkeley: University of California Press, 1983), 361–62.
53. See Immanuel Kant, "Duties to Animals and Spirits," in *Lectures on Ethics* (Cambridge: Cambridge University Press, 1997); and see Regan's discussion in *The Case for Animal Rights*.
54. Jeremy Bentham, *Introduction to the Principles of Morals and Legislation* (1789), chap. 17.
55. Martha C. Nussbaum, *Frontiers of Justice: Disability, Nationality, and Species Membership* (Cambridge, MA: Harvard University Press, 2006), 351.
56. Reported by Holmes Rolston III in *Environmental Ethics: Duties to and Values in the Natural World* (Philadelphia: Temple University Press, 1988), 50.
57. David De Grazia, *Taking Animals Seriously: Mental Life and Moral Status* (Cambridge: Cambridge University Press, 1996), 46.
58. Peter Singer, *Animal Liberation: A New Ethic for Our Treatment of Animals* (New York: Random House, 1975). Singer was not the first to use the term *speciesism*. Ryder also used it in his work *Victims of Science* (London: Davis-Poynter, 1975).
59. Bonnie Steinbock, "Speciesism and the Idea of Equality" *Philosophy* 53, no. 204 (April 1978): 253.
60. Joel Feinberg, "The Rights of Animals and Unborn Generations," op cit., 195.
61. Tom Regan, *The Case for Animal Rights* (Berkeley: University of California Press, 1983).
62. Peter Singer, "Animal Liberation at 30," *New York Review of Books*, May 15, 2003, accessed April 5, 2013, http://www.nybooks.com/articles/archives/2003/may/15/animal-liberation-at-30/?pagination=false#fn5-501709338

REVIEW EXERCISES

1. In your view, is it acceptable to hunt animals? Which animals: bears, wolves, elephants, or whales? Does the method matter? Is trapping or aerial hunting acceptable? Justify your answers using concepts from the chapter.
2. Evaluate moral arguments in defense of vegetarianism. Are these arguments persuasive?
3. What counts as cruelty to animals? What's wrong with cruelty to animals?
4. What is the meaning of the term *rights*? Does it make sense to apply this term to animals? Why or why not?
5. For a being to be the kind of being that can have rights, is it necessary that it be able to claim them? That it be a moral agent? Why or why not? What about infants and cognitively disabled humans?
6. Do animals have interests? Are these interests worth consideration? Support your answer, drawing on the discussion of interests in the text.
7. Describe the issues involved in the debate over whether nonhuman animals' interests ought to be treated equally with those of humans.
8. List some anthropocentric reasons for preserving animal species.
9. What problems does the meaning of the term *species* raise for deciding whether animal species have moral standing of some sort?
10. What reasons do supporters give for using nonhuman animals in experimental research? What objections to this practice do their opponents raise? Be sure your answer makes reference to issues such as the extent and purpose of pain.

DISCUSSION CASES

1. **Animal Experimentation.** Antonio wants to become a doctor and is pursuing a premed major. He has dissected frogs and worms in some of his biology classes. He knows that animal research has produced good outcomes for human beings, including antibiotics and other cures for diseases. Antonio's roommate, Joseph, is a vegetarian who is opposed to all animal research. One night, as Joseph is cooking some tofu, he says, "Look Antonio, there are all kinds of healthy alternatives to eating

meat. There are also alternatives to using animals in research. You can now use computer models to accomplish most of the same outcomes." Antonio disagrees. "Maybe vegetarian food can be nutritious. But even if there were other ways to do medical research, I'd want to be sure that a drug or treatment really worked on an animal before I used it on a human being."

Whose position is closest to your own? Which ways of treating animals do you find acceptable, and which do you find unacceptable? Is animal experimentation ever justified? If so, on what grounds? What about eating meat?

2. **People Versus the Gorilla.** Many of the world's few remaining mountain gorillas are located in the thirty-thousand-acre Parc des Volcans in the small African country of Rwanda. Rwanda has the highest population density in Africa. Most people live on small farms. To this population, the Parc des Volcans represents valuable land that could be used for farming to feed an expanding human population. Opening the park to development could support thirty-six thousand people on subsistence farms. But it would have an adverse impact on the gorilla population.

Should the park be maintained as a way to preserve the gorillas, or should it be given to the people for farming? To what extent, if any, do humans have an obligation to look for new and creative ways to meet their own needs in order to protect the interests of animals?

3. **What Is a Panther Worth?** The Florida panther is an endangered species. Not long ago, one of these animals was hit by a car and seriously injured. He was taken to the state university veterinary medical school, where steel plates were inserted in both legs, his right foot was rebuilt, and he had other expensive treatment. The panther was one of dozens that had been injured or killed on Florida's highways in recent years. As a result, some members of the Florida legislature introduced a proposal that would allocate $27 million to build forty bridges that would allow panthers to move about without the threat of car injuries and death. Those who support the measure point out that the Florida panther is unique and can survive only in swampland near the Everglades. Those who oppose the measure argue that the money could be better spent on education, needed highway repairs, or other projects.

Should the state spend this amount of money to save the Florida panther from extinction? Why or why not?

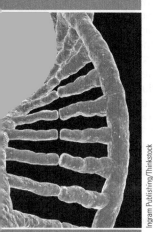

Ingram Publishing/Thinkstock

18 Biotechnology and Bioengineering

Learning Outcomes

After reading this chapter, you should be able to:

- Understand current issues in biotechnology and bioengineering including athletic and cognitive enhancements, stem cell research, cloning, genetic engineering, and genetically modified organisms.

- Draw connections between the ethical challenges of biotechnology and ethical issues related to abortion, animal welfare, and personal privacy.

- Examine the difference between a therapy and an enhancement, with respect to various applications of biotechnology and bioengineering.

- Explain how consequentialist arguments about costs and benefits apply to bioengineering and biotechnology.

- Critically examine moral objections to "playing God" and the idea of the "wisdom of repugnance."

- Analyze concerns and hopes for a future in which human beings have more control over biology.

- Defend a thesis with regard to biotechnology and bioengineering.

For more than seventeen years, Jan Scheuermann has suffered from degenerative brain disease that has left her paralyzed from the neck down. In 2012, however, a revolutionary new technology allowed Scheuermann to use a robotic arm to feed herself for the first time in years. By implanting special electrodes in Scheuermann's brain, her doctors were able to create a "brain-computer interface" and connect it to the robotic arm. With practice, Scheuermann learned to control the arm using only her thoughts. This technological feat might sound like science fiction. But it is part of a set of rapidly advancing technologies produced by engineers and doctors who are finding ways to cure disease and improve human capacities. Another example is the development of an artificial eye—a retinal implant—that allows blind people to see.[1] Other surgeries and interventions allow us to radically alter our bodies, including, for example, sex reassignment surgery. In the future, **regenerative medicine** and genetic interventions may be able to extend our life spans, screen out deadly genetic mutations, or allow us to grow replacement organs. Performance- and mood-enhancing drugs may make us stronger, improve memory and concentration, and help us achieve better emotional health. Other biotechnologies may make it possible to extend our physical capacities—to walk, run, or swim—as the human body has never done before.

While many emerging biotechnologies, such as the brain-computer interface that allowed Jan Scheuermann to feed herself, have obvious therapeutic applications, some worry that these technologies will be abused in ways that are unethical. Others argue that a new form of humanity is looming on the horizon—one that is genetically, chemically,

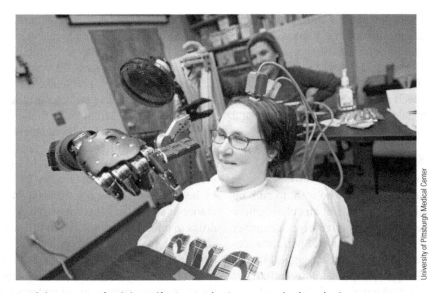

University of Pittsburgh Medical Center

Jan Scheuermann feeds herself using a robotic arm attached to a brain-computer interface.

and mechanically enhanced. Some view the "transhuman" or "posthuman" future as a positive development; others worry that we are not wise or virtuous enough to properly handle these new technologies.

Consider, for example, the speed and variety of recent advances in mind-computer interfacing. One recent technological feat allowed one rat to control the actions of another rat by way of implants connecting the two animals' brains.[2] And researchers at Harvard have found a way to connect human brain waves—detected by electrodes placed on the human's skull—to the nerves of a rat so that the human subject is able to make the rat's tail move by thought-power.[3] While such experiments might raise concerns from the standpoint of animal ethics, they also suggest other moral concerns. What if biotechnology and bioengineering could be used in ways that provide control over other human beings? This is related to a concern of those who oppose human cloning; that biotechnologies should not be used in ways that engineer human beings or that create human beings for the purpose of organ harvesting. The worry is that in our pursuit of medical advancement, we will lose sight of those features of humanity that give life its worth and dignity.

Biotechnology can be broadly defined as the manipulation of biological systems and organisms through technological means. Biotechnology includes performance-enhancing drugs, **stem cell research**, genetic engineering, cloning, and **genetic screening**. These technologies can be applied, for example, in human reproduction to select or even engineer desired offspring. They can also be applied to animals, in scientific breeding practices to increase meat production. And plants grown for food can be genetically modified in ways that improve crop yields. **Bioengineering** uses biological science to design machines and alter biological systems for a range of purposes, including the use of machines to supplement or enhance biological organisms as in the case of the brain-computer interface discussed previously.

Some biotechnologies have strikingly therapeutic effects, for example, giving paralyzed people the ability to feed themselves. A **therapy** is an intervention that helps restore normal function to an organism that is suffering from an impairment due to disease or injury. But other technologies may be viewed as enhancements, which may be seen to give some people (fair or unfair) advantages over others. An **enhancement** is the result of a technology that provides more than merely normal function. One of the ethical questions to be discussed here is whether there is anything wrong with enhancements. While we might accept such uses of technology out of respect for individuals' rights to control their own bodies, some biotech enhancements appear to raise serious ethical questions about what is "natural" and about the value and nature of human life.

CURRENT ISSUES
Athletic and Cognitive Enhancement

The use of steroids by athletes who want to bulk up and build strength is a clear case of an enhancement rather than a therapy. There have been a number of controversies regarding the use of performance-enhancing substances by some of the biggest names in sports, such as baseball superstar Barry Bonds and Olympic sprinter Marion Jones. In 2013, cyclist Lance Armstrong admitted that he had used performance enhancements, including blood doping, in his seven triumphs in the Tour de France. Most athletic organizations view the use of performance enhancements as an immoral action that undermines fair play and allows some athletes with sufficient money and connections to buy their victories. But consider the case of Oscar Pistorius, the so-called "blade runner" of track and field sports. Pistorius was born without fibulas, the bones in his lower legs. On the track, he uses prosthetic legs made out of carbon fiber blades, which have allowed him to compete (and win medals) in world events for able-bodied athletes. After some controversy, the International Olympic Committee permitted him to run the 400-meter race in the London Olympics of 2012. Some critics have complained that Pistorius's prosthetic legs give him an unfair advantage. *Scientific American* examined the issue and concluded that Pistorius uses less energy, due to the elastic action of the blades.[4] His lower "legs" are lighter than those of other runners, and they do not tire. On the other hand, Pistorius must compensate for the light springiness of his blades by bearing down on his prostheses in a way that no other runner must do. The question of whether Pistorius gets *unfair* advantage is not easy to determine. The distinction between therapy and enhancement is a bit fuzzy, as we can see in the Pistorius case. Are Pistorius's blades merely a therapeutic treatment or do they enhance his abilities in immoral ways? (As of February 2013, a more serious moral question surrounded Pistorius and may prevent him from competing in future athletic events: he was charged with the murder of his girlfriend, Reeva Steenkamp.)

There is no denying that therapeutic technologies can be used or abused in ways that enhance performance. One controversial development is in the field of so-called "cognitive enhancements" or "smart drugs." Drugs such as Ritalin and Adderall, which are prescribed for diseases such as ADHD, can be used by healthy people in ways that may improve performance at school and at work. It is illegal to use these drugs to enhance performance in this way, and critics warn that such nontherapeutic use is addictive and dangerous. At least one suicide has been connected with abuse of Adderall.[5] But defenders argue that these drugs can provide an advantage in highly competitive fields such as academia and business. Others argue that smart drugs are less like steroids than they are like caffeine or nicotine. In any case, there is no clear proof that such drugs actually work to consistently improve cognitive performance. "As useful as they may be during the occasional deadline crunch, no study has linked Ritalin or Adderall use in people without ADHD to sustained increases in things like grades or performance reviews."[6]

Nevertheless, other nonpharmaceutical technologies have been developed that purport to stimulate cognitive ability. One of these is the use of *transcranial direct-current stimulation*—the application of electric current to the brain. This technology has therapeutic applications, for example, in treating depression or helping cognitive recovery after a stroke. But apparently electric stimulation of the brain can also be used to enhance the cognitive abilities of healthy individuals. Some studies suggest that transcranial stimulation can help increase memory and learning, producing, for example, a greater capacity to learn a new language or mathematical skill.[7] Would it be ethical to use such a technology to enhance your ability to learn new information?

Stem Cell Research

Another current issue in bioethics is embryonic stem cell research. In recent years, several public figures have made public appeals for the funding of stem cell research with its potential for treating or curing certain serious diseases. For example, Mary Tyler Moore, who has type I (insulin-dependent) diabetes and chairs the Juvenile Diabetes Foundation, brought children with this condition to testify in hearings before Congress. These children are not able to produce enough insulin to change nutrients into the energy needed for life; they must monitor their blood sugar and be injected with manufactured insulin every day. Other advocates hope that stem cell research could lead to a cure for Alzheimer's disease, and the actor Michael J. Fox has promoted this research as a possible cure for Parkinson's disease, with which he is afflicted. Before he died, *Superman* star Christopher Reeve lobbied for this research as a possible treatment for spinal cord injuries such as his.

Stem cell research is part of the field of *regenerative medicine*. One long-term goal of such research is to produce new cells, tissues, and organs that can be used to treat disease or injury. Certain stem cell therapies have been around for some time. One example is the transplantation of the stem cells present in bone marrow to treat certain forms of leukemia. Another more recent example is the extraction from cadavers of certain parts of the human pancreas for an experimental treatment of diabetes.[8]

In 2012, scientists were able to find a way to grow a replacement windpipe for a patient with a tracheal tumor. They induced stem cells from the patient's own bone marrow to grow on an artificial windpipe scaffolding, which ensured that the plastic scaffolding would not be rejected by the body's immune response. The stem cells went on to develop into the kind of tissue that is found in normal windpipes. The patient has gone on to recover with the plastic scaffolding in place and the stem cells developing into the appropriate form of tissue.[9] A similar procedure was recently employed to grow a replacement windpipe for a two-year-old girl who was born without a windpipe—the youngest person ever to undergo the procedure and the first in the United States.[10] Unfortunately, the child died of complications in July 2013.[11]

Stem cells are found in bone marrow and in other parts of the body. These cells have not yet developed into specific skin, muscle, or other types of body cells and tissues. The most potent or flexible type of stem cells are embryonic stem cells. These are the undifferentiated cells of the early embryo in the first weeks of development, called a *blastocyst*. In human beings, these cells remain undifferentiated for approximately five to seven days after an egg is fertilized. They can be removed and placed in a culture where they will continue to divide. They are the cells from which all of the body's organs develop. For this reason, they are called *pluripotent*, which means that they have the potential to develop into a variety of cells and tissues. However, once removed in this manner, these cells can no longer develop into a fetus.

In the case of these embryonic stem cells, researchers hope to be able to learn how to control the process of their differentiation so as to be able to provoke them to become, for example, the insulin-producing beta cells of the pancreas (thus effecting the cure of diabetes) or neurons for the treatment of spinal cord injuries. Stem cells themselves cannot be directly implanted into the pancreas, however, because they can cause cancerous tumors to develop. Thus it is necessary to take steps to direct the development of the cells, to ensure they become the specialized cells that are needed.

There are many practical challenges with stem cell treatments, among which are efficiently obtaining the cells and directing and controlling their specialization. Some researchers have pointed out that in the case of some diseases such as Lou Gehrig's disease (amyotrophic lateral sclerosis, or ALS) and other autoimmune diseases, replacing the damaged cells may not help the patient because it is "the cellular environment" that is the problem, and the newly added cells could be damaged as well. In these cases, the source of the problem with other bodily systems might need first to be addressed before regenerative stem cell treatments could be effective.[12]

Embryonic stem cell research has generated substantial political and ethical controversy in recent years. Among the central ethical issues is the moral status of the early embryo. Those who believe that a human being exists from the time of conception also hold that the blastocyst—although a ball of cells smaller than a grain of sand—has the full moral status of a person.

Therefore, they believe it wrong to interrupt the development of such embryos, even to save another life. (See Chapter 11 on abortion for the arguments regarding the moral status of the embryo.) Supporters of stem cell research, however, point out that leftover embryos now stored in fertility clinics (approximately half a million are now frozen in the United States) could be used because they are often otherwise destroyed, and using these embryos could do some good. New techniques have also been developed to "reprogram" adult stem cells to behave like embryonic stem cells, which may defuse some of the controversy.[13]

Cloning

A separate but related issue is cloning. A clone is a genetically identical copy, produced asexually from a single living being. Since the birth of Dolly the sheep at the Roslin Institute near Edinburgh, Scotland, in March 1996, people have wondered whether it also would be possible to produce humans by cloning. Dolly was a clone or generic copy of a six-year-old ewe. She was created by inserting the nucleus of a cell from the udder of this ewe into a sheep egg from which the nucleus had been removed. After being stimulated to grow, the egg was implanted into the uterus of another sheep from which Dolly was born. Dolly was produced from a somatic cell of an adult sheep with already-determined characteristics. Because the cells of an adult are already differentiated, that is, they have taken on specialized roles, scientists had previously assumed that cloning from such cells would not be possible. Now, for the first time, producing an identical, although younger, twin of an already existing human being seemed possible.

The type of cloning described above is called *somatic cell nuclear transfer* (SCNT) because it transfers the nucleus of a somatic or bodily cell into an egg whose own nucleus has been removed. Cloning can also be done through a *fission,* or cutting, of an early embryo. Through this method it may be possible to make identical human twins or triplets from one embryo.

In the past two decades, many higher mammals have been produced through cloning, including cows, sheep, goats, mice, pigs, rabbits, and a cat named "CC" for "carbon copy" or "copy cat." CC was produced in a project funded by an Arizona millionaire, John Sperling, who wanted to clone his pet dog, Missy, who had died. The company that he and his team of scientists established, Genetic Savings and Clone, was based in Sausalito, California, and Texas A&M University at College Station, Texas.[14] In 2004, it was charging $50,000 for a cloned cat and $295 to $1,395 to store genetic material from a cat. Two kittens, Tabouli and Baba Ganoush, who were cloned from the same female Bengal tiger cat, were displayed at the annual cat show at Madison Square Garden in October 2004. According to the owners, the kittens have personality similarities as well as differences.[15] Genetic Savings and Clone shut down in 2006.[16] However, Sperling established a new company, BioArts, in 2007. He then again attempted to clone the dog, Missy, using samples he had saved and frozen. This time he was successful and produced three clones, Mira, Chin-Gu, and Sarang, all born in February 2008. Sperling said that "cloning techniques had become more efficient over the years" such that "1 percent to 4 percent of embryo transfers now result in a puppy."[17] Cloned animals have themselves produced offspring in the natural way. Dolly had six seemingly normal lambs. Several generations of mice have also been produced through SCNT, using cells from mouse embryos and fetuses, as well as from mice tails and cumulus cells.

Unfortunately, animal cloning has not always been efficient or safe. In the case of Dolly, for example, 277 eggs were used but only one lamb was produced. Moreover, cloned animals also have exhibited various abnormalities. In one study, all twelve cloned mice died between one and two years of age. Six of the cloned mice had pneumonia, four had serious liver damage, and one had leukemia and lung cancer. Dolly may have had arthritis, although this claim has been disputed. Some scientists suggest that this may be because she was cloned from the cell of an already aged adult sheep. In February 2003, Dolly was euthanized because she had developed an infectious and terminal lung disease.

Some proponents of cloning argue that the use of cloning technologies on animals might help farmers to more efficiently produce livestock herds. Others argue that cloning could provide a way to save endangered species. Cloning works about 5 percent of the time for domestic animals and less than 1 percent of the time with wild animals.[18] The reason for this low success rate has to do with the complexity of the process of reprogramming a cell with new genetic material. Critics argue against animal cloning by appealing to concepts about animal welfare and animal rights (see Chapter 17). These critics complain that animal clones have high rates of abnormalities and that the risk of animal suffering and illness outweighs potential benefits.[19]

Given the controversy surrounding animal cloning, it is not surprising that human cloning is subject to even more scrutiny. However, proponents of cloning for human beings point to potential benefits of cloning technologies for both therapeutic and reproductive goals. **Therapeutic cloning** is the use of cloning for medical purposes. One such use of cloning might be in conjunction with stem cell therapy, to help avoid the immunological rejection by a patient's body of "foreign" tissues or organs grown from stem cells. In this type of cloning, the nucleus of a somatic or bodily cell from the patient, such as a skin cell, would be inserted into an unfertilized egg that had its own nucleus removed. The egg would then be stimulated to develop into an embryo. The stem cells in this blastocyst would be genetically identical with the patient, and tissue grown from them would not then be rejected by the patient's immune system as foreign. The ethical issues raised by this type of cloning mirror those of stem cell research, especially the question of the moral status of the human embryo.

Reproductive cloning aims to produce a new human being who would be the genetic twin of the person whose cell was used in the process. Reproductive cloning may be thought of as one of several reproductive technologies that have been developed in recent decades. Among these are artificial insemination, in vitro fertilization with its resulting "test-tube babies," donated and frozen embryos and eggs, and the use of surrogate mothers. Although these other methods of reproduction have been widely accepted, there is almost universal objection to reproductive cloning, even among those countries that allow and support stem cell research or therapeutic cloning. Some countries, such as the United Kingdom, have laws prohibiting reproductive cloning while

still actively supporting therapeutic cloning. Japan, China, Singapore, and South Korea have similar laws. However, Germany, Austria, France, and the Netherlands have banned both types of cloning. Countries in South America, the Middle East, and Africa also have a diversity of regulation. In the United States, bills to regulate or prohibit human cloning have been proposed, including the Human Cloning Prohibition Act introduced into the House of Representatives in November 2012. Meanwhile, one of the leading scientists in the field, John Gurdon—the 2012 cowinner of the Nobel Prize for medicine—has predicted that we will be able to safely clone human beings within fifty years.[20] Gurdon suggests that one reason to develop such techniques would be so that parents of children who die could replace their lost child with a copy. Gurdon further suggests that just as the public has gotten used to in vitro fertilization, the public will eventually come to accept the practice of reproductive cloning.

Others worry that such concepts of "replacing" individuals through cloning could lead to a devaluation of human life and a mechanistic "mass production" of babies. They point to the growing acceptance of paying surrogate mothers to bear children and argue that we are already commercializing reproduction, allowing (often wealthy and Western) couples to "rent" the wombs of women (often poor and in the developing world). When combined with cloning, such practices might seem to spring from the dystopia of Aldous Huxley's novel *Brave New World* in which the production of children was outsourced and managed for sinister eugenic purposes. Huxley's novel is often invoked as a cautionary tale about the totalitarian dangers of cloning and technologized reproduction.

Genetic Engineering and Genetic Screening

Developments in modern genetics can create new ethical problems. The controversial history of the eugenics movement mentioned above is an important concern. **Eugenics** can be defined as the science of finding ways to improve the genetic components of a species. Livestock breeders have worked for centuries to create such genetic changes in animals. But eugenic practices become more problematic when attempted with human beings, especially given the history of human eugenics efforts, which includes forced sterilizations and abortions and other practices that violated people's liberty in the name of producing good offspring. There is a long history of eugenic projects, going back to Plato's plan for breeding good citizens in the *Republic*. There were eugenic laws enforced in the United States in the early part of the twentieth century, which included the forced sterilization of thousands of people deemed "mentally defective." Nazi Germany took eugenic projects to another level of sophistication and cruelty. The efforts to "purify" the Aryan race involved the killing of more than 200,000 people—many of them children—who were deemed disabled, degenerate, homosexual, or insane by Nazi doctors and therefore "unworthy of life."[21] Hundreds of thousands more were sterilized against their will. And eventually millions were slaughtered in the Holocaust.

For the most part, contemporary societies view eugenics as fundamentally immoral. But contemporary genetic research may open the door toward a different form of eugenic outcome—such as occurs when parents are able to select the genes of their children.

Consider what decisions you might make if it were possible for you to engineer a "designer baby" or to screen out an embryo with an unwanted genetic mutation. Take the process known as *preimplantation genetic screening,* by which embryos with harmful or perhaps even simply unwanted genetic mutations can be selected out during the in vitro fertilization process. Or take the controversy surrounding a Maryland couple—both born deaf—who opted to increase the likelihood that their child would also be born deaf. The couple (two women who had been together for eight years) sought out a sperm donor with hereditary deafness out of a conviction that deafness is not a disability and that they wanted to share deaf culture with their children. "A hearing baby would be a blessing," one of the mothers said. "A deaf baby would be a special blessing."[22] After one of the women did, in fact, give birth to a deaf baby, some critics argued that the selection of a deaf donor was an abuse of genetic screening practices. But one of the mothers argued in reply that if black parents were able to choose black sperm donors, a deaf mother should be allowed to choose a deaf sperm donor.[23]

Many of the ethical controversies surrounding genetic engineering and screening have been intensified by the great progress scientists have made in recent decades in understanding the human genetic structure. The Human Genome Project, an effort to map the entire human genome, was completed in the summer of 2000 and its results first published in early 2001. The project found that humans have approximately twenty thousand genes—roughly the same number as most other animals—and helped scientists determine that "we have only 300 unique genes in the human [genome] that are not in the mouse."[24] However, although humans have approximately the same number of genes as a spotted green puffer fish, it is surmised that human capacity comes from "a small set of regulatory genes that control the activity of all the other genes." These would be different in the puffer fish.[25]

Two entities competed in the race to map the entire human genome. One was a public consortium of university centers in the United States, Great Britain, and Japan. It made its findings publicly available and used the genome from a mosaic of different individuals. The other research was done by Celera Genomics, a private company run by Dr. Craig Venter. It used a "shotgun" strategy, with genetic source material from Venter and four others. Celera performed an analysis of the DNA—identifying where the genes lay in the entire DNA sequence—and in 2007 Venter published his entire genetic sequence.[26] Although initially the cost to have one's complete genome sequenced was quite high, the cost has dropped to under $10,000.[27] A few companies have begun charging much less, sometimes less than $500, for a genetic screening of roughly twenty medical conditions. These companies include 23 and Me, Navigenics, and deCODE genetics. The customer simply sends them a tube of saliva or a cheek swab and they "match the results with the latest publications on traits, common diseases, and ancestry."[28]

Since the initial mapping of the human genome, various scientific projects have attempted to determine the precise role that hereditary elements, including the genes, play in human development, health, personality, and other characteristics. In this effort, one focus has been on individual differences. The human genome, "a string of 3 billion chemical letters that spell out every inherited trait," is almost identical in all humans—99.99 percent. But some differences, so-called genetic misspellings that are referred to as *single nucleotide polymorphisms* (SNPs or "snips"), can be used to identify genetic diseases. The SNPs give base variations that contribute to individual differences in appearance and health, among other things. Scientists look for differences, for example, by taking DNA samples of five hundred people with diabetes and a similar number from people without the disease and then looking for contrasting DNA patterns.[29] SNPs also influence how people react differently to medications. Some people can eat high-calorie and high-fat foods and still not put on weight, while others are just the opposite. Some have high risks of heart disease, whereas others do not. With genetic discoveries based on the Human Genome Project and more recent efforts, one hope is that diets can be tailored to individual human genetic makeups.

Since the early 2000s, an international consortium of scientists has been working on the "hapmap" project, a $100 million endeavor "to hasten discovery of the variant genes thought to underlie common human diseases like diabetes, asthma, and cancer."[30] Scientists use the Human Genome Project map as a master reference and compare individual genomes to it. Some diseases are caused by single genes, such as that producing cystic fibrosis, but others are thought to be caused by several genes acting together.

Other efforts are directed to finding genes that relate to certain beneficial human traits. For example, some scientists are working on locating what they call the "skinny gene." Using mice from whom a single gene has been removed, scientists at Deltagen, a company in Redwood City, California, have been able to produce mice that remain slim no matter how much they are fed.[31] According to geneticist David Botstein, the impact of the Human Genome Project on medicine "should exceed that 100 years ago of X-rays, which gave doctors their first view inside the intact, living body."[32]

Our growing knowledge of the human genome may lead to powerful new medical treatments but also raise new ethical questions. Consider, for example, gene therapies that could impact the growth of muscle. Myostatin is a hormone that curbs the growth of muscles. Gene therapies might be able to block myostatin, which could promote muscle growth. As a therapy this could be useful for treating muscular dystrophy or frailty in older persons. Myostatin mutations are already responsible for the development of a breed of cattle called the Belgian Blue that has huge muscles and very little fat. And some human beings have a myostatin mutation, which promotes muscle growth—a natural abnormality that has helped produce exceptional athletes, including a gold medalist in cross-country skiing.[33] While myostatin treatments could save lives, there is also concern that athletes and other healthy individuals might purchase them to gain an advantage in competition or for cosmetic purposes. Such genetic enhancements might not leave traces in urine or blood the way that other performance-enhancing drugs do. However, in recent years the World Anti-Doping Agency has begun to develop new blood tests to detect so-called "gene doping," including other genetic enhancements that allow the human body to produce extra red blood cells.[34]

Ethical issues have also arisen over new genetic screening procedures made possible by the genome map. While such screenings may benefit health, insurers and prospective employers might also use genetic screening to their own advantage but not necessarily to the advantage of the person being screened. Although the procedures may be new, the ethical issues are similar to those raised by other types of screening, including drug screening. While we may agree that athletes and airline pilots should have their blood and urine screened for the use of performance enhancements and recreational drugs, do we also agree that students and retail employees should be subject to similar screenings? Related to this is the question of whether insurance companies or employers should be able to obtain information about an individual's genetic code. In 2013, scientists published the results of a study that showed that it was finally possible to identify individuals based upon an analysis of genetic codes in comparison with publicly available databases containing the genetic information of individuals whose genes have been sequenced.[35] This technology could be useful for tracing out genealogies. But it could also raise privacy concerns, for example, among people who fear being stigmatized because of a genetic abnormality or disease.

Genetically Modified Plants and Animals

During the past few decades, a lively debate has sprung up in the United States and beyond about **genetically modified organisms**, or GMOs. While, strictly speaking, humans have been modifying the genes of plants and animals for centuries—through such practices as plant hybridization and selective animal breeding—GMOs are created through new biotechnologies such as gene splicing, radiation, or specialized chemicals. These technologies often change the genetics of plants and animals that humans grow for food, in an attempt to make them hardier, larger, more flavorful, or more resistant to drought or freezing temperatures. Although some of these traits could be established through traditional breeding methods, some could not, and a highly profitable new industry now revolves around creating (and usually patenting) these new forms of life.

Critics of GMOs argue that they open a "Pandora's box" of potential risks to ecosystems and to human health. (In Greek mythology, Pandora's seemingly minor act of opening a beautiful box releases a host of evils into the world.) In 2004, the National Academy of Sciences determined that, "genetically engineered crops do not pose health risks that cannot also arise from crops created by other techniques, including conventional breeding."[36] It is not the method of production that should be of concern, the NAS argued, but the resulting product. Nevertheless, there is much that the general public does not understand about so-called genetically modified food.

Strictly speaking, genetic engineering involves inserting a specific gene from one organism into another in order to produce a desired trait. In a broader sense, "nearly every food we eat has been genetically modified" as crops and domesticated animals have been bred by humans for centuries.[37] Cross-breeding crops "involves the mixing of thousands of genes, most unknown," and trying to select desirable mutations.[38] In the case of some contemporary GMOs,

such mutations are now often caused by "bombarding seeds with chemicals or radiation" and seeing what comes of it. For example, lettuce, beans, and grapefruit have been so modified.[39]

An increasing number of crops have been genetically modified in recent decades. A report of the International Service for the Acquisition of Agri-Biotech Applications concludes, "Biotech Crop hectares increased by an unprecedented 100-fold, from 1.7 million hectares in 1996, to 170 million hectares in 2012."[40] According to the Non-GMO Project, "In North America, 80 percent of our foods contain GMOs."[41] The Non-GMO Project has spearheaded a campaign to certify foods that do not contain GMOs. In 2013, the grocery chain Whole Foods announced that it would label products that contain GMOs in its stores.[42] While some are pushing back against GMOs, mainstream science tends to hold that these products are beneficial or at least not harmful. GMO crops are easier and cheaper to grow and can provide more food from less land. They may be engineered to survive the use of herbicides and insecticides or to be more resistant to pests. Critics argue, however, that herbicide- and pesticide-resistant crops will lead to more toxic chemicals in agriculture, which may have long-term negative impacts on the environment and human health. One article claims that the use of genetically modified crops has unleashed a "gusher" of pesticides.[43] But proponents of GMOs explain things differently. One technique has inserted *Bacillus thuringiensis* (B.t.) genes into corn, which enables it to resist a devastating pest called the corn borer. With this mutation, the use of environmentally damaging herbicides intended to combat the corn borer can then be reduced.

Other benefits of GMOs include the possibility of engineering crops so that they contain more nutritional value. New strains of rice have been developed specifically to combat famine and to reduce a vitamin A deficiency that commonly causes blindness and other infections among the world's poorest children. Plans for GMOs include "edible vaccines" in fruits and vegetables that would make them more easily available to people than injectable ones.[44] Perhaps most significant for global public health, genetically modified foods offer a chance to "produce more food on less land—using less water, fewer chemicals, and less money."[45] And opposition to GMOs in the wealthy West may have negative consequences for developing countries where famine and malnutrition are serious problems. For example, opposition to genetically modified food has led Uganda to prohibit efforts to develop a fungus-resistant banana, even though fungus has seriously damaged its banana crop, one of its most important.[46]

At the same time, protests against genetically modified foods have grown, especially in Europe and Japan, but also in the United States. One significant concern is food allergies that could result from products containing new genetic information.[47] Some of the criticism may be based on ungrounded fears about new technologies, but some GMO-related hazards may be real. There is some evidence, for example, that crops genetically modified for antibiotic resistance may transfer that resistance to humans who eat them, raising serious health concerns.[48] There is also evidence that herbicide-resistant crops may help create "superweeds" that require ever more toxic chemicals to try to control them. Neighboring non-GMO crops may become contaminated by GMO crops, which has, ironically, allowed giant GMO producers such as Monsanto to sue farmers for patent infringement when pollen from GMO crops blows onto their land. It may well be possible to reduce some of these risks, for example, by creating sterile plants that do not produce pollen. But clearly we are in the early days of human experimentation with GMOs. So far, many of the dangers that people associate with GMOs have not materialized, but this does not prove their safety for humans and the environment.

LEGAL AND ETHICAL ISSUES

A variety of legal and ethical issues arise in thinking about biotechnology and bioengineering. In general, there is a tension between valuing our liberty to pursue biotechnologies for their immediate utility, on the one hand, and concerns over the potential negative impacts of such technologies in the long run. There are also tensions between the liberty of individuals and groups to modify biology and concerns about the moral problems involved in such modification, including the risk of "playing God." There is also a concern that new technologies will diminish

human dignity by turning human beings into products that are created and engineered. One significant argument, associated with the work of bioethicist Leon Kass, is that there is a kind of wisdom in our "repugnance" for certain forms of bioengineering. When a new technology makes us pause and say "yuck," we may be tapping into a deeper insight about human nature. Of course, others reject such repugnance as little more than taste and inclination without any deeper moral basis. Indeed, some theorists argue that what one generation finds to be yucky and repugnant is easily accepted by the next generation, as people get used to new norms and new ideas about what is natural and possible.

Athletic and Cognitive Enhancement

The issues arising around athletic and cognitive enhancement involve the conflict between liberty and negative consequences. In terms of liberty, defenders of biotechnology will argue that individuals have a right to do whatever they want to their own bodies, a right to enhance their performance, a right to use technology to choose their own offspring, and a right to find ways to profit and benefit from technology so long as they do not hurt other people. Therapeutic technologies can be defended in terms of their immediate positive impact on impaired and disabled people. Those who want to use these technologies in ways to go beyond mere therapy will argue that the benefits are obvious and that individuals should be free to take the risks that might be associated with the use of performance-enhancing drugs. Arguments along these lines might parallel ethical considerations regarding the use of other drugs, such as marijuana or nicotine. Defenders will argue that so long as no one else is harmed, individuals should be allowed to choose to use these substances because of a basic right to do what one wants with one's own body.

On the other hand, critics will argue that the benefits are not obvious. Steroid use by athletes has been proved to produce long-term negative health effects. Athletes may need to be protected from competitive or organizational pressures to alter their bodies in ways that are not healthy. Indeed, the international agreements that prohibit the use of performance enhancements in sports are partly intended to benefit the athletes themselves. If steroid use were allowed, for example, there is a worry that there would be an "arms race" among athletes, which might increase performance but would result in serious health problems. Furthermore, critics of performance enhancements argue that these drugs and technologies create unfairness, as those who are willing to use these drugs (or those who can afford them) will have an unfair advantage over those who restrict themselves to developing their own natural talents and abilities. There is a worry, for example, that affluent students will benefit from smart drugs, giving them an unfair advantage over less fortunate students.

Furthermore, critics will argue that we may not yet understand the potential long-term impacts of these biotechnologies. Just as genetically modified organisms may produce food allergies and contribute to the growth of superweeds, so too, the use of performance enhancements may create future impacts that we might come to regret. Critics may also argue with regard to biotechnology and bioengineering in general that we are not wise enough or benevolent enough to be entrusted with technologies that could be easily abused. This is related to a naturalistic argument, which suggests that we ought to leave natural things alone and not risk dangerous perversions of Nature.

Stem Cell Research

As we have seen, ethical debate over stem cell research is often—but not always—rooted in the contentious debate about the moral status of the human embryo. In 2001, President George W. Bush introduced a ban on federally funded research using stem cells from new embryos, stating that, "[l]ike a snowflake, each of these embryos is unique, with the unique genetic potential of an individual human being."[49] In 2009, President Obama expanded the number of stem cell lines available for use and allowed federal grant money to be used for research on these lines. These stem cell lines are to be derived from excess embryos created in fertility clinics and donated for research purposes with the consent of the donor. (If not used in this way, these excess embryos would be thrown away.) In 2013, the U.S. Supreme Court overruled a lower court decision

that would have prevented federal funding for embryonic stem cell research. The plaintiff in that case, Dr. James Sherley, said that his goal was to "emancipate human embryos from research slavery."[50]

To overcome such ethical concerns about the moral status of the early embryo, some people have suggested that only adult stem cells be used in research. Adult stem cells exist in bone marrow and purportedly in other parts of the body such as the brain, skin, fat, and muscle. The therapeutic use of these cells seems to work in some situations, such as the case of the reconstructed windpipe mentioned previously. Adult stem cells have been used to grow different types of cells, including heart cells, which could be useful for treating heart disease.[51] However, adult stem cells may be limited in their ability to develop into tissues. They may only be *multipotent* rather than pluripotent.

Nevertheless, some recent scientific developments suggest that researchers may find a way out of the moral impasse over embryonic stem cells. Several studies have found that the stem cells present in amniotic fluid (the fluid that surrounds the fetus in the uterus) can be used for many of the same therapies as embryonic stem cells. This would constitute a plentiful source of stem cells and would perhaps be less controversial than obtaining the cells directly from embryos. In 2012, the Nobel Prize for Medicine was given to two researchers, Shinya Yamanaka and John Gurdon (mentioned previously), whose work showed how mature cells could be "reprogrammed" into an immature state capable of growing into various kinds of tissue—a capacity that resembles the pluripotency of embryonic stem cells.[52] Such new techniques may change the ethical conversation about stem cells, especially if it is possible to create therapies that use adult cells instead of embryonic cells. Such work would circumvent the complaints of those who view embryos as incipient human life that ought not be destroyed in the name of research. Scientists continue to make rapid progress along these lines. In April 2013, scientists announced that they had perfected a technique for creating and growing induced pluripotent cells that allows for successful cultivation of large numbers of these cells.[53]

Not all moral concerns about stem cell research, however, are narrowly focused on the individuality and potential personhood of the human embryo. Another significant concern raised, for example, in the National Academy of Sciences (NAS) recommendations for stem cell research is the possible creation of *chimeras*, or new creatures that cross species borders. The NAS guidelines prohibit research in which human embryonic stem cells "are introduced into nonhuman primate blastocysts or in which any embryonic stem cells are introduced into human blastocysts." Furthermore, the guidelines maintain, "no animal into which human embryonic stem cells have been introduced such that they could contribute to the germ line should be allowed to breed."[54]

The possibility of creating and breeding partially human or cross-species genetic mutants raises a number of serious ethical worries about how such creatures might be treated, about just *how* human such beings would need to be to deserve human rights and personhood, and, more generally, what it means for scientists to "play God" and create unprecedented new life forms. Such moral questions are not merely speculative or limited to the realm of science fiction. Some medical therapies already do include tissues and genes taken from animals, for example, pig heart valves that contain some human cells have been used to treat human patients with cardiac diseases. While recommending that these therapies and research programs be allowed, the NAS also recommended that: (1) chimeric animals not be allowed to mate because, if human cells invaded the sperm and eggs of an animal host, this could lead to the remote possibility of a being with human DNA being conceived in a nonhuman host; (2) human stem cells not be allowed to become part or all of an animal's brain and not be injected into other primates because this could have the possible result of a human mind trapped in a nonhuman body; (3) embryos used in stem cell research should not be allowed to develop for more than fourteen days; and (4) women who donate eggs not be paid in order to avoid financial inducement.[55]

In 2007, a task force of the International Society for Stem Cell Research published its own guidelines for embryonic stem cell research. These guidelines were developed by ethicists, scientists, and legal experts from fourteen countries. Like the NAS recommendations, these guidelines do allow some research on chimeric animals—those that could carry human gametes—but only if such research passes the review of an oversight committee. The guidelines also affirm the fourteen-day limit for embryo development, arguing that it is not until this point in the development of a "primitive streak" that the embryo "has begun to initiate organogenesis."[56] The idea is that prior to that point, the embryo has not yet reached a point of development that would qualify it for moral concern—a claim that is connected to the discussion of the ethics of abortion (see Chapter 11).

Cloning

Perhaps no issue related to biotechnology raises more ethical controversy than the prospect of cloning human beings. Although much of the reaction to cloning humans has been the product of both hype and fear, serious ethical questions also have been raised. One of the most serious concerns is that cloning might produce medical problems for the individuals produced in this way, just as it has in some cases of animal cloning. For this reason alone, we might raise ethical objections to human cloning. Some have pointed out, though, that fertility clinics have had broad experience in growing human embryos, and thus cloning humans might actually be less risky than cloning animals. However, moral objections to cloning are also based on other considerations.

One classic objection to human cloning is that it amounts to "playing God." The idea is that only God can and should create a human life. Those who hold this view might use religious reasons and sources to support it, but although this looks like a religious position, it is not necessarily so. For example, it might just mean that the coming to be of a new person is a *creation*, rather than a making or production. According to this view, the creation of a human is the bringing into being of an individual, a mysterious thing and something that we should regard with awe. When we take on the role of *producing* a human being, as in cloning, we become makers or manipulators of a product that we control and over which we have some kind of power. Another version of this objection stresses the significance of Nature and the natural. In producing a human being through cloning, we go against human nature. For example, in humans, as in all higher animals, reproduction is sexual. Cloning, by contrast, is asexual reproduction, and thus may be seen to go beyond the "natural" boundaries of human biology. Leon Kass, whom we mentioned earlier, is one of the strongest proponents of the view that in cloning someone, we would wrongly seek to escape the bounds and dictates of our sexual nature. According to another related criticism, attempting to clone a human being demonstrates *hubris,* an arrogant assumption that we are wise enough to know and handle its potential consequences. Tampering with a process as fundamental as human reproduction should only be undertaken with the utmost caution, this argument claims. Above all, we should avoid doing what unknowingly may turn out to be seriously harmful for the individuals produced as well as for future generations.

Those who defend human cloning respond to this sort of objection by asking how cloning is any different from other ways we interfere with or change Nature in accepted medical practices such as in vitro fertilization, for example. Others argue from a religious perspective that God gave us brains to use, and that we honor God in using them, especially for the benefit of humans and society. Cloning advocates also point out that in using technology to assist reproduction, we do not necessarily lose our awe at the arrival of a new being, albeit one who comes into being with our help.

A second objection to the very idea of cloning a human being is that the person cloned would not be a *unique individual*. He or she would be the genetic copy of the person from whom the somatic cell was transferred. He or she would be the equivalent of an identical twin of this person, although years younger. Moreover, because our dignity and worth are attached to our uniqueness as individuals, this objection suggests that cloned individuals would lose the unique value we believe persons to have. We might find that the difficulties that clones have in maintaining their individuality would be a more confusing and troubling version of the difficulties that identical twins sometimes have. Sometimes they are dressed alike,

and often they are expected to act alike. The implication is that they do not have the freedom or ability to develop their own individual personalities. A related objection is sometimes expressed as the view that a cloned human being would not have a soul, or that he or she would be a hollow shell of a person. The idea is that if we take on the role of producing a human being through cloning, then we prevent God or Nature from giving it the spiritual component that makes it more than a material body.

One response to this objection points out how different the cloned individual would be from the original individual. Identical twins are more like each other than a clone would be to the one cloned. This is because twins develop together in the same mother's body in addition to sharing the same genetic code. Clones would develop in different uteruses and would have different mitochondria—the genes in the cytoplasm surrounding the renucleated cell that play a role in development. They would also likely grow up in very different circumstances and environments. Developmental studies of plants and animals give dramatic evidence of how great a difference the environment makes. The genotype (the genetic code) does not fully determine the phenotype (the genes' actual physical manifestations). CC, the cloned cat mentioned previously, does not quite look like its genetic donor, Rainbow. They have different coat patterns because genes are not the only things that control coat color. There are other differences. "Rainbow is reserved. CC is curious and playful. Rainbow is chunky. CC is sleek."[57] Although genes do matter, and thus there would be similarities between a human clone and the person who was cloned, they would not be identical. On the matter of soul, cloning defenders ask why could God not give each person, identical twin or clone, an individual soul; any living human being, cloned or not, would be a distinct being and so could have a human psyche or soul, they suggest.

Another objection to human cloning is that while any person born today has a *right to an open future,* a cloned human being would not. He or she would be expected to be like the originating person and thus would not be free to develop as he or she chose. The genetic donor (or his or her life story) would be there as the model of what he or she would be expected to become. Even if people tried not to have such expectations for the one cloned, they would be hard-pressed not to do so. Critics of this argument point out that while there might indeed be certain expectations for a clone, this undue influence is a possibility in the case of all parents and children, and thus a possibility that is not limited to clones. Parents select their children's schools and other formative experiences and promote certain activities, perspectives, and tastes. Thus any child, cloned or sexually reproduced, would seem to run the risk of being unduly influenced by those who raise them or contribute to their genetic makeup.

Related to the previous objection to cloning is one that holds that cloned children or adults would tend to be *exploited*. If one looks at many of the potential motivations for cloning a person, the objection goes, they indicate that cloning would often be undertaken for the sake of others, rather than for the sake of the new cloned person. For example, the cloned child could be viewed as a potential organ or blood donor—a so-called "savior sibling"—or to "replace" a child who has died. A more far-fetched scenario might include making clones who were specifically produced for doing menial work or fighting wars. We might want to clone certain valued individuals, such as stars of the screen or athletics. In all these cases, the clones would neither be valued for their own selves nor respected as unique persons. They would be valued for what they can bring to others. As discussed in Chapter 6, Kant's basic idea is that persons ought not simply be used but ought to be treated as ends in themselves, and such practices would seem to be condemned by this Kantian principle.

Critics of these objections could agree with Kant but still disagree that a cloned human being would be more likely than anyone else to be used by others rather than valued as an individual. Just because a child was conceived to provide bone marrow for a sick sibling would not prevent her from also being loved for her own sake. Furthermore, the idea that we would create and confine a group of human beings while training them to be workers or soldiers must presuppose that we abandon a host of legal protections against such treatment of children or other individuals. Equally far-fetched, these critics

say, is the notion of a eugenic "brave new world" in which children are produced only through cloning.

Some people believe that if human cloning were widely practiced, then it would only add to the *confusion within families* that is already generated by the use of other reproductive technologies. When donated eggs and surrogate mothers are used, the genetic parents are different from the gestational parents and the rearing parents, and conflicts have arisen regarding who the "real" parents are. Cloning, objectors contend, would create even more of a problem, adding to this confusion the blurring of lines between generations. The birth mother's child could be her twin or a twin of the father or someone else. What would happen to the traditional relationships with the members of the other side of the family, grandparents, aunts, and uncles? And what would be the relationship of a husband to a child who is the twin of his wife or of a wife to a child who is the twin of her husband?

Critics of these arguments respond that, although there is a traditional type of family that, in fact, varies from culture to culture, today there are also many different kinds of nontraditional families. Among these are single-parent families, adopted families, blended families, and lesbian and gay families. It is not the type of family that makes for a good loving household, they argue, but the amount of love and care that exists in one.

A final objection to human cloning goes something as follows: Sometimes we have a *gut reaction* to something we regard as abhorrent. This is the "yuck" objection, mentioned previously. We are offended by the very thought of it. We cannot always give reasons for this reaction, yet we instinctively know that what we abhor is wrong. Many people seem to react to human cloning in this way. The idea of someone making a copy of themselves or many copies of a famous star is simply bizarre, revolting, and repugnant, and these emotional reactions let us know that there is something quite wrong with it, even if we cannot explain fully what it is.

Any adequate response to this argument would entail an analysis of how ethical reasoning works when it works well. Emotional reactions or moral intuitions may indeed play a role in moral reasoning. However, most philosophers would agree that adequate moral reasoning should not rely on intuition or emotion alone. Reflections about why one might rightly have such gut reactions are in order. People have been known to have negative gut reactions to things that, in fact, are no longer regarded as wrong—interracial marriage, for example. It is incumbent on those who assert that something is wrong, most philosophers believe, that they provide rational arguments and well-supported reasons to justify these beliefs and emotional reactions.

There is currently no federal law banning human cloning, although as we saw previously, several laws have been proposed to ban the practice or to prohibit federal funding for research that involves it. Under President George W. Bush, the President's Council on Bioethics recommended a moratorium on all types of human cloning. In 2009, President Barack Obama replaced the council with the Presidential Commission for the Study of Bioethical Issues, chaired by philosopher Amy Gutmann and focused on specific policy recommendations.[58] This commission has yet to issue a specific recommendation on cloning. Meanwhile state legislatures have weighed in on the issue. As of 2011, eight states ban human cloning for any purpose, while ten other states explicitly allow research in which clones are created and destroyed for therapeutic purposes.[59]

Some critics of state cloning laws argue that it is too difficult to ban one type of cloning without the other. For example, if reproductive cloning were prohibited but research or therapeutic cloning were allowed, it would be difficult to know for certain that cloned embryos were not being produced for reproductive purposes. With regard to proposed federal bans, some have pointed out that if there are no federal funds provided for research cloning, then there also will be no oversight. We will not know what types of cloning that corporations or other private entities engage in. Scientists also point out how essential federal research funds have been for new developments in biotechnology.

Genetic Engineering and Genetic Screening

The ethical debate over the genetic engineering of human offspring has substantial overlap with the debate outlined previously with regard to reproductive human cloning. Those who oppose the prospect of "designer babies" argue that exercising control over these aspects of traditional human reproduction would be both unnatural and an affront to human dignity. Those on the other side argue on consequentialist grounds for giving parents the opportunity to choose to produce the healthy children they desire, even if that involves selection of preferred physical and mental characteristics beyond the merely healthy. So long as there is no coercion involved and no one is harmed in the process, one might think that people should be free to reproduce in accord with their own interests and in ways that would be beneficial to society. Again, the worry is that this could easily slide toward a eugenic project in which reproduction is regulated in more insidious ways. Defenders of genetic engineering will respond by claiming that the slope is not really that slippery.

There are some obvious benefits of genetic engineering of humans. If it were possible to use gene therapy to activate, replace, or change malfunctioning genes before a baby is born, then this could greatly reduce human suffering from genetic diseases. Using genetic techniques to manipulate cells or organisms in order to provide human blood-clotting factor for hemophiliacs, manufactured human insulin for diabetics, human growth hormone for those who need it, and better pain relievers for everyone is surely desirable and ethically defensible. However, use of the technology also raises ethical concerns. Among these questions are those related to the risks that exist for those who undergo experimental genetic therapies and the issue of informed consent in such experiments.[60]

Related to the issue of informed consent are a variety of ethical questions that arise with regard to genetic screening, the process of searching for and screening out genetic defects. For example, what limits should be placed upon the ways that genetic information is used? Do people have a right to know their own genetic predispositions? And is there a right to privacy with regard to our genetic information?

We also should be concerned about access to these procedures and whether only the well-off will benefit from them. The biotechnology industry continues to grow. Should information and products of great medical benefit be kept secret and patented by biotech companies and developers? For example, the company Myriad Genetics found a gene linked with breast cancer and attempted to patent the gene.[61] In another example, therapeutic techniques now allow the alteration of genes in sperm, which affect not the individual himself but his offspring and thus alter human lineage.[62] It is one thing to do this in the interest of preventing genetic disease in one's offspring, but it is quite another to add new genetically based capabilities for one's children or to the human race. Such capabilities raise serious moral concerns. Are we wise enough to do more good than harm with these methods? Can we legitimately deny access to such technologies to individuals who may benefit from them, without also violating those individuals' rights to do what they want with their own bodies and reproductive capabilities?

The Value of Privacy As in our discussion of abortion in Chapter 11, arguments about our rights to employ biotechnologies in our own bodies often involve the value of privacy. We might want to say that decisions that people make about their own health and reproductive lives is no one's business but their own. We think that people generally have a right to privacy, but we are less sure what this means and what kinds of practices would violate privacy. Suppose, for example, that a technology existed that could read a person's mind and the condition of various parts of her body, or could hear and see what goes on in one's home—his bedroom or bathroom—and could record all of these in a data bank that would be accessible to a variety of interested parties. What, if anything, would be wrong with this?[63] One of the things that we find problematic about others having access to this knowledge is that they would have access to matters that we would not want anyone else to know. According to Thomas Scanlon, this is what the right to privacy is—a right "to be free from certain intrusions."[64] Some things, we say, are just nobody else's business.

If this definition of privacy seems reasonable, then we can ask for reasons why we would not want certain intrusions like those in the hypothetical example. Many reasons have been suggested, and you may sympathize with some more than others. Four are provided here.

The first concern is the basic idea of shame. Shame and embarrassment are feelings we have when certain private things become known or observed—one's thoughts, bathroom behavior, or sexual fantasies, for example. Some private thoughts and behaviors are thought to be shameful—something that should remain private and not shared in public. Could there be reasons to be ashamed of our genetic inheritance or genetic disease susceptibilities, for example?

A second reason why we might want certain things kept to ourselves is our desire to control information about us and to let it be known only to those to whom we choose to reveal it. Such control is part of our ability to own our own lives. We speak of it as a form of autonomy or self-rule. In fact, the loss of control over some of these more personal aspects of our lives is a threat to our very selfhood, some say. For example, in his classic study of what he calls "total institutions" such as prisons and mental hospitals, the sociologist Erving Goffman describes the way that depriving a person of privacy is a way of mortifying (literally killing) the self.[65] Having a zone of privacy around us that we control helps us define ourselves and marks us off from others and our environment. Perhaps our genetic endowment should be kept private so that we have a zone of control in this sphere.

Third, privacy helps in the formation and continuation of personal relations. We are more intimate with friends than with strangers, and even more so with lovers and spouses than with mere acquaintances. The private things about ourselves that we confide to those closest to us are an essential part of those relationships. According to legal theorist Charles Fried, "privacy is the necessary context for relationships which we would hardly be human if we had to do without—the relationships of love, friendship, and trust."[66] Sexual intimacies are thus appropriate in the context of a loving relationship because they are private sharings that also help to establish and further that relationship. It may be that our genetic heritage is only the business of our potential sexual partners, those with whom we may choose to have children. Potential mates might actually have a right to access our genetic information, in this view.

Fourth, we want to keep certain things private because of the risk that the knowledge might be used against us to cause us harm. Screening procedures in particular come to mind here. Drug screening, HIV testing, or genetic disease scans all make information available to others that could result in social detriment. For example, we could be harmed in our employment or our ability to obtain medical insurance. The problem of data banks is also at issue here. Our medical records, records of psychiatric sessions, histories of employment, and so forth could be used legitimately by certain people. However, they also may be misused by those who have no business having access to them. In a particularly problematic example, the managed care company that was paying for the psychological counseling of one patient asked to inspect his confidential files. The psychologist was concerned. "The audit occurred, they rifled through my files," he said, and "made copies and went. But it changed things. He [the patient] became more concerned about what he was saying.... A few visits later he stopped coming."[67] Another notorious case is also illustrative of the harm that can be caused by the invasion of privacy. During a contentious New York congressional campaign, someone obtained a copy of the hospital records of one of the candidates and sent them anonymously to the press. *The New York Post* published the material, including notes about the candidate's attempt to kill herself with sleeping pills and vodka. Despite this, the candidate won the election and she successfully sued the hospital for invasion of privacy.[68] Similar concerns about privacy and reputation may arise with regard to genetic information.

Screening and Conflicting Interests As we have seen, the value of privacy is particularly relevant in the context of genetic screening and screening procedures in general. Ethical debates over screening often revolve around a conflict between the privacy interests of those being screened, on the one hand, and the legitimate interests of others in obtaining relevant information, on the other. An employer may have a legitimate interest in having a drug-free workplace, for example. It may have a valid economic interest, for one's employees may not be able to do an effective job if they have drug-use problems. Passengers on public transportation may also have a legitimate interest in seeing that those who build and operate the bus, train, or plane are able to function well and safely. Airline passengers may have an interest in having other passengers and their bags scanned to prevent dangerous materials from being carried on board. Drug screening in professional athletics might be justified with reference to the interests of several different parties. In some cases, it may be in the legitimate economic interests of the owners; in collegiate athletics and nonprofessional competitions such as the Olympics, it might be justified by the fans' interests in fair competition as well as by an interest in the health of the athletes themselves. But in all these cases, we also need to consider the privacy interests of the parties being screened.

In cases of conflicting interests generally, as in the more specific examples given here, we want to know on which side the interest is stronger. In the case of drug testing of airline pilots, the safety of the passengers seems clearly to outweigh the legitimate interest that pilots might have in retaining their privacy. In many other cases of employee drug screening, it is not so clear that employers' economic interests outweigh the employees' privacy interests. In these cases, one might well argue that unless there is observable evidence of inefficiency, drug testing should not be done, especially mandatory random drug testing. In the case of genetic screening by life or health insurance providers, the answer also seems less clear. If a person has a genetic defect that will cause a disease that will affect his life expectancy, is his interest in keeping this information secret more important than the financial interests of the insurer knowing that information? A person's ability to obtain life insurance will affect payments to others on his or her death. In the case of health insurance coverage, where it is not socially mandated or funded, the stronger interest might seem to lie with the person to be insured rather than the insurer—in part because being able to afford health care or not plays such a major role in a person's health and well being. In fact, some state legislatures have moved to prevent health insurers from penalizing individuals who are "genetically predisposed to certain diseases."[69] In arguing for these laws, supporters sometimes frame them as a matter of preventing "genetic discrimination." The phrase is apt in the sense that it seeks to prevent people from being singled out and penalized for things that are not in their power to control—their genes. On a national level, the "Genetic Information Nondiscrimination Act...makes it illegal for insurers and employers to discriminate against people with genetic markers for diseases like cancer, Alzheimer's disease, and diabetes." This act took full effect on November 21, 2009.[70]

With genetic screening, as with many other controversial issues, ethical analysis of conflicting interests can be consequentialist, deontological, or some mixture of the two. On consequentialist grounds, we might ask whether mandatory screening in a particular situation would really produce more harm than good or more good than harm overall. We might weigh the harm done to individuals through intrusions into their privacy against the benefits to the public or employers. On deontological grounds, we might compare the rights of individuals to be "free from certain intrusions" with their duties as employees, soldiers, or citizens. Or we might need to factor in both consequentialist and deontological concerns as we try to determine whose interest is stronger or more important morally.

Genetically Modified Organisms

In general, the ethical debate over genetically modified food and crops has involved a consequentialist analysis of costs and benefits. Cost–benefit analysis first involves estimating risks and potential benefits—an empirical matter—and then a comparative evaluation in which one tries to analyze and weigh the various values involved. Longer and healthier lives for more people clearly go on the positive side, and risks to longevity and health go on the negative side, but we must also try to determine the relative value of life, health, well-being, and so on. There is also the problem of how to count speculative and unknown risks. If we are risk-averse and come down on the side of conservatism, then we may avoid unknown risks but also eliminate possible benefits, including that of saving lives.

Such problems are particularly vexing when it comes to GMOs, which appear to have striking potential benefits—such as increased crop yields in the developing world—as well as some potential risks—such as increased resistance to herbicides

or antibiotics. As we saw previously, benefits to genetically modifying animals can include the production of "pharmaceutical" milk from cows, sheep, and goats that can provide more effective treatments for cystic fibrosis and hemophilia.[71] And through *xeno-transplantation,* animal organs (such as those from pigs as described previously) may be modified with human genes and given to humans with reduced risk of immune rejection. In other cases, GMOs may promote economic efficiency, as animals are modified to produce more meat or meat with less fat or to have better resistance to disease. Still, GMOs may also pose risks. For example, some critics worry that farm-raised and genetically altered salmon, if released into the wild, might harm other species of fish.[72] Weighing potential benefits and risks of GMOs will likely be an ongoing process in the decades to come—one that may reach different conclusions about different techniques of modifying organisms along the way.

A different ethical debate over GMOs involves the idea that humans should not modify or interfere with the fundamental design of nature. Shouldn't the world of plant and animal species as we find them inspire our respect and awe and place some limits on our efforts to manipulate or change them? One problem with this line of criticism is that it is difficult to distinguish good forms of manipulating nature from unacceptable ones. Some critics of GMOs argue that we ought to leave species as we find them, and that it is the cross-species transfers of genetic material involved in some GMOs that make them unacceptable. One problem with this objection is that similar transfers have occurred in nature—from basic plant genetics to the long-term patterns of evolution.

In addition, the "yuck" objection introduced earlier is sometimes also raised in this context. For example, just the thought of having a pig heart or lung within one's own body might provoke this reaction in some people. As with similar objections to human cloning, however, we must question whether such reactions are, by virtue of their intuitive force alone, legitimate moral insights. Even more important, in the case of genetically modified animals, is the question of their ethical or humane treatment and potential violations of their dignity or rights. This may involve not only the engineering of such animals but also their suffering and death as in the case of pigs whose organs would be transplanted or mice who would be given a human cancer. Animal welfare and rights arguments (as discussed in Chapter 17) should be considered with regard to such cases.

As we have seen in this chapter, biotechnology and bioengineering raise a host of ethical issues—something that should probably come as no surprise. With every new scientific advance and development come new ethical problems, for there are new questions about what we ought and ought not to do. To judge well with regard to these issues, we need to understand the facts, including facts about possible benefits and adverse consequences. We also need to clarify our values about issues such as autonomy, liberty, and privacy. And we need to consider whether there is anything wrong with "playing God" and using technology to alter natural beings, including ourselves.

NOTES

1. Judy Lin, "Farsighted Engineer Invents Bionic Eye to Help the Blind," *UCLA Today*, March 21, 2013, accessed April 11, 2013, http://today.ucla.edu/portal/ut/wentai-liu-artificial-retina-244393.aspx

2. James Gorman, "In a First, Experiment Links Brains of Two Rats," *New York Times*, February 28, 2013, accessed April 11, 2013, http://www.nytimes.com/2013/03/01/science/new-research-suggests-two-rat-brains-can-be-linked.html?_r=0

3. "Man Wriggles Rat's Tail Using Only His Thoughts," *Discovery News*, April 9, 2013, accessed April 11, 2013, http://news.discovery.com/tech/biotechnology/man-wriggles-rats-tail-using-thoughts-130409.htm

4. Rose Eveleth, "Should Oscar Pistorius's Prosthetic Legs Disqualify Him from the Olympics?" *Scientific American*, July 24, 2012, accessed April 22, 2013, http://www.scientificamerican.com/article.cfm?id=scientists-debate-oscar-pistorius-prosthetic-legs-disqualify-him-olympics

5. Alan Schwarz, "Drowned in a Stream of Prescriptions," *New York Times*, February 2, 2013, accessed April 22, 2103, http://www.nytimes.com/2013/02/03/us/concerns-about-adhd-practices-and-amphetamine-addiction.html

6. Will Oremus, "The New Stimulus Package," *Slate*, March 27, 2013, accessed April 22, 2013, http://www.slate.com/articles/technology/superman/2013/03/adderall_ritalin_vyvanse_do_smart_pills_work_if_you_don_t_have_adhd.2.html

7. Will Oremus, "Spark of Genius," *Slate*, April 1, 2013, accessed April 22, 2013, http://www.slate.com/articles/technology/superman/2013/04/tdcs_and_rtms_is_brain_stimulation_safe_and_effective.html

8. *Scientific American*, July 2005, A6–A27.

9. Henry Fountain, "A First: Organs Tailor-Made with Body's Own Cells," *New York Times*, September 15, 2012, accessed April 11, 2013, http://www.nytimes.com/2012/09/16/health/research/scientists-make-progress-in-tailor-made-organs.html?_r=1&pagewanted=all

10. Henry Fountain, "Groundbreaking Surgery for Girl Born without Windpipe," *New York Times*, April 30, 2013, accessed May 8, 2013, http://www.nytimes.com/2013/04/30/science/groundbreaking-surgery-for-girl-born-without-windpipe.html?pagewanted=all&_r=0

11. "Young Girl Given Bioengineered Windpipe Dies," *New York Times*, July 7, 2013, accessed July 25, 2013, http://www.nytimes.com/2013/07/08/science/young-girl-given-bioengineered-windpipe-dies.html

12. Carl T. Hall, "Stem Cell Research Opens New Doors," *San Francisco Chronicle*, April 16, 2007, A1, A9.

13. "Stem Cell Information," National Institutes of Health, accessed June 16, 2013, http://stemcells.nih.gov/info/pages/faqs.aspx#besttype

14. Jason Thompson, "Here, Kitty, Kitty, Kitty, Kitty, Kitty!" *San Francisco Chronicle*, February 24, 2002, D6.

15. *New York Times*, October 8, 2004, A24.

16. Peter Fimrite, "Pet-Cloning Business Closes—Not 'Commercially Viable,'" *San Francisco Chronicle*, October 11, 2006, B9.

17. James Barron, "Biotech Company to Auction Chances to Clone a Dog," *New York Times*, May 21, 2008, A17.

18. Ferris Jabr, "Will Cloning Ever Save Endangered Animals?" *Scientific American*, March 11, 2013, accessed April 22, 2013, http://www.scientificamerican.com/article.cfm?id=cloning-endangered-animals

19. "Fast Facts about Animal Cloning," End Animal Cloning.org, accessed April 22, 2013, http://www.endanimalcloning.org/factsaboutanimalcloning.shtml

20. Nick Collins, "Human Cloning 'within 50 Years,'" *Telegraph*, December 18, 2012, accessed April 22, 2013, http://www.telegraph.co.uk/science/science-news/9753647/Human-cloning-within-50-years.html

21. "Close-up of Richard Jenne, the last child killed by the head nurse at the Kaufbeuren-Irsee euthanasia facility," United States Holocaust Memorial Museum, accessed June 16, 2013, http://tinyurl.com/ke3kj6e

22. Discussed in Michael J. Sandel, *The Case against Perfection: Ethics in the Age of Genetic Engineering* (Cambridge, MA: Harvard University Press, 2009), chap. 1.

23. "Couple 'Choose' to Have Deaf Baby," BBC, April 8, 2002, accessed April 22, 2013, http://news.bbc.co.uk/2/hi/health/1916462.stm; also see Darshak M. Sanghavi, "Wanting Babies Like Themselves, Some Parents Choose Genetic Defects," *New York Times*, December 5, 2006, accessed June 15, 2013, http://www.nytimes.com/2006/12/05/health/05essa.html?_r=0

24. Tom Abate, "Genome Discovery Shocks Scientists," *San Francisco Chronicle*, February 11, 2001, A1.

25. *New York Times*, October 21, 2004, A23.

26. "In the Genome Race, the Sequel Is Personal," New York Times, September 4, 2007, accessed July 25, 2013, http://www.nytimes.com/2007/09/04/science/04vent.html?pagewanted=all

27. K. A. Wetterstrand, "DNA Sequencing Costs: Data from the NHGRI Genome Sequencing Program (GSP)," accessed July 25, 2013, www.genome.gov/sequencingcosts

28. "Breakthrough of the Year: The Runners-Up," *Science*, December 21, 2007, 1843.

29. Tom Abate, "Proofreading the Human Genome," *San Francisco Chronicle*, October 7, 2002, E1; Nicholas Wade, "Gene-Mappers Take New Aim at Diseases," *New York Times*, October, 30, 2002, A21.

30. Wade, "Gene-Mappers."

31. "Decoding the Mouse," *San Francisco Chronicle*, February 24, 2002, G2.

32. Nicholas Wade, "On Road to Human Genome, a Milestone in the Fruit Fly," *New York Times*, March 24, 2000, A19.

33. Nicholas D. Kristof, "Building Better Bodies," *New York Times*, August 25, 2004, accessed April 22, 2013, http://www.nytimes.com/2004/08/25/opinion/building-better-bodies.html

34. "WADA-Funded Researchers Achieve Gene Doping Breakthroughs," World Anti-Doping Agency, accessed April 22, 2013, http://www.wada-ama.org/en/Media-Center/Archives/Articles/WADA-Funded-Researchers-Achieve-Gene-Doping-Breakthroughs/

35. "Genetic Privacy," *Nature*, January 17, 2013, accessed April 22, 2013, http://www.nature.com/news/genetic-privacy-1.12238

36. *New York Times*, July 28, 2004, A13.

37. *New York Times*, January 11, 2005, D7.

38. *New York Times*, July 28, 2004, A13.

39. *New York Times*, January 11, 2005, D7.

40. International Service for the Acquisition of Agri-Biotech Applications, *Global Status of Commercialized Biotech/GM Crops: 2012*, accessed April 22, 2013, http://www.isaaa.org/resources/publications/briefs/44/executivesummary/pdf/Brief%2044%20-%20Executive%20Summary%20-%20English.pdf

41. "GMOs and Your Family," Non-GMO Project, accessed April 22, 2013, http://www.nongmoproject.org/learn-more/gmos-and-your-family/

42. Stephanie Strom, "Major Grocer to Label Foods with Gene-Modified Content," *New York Times*, March 8, 2013, accessed April 22, 2013, http://www.nytimes.com/2013/03/09/business/grocery-chain-to-require-labels-for-genetically-modified-food.html?pagewanted=all&_r=0

43. Tom Philpott, "How GMOs Unleashed a Pesticide Gusher," *Mother Jones*, October 3, 2012, accessed April 22, 2013, http://www.motherjones.com/tom-philpott/2012/10/how-gmos-ramped-us-pesticide-use

44. See "Genetically Modified Foods: Harmful or Helpful," ProQuest, http://www.csa.com/discoveryguides/gmfood/overview.php

45. *New York Times*, January 1, 2005, D7.

46. Ibid.

47. "Genetically Engineered Foods May Cause Rising Food Allergies—Genetically Engineered Soybeans," Institute for Responsible Technology, accessed April 22, 2013, http://www.responsibletechnology.org/gmo-dangers/health-risks/articles-about-risks-by-jeffrey-smith/Genetically-Engineered-Foods-May-Cause-Rising-Food-Allergies-Genetically-Engineered-Soybeans-May-2007

48. Sean Poulter, "Can GM Food Cause Immunity to Antibiotics?" *Daily Mail*, accessed June 25, 2013, http://www.dailymail.co.uk/health/article-128312/Can-GM-food-cause-immunity-antibiotics.html

49. "Text: Bush Announces Position on Stem Cell Research," accessed June 28, 2013, http://www.washingtonpost.com/wp-srv/onpolitics/transcripts/bushtext_080901.htm

50. Meredith Wadman, "High Court Ensures Continued US Funding of Human Embryonic-Stem-Cell Research," *Nature*, January 7, 2013, accessed April 20, 2013, http://www.nature.com/news/high-court-ensures-continued-us-funding-of-human-embryonic-stem-cell-research-1.12171

51. "Adult Stem Cells: A Piece of My Heart, From Cells in My Arm," ABCNews January 28, 2013, accessed July 25, 2013, http://abcnews.go.com/Health/stem-cells-bill-weir-nightline-sees-cells-turned/story?id=18252405

52. "Nobel Prize in Physiology or Medicine," Nobelprize.org, press release, October 8, 2012, accessed April 20, 2013, http://www.nobelprize.org/nobel_prizes/medicine/laureates/2012/press.html

53. "New Protocol to Ready Clinical Applications of Induced Pluripotent Stem Cells," *Science Daily*, April 3, 2013, accessed April 20, 2013, http://www.sciencedaily.com/releases/2013/04/130403092655.htm

54. "Final Report of The National Academies' Human Embryonic Stem Cell Research Advisory Committee and 2010 Amendments to The National Academies' Guidelines for Human Embryonic Stem Cell Research" (2010), Appendix C, p. 23, National Academies Press, accessed April 20, 2013, http://www.nap.edu/openbook.php?record_id=12923&page=23#p2001b5399970023001

55. "Group of Scientists Drafts Rules on Ethics for Stem Cell Research," *New York Times*, April 27, 2005, accessed July 25, 2013, http://www.nytimes.com/2005/04/27/health/27stem.html?pagewanted=print&position=

56. George Q. Daley et al., "The ISSCR Guidelines for Human Embryonic Stem Cell Research," *Science*, February 2, 2007, 603–04.

57. "Copied Cat Hardly Resembles Original," CNN.com, January 21, 2003.

58. The Commissions website is found here: http://www.bioethics.gov/

59. Bioethics Defense Fund, *Human Cloning Laws: 50 State Survey*, (2011), accessed April 22, 2013, http://bdfund.org/wordpress/wp-content/uploads/2012/07/CLONINGChart-BDF2011.docx.pdf

60. See Barbara MacKinnon, "How Important Is Consent for Controlled Clinical Trials?" *Cambridge Quarterly of Healthcare Ethics* 5, no. 2 (Spring 1996): 221–27.

61. Reported in *New York Times*, May 21, 1996.

62. *New York Times*, November 22, 1994, A1.

63. This is modeled after a "thought experiment" by Richard Wasserstrom in "Privacy," *Today's Moral Problems*, 2nd ed. (New York: Macmillan, 1979), 392–408.

64. Thomas Scanlon, "Thomson on Privacy," in *Philosophy and Public Affairs* 4, no. 4 (Summer 1975): 295–333. This volume also contains other essays on privacy, including one by Judith Jarvis Thomson on which this article comments. W. A. Parent offers another definition of privacy as "the condition of not having undocumented personal knowledge about one possessed by others." W. A. Parent, "Privacy, Morality, and the Law," *Philosophy and Public Affairs* 12, no. 4 (Fall 1983): 269–88.

65. Erving Goffman, *Asylums* (Garden City, NY: Anchor Books, 1961).

66. Charles Fried, *An Anatomy of Values: Problems of Personal and Social Choice* (Cambridge, MA: Harvard University Press, 1970), 142.

67. "Questions of Privacy Roil Arena of Psychotherapy," *New York Times*, May 22, 1996, A1.
68. "Who's Looking at Your Files?" *Time* (May 6, 1996): 60–62.
69. "Bill in New Jersey Would Limit Use of Genetic Tests by Insurers," *New York Times*, June 18, 1996, A1.
70. Tracey Neithercott, "A Victory for Your Genes," *Diabetes Forecast*, August 2008, 35.
71. Tom Abate, "Biotech Firms Transforming Animals into Drug-Producing Machines," *San Francisco Chronicle*, January 17, 2000, B1.
72. See www.greennature.com

REVIEW EXERCISES

1. What is the basic difference between a therapy and an enhancement?
2. How do bioengineering and biotechnology provide opportunities for the disabled? How might these techniques point toward a posthuman future?
3. How does your thinking about animal ethics, the ethics of abortion, and even sexual ethics connect with your thinking about the ethics of biotechnologies? What concepts overlap among these issues?
4. Summarize the arguments for and against cloning and other reproductive technologies based on the idea that it would be "playing God" and would undermine human dignity.
5. Summarize the idea that cloning might pose a threat to the clone's individuality.
6. Summarize the arguments regarding human cloning related to exploitation, confusion of families, and the "yuck" factor.
7. Summarize arguments for and against genetic screening and genetic engineering of offspring.
8. What ethical issues have been raised regarding the production and use of genetically modified plants and crops?
9. Discuss the value of privacy and how it relates to genetic and other types of screening.
10. Should we pursue a "posthuman" future or are there reasons to remain more conservatively connected to more traditional ideas about human nature? Why or why not?

DISCUSSION CASES

1. **Human Cloning.** Victor and Jenny have one son, Alan, who was hit by a car at age four and then lapsed into a coma. The prognosis is bleak for Alan, but Jenny cannot bear to see him die and so they have kept him on life support. Victor has heard that scientists working at a secret lab have been successfully cloning human beings. Victor suggests that they contact the scientists to see if they can clone Alan—using Alan's DNA to grow a new baby, which would be a genetic copy of him. Jenny is appalled at this idea. "But it wouldn't be Alan. It would be a totally different person." But Victor suggests that the clone would be very similar. "The new baby would be created to honor Alan. Of course it wouldn't literally be *him*. But we could honor Alan's memory and keep Alan's unique genetic gifts alive by cloning him."

   What do you think? To what extent would a clone be the same person as the original? Would it be unethical to clone Alan? Why or why not?

2. **Smart Drugs.** Ramsey has obtained a "smart drug" from someone else in the dorms. He's heard that it may be possible to increase cognitive ability through the use of this drug and hopes it will help him on his upcoming finals. He knows it is illegal to use the drug in this way. But he does not believe that it would be unethical. "I think they ought to legalize marijuana too," he says to his roommate, Marc. "That's not the same, man," Marc replies. "Marijuana is just for fun. You're talking about using a drug to get an edge over other people on tests and in studying. That's just not fair. It's cheating." Ramsey rolls his eyes. "That's ridiculous. It's not really cheating," he says. "The drug won't make me smart. I still have to study. The drug will just make me more effective at studying. It's like coffee but stronger. Besides, the guy I got the drugs from has a prescription for them because he's got ADHD. If he gets to use the drugs to improve his performance, why can't I?"

Who do you agree with here: Ramsey or Marc? Is it "cheating" to use a "smart drug"? Explain your answer using concepts discussed in the chapter.

3. **Designer Babies.** Steven and Marisol are a young married couple who are concerned about passing genetic diseases on to their children. Members of Steven's family have been diagnosed with Huntington's disease, an incurable genetic disorder that causes cognitive problems, difficulties with movement that ultimately require full-time nursing care, and reduced life expectancy. Members of Marisol's family have tested positive for a mutation of the BRCA genes that are strongly associated with breast and ovarian cancer. At a family reunion, they are discussing their decision to use in vitro fertilization and preimplantation genetic screening of embryos. Steven's cousin, Valerie, is appalled. She is opposed to the idea of in vitro fertilization and to the entire idea of genetic screening. Valerie says, "You can't just choose the babies you want to have. God will only give you the challenges that He knows you can handle. And if a child is born with a disease, your job is to love that child, no matter what." Steven is speechless. But Marisol is not. "But if we can guarantee that our child is healthy and will live a happy life, shouldn't we do that? We don't want to raise a child who is doomed to genetic diseases." Valerie shakes her head. "There is no way to know," she says. "Kids get sick and die. Some who have diseases get better. You can't control everything. And besides, that test-tube baby stuff is really expensive. How can you afford it?" Now Steven replies, "We want to invest in this procedure now because it might save money in the long run. I've seen how much Huntington's costs a family—so have you. I'd rather pay to prevent it now than have to deal with the costs later." Valerie responds, "That sounds really rude. It sounds like you resent people who get sick and need your help. The whole thing is very selfish."

Whom do you agree with here: Steven and Marisol or Steven's cousin, Valerie? Is it wrong to want to prevent genetic disease? Is it a wise investment? Is it selfish to want to control your child's genes? Explain your answer.

19 Violence and War

iStockphoto/Thinkstock

Learning Outcomes

After reading this chapter, you should be able to:

- Describe issues arising in the context of the war on terrorism including the use of drones and targeted assassination, and the morality of terrorism and torture.
- Articulate arguments for pacifism.
- Articulate arguments for realism.
- Understand basic distinctions made within the just war theory between *jus ad bellum* and *jus in bello*.

- Explain and apply key terms employed in the just war tradition including *just cause*, *legitimate authority*, *discrimination*, and *noncombatant immunity*.
- Demonstrate how the doctrine of double effect applies within the just war theory to deal with the problem of collateral damage.
- Understand the history and concept of war crimes and crimes against humanity.
- Defend your own ideas about the ethics of war.

For most Americans, terrorism became an inescapable moral issue after September 11, 2001. On that day, Al Qaeda terrorists crashed loaded passenger jets into the World Trade Center in New York, the Pentagon in Washington, D.C., and a field near Shanksville, Pennsylvania, killing nearly three thousand people. The U.S. administration of President George W. Bush came to call its response to these attacks "the war on terrorism," a war that has grown and changed in a variety of ways. It began as the United States and its allies invaded Afghanistan in late 2001, in an unsuccessful effort to capture or kill the leadership of the Al Qaeda terrorist group, including Osama bin Laden. Afghanistan was viewed both as a failed state being ruled by an extremist religious faction—the Taliban—and as the haven from which Al Qaeda masterminded the September 11 attacks. Within two years, another front in the war on terrorism opened in Iraq, as the United States invaded the country in March 2003. Although Iraq had nothing to do with the September 11 terrorist attacks, President George W. Bush argued that the leader of Iraq, Saddam Hussein, was a malicious dictator who was a threat to stability in the region, that he had used chemical weapons against his own people, and—quite controversially—that he was currently stockpiling other weapons of mass destruction or WMDs. (After the U.S. invasion of Iraq, no such weapons were ever found, but the country did descend into a bloody and destructive civil war.) Bush also identified Iraq and two other countries—Iran and North Korea—as part of an "axis of evil" and argued that they were all sponsoring terrorism and pursuing weapons of mass destruction, including nuclear weapons. His administration threatened to use military means to prevent these countries from obtaining WMDs, although no direct military confrontation occurred. In more recent years, under the administration of Barack

Obama, battles in the war on terror have been waged in other countries such as Yemen and Pakistan, fought by drone aircraft and special operations forces. The U.S. forces have targeted the leaders of Al Qaeda and other terrorist groups, although substantial numbers of civilians have also been killed in these attacks.

As of 2013, the war in Iraq has ended and the U.S. involvement in the Afghanistan war is coming to a close. But terrorism remains an issue of grave concern throughout the world. As of this writing, Syria is embroiled in a brutal civil war, involving suicide car bombings and chemical and mortar attacks on civilians and causing more than 100,000 deaths.[1] Recent and ongoing conflicts in Israel, Lebanon, Libya, Pakistan, Mali, and Egypt have been marked by high civilian death tolls, both as a result of terrorist attacks and the actions of conventional armies. And the United States remains concerned that Iran is pursuing nuclear weapons technologies. More than a decade of war in the Middle East and North Africa has had a profound impact on the world. Estimates for civilians killed in the war on terrorism are as low as 140,000, with other estimates putting civilian casualties at well over 1.1 million. Military deaths include nearly 7,000 Americans killed, more than 1,300 coalition forces killed, and 60,000 to 80,000 enemy fighters killed.[2] Instability remains across the region.

Since 2001, there have been several attempted terrorist attacks in the United States—and one notoriously successful attack: the bombing of the Boston Marathon in April 2013, which we discussed in Chapter 15. We continue to worry about attacks on water supplies, transportation systems, computer systems, and fuel depots. Attacks in Europe, the Middle East, and Asia have targeted civilians in crowded markets, shopping malls, and buses. While Americans remain concerned about terrorism employed by foreigners, we should note that terrorism can be employed by homegrown domestic terrorists. One of the brothers involved in the Boston Marathon bombing was a naturalized American citizen; the perpetrator of the far more deadly Oklahoma City bombing, in 1994, was a native-born citizen. Terrorists do not need complicated or high-tech mechanisms to cause serious damage and

widespread fear. And terrorists do not wear uniforms or announce their plans in advance.

Some claim that it is difficult to define terrorism, pointing out that one person's "freedom fighter" is another person's "terrorist." But terrorism is generally agreed to involve violent acts that deliberately intend to inflict harm on those who do not deserve to be harmed. We'll discuss this further below. But note that according to that definition, school shootings—such as the one that occurred at Sandy Hook Elementary School in Newtown, Connecticut, in 2012 and at Virginia Tech University in 2007—can be described as terrorism. These acts may not have been politically motivated. But they certainly inflicted harm on the innocent. Most would agree that violence of this sort is wrong. And many would also agree that the police and the military would be justified in using violent force to disable or kill those who kill children. But are there moral limits on how much violence might be employed in such circumstances?

Most people assume that there is a right to use violence in self-defense. And many also think that we are *permitted* (some may say *required*) to use violence in defense of innocent children. The natural law tradition maintains that individuals have a right to life and liberty—and that violence can be employed to defend life and liberty against those who threaten it, including the life and liberty of defenseless and innocent others. A consequentialist argument could also be used here. More happiness will be produced for more people when such threats are eliminated. For a strict consequentialist, if the goal is to eliminate threats, the means employed are irrelevant. If war or other forms of violence work to produce good outcomes, then these can be used as a tool to defend social welfare.

In this chapter, we discuss three alternative approaches to the justification of violence. One maintains that violence is always wrong—this is **pacifism**. Another approach, often called **realism**, maintains that there are no *moral* limits on violence in warfare, even though there may be *pragmatic* or *strategic* reasons to limit violence. In the middle between these two extremes is an idea known as **just war theory**, which holds that violence can be justified when it is employed in limited and focused ways. The just war

Parents leave a staging area after being reunited with their children following a December 2012 shooting at the Sandy Hook Elementary School in Newtown, Connecticut—where Adam Lanza fatally shot twenty-seven people, including twenty children.

theory is grounded on a fundamental claim about the justification of violence in self-defense, and it extends this to a consideration of violence used in defense of others. While the just war theory is not directly applicable to the issue of domestic law enforcement, there are clear parallels between the idea that war can be justified and the idea that violence can be employed by armed guards to defend people against domestic criminals and terrorists. If we have a right to use violence to defend ourselves against those who would do violence to us, then we can also delegate defense to others—the police or the army. Furthermore, we might claim that while we are entitled to defend ourselves against violence, we are also entitled (or even obliged) to defend innocent and defenseless others from those who would do them harm. Realists will claim that in such circumstances, anything goes. We are entitled to pursue our own interests and defense in whatever way works. Pacifists have a difficult choice to make about the right to use violence in self-defense. But they tend to maintain that nonviolent alternatives should be developed and employed in a sustained and deliberate fashion.

Central to the discussion of the justification of violence is the question of what violence is. Violence is generally thought of as the use of physical force to cause injury to another. Physical assaults, shooting, and bombing are examples. However, we would not say that someone who pushed another out of the way of an oncoming car had been violent or acted violently. This is because violence also implies infringement of another in some way as well as the intent to do harm. It also has the sense of something intense or extreme. A small injury to another may not be considered an act of violence. Whether some sports—for example, football—can be considered violent games is something to think about. But we would certainly want to say that the destruction and harm of war is violent. The three moral approaches to thinking about the justification of violence—realism, pacifism, and the just war theory—are primarily focused on the morality of war, which may be defined as sustained and organized political violence. But the arguments presented here can be expanded and applied to the justification of other sorts of violence (for example, as Lloyd Steffen did in his discussion of the death penalty in Chapter 15). To get a better sense of these implications, let's turn to a more detailed exposition of realism, pacifism, and just war theory.

REALISM

Realism is the idea that in the "real world" of social and political life, violence is one tool among others to be employed strategically to get things done. Realists tend to be consequentialists, who are primarily focused on outcomes and results—and who are not as concerned with the morality of the means employed to achieve such results. Realism is often characterized as holding an "anything goes" approach to the question of violence. The idea of realism has roots in the thinking of Thucydides, the ancient Greek historian of the Peloponnesian War. In his account of a battle between the Athenians and the inhabitants of the island of Melos, Thucydides describes an attempted negotiation prior to the battle. The Athenians argue that since they have the more powerful military, the Melians ought to surrender, since it is useless for them to fight. The Athenians explain that the stronger party does whatever it can get away with, while the weaker party is prudent to acquiesce. The Athenians go on to say that the strong sometimes have to use violence to establish their supremacy and as a warning against those who might challenge them. The Melians do not submit to the Athenian threat. The Athenians attack, killing or enslaving all the inhabitants of the island of Melos. One moral of this story is that it is better to be strong than to be weak. Another moral is that there are no limits in war. From this perspective, war is understood as an existential struggle for supremacy. Perhaps it is possible to achieve a balance of power between equal powers. But if another power is threatening you, the realist would argue that in a life or death struggle it is necessary to do whatever it takes to defend against the threat of annihilation. Realists are opposed to the idea that there are inherent or intrinsic moral limits on the justification of violence. Indeed, they may argue that adherence to limitations on violence can make a nation look weak and ineffectual and produce more harm than good.

Realism is sometimes related to "militarism," which is a social and ethical system that celebrates martial power and military might. Some militarists argue that the highest glory is to be found in military adventures—an idea with a deep history that goes back to Achilles, the warrior hero in Homer's *Iliad*. Achilles and other heroes in warrior cultures view warfare as a test of manhood, which produces virtues such as loyalty, courage, and steadfastness (see Chapter 8 for discussion of virtue). Some continue to celebrate this spirit of masculine sacrifice and the glory of military service. But in modern culture, we have also expanded the definition of service and sacrifice to include gender-neutral virtues: it is not manhood that is tested but dedication and valor. Indeed, in the American military, women have been active participants for decades, and a recent policy change allows women to serve in combat.

Critics of militarism argue that there should be nonviolent ways to produce the same sorts of virtues. In his essay "The Moral Equivalent of War," American pragmatist philosopher William James called for a substitute for war. He wanted to find a way to develop virtues such as heroism and loyalty without the destruction of armed conflict.[3] But James was generally an opponent of war—especially the expansive American war in the Philippine islands. He and other philosophers—including the American feminist and pacifist author Jane Addams—were actively involved in the antiwar movement during the early part of the twentieth century.

Realists generally deny that moral ideas can be applied in warfare or that moral concerns should inhibit us from doing what is necessary to achieve victory. If we must bomb civilians or use torture to win a war, then that is what we must do. But realists are not simply bloodthirsty. They might agree that there are good pragmatic reasons to limit the use of violence. Violence can provoke a backlash (as enemies fight harder and unite against a dominant power). For realists, the central question is about what works. If terror bombing works, then it should be used, but if it does not work, then it should be avoided. Realists also have to consider the costs and benefits of warfare. War can be expensive. Realists do not advocate war at any cost. Instead, realists want to be strategic about the use of violence. It is not prudent to get involved in battles that cannot be won or that are so costly that they leave us in a weakened state.

Note here that realism is focused on the question of prudence, strategy, and pragmatism—it is a consequentialist approach that is not concerned with moral questions about the means employed. From a utilitarian perspective, war may be employed as a way of pursuing the greatest happiness for the greatest number of those living within a polity. (Note that such a use of the utilitarian calculus ignores suffering on the other side.) Realism may also be criticized as being amoral, as when it simply denies that morality applies in the context of war. This version of realism will hold that "all's fair in love in war" or that "war is hell"—both clichés point in the direction of the realist idea that in war, there is no morality at all.

PACIFISM

Pacifism lies on the opposite end of the spectrum from realism. While extreme realists argue that there are no moral limits in warfare, extreme pacifists argue that war is always wrong. Pacifism is often grounded in a deontological claim that focuses on the morality of killing. Deontological pacifists will maintain that there is an absolute moral rule against killing. Pacifism is also grounded in a more positive commitment to active nonviolence. Some forms of pacifism extend the idea of nonviolence in a very general way that condemns violence done to sentient beings in general, including nonhuman animals. Other forms of pacifism are narrowly focused on a condemnation of war as the most horrible form of violence, which must be opposed. Not all pacifists oppose the use of all types of force. After all, there are nonphysical means of exerting force, and even nonviolent social protest is a way of mobilizing social force. One can think of there being degrees of pacifism—that is, in terms of the degree and type of force thought acceptable. Some pacifists may reluctantly allow the use of physical and even lethal physical force when it is absolutely necessary, such as to defend oneself.

Pacifists generally maintain that nonviolent alternatives to violence are preferable and should be actively pursued in a creative and sustained fashion. Prominent pacifists include Mohandas Gandhi and Martin Luther King Jr., whose ideas we encountered in Chapter 2. Both were actively engaged in trying to change the world by using nonviolent social protest,

including nonviolent civil disobedience. While Martin Luther King Jr. is best known as a civil rights activist, he was also a critic of war. He opposed the Vietnam War, for example, arguing that using war to settle differences is neither just nor wise.[4]

The reasons given in support of pacifism vary. Some—like Gandhi and King—grounded their commitment to nonviolence in a religious perspective. Gandhi was dedicated to the idea of *ahimsa* (Sanskrit for nonviolence), which is a common value in South Asian traditions such as Hinduism, Buddhism, and Jainism. King developed his ideas about nonviolence from reading Gandhi. But as a Baptist minister, he also appealed to a pacifist interpretation of the Christian Gospels, an interpretation that is shared by such groups as Mennonites and Quakers. These Christians view Jesus as a pacifist who maintained (in the Sermon on the Mount found in the Gospel of Matthew 5, for example) that peacemakers are blessed, that one should not return evil for evil, and that we should love even our enemies.

Nonreligious arguments for pacifism can also be found—many derived from consequentialist considerations. Consequentialist pacifists believe that nonviolent means work better than violence to produce social goods. Violence does more harm than good, they argue, because violence begets violence. How can we determine whether or not this is true? We can look to see whether historical examples support the generalization. We also can inquire whether this may result from something in human nature. Are we overly prone to violence and bloodlust? Are we able to restrain ourselves when we turn to war? Our judgments will then depend on adequate factual assessments. We should note that it is difficult to weigh the benefits and costs of war—because we would have to engage in counterfactual speculation, asking what would have happened if we had (or had not) gone to war. War does cause substantial damage; however, it is an open question as to whether the damage of war is worse than the damage that would result if we did not use war to respond to aggressive dictators or genocidal regimes.

Most pacifists argue that killing is wrong. But critics of this view argue that if killing is wrong, there may be times when we need to kill to prevent killing from occurring. Consider, for example, whether it is justifiable to kill those who threaten the innocent. Should an exception to the rule against killing be made to prevent such killing? Would it be acceptable to kill in self-defense? Or in defense of innocent children, such as the children killed at Sandy Hook Elementary School? Or in defense of those who are being slaughtered by genocidal or racist governments? Pacifists must address the criticism that it seems inconsistent to hold that life is of the highest value and yet not be willing to use force to defend it. One way they might address this objection is to clarify that pacifism is not passive—pacifists do not advocate doing nothing in response to atrocity. Rather, pacifists can be committed to active, creative, and sustained efforts to help people and defend the innocent, so long as such efforts do not involve killing. Pacifists will also argue that the problem of war is that innocent people are accidentally killed even by the "good guys" and that it is very difficult to focus the destructive power of war in a way that does not harm the innocent.

JUST WAR THEORY

Intermediate between pacifism and realism is the idea that the use of force, including military force, is justified in limited and specific circumstances. The just war theory attempts to clarify when it is justifiable to resort to the use of lethal force. The just war approach is more or less the mainstream theory of the American military and political system. While some critics may argue that American military strategy includes a realist element—that the United States is engaged in asserting force and displaying strength around the globe—the rhetoric used to explain American military power is generally grounded in just war language. In a speech to the U.S. Military Academy at West Point on January 5, 1992, President George H. W. Bush put forth the following criteria: "Using military force makes sense as a policy where the stakes warrant, where and when force can be effective, where its application can be limited in scope and time, and where the potential benefits justify the potential costs and sacrifice."[5] President Barack Obama reiterated this idea nearly twenty years later when he delivered his Nobel Peace Prize acceptance speech. According to Obama, philosophers and theologians developed the just war idea over time as they attempted to find

moral language to criticize and limit the destructive power of war. "The concept of a 'just war' emerged, suggesting that war is justified only when certain conditions were met: if it is waged as a last resort or in self-defense; if the force used is proportional; and if, whenever possible, civilians are spared from violence."[6]

As Obama noted, the just war theory is not new. Indeed, the just war theory has a long history. Its origins can be traced to the writings of Augustine, one of the ancient fathers of the Catholic Church. Augustine wanted to reconcile traditional Christian views about the immorality of violence with the necessity of defending the Roman Empire from invading forces.[7] He asked what one should do if one sees an individual attacking an innocent, defenseless victim. His response was that one should intervene and do whatever is necessary (but only so much as was necessary) to protect the victim, even up to the point of killing the aggressor. Further developments of the theory were provided by Thomas Aquinas, who provides a natural law justification of the violence used in self-defense. Medieval codes of chivalry also have something in common with just war ideas. But the theory gets its most systematic exposition in the work of early modern theologians and jurists such as Francisco de Vitoria, Francisco Suarez, and Hugo Grotius. In more recent times, just war ideas have been instituted in international law, which asserts the right of a nation to defend itself against aggression, while also calling for protections for civilians and prisoners of war. These ideas can be found in international conventions, as well as in the Charter of the United Nations and other treaties signed by world powers.

There is general agreement that just war theory includes two basic areas: principles that would have to be satisfied for a nation to be justified in using military force, or initiating a war, and principles governing the conduct of the military action or war itself. These have been given the Latin names of *jus ad bellum* (the justness of going to war) and *jus in bello* (justness in war).

Jus ad Bellum

Just Cause   To use force against another nation, there must be a serious reason to justify it. Defense of one's territory against an invader is a prime example of a just cause for war. Nations have the right to defend themselves against aggression. But war is not justified to right a minor wrong or to respond to an insult. A newly developing concept of just cause includes the idea of intervening to prevent another nation from harming its own population. This idea is known as humanitarian intervention—the idea of using limited military force for humanitarian purposes. The United Nations has expanded this idea recently under the idea of a "responsibility to protect" (sometimes called "R2P"). The R2P idea holds that the international community has a responsibility to intervene to protect people from their own governments and to prevent war crimes and crimes against humanity (which we discuss in more detail below).

Other causes for war have been proposed. Could war be employed to prevent the spread of communism, to rid another country of a despotic leader, to prevent a nation from obtaining nuclear weapons, or to protect the world's oil supply? These may be viewed as cases of self-defense, using a broad definition of what is in a nation's vital interest. But the just war theory in general attempts to limit the causes of war.

One contentious issue related to just cause is the justification of preventive and preemptive strikes. If a neighboring nation is about to invade one's territory, preemptive defense against threatened aggression would seem to be a just response. A nation need not wait to be attacked when it knows an invasion is impending. The principle of "only if attacked first" may be too strict. Traditionally, preemptive attacks were thought to be justified if an attack was *imminent*. However, in the age of terrorists with weapons of mass destruction, some have argued that to wait until an attack is imminent is to wait too long. This logic has been employed to justify a variety of attacks. For example, Israel has attacked weapons sites in Iraq (in 1981) and in Syria in more recent years in an effort to prevent its enemies from developing deadly weapons. The U.S. invasion of Iraq in 2003 was justified as an attempt to prevent Iraq from using, developing, and disseminating weapons of mass destruction. While some just war theorists supported this invasion, others argued that preventive

war was an immoral use of war.[8] The danger of preventive war is that it can cause an escalation in violence, as each side may feel justified in attacking first.

Legitimate Authority If we assume that we can agree upon the question of what counts as a just cause for war, another concern is the question of who has the authority to declare war. Traditionally, it was thought to be the sovereign power who had the right to declare war. In the era of kings and princes, it was the monarch who declared war. In democracies, however, we presume that the power to declare war rests in the hands of the duly elected government. In the United States, there has been some concern about where the power to declare war resides: in Congress or in the president. The Constitution (Article I, Section 8, Clause 11) stipulates that the power to declare war rests in the hands of the Congress. However, in recent decades, the president has sent military forces into battle without explicit declarations of war. Leaving aside this constitutional question, we might wonder whether it makes sense for the civilian leadership to declare war. Wouldn't it be wiser to let the military decide when and where to fight? After all, soldiers are the experts in war. However, the idea of civilian control of the military is a central idea for democratic nations, which believe that warfare must be approved by the people through duly elected representatives. This can lead to a difficulty, however, as military priorities may conflict with the concerns of the civilian leadership.

The issue of **legitimate authority** points toward other problems. Who has a claim to legitimate authority in a civil war or a revolution? That's a difficult question to answer. Another problem has to do with the development of international institutions such as the United Nations. Should the United States defer to the judgments of the United Nations Security Council about wars and interventions? Or do the United States and other nations have the right to "go it alone" when it comes to war? In 2004, the secretary-general of the United Nations, Kofi Annan, declared that the United States had violated the United Nations Charter by going to war against Iraq and that the war was illegal.[9] But the United States maintained that it had a moral right to go to war without United Nations approval.

The issue of legitimate authority remains an important concern for thinking about the justification of war.

Proportionality Not only must the cause be just, according to the theory, but also the probable good to be produced by the intervention must outweigh the likely evil that the war will cause. Before engaging in warfare, we should consider the probable costs and benefits and compare them with the probable costs and benefits of doing something else or of doing nothing. Involved in this utilitarian calculation are two elements: one assesses the likely costs and benefits, and the other weighs their relative value. The first requires historical and empirical information, whereas the second involves ethical evaluations. In making such evaluations, we might well compare lives that are likely to be saved with lives lost, for example. But how do we compare the value of freedom and self-determination, or a way of life with the value of a life itself? How do we factor in the long-term impacts of war, including the possibility of post-traumatic stress for soldiers and civilians? Moreover, there is the difficulty of assessing costs and benefits with regard to a complex and chaotic activity such as fighting a war.

Last Resort The just war theory holds that war should be a last resort. Military interventions are extremely costly in terms of suffering, loss of life, and other destruction, so other means must be considered first. They need not all be tried first, for some will be judged useless beforehand. However, nonviolent means should be attempted, at least those that are judged to have a chance of achieving the goal specified by the just cause. Negotiations, threats, and boycotts are examples of such means. When is enough finally enough? When have these measures been given sufficient trial? There is always something more that could be tried. This is a matter of prudential judgment and therefore always uncertain.[10]

Right Intention Military action should be directed to the goal set by the cause and to the eventual goal of peace. Thus, wars fought to satisfy hatred and bloodlust or to obtain wealth are unjustified. The focus on intentions is a deontological element in the *jus ad bellum* consideration. Recall that Kant's deontological theory focused on the intention behind an act (what Kant called the "good will" and the nature of the maxims of action). In thinking about going to war, this principle would remind us that we ought to intend good things even as we employ violent means. The right intention principle seems to imply that there should be no gratuitous cruelty such as would follow from malicious intentions. This moves us into discussion of the conduct of a war, the second area covered by the principles of just war theory.

Jus in Bello

Even if a war were fought for a just cause and by a legitimate authority, with the prospect of achieving more good than harm, as a last resort only, and with the proper intention, it still would not be fully just if it were not conducted justly or in accordance with certain principles or moral guidelines. The *jus in bello* part of the just war theory consists of several principles.

Proportionality The principle of proportionality stipulates that in the conduct of the conflict, violence should be focused on limited objectives. No more force than necessary should be used. And the force or means used should be proportionate to the importance of the particular objective for the cause as a whole. This principle is obviously similar to the principle of proportionality discussed previously in thinking about *jus ad bellum*; however, within the *jus in bello* consideration of proportionality, the cost–benefit analysis is focused on limited war aims and not on the question of the war itself.

Discrimination Just warriors should not intentionally attack noncombatants and nonmilitary targets. While this principle sounds straightforward, there are complex issues to sort out in terms of what counts as a nonmilitary target or who is a noncombatant. Are roads, bridges, and hospitals that are used in the war effort military targets? The general consensus is that the roads and bridges are targets if they contribute directly and in significant ways to the military effort, but that hospitals are not legitimate targets. The principle to be used in making this distinction is the same for the people as for the things. Those people who contribute directly are combatants, and those who do not are not combatants. There is some vagueness here. Is a soldier at home on leave a legitimate target? One writer suggests that persons who are engaged in doing what they do ordinarily as persons are noncombatants, while those who perform their functions specifically for the war effort are combatants.[11] Thus, those who grow and provide food would be noncombatants, whereas those who make or transport the military equipment would be combatants.

Note, too, that although we also hear the term *innocent civilians* in such discussions, it is noncombatants who are supposed to be out of the fight and not people who are judged on some grounds to be "innocent" in a deeper moral sense. Soldiers fighting unwillingly might be thought to be innocent but are nevertheless combatants. Those behind the lines spending time verbally supporting the cause are not totally innocent, yet they are noncombatants. The danger of using the term *innocents* in place of *noncombatants* is that it also allows some to say that no one living in a certain country is immune because they are all supporters of their country and so not innocent. However, this is contrary to the traditional understanding of the principle of discrimination.

One way of describing the discrimination principle is to say that noncombatants should have immunity from harm. The idea of *noncombatant immunity* says that noncombatants should not be intentionally harmed. Combatants are not immune because they are a threat. Thus, when someone is not or is no longer a threat, as when they have surrendered or are incapacitated by injury, then they are not to be regarded as legitimate targets. The discrimination principle does not require that no noncombatants be injured or killed, but only that they not be the direct targets of attack. Although directly targeting and killing civilians may have a positive effect on a desired outcome, this would not be justified. The principle of discrimination is a deontological principle that stipulates a duty not to deliberately target noncombatants.

Nonetheless, some noncombatants are harmed in modern warfare—as bombs go astray and battles rage within cities. Noncombatant harms can be permitted by application of the *principle of double effect* (also discussed in Chapter 10). Noncombatant harms can be permitted if they are the foreseen but unintended and accidental result of a legitimate war aim. Not only must the noncombatants not be directly targeted but also the number of them likely to be injured when a target is attacked must not be disproportionately great compared to the significance of the target. Thus if a bomb goes astray and kills some children, this could be permitted by the principle of double effect if the intended target was a legitimate one, if the numbers harmed were minimal, and if the death of the children was not directly intended. In such a case, these children would be described as *collateral damage*, that is, as harms that are accidental and unintended.

Intrinsically Evil Means   A final concern of *jus in bello* is a strictly deontological prohibition on the use of means that are viewed as being evil in themselves (or *mala in se*, as this is expressed in Latin). One obvious inherently evil act is rape. Rape has long been a weapon of war, employed by conquering armies as a way of degrading and terrorizing a conquered people. But just warriors ought not engage in rape. We should also prohibit slavery as a means of warfare—for example, forcing captured enemies to engage in hard labor or using them as human shields. We might also think that the use of poisons—including poison gas—is intrinsically wrong. And most just war accounts maintain that torture is intrinsically wrong, although (as we shall see) in recent years there has been an open debate about the morality of torture in American war-making. To say that these things are wrong in themselves creates a deontological prohibition on such weapons and actions: just warriors may not use such weapons even if they might work to produce good outcomes.

According to just war theory, then, for a war or military intervention to be justified, certain conditions for going to war must be satisfied, and the conduct in the war must follow certain principles or moral guidelines. We could say that if any of the principles are violated, that a war is unjust, or we could say that it was unjust in this regard but not in some other aspects. Just war ideas have become part of national and international laws, including the U.S. Army Rules for Land Warfare and the UN Charter. Its principles appeal to common human reason and both consequentialist and non-consequentialist concerns.

Realists will maintain that the moral limits imposed by the just war theory can get in the way of victory and the goal of establishing power and supremacy. Pacifists will maintain that the just war theory is too permissive. Pacifists might reject, for example, the way that the doctrine of double effect allows noncombatants to be harmed. To evaluate realism, pacifism, and the just war theory, you must think about how you evaluate the various consequentialist and deontological principles and ideas appealed to by each approach. Let's apply these principles to some current issues.

CURRENT ISSUES

Terrorism

Terrorism would be condemned by pacifists, along with other acts of killing. **Just war theory** would condemn terrorism that kills noncombatants as violating the *jus in bello* principle of discrimination. Realists may argue that terrorism is acceptable if it works as a strategy.

We can describe an act of violence as terrorism when this violent act causes or intends to cause widespread terror. Usually this terrifying act has a political goal (although there may be nihilistic terrorists who blow up things just for fun). Some maintain that terrorism is a politically loaded term, employed to denigrate one's enemies. Some say that one person's terrorist is another person's freedom fighter. But the common element in a definition of terrorism is the use of attacks on noncombatants. The first known use of the term *terrorism* was during the French Revolution for those who, like Maximilien Robespierre, used violence *on behalf* of a state. Only later was the term used to categorize violence *against* a state. The U.S. Code of Justice (Title 22, section 2656f(d)) defines terrorism as "premeditated, politically motivated violence perpetrated against noncombatant targets by subnational groups or clandestine agents, usually intended to influence an audience." The FBI defines terrorism as, "the unlawful use of force or violence against persons or property to intimidate or coerce a government, the

civilian population, or any segment thereof, in furtherance of political or social objectives."[12]

By combining these definitions, we see that terrorism is, first of all, a particular kind of violence with particular aims and goals. The more immediate goal is to create fear. This is why civilians simply going about their daily routines are targeted at random. The more distant goals vary. Terrorists may use such violence to achieve some political goal such as independence from a larger national unit or to fight back against occupying armies or to protest against particular injustices. A terrorist may be motivated by religious or political ideology. Although we often read about Islamic militants employing terror tactics, it is important to note that terrorism can be employed by people from a variety of religions, and it can be used by secularly minded political groups. Christians have employed terror tactics (as in the struggles in Northern Ireland or as in the antiapartheid violence in South Africa). And Marxist revolutionaries have employed terrorism in pursuit of atheistic and communistic goals.[13] One could argue that the Ku Klux Klan used terrorism to subjugate the black population in the American South. And black militants in the 1960s advocated terrorism against white supremacy. One could argue that Native Americans used terrorism against the white settlers of the American West. And one could argue that colonial powers used terror tactics against the Natives. And so on. Any time there is an attempt to manipulate a political situation by applying indiscriminate force, it is possible that there is terrorism. We might even suspect that the use of firebombing and atomic bombing during the Second World War was a sort of terrorism—terror bombing that aimed to force the enemy to surrender by indiscriminately bombing civilian population centers.

Some terrorists commit suicide while killing others. We hear quite a bit about Muslim terrorists who employ the tactic of suicide attack. But we should note that suicide attacks have been employed by a variety of religious (and nonreligious) groups. The Japanese kamikaze pilots of World War II were, for example, suicide attackers (although since they attacked military targets, they may not be considered terrorists). Indeed, we might note that those American soldiers who launched themselves on the beach of Normandy on

D-Day also were involved in a kind of suicidal attack—although again, such a military onslaught is not terrorism. Suicidal terrorism is especially frightening, however, because the suicide bomber is not subject to a rational calculus of deterrence. The suicidal bomber is willing to die and wants to kill others in order to produce terror. Most suicide bombers are young (as are most soldiers) and thus may be more idealistic and easily influenced and manipulated. While some blame fundamentalist preaching and religious schools for the rise of suicidal terrorism, those who have investigated the background of known terrorists find that most of them are at least middle class and most often well educated.[14] Some terrorists are more rational in their goals than others, in having sufficient historical and political sense to know what will and will not work. In other cases, it seems that terrorists simply strike out in frustration, not caring about the long-term strategic consequences of their actions.

Terrorists seem to lack the ability to empathize with the innocent victims of their attacks. Terrorists may demonize entire nations and peoples, killing out of hatred. But terrorists may also be engaged in a consequentialist calculation that has much in common with the thinking of realism. From a realist perspective, there is nothing inherently wrong with targeting innocent civilians for attack. And if one is on the losing end of a military conflict, it might be necessary to resort to terror attacks as a way of continuing the fight. Those who resort to terror may be motivated by political or religious ideology. But they may also feel they have no other way to influence the state of affairs than to resort to terrorism.

In evaluating terrorism we might reject it outright as a form of unjustified killing. From this standpoint, terrorism is like murder—by definition wrong. Terrorism would be condemned in this way by pacifists, who maintain that all violence is wrong. Pacifists would also maintain that a war against terrorism is also wrong, since pacifists maintain that war is wrong. Pacifists may also view terrorism as an example of what is wrong with war and violence—it tends to spread toward the deliberate targeting of noncombatants. Moreover, pacifists might point out that terrorism produces backlash and escalation, which only tends to beget more violence.

Could there be an ethical justification of terrorism? The reasoning that supports terrorism is most often basically consequentialist. This is connected with the realist approach to the justification of violence, which holds that the end justifies the means. If one supported this type of reasoning, then one would want to know whether, in fact, the benefits outweighed the harm and suffering caused by the means. One could do empirical studies to see whether terrorism actually produces desired outcomes. Did the terror bombing of Japan during World War II result in the surrender of the Japanese? Did the September 11 attacks bring down the U.S. government or change its international behavior? Did terror attacks on American military forces in Iraq and Afghanistan lead Americans to retreat? These sorts of questions point toward the primary realist concern, which is the prudential and strategic application of power.

One might, however, question the consequentialist nature of realist reasoning by appealing to the just war theory's ideas about **noncombatant immunity** and discrimination. Indiscriminate violence can be rejected on realist grounds as simply being an inefficient use of power and resources. But in the just war tradition, the principle of discrimination is a non-consequentialist or deontological prohibition. Noncombatants cannot be intentionally or directly targeted, their deaths being used to send a message to others (no matter the importance of justification of the cause for which we are fighting). International law also condemns terrorism. The Geneva Conventions, including the fourth (adopted on August 12, 1949—more than sixty years ago), enunciated principles that aim to protect civilian populations from the worst effects of war. These conventions hold that civilians should not be directly attacked. From the standpoint of international law and the just war theory, terrorism is a war crime.

Targeted Killing and Drones

Terrorists are not necessarily part of any recognized state. Often they are loosely affiliated, acting alone or organized in small cells. They may be motivated by radical ideology read online or viewed in videos. And terrorists do not declare war or put on uniforms that distinguish them as combatants. For these reasons, some argue that the weapons and rules of traditional just war theory may not apply. Others argue that terrorists are simply criminals and that domestic and international law enforcement should be employed to bring them to justice.

Should terrorists be viewed as criminals, who ought to be captured if possible and put on trial so that they might be punished? Or are terrorists *enemy combatants* who may be killed or captured without a trial and held as prisoners of war until an eventual peace treaty is concluded? Or are terrorists *unlawful combatants* whose actions and ideology put them outside of the established moral and legal framework for dealing with enemy combatants? The term *unlawful combatant* has been employed by the United States to indicate that the normal rules for dealing with criminals and enemy fighters do not apply to those suspected of terrorism. For example, American policy is that terrorist suspects can be killed without trial. And when captured, terrorism suspects have been held without trial in extraterritorial prisons such as the American prison at Guantanamo Bay in Cuba (discussed in Chapter 7). Terror suspects have been tortured. And Americans have been engaged in targeted killing of terrorists, hunting them down in foreign lands (often in violation of the sovereignty of foreign nations).

The most famous case of targeted killing is that of Osama bin Laden. Osama bin Laden was the leader of Al Qaeda at the time of the September 11 attacks. He was killed by an American military attack on his compound in Abbottabad, Pakistan, on May 2, 2011. The operation that killed him was in violation of Pakistani sovereignty. When he was killed, he was accompanied by his wives and children. He was not actively engaged in military operations. Some claim that he was unarmed, with a recent book by one of the Navy SEALs involved in the raid maintaining that bin Laden was shot in the head as he peered down a dark hallway and again in the chest as he lay convulsing in a pool of his own blood.[15] The SEALs feared bin Laden could have had a booby trap or suicide vest at his disposal. President Obama explained in a speech to the nation celebrating the death of bin Laden that there was a firefight, which led to bin Laden being killed.

Whether bin Laden posed an active threat to the Navy SEAL team that attacked him or not, Obama and others maintain that the killing of bin Laden was justified. Obama explained that bin Laden was responsible for killing Americans and that he was also, as Obama explained, "a mass murderer of Muslims." Obama concluded, "[H]is demise should be welcomed by all who believe in peace and human dignity."[16] Eric Holder, the attorney general of the United States, further explained, "The operation against bin Laden was justified as an act of national self-defense. It's lawful to target an enemy commander in the field."[17] Critics objected that the killing was a violation of international law and that Americans had an obligation to work to try to extradite bin Laden and put him on trial. Critics might also object to Holder's claim that bin Laden was a "commander in the field." Is a terrorist who is resting at home in the middle of the night a commander in the field?

The justification of the killing of bin Laden points toward the broader question of whether it is morally and legally permissible to employ targeted killing as a method of warfare. The larger question from the standpoint of the just war theory is whether it is permissible to target an enemy commander or other soldier who is not actively engaged in fighting. The just war idea of discrimination may encourage us to distinguish between soldiers who are actively fighting and those who are in hospitals, on leave, or engaged in nonlethal support operations. One reason to avoid targeting soldiers behind the lines is to keep violence contained on the battlefield. But some may argue that this convenient distinction between combatants who are fighting and soldiers on leave does not hold in the war on terrorism where there are no specified fields of battle and where terrorists themselves refuse to adhere to the distinction between combatants and noncombatants. A realist would have no problem with targeting a terrorist mastermind or a political leader, except for pragmatic concerns about potential blowback from such attacks. The just war theory may also permit assassinations of terrorist masterminds and political leaders, if such attacks are discriminate and proportional. One concern, however, is that by employing targeted assassination, the door is open for similar attacks coming from the other side. Could Al Qaeda make similar arguments in attempting to justify attacks on American political or military leaders? The presumption here is that the "good guys"—those who fight justly and who have a just cause—are permitted to employ targeted killing, while the "bad guys" are not.

The issue of targeted killing has come to prominence lately with regard to the use of unmanned drones. Drone aircraft, piloted by remote control, can attack terrorist suspects around the world, easily crossing borders. Drones have been used to attack targets in a variety of countries: Afghanistan, Pakistan, Yemen, Somalia, and elsewhere. One advantage of drones is that they are more precise than other sorts of bombing, allowing for more discriminate and proportional killing. However, civilian noncombatants have been killed by the use of drones. One estimate is that in Pakistan, American drones have killed 1,600 people. At one point, early in the drone program in Pakistan, nearly half of the casualties were noncombatants. But the drone program has become more precise, with civilian deaths accounting for only 10 to 15 percent of casualties from more recent drone attacks.[18] Such killing may be justifiable on just war grounds as **collateral damage**.

Another advantage of using drones is that drones are cheaper than manned aircraft. And they do not put pilots at risk. However, they return us to the problem of who counts as a combatant. Would the remote control drone pilots, who fly these drones from facilities based in the United States and who thus never come near the battlefield, be considered "combatants"? One worry along these lines is that remote control piloting of drones extends our idea of what counts as "the battlefield" in a way that undermines the just war effort to constrain violence to a confined space of battle.

Defenders of drones will argue that they are an essential response to terrorism. The war on terrorism is not a traditional war, with armies fighting each other on clearly marked battlefields. Terrorists do not wear uniforms. Indeed, they try to blend into the local populace. And they employ mundane objects and camouflaged devices as part of their weaponry: car bombs, suicide vests, and, most notoriously, commercial jet airliners. Perhaps the rules have changed for a war on terrorism, which leads to a changed evaluation of the use of targeted killing. And since terrorists

plan their operations in cities and villages around the globe, it might be necessary to use drones to cross borders and kill terrorists where they are doing their planning.

Another problem arises when we think about the justification of targeted killing of terrorists—whether by drones or by other means—and that is the question of preventive violence. We might think that the killing of Osama bin Laden is justifiable because he was responsible for terrorist attacks in the past. But the drone and targeted killing policy of the United States allows for targeted killing of terrorists who have not themselves committed terrorism and who may not be an imminent threat. A Justice Department memo outlining the justification of targeted killing explains that the policy "does not require the United States to have clear evidence that a specific attack on U.S. persons and interests will take place in the immediate future."[19] In other words, it may be enough to be thinking about terrorism to be liable for targeted killing. Such an idea might make sense from a standpoint that advocates preventive warfare, as discussed previously. If the U.S. invasion of Iraq was justified as a war aiming to prevent Iraq from obtaining or using weapons of mass destruction to terrorize the world, couldn't a drone attack on a terrorist in Yemen be justified by the same logic? A defender of the drone program will argue that it is better to prevent terrorist attacks before they happen. But a critic will argue that it is a disproportionate escalation of hostilities.

The discussion of drones has become even more contentious due to the government policy of allowing targeted killing of American citizens. The Department of Justice memo mentioned above was used to justify the killing of American citizens who are actively involved in Al Qaeda and who are residing in foreign countries. This policy was employed in the killing of four Americans in Yemen and Pakistan in 2011.[20] Among those killed was a radical Muslim cleric, Anwar Al-Awlaki, who was born in New Mexico and attended college in Colorado. He was killed along with his son and another American associate. The U.S. government claims that Al-Awlaki was actively involved in planning terrorist operations against the United States and thus that his killing was justified.

Such a justification might appeal to just war ideas about the killing of aggressive combatants. Or targeted killing might be justified by realists as part of the struggle for supremacy in the world of power and politics. Critics have argued that it is illegal for the government to execute American citizens without attempting to capture them and put them on trial, perhaps maintaining that domestic and international law enforcement standards should be employed. But President Obama defended the drone program by maintaining that it was part of a just war against terrorism, which is discriminate and proportional in its approach to targeted killing.[21]

Weapons of Mass Destruction

One of the central concerns of the war on terrorism is the issue of weapons of mass destruction. Recall that the proliferation of weapons of mass destruction was a primary reason given by George W. Bush as a cause for the invasion of Iraq in 2003. The Bush administration maintained that the invasion was necessary to prevent Saddam Hussein from obtaining weapons of mass destruction, especially nuclear weapons. The issue of weapons of mass destruction remains a concern with regard to Iran and North Korea. Continuing hostilities with Iran are oriented around Iran's nuclear program. And the Korean peninsula remains tense due to North Korea's nuclear capabilities. In 2013, there was evidence that the Syrian government had used chemical weapons against rebels. This was widely condemned by the international community, leading to a change in U.S. policy toward the civil war in Syria. As a result of the chemical weapons attacks, the United States began actively arming rebel forces in Syria, while also threatening a military strike on the country.

The category of weapons of mass destruction usually includes biological, chemical, and nuclear weapons. Biological weapons are living microorganisms that can be used as weapons to maim, incapacitate, and kill. Among these weapons is anthrax, which infects either the skin or the lungs. Breathing only a small amount of anthrax causes death in 80 to 90 percent of cases. Smallpox, cholera, and bubonic or pneumonic plague are other biological agents that might be used. Genetic engineering may also be used to make more

virulent strains. There have been no proven usages of biological weapons in modern wars. One hundred sixty-three states have ratified the Biological Weapons Convention (1975), which prohibits the production, stockpiling, and use of such agents as weapons.

Chemical weapons include blister agents such as mustard gas, which is relatively easy and cheap to produce. It produces painful blisters and incapacitates rather than kills. Iraq used mustard gas in its 1980 to 1988 war with Iran as well as some type of chemical weapon on the Kurdish inhabitants of Halabja in 1988. Through low-level repeated airdrops, as many as five thousand defenseless people in that town were killed. Phosgene is a choking agent, and hydrogen cyanide "prevents transfer of oxygen to the tissues." Large quantities of the latter, however, would be needed to produce significant effects.[22] Hydrogen cyanide is a deadly poison gas, as is evidenced by its use in executions in the gas chamber. Sarin is called a nerve "gas," but it is actually a liquid. It affects the central nervous system and is highly toxic. In 1995, the Japanese cult group Aum Shinrikyo deployed sarin in the Tokyo subway. It sickened thousands and killed twelve people. Sarin is the gas employed in attacks in Syria that killed more than 1,000 people. Chemical weapons were also used in both world wars. For example, in World War I, the Germans used mustard gas and chlorine, and the French used phosgene. Although it might not be usually classified as the use of a chemical weapon, in 1945, American B-29 bombers "dropped 1665 tons of napalm-filled bombs on Tokyo, leaving almost nothing standing over 16 square miles." One hundred thousand people were killed in this raid, not from napalm directly but from the fires that it caused.[23] One hundred eighty-eight nations are party to the Chemical Weapons Convention (1994). Because such weapons can be made by private groups in small labs, however, verifying international compliance with the convention is highly problematic. Furthermore, Angola, Egypt, Syria, Somalia, and North Korea have refused to sign the convention, some arguing that they should do this only if all weapons of mass destruction were banned, implying nuclear as well.[24]

Nuclear weapons, including both fission and fusion bombs, are the most deadly weapons.

They produce powerful explosions and leave radiation behind that causes ongoing damage. The effects were well demonstrated by the U.S. bombings of Hiroshima and Nagasaki in August 1945. It is estimated that 150,000 people perished in these two attacks and their immediate aftermath, with an eventual total of nearly 300,000 deaths caused by these bombs (as survivors died of subsequent maladies attributed to the bombing).[25] Among the casualties at Hiroshima were American citizens—including American prisoners of war and Japanese Americans who were unable to escape from Japan once the war began. Some 3,000 Japanese Americans were in Hiroshima when the bomb was dropped; 800 to 1,000 survived and returned to the United States.[26]

Since the bombings of Hiroshima and Nagasaki, no other nation has ever employed nuclear weapons in wartime. Perhaps we learned a moral lesson from the sheer destructive power of these bombings. But for many decades after World War II, we continued to stockpile weapons. The world's nuclear arsenals grew to include unimaginable destructive power throughout the Cold War. Recognizing that nuclear weapons were pointing toward the nihilistic conclusion of mutually assured destruction, the nuclear powers have attempted to limit nuclear arsenals. There have been many nuclear weapons treaties—for example, the Nuclear Non-Proliferation Treaty (1968), the Strategic Arms Limitation Treaties (SALT I in 1972 and SALT II in 1993), and the Strategic Offensive Reductions Treaty (2002). Nations known to have nuclear weapons now include China, France, India, Israel, North Korea, Pakistan, Russia, the United Kingdom, and the United States. Although the parties to the 1968 agreement promised to pursue negotiations in good faith and move to a future treaty on general and complete disarmament, none of them has made real efforts in this regard. On the other hand, there has been some progress made regarding the agreement to reduce their stockpiles and the numbers of deployed warheads in the 2002 treaty.[27] On April 8, 2010, in a new START treaty, President Barack Obama and Russian President Dmitry Medvedev agreed to limit the number of nuclear warheads in each arsenal to 1,550.[28]

The global community continues to be concerned about nuclear proliferation. There is a worrisome global black market in nuclear materials and know-how. These weapons are difficult but not impossible to make. And many fear so-called "loose nukes," nuclear weapons that are not carefully guarded (for example in the former Soviet Union) and that are sold on the black market to terrorists. There was an attempt to confine possession of nuclear weapons to the original nuclear powers: the United States, the United Kingdom, France, the Soviet Union (now Russia), and China. But in recent decades nuclear weaponry has been developed by Israel and India, with Pakistan joining the nuclear club in 1998 and North Korea successfully detonating a nuclear device in 2006. Other states have agreed not to pursue nuclear weapons by signing on to the Nuclear Non-Proliferation Treaty. At least one state has voluntarily given up its nuclear weapons: South Africa dismantled its nuclear weapons in the 1990s.

In calling these nuclear, chemical, and biological devices *weapons of mass destruction*, we imply that they are of a different order of magnitude than the usual means of modern warfare. It is clear why nuclear weapons are labeled in this way, but it is not so clear why the others are. Even when used somewhat extensively in World War I, "fewer than 1 percent of battle deaths" during that war were caused by gas, and only "2 percent of those gassed during the war died, compared with 24 percent of those struck by bullets, artillery shells, or shrapnel."[29] For gas to work well, there can be no wind or sun, and it must be delivered by an aircraft flying at very low altitude. If delivered by bombs, the weapons would be incinerated before they could become effective. Today's gas masks and antibiotics and other preventives and treatments lessen the lethality of such weapons even more. In 1971, smallpox accidentally got loose in Kazakhstan but killed only three people; and in 1979, a large amount of anthrax was released through the explosion of a Soviet plant, but only sixty-eight people were killed.[30] There have been subsequent scares with regard to chemical and biological agents. In 2001, Americans were frightened by anthrax scares, as suspicious white powder was sent by the mail. In 2013, federal authorities arrested domestic terrorists who sent letters laced with the poison ricin through the mail to judges and politicians, including one to the president. Ricin is made from castor beans and it is quite deadly: a dose about the size of a grain of salt can cause death.

Realists would have no moral problem with weapons of mass destruction, provided that they work. One concern is that such weapons are difficult to use without harming your own soldiers. The wind can blow chemical and biological weapons in the wrong direction, and nuclear weapons leave deadly radiation that can harm one's own troops. On the other hand, just war theorists may argue that weapons of mass destruction are *mala in se* or evil in themselves (and so prohibited). But we need not appeal to intrinsic qualities of the weapons to form a moral critique of weapons of mass destruction. Principles from the just war theory that are used to evaluate terrorism and other warfare can be employed to evaluate the use of weapons of mass destruction. The principle of discrimination tells us that it is morally wrong to deliberately target innocent civilians with firebombs, nuclear bombs, or chemical weapons. And massive destruction caused by these weapons might fail the proportionality test as well. One wonders, however, whether ordinary bombs and bullets that explode and kill many more people than biological or chemical weapons are less objectionable. During the Second World War, more civilians were killed by conventional bombs than were killed by atomic bombs. And land mines continue to be a cause of harm—left behind in battlefields to harm civilians after conflicts end. Nevertheless, people seem to fear biological and chemical weapons more than conventional weapons. Possibly it is the thought of being killed by something invisible—radiation sickness or poison gas—that makes them so feared and is behind the desire to call them weapons of mass destruction, with the implication that they are morally abhorrent and are intrinsically evil.

War Crimes and Universal Human Rights

One of the difficulties of thinking about the morality of war is that, as the realists may insist, there is no international authority that could regulate behavior in war. Realists will argue that victors dispense so-called "victor's justice." Usually the term *victor's justice* is thought of as an accusation of unilateral and hypocritical judgment, as the victors punish the losers, while failing to prosecute or condemn their own unjust or immoral actions. Consider, for example, a scene from the 2003 documentary *The Fog of War* in which former Defense Secretary Robert S. McNamara is interviewed about his participation in the bombing of Japan during World War II. McNamara worked with General Curtis LeMay to coordinate the bombing of Japan. In addition to the atomic bomb attacks mentioned previously, American planes dropped incendiary bombs on a large number of Japanese cities, causing massive damage and killing millions. As McNamara reflects on this in the film, he acknowledges that the bombing would have been viewed as a war crime if the Americans had lost. He said that LeMay suggested, "If we had lost the war, we'd all have been prosecuted as war criminals." McNamara continued, "And I think he's right. He ... and, I'd say, I ... were behaving as war criminals. LeMay recognized that what he was doing would be thought immoral if his side had lost. But what makes it immoral if you lose and not immoral if you win?"[31] The realist will argue that this shows us that moral judgments do not apply in wartime and that the goal is to win so that one can be the victor dispensing victor's justice.

On the other hand, there is a growing consensus in the international community that moral judgment should apply to behavior in war. International agreements, treaties, and institutions have developed in the past centuries that aim to limit warfare and prosecute immoral actions done in war. These efforts in international law are grounded upon ideas that are closely connected to ideas found in the just war theory—most important, the idea that civilians should not be targeted and the idea that certain actions—rape, for example—are always immoral. Many of the elements of the laws of war and the nature of war crimes have been developed in the various declarations of the Geneva Conventions and in other international treaties and agreements. For example, the 1984 UN Convention against Torture, which was ratified by the United States, requires that all signatory nations avoid cruel, inhuman, or degrading treatment.[32]

Those who violate these conventions and protocols may be held to be guilty of "war crimes." One important source for the conventions regarding war crimes were the war crimes tribunals conducted after World War II—both the Nuremberg trials and the Tokyo trials. There have been questions about the legal procedures and standards of proof employed in these trials. But in general, they are viewed as examples of the developing moral consensus about the rules of war. The Nuremberg trials established three categories of crimes: *crimes against the peace* (involving aggression and preparation for war), *war crimes* (including murder, maltreatment of prisoners, etc.), and *crimes against humanity* (involving racial, religious, or political persecution of civilians). The last category, *crimes against humanity*, included a newly developed concept—that of *genocide*, the deliberate effort to exterminate a people. As is well known, the Nazis were engaged in a genocidal campaign of extermination against Jews, Gypsies, and others. Nazi death camps were employed in an efficient and mechanized effort to annihilate the Jewish people, resulting in the deaths of six million Jews (out of a prior population of nine million Jews in the German-controlled parts of Europe). This event is referred to as the Holocaust. The mass extermination of civilians is a war crime and a crime against humanity.

The idea of a crime against humanity and of war crimes in general can be understood in relation to the natural law and natural rights theories discussed in Chapter 7. Certain actions violate the natural value and dignity of persons, and all human beings should know this based upon a common moral sense, no matter what orders they receive. The important point here is that soldiers cannot be excused for criminal behavior by claiming that they are merely following orders. Principle IV of the Nuremberg trials stipulates, "The fact that a person acted pursuant to order of his Government or of a superior does not relieve him from responsibility under international law, provided a moral choice was in fact possible to him."[33] Moreover, Principle III of the Tribunal stipulated that heads of state and other political leaders were not excused from prosecution. The Nuremberg trials put twenty-two Nazi leaders on trial (Hitler, Himmler, Goebbels, and other Nazi leaders were already dead), resulting in convictions for nineteen of them and death sentences for twelve. While the Nuremberg trials are viewed as an important step in the development of war crimes tribunals and international law, some still worry that they remained examples of victor's justice—since there was no similar accounting for war crimes committed by the Allied powers.[34]

Since Nuremberg, the international community has worked to create a more impartial system for dealing with war crimes and crimes against humanity, including the development of an International Criminal Court in the Hague. But egregious attacks on civilians continue to occur, attacks that are referred to as "ethnic cleansing" or genocide. These attacks have occurred in Kosovo, in Rwanda, in Sudan, in Syria, and elsewhere. The international community condemns such atrocities. But it is often at a loss as to what to do about them. Military intervention is risky—and pacifists will argue for nonviolent responses. A significant problem is whether a war of intervention intended to rescue civilians will produce more harm than good in the long run. Although there is a developing international consensus about war crimes, the world is still not able to agree on strategies for responding to such crimes.

Torture

Torture is viewed as a criminal activity, outlawed by the Geneva Conventions and by other international treaties such as the UN Convention against Torture. But some have argued that torture could be justified in the fight against terrorism. And others in the U.S. government have sought to justify techniques that have traditionally been viewed as torture, in part by calling them "enhanced interrogations methods." In congressional testimony in February 2007, the director of the CIA, Michael Hayden, admitted that the United States has used waterboarding on prisoners. Waterboarding is a technique in which a prisoner's head is strapped to a board with his face drenched in water to produce a sensation of drowning. The CIA admitted that it used waterboarding on one particular terror suspect, Khalid Shaikh Mohammed, 183 times; another suspect was waterboarded 83 times.[35] These prisoners were subjected to other so-called "enhanced interrogation techniques": they were kept disoriented, naked, and cold. We have learned that prisoners were slammed against walls, given suppositories, prevented from sleeping, and kept in stress positions.

The Red Cross concluded that this treatment was torture and that it was cruel, inhuman, and degrading.[36]

But the government under George W. Bush argued that this use of torture was justified. Former Vice President Dick Cheney explained,

> No moral value held dear by the American people obliges public servants to sacrifice innocent lives to spare a captured terrorist from unpleasant things. And when an entire population is targeted by a terror network, nothing is more consistent with American values than to stop them. The interrogations were used on hardened terrorists after other efforts had failed. They were legal, essential, justified, successful, and the right thing to do.[37]

Cheney's justification of torture is a straightforwardly utilitarian justification: it works to prevent terrorism and should not be prohibited by a "moral value." The Bush administration's legal staff provided legal and moral justifications of torture. The Office of Legal Counsel in the Justice Department issued a number of memos suggesting that certain methods of trying to extract information from prisoners suspected of terrorism were not torture. The author of a number of these was a lawyer named John Yoo. Yoo argued that "inflicting physical pain does not count as torture unless the interrogator specifically intends the pain to reach the level associated with organ failure or death."[38] This definition was given to allow certain enhanced interrogation techniques while avoiding the legal prohibition on torture. According to this definition, waterboarding—simulated drowning—does not count as torture. Critics complained loudly that waterboarding was indeed torture and that this was not consistent with American law or international law and that the use of torture was contrary to American values.[39] For example, the U.S. Uniform Code of Military Justice makes "cruelty, oppression, or maltreatment of prisoners a crime."[40] Senator John McCain—who was himself tortured as a prisoner of war in Vietnam—spoke out against torture. And when Barack Obama became president, he banned the use of these "enhanced interrogation methods."

Pacifists will condemn torture as another example of unjustified violence. They may also point out that this episode from recent history indicates the ugly logic of war—that we can end up betraying our own values in the name of victory and power—and that this shows us why war is a corrupting and immoral force. Realists may nod in agreement with Dick Cheney's consequentialist justification of torture. Realists are not opposed to using supposedly immoral means to achieve other goals. Indeed, realists may also add that our enemies are not opposed to using torture and to employing other cruel techniques, including beheading prisoners. Realists may argue that the best way to fight cruelty is to employ cruelty in return. Just war theorists will not agree to that line of reasoning. Instead, they may argue that torture ought to be considered as one of those actions that are considered as evil in themselves and that are prohibited by principles of *jus in bello*. They may argue that even if torture works, there are some things we simply ought not do in pursuit of justified causes.

NOTES

1. Alan Cowell, "War Deaths in Syria Said to Top 100,000," *New York Times*, June 26, 2013, accessed July 11, 2013, http://www.nytimes.com/2013/06/27/world/middleeast/syria.html
2. Combining several sources: http://costsofwar.org; www.icasualties.org; www.iraqbodycount.org; and Wikipedia
3. William James, "The Moral Equivalent of War," *Popular Science Monthly*, October 1910.
4. Martin Luther King Jr., "Beyond Vietnam" (speech from April 4, 1967) at Martin Luther King Papers Project (Stanford), accessed May 21, 2013, http://mlk-kpp01.stanford.edu/index.php/encyclopedia/documentsentry/doc_beyond_vietnam/
5. *New York Times*, January 6, 1993, A5.
6. "Remarks by the President at the Acceptance of the Nobel Peace Prize," The White House, press release, December 10, 2009, accessed May 21, 2013, http://www.whitehouse.gov/the-press-office/remarks-president-acceptance-nobel-peace-prize
7. Robert W. Tucker, *The Just War* (Baltimore: Johns Hopkins University Press, 1960), 1.
8. See Andrew Fiala, *The Just War Myth* (Rowman & Littlefield, 2008), chap. 6.
9. "Lessons of Iraq War Underscore Importance of UN Charter—Annan," UN News Centre, September 16, 2004, accessed July 25, 2013, http://www.un.org/apps/news/story.asp?NewsID=11953&#.UfMBmWTEo_s
10. We might consider this particular principle as what is called a regulative rather than a substantive principle. Instead of telling us when something is enough or the last thing we should try, it can be used to prod us to go somewhat further than we otherwise would.
11. James Childress, "Just-War Theories," *Theological Studies* (1978): 427–45.

12. Both definitions found at "Terrorism," National Institute of Justice, September 12, 2011, accessed May 21, 2013, http://www.nij.gov/topics/crime/terrorism/

13. Max Rodenbeck, "How Terrible Is It?" *New York Review of Books*, November 30, 2006, 35.

14. Peter Bergen and Swati Pandey, "The Madrassa Myth," *New York Times*, June 14, 2005, A19.

15. Mark Owen, *No Easy Day: The Firsthand Account of the Mission That Killed Osama Bin Laden* (New York: Dutton, 2012).

16. "Remarks by the President on Osama Bin Laden," The White House, press release, May 2, 2011, accessed May 21, 2013, http://www.whitehouse.gov/the-press-office/2011/05/02/remarks-president-osama-bin-laden

17. Erik Kirschbaum and Jonathan Thatcher, "Concerns Raised over Shooting of Unarmed bin Laden," Reuters, May 4, 2011, accessed May 22, 2013, http://www.reuters.com/article/2011/05/04/us-binladen-legitimacy-idUSTRE74371-H20110504

18. Peter Bergen and Jennifer Rowland, "9 Myths about Drones and Guantanamo," CNN, May 22, 2013, accessed May 22, 2013, http://www.cnn.com/2013/05/22/opinion/bergen-nine-myths-drones-gitmo/index.html

19. Department of Justice White Paper (published by NBC News February 2013), accessed May 22, 2013, http://msnbcmedia.msn.com/i/msnbc/sections/news/020413_DOJ_White_Paper.pdf

20. "Obama, in a Shift, to Limit Targets of Drone Strikes," *New York Times*, May 22, 2013, accessed July 26, 2013, http://www.nytimes.com/2013/05/23/us/us-acknowledges-killing-4-americans-in-drone-strikes.html?_r=0

21. "Obama Speech on Drone Policy," *New York Times*, May 23, 2013, accessed May 23, 2013, http://www.nytimes.com/2013/05/24/us/politics/transcript-of-obamas-speech-on-drone-policy.html?pagewanted=all&_r=0

22. "Introduction to Chemical Weapons," Federation of American Scientists, www.fas.org/cw/intro.htm

23. Howard W. French, "100,000 People Perished, but Who Remembers?" *New York Times*, March 14, 2002, A4.

24. Daniel J. Kevles, "The Poor Man's Atomic Bomb," *New York Review of Books*, April 12, 2007, 60–63; also see http://treaties.un.org

25. John W. Dower, "The Bombed: Hiroshimas and Nagasakis in Japanese Memory," in *Hiroshima in History and Memory*, ed. Michael J. Hogan (Cambridge: Cambridge University Press, 1996).

26. Rinjir Sodei, *Were We the Enemy?: American Survivors of Hiroshima* (Boulder, CO: Westview Press, 1998).

27. *Time*, August 1, 2005, 38–39.

28. U.S. State Department, "New START," accessed July 26, 2013, http://www.state.gov/t/avc/newstart/index.htm

29. Gregg Easterbrook, "Term Limits, The Meaninglessness of 'WMD,'" *New Republic*, October 7, 2002, 23.

30. Ibid.

31. Errol Morris, *The Fog of War* transcript, accessed May 21, 2013, http://www.errolmorris.com/film/fow_transcript.html

32. "UN Convention against Torture and Other Cruel, Inhuman or Degrading Treatment or Punishment (December 1984)," Audiovisual Library of International Law, accessed May 21, 2013, http://untreaty.un.org/cod/avl/ha/catcidtp/catcidtp.html

33. "Principles of the International Law Recognized in the Charter of the Nüremberg Tribunal and the Judgment of the Tribunal, 1950," Principle IV, at International Committee of the Red Cross, accessed May 21, 2013, http://www.icrc.org/applic/ihl/ihl.nsf/ART/390-550004?OpenDocument

34. See Michael Biddiss, "Victors' Justice? The Nuremberg Tribunal," *History Today* 45, no. 5 (1995), accessed May 21, 2013, http://www.historytoday.com/michael-biddiss/victors-justice-nuremberg-tribunal

35. Scott Shane, "Waterboarding Used 266 Times on 2 Suspects," *New York Times*, April 19, 2009, accessed June 16, 2013, http://www.nytimes.com/2009/04/20/world/20detain.html

36. Mark Danner, "U.S. Torture: Voices from the Black Sites," *New York Review of Books*, April 9, 2009, http://www.nybooks.com/articles/22530

37. Dick Cheney speaking on *The McLaughlin Group*, May 22, 2009, accessed June 18, 2013, http://www.mclaughlin.com/transcript.htm?id=725

38. David Luban, "The Defense of Torture," *New York Review of Books*, March 15, 2007, 37–40.

39. Ibid.

40. Uniform Code of Military Justice Sec. 893, Art. 93, accessed May 21, 2013, http://www.au.af.mil/au/awc/awcgate/ucmj2.htm

REVIEW EXERCISES

1. Explain realism and how it is related to consequentialist concerns.

2. Explain pacifism and how it is related to deontological concerns.

3. Why is the just war theory considered a middle path between realism and pacifism?

4. What is just war theory, and how did it come to be developed?

5. List and explain the basic principles of *jus ad bellum* and *jus in bello*.

6. What are the challenges for thinking about the application of just war principles in the contemporary world?

7. Can terrorism be justified? On what grounds?

8. What is a weapon of mass destruction?

9. How does the principle of double effect apply in just war thinking?

10. What counts as a "war crime" or a "crime against humanity"?

11. Can torture be justified or is it always wrong?

D I S C U S S I O N   C A S E S

1. **Military Service.** Although military service is no longer compulsory in the United States, American males age eighteen to twenty-five have to register with the Selective Service. If you do not register, you may be denied benefits and employment opportunities. James recently turned eighteen. He is opposed to war and is considering not signing up. He is explaining this to his parents. James says, "Look, I don't want to support a system that fights unjust wars and I won't fight in one. So I'm not going to sign up." James's father is a military veteran. He responds, "We've all got a duty to serve our country, whether just or unjust. And anyway, you're wrong to claim we fight unjust wars. Our military fights justly. Do your duty and register." James's brother has a different opinion. He says, "Your moral principles don't apply in war. There are no just or unjust wars. There are only winners and losers. It's better to be on the winning side. You should register because you want the benefits and don't want to get busted."

   Whom do you agree with here: James, his father, or his brother? Should a person register to fight if he doesn't believe in the justice of the wars that are being fought? How should moral principles apply in this case?

2. **Terrorism.** Marta has expressed sympathy for rebels fighting in country X. These rebels have been fighting against an unjust and malicious regime. The regime has killed innocent civilians and has an awful record of human rights violations. The rebellion started as a nonviolent protest in the streets. But now the rebels have taken up arms and are actively fighting government forces. They have begun to employ terror tactics, exploding car bombs in the city center in the capital. Marta supports the rebel cause and has even bought a T-shirt with a slogan from the rebel campaign on it. Marta's roommate, Andrea, is appalled. Andrea tells her, "How can you wear a T-shirt celebrating terrorists? They kill innocent people. Even if their cause is just, the rebels have crossed the line. They're murderers. All terrorists are simply murderers." Marta replies, "That's easy for you to say because you're not suffering under a repressive government. The rebels are justified in doing whatever it takes to bring down the government. The government forces are ruthless and strong—the rebels have to use terrorism: it's their only tool."

   Whom do you agree with here: Marta or Andrea? Is terrorism justified as a tool of last resort? Or is terrorism always murder? Explain your answer, making use of concepts employed in discussions of realism, just war theory, and pacifism.

3. **Military Intervention.** The ruler of country Z has a terrible record of human rights violations. He has ordered the slaughter of civilians and has threatened to invade neighboring states. He has been working with known arms dealers to develop his military capacity. And he has worked to spread his influence by supporting insurgent fighters and terrorist groups in other countries. Three students are debating this case and what the United States should do in response. Roxanne is a realist. She argues that we should attack country Z with massive force as soon as possible with the goal of decapitating the regime. "That's what we did in Japan during World War II. And now Japan is a peaceful and stable ally." Patrick is a pacifist. He disagrees. "You know that we dropped atomic weapons on Japan and firebombed cities. It was immoral to do that. The end doesn't justify the means. We have to find nonviolent alternatives to deal with Z." Justin advocates limited use of military force. He says, "The just war tradition might allow for preemptive force and may allow for limited war in defense of human rights. But we have to be careful not to kill civilians." Roxanne shakes her head. "Sorry, but you can't win a war without killing civilians. And the faster you win, the better for everyone." Patrick sighs. "Have we even tried all of the nonviolent alternatives?" Justin shrugs. "If we go to war, it can only be a last resort. But, Roxanne, you can't just kill the innocent. You've got to win hearts and minds, as well."

   Whom do you agree with in this debate? Why? What do you suggest we do about brutal dictators and aggressive regimes?

valentina anguli photografie/Flickr/Getty Images

20 Global Justice and Globalization

Learning Outcomes

After reading this chapter, you should be able to:

- Understand contemporary debates over global justice.
- Explain the idea of ethical consumerism and fair trade.
- Describe some of the ethical challenges involved in responding to global poverty.
- Apply concepts such as utilitarianism, justice, and rights to the problem of global poverty.

- Explain criticisms and defenses of economic globalization.
- Describe connections between globalization and the challenges posed by cultural diversity and relativism.
- Evaluate levels of international aid and the role of international institutions.
- Defend a thesis about the ethical issue of global poverty.

In 2013, a garment factory in Bangladesh collapsed, killing more than 1,120 workers. The previous year, a fire at another Bangladeshi garment factory resulted in more than a hundred deaths. In 2013, a shoe factory caved in on workers in Cambodia, killing two and injuring dozens of others.[1] In 2011, two explosions at plants manufacturing iPads in China killed four workers, injured seventy-seven others, and raised serious questions about safety conditions throughout Apple's supply chain.[2] These industrial disasters prompted call for more equitable and just treatment of workers across the globe. The Walt Disney company announced that it was going to stop producing Disney brand products in developing countries that have lax labor standards and poor regulation, including Bangladesh, Pakistan, Belarus, Ecuador, and Venezuela.[3] Some viewed this as a good move on the part of Disney, motivated by a sense of moral responsibility. But critics worry that if big corporations pull out of the developing world, it will cause unemployment and create negative outcomes for the workers there. Some brands and retail chains are working with local labor and business leaders in the developing world to forge agreements on fire and other safety codes for the factories they do business with.

Of course, if working conditions in the developing world are improved, consumer prices in the developed world may rise. While rising prices of consumer goods would create hardship for many, some consumers may not mind paying more for products that are produced and traded in nonexploitative markets. Indeed, some people conscientiously choose to pay more for clothing and other products that are not produced in sweatshops, pursuing a path called variously, *ethical consumption*, *ethical consumerism*, or *shopping with conscience*. This approach to consumption aims to channel consumer choices in morally responsible and sustainable directions. Would you be willing to pay more for a product to ensure that the product is not produced in a sweatshop or by other exploitative labor practices?

One concept associated with the idea of ethical consumerism is the idea of *fair trade practices*. Fair trade aims to help disadvantaged people in the developing world by buying goods that are produced in beneficial and nonexploitative conditions.[4] You may have seen fair trade items advertised in stores or on websites. Fair trade coffee, for example, is typically certified by one of several nonprofit organizations (such as Fair Trade USA) to be grown and harvested by workers who are able to earn a living wage under safe working conditions. (See the discussion of living wage in Chapter 14.) But some critics worry that the fair trade label simply makes consumers feel good, while being used as a marketing ploy by big corporations.[5] Similar worries have been voiced about contributions to aid organizations. How can we be sure that those we intend to help actually receive the help we intend to give? There is an important practical question here, one that does not, however, change the moral question of whether we should help others in need—especially very poor people in other parts of the globe.

Not everyone agrees we should go out of our way to help others. And many will argue that it is perfectly fine to maximize one's own self-interest by seeking out bargains no matter how they are produced, or by refusing to donate to charities. For many, it just does not seem rational to pay more for fair trade coffee or sneakers or T-shirts, when cheaper products can be found. Why should we be concerned with the deaths of garment workers in distant countries? Why should we care whether foreign peasants earn a living wage? Those questions are part of a larger question about the sorts of obligations we have to those who suffer and die in distant lands. These sorts of ethical questions arise in the context of thinking about globalization; they are the concerns of global justice.

Globalization is the process through which the world's business, cultural, and political systems are becoming more integrated. **Globalization** can be defined as a historical process that includes the growing interconnection of local and national economies from all corners of the world, which occurs as capital,

Civilians try to put out a fire at the Sir Denim Limited garment factory in Bangladesh.

goods, services, labor, technology, ideas, and expertise move across international borders. Globalization is a fact; the world is increasingly integrated. **Global justice** is focused on the moral question of the underlying fairness and justice of the current globalized situation. Proponents of global justice are focused broadly on the question of what sort of concern we ought to have for all human beings, regardless of national status or citizenship. In this sense, global justice is *cosmopolitan*—directed toward the universal concerns of all citizens of the world. We discussed cosmopolitan concerns in Chapter 2, where we dealt with the problem of relativism and religious difference. Those issues remain in the background of the consideration of global justice. Is there a moral framework that can encompass the entire globe, despite global diversity? Or is the world fragmented into rival nations, economies, and civilizations that each ought to fend for themselves? What sorts of obligations do individuals have toward each other in the context of a world that is controlled by national governments, international treaties, nongovernmental organizations, and multinational corporations?

One of the issues of concern from the standpoint of global justice is poverty and gross inequalities across the globe. This topic is connected to our discussion of economic justice and inequality in Chapter 14. But the issue of global economic inequality is complicated by the fact that many current inequities can be traced to past colonial and imperial injustices. Some nations have built up their present economic power by exploiting other nations. A further problem is the presence of national and cultural differences, as well as local governments of various types, which operate as intermediaries between individual citizens and the demands of global justice. We have to figure out which theory of economics and politics makes sense in thinking about global justice. We also have to figure out how that moral theory should be applied in a world of vast cultural differences.

MORAL ARGUMENTS ABOUT GLOBAL POVERTY

In 2013, the president of the World Bank, Jim Yong Kim, announced the goal of eliminating extreme poverty across the globe by the year 2030. He linked the moral goal of eliminating global poverty to the goal of sustainable development for all peoples: "Assuring that growth is inclusive is both a moral imperative and a crucial condition for sustained economic development."[6] Kim suggested that sustainable development for everyone requires us to address global poverty and inequality—and that it is beneficial for those in affluent nations when those in the developing world are also doing better. But we should note that Kim also used strong moral language here, claiming that helping the global poor is a moral imperative. If there is a moral duty to help the poor, then it would be wrong not to help them. And if it is wrong not to help the poor, then we should feel guilty if we do not help them. With billions of people living on a few dollars per day, should we feel guilty if we are enjoying a $4 café latte or a $5 ice cream treat? For the price of one of those luxuries, we could be helping children who might die from poverty. If you don't feel guilty

when you enjoy your tasty treat, is there something morally wrong with you?

A critic may reply that the fact that we do not feel guilty about our indulgences is a sign that there is no moral obligation to care about the suffering of distant people. Of course, it might be that our feelings are poor guides for morality and we really should feel guilty. A further argument is needed. The critic might provide one by claiming that our individual choices can have little effect on something as complex as the global economy. There is no guarantee that by donating to charity instead of enjoying a luxury good, we will actually help anyone. And besides, the critic may continue, the old saying holds that if you give a man a fish, you only feed him for a day but when you give a man a fishing pole, you feed him for a lifetime. Following that line of reasoning, the critic may argue that giving to the poor only makes them dependent on handouts. It is better, from this perspective, to buy commodities produced by the poor than to give to them directly, since trading on the market is the key to long-term economic well-being.

Another criticism of the idea of donating to the poor focuses on the nature of obligation and duty. Many feel that although it would be nice to help poor people, charity is supererogatory—something that goes above and beyond what is required. And furthermore, some might argue, charity should begin at home, as the saying goes. In this view, we have obligations to care for our close relations, our friends, and our co-citizens, and those obligations are more important than any charitable obligation we might have to suffering foreigners. These critics may also argue that global poverty is simply not our fault. Guilt and responsibility are appropriate if you have done something wrong. But there is nothing wrong with buying a latte or a pair of sneakers, and my consumer choices do not actively harm the poor. In fact, some may argue, by buying sneakers produced in sweatshops in Cambodia, I am helping the Cambodians who produce them by purchasing their products. Without the purchases of consumers in affluent countries, those workers may have no jobs at all.

One response to that argument has been given by the philosopher Thomas Pogge, an important proponent of the idea of global justice. Pogge argues that the international system unjustly violates the rights of the world's poor. He claims that the international system is rigged against the poor—as large corporations and conditions created by historical injustices contribute to the continuing plight of the disadvantaged. Pogge acknowledges that there is a difference between failing to save people and actively killing them. But he claims that we are not merely failing to save the poor; he also claims that we are actively perpetuating their predicament because historical and international structures create a "massive headwind" that the poor cannot overcome. He concludes that affluent nations and citizens of affluent nations owe compensation to the poor.[7] He has proposed, for example, a "global resource dividend" as one aspect of a global scheme for compensating the poor. This is a sort of tax on resources, which would be used to help the poor. One example he proposes is a $3 per barrel charge on oil. This would raise the price of oil by about 7 cents per gallon; but the revenue generated would create sufficient funding to eradicate world hunger within a few years.[8] There are practical and political details to be worked out for such a proposal. For example, how do we institute and collect such resource dividends? But the practical concerns do not change the nature of Pogge's moral claim—that we owe compensation to the poor and that we ought to find ways to help alleviate world hunger.

A similar argument has been made by the utilitarian philosopher Peter Singer—an author whom we've discussed in previous chapters (with regard to animal welfare, for example, in Chapter 17). Singer maintains that giving to victims of famines is not charity but, rather, a duty. Singer stipulates that, "if it is in our power to prevent something very bad from happening, without thereby sacrificing anything morally significant, we ought, morally, to do it." Singer uses an analogy of saving a child from drowning in a mud puddle to make his point: "if I am walking past a shallow pond and see a child drowning in it, I ought to wade in and pull the child out. This will mean getting my clothes muddy, but this is insignificant, while the death of the child would presumably be a very bad thing."[9] Singer maintains that proximity does not matter—if the

dying child is far away or nearby, we still have the same obligation. And he denies that our individual responsibility can be diffused by the fact that there are lots of others who could also help; each should help, whether there are others who could help or not. Singer believes that we have an obligation to help those less well off than ourselves to the extent that helping them leaves us less well off than they are. He explains that we ought to give up to the point of "marginal utility," that is up to the point at which giving causes us to suffer significantly so that by giving we end up in as bad a state as those we are trying to help.

Singer's idea is very demanding. It implies that I must always justify spending money on myself or my family or friends. Whether I am justified in doing so, in this view, depends on whether anything I do for myself or others is of comparable moral importance to saving the lives of others who are starving and lacking in basic necessities. But Singer's arguments have resonated with a number of people. The *Washington Post* reported on a number of people who have pursued big salaries on Wall Street and in other ventures with the goal of earning lots of money precisely so they can give much of it away to help the poor. The phenomenon has been described as "earning to give." Several of the individuals who are "earning to give" explain that they were motivated by Singer's concerns.[10]

Of the opposite point of view is Garrett Hardin, who believes that we have no obligation to give to the poor because to do so will do no good.[11] We discussed Hardin (in Chapter 16) with regard to the problem of the tragedy of the commons—the problem that arises when everyone pursues their own self-interest without regard for common environmental goods. Hardin's ideas about global justice are linked to a related worry about growing populations and lack of adequate resources to feed everyone. Hardin maintains that the nations of the world are struggling for existence as if each nation is an individual lifeboat on a stormy sea. Each of these lifeboats has a limited carrying capacity and is subject to environmental threats, which means that the members of each lifeboat have to look out for themselves by building up reserves and avoiding overuse of their own resources.

Hardin further suggests that famine relief only postpones the inevitable—death and suffering. According to Hardin, this is because overpopulation produced by famine relief will lead to more famine and even worse death in the future. From Hardin's perspective, there is a natural process of boom and bust, binge and purge that follows along lines outlined by Thomas Malthus, the eighteenth-century author and economist. Malthus predicted that populations grow until they outstrip their resources, after which they die back. Hardin maintains—as Malthus did—that it is wrong to help starving people because such help only causes them to live longer and reproduce, which will produce more mouths to feed and more suffering and a worse die-back in the future.

Whether Hardin's Malthusian predictions are correct is an empirical matter. These predictions would need to be verified or supported by observation and historical evidence. And many factors must be considered. For example, will all forms of famine relief, especially when combined with other aid, necessarily do more harm than good as Hardin predicts? Is it possible to provide assistance to the impoverished while also encouraging birth control, responsible farming practices, liberation for women, and sustainable industrial development—all of which would prevent overpopulation and subsequent die-back?

Answering such questions is difficult because it requires knowledge of the effects of aid in many different environmental, cultural, and political circumstances. It is worthwhile reflecting, however, on the consequentialist nature of these arguments. The primary focus of most discussions of global poverty is a sort of global utilitarianism, which is concerned with the suffering of mass numbers of the global poor. A different sort of concern can be grounded in the natural law tradition associated with the Catholic Church. Thomas Aquinas suggests, for example, that when people are in severe need, they have a natural right to be fed and that it is immoral for those with a superabundance of food to withhold assistance to the needy: "whatever certain people have in superabundance is due, by natural law, to the purpose of succoring the poor." Aquinas quotes Saint Ambrose who says of rich people who hoard their wealth: "it is the hungry man's bread that you withhold."[12]

Claims about the need to alleviate poverty can also be derived from other non-consequentialist arguments that rely on notions of justice and fairness. Objections to these sorts of arguments may also appeal to non-consequentialist concerns such as concern for property rights. My right to my own property, for example, might trump another person's entitlement to be helped. Other non-consequentialist considerations may involve claims about the importance of proximity and relatedness. For example, I may have stronger obligations to my own kin or to members of my own country than I do to distant strangers.

Before we move on to examine the practical implications of this debate, let's consider in greater detail a few other basic ethical ideas that could be appealed to in thinking about global poverty and global justice.

Self-Interest
On the one hand, our own interests may dictate that we should do something to lessen the gap between rich and poor nations and alleviate the conditions of the less fortunate. In terms of trade alone, these nations can contribute much to our economic benefit by the goods they could purchase from us. Moreover, the worldwide problems caused by the migration of desperate people from poorer to wealthier countries could be moderated. Furthermore, the problem of terrorism might be dramatically reduced if we could reduce poverty and suffering abroad. Some critics argue that it is not poverty that breeds terrorism but "feelings of indignity and frustration."[13] Nonetheless, poverty is destabilizing and inequality breeds resentment. In the long run, other people's poverty can have negative consequences for our own self-interested concerns.

In terms of self-interest, we may also be concerned about the impact of global poverty on the environment and with regard to other social issues that affect us. Global poverty causes stress on the environment. Poor people in the Amazon region, for example, cut down trees to make farms and charcoal to sell. Impoverished people burning wood for cooking and warmth produce pollution. Because we are all affected by damage to the environment, it is in our best interest to find ways to eliminate the poverty that leads to some of this damage. Furthermore, new infectious diseases often break out in impoverished areas, which can then spread across the globe. And mass migrations of the poor and dispossessed can put pressure on political and social institutions, as affluent nations are forced to deal with the needs of so-called economic refugees.

Justice

Apart from self-interest, there may be requirements of justice that tell us we ought to care for the poor. Justice is not charity. It may well be that *charity* or altruistic concern for the plight of others ought to play a role in how we relate to distant peoples. It is nice to help people, and charity is certainly an ethically important notion, but a more difficult consideration is whether we have any obligation or duty to help those in need in faraway places. Charity, in some sense, is optional. But if we are obligated to help others, then this is not an optional matter. Are we under any obligation to help those faraway persons in need, and why or why not? Recall from Chapter 14 that considerations of justice play a role in evaluating the distribution of goods. In that chapter, we discussed this in relation to such a distribution within a society. However, it can also be used to evaluate the distribution of goods in the human community as a whole. We can then ask whether a particular distribution of goods worldwide is just. As noted in Chapter 14, there are differences of opinion as to how we ought to determine this.

One idea of justice is the *process view*, according to which any distribution can be said to be just if the process by which it comes to be is just. In other words, if there was no theft or fraud or other immoral activity that led to the way things have turned out, then the resulting arrangement is just. In applying this at the global level, we can ask whether the rich nations are rich at least partly because of wrongful past actions, such as colonialism, the slave trade, or other forms of exploitation. If affluent nations caused poverty in poor nations through colonial exploitation, then the affluent countries might owe some sort of reparation to the poor. But a critic may respond by saying that even if past exploitation was wrong, at some point history is over and we have to move forward.

Another idea of justice is called *end-state justice*. According to this view, the end state, or how things have turned out, is also relevant. Egalitarians argue that the gap between rich and poor is something wrong in itself because we are all members of the same human family and share the same planet. On the one hand, some argue that it is morally permissible for some people to have more than others if the difference is a function of something like the greater effort or contributions of the affluent. From this perspective, those who work harder and who are thrifty are entitled to what they've got. They sacrificed and saved while others did not. On the other hand, if the wealth of some and the poverty of others result instead from luck and fortune (or exploitation of the poor), then it does not seem fair that the lucky have so much and the unlucky so little. Is it not luck that one nation has oil and another does not? But the primary concern for the defenders of end-state justice is the actual distribution of things; if it is too unequal, then it is wrong.

Justice is also a matter of *fairness*. People in affluent nations consume a much larger proportion of goods and resources than people in less affluent nations. According to one estimate, people in affluent nations such as the United States, Japan, and countries in Western Europe consume on average thirty-two times more resources per person than do people in underdeveloped countries.[14] The ecological footprint of affluent nations is also larger than that of underdeveloped countries. People in affluent countries consume more, use more resources, and produce more pollution. We could ask whether this is a fair distribution. How would we determine an equal or fair share of resource use or pollution production, while also taking into account global diversity? Do people in very hot or very cold climates deserve more or less energy usage? Are people in cities entitled to more or less pollution than people who live in rural or in wilderness areas? To address this issue more fully would require complex analysis of the idea of fair shares of world resources.

Rights

Most Western governments and international organizations agree that political freedoms, civil rights, and labor standards are not separable from economic progress. They stress that prohibitions on child labor, enforcement of women's rights, prevention of deforestation and pollution, and the enhancement of intellectual property rights, freedom of the press, and other civil liberties must be central to economic development. As the global economy is becoming more integrated, many would argue that this integration must be based upon ideas about human rights, which are supposedly universally valid and applicable.

The issue of rights is not that simple. There are positive rights—to welfare—and negative rights—to liberty and property (as discussed in Chapter 14). Some proponents of globalization will argue that every person has a positive right to subsistence—a basic right to clean water, basic food, and freedom from want. It is not enough, from this perspective, to avoid harming others or exploiting them. Rather, such a positive right to subsistence implies a positive obligation on the part of those who have surplus wealth. Others will maintain that the negative rights to liberty and property are primary. From this perspective, we only have an obligation not to exploit others, steal their property, or enslave them.

PRACTICAL CONSIDERATIONS

Responses to global poverty should be guided by moral concepts, such as the ones we've discussed previously. But, as we've seen with regard to many of the applied topics in this book, moral questions also depend on circumstantial and factual matters. This is especially true with regard to consequentialist reasoning, where the goal is to produce good outcomes in the world. If we are going to produce good outcomes, we have to understand the circumstances and empirical issues. Here are some issues to consider.

Global Inequality

At the heart of many arguments about the need to help the poor is the claim that gross inequalities across the globe are unjustified. A related claim is that there is an obvious moral demand for the affluent to respond to the abject suffering of those who are on the bottom. Singer, Pogge, and others argue that our relative wealth means that we can alleviate lots of suffering for a minor cost—an empirical

claim that should prompt us to examine the severity of global inequality.

Consider, for example, that workers in the Bangladeshi garment factories that have burned and collapsed typically earn between $37 and $50 per month—that amounts to just over a dollar per day.[15] This means that if you donate a dollar and change per day, you could double someone's income. Across the globe there are more than one billion people living in that level of extreme poverty (classified as living on less than $1.25 per day) with a billion more living on between $1.25 and $2 per day. There are 870 million people who go hungry every day; 6.9 million children under five die every year as a result.[16] Extreme poverty is also "poverty that kills." People in extreme poverty are "chronically hungry, unable to get health care, lack safe drinking water and sanitation, cannot afford education for their children, and perhaps lack rudimentary shelter ... and clothing."[17] Children of the global poor are particularly vulnerable, dying from various causes including easily preventable diseases and illnesses.[18] For example, more than 200 million people come down with malaria every year, with 600,000 people dying of the disease each year. People living in the poorest countries are especially vulnerable to malaria, which can be easily prevented by the use of mosquito nets and other prophylactic measures. There has been an improvement over past mortality rates as a result of an active campaign to prevent and treat malaria.[19] Nonetheless, the disease still preys upon the poor.

Poverty in the developing world undermines opportunities. It is connected to a variety of issues including the oppression of women, illiteracy, governmental corruption, and so on. There are vast inequalities across the globe. One obvious measure of inequality is found in mortality rates and life expectancy. Life expectancy in rich countries is substantially higher than in poor countries. In Japan, Switzerland, Germany, and Norway, life expectancy is above 80 years. In the United States, life expectancy is 78 years. But in Kenya, life expectancy is 63 years; it is 70 years in Bangladesh; and 63 years in Cambodia. The country of Chad has the lowest life expectancy, 49 years.[20] Those who argue that we ought to take action to alleviate global poverty will point out the injustice of these sorts of inequalities. Is it fair that Americans and Europeans live long and live well while others suffer and die young?

Another measure of inequality is in economic terms. According to the World Bank, the United States is the world's richest country in terms of gross domestic product (GDP), with China, Japan, Germany, and France following. The GDP in the United States in 2012 was over $15.6 trillion, compared, for example, to Kenya, with a GDP of $37.2 billion or with some smaller nations such as the Marshall Islands, with a GDP of $187 million.[21] A more precise measure of inequality is to compare per capita GDP, which divides the gross domestic product of a nation by its population. Using that measure, Burundi had the lowest per capita GDP in 2012, at $251. By comparison, Kenya's per capita GDP in 2012 was $862 and Chad's was $885. The per capita GDP for Bangladesh was $747, while in the United States, per capita GDP was $49,965. The per capita GDP in the United States was lower than that of a number of other countries, including Sweden, Denmark, Switzerland, and Norway.[22]

Levels of International Aid

The rich nations of the world do allocate some of their budgets to the alleviation of global poverty and inequality. Most affluent nations acknowledge that there is some need to help the poor, either because they see a moral imperative to help or believe that helping is in everyone's interest, since poverty and inequality are destabilizing forces in the global economy. International agreements have established a goal for rich countries to donate 0.7 percent of their gross national product (GNP) to alleviate poverty. (GNP is calculated in ways that are similar to GDP, or gross domestic product.) This international effort has been established in a variety of treaties in recent decades including the UN Millennium Development Project and the Monterrey (Mexico) Conference on Financing for Development and a subsequent agreement in Johannesburg, South Africa.[23] President Obama has recently reiterated the United States' commitment to foreign aid. In 2013, Obama took a trip across Africa, where he called for an increase in foreign aid. According to Obama, "Our foreign aid budget is around 1 percent of our total federal budget.

It's chronically the least popular part of our federal budget."[24] One of the difficulties for discussing foreign aid is that many Americans think that the United States gives much more in aid. A poll in 2011 reported that Americans think that 25 percent of the federal budget goes to foreign aid. When asked what they considered the appropriate amount of foreign aid to be, the typical response was about 10 percent of the budget—which is actually ten times the amount of aid actually allocated in the federal budget.[25]

Even at 1 percent of the federal budget, the United States falls short of the 0.7 percent of GNP target set by the United Nations. The United States continues to be the world's largest donor in raw terms, giving a total of $30.5 billion in 2012. This was a decline of 2.8 percent when compared to 2011. In terms of percentages, however, the United States has never gotten close to the 0.7 percent target. U.S. donations fell from 0.20 percent of GDP in 2011 to 0.19 percent in 2012.[26] This means that U.S. aid donations amount to about 20 cents for every $100 of income, while the United Nations' target would have the United States donating 70 cents for every $100. If the United States hit the 0.7 percent target, its aid budget would increase from its current $30.5 billion to around $100 billion. That extra $70 billion could go a long way toward solving the problem of global poverty.

Some rich nations have made an effort to reach the target of donating 0.7 percent, with European nations in the lead. However, the economic crisis of the past decade has had a negative impact on donor countries. The Organization for Economic Cooperation and Development reports that in 2012, the world's largest donors in raw terms were the United States, the United Kingdom, Germany, France, and Japan. While the economic crisis caused some European nations such as Spain and Greece to cut back on donations, other European countries—Denmark, Luxembourg, the Netherlands, Norway, and Sweden—continued to exceed the UN's 0.7 percent donation target.[27]

Causes of Global Poverty

The causes of extreme poverty and lack of development in a nation are many and complicated. Among them are said to be geographic isolation, epidemic disease, drought and other natural disasters, lack of clean water, poor soil, poor physical infrastructure, lack of education and a decent health care system, civil war and corruption, and the colonial and trade practices of Western nations.

Colonialism   In one view, it is colonialism that has been the cause of poverty in many of the world's poorest countries. Among those who hold this to be the case is Frantz Fanon, a North African intellectual who was born in the Caribbean. Fanon's work *The Wretched of the Earth* is a seminal text in post colonial studies.[28] Fanon's idea is that the Western nations stole the riches of their colonies, thus enhancing their own wealth while depressing the wealth of the colonies. According to Fanon, "European opulence is literally scandalous, for it has been founded on slavery, it has been nourished with the blood of slaves and it comes directly from the soil and from the subsoil of that underdeveloped world. The well-being and the progress of Europe have been built up with the sweat and the dead bodies of Negroes, Arabs, Indians, and the yellow races."[29] From this standpoint, the poverty of much of the world is due to a long history of European intervention, colonial domination, slavery, and theft. Moreover, the argument continues, deprivation in what Fanon calls the "Third" or underdeveloped world can be attributed to continued exploitation of the poor by the rich. Even though outright colonialism ended in the twentieth century, as former colonies gained their independence, Fanon argues that the institutions, corporate structures, military treaties, and trade relations left behind continue to favor the First World to the detriment of the Third World.

One response to this sort of argument is to claim that colonialism was not the evil it is made out to be. Dinesh D'Souza—an Indian-born American intellectual—has argued, for example, that "colonialism has gotten a bad name in recent decades."[30] D'Souza maintains that in some ways colonialism may have been good for the colonized countries. In a book in which he accuses President Obama of being a proponent of Fanon-style anticolonialism, D'Souza concludes,

> When the British came to India and Kenya, they came for selfish reasons: they came to rule and to benefit from that rule. Nevertheless, in order to rule effectively the British introduced Western ideas and Western

institutions to the subject peoples. Eventually those people used British ideas of self-determination and freedom to combat British rule. As a native-born Indian, I have to say that even our freedom was a consequence of what we learned from our Western captors.[31]

D'Souza has also pointed out that Western colonialism is only part of a much larger history that includes a long litany of colonial interventions, including colonizing by the Egyptians, the Persians, and so on. D'Souza concludes that to blame European colonialists for stealing and exploitation in the Third World is to "relieve the Third World of blame for its wretchedness."[32] From D'Souza's perspective, the corruption, injustice, and poverty found in the Third World are not the result of European exploitation. Rather, they are the result of insufficient Westernization. D'Souza argues that the solution is further expansion of Western European ideas about human rights, technology, and free markets.

Farm Subsidies and Other Trade Barriers   Subsidies for the farms of Western countries have also been blamed by some critics for the poverty in developing countries. In the United States, these subsidies originally were intended to help farmers hurt by the Great Depression. But they have been maintained and expanded. Between 1995 and 2012, farmers in the United States received $292.5 billion in subsidies—both by direct payments and through crop insurance.[33] In other countries, subsidies are given to small specialty farms, for example, those in the grape-growing or cheese-producing regions of France. Such distortions of the international agriculture market can make it extremely difficult for poor farmers in Mexico or in sub-Saharan Africa to compete. Moreover, in some cases (especially in the United States) such subsidies go to large industrialized farms that then produce huge crop surpluses for cheap export—undercutting the sale of local agricultural products in the developing world. Substantial evidence suggests that reducing subsidies and removing trade barriers would help end poverty. Economist Gary S. Fields points out, "Agricultural subsidies by the United States, Europe, and Japan total $350 billion a year—seven times the foreign aid provided by all developed countries."

He concludes that ending farm subsidies could lift 140 million people out of poverty.[34] Other people argue, however, that there is no guarantee that eliminating these subsidies would help poor farmers. Moreover, perhaps all nations should have a right to protect and support their own farmers, whatever the consequences abroad.

One of the issues with regard to subsidies is fairness. The International Monetary Fund and the World Bank often ask developing countries that receive loans and other aid to eliminate subsidies for their exports. However, developed countries such as the United States continue to subsidize their own agricultural products. As a result, foreign farmers frequently cannot compete on the global market with products grown on American farms. At the same time, American producers lobby against trade barriers enacted by foreign countries, which prevent Americans from selling American products in foreign markets. It makes sense for nations to want to protect their own farmers and producers. And it also makes sense that farmers and producers would want to have access to markets abroad. The reality of globalized business is complicated and there is a constant struggle to maximize profit and minimize risk. All this results in unequal outcomes across the globe. Consider the North American Free Trade Agreement (NAFTA), which links Canada, Mexico, and the United States in a Free Trade Zone. As a result of this agreement, Mexico was flooded with cheap corn and corn products, such as animal feed, from the United States. (Corn is one of the most heavily subsidized crops in the United States.) This had a devastating impact on small Mexican farmers. According to one estimate, nearly two million farm jobs were lost in Mexico as a result. Many of these small farmers abandoned their fields and headed north to work as illegal laborers in the United States. The general cross-border economy is doing well. But the chief beneficiaries of NAFTA have been big companies, while the small operations have been hurt.[35] The moral ideal of fair competition is certainly relevant in such discussions. Just how to make competition fair is, however, a matter for debate.

Institutional Issues Debate also continues about the role played by international financial institutions.

The International Monetary Fund (IMF) and World Bank were both established in 1944 to preserve international financial stability. A newer international organization is the World Trade Organization (WTO), and there are other organizations such as the G8 or "Group of Eight," which represents the interests of eight of the world's largest economies, accounting for half of global GDP. The G20 includes twenty finance ministers and central bank governors and represents the financial interest of nations that account for about 80 percent of world trade. In recent years, there have been massive protests at meetings of these organizations and others like them. Pro-labor and environmental groups have protested against economic globalization at meetings of the WTO, the G8, the G20, the IMF, and the World Bank. These antiglobalization protests culminated in police crackdowns, mass arrests, vandalism, and street fighting in Seattle in 1999; in Genoa, Italy, in 2001; and in Geneva in 2009. In Toronto, Canada, in 2010, more than 1,100 people were arrested in anti-G20 protests.[36]

The antiglobalization protesters have a variety of specific concerns. But among them is a feeling that economic decisions are being made by bureaucrats and bankers without concern for the interests of working people. Canadian journalist and author Naomi Klein has explained the antiglobalization movement as developing out of a perceived "crisis of democracy."[37] Critics of the economic institutions of globalization insist that they are not opposed to international integration and cooperation. Rather, they say that they are opposed to that type of globalization that is more concerned about the rights of investors than the rights of workers. Noam Chomsky, a well-known critic of globalization and of American foreign policy, argues, "the term 'globalization' has been appropriated by the powerful to refer to a specific form of international economic integration, one based on investor rights, with the interests of people incidental."[38] The alternative would be a form of economic integration that was more concerned with human development and the concerns of ordinary people than with the bottom line of banks and corporations.

In response, defenders of the international finance and business system argue that investing in and supporting the current economic system is the best (and possibly only) way to help poor people around the globe—by using banks and other global economic infrastructure to invest in opportunities for the impoverished. We've already seen that the World Bank is concerned with poverty reduction across the globe. And international agreements (such as the 0.7 percent aid target) are aimed at reducing poverty by increasing foreign aid.

However, some criticize the methods employed by international institutions such as the World Bank, IMF, and WTO. According to Joseph Stiglitz, a Nobel Prize–winning economist, the key to problems in developing nations has been these international financial institutions' ideological support of strict capitalism. He argues that free markets and global competition are not the solution to all problems. And he worries about the lack of representation of poorer countries: "these institutions are not representative of the nations they serve."[39] Some IMF and World Bank policies, for example, have harmed rather than helped the development of Third World countries. High interest rates harmed fledgling companies, trade liberalization policies made poorer countries unable to compete, and liberalization of capital markets enabled larger foreign banks to drive local banks out of business. Privatization of government-owned enterprises without adequate local regulation also contributed to the increasingly desperate situation of some developing countries. According to Stiglitz, these international financial institutions have ignored some of the consequences of their policies because of their belief in unfettered capitalism. He writes,

> Stabilization is on the agenda; job creation is off. Taxation, and its adverse effects, are on the agenda; land reform is off. There is money to bail out banks but not to pay for improved education and health services, let alone to bail out workers who are thrown out of their jobs as a result of the IMF's macroeconomic mismanagement.[40]

In response to Stiglitz and others, defenders of the international economic system have argued that these worries are overblown and based on a limited analysis that does not take economic realities into account. Moreover, defenders of economic globalization argue that the critics of globalization have actually made things worse by encouraging developing countries to feel that they are being taken advantage of and that the global institutions that are the best hope for development are hypocritical and mercenary. The economist Jagdish Bhagwati has argued, for example, that globalization actually does have a human face. He argues that economic globalization—by promoting competition in wages across international borders—has benefited women by equalizing gender-based wage disparities, which were more typical of countries where the wage gap was protected against global competition.[41] To assess these arguments would require a much deeper examination of economic issues.

A further criticism should be mentioned here, which is the concern for corruption and self-interest. Just as the antiglobalization movement suspects that the global financial sector is interested only in profit, a similar suspicion is held by some who worry that local governments and aid organizations are corrupt. Not all financial aid given to poor countries actually gets directly to the people. Much of it, for example, covers consultants, administrative costs, and debt relief. Furthermore, aid dollars are used to purchase supplies and hire experts from the developed world. Journalist Loretta Napoleoni argues that "foreign aid is mostly beneficial to those who give it" because aid creates a market for Western products.[42] One of the difficult practical challenges to be confronted is how we can best provide aid in a global economy that includes corrupt local politicians as well as international corporations and banks that are seeking to make a profit.

Poor countries suffer from serious political problems: continuing civil wars and corrupt and unstable governments. Corruption and mismanagement have contributed not only to the poverty of the people but also to the hesitancy of wealthy countries to give aid. Any solution to the issue of global poverty will have to deal with a variety of concerns: the problem of local corruption, the challenge of making sure that aid is effective, and the concern that large multinational banking and corporate concerns are seeking profit. But it is important to note that none of these empirical concerns changes the moral question of whether we ought to be concerned about the suffering of others in distant lands.

Solutions and Progress

The issues discussed in this chapter are complex. It will be difficult to solve issues like global poverty and to deal with the ongoing cultural, political, and economic conflicts that are part of the era of globalization. Nonetheless, some thinkers argue that there are some fairly obvious solutions to the most pressing issues, such as poverty. We saw that Thomas Pogge proposed a resource tax and that Peter Singer thought that we have a duty to donate to charity. Development economist Jeffrey Sachs has argued that we should focus on five "development interventions": (1) boosting agriculture, with improvements in fertilizers and seeds; (2) improving basic health, in particular through bed nets and medicines for malaria and treatments for AIDS; (3) investing in education, including meals for primary school children; (4) providing power, transportation, and communications technologies; and (5) providing clean water and sanitation.[43] Others argue that changing intellectual property laws and freeing up patents would help to make new technologies— such as better seeds for growing crops or beneficial medicines—available to poor people who could use them.[44] Some suggest that money is the most basic solution and that rich nations should live up to the standard of donating 0.7 percent of GNP.

The global poverty numbers have been improving, thanks to a concerted effort by international organizations such as the United Nations and the World Bank. According to the president of the World Bank, Jim Yong Kim, poverty is in retreat and we are making progress in dealing with other issues such as malaria control, AIDS, and education. According to Kim, the global poverty rate dropped from 43 percent to 21 percent in the past two decades; in the past decade the annual number of malaria deaths has dropped by 75 percent; and AIDS drugs and education are more easily available to more people.[45] The good news is that we are making progress. But we still have a long way to go in a world where 21 percent of the people on earth live in extreme poverty. If we are going to make further progress, we will have to take the problem of global justice seriously. But as we've seen, there are others who think that helping the global poor is not a matter of justice but only a matter of charity. And there are other critics, such as Hardin, who appeal to Malthusian logic to argue that it is not a good idea to help the poor.

GLOBALIZATION AND ITS CRITICS

Questions of global justice are complicated by the fact of globalization. As the world's economic and cultural forces become more interconnected, our understanding of our obligations to distant others may be shifting in a more global direction. But one might argue, to the contrary, that our primary obligations to members of our own nation or culture remain more important than obligations to distant others. To think about global justice, it is useful to understand the causes and effects of globalization.

One key causal factor in globalization is the development of technologies that improve economic efficiency and allow for broader economic and cultural influence. According to the journalist and scholar Robert Wright, "globalization dates back to prehistory, when the technologically driven expansion of commerce began."[46] Technological innovations—from roads and boats to writing, airline travel, and the Internet—allow for commercial and cultural interchanges among formerly isolated peoples. The journalist Thomas Friedman described globalization as a process that has made the world "flat."[47] People around the world are now connected in ways unimaginable twenty years ago, and the playing field in which they operate is now more even—provided that they have access to computers, Internet connections, and email. This increases opportunities for collaboration and development. It also changes the nature of the economy.

According to Jan Scholte, a leading expert on globalization, there are at least five different interpretations of globalization, some of which are overlapping: internationalization, liberalization, universalization, modernization or Westernization, and deterritorialization or respatialization.[48] *Internationalization* refers to "cross-border relations between countries." Among these are trade, finance, and communication, which create international interdependence among nations and peoples. *Liberalization* focuses on the free and "open, borderless world economy." Trade and foreign exchange, as well as travel barriers, are abolished or reduced, making it possible to participate in the world as a whole. *Universalization* refers to the various ways in which a synthesis of cultures has taken place. This covers such things as having a common calendar; shared communication technologies; and similar methods of manufacturing, farming, and means of transportation. *Modernization* or *Westernization* refers to the ways that "the social structures of modernity"—capitalism, science, movies, music, and so forth—have spread throughout the world. Among the characteristics of modernity is an emphasis on scientific rational thought in combination with technological innovation—as well as a move toward secular institutions that are independent of traditional religious organization. *Deterritorialization* or *respatialization* refers to the fact that in the globalized world "social space is no longer wholly mapped in terms of territorial places ... and borders."[49] Thus corporations as well as nongovernmental organizations transcend local geographic constraints.

Sometimes the processes of globalization have increased people's understanding and sympathy for other peoples, while fostering tolerance, respect, and concern for human equality. The economic integration of isolated communities often brings with it greater peace as people of different races and cultures trade and rub shoulders with one another. But this globalizing process can also be the basis of resentment and antipathy. One source of complaint is the way that globalization affects local economies. Another complaint involves the problem of cultural diversity.

Economic Impacts

Many argue that globalization will increase productivity and produce profit and innovation. But others complain that this produces certain costs that may not be outweighed by such benefits. *Outsourcing* is one example. Outsourcing occurs when part of a process—say, tax preparation or customer service information—is contracted out to workers in other countries where labor costs are cheaper. A related issue is *offshoring*. This differs from outsourcing in that rather than taking some specific function and hiring it out, entire factories or operational units are moved to cheaper offshore locations. Outsourcing and offshoring may help to produce profit and lower the

price of commodities. But they also undermine opportunities in countries that lose jobs to cheaper countries. Furthermore, if jobs are allowed to go where the lowest-priced workers are located, this produces a "rush to the bottom" in which labor, safety, and environmental standards are constantly being undermined. Defenders of these practices argue that in the long run globalization is good for everyone as products become cheaper, capital flows toward labor markets, and jobs and wealth are created.

Globalization will be evaluated in different ways by those who think in different ways about economic and political issues. Proponents of free-market capitalism see globalization as a further stage of economic development as markets go global and capital, labor, and commodities are free to flow around the world. Others worry that the development of global capitalism will come at the expense of social welfare and the interests of the global poor and working classes. Some praise the development of cosmopolitan social concern and international laws that regulate wars, environmental impacts, and economic development. Others rue the demise of state sovereignty and the autonomy of the more traditional nation-state. Another critical perspective is more concerned that the development of global culture poses a threat to traditional familial, cultural, and religious values.

Cultural Diversity

This last issue points toward cultural problems created by modernization, Westernization, and secularization. Some have argued that there is a clash of civilizations in the world today—most notably between secular Westernized democracies and more conservative, traditional societies.[50] Those who focus on such civilizational conflict may argue that there are deep cultural and historical values found in various "civilizations." From this perspective, the process of globalization will be fraught with conflict, instead of being a process of harmonious integration and global development.

One supposed civilizational fissure is that between Western and Asian values. But some have argued that "Asian values" do not fit well with the values of Western liberal democracy and capitalism. Defenders of

"Asian values" may claim, for example, that the welfare of society and economic development ought to come first before political rights. They may claim that human rights may temporarily be put on hold for the sake of economic growth. Thus it would be better, they say, to give a starving person a loaf of bread than a crate on which to stand and speak his mind. This idea was propounded in the 1990s by Lee Kuan Yew, the former prime minister of Singapore. Lee maintained that Asian values were founded on a communitarian approach that could be traced back to Confucian ethics. (See the discussion of communitarianism in Chapter 14.) He held that there was a social pyramid with a good leader at the top, good executives in the middle, and civic-minded masses at the bottom.[51]

Some critics worry that these sorts of relativist appeals to culturally specific value systems provide a justification for the continued exploitation of oppressed groups within countries that are reluctant to democratize and modernize. Criticism of democratic values may be used to serve the ideological purposes of those in charge and those who benefit from inequality. Others maintain that an idea such as "Asian values" is so broad and obscure as to be meaningless. The economist Amartya Sen concludes, for example, that we must recognize diversity within different cultures and that we should avoid simplifying concepts such as "Western civilization," "African cultures," or "Asian values." He concludes, "the grand dichotomy between Asian values and European values adds little to our understanding, and much to the confounding of the normative basis of freedom and democracy."[52] There are liberal-democratic and capitalist elements in Asian cultures just as there are antiliberal and authoritarian strands in Western cultures.

Another line of supposed civilizational conflict is that between the Arab/Muslim world and the European/Christian world. Some claim that "Islamic values" do not fit within the increasingly globalized and Westernized economic system. Proponents of Islamic values claim that Western market-oriented economics does not help the poor and that the secular nation-states of the West sacrifice a more valuable religiously structured social system. Some argue that Islamic culture emphasizes a more collectivist and communitarian approach to social norms and structures and is thus at odds with Western individualism.[53]

A more concrete issue is whether there are cultural or "civilizational" issues that exacerbate inequality and the challenge of global poverty. As of 2011, the combined gross domestic product of all twenty-two Arab nation-states was about $2.8 trillion with a population of more than 350 million. By comparison, Germany's GDP is higher at around $3 trillion with a much smaller population of 81 million.[54] This wealth disparity may help explain why poverty and food insecurity are problems in some parts of the Arab world. Of course, one might respond by pointing out that even within the richest nation on earth—the United States—there are gross inequalities, hungry people, and people living in poverty (we discussed some of this in Chapter 14). It may be that cultural differences do not make all that much difference when it comes to economics.

A further problem may have to do with political institutions. Poverty and food insecurity may have been exacerbated by political instability since the "Arab Spring" (revolutions across the Arab world in 2011). One recent report indicates that official poverty numbers are untrustworthy and that economic inequality including high unemployment was a chief cause of the uprising of Arab people in 2011. Political turmoil has led to even further unemployment and food insecurity. Youth unemployment is at 50 percent in a number of Arab nations.[55] Political instability makes it difficult to develop natural resources, create educational opportunities, and build businesses.

Moreover, defenders of the clash of civilization idea argue that there are cultural reasons that unemployment is high and the economy is shaky in Muslim and Arab countries. As an example, some cite a 2002 report from the United Nations Development Programme in coordination with the Arab Fund for Economic and Social Development, which held that Arab countries have not advanced economically in modern times because of "a shortage of freedom to speak, innovate, and affect political life, a shortage of women's rights, and a shortage of quality education."[56] That report criticized education in the Arab world with remaining illiteracy and educational gaps.

Literacy in the Arab world has hovered at around 70 percent compared to the literacy rate of the developed world, which is around 95 percent. Some will attribute these kinds of disparities to cultural and religious differences. And similar disparities and challenges are found in other parts of the world, with literacy rates in sub-Saharan Africa even lower than rates in the Arab world—at around 65 percent.[57]

The general issue of cultural relativism shows up here. Are we employing Eurocentric values when thinking about development issues? Is it possible to focus on helping impoverished people, while also respecting cultural practices that may be contributing to poverty? And how can we encourage and support indigenous cultural values that can help deal with these problems? Muslims practice *zakat* or alms-giving, for example. How can aid to the poor be coordinated with traditional religious practices such as this? A further problem involves cultural and political conflicts of the past. Will predominantly Muslim countries welcome aid that comes from the United States, when, in the past, this aid has been used to prop up unpopular governments as in Egypt, where the United States supported the former president, Hosni Mubarak, who was driven from power by the Egyptian people who gathered in protest during the Arab Spring. Similar political and historical problems haunt aid efforts in the rest of the world, with former colonial powers in the developed world dealing with residual political issues as they also try to fulfill obligations to assist. Do the British have more of an obligation to help in India, or do the French have more of an obligation to help in North Africa because of their past colonial relations? And how will assistance be perceived by former colonies?

There is no denying that Western values dominate global culture. Western-style clothing, advertising, and products are becoming more and more pervasive. Coca-Cola, McDonald's, American pop music, and American computer and Internet technologies seem to be everywhere. Do people around the world admire or want American goods? Or are these goods somehow foisted upon them by the forces of corporate globalization?

There is also cultural backlash against the values of Western consumerism and individualism. These values are viewed with antipathy and resentment by some people who hold other traditional cultural or religious values. For example, some traditional cultures reject the lack of modest dress in women and graphic and sexualized forms of popular entertainment and music. Clearly, there are criticisms to be made of some elements of Western societies that are showing up around the world. On the other hand, we may want to argue that other elements of modern culture ought to become universally accepted. Take, for example, the position of women. Should modern notions of individual rights and freedoms and equality for women become the norm? There are those who argue against this. They would retain individual cultural and religious practices regarding the position of women. Is it colonialist or Eurocentric to want to encourage development toward a more secular and liberal social and political system?

Can we actually judge the practices of another culture? Are one culture's values as good as any other? This is the issue of ethical relativism discussed in Chapters 2 and 3. We surely want to say that if some culture has a practice of enslaving some of its members, this is not morally acceptable. Which elements of globalization are good and bad is not always an easy matter to judge. Hopefully, however, the ethical signposts, values, and principles discussed here and elsewhere in this text can help determine the way we should go in a world that is, in ever-increasing ways, becoming one.

Let's conclude this section by mentioning the conflict between modernization and globalization and traditional religion. The modernized world is a secular one, which keeps traditional religious values distinct from the public values of the political sphere. While religions have "gone global" during the past millennia—spreading around the globe through conquest and missionary work—economic and political globalization pose a threat for traditional religion. The modern Western nation-state is grounded upon basic claims about human rights including the right of freedom of religion. And the modern economy is a 24/7 activity oriented toward progress and development, ignoring the ritual time frames and Sabbath days of rest in traditional religions.

Some critics of globalization, modernization, and secularization will argue that all of this is heading in the wrong direction. Some will want to return to tradition—as religious fundamentalists do—withdrawing from the global economy and finding a separate peace with the secular, modern world. Some other fundamentalists may take up arms against the global system—as religious terrorists do. Others will want to find ways to humanize and universalize traditional religious values. And others will insist that the way forward must be to find universal human values that can transcend cultural and religious differences and that can be used to deal with the difficult challenges of the future, such as we've discussed in the course of this book.

NOTES

1. Thomas Fuller, "Deadly Collapse in Cambodia Renews Safety Concerns," *New York Times*, May 16, 2013, accessed June 25, 2013, http://www.nytimes.com/2013/05/17/world/asia/cambodia-factory-ceiling-collapse.html?_r=0

2. Charles Duhigg, "In China, Human Costs Are Built into an iPad," *New York Times,* January 25, 2012, accessed July 14, 2013, http://www.nytimes.com/2012/01/26/business/ieconomy-apples-ipad-and-the-human-costs-for-workers-in-china.html?pagewanted=all

3. Peter Grier, "The Walt Disney Company Pulls Out of Bangladesh: Will That Make Workers Safer?" *Christian Science Monitor*, May 3, 2013, accessed June 25, 2013, http://www.csmonitor.com/USA/2013/0503/The-Walt-Disney-Company-pulls-out-of-Bangladesh-Will-that-make-workers-safer

4. See Alex Nicholls and Charlotte Opal, *Fair Trade: Market Driven Ethical Consumption* (London: SAGE Publications, 2005).

5. See Peter Griffiths, "Ethical Objections to Fair Trade," *Journal of Business Ethics* 105 (2012): 357–73.

6. "Within Our Grasp: A World Free of Poverty - World Bank Group President Jim Yong Kim's Speech at Georgetown University," April 2, 2013, accessed June 25, 2013, http://www.worldbank.org/en/news/speech/2013/04/02/world-bank-group-president-jim-yong-kims-speech-at-georgetown-university

7. Thomas Pogge, "Are We Violating the Human Rights of the World's Poor?" *Yale Human Rights & Development Journal* 14, no. 2 (2011): 1–33.

8. Thomas Pogge, *World Poverty and Human Rights* (Cambridge, UK: Polity Press, 2008), 211–12.

9. Peter Singer, "Famine, Affluence, and Morality," *Philosophy and Public Affairs* 1, no. 3 (1972): 231.

10. Dylan Matthews, "Join Wall Street, Save the World," *Washington Post*, May 31, 2013, accessed June 25, 2013, http://www.washingtonpost.com/blogs/wonkblog/wp/2013/05/31/join-wall-street-save-the-world/

11. Garrett Hardin, "Living on a Lifeboat," *Bioscience* (October 1974).

12. Thomas Aquinas, *Summa Theologica*, trans. by the Fathers of the English Dominican Province, Online Edition Copyright © 2008 by Kevin Knight, II–II, Q 66, Art. 7, http://www.newadvent.org/summa/3066.htm, accessed July 26, 2013

13. Alan B. Krueger and Jitka Maleckova, "Does Poverty Cause Terrorism?" *New Republic*, June 24, 2002, 27.

14. Jared Diamond, "What's Your Consumption Factor?" *New York Times*, January 2, 2008, accessed June 25, 2013, http://www.nytimes.com/2008/01/02/opinion/02diamond.html?pagewanted=all

15. Jim Yardley, "Made in Bangladesh: Export Powerhouse Feels Pangs of Labor Strife," *New York Times*, August 23, 2012, accessed June 20, 2013, http://www.nytimes.com/2012/08/24/world/asia/as-bangladesh-becomes-export-powerhouse-labor-strife-erupts.html?pagewanted=1; "Worker Safety in Bangladesh and Beyond," *New York Times*, May 4, 2013, accessed June 20, 2013, http://www.nytimes.com/2013/05/05/opinion/sunday/worker-safety-in-bangladesh-and-beyond.html

16. Data from World Bank, United Nations World Food Programme, and World Health Organization, accessed June 26, 2013, http://www.worldbank.org/en/topic/poverty/overview; http://www.wfp.org/hunger; http://www.who.int/mediacentre/factsheets/fs178/en/

17. "The End of Poverty," *Time*, March 14, 2005, 47.

18. "Today, Around 21,000 Children Died around the World," Global Issues, http://www.globalissues.org/article/715/todaay-over-24000-children-died-around-the-world

19. "10 Facts on Malaria," March 2013, World Health Organization, accessed June 25, 2013, http://www.who.int/features/factfiles/malaria/en/

20. CIA World Factbook: Life Expectancy (2013), accessed June 25, 2013, https://www.cia.gov/library/publications/the-world-factbook/rankorder/2102rank.html

21. World Bank, "Gross Domestic Product 2012," accessed July 26, 2013, http://databank.worldbank.org/data/download/GDP.pdf

22. World Bank, GDP Per Capita, 2012, accessed July 26, 2013, http://data.worldbank.org/indicator/NY.GDP.PCAP.CD

23. See "The 0.7% Target: An In-Depth Look," Millennium Project, accessed June 25, 2013, http://www.unmillenniumproject.org/press/07.htm

24. "Press Gaggle by President Obama aboard Air Force One," White House, June 28, 2013, accessed July 26 2013, http://www.whitehouse.gov/the-press-office/2013/06/28/press-gaggle-president-obama-aboard-air-force-one

25. Ken Hackett, "Surprise! Americans Want to 'Slash' Foreign Aid – to 10 Times Its Current Size," *Christian Science Monitor*, March 7, 2011, accessed June 30, 2013, http://www.csmonitor.com/Commentary/Opinion/2011/0307/Surprise!-Americans-want-to-slash-foreign-aid-to-10-times-its-current-size

26. "Aid Statistics," Organization for Economic Cooperation and Development, accessed June 25, 2013, http://www.oecd.org/dac/stats/aidtopoorcountriesslipsfurtherasgovernmentstightenbudgets.htm

27. Ibid.

28. Frantz Fanon, *The Wretched of the Earth* (New York: Grove Press, 1968).

29. Fanon, *Wretched of the Earth*, 96.

30. Dinesh D'Souza, "Two Cheers for Colonialism," *Chronicle of Higher Education*, May 10, 2002.

31. Dinesh D'Souza, *Obama's America: Unmaking the American Dream* (Washington, DC: Regnery Publishing, 2012), 219.

32. D'Souza, "Two Cheers for Colonialism."

33. "United States Summary Information," Environmental Working Group, Farm Subsidies, accessed July 16, 2013, http://farm.ewg.org/region.php?fips=00000

34. Gary S. Fields, *Working Hard, Working Poor: A Global Journey* (Oxford: Oxford University Press, 2011), 114.

35. Tim Johnson, "Free Trade: As U.S. Corn Flows South, Mexicans Stop Farming," McClatchy News, February 1, 2011, accessed June 25, 2013, http://www.mcclatchydc.com/2011/02/01/107871/free-trade-us-corn-flows-south.html#.UcyNyz7Eo_s#storylink=cpy

36. Adrian Morrow, "Toronto Police Were Overwhelmed at G20, Review Reveals," *Globe and Mail*, June 23, 2011, accessed July 1, 2013, http://www.theglobeandmail.com/news/toronto/toronto-police-were-overwhelmed-at-g20-review-reveals/article2073215/

37. Naomi Klein, interview on PBS, April 21, 2001, accessed July 1, 2013, http://www.pbs.org/wgbh/commandingheights/shared/minitext/int_naomiklein.html

38. Noam Chomsky, quoted in Jack Lule, *Globalization and Media: Global Village of Babel* (Lanham, MD: Rowman & Littlefield, 2012), 11.

39. Joseph E. Stiglitz, *Globalization and Its Discontents* (New York: Norton, 2003), 19.

40. Ibid., 80–81.

41. Jagdish Bhagwati, *In Defense of Globalization* (Oxford: Oxford University Press, 2007), see especially the Afterword.

42. Loretta Napoleoni, *Rogue Economics* (New York: Seven Stories Press, 2011), 195.

43. Jeffrey Sachs, *The End of Poverty: Economic Possibilities for Our Time* (New York: Penguin Press, 2005), chap. 12.

44. See Thomas Pogge, *World Poverty and Human Rights* (op. cit.), Section 9.2.

45. "Within Our Grasp: A World Free of Poverty—World Bank Group President Jim Yong Kim's Speech at Georgetown University," April 2, 2013, accessed June 25, 2013, http://www.worldbank.org/en/news/speech/2013/04/02/world-bank-group-president-jim-yong-kims-speech-at-georgetown-university

46. Robert Wright, "Two Years Later, a Thousand Years Ago," *New York Times*, Op-Ed., September 11, 2003.

47. Thomas L. Friedman, *The World Is Flat: A Brief History of the Twenty-First Century* (New York: Farrar, Straus, and Giroux, 2005), 8.

48. Jan Scholte, *Globalization: A Critical Introduction*, 2nd ed. (New York: Palgrave MacMillan, 2005), 15–17.

49. Ibid.

50. Samuel P. Huntington, *The Clash of Civilizations* (New York: Simon and Schuster, 1996).

51. Michael D. Barr, *Cultural Politics and Asian Values: The Tepid War* (London: Routledge, 2002), chap. 3.

52. Amartya Sen, *Human Rights and Asian Values* (New York: Carnegie Council on Human Rights, 1997), 31.

53. See essays in Ali Mohammadi, *Islam Encountering Globalization* (London: Routledge, 2002).

54. Eman El-Shenawi, "Poking at the Arab Beast: How Much Is the Arab World Worth?" *Al-Arabiya News*, May 5, 2011, accessed June 25, 2013, http://english.alarabiya.net/articles/2011/05/05/147980.html

55. International Food Policy Research Institute, "Beyond the Arab Awakening: Policies and Investment for Poverty Reduction and Food Security" (February 2012), accessed June 30, 2013, http://www.ifpri.org/sites/default/files/publications/pr25.pdf

56. Thomas L. Friedman, "Arabs at the Crossroads," *New York Times*, July 3, 2002, A19.

57. "Human Development Data for the Arab States," United Nations Development Programme, accessed July 2, 2013, http://www.arab-hdr.org/data/indicators/2012-18.aspx

REVIEW EXERCISES

1. What are some of the current contrasting conditions between rich and poor nations described in the text?

2. Explain how the history of colonialism might be connected to current inequalities. Explain a criticism of this idea.

3. What self-interested reasons can be given for doing something to remedy the situation of poor countries?

4. What is justice, and what role does it play in determining what ought to be done about global poverty?

5. Why is cultural relativism a concern when thinking about global justice?

6. Why might we think that we have obligations to be concerned with the suffering of those in distant lands? Explain one criticism of this idea.

7. Contrast Singer's and Hardin's views on how we ought to deal with famine.

8. Summarize different meanings of *globalization* given in the text.

9. Describe some positive and some negative aspects of globalization.

1. **Ethical Consumption.** Chris is an advocate of ethical consumption. He tries to buy only fair trade products, and he is willing to pay more for an item when he is certain that the item is produced without exploitation. This means that he often pays 10 to 25 percent more for certain products. His father thinks this is a dumb idea. He tells Chris, "You could buy cheaper stuff and, with the money you save, you could save for your own future and retirement. Heck, you could even give that money to the poor." Chris is not concerned with his retirement fund. But he is concerned about alleviating poverty. He's puzzled by his father's response.

   Should Chris try to find the cheapest products and save money, which he would then donate to charity? Or should he continue to seek out fair trade items, which would leave him with less to donate to charity? What is the solution to this problem? Explain your thinking.

2. **Which Poverty Matters?** Madison is a successful businesswoman who has become convinced that she ought to give a substantial amount of her earnings to help those in extreme poverty in the developing world. Her brother, Thomas, a local college student, is not persuaded that such donations are a good idea. "It just makes people ask for more handouts later," he says. "And besides," he adds, "there are a lot of poor people here in our city: homeless people living on the streets. And I'm not doing too well myself. You ought to give me some of your charity so I can pay for college. I'm going to be swamped with student loan debt."

   How should Madison reply? Does she have an obligation to help her brother pay for school, to help the homeless in her city, or to help those in poverty in other countries? Should her proximity or relationship to these various people make a difference here? Or is Thomas right that handouts don't help?

3. **Global Culture.** Sam and Jane have been arguing about the effects of globalization as a form of modernization or Westernization of the world. Sam points out all of globalization's crass and commercialized aspects—the same McDonald's, consumer electronics, and pop culture icons all over the world—and the negative impact that Western culture has on local and indigenous cultures. Jane argues that Western personal and political freedoms ought to be made universal and that a more homogenous culture is a small price to pay for democracy and the liberation of women and minority groups.

   With whom do you agree, Sam or Jane? Can economic and political modernization be divorced from cultural globalization?

4. **Colonialism and Globalization.** Robert is excited about the recent focus on global justice within institutions such as the United Nations and the World Bank. His family emigrated from Africa to the United States to escape the poverty and political instability of his home country. He thinks these new initiatives will be helpful to those they left behind. But his brother, Daniel, is not convinced. Daniel complains, "Nobody helps without asking for something. Most of those international organizations serve the interests of the countries who caused our unhappiness to begin with. The rich countries are always taking advantage of the poor. They enslaved and marginalized lots of us and exploited our countries' resources. Then they left us with a mess." Robert disagrees. "I don't know why you blame others for the poverty back home. Anyway, I'm glad that the rich countries are finally helping. Our people need any help they can get." Daniel responds, "They owe us for what they did to us. But I still don't trust them."

   What do you think? Do rich countries owe something to poor countries? Do rich countries offer their help without strings attached? Or is Daniel right to be cynical?

Appendix

How to Write an Ethics Paper

WRITING a paper does not have to be difficult. It can at least be made easier by following certain procedures. Moreover, you want to do more than complete the assignment—you want to write a *good* paper. You can do several things to improve your paper, changing it from a thing of rags and patches to a paper that you can be proud of. If it is a good paper, then you also will have learned something from producing it. You will have improved your abilities to understand and communicate, and you will have come to appreciate the matters about which you have written.

Writing philosophy papers, in particular, has a value beyond what one learns about the subject matter. As you know, philosophy is a highly rational discipline. It requires us to be clear, precise, coherent, and logical. Skill in doing this can be improved through practice and care. By trying to make your philosophy paper excel in these aspects, you will build skills that should carry over to other areas of your life. You may find that you are less likely to engage in sloppy and careless thinking, speaking, and writing.

This appendix reviews general procedures for writing papers and then outlines elements that are particularly important for writing ethics papers. By following the suggestions given here, you should be able to produce a good ethics paper and further perfect your reasoning skills.

Several elements are basic to any paper. Among these are its content; the content's structure and format; and correct usage of grammar, spelling, and gender-neutral pronouns.

THE CONTENT OF THE PAPER

Your paper's subject matter is partly determined by the course for which it is assigned. Sometimes the topic will be chosen for you. If the paper is for an ethics course, then it will deal with matters of right and wrong, good and bad, or just and unjust. It also probably will be assigned as a certain type of paper: a summary or critical analysis of some article or other writing, an exploration of a thesis or idea, or a research paper (more on this later). At other times, you will choose a topic yourself from a list or be asked to choose something specific from some more general area. You can select something that particularly interests you or something you would like to explore. It may be a topic you know something about or one about which you know little but would like to know more. Sometimes you can begin with a tentative list that is the result of brainstorming. Just write down ideas as you think of them. Sometimes you will have to do exploratory reading or library or Internet research to get ideas. In any case, choosing a topic is the first order of business in writing a paper. This is true of papers in general and ethics papers in particular.

THE PAPER'S STRUCTURE

Here are two simple bits of advice.

1. A paper should have a beginning, a middle, and an end.
2. First you should tell what you are going to do in the paper. Then you should do it. Finally, you should tell what you have said or done.

This may seem overly simplistic, but you would be surprised at how many papers suffer from not including one or both of these elements.

You can develop the structure of your paper with an outline. Here is a sample using the advice just discussed.

1. *Beginning paragraph(s)*. Tell what you are going to do or say. Explain what the problem or issue is and how you plan to address it. You should make your reader want to read further. One way to do this is by showing why there is a problem. You can do this by giving contrasting views on a topic, for example. This is a particularly good way to begin an ethics paper.
2. *Middle paragraph(s)*. Do what you said you were going to do. This is the bulk of the paper. It will have a few divisions, depending on how you handle your subject matter. (A more detailed outline of an ethics paper is given at the end of this appendix.)
3. *End paragraph(s)*. Tell what you have done or said or concluded. More often than not, students end their papers without really ending them. Perhaps they are glad to have finished the main part of the paper and then forget to add an ending. Sometimes they really have not come to any conclusion and thus feel unable to write one. The conclusion can be tentative. It can summarize what you have learned, for example, or what questions your study has raised.

Some word processing programs provide an outlining function. These are helpful because they provide templates that allow you to set out your main points first and then fill in the details. Parts can be expanded, moved, and reoriented. You can look at your paper as you progress with just the main headings or with as much detail as you like. In this way, you can keep your focus on the logic of your presentation. If you have access to such a program, you may want to get acquainted with and use it. Or you might try printing out your draft and marking the different sections by hand, checking it against a separate outline.

Format

How you arrange and present your ideas is also important. Among the elements you should examine are the following: length, notes, Internet citations, and title page and bibliography.

Length This is most often the first, and perhaps the most significant, question asked by students when a paper is assigned: "How long does it have to be?" To pose the question of length in this way may suggest that the student wants to do no more than the minimum required. Although an excellent paper of the minimum length may fetch a top grade, it is probably a good idea to aim at more than the minimum length—although be careful of including extraneous material that does not directly relate to your argument. Your professor may assign a maximum paper length as well, to help you keep your paper narrowly focused on a clear and logical argument.

It is also not enough just to know how many pages within a range are expected. If you use a large font, then you will write much less in five pages than if you use a small one. A word-count estimate is more definite. For example, you could be told that the paper should be between eight and ten pages with approximately 250 typed words per page. In some cases, professors have very specific requirements, expecting, for instance, ten pages of Times-style font, point size 12, with one-inch margins all around! You should have definite information as to what is expected in this regard.

Footnotes and Endnotes Most instructors will expect your paper to include notes or citations. If so, you should find out whether they should be at the bottom of the page (*footnotes*) or if it is permissible to place them at the end of the paper (*endnotes*). Be sure to ask whether a specific format must be followed for citations.[1] Failing to document sources that you have used may be a form of *plagiarism*. Plagiarism is not acknowledging the source of ideas you include and attempting to pass them off as your own. This is not only deceitful but also often seen as a form of stealing. The use of proper citations avoids this.

Footnotes and endnotes have three basic purposes. The first purpose is to give the source of a direct quotation. This gives proper credit to other authors for their ideas and statements. You use quotations to back up or give examples of what you have said. You should always introduce or comment on the quotations that you use. You can introduce a quotation with something like this:

> One example of this position is that of Jack Sprat, who writes in his book *Why One Should Eat No Fat* that "… eating lean is not only good for you, it's the right thing to do."[1]

This quotation is followed by a footnote marker that would lead to the full citation. Sometimes, you will want to follow a quote with your own interpretation of it, such as "I believe that this means...." In other words, you should always put the quotation in a context.

The second purpose of footnotes or endnotes is to give credit for ideas that you have used but summarized or put into your own words. Sometimes students think that the instructor will be less pleased if they are using others' ideas and are tempted to treat them as their own without giving a footnote reference. Actually, these attempts are often suspicious. Thus, the student who says that "Nowhere in his writings does Descartes mention x, y, or z" obviously strains credibility; it is unlikely that the student will have read all of the works of Descartes or know this on his or her own. It is one sign of a good paper if it gives credit for such indirect references. It shows that the student has read the source that is cited and has attempted to put it into his or her own words. This is a plus for the paper.

The third purpose of footnotes and endnotes is to give further information or clarification. For example, you might want to say that you mean just *this* in the paper and not *that*. You might also want to say something further about a point in the paper but you don't want to markedly interrupt the current line of thought.

Citing Internet Sources The Internet has become a major source of information for students and scholars in the writing of papers and monographs. But some of these sources are more reliable and suitable for your ethics papers than others. According to Jim Kapoun, a reference and instruction librarian, you should base your "Web evaluation on five criteria... racy, authority, objectivity, currency, and cover- You should consider who wrote the material, what the author's credentials are, whether the source of publication is a respected institution, whether the presentation is objective or is a mask for advertising or a specific political agenda, whether it is up to date, and whether the article is whole and intact or has elements that you must find elsewhere. Your instructor or librarian may be able to suggest reliable sources. Google, Bing, and other search engines can be exceptionally helpful if used correctly. Your job as a critical reader and writer is to sift and compare—and actually think about—the information you get from Google or elsewhere. Does it come from an authoritative or scholarly source or is it simply one writer's opinion expressed on her blog? Can you find the same information repeated on other reputable websites or does it contradict what most writers say about the topic?

You can learn a lot about your topic this way. But remember that if you include any of your research material in your paper, you need to be sure that you credit your source—otherwise you are plagiarizing the material. You should cite your source and use quotation marks when you make a direct quote. But you should also cite it if you are putting the ideas in your own words (as noted previously). You may think you will not be found out, but most professors now have sophisticated tools to check suspicious aspects of any paper.

Using and then showing how you used the Internet itself requires some detail and direction. You should supply the *uniform resource locator* (URL) of the site you use. Because these frequently change, you can also use the site's author, date you visited, and title. Giving the URL involves giving the whole reference, along with some indication of the date when you accessed the website.[3]

Depending on your instructor's directions for your paper, you probably should not limit your research or sources to the Internet, however, especially if you are doing something in depth or on historical topics such as the philosophy of Kant. You will most likely need to make use of your college or university library to obtain important books on the topic and access scholarly journals.

Title Page and Bibliography You also will want to know whether your instructor expects a title page, a bibliography, and so forth. A bibliography will be fitting for certain types of papers—namely, research papers—and unnecessary for others. A paper in which you are mainly arguing for a point and developing ideas of your own may not require a bibliography. If a bibliography is required, then just how extensive it should be will depend on the paper's purpose, type, and length.

Grammar, Spelling, and Gender In many cases, your paper will be graded not only on its content but also on mechanics such as grammar, spelling, and punctuation. It is always advisable to reread your paper for grammatical mistakes before you hand in the final version. For example, make sure all of your sentences are complete sentences. In the initial writing or revision, a sentence may lose its verb, the subject and predicate may no longer match, nouns and pronouns may not match, and so forth. You should review the paper to correct such mistakes.

Misspelling often is a sign of carelessness. We know how to spell the words, but we do not always take care to do so. Sometimes we are uncertain and do not take the time to look up the word in a dictionary. In using a word processor, spell-checking is easy. However, even here spelling mistakes can be missed. For example, a spell-checker cannot tell that you mean to say "to" instead of "too" or that you wanted to write "he" rather than "hell."

Today, we are also much more conscious of gender issues and gender bias than in decades past. In writing your ethics paper, you should be careful to avoid gender bias or sexist assumptions. For example, you should avoid such general terms as *mailman* and *policeman,* unless you are referring to a specific individual. Acceptable substitutes are *mail carrier* and *police officer.* You also can avoid gender bias by not reinforcing traditional gender roles in your writing. You might, for instance, speak of the business executive as a "she" and the nurse as a "he."

In times past, it also may have been acceptable to use *he* as a generic pronoun throughout a paper. Today, this is often less acceptable or even unacceptable. It is not always easy to remedy the situation, however, even when one wants to be fair and nonsexist. If one is referring to a particular male or female, then choosing the proper pronoun is easy. But if the

reference can be either male or female, then what should one do with the pronouns? One can say "she or he" or "he or she," although this usage can get cumbersome. You can also alternate pronouns throughout the paper, sometimes using "he" and sometimes "she." You can also use the gender-neutral "you," "one," or "they," "their," or "them" when possible.

TYPES OF ETHICS PAPERS

Several different types of ethics papers may be assigned in a philosophy class. You should be clear from the beginning which type you have been assigned or which you intend to pursue if you have a choice. According to one writer, there are five types of philosophy papers[4]:

1. A thesis defense paper in which one "state[s] a position and give[s] reasons for believing it is true"[5]
2. A paper that compares and contrasts two viewpoints
3. An analysis paper in which some particular viewpoint is examined more closely
4. A paper that summarizes an article or a book
5. A research paper or survey on a specific topic[6]

Our discussion of ethics papers overlaps this five-fold division. The following sections describe three types of ethics papers. Short examples of each can be found at the end of this appendix.

A Historical Approach

If you have already covered at least part of the beginning of this text, you have some background in the history of ethics. If you are interested in exploring the ethical views of any of the philosophers we've discussed, you can start with an overview of their philosophies as given in some of the more general scholarly sources on philosophy. The *Stanford Encyclopedia of Philosophy* (at http://plato.stanford.edu) is useful as an initial starting point. From this, you can determine whether a philosopher's views interest you, and you can see in general what type of ethical theory he or she espouses.

The main point of a historical exposition is to summarize or analyze a philosopher's views. It involves learning and writing down in some structured way your own understanding of those views. Your own views and interpretive comments can be added either as you go along or in some final paragraphs. You also can add your own critical or evaluative comments (positive or negative or both), possibly saving them for the end of the paper. Alternatively, and depending on your instructor's preferences, you might make the paper entirely exposition, without adding your own views or critical comments.

A Problem in Ethical Theory

Another type of ethics paper is one that examines some particular issue or problem in ethical theory. Part One of this text addresses several of these. Among these problems are the following:

> The Nature of Ethical Reasoning
> An Ethics of Rights versus an Ethics of Care
> Ethical Relativism
> Moral Realism
> Moral Pluralism
> Ethical Egoism
> Why Be Moral?
> The Nature of a Right
> Charity versus Obligation
> What Is Justice?
> What Is Virtue?

The point of a paper that treats a matter of ethical theory is to examine the problem itself. One approach is to start with a particular view on the issue, either in general or from some philosopher's point of view, and then develop it using your own ideas. Another approach is to contrast two views on the issue and then try to show which one is more reasonable, in your opinion. For example, you could contrast two views on the nature of justice. One might hold that justice requires some kind of equality. Thus, a just punishment is one that fits the crime, or a just distribution of wealth is one that is equal. Then contrast this with another view and follow that with your own comments. For another approach, you might provide a general presentation that simply tries to state the gist of the issue or problem and then give your own position on it. To summarize these, you could:

ate a view, then develop it with your own

2. Contrast two views on a subject, then say which, if either, you find more persuasive.
3. Explain the problem and present your views on it.

A Contemporary Moral Issue

A third type of ethics paper focuses on some practical moral issue that is currently being debated. Part Two of this text presents a selection of such issues. However, in each chapter in Part Two, there are several issues from which you could choose. You might, for example, focus just on the issue of active euthanasia or physician-assisted suicide. You might write about the ethical issues that arise in our treatment of endangered species. All of these issues are treated as part of chapters in this text. You might want instead to address some ethical issue that is not extensively discussed in this text: gun control, for example. However, on this topic as well as the others just mentioned, you should be certain to focus on the specific ethical concepts involved, rather than merely discussing the current political landscape or debate.

One useful method of approaching a contemporary moral issue is to distinguish among conceptual, factual, and ethical matters. *Conceptual matters* are matters of meaning or definition. *Factual matters* refer to what is the case about something. *Ethical matters* are matters of good and bad, better and worse, and they involve evaluation. Thus, regarding the issue of abortion, we could distinguish conceptual problems related to the attempt to say what it is as well as categorizing various forms of it, as well as its prevalence and legal status. The majority of an ethics paper should, however, be the attempt to evaluate it and give reasons for the evaluation that are based on some normative theory—such as utilitarianism, egoism, or Kantian deontology.

IS IT AN ETHICS PAPER?

An ethical problem can be approached in different ways. Not all of them are ethical approaches or would make the basis of an ethics paper. Take problems of violence in this country. Many people believe that the United States is too violent. One approach to examining the problem is to focus on questions about the causes of violence. Is it something in the American history or psyche? Do the media cause violence or reflect it or both? To make either of these issues the focus of one's paper, however, is not to do ethics or an ethics paper but a sociological analysis or descriptive account of the situation.

An ethics paper requires that you take a *normative* approach and ask about what is better or worse, right or wrong, good or bad, just or unjust, and so on. (See Chapter 1 on the distinction between a normative and descriptive approach.) Therefore, regarding violence, an ethics paper might begin with a clarification of what is meant by violence and a description of different categories of violence. Next, it might discuss what kinds of violence are justified or unjustified, for example. It might address the question of whether social or legal force is justified to diminish violence. This latter discussion could raise issues of the morality of legal force or the importance of individual liberty. In such discussions, one would be doing ethics because one would be addressing the ethical issues about just and unjust behavior or the moral justification of some practice or the moral value of liberty.

To be sure that your presentation is one that strictly addresses an ethical issue as an ethical problem, make sure you do not primarily draw on sources that are not authoritative on ethical matters. For instance, if you are addressing the issue of gun control, then you should not appeal simply to legal sources such as the U.S. Constitution to back up your ideas. You may appeal to ethical values that are part of the Constitution, such as the value of life or freedom of speech, but then you are using them as ethical values apart from whether or not the law values them. If you are considering whether the law ought to permit active euthanasia or physician-assisted suicide, then you may consider whether having such a law would or would not promote certain ethical values. This is an approach that could be used in an ethics paper.

STRUCTURING OR ANALYZING AN ETHICAL ARGUMENT

Most ethics papers either present or analyze ethical arguments, so you should consider some of the elements and types of ethical arguments. (Review the sections on ethical reasoning and ethical arguments from Chapter 1.) Among these are the following:

Reasons and Conclusions

It is important to notice and to be clear about what follows from what. Sometimes, key words or phrases will indicate this. For example, consider this statement: "Because X has better results than its alternative Y, we ought thus to adopt X." In this statement, the conclusion is that we ought to adopt some practice. The reason for this is that it has better results than its alternative. The key to knowing what follows from what in this example are the words *thus* and *because*. Being clear about this distinction enables you to make a better argument, for you can then back up your conclusion with other reasons and fill in the conclusions with more details.

Types and Sources of Evidence

As just noted, if you are to make an ethical argument, strictly speaking, you should not appeal to legal sources as such in order to make your case. You also cannot appeal to scientific sources for the ethical values or principles that you want to stress. For instance, although physicians are experts in diagnoses and prognoses, such medical expertise does not make them experts in knowing what kind of life is worthwhile or valuable, or how important rights or autonomy are. So, also, natural scientists can give us valuable information about the results of certain environmental practices, but this information and knowledge does not determine the importance or value of wilderness or endangered species. Sometimes, religious sources or authorities can be used in ethical arguments. When this is acceptable in an ethics or moral philosophy paper, however, it is usually because the values supported by religious sources are ethical values. For example, respect for one's parents might be promoted by a religion, but it also can be reasoned about by those who are not members of this particular (or any) religion.

Types of Reasons

As noted throughout this text, one primary distinction in ethical reasoning is the difference between an appeal to the consequences of some action or practice, and a judgment of actions and practices as right or wrong regardless of the consequences. It is important to be clear about which type of reason you or your source uses or critically evaluates.

Consequentialist Reasoning Your argument or the argument that you are summarizing or evaluating may be one that appeals to consequences. For example, you or the argument may assert that if we do such and such it will produce certain bad results. The argument can demonstrate these results by appeal to a scientific or other empirical source. The argument also must show why these results are bad—they may result in loss of life or produce great suffering, for example.

Non-consequentialist Reasoning If your argument appeals to some basic moral value or what is alleged to be a moral right, then it is non-consequentialist. For example, it might be based on the idea that we ought to be honest no matter the consequences. It may appeal to certain basic rights that ought to be protected whatever the consequences. To complete the argument or our evaluation of it, we should show or ask what the basis is for this type of assertion. For example, we might want to ask why autonomy is said to be a value or why liberty of action is a moral right.

Other Types of Reasons Consequentialist and non-consequentialist are not the only types of reasons that can be given. One might say that something is just or unjust because all persons, when they think about it in the proper light, would agree that this is just. This is an appeal to something like common moral rationality or a common moral sense. Although this is problematic, the appeals to other types of reasons are also not without their critics.

Some people believe that persons of good character or virtue or of caring temperaments will best be able to judge what is right. To give a moral reason appealing to this sort of belief will also need some explanation. But it will be a start to notice that this is the type of reason that is being given.

Top-to-Bottom or Bottom-to-Top Reasoning? Another way to construct or analyze ethical arguments is to first decide whether your reasoning will move from top to bottom or from bottom to top.

The top-to-bottom argument starts with a particular moral principle or moral value, and then applies

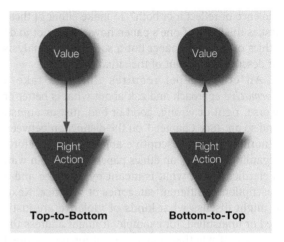

the principle to a specific situation. For example, you might do the following:

1. Start with the assertion that happiness is the most important value, or the principle that we always ought to do whatever promotes the greatest amount of happiness (the utilitarian moral principle).
2. Then you would examine which action or practice among those that you are analyzing would promote the most happiness.

The bottom-to-top argument starts with a situation in which we intuitively feel that a certain course of action is right. We take a concrete case and our judgment about it, and then ask what moral value or principle leads us to make this judgment. For example, one might take the following approach:

1. Start with a case in which we believe that if someone is in great danger of drowning and we can save him, then we ought to do so.
2. Then we proceed to ask why we believe we have this obligation. What value does it promote or what rights or principles? We ask why we believe that we ought to save this person from drowning. We might conclude that it flows from a moral principle that says that we always ought to help others in great need when we can do so without much cost to ourselves, and that this is a matter of obligation rather than of charity.

Although one can construct an argument that uses one or the other of these types of reasoning, actual moral reasoning often does both. Thus, your ethics paper also could incorporate both patterns, as long as you are careful to distinguish between them.

Using Examples and Analogies

Many philosophers use real or imaginary examples or analogies in their arguments. Among the more famous ones are Judith Thomson's violinist analogy (described in Chapter 11, on abortion) and James Rachels's Smith/Jones example (in Chapter 10, on euthanasia). There are also innumerable lifeboat and trolley examples, as discussed in Chapters 5 and 16. The method of arguing by analogy is as follows: If I start with some case and reach a certain moral conclusion about it, and if there is another case that is like it in the relevant respects, then I should conclude the same about it. Consider this example:

If we are dividing a pie and one person is hungrier than another, then that person should get the bigger piece. This is only fair. So, also, then we should say that in society at large the fair distribution of wealth is one in which those people who have greater needs should have a greater share of the wealth.

We can critically evaluate an analogy by considering whether the analogy fits. We ask whether the two situations or scenarios are similar in the relevant respects. Thus, in the previous example, we might ask whether being hungrier than another is the same as having greater needs. We might also wonder whether there is anything crucially different between what is fair among individuals in sharing some good and what is fair in society with regard to sharing a nation's wealth. We might say that nothing else matters so much in the pie-sharing situation, but that additional things do matter in the situation of sharing a nation's wealth.

Many other considerations go into making an ethical argument a strong argument. However, these few given here should help you construct and critically analyze ethical arguments, which are the heart of an ethics paper.

SAMPLE ETHICS PAPERS

Here follow three shortened versions or outlines of the three types of ethics papers just described. The first gives an outline of a historical ethics paper. The other two give partial examples of papers that address issues in ethical theory and practice. Although there are a few sample footnotes and endnotes included in the sample ethics papers, other examples of endnotes can be found throughout this text.

NOTES

1. See, for example, Modern Language Association, *MLA Handbook for Writers of Research Papers*, 7th ed. (New York: The Modern Language Association of America, 2009), for detailed help on forms of citation.
2. Jim Kapoun, "Questioning Web Authority: How a Librarian Trains Students to Assess Web Page Credibility," *On Campus* (February 2000): 4
3. See the current edition of the *MLA Handbook, The Chicago Manual of Style,* and other style guides, for more details on proper Internet citations.
4. Zachary Seech, *Writing Philosophy Papers*, 3rd ed. (Belmont, CA: Wadsworth, 1997).
5. Ibid., 5.
6. Ibid.

Historical Approach

Kant's Theory of the Good Will

I. The Problem: Is it always good to do what you yourself think is right?

Sometimes people seem to act out of conscience and we like to praise this. However, sometimes they then do things that turn out to hurt others. How can we praise such behavior? Is it enough to have a good intention or a good will?

In this paper I plan to consider this issue from the perspective of the modern philosopher Immanuel Kant, who is known for his views on the importance of motive in ethics. I will look briefly at who Kant was and then proceed to examine his views on the good will. Finally, I will see whether his views help me to answer the question I have posed in this paper.

II. Kant's Theory of the Good Will

A. Who was Kant?

B. What Kant holds on the good will

1. It is always good

2. To act with a good will is to act out of duty

3. To act with a good will is to act out of respect for the moral law

C. How this position relates to the initial problem

III. In this paper I have described Kant's views on the good will. I have found that, according to Kant, it is always good because the person who acts with a good will acts with the motive to do what morality requires. I then returned to the original questions that I posed to see how Kant answered them.

Finally, in my view Kant does (not) give a reasonable answer to my question, because . . .

A Problem in Ethical Theory

Moral Relativism

Many people today seem to be moral relativists. We tend to believe that what is good for some people is not necessarily also good for others. In some circumstances it seems that it is permissible to lie, and at other times it seems that we ought to tell the truth. On the other hand, we also argue with one another all the time about what actually is right and wrong. We do not seem to always accept the view that there is no better way. Are we then moral relativists or not? What is moral relativism? This paper will address these questions. It will begin with an attempt to determine what ethical relativism is. Then it will look at some of the arguments about whether it is true. Finally it will draw some conclusions about whether we actually do believe in ethical relativism.

What Ethical Relativism Is

According to the philosopher Richard Grace, ethical relativism is a theory that holds that "…."[1] He goes on to explain that…. As I understand it, this would mean….

Two Views of Ethical Relativism

Professor Grace believes that what ethical relativism asserts is not correct. The reasons he gives for his view are….[2]

A contrasting view is held by the philosopher Eleanor Brown. She writes that "…."[3] The reasons that Professor Brown believes that ethical relativism is a valid theory are….

My Views

I believe that Professor Grace has given reasonable arguments against ethical relativism. In particular I agree with his argument that….

My reason for doing so is that this is true to my experience. For example, ….

Notes as Footnotes

1. Richard Grace, "What Relativism Is," Journal of Philosophy, vol. 3, no. 2 (June 1987): 5–6.

2. Ibid., 6.

3. Eleanor Brown, Relativism (Cambridge, Mass: Harvard University Press, 1988), 35.

My Conclusions

In this paper, I have looked at two views on ethical relativism, one critical of it and one supporting it. Now that I have become clearer about what relativism is and have looked at opposing views on it, I conclude that it is not a reasonable view. Additionally, I believe that if we understand relativism in the way that these philosophers have explained it, we generally do not behave as though we were ethical relativists. For example, …. On the other hand, there are some things that are still questions in my mind about ethical relativism. Among these are…. I look forward sometime to finishing my inquiry into this difficult problem.

| **Notes as Endnotes** |

Notes

1. Richard Grace, "What Relativism Is," *Journal of Philosophy* 3, no. 2 (June 1987): 5–6.

2. Ibid., 6.

3. Eleanor Brown, *Relativism* (Cambridge, MA: Harvard University Press, 1988), 35.

A Contemporary Ethical Issue

The Ethics of Cloning

Just the other day in the newspaper there was a report of a case of the cloning of a human being.[1] According to this report, while we have cloned vegetables and some small animals in the past, there has never before been a published report of a case of a human being being cloned. This case has raised quite a stir. In particular many people have raised ethical questions about this case. There is a diversity of opinion about whether such a practice is right or wrong. In this paper I will examine the ethical debate over the cloning of human beings. I will begin with a description of the process and this case. Next I will summarize the arguments for and against this practice. Finally I will present my own conclusions about the ethics of cloning human beings.

What Is Cloning?

There are two types of cloning.[2] One is…. The other is…. In this case the second type was used. What these scientists did was….

The Case against Cloning

Many people wonder about the ethics of cloning human beings. Some express fears that it would be abused. For example, Professor … is quoted in the news article saying that….[3] The idea seems to be that many people might have themselves cloned so that they could use this clone for organ transplants. Others worry that….

The arguments of Professor … seem reasonable. I especially agree with him that….

The Case in Favor of Cloning

On the other hand, Doctor … and others argue that with the right kinds of safeguards the cloning of humans would be just as ethically acceptable as the cloning of carrots. Among the safeguards that they list are….[4]

One of the problems that I see with this position is….

My Conclusions

In this paper I have found that the project to clone human beings consists of a process of…. I have looked at ethical arguments in support of and critical of this procedure when applied to humans. I conclude that while there may be some advantages to be gained from this method of producing babies, what worries me about cloning humans is…. I will continue to follow this issue as it develops, for I'm sure that this is not the last time we will hear of the cloning of humans nor the last of the debate about its ethical implications.

Notes

1. *The Sue City Daily News*, January 17, 1993, C7.

2. Jane Gray, *Modern Genetics* (New York: The American Press, 1988), 5–10.

3. *The Sue City Daily News*, C7.

4. See one of the Chapters in Martin Sheen and Sam Spade, *Cloning* (San Francisco: The Free Press, 1991), 200–48.

Glossary

A

Absolutism metaethical idea that there are eternal and unchanging values and rules (vs. *relativism*).

Act utilitarianism utilitarian theory that focuses on judging whether individual acts create the greatest happiness for the greatest number (compare: *rule utilitarianism*).

Active euthanasia actively killing someone for the benefit of the one being killed (vs. *passive euthanasia*).

Actuality ontological consideration focused on what a thing is at the present moment (vs. what it has the potential to become); often employed in discussions of the ethics of abortion; see also *ontological status* and *potentiality*.

Ad hominem a phrase meaning "to the person"; ad hominem arguments are (usually) fallacious arguments that attack a person rather than the person's idea or logical reasoning.

Advance directive a health care directive that stipulates in advance what sort of care a patient wants or does not want in case of incapacity; see also *living will* and *durable power of attorney.*

Aesthetics the study of beauty and taste.

Affirmative action social programs that take positive steps to remedy past injustice and inequality (usually racial); for example: *preferential treatment*; criticized as *reverse discrimination.*

Ahimsa term meaning nonviolence; associated with South Asian traditions such as Hinduism and Buddhism.

Akrasia see *weakness of will.*

Altruism behavior that is oriented toward the well-being of others (vs. egoism); see also *pro-social behaviors.*

Animal rights idea that individual animals have an interest in their lives and a corresponding right not to suffer or be killed (associated with Regan); see also *animal welfare.*

Animal welfare idea that animal suffering matters and that we should not cause unnecessary harm to animals (associated with *utilitarianism* and Singer); see also *animal rights.*

Anthropocentrism approach to environmental ethics (and *animal welfare*) that maintains that human interests alone are the proper focal point (vs. *biocentrism* and *ecocentrism*).

Arguments from analogy arguments based upon a comparison between items; relevant similarities among things are intended to incline us to accept conclusions about these things that are also relevantly similar.

Autonomy self-rule or self-control; a central concern for Kantian ethics, which emphasizes respect for the autonomy of rational persons.

B

Begging the question a fallacious argument in which the conclusion is assumed in the premises (also called a *circular argument*).

Biocentrism approach to environmental ethics that is focused on the value of biotic systems and all life (vs. *anthropocentrism*); see also *ecocentrism.*

Bioconservativism idea that we should not be "playing God" with regard to biotechnologies, sometimes based upon repugnance toward new technologies (associated with Kass).

Bioengineering projects aiming to develop mechanical supplements for biological systems, which can be used for therapy or enhancement.

Biotechnology interventions and manipulations of biological systems and organisms through the use of technological means including genetic engineering, cloning, the use of drugs, surgeries, and so on.

Biotic pyramid the interrelated food chains that unite plants, grazing animals, prey animals, predators, and human beings (associated with Leopold's *land ethic*).

C

Capitalism a social and economic system based on private property and freedom to make profit; see also *laissez-faire capitalism* (vs. *socialism* and *communism*).

Cardinal virtues primary virtues; the four cardinal virtues in the ancient Greek tradition are justice, wisdom, moderation, and courage.

Care ethics ethical theory that emphasizes nurturing relationships, while downplaying autonomy and individualism (associated with Noddings).

Categorical imperative Kantian idea about the universal form of the moral law, which is not based on hypothetical or conditional interests; Kant's formulation: "act only according to that maxim, whereby you can will that it should also be a universal law" (vs. *hypothetical imperative*).

Circular argument a fallacious argument that assumes what it seeks to prove (also called *begging the question*).

Civil disobedience breaking a law in a civil manner that retains fidelity to the system of justice and accepts punishment as an act of protest.

Civil union a legally recognized relationship between same-sex partners; similar but not identical to marriage (also called civil partnership or domestic partnership).

Collateral damage term used in just war ethics to describe unintended noncombatant harm that is justified by application of the *principle of double effect*; see also *noncombatant immunity*.

Communism a social and economic system focused on communal ownership of the means of production, radical equality, and the abolition of social classes; see also *socialism* (vs. *capitalism*).

Communitarianism a theory of society that emphasizes communal belonging and is critical of the individualistic focus of *liberalism* and *libertarianism*.

Consequentialism normative theories that focus on the consequences of actions; examples include *egoism*, *altruism*, *utilitarianism* (vs. *non-consequentialism*).

Contractarianism normative theory that holds that moral norms arise from a contract or agreement between rational parties (associated with Hobbes and Rawls); see also *reciprocal altruism*.

Cosmopolitanism idea that there are (or ought to be) universal norms that unite people across the globe.

Criminal justice justice that is focused on punishment and correction (vs. *social justice*); see also *retributive justice*, *deterrence*, *restorative justice*.

D

Deep ecology extreme ecocentric idea in environmental ethics that emphasizes human belonging to nature and the intrinsic value of natural things (associated with Devall and Sessions).

Deontological ethics normative theory that morality ought to be focused on duties and adherence to rules and imperatives (associated with Kant).

Descriptive claims propositions that state true or false claims about facts in the world.

Descriptive egoism (*defined under *egoism*).

Descriptive ethical relativism descriptive claim that values differ depending upon culture and perspective.

Deterrence a focal point for consequentialist approaches to *criminal justice*, which is concerned with deterring criminals from committing crime (vs. *retributive justice* and *restorative justice*).

Discrimination (in just war) principle of the just war theory that stipulates that just warriors should target only combatants and protect noncombatants; see also *noncombatant immunity*.

Discrimination (as injustice) to treat someone unfairly and unequally based upon racial, ethnic, gender, or other identity claims (not to be confused with discrimination in just war theory).

Distributive justice a theory of justice concerned with the fair distribution of benefits and harms within society (vs. *retributive justice* and *procedural justice*).

Divine command theory idea that ethical norms are ultimately based upon the authoritative decrees of God.

Double effect the principle or doctrine of double effect is the idea in deontological ethics that holds that if the intention behind an action is morally appropriate, unintended (but foreseen and accidental) negative effects may be permissible.

Durable power of attorney used to appoint or empower someone to make health care decisions for you in the case of incapacity; see also *advance directive* and *living will*.

E

Ecocentrism approach to environmental ethics that is focused on the value of the ecosystem as a whole and not merely on its relation to human beings (vs. *anthropocentrism*); see also *biocentrism.*

Ecofeminism a critical version of environmental ethics that emphasizes the way that patriarchal systems have abused nature and a more productive feminine connection with nature.

Ecosystem a concept used in environmental ethics that refers to the broad, integrated, coordinated, and organized whole, including plants, animals, and human beings.

Egoism normative or *ethical egoism* claims that we ought to pursue our own self-interest; *descriptive egoism* (also called *psychological egoism*) maintains that as a matter of fact we can pursue only our own self-interest (vs. *altruism*).

Embryonic stem cells cells, removed from a developing embryo, that can develop into multiple tissues; controversial because the embryo is destroyed to harvest them.

Emotivism metaethical idea that ethical propositions express emotional states (associated with Stevenson).

Enhancement an intervention that goes beyond natural/normal function and creates superior performance, employed in discussions of biotechnology (vs. *therapy*).

Enlightenment period of fertile development of Western culture and philosophy, during the seventeenth and eighteenth centuries.

Environmental ethics field of ethical inquiry that is concerned with the question of the value of ecosystems, the natural environment, and the distribution of benefits and harms in relation to the environment.

Environmental justice a concern in environmental ethics that is focused on the fair distribution of harms and benefits to human beings in relation to environmental impacts such as pollution (related to *distributive justice* and *social justice*).

Epicureanism theory of Epicurus, which holds that pleasure and happiness are primary (also called *hedonism*).

Epistemology theory of knowledge.

Ethical egoism see *egoism.*

Eudaimonia Greek term for human flourishing and happiness that is more than simply pleasure; associated with Aristotle and *virtue ethics.*

Eugenics goal of producing genetically superior offspring, either through genetic screening or through more forceful interventions including forced sterilization.

Eurocentrism attitude or practice of interpreting the world from a perspective that focuses primarily on European interests, values, and history.

Euthanasia literally good death; also called mercy killing; forms include *active*, *passive*, *voluntary*, *involuntary*, and *nonvoluntary.*

Exoneration to be found innocent of a crime for which one was previously convicted and found guilty.

Extraordinary measures in discussion of end of life care and euthanasia, extraordinary measures are medical interventions that are not proven to be reasonably beneficial—may include, for example, experimental treatments or risky interventions (vs. *ordinary measures*).

F

Fair chase idea in hunting ethics that the animal should stand some chance and the hunter requires some skill and good luck.

Female genital mutilation/ FGM removal of parts of the female genitals (includes a variety of procedures); also called female circumcision.

Feminism intellectual commitment and a political movement that seeks justice for women and the end of sexism in all forms.

Feminist ethics a critical theory of ethics that rejects male-dominant ideas; can include "feminine" ethics emphasizing community and caregiving (associated with Noddings).

Fundamentalism idea that truth is grounded in religious texts, traditions, and prophets.

G

Gay marriage marriage of homosexual couples; also called same-sex marriage; see also *civil union.*

Genetic screening process of choosing embryos based on their genetic assets prior to implantation; can include efforts to modify genes to eliminate disease or produce enhanced capacities.

Genetically modified organisms plants or animals that have been genetically altered by scientists in an effort to improve the stock and increase yield.

Global justice concern for distributive justice, environmental justice, and social justice across the globe.

Globalization process of increasing integration of global markets and ideas, by way of growing international cooperation and international business.

Golden Mean idea associated with virtue ethics that virtue is found in the middle between excess and deficiency.

Golden Rule idea that one ought to love one's neighbor as oneself or do unto others as we would have them do unto us.

Greatest happiness principle utilitarian idea that we ought to work to achieve the greatest happiness for the greatest number of people; see also *principle of utility*.

H

Hate crime a crime that is accompanied by bias (racial, religious, gender, sexuality) against the individual who is the victim of the crime.

Hedonism theory that holds that pleasure is the highest good; as a normative theory tells us we ought to pursue pleasure; see also *Epicureanism*.

Hippocratic Oath medical ethics pledge rooted in ancient Greek tradition; primary tenet is to do no harm.

Human rights rights that are basic to human beings, often described in universal terms that transcend national and cultural differences; see also *rights, natural rights*.

Humanism orientation to human concerns and interests (as opposed to theistic or religious orientation); see also *secular ethics*.

Hume's law the claim (derived from David Hume's thinking) that it is illegitimate to derive an "ought" from an "is"; see also *naturalistic fallacy*.

Hypothetical imperative Kantian idea of a conditional rule that governs prudential behaviors and skilled activities aimed at procuring or producing some conditional good (vs. *categorical imperative*).

I

Imperfect duties Kantian idea about duties of virtue that are admirable and praiseworthy but not always necessary (vs. *perfect duties*).

In vitro fertilization a process by which egg and sperm are united outside of the uterus, the consequent embryo is implanted into the uterus—a way to create pregnancy for infertile couples.

Individual relativism idea that ethical claims are relative to an individual's values and perspectives; see also *subjectivism*.

Inherent value value residing by nature in something and without reference to any other value or good; see also *intrinsic value/goods*.

Institutional racism see *structural racism*.

Instrumental value/ goods things that are useful or good as tools or as means toward some other good (vs. *intrinsic value/goods*).

Intrinsic value/goods things that have value in themselves and not merely as tools or means (vs. *instrumental value/goods*); see also *inherent value*.

Intrinsically evil means concept in just war theory that rules out some weapons and methods of war as being evil in themselves (or *mala in se*).

Intuitionism metaethical idea that ethical truths are objective and irreducible and can be known by faculty of intuition (associated with Moore).

Involuntary euthanasia euthanasia that is done against an individual's will (vs. *voluntary euthanasia* and *nonvoluntary euthanasia*).

J

Jus ad bellum just war concern for ethical issues arising in deciding to go to war, including *just cause, legitimate authority*, and *proportionality*.

Jus in bello just war concern for ethical issues arising within warfare, including *proportionality, discrimination*, and prohibition on *intrinsically evil means*.

Just cause concern of *jus ad bellum*, which holds that a war is justified only if there is a just cause, including defending the innocent or repelling aggression.

Just war theory a theory about the justification of war that maintains that war should be limited by moral concerns; see also *jus ad bellum* and *jus in bello*.

K

Kingdom of ends Kantian ideal of a rational, moral society in which persons are respected as ends in themselves.

L

Laissez-faire capitalism form of economic and social organization that emphasizes leaving the market alone to regulate itself.

Land ethic an ecocentric idea in environmental ethics that views the land as a whole and claims that good actions contribute to the well-being of the whole (associated with Leopold).

Law of peoples idea of international law that transcends national borders.

Legitimate authority concern of *jus ad bellum* that holds that a war is justified only if the entity declaring war holds power legitimately.

Lex talionis an idea of *retributive justice*, which is focused on equivalence or proportionality between the crime and the punishment, often described as "eye for an eye" justice.

Liberalism a political theory that emphasizes a combination of concern for liberty and concern for social justice and distributive justice (associated with Rawls) (vs. *libertarianism* and *socialism*).

Libertarianism a political theory about both the importance of liberty in human life and the limited role of government (associated with Rand) (vs. *liberalism* and *socialism*).

Liberty rights see *negative rights*.

Living wage a minimum wage standard indexed to the cost of living (vs. *minimum wage*).

Living will a form of advance health care directive; see also *advance directive* and *durable power of attorney*.

M

Metaethical relativism metaethical claim that there are no objective or nonrelative values that could mediate disputes about ethics.

Metaethics study of moral concepts and the logic of ethical language.

Minimum wage legally mandated minimum hourly wage for labor (vs. *living wage*).

Modernization theory of development that emphasizes increased secularization, spread of capitalism, and liberalization of economics and politics.

Moral agent a being who is able to express ethical concern and take responsibility for behaviors, attitudes, and actions (vs. *moral patient*)

Moral patient an object of ethical concern, a recipient of moral concern, or a being that is viewed as having value (vs. *moral agent*).

Moral pluralism see *value pluralism*.

Moral realism idea that there are ethical facts and that moral judgments can be said to be true or false; see also *objectivism*.

N

Natural law theory a theory of law that is grounded in claims about nature; natural law ethics is a normative theory that holds that reason can discover objective ethical norms by examining natural human functions (associated with Aquinas).

Natural rights rights or entitlements that we have by nature, which are not created by positive laws and which create a limit to legal intervention; see also *rights*, *human rights*.

Naturalistic fallacy argument that inappropriately derives normative claims from descriptive claims (associated with Moore); see also *Hume's law*.

Negative rights rights of noninterference and prevention of harm, often called *liberty rights* (as opposed to *welfare rights* and *positive rights*).

Noncombatant immunity idea in just war theory that noncombatants should not be deliberately targeted; see also *collateral damage*.

Non-consequentialism normative theories that do not focus on consequences of actions but instead on intentions, rules, or principles; examples include deontology, divine command, and natural law (vs. *consequentialism*).

Nonvoluntary euthanasia euthanasia that is done when the patient is incapacitated and unable to express her wishes or give consent (vs. *voluntary euthanasia* and *involuntary euthanasia*).

Normative ethics study of prescriptive accounts of how we ought to behave.

Normative judgments evaluative or prescriptive claims about what is good, evil, just, etc.

O

Objectivism metaethical idea that ethical propositions refer to objective facts (vs. *subjectivism*); see also *moral realism*.

Ontological status related to a theory of being (ontology); questions about the moral status of things (fetuses, ecosystems, etc.) depend upon deciding what sorts of beings these things are; see also *actuality* and *potentiality*.

Ontology theory of being or beings; an account of what exists or about the sort of being a thing is.

Ordinary measures in discussions of end of life care and euthanasia, ordinary measures are those medical interventions that are proven to be reasonably beneficial in most cases (vs. *extraordinary measures*).

Original position idea used in John Rawls's theory of justice that asks us to imagine ourselves as original or founding parties to the social contract; see also *veil of ignorance*.

Original sin Christian idea that human beings inherit a tendency to do evil from the original sin of Adam and Eve.

P

Pacifism commitment to nonviolence and opposition to war (associated with Gandhi and King).

Palliative care health care that is aimed at pain management and dealing with suffering.

Palliative sedation sedation employed to provide pain management at the end of life (related to *terminal sedation*).

Paradox of hedonism problem for hedonism: when pursuing pleasure directly, we fail to obtain it; but pleasure occurs when we do not directly pursue it.

Paradox of toleration problem of whether one should tolerate those who are intolerant or who reject the idea of toleration.

Passive euthanasia allowing someone to die ("letting die") for the benefit of the one who is dying (vs. *active euthanasia*).

Perfect duties Kantian idea about duties of justice that we always ought to do or that we always ought to avoid (vs. *imperfect duties*).

Persistent vegetative state (PVS) a condition of permanent brain damage, characterized by lack of awareness and loss of higher brain functions; patient remains alive but has lost cognitive function; see also *whole brain death*.

Perspectivism relativist idea that there are only perspectives and interpretations, which cannot be reduced to a fundamental fact of the world.

Physician-assisted suicide closely related to euthanasia; doctor prescribes lethal medication but the patient takes the medication, killing himself.

Positive rights rights of entitlement to basic subsistence and other means of living sometimes called *welfare rights* (as opposed to *liberty rights* and *negative rights*).

Post-structuralism a philosophical movement of the late twentieth century that emphasizes the social construction of categories of thought.

Potentiality ontological consideration focused on what a thing has the potential to become; often employed in discussions of the ethics of abortion; see also *ontological status* and *actuality*.

Preferential treatment a form of affirmative action that intends to give preference to members of groups who were previously unjustly discriminated against; see *affirmative action*.

Premises the reasons given in an argument that provide support for the argument's conclusion.

Prima facie term meaning "on the face of it" or "at first glance."

***Prima facie* duties** pluralist idea that there are several duties, each of which is valuable but which can end up in conflict (associated with Ross).

Principle of equality idea that we should treat equal things in equal ways and that we ought to treat different things in unequal ways.

Principle of utility utilitarian idea that what matters is the pleasure produced by an action, especially the pleasure produced for the greatest number of people; see also *greatest happiness principle*.

Prisoner's dilemma problem for rational self-interest and social contract: self-interested parties who do not trust one another will be unable to cooperate and thus will end up with less than optimal outcomes.

Problem of evil argument against the existence of God that claims that a good God would not permit evil, but since evil exists, God must not exist (vs. *theodicy*).

Procedural justice a theory of justice focused on the fairness of the procedures used to distribute benefits and harms (vs. *distributive justice*).

Proportionality concern of just war theory that maintains that war should be a proportional last resort and that limited and proportional means should be employed during the course of war.

Pro-social behaviors behaviors that intend to help others (vs. antisocial behavior).

Psychological egoism (*defined under *egoism*).

Q

Queer theory a post-structuralist approach to thinking about gender and sexuality that maintains that sex and gender roles are socially constructed (associated with Butler).

Quickening the point in pregnancy at which the mother is able to detect movement of the fetus; sometimes viewed as the time when the fetus attains moral status.

R

Racial profiling law enforcement technique that targets individuals based upon suspicion resulting from the individual's racial or ethnic identity.

Racialism idea that there are firm biological distinctions between human beings based on racial categories (critiqued by Appiah).

Racism unjust use of racial or ethnic categories to classify individuals and distribute social benefits and harms.

Realism view on ethics of war that maintains that limits on warfare are merely pragmatic or prudential and that the goal is strength and victory.

Reciprocal altruism idea that altruistic behavior is traded with others in a mutually beneficial exchange; see also *contractarianism.*

Regenerative medicine an approach to medical therapy that aims to regrow damaged tissues and organs using stem cells—both embryonic stem cells and other forms of stem cells.

Relativism a variety of claims that deny the objectivity of values including: *descriptive relativism*, *individual relativism* (or *subjectivism*), *metaethical relativism*, and social or cultural relativism.

Relativism, social *or* **cultural** idea that ethical claims are relative to a social or cultural matrix.

Religious pluralism idea that diverse religions provide multiple paths toward a common truth (associated with Gandhi).

Reproductive cloning a cloning procedure that aims to develop an individual organism as a substitute for ordinary reproduction (vs. *therapeutic cloning*).

Restorative justice an approach to *criminal justice* that seeks to make criminals take responsibility and make amends, while restoring the community that they have broken (vs. *retributive justice* and *deterrence*).

Retributive justice a theory of *criminal justice* that focuses on giving criminals what they deserve and forcing them to pay back what they owe to victims or to society (vs. *restorative justice* and *deterrence*); see also *lex talionis.*

Reverse discrimination an idea used to criticize affirmative action, which claims that actions aiming to help those who were previously discriminated against result in discrimination against those who were the beneficiaries of past discrimination.

Rights basic entitlements, which ordinarily cannot be taken away or overridden; can be positive entitlements (*positive rights*) or negative protections (*negative rights*) (associated with Locke); see also *natural rights* and *human rights*

Rule utilitarianism utilitarian theory that focuses on postulating general rules that will tend to produce the greatest happiness for the greatest number (vs. *act utilitarianism*).

S

Secular ethics approach to ethics that locates ethical norms in nonreligious principles acceptable to people from a variety of religions (vs. *divine command theory*); see also *humanism.*

Secularization movement away from religious culture and toward a nonreligious public sphere; see also *modernization.*

Sentience the ability to feel, perceive, and be conscious of the world, used in discussions of animal welfare and abortion in considering the moral status of animals and fetuses.

Sex trafficking trading sex for money; also called prostitution.

Sex-selective abortion abortion performed for the purpose of selecting the gender of the baby.

Skepticism questioning and doubting attitude.

Social contract theory idea that social norms and political agreement are derived from a mutually beneficial contract to which the parties would consent (associated with Hobbes, Locke, and Rawls).

Social Darwinism idea of applying Darwinian evolution to society as a way of improving the genetic stock of humanity (widely repudiated as immoral).

Social justice an approach to justice that is concerned with the fair distribution of goods in society, often associated with natural law theories (vs. *criminal justice*).

Socialism a social and economic system focused on developing shared social assets and a social safety net; see also *communism* (vs. *capitalism*).

Sociobiology a field of study that applies evolutionary and comparative biology to understanding social phenomena including ethical behaviors.

Sound argument a valid argument with true premises.

Speciesism a pejorative term used to describe anthropocentrists, who maintain that human beings are superior to nonhuman animals (associated with Singer).

Stem cell research a promising line of research that could help to regenerate damaged tissues; controversial when it employs human *embryonic stem cells.*

Stoicism theory of ancient Stoic philosophers, which holds that obedience to natural law and duty is essential (despite pain).

Straw man argument fallacious argument that describes an opponent's position in such a way as to easily dismiss it.

Structural racism idea that social structures are constituted in ways that create disparate racial outcomes (also called *institutional racism*).

Subjectivism metaethical idea that ethical propositions refer to subjective dispositions or values (vs. *objectivism*); see also *individual relativism, descriptive relativism, metaethical relativism.*

Supererogatory a term used to describe actions that go above and beyond the call of duty.

T

Teleological adjective used to describe ideas and theories that are focused on goals, purposes, or outcomes (related to *consequentialism*).

Terminal sedation use of sedatives in palliative care, which aims to reduce suffering at the end of life but may also contribute to death and be considered as part of euthanasia.

Theodicy theoretical explanation of why a good God would permit evil; response to the *problem of evil.*

Therapeutic cloning a cloning procedure that is used to grow stem cells or tissues, which could be used for organ donation or regenerative medicine (vs. *reproductive cloning*).

Therapy an intervention employed to return something to natural/normal function, employed

in discussions of biotechnology (vs. *enhancement*).

Toleration attitude of forbearance or permission for attitudes or behaviors that are disapproved; an open and nonjudgmental attitude.

Totipotent term describing the ability of embryonic stem cells to develop into any kind of tissue; see also *stem cell research.*

Tragedy of the commons worry about degradation of common resources when no one owns them, associated with concerns for environmental degradation (associated with Hardin).

Transhumanism a movement aiming to improve human abilities, extend human life span, and increase cognitive capacity; sometimes referred to as post-humanism (associated with Bostrom).

Trolley Problem a thought experiment that asks one to compare the numbers of those killed or saved in the face of a run away train or trolley; useful for discussions of utilitarianism.

U

Utilitarianism normative theory that we ought to concern ourselves with the greatest happiness for the greatest number of people (associated with Bentham and Mill).

V

Valid argument an argument in which the conclusion necessarily follows from the premises.

Value pluralism the metaethical idea that there is more than one

objective value (associated with Ross); see also *prima facie duties.*

Vegetarianism commitment to avoiding eating meat including *veganism*, which avoids consuming any animal product including eggs, milk, and leather.

Veil of ignorance idea used in John Rawls's version of the social contract that asks us to ignore concrete facts about our own situation as we imagine the ideal social contract.

Viability the point at which a fetus might live outside of the womb if delivered early; sometimes used as a criteria for determining the permissibility (or not) of abortion.

Virtue ethics normative theory that maintains that the focus of morality is habits, dispositions, and character traits (associated with Aristotle).

Voluntary euthanasia euthanasia that is done with consent of the one being killed or dying (vs. *involuntary euthanasia* and *nonvoluntary euthanasia*).

W

Weakness of will problem in moral psychology: we sometimes will things that we know are not in our own self-interest or are unable to do things we know are good (also called *akrasia*).

Welfare rights see *positive rights.*

Whole brain death legal criteria for death focused not on respiration and heartbeat but on the presence of brain activity; see also *persistent vegetative state.*

Index